GW01374858

THE
ELECTRIC INTERURBAN RAILWAYS
IN AMERICA

THE ELECTRIC INTERURBAN RAILWAYS IN AMERICA

GEORGE W. HILTON and JOHN F. DUE

Second Printing, 1964
with corrections and additions

STANFORD UNIVERSITY PRESS
STANFORD, CALIFORNIA

Stanford University Press
Stanford, California
© 1960 by the Board of Trustees of the
Leland Stanford Junior University
Printed in the United States of America
ISBN 0-8047-0553-4
Original printing 1960
Second printing 1964
Last figure below indicates year of this printing:
95   94   93   92   91   90   89   88   87   86

To
JAMES EDWARD DILLON COLEMAN
(1925–1944)

who was killed in France in the Second World War. He would have found in this book little that he did not know.

Preface

THE ELECTRIC interurban railway played a major but short-lived role in the development of intercity passenger transport. Basically, it provided a transitional step from almost sole reliance upon the steam railroad to an almost equally complete dependence on the automobile. Offering greater convenience and flexibility for short-distance travel than the railroad, the interurban greatly increased passenger mobility in the areas that it served, but it quickly gave way to the motor vehicle, which offered still greater flexibility. The interurban and the motor vehicle were first developed in roughly the same period; had the latter been perfected more rapidly, the interurban would have been killed in infancy. As it was, the interurban initially far outpaced its competitor, only to have the motor vehicle surpass and eventually destroy it. The intercity electric railway was a peculiarly American institution; although substantial mileage was built in parts of continental Europe, especially in the Low Countries and in Germany, only in the United States did a widespread network develop.

The interurbans have received much less attention than their significance in American economic history warrants. The Lynds' comprehensive studies of the society of Muncie, Indiana, are in a sense typical; although Muncie was a major interurban junction, there is barely a mention of the interurban in *Middletown* and *Middletown in Transition*. Even general transportation histories have only incidental references to the interurbans, and local historians have ignored the industry almost entirely. To some extent, this neglect is compensated for by the publication of detailed histories of a number of interurbans by groups specifically interested in the technology and history of electric railways. Many of these studies are of high quality, and have preserved substantial amounts of detailed information which would otherwise have been lost. They are, however, almost purely descriptive, and they have never achieved a wide audience.

This general history of the interurbans was made possible in large measure by the availability of sets of the *Electric Railway Journal* and its predecessors, the principal trade journal of the street railway and interurban industries. The excellence and comprehensiveness of the *Electric Railway Journal* were mainly due to the high standards of its editor for many years, Henry W. Blake. An electrical engineer trained at Yale and MIT, Blake was an associate of Frank Sprague in the development of the electric streetcar. In 1891, Blake became associated with the *Street Railway Journal*, which in 1908 became the *Electric Railway Journal*. He was its editor until January 1, 1925, and remained associated with the magazine until his death in 1929.

The authors are also greatly indebted to a number of authorities for their assistance. In particular, indebtedness is due Dr. Thomas Conway, Jr., sometime Professor of Finance in the Wharton School of the University of Pennsylvania, and successively President of the Chicago Aurora and Elgin, the Cincinnati and Lake Erie, and the Philadelphia and Western, for his suggestions and his kindness in reading a portion of the manuscript. The authors are also very grateful to George Krambles, Operations Planning Engineer of the Chicago Transit Authority, for his comments on the manuscript, discovery of a number of errors, and assistance in providing illustrations. Stephen D. Maguire, Electric Lines Editor of *Railroad Magazine*, read the manuscript and assisted in obtaining information. Dr. George T. Oborn, Vice-President of Illinois Wesleyan University, kindly made available to us extensive material he had compiled on the Indiana interurbans, and permitted us to use his data on these companies.

Other men who have been of particular assistance are Charles W. Hoke, President of Norwalk Truck Lines; Felix E. Reifschneider, who has long been active in electric railway historical circles; Professor J. W. Martin, Director of the University of Kentucky Bureau of Business Research; Professor R. W. Harbeson of the University of Illinois; Professor Robert L. Rivers of the University of Massachusetts; Professor Carl Shoup of Columbia University, whose father headed the Pacific Electric during its peak years; Robert E. Lee of the Detroit Historical Commission; Julian M. Bamberger of Salt Lake City; Professor Elvis L. Eckles of Alleghany College; Mr. Terence W. Cassady; and Mr. Philip T. Clark, Comptroller of Revenue of the Province of Ontario. A number of people provided information on individual interurbans, and we appreciate the courtesy of *Trains* magazine in making their library available to us. Several railroads, electric railways, bus lines, and power companies have provided information; these include the Western Pacific, the Southern Pacific, the Spokane Portland and Seattle, the Pennsylvania, the Illinois Terminal, the Altoona and Logan Valley, the Conestoga Transportation Company, the Chicago North Shore and Milwaukee, the Chicago South Shore and South Bend, the Salt Lake Garfield and Western, the Bamberger, the Detroit Toledo and Ironton, the Chesapeake and Ohio, the Soo Line, the Canadian Pacific, the Canadian National, the Ontario Northland, the Idaho Power Company, the Ohio Power Company, the Georgia Power Company, the Virginia Electric Power Company, the Central Louisiana Power Company. City librarians and secretaries of chambers of commerce in a number of communities were also of assistance.

The authors are grateful to Mrs. Linda Brownrigg of the Stanford University Press for her assistance.

Maps were drawn by Mr. James Bier of the Department of Geography of the University of Illinois.

Preface

Articles based in part on the material from which this book has been prepared have appeared in the *Bulletin of the Upper Canada Railway Society,* No. 50 (1958), and in the *Journal of Finance,* XIV (1959).

The study was facilitated by grants from the University Research Board of the University of Illinois and from the faculty research fund of the Department of Economics of Stanford University.

In a work of this character, it is all but impossible to avoid errors and imprecisions. Accordingly, the authors have arranged to publish factual errors brought to their attention in *Headlights,* which is the closest remaining approximation to a trade journal for the interurbans (see p. 436). The authors are indebted to the Electric Railroaders' Association, publishers of *Headlights,* and to its editor John Baxter for agreeing to this arrangement.

GEORGE W. HILTON
JOHN F. DUE

Stanford University
University of Illinois
January 1960

Preface to the Second Printing

The interurbans were so nearly extinct by 1960 that little need be said to bring our book up to date. Of the four lines that remained in 1960, only the South Shore Line and the Philadelphia Suburban Transportation Company survive; the Long Beach line of the old Pacific Electric was discontinued in 1961, and the North Shore Line was abandoned in 1963. The transfer of equipment between companies was not quite ended, for the Philadelphia Suburban Transportation Company bought the North Shore Line's Electroliners.

Beyond noting these developments, we have corrected the errors brought to our attention since the first printing appeared. We are grateful to readers who pointed out errors to us.

Finally, on p. 426 we have added histories of three small lines which we feel deserve inclusion.

G.W.H.
J.F.D.

University of California, Los Angeles
University of Illinois
May 1964

Contents

Part One: THE INDUSTRY

1	The Rise of the Industry	3
2	The Technology of the Interurbans	45
3	Passenger Traffic	91
4	Freight Traffic	119
5	The Interurbans and Government Regulation	149
6	Finance	183
7	The Decline of the Industry	208
8	The Decision to Abandon	240

Part Two: THE INDIVIDUAL INTERURBANS

Ohio	255	Nebraska	365
Indiana	275	Missouri, Kansas, and Oklahoma	365
Michigan	287	Texas	376
Kentucky	291	Colorado	380
Pennsylvania	293	Wyoming	383
Delaware	302	Utah	383
West Virginia	302	Idaho	387
New Jersey	306	Montana	388
New York	309	Arizona	389
New England	319	Washington	389
The Southern States	326	Oregon	394
Illinois	335	California	398
Wisconsin	353	Canada	413
Minnesota and the Dakotas	357	Three Late Discoveries	426
Iowa	359		

Principal Interurban Car Builders	424
Notes	427
Bibliographical Note	437
Index	439

Part I

THE INDUSTRY

I
The Rise of the Interurbans

IN THE FIRST decade of the twentieth century, America witnessed a great technological revolution, with the rapid development of the electric interurban railway, closely followed by the introduction of the first successful mass-produced automobile, Ford's model T. Both threatened the position of the railroad train as the principal means of passenger transportation; by 1960 the automobile was providing 90 per cent of intercity passenger miles, and had replaced the passenger train as the chief intercity vehicle. In the early days of the automobile's history, however, few people anticipated the turn that transportation history was to take; indeed, there have been few examples of such faulty prediction on the part of the capital market. When Henry Ford sought $100,000 to found the Ford Motor Company in 1903, he was able to raise only some $28,000 in cash;[1] and when W. C. Durant, founder of General Motors, told an investment banker in 1908 that eventually 500,000 automobiles per year would be produced, the banker had Durant shown out.[2] Owing to the inadequate prediction of the success of the automobile, men who joined the industry early and chose the right company made fortunes.

The great investment boom in this decade was not in automobile factories but in electric interurban railways. Although some interurban lines were built in the 1890's, and a few were opened as late as the 1920's, most were built in two great bursts, the first between 1901 and 1904 and the second between 1905 and 1908. The first was ended by the panic of 1903, and the second by the panic of 1907. There was a smaller revival of construction after 1908, but by 1912 the American interurban network on the whole had taken its final shape. A marked decline set in about 1918, and in the decade 1928–37 the industry was virtually annihilated. By 1960, no trace of it remained in its original form. A very small amount of the mileage remains in suburban passenger service, and a somewhat larger amount in freight service, integral with the steam railroad system, but fully 85 per cent of the peak interurban mileage is evidenced only by abandoned rights-of-way, decaying wayside structures, and terminals long since diverted to other uses.

Most of what can be said of the rise of the automobile industry is true in reverse of the interurbans. Those who had faith in them paid dearly. Few industries have arisen so rapidly or declined so quickly, and no industry of its size has had a worse financial record. The interurbans were a rare example of an industry that never enjoyed a period of prolonged prosperity; accordingly, they played out their life cycle in a shorter period than any other important American industry. The impersonal forces of the market reward those who predict accurately the future course of the public's tastes and penalize those who predict badly. Economic history, naturally, has concerned itself mainly with success, but the study of failure is no less illustrative of the processes of capitalism.

THE INCEPTION OF THE INTERURBANS

The building of the interurbans, which must be looked upon from the vantage point of history as unfortunate, occurred because the electric streetcar was developed to a high degree of technological perfection only a little more than a decade before the automobile. Like most technological advances, the streetcar was the product of many minds engaged in bringing together relevant knowledge and assembling it in some effective fashion. The electric motor had been in existence, at least in rudimentary form, as early as the 1830's; in 1835 the Vermont blacksmith Thomas Davenport exhibited an electrically propelled toy train in Boston and Springfield. In 1842, the Scottish engineer Robert Davidson operated an electric locomotive from a battery at four miles per hour on the railway between Edinburgh and Glasgow.[3] In 1851, a battery car built by Professor Charles G. Page of the Smithsonian Institution achieved a speed of nineteen miles per hour between Washington and Bladensburg, Maryland, before it failed. A series of improvements occurred beginning around 1845 that culminated in Pacinotti's development of the continuous-current dynamo in 1860, and in the announcement of the self-excitation of field magnets in 1866–67 by several independent inventors: Sir Charles Wheatstone, C. F. Varley, William Ladd, Werner von Siemens, and Moses Farmer. About 1870 Zenobe Gramme combined these developments into a commercially practical generator, and by 1872 the reversibility of motors and generators had been demonstrated. At the Berlin exhibition of 1879 Siemens operated a small electric locomotive by third rail on a track about a third of a mile long. Hauling twenty people on three small cars, the locomotive could reach speeds of about eight miles per hour.

Thus, by 1880 the basic technological knowledge for electric traction was available. For various reasons, the need to apply electric power to street railways became increasingly urgent in the 1880's. The horsecar remained the principal means of public street transportation, but its inadequacy was all but universally recognized.[4] Schedule speed was under six miles per hour, derailments were frequent, gradients were a serious problem, and operation in the snow was difficult. Horses cost from $125 to $200 each, and a transit company had to own some five to eight times as many horses as cars. Horses averaged only four or five hours of service per day, usually in teams, and consumed about 30 pounds of hay and grain daily. Hostlers, blacksmiths, and veterinarians had to be provided. The life expectancy of a horse in street railway service was particularly low; thus a horse sold for lighter duty after four or five years' experience was likely to fetch a very low price. Finally, the industry faced the constant danger that its horses would be decimated by disease. In 1872 the North American continent was ravaged by an epidemic of an equine respiratory disease called the Great Epizootic. In Philadelphia the Great Epizootic killed over 2,250 horses in a period of three weeks and in New York 18,000 horses were reported to be either dead or too ill for service. Fear that this disaster might recur was in the minds of street railway operators as they sought alternatives to the horsecar.

Until the coming of the electric streetcar, each alternative to the horsecar had serious disadvantages. Steam dummy engines, which were used to pull cars in some cities, were expensive and dirty, and frequently frightened horses. They were considered appropriate for suburban areas, but not for the hearts of cities. Trams operated by compressed air and internal-combustion engines were developed but never perfected. Battery cars suffered from a severe limitation of speed unless the battery was charged or replaced very frequently. Accordingly, battery cars proved moderately successful on crosstown lines on Manhattan Island, where they operated until 1933, but not elsewhere. By far the most successful replacement for the horsecar in the early 1880's was the cable car, developed by Andrew S. Hallidie in 1873 as a means of climbing the hills of San Francisco.[5] Cable lines were built in most major American cities in the 1880's; the largest system was in Chicago, where three companies owned 82 miles of track and 710 grip cars.[6] Cable railways entailed heavy initial expenditures and the underground construction tended to deteriorate quickly because of the heavy weight of the moving cable. An entire line was tied up when a cable broke; and when a grip became entangled with a loose strand of the cable, the car was often uncontrollable. But with all its disadvantages, the cable car was much superior to the horsecar on lines of heavy traffic density, particularly in hilly cities.

The two principal problems involved in developing an electric streetcar were designing motors that could withstand the shocks of ordinary travel, and discovering a way to transmit current from a central powerhouse to the cars. In the 1880's, several engineers addressed themselves to these tasks. Thomas A. Edison had built the first American dynamo-driven electric locomotive in 1880 at Menlo Park, New Jersey, but he made no effort to adapt it to economic use. In 1884 a former farmer, John C. Henry, strung a dual overhead wire over a horsecar track in Kansas City and installed an electric motor in a mule car. But Henry was unable to develop an adequate speed control for his car and fell into bankruptcy. In the same year, two former patent examiners, Bentley and Knight, built an unsuccessful line in Cleveland, using a conduit system to transmit power.

In 1883 experimental locomotives were exhibited independently by two inventors, Leo Daft at Greenville, New Jersey, and Charles J. Van Depoele at Chicago. Each of these men developed streetcars that were successful enough to be put into commercial use. Daft installed a 120-volt third-rail system about three miles long in Baltimore, drawing horse cars through the streets with small electric locomotives. The system failed, largely because of the hazard of an exposed third rail in the streets, but in

1885 Daft undertook a similar low-voltage third-rail electrification of the Ninth Avenue Elevated in New York. In 1887 and 1888 Daft installed several street railways of the same sort, this time with the power distributed by a dual overhead of the kind that was standard in most early electrifications. The cars picked up power with a small four-wheeled truck that rode on the overhead wires, dragged along by a flexible cable. This truck, called a troller—shortly corrupted into "trolley," a word that was to become the generic term for electric streetcars—was easily dislodged from the wires and was not easily replaced. Switching operations were very difficult, and in order to pass on a single-track line, cars had to exchange trollers at the siding. Daft installed car lines in Asbury Park, New Jersey, in several cities in Connecticut, and elsewhere.

In 1884 Van Depoele installed one of his cars, fed by a conduit system, at the Toronto Agricultural Fair. In 1885, at the same exhibition, Van Depoele operated a car from an overhead wire, using an under-running trolley wheel at the end of a weighted pole to make contact. Van Depoele's success at the Canadian expositions led to orders for his system at South Bend, Minneapolis, Windsor (Ontario), Appleton (Wisconsin), Port Huron, Lima, Scranton, Wheeling, Montgomery, and elsewhere. In the Montgomery installation, Van Depoele's largest, the cars carried front-mounted pole trolleys, although some of his earlier systems had used trollers similar to Daft's. Van Depoele's system used a voltage of about 1,400, and its motor was mounted on the front platform in the same housing as the control mechanism. Although the higher voltage gave Van Depoele an advantage over Daft, mounting the motor on the platform was unwise, since the frames of the wooden cars of the time were ill equipped to stand the weight. Thus, slack typically appeared in the chain drive mechanism as the car grew older, and failures from chain slippage became common. Van Depoele's motors and control mechanisms were crude, but his system was universally looked upon as promising.

It was neither from Daft's system nor from Van Depoele's that the streetcar and interurban sprang, but rather, from the work of a young naval officer, Frank J. Sprague. Sprague graduated from the United States Naval Academy in 1878 and spent five years in active naval duty, almost wholly engaged in electrical experimentation. Assigned to the Newport Torpedo Station in 1881, Sprague was associated with Professor Moses Farmer, himself a pioneer in development of a battery car. In 1882, while Sprague was on leave to visit the British Electrical Exhibition at Sydenham, England, his experiences on the coal-burning London Underground interested him in the possibilities of electric traction. Upon resigning from the Navy in 1883, Sprague became an assistant to Thomas A. Edison for work on electric lighting, but after less than a year left to found the Sprague Electric Railway and Motor Company. Sprague carried on experiments in New York, mainly with a view toward electrification of the elevated lines, but he failed to interest the management. In this period, however, he developed a reliable motor for direct current at about 500 volts, and designed a method of mounting it that resolved the dilemma faced by earlier designers: hitherto, the motor had been mounted either on the axle, where it suffered from shocks and jarring, or in some other fashion, so that gears or belts presented problems of a proper mesh. Sprague mounted his motor between the axle and a spring, wheelbarrow fashion, and secured a sure mesh by having his motor engage with a cogwheel on the axle. The spring permitted the motor to move in the same arc as the cogwheel and thus secured both minimization of shock and a sure engagement of the cogwheels. Sprague used an under-running pole trolley with a single overhead and rail return.

In May 1887, Sprague received an order for installation of his system on the Richmond Union Passenger Railway in Virginia. His firm was to build about 12 miles of track, a powerhouse, and 40 double-motored cars. The line included an 8 per cent grade and presented other formidable operating problems. Sprague's installation was a great success from its opening in 1888, and it attracted wide notice. After Henry M. Whitney adopted the Sprague system for his West End Railway of Boston, Sprague received an avalanche of orders; within three years 200 streetcar systems were built or ordered, about half built by Sprague himself and 90 per cent based on Sprague's patents. Few inventions have ever achieved a more rapid and complete acceptance. The superiority of the electric car to the horsecar was obvious from the outset, and by 1893 the cable car was demonstrably inferior except on very heavy grades. By 1902 97 per cent of street railway mileage was electrically operated; only twelve years earlier, 70 per cent of street railways had used animal power. In 1901 there were some 15,000 miles of electric railway in the United States.[7]

The remarkable success of the electric car in urban service inevitably led to its consideration for rural and intercity operation. For various reasons, extension of electric railways into rural areas appeared particularly attractive around the turn of the century. The American population was increasing at a rate of about a million and a third per year as a result of heavy immigration, greater life expectancy, and a relatively high birth rate. The period beginning about 1897 and extending through the First World War witnessed a generally rising price level and almost unparalleled agricultural prosperity. The great increase in farm incomes in this period was accompanied by an increase in literacy in rural areas, brought about by an improvement in educational facilities. The establishment of the Department of Agriculture in 1862, and the federal provision of the same year for aid in establishing land-grant agricultural colleges, resulted in wider dissemination of agricultural knowledge in the late nineteenth century than at any previous time. Commercial newspapers designed for farmers were expanding in circulation. The inauguration of rural free delivery of mail in 1896 contributed greatly to the general decline of the traditional isolation of the rural population.

A concomitant of the increase in incomes and literacy among farmers was a demand for greater mobility and more frequent access to towns and cities. All available transportation media were in some measure inadequate for this purpose. The horse-drawn buggy was limited in range to a few miles both by its speed over dirt roads and by the fatigue of the horse. At the opposite extreme, railroad trains typically stopped only in towns, often miles from a farmhouse. Local steamboats stopped virtually anywhere, but they were slow and could serve only areas close to navigable streams.

In New England, electric railways came to rural areas mainly by way of the extension of city streetcar systems along country roads. Usually there was little or no differentiation between urban and rural lines, since both typically shared the thoroughfare with horse-drawn vehicles. Equipment of the street railway sort was used, open cars in the summer and closed in the winter. Zone fare systems were all but universal, and running times in the country were only slightly better than in the city, usually not over 12 to 14 miles per hour.

In the rest of the United States, the electric railway came to the country in more substantial form. In cities and towns track was laid in the streets; in the rural areas it was laid either a few feet to the side of the highway or on a private right-of-way. Equipment was larger, heavier, and faster; closed equipment was used throughout the year. Tickets were sold at tariff rates and baggage was checked, as on the railroads. Speeds almost always exceeded 15 miles per hour. The two systems were at least as different as present-day extensions of city transit companies and intercity bus lines.

The intercity electric railways of the heavier sort were the interurbans; it is to them that this study is directed. The electric railways of the New England style have not customarily been considered interurbans, although usage on this point has never been unambiguous. The Bureau of the Census, which from 1902 collected data on electric railways at five-year intervals, at first classified as interurbans all electric lines providing intercity or rural services. Under this classification, the extensive network of electric lines built in Massachusetts in the 1890's and in the early years of the twentieth century was considered almost wholly interurban, even though its technology was essentially identical to that of street railways elsewhere. Because this initial taxonomy was clearly unrealistic, beginning in 1912 the Bureau of the Census let the reporting officer of each railway make his own classification of the property.[8] At the opposite extreme, Edward S. Mason has used the style of right-of-way for a criterion, and has defined as street railways all lines that used the public highway, even in rural areas. By this standard, only 9.2 per cent of the electric railway mileage in Massachusetts could be considered interurban.[9] There were many intermediate lines, particularly in Pennsylvania, that had elements of both the street railway and the interurban. Zone fares and off-the-road rights-of-way were equally characteristic of the Pennsylvania electric lines, but some used open cars and others did not.

The intercity electric lines actually formed a continuum from suburban operations of city systems to heavy electric railways that interchanged freight with steam railroads and differed from them only in type of motive power. Since some definition is necessary, the term interurban may be applied to railways that shared most or all of the four following characteristics: electric power, primary emphasis on passenger service, equipment that was heavier and faster than city streetcars, and operation on streets in cities but at the sides of highways or on private rights-of-way in rural areas.

The fact that a rigorous definition of an interurban is impossible makes it difficult to identify the first. Probably the earliest line having the interurbans' general characteristics was the Giant's Causeway Electric Tramway, installed by the Siemens brothers between Portrush and the Giant's Causeway in Ireland in 1883. It was about seven miles long, built in the streets in Portrush, but at the side of the highway elsewhere. The gauge was 3'-0"—the standard in County Antrim—and power was distributed by means of an elevated third rail at 250 volts. Speeds of ten miles per hour were reached.[10] In Canada, Van Depoele's installation on the St. Catharines Street Railway in 1887 included an extension to Thorold, Ontario, probably the first intercity electric line of importance in North America.

The first American line to become part of the general network of interurbans was an Ohio road, the Newark and Granville Street Railway. This company considered building a conduit system, but installed an orthodox overhead instead. The first car ran on December 28, 1889, and operation with a full set of equipment began on September 1, 1890.[11] It was a small line, beset with technological problems (especially of speed control), and it was not particularly profitable. Accordingly, it attracted little notice. In 1891, as part of a real estate promotion in the state of Washington, an 11-mile line, the Fidalgo City and Anacortes Railway, was built. This road, running by the shore of Puget Sound, was even more obscure. In 1892 Canton and Massillon, Ohio, were connected by an interurban.

Two lines of greater importance were built in 1893, one in Oregon and the other in Ohio. In February, the East Side Railway Company began service between Portland and Oregon City.[12] This line proved quite successful in the long run; it is the only one of the early interurbans still extant as a freight carrier. The road in Ohio, the Sandusky Milan and Norwalk Electric Railway, opened its 19.5 miles of line between July and December.[13] Of all the early lines, this was the most important to the development of the industry, if only for its location. Ohio, apart from its southeastern quarter, is an area of many medium-sized towns at no great distance from one another. The rural area is fairly densely populated, and farm income relatively high. Much of the terrain is flat, and there are few impediments to railway construction. In the 1890's local railroad service in the Midwest was generally inferior to that of the New England railroads. For these reasons Ohio and central Indiana (which shared Ohio's characteristics) were the most promising areas for development of intercity electric lines.

The financial history of the early interurbans gave little cause for optimism. The Fidalgo City and Anacortes failed with its real estate development and was abandoned in 1893. The Oregon City line had fallen into receivership before it completed a year of operation. The Sandusky–Norwalk road went bankrupt during construction, but afterward proved moderately profitable and paid a 3 per cent dividend in 1895. Equipment on the early lines depreciated quickly, and maintenance expenditures were large because the electric car was still highly imperfect. Breakdowns were frequent, and means of transmitting power over long distances were still to be found.

The great proliferation of street railways in this period stimulated engineering development, and the electric car was steadily improved as the 1890's wore on. The Sandusky Milan and Norwalk used Westinghouse equipment and was considered relatively advanced. In 1893, General Electric introduced a speed control much superior to any of its predecessors—the type-K controller. The development of the substation in 1897 made possible fairly satisfactory power transmission for considerable distances.

The interurban received its greatest early impetus in 1895, when Henry A. Everett and Edward W. Moore built the Akron Bedford and Cleveland Railroad. It served a populous area, and was built, by the standards of the time, to heavy and substantial specifications. The line proved profitable. In 1896 it earned $16,030 and in 1897, $8,987.[14] Everett and Moore were well-known figures in the local public utility industries; they were engaged in promoting several local telephone systems in Ohio, and were jointly and individually interested in a large number of street railways. Everett had invested in Canadian streetcar systems in Winnipeg, London, Toronto, and Montreal; and Moore, who was cashier of the Dime Savings Bank of Cleveland, controlled systems in Wheeling and Syracuse. They had joint interests in city lines in Detroit, Toledo, Akron, Sandusky, and Cleveland.

Together with several of the directors and officers of the Cleveland Electric Railway Company, Everett and Moore formed a syndicate that was active for about a decade in building and operating interurbans. By the turn of the century, they were operating over 500 miles of electric line, and were building or planning over 500 more.[15] Their Cleveland Painesville and Eastern paralleled Lake Erie eastward to Painesville, and they had plans for an extension to Ashtabula. They were interested in two closely related lines that served what is now the Cleveland east suburban area: the Cleveland and Eastern and the Cleveland and Chagrin Falls. Their Northern Ohio Traction Company, successor to the Akron Bedford and Cleveland, was building south to Canton and Massillon, and plans were made for an extension to connect with Moore's city system in Wheeling. West of Cleveland, they controlled the Lorain and Cleveland Railway, the Sandusky and Interurban, which ran between Sandusky and Huron, and the Toledo Fremont and Norwalk Street Railroad. In the summer of 1901, they amalgamated these lines into the Lake Shore Electric Railway, which connected the trackage and opened through service from Cleveland to Toledo in December. The Lake Shore Electric also acquired the pioneer Sandusky Milan and Norwalk. In January 1901, Moore had said that the syndicate intended to control every paying interurban in northern Ohio.[16]

In Michigan Everett and Moore engaged in similar consolidation to form the Detroit United Railway, and by 1901 they were operating interurbans to Port Huron, Pontiac, and Flint.[17] In Canada, the Detroit United controlled the Sandwich Windsor and Amherstburg Railway, which provided city and suburban service in the Windsor area. Everett and Moore sought to connect their Ohio and Michigan properties with the Detroit and Toledo Shore Line, and they also controlled the Toledo and Monroe Railway, which had been begun as a rival Detroit–Toledo connection. By 1902 Everett and Moore were also building the Scioto Valley Traction Company southward from Columbus and the Cleveland Painesville and Ashtabula east from Painesville. Elsewhere, the syndicate was interested in the Illinois Central Traction Company, the Aurora Elgin and Chicago, the Washington and Baltimore, and several other properties. On January 1, 1902, the syndicate was said to have had 1,500 miles of electric railway in service with several hundred miles more under construction. Their telephone properties included over thirty exchanges in Ohio and Michigan and an independent long-distance network of 9,000 miles.[18]

The reported earnings of some of the Everett-Moore properties around the turn of the century were, at least superficially, very impressive. The Detroit United in 1900 reported gross receipts from city and interurban passenger service of $2,351,317, and carried $519,751 into net income. In the same year, the Northern Ohio Traction Company earned a net income of $39,508 on gross receipts of $425,887.[19] In 1901 the Northern Ohio grossed $617,011, and reported a net of $80,004.[20] In November 1901, the *Street Railway Journal* reported that the Lake Shore and Michigan Southern, a major railroad controlled by the New York Central, was capitalized at $75,000 per mile and was grossing $1,600 per mile, but that the Toledo Fremont and Norwalk interurban, which paralleled it, was capitalized at $45,000 per mile and was grossing $3,800.[21] A year later, the Detroit United interurban lines were said to be capitalized at about $40,000 per mile—a figure widely claimed to be typical of the Midwestern interurbans—and to be grossing around $3,500.[22] The Everett-Moore properties as a whole were said to be capitalized at $47 million and to have netted $5.5 million in 1900.[23]

To a considerable extent, it was the favorable earnings of the Everett-Moore properties in this period that engendered the great booms in interurban building between 1900 and 1908. Many projects conceived in the 1890's could not be executed until the period of ease in the money market that began about the turn of the century. It is tempting to argue that all this investment was misguided, but, in the light of the expectations of the time, this is not an entirely fair and accurate interpretation. Certainly, the earnings of the interurbans about 1900 and 1901 were greatly overstated in their reports. The *Street Railway Journal*, a spokesman for moderation and restraint throughout the years of interurban building, pointed out that the earnings data of the time typically made little or no allowance for depreciation. The *Journal* argued that 10 to 20 per cent of the gross receipts should be earmarked for depreciation. Moreover, because the equipment was new, repairs and other maintenance costs were abnormally low in this period.[24]

The fact remains, however, that the actual earnings at least of the major interurbans about 1901 were great enough to attract investment rationally into the industry. There was reason to expect a secular increase in traffic as a result of population growth. The automobile was in its infancy, and not even Ford and Durant predicted accurately its enormous development. The network of hard-surfaced highways that was to be built in the 1920's had not even been conceived. To the vast majority of investors in 1902, the Lake Shore Electric looked infinitely more attractive than the motor company Henry Ford was trying to promote. And yet, even though the interurbans built to connect major cities or to tap rural areas of considerable population density were not, in light of the expectations of the time, irrationally conceived, their construction was accompanied by an outpouring of optimism and a rash of ill-considered projects that, in retrospect, can only be called one of the classic manias. As the *Street Railway Journal* noted:

the very fact that the greater part of the interurban roads which have been built have shown an excellent profit has led to the impression, more or less widely diffused, that all roads of this kind are Golcondas, which need only to be built to turn into the pockets of their promoters and stockholders inexhaustible streams of wealth. Nothing is further from the truth.[25]

It was in Ohio that the largest number of projects were conceived and the greatest mileage actually laid. In addition, the early financial history of the Ohio lines largely determined the pattern of ownership of the major Midwestern interurbans for virtually their entire life cycle. Finally, in so far as the interurbans engaged in concerted action of any sort, it was almost wholly carried on by the lines in Ohio and its neighboring states, Indiana and Michigan. For all these reasons, we shall be concerned in this chapter primarily with the Ohio lines.

The Secretary of State of Ohio reported that 144 electric railway companies had been chartered between November 1898 and July 1901, about half of which were probably interurbans. Interurban trackage comprised about 54 per cent of all electric railway track built in Ohio during the building booms.[26] About 92 interurban projects were incorporated in Ohio in 1901, 47 in 1902, and 46 in 1903.[27] The number of projects conceived but never brought as far as incorporation cannot even be estimated. If all the incorporated projects had been executed—to say nothing of the rest—the interurban trackage would have rivaled the 9,000 miles of railroad in Ohio. It is safe to say that there was no route between points of any considerable population that was not projected—and frequently several times over.

At least eleven interurban companies proposed to build into Tiffin, although only one, the Tiffin Fostoria and Eastern, ever did so. No fewer than three companies, none of which ever built track, were reported in 1901 to be grading rights-of-way from Tiffin to Port Clinton, and another was said to be grading from Tiffin to Sandusky.[28] Other companies subsequently considered building on the same route. At least four firms proposed to build from Coshocton to Newark or Zanesville, but none did so.

The promoters of the interurbans ranged from relatively well financed syndicates to local businessmen with no real prospect of raising enough funds to build. The most important rival to the Everett-Moore interests was a syndicate led by F. J. Pomeroy and M. J. Mandelbaum. By 1901 their principal early property, the Cleveland Elyria and Western Railway, was operating west from Cleveland to Elyria, Oberlin, and Wellington, and building toward Norwalk. In January 1903, it absorbed the Cleveland and Southern, another Pomeroy-Mandelbaum line, which was operating from Cleveland to Berea and building south to Seville and Wooster.[29] At the same time, the property changed its name to the Cleveland and Southwestern Traction Company. The Pomeroy-Mandelbaum syndicate simultaneously promoted the Western Ohio Railway, which was building from Piqua north to Findlay via Lima and Wapakoneta. The syndicate hoped to connect the Cleveland and Southwestern with the Western Ohio, but was never able to do so. It also hoped to join the Southwestern with the independent Columbus Delaware and Marion, which reached Marion from the south in 1903. Five years elapsed before a connection was made at Bucyrus. Pomeroy and Mandelbaum also controlled the Cincinnati Dayton and Toledo Traction Company, a line between Cincinnati and Dayton that the syndicate hoped to link with the Western Ohio as part of a through route to Toledo. The syndicate operated several minor properties, and promoted one particularly unfortunate project, an electric railway built on the towpath of the Miami and Erie Canal for towing barges between Cincinnati and Dayton.

The third major builder of interurbans in Ohio was Arthur E. Appleyard, of Boston, who promoted a system centering around Columbus. Appleyard was principally interested in an east-west line between Dayton and Zanesville. His Dayton Springfield and Urbana Railway was completed in 1899 and his Columbus London and Springfield in 1902. East of Columbus, his Columbus Buckeye Lake and Newark Traction Company reached Newark in 1902, and its affiliate, the Columbus Newark and Zanesville Electric Railway, reached Zanesville in 1904. Appleyard also acquired a narrow-gauge steam line between Zanesville and Wheeling—the Ohio River & Western—which he proposed to electrify.

The three major syndicates were never distinct. Membership in the boards of directors of individual roads varied, and there was occasional overlapping between syndicates. Men identified with both the Pomeroy-Mandelbaum and Everett-Moore organizations, for example, were interested in the Aurora Elgin and Chicago.

Some of the independent lines were financed by wealthy local businessmen and were completed without difficulty. The Toledo Port Clinton and Lakeside, a relatively strong interurban, was financed by Toledo businessmen, and in New York the lines on both sides of Chautauqua Lake were financed by the prosperous Broadhead family of Jamestown. The prospect of frequent, low-cost transportation was so attractive to residents of small towns that there were innumerable local projects to build interurbans. As one writer has described it: "It is impossible for anyone who was not living in the rural community where there was no thought or knowledge of automobiles, but where the community had the possibility of getting an electric line, to realize the vision which such a possibility encouraged."[30] Residents of the little town of Bono (1910 population: 160) proposed to buy four cars and to build the Toledo and Eastern Railway in order to provide access to Toledo, 13 miles away. Most such projects were stillborn (this was true of the Toledo and Eastern), but some were executed, usually with disastrous consequences. Local lines that served no large communities proved the weakest firms in a weak industry, and were the most quickly destroyed by adverse circumstances. The best example of such a line is the Lake Erie Bowling Green and Napoleon, built mainly to provide Bowling Green (1910 population: 5,222) with a connection to Cleveland via the Lake Shore Electric. This company, whose history appears in Part II, survived only until 1916 and was such a total failure that even the optimists in the industry agreed it should never have been built.

Some promoters made serious efforts to predict the expected level of traffic, but the profusion of projects indicates that there was little genuine research on the actual prospects of the lines. Even the most crude estimates of prospective traffic would have indicated that projects such as the Lake Erie Bowling Green and Napoleon and the Sandusky Norwalk and Mansfield were hopeless. Ernest Gonzenbach, a writer who counseled conservatism in promotion and high standards in construction, proposed that the population considered tributary to an interurban be limited to people living within two and a half to three miles from the track. If only one terminus of a line was to be a major city, its population, Gonzenbach thought, should not be considered as part of the traffic potential.[31]

Riding habits varied from one area to another, and a promoter might anticipate receipts anywhere from about five dollars to more than nine dollars a year per person from his tributary area. Traffic could be predicted by analogy to interurbans serving similar territories, and by observation of the railroad the interurban was to parallel. (There were few interurbans—usually the weaker ones—that did not parallel railroad tracks.) W. C. Gotshall, a well-known railway engineer and writer recommended a simple device for sampling railroad traffic: the promoter should buy a ticket from the railroad station in every town on his proposed line to every other town on the line. He should repeat the process at ten-day intervals for a few months, and then, by comparing serial numbers on the tickets, he would have a sample of travel between all the towns he proposed to serve.[32] The railroads were aware that promoters used this system, but any deviation from selling tickets in numerical order caused difficulties in their own accounting processes. Dr. Thomas Conway, Jr., a lifelong student of the industry, felt that this sampling method and the informal analogies to railroad traffic caused interurban promoters to overestimate their prospective returns from long-distance traffic. Virtually no interurban promoter was discouraged by the adequacy of competing railroad service; the Kansas City Clay County and St. Joseph was built even though six railroads operated passenger trains between the termini. Ten efforts to promote a line between Kansas City and St. Joseph had failed before this road was opened.

An interurban promoter could reasonably expect to attract about 75 per cent of the local traffic from a parallel railroad line, and to generate a considerable amount of additional short-haul traffic. The interurban between Detroit and Ann Arbor carried well over ten times as much traffic as the Michigan Central had formerly handled, but because of the growth of the University of Michigan at Ann Arbor, this line's experience was a special case.[33] The Monon reported that its local business on one line declined 78 per cent in the first year an interurban operated parallel to it. Between 1895 and 1902, owing to the opening of interurbans, traffic on the Lake Shore & Michigan Southern between Cleveland and Painesville fell from 199,292 passengers per year to 28,708, and on the Nickel Plate between Cleveland and Lorain from 42,526 to 9,795. Interurbans had greatest success in attracting traffic from towns ten to forty miles from a major city; they offered service at two-thirds the speed of the railroads, but with at least four to six times the frequency, and at half to two-thirds the fare. Some interurbans with high-speed rights-of-way or exceptionally high frequency were able to attract as much as 95 per cent of the local traffic.[34] The mere fact of this success was enough to stimulate a great deal of uncritical promotion of interurbans. There was little explicit recognition among the interurbans that the industry was attracting the railroads' least profitable passenger traffic, but the fact was not lost on the railroads: an anonymous official of the Lake Shore & Michigan Southern pointed out that the traffic being lost to the electric lines was barely profitable at best.[35] This realization, however, did little to mollify the hostility with which the railroads viewed the spread of the interurbans.

BUILDING THE INTERURBANS

The first step in promoting an interurban was to amass enough initial capital to demonstrate substantiality to the Secretary of State, who was responsible for issuing charters. A few interurbans, notably the Lackawanna and Wyoming Valley in Pennsylvania, were organized under the statutes for incorporation of railroads. The Lackawanna and Wyoming Valley planned to use private rights-of-way in cities, and therefore wanted the power to condemn urban land, which incorporation as a railroad would give it. For most interurbans, urban condemnations would have been unthinkably expensive, and thus most were incorporated under the statutes regulating the organization of street railways. Accordingly, the promoters' next step was to secure franchises for operation in the streets of towns along their route.

Given the strong local pressure for the building of interurbans, the promoters usually had little difficulty securing the right to lay track in the main streets of small towns. To be sure, sometimes there was organized opposition, usually led by local merchants in dry goods, clothing, and other nonperishable items, who feared they would lose trade to stores in larger towns as mobility of the population increased. Oberlin merchants published handbills opposing entry of the interurban from Cleveland, but on the whole little came of this sort of resistance. In contrast, dealers in perishables were typically enthusiastic at the entry of an interurban; and to hardware merchants the prospect made little difference.

Some municipal governments were hostile, particularly in Massachusetts. Lenox and Stockbridge both refused to permit the Berkshire Street Railway to build in their main streets. Massachusetts enacted a statute known to the trade as "the missing link law," empowering state authorities to grant a franchise to build in the streets of a town if the electric railway had secured franchises in its terminal cities and in all other intermediate towns. In connection with a proposed branch, the Boston and Worcester Street Railway threatened to invoke this law at Weston, which had blocked efforts of all street railways to build in its streets.[36] The Columbus London and Springfield in Ohio avoided franchise problems by running past the outskirts of several towns.

The Midwestern lines rarely encountered outright refusal to permit interurbans in the streets, but frequently promoters were presented with terms they considered to be quite unfavorable. The terms agreed upon depended mainly on the alternatives open to each party. A promoter fared best when the existing transportation was inadequate and when no other interurban was being projected. Under such circumstances, he could expect lenient franchise terms and might even secure a subsidy. The village of Almont, Michigan, is a case in point. Although Almont is only 43 miles north of Detroit, its railroad line, a branch of the Pere Marquette, ran due east to Port Huron, and the town had no direct route south. Residents were so eager for the Detroit United to build north nine miles from Romeo that in 1904 they were reported to have raised $10,000 as a subsidy. The line was built, but not until 1915.

It was common for residents of towns, including municipal officials, to buy bonds in a proposed interurban—a practice that proved to be more in the nature of a subsidy than they anticipated. There were some examples of outright municipal subsidies and municipal guarantee of bonds. Such arrangements were more common in Canada than in the United States; many Ontario electric lines were aided in this fashion. In 1910 the Arkansas Valley Interurban demanded a subsidy of $100,000 to build a branch into Newton, Kansas. When Newton businessmen were unable to raise the amount, the city government, after a referendum, agreed to contribute to it. The branch was then quickly built.[37] The town of Chrisney, Indiana, offered the Evansville and Eastern a subsidy of $20,000, a free right-of-way, and free grading in return for building a branch into the community. Hammond township voted a subsidy of $14,000 if the branch would be extended north to Jasper or Huntingburg, but the line was never built.

In contrast, a promoter was likely to be faced with difficult terms if he was contesting with a rival for a given route. A great favorite among promoters was a line from Toledo to Napoleon and Defiance, Ohio, along the Wabash Railroad and the Maumee River. Twelve projects to build between these points are known to have been incorporated, or at least to have progressed far enough to be mentioned in the trade journals. There is no reason to believe that there were not others. The two principal early projects, the Toledo Napoleon and Defiance Railroad and the Toledo Waterville and Southern Railway, were both incorporated January 21, 1901, and immediately engaged in heated rivalry for franchises. One of them was so eager to get a franchise that it was reported to have agreed to carry local traffic free within one town. Each company secured about half the needed franchises, but they never came to agreement with one another and neither line was built. The Toledo Waterville and Southern opened six miles of interurban between Maumee and Waterville, which was in operation until 1913, but otherwise none of the companies that proposed to build along the Toledo–Defiance route ever put track in service. Several later companies graded short distances.

When the Columbus Delaware and Marion and the Columbus Delaware and Northern were trying to build between Columbus and Marion, the former gained control of the Worthington Clintonville and Columbus, which had an entry into the capital; however, the CD&N took control of the local franchise holder in Delaware, the principal intermediate town. This conflict, like most, ended when the stronger company, in this instance the Columbus Delaware and Marion, bought out its rival. Even some of the least successful properties had substantial competition during construction; the Lake Erie Bowling Green and Napoleon had to compete for franchises with the Lakeside Napoleon and Western. In only one major instance, the route between Dayton and Xenia, were two projects built simultaneously, side by side.

The length and content of franchises were considerations of some importance to interurban promoters. Although in retrospect it seems strange that enterprises lasting an average of only about thirty years should have been concerned about the length of their franchises, interurbans that secured long franchises for street running were looked upon more favorably in the capital market, and were thus able to finance construction more easily. Perpetual franchises were, of course, most attractive, and some interurbans secured perpetuity for almost all their street running. The Toledo and Indiana had perpetual franchises throughout, except for a single highway crossing. Most interurbans received franchises of 25 or 50 years, but a few received longer ones. The Western Ohio, the Sandusky Norwalk and Mansfield, and the Lima and Toledo were all built with 25-year franchises, the Indianapolis Crawfordsville and Western 50 years, and the Indianapolis and Northwestern with various periods from 31 to 50 years. Twenty-five-year franchises, which were the most common, proved also to be the most undesirable, for they terminated by chance in the period when the interurbans were declining most rapidly. The decade 1925-35, therefore, saw many interurbans involved in disputes with municipalities concerning franchise extensions, just at the time when the industry was dying from highway competition.

Certain franchise provisions were quite standard, especially maintenance of the pavement between the rails and for a certain distance, usually two feet, on either side. At first, many interurbans were irritated at having to pave the center of a street otherwise unimproved, but eventually most found themselves operating in entirely paved streets. Towns that had paved their main streets before the interurbans arrived were reluctant to let them tear up pavement to lay track. In 1906 the town council of Celina, Ohio, announced that it was willing to give the Muncie and Portland Traction Company a franchise, but not for the main street, which it had recently paved. Maintenance of track in the streets was to become the greatest source of controversy between the interurbans and municipalities; as early as 1905 the village of Milford, Ohio, initiated legal action to oust the Cincinnati Milford and Loveland from its streets for failure to maintain the pavement.

A typical franchise was granted by the town of Defiance to the Toledo and Defiance Railway, one of later lines to make an unsuccessful attempt to build along the Maumee River. The company was to be permitted to run in the streets for 25 years under electric power. It might move railroad freight cars in the streets only between 9:00 P.M. and 5:00 A.M. Local passengers were to be carried for a cash fare of 5 cents or at six fares for 25 cents. The company was to furnish a bond of $10,000 for failure to build to Defiance and to operate under terms of the franchise.

Limitations on length of trains and prohibitions on certain types of freight, livestock in particular, were common. The Milwaukee Northern had to sprinkle streets on its long entry into Milwaukee, and several lines obligated themselves to provide street lighting in small towns. In order to secure permission to build in Bellefontaine in 1908, the Ohio Electric had to pay $5,000, widen and lengthen several streets, and build a spur to the local waterworks. The city of Kalamazoo, Michigan, endeavored to charge the Kalamazoo Lake Shore and Chicago Traction Company $1,000 a year for the right to a mile of street running, but the company refused and the track was never laid. Many of the abortive projects ended with similar failures to secure a crucial franchise. Another typical feature was that franchises lapsed if the interurban were not put in service by a specified date, often December 31 of the following calendar year; innumerable projects failed to be completed—or even begun—within the time allotted. The interurbans' franchise problems were anything but unique; in this same period, telephone companies, gas and electric systems, and other public utilities were engaged in similar controversies with municipalities.

With franchises in hand, a promoter proceeded to raise funds for construction and to arrange for his rural right-of-way. Interurbans were characteristically financed by the sale of mortgage bonds to the public, usually at 5 per cent interest. Stock was issued, but all too often it was given away to bondholders as an additional inducement to invest. Similar arrangements had been very common in railroad finance in the nineteenth century, but little can be said in defense of the practice. As a consequence, the interurbans were saddled with heavy fixed charges that threatened them with bankruptcy should there be even minor declines in traffic; and the identity of the bondholders and stockholders offered little incentive to try to avoid reorganization. The initial capital structures of the interurbans were inflated by the arbitrary and excessive values assigned to the stock; the typical capitalization per mile of the Ohio-Indiana lines was considerably in excess of the average cost per mile of building the interurbans. Watered stock was by no means unusual in the United States at that time, but in the case of the interurbans, the anticipated increases in earnings never materialized to make good the expectations of the issuers of the stock.

Everett, Moore, Pomeroy, and Mandelbaum operated primarily in the Cleveland money market; Appleyard operated in Boston. Chauncey Eldridge and C. L. Saltonstall of Boston and Jay Cooke III of Philadelphia participated in the Everett-Moore financing. Surprisingly little interurban finance was carried on in the New York money market. Many major investment bankers looked upon the interurbans as highly speculative, and many were closely affiliated with the railroads, which looked upon the spreading interurban lines with unconcealed malevolence. The *Wall Street Journal* paid little attention to the investment boom in the interurbans, but continued to devote most of its space to railroad finance. Particularly after the panic of 1903, the Philadelphia money market became important in financing the interurbans. Financing was generally done through lesser brokerage houses—firms that dealt heavily in speculative enterprises. The smaller lines were financed mainly by security sales in their home areas, but securities of the larger companies were widely held. Only a very few companies — notably the important Portland-Lewiston Interurban in Maine and the hapless St. Joseph Valley Railway in Indiana—were financed without public sale of securities. Some savings banks and other financial institutions, particularly those that had direct connections with the promoters, invested in interurban bonds, frequently with dire consequences. Hardly any identifiable class of securities had a worse record than bonds and stocks of newly built interurban lines.

The interurbans adopted various methods for acquiring rights-of-way in rural areas. Simplest and cheapest was to secure permission from the county road authorities to operate on part of the highway right-of-way. By building on the highway itself, as the New England lines did, a road might be built for as little as $10,000 per mile, but the resulting physical plant was of the least satisfactory sort. In the Midwest there was usually room at the side of the highway for a single track. The Lake Shore Electric built about a third of its original right-of-way on a strip ten feet wide at the side of the Perrysburg turnpike secured from the county highway authorities.[38] The Marion County Commissioners in 1906 granted the Findlay Forest and Marion Railway a franchise to build along the Garden City Pike on a strip of 13.5 feet. The promoters considered this right-of-way adequate, but for other reasons the interurban was never built.

Apart from the operating problems entailed by a right-of-way on or adjacent to a highway, building on public property generally involved further dependence on a franchise. Having rural mileage at the mercy of the public authorities after 25 years was a much more serious prospect than merely risking an entry into a town. At worst, an interurban could relocate around a town, as the Dayton and Western did at New Lebanon, Ohio, in 1923 after a franchise dispute, but relocation of long stretches of rural track was likely to be prohibitively expensive. Consequently, promoters generally preferred to acquire their rights-of-way privately, if they possibly could. Fortunately, most farmers were so eager to have local transportation virtually to their doors that they were usually cooperative. Many farmers gave land (or sold it for one dollar) in return for a promise that cars would stop nearby, and for an agreement that the property would revert to them in the event of abandonment. An interurban promoter could argue quite truthfully that the proximity of an interurban would increase the worth of a farm by much more than the value of a marginal strip of land of ten or twenty feet. E. L. Bogart estimated that an adjacent interurban raised land values by 20 to 50 per cent at the height of the building boom, but some of the extreme enthusiasts for interurban building promised a doubling of farm values.[39] Some farmers were paid in cash for land, others accepted bonds of the interurban in payment, and many farmers were induced to put their own savings into the securities of the companies. Farmers along the proposed right-of-way of the Indianapolis Martinsville and Southern Railroad, which was never built, subscribed $50,000 in tickets for future transportation.[40]

It was rarely possible to make amicable arrangements with every farmer along a projected route of any length, and so, rather as a last resort, the interurbans turned to condemnation proceedings. The Lafayette and Indianapolis Rapid Transit Company, a line that was never constructed, instituted 105 condemnation actions in an effort to secure a right of way of some 65 miles, but most interurbans used condemnation more sparingly.[41] Because the interurbans usually did not condemn urban land, and because they acquired most of their rural land cheaply or free, they needed far less investment to begin construction than most of the railroads. Railroad officials knew this very well, and it irritated them no less than the alleged subsidies of trucks and buses from highway appropriations in later decades.

The building of an interurban was almost always carried on by a contracting company. Most of these companies were organized by the promoters of the interurbans themselves, but there were several firms, such as Tucker, Anthony and Co., that specialized in interurban building for promoters. A. E. Appleyard usually organized his own contracting companies. The Toledo Port Clinton and Lakeside was built by the Toledo Interurban Construction Company, organized by the officers of the interurban, and the Springfield Construction Company was organized in similar fashion to build the Springfield Washington Court House and Chillicothe Traction Company. Such companies generally employed subcontractors. The Patrick Hirsch Construction Company, which built the Toledo and Indiana and the stillborn Toledo Ann Arbor and Detroit, subcontracted for the latter to the Fidelity Construction Company. Will and James Christy, Jr., were the principal builders of Ohio interurbans. The Newark and Granville and much of the later mileage in Ohio was built by their Cleveland Construction Company. The Christy brothers also participated in the ownership and operation of interurbans, mainly in connection with the major syndicates. The Electrical Installation Company of Chicago was known for its work in building power systems, as was another Chicago firm, the Arnold Electric Power Station Company, run by the well-known electrical engineer Bion J. Arnold. The J. G. White Engineering Company of New York built several properties, including the Oakland Antioch and Eastern in California. Tucker, Anthony and Co. was a major builder of electric lines in New England. To some extent, participation of the major contractors in interurban management was involuntary; if an interurban failed about the time of completion, as many did; the contractor was one of the principal creditors when the property went into reorganization. Some subcontractors, to avoid this situation, accepted payment in the bonds of the interurban. In a famous incident, described in Part II,[42] the Electrical Installation Company forced the Winona Interurban to operate on Sundays (despite the sabbatarian belief of its fundamentalist founders and directors) in order to preserve it from bankruptcy.

Construction techniques were orthodox. Grading was most often done by gangs of men with teams of horses or mules using slip scrapers, but steam shovels were employed for heavy construction work. When track had been laid, it was customary to use small steam locomotives for construction work until wire was strung and the powerhouse completed. Interurban building constituted a modest market for second-hand steam locomotives, chiefly six-wheel switchers and Americans. Many of the construction gangs, as well as some of the contractors, had been engaged in railroad building in the 1880's and 1890's. Mrs. W. M. Smith, a subcontractor who built much of the Salt Lake and Utah, had previously built track for the Western Pacific, Union Pacific, and Southern Pacific, and many in her crew had had similar experience. Mrs. Smith was reported to be the only female contractor in the industry.

Speed of construction varied with the difficulty of the terrain and the heaviness of the grading. Building along the side of the road following the highway grade was not difficult, but building private right-of-way involved establishing a new drainage pattern, and thus entailed a considerable amount of earth-moving. Interurbans were not built with spectacular speed. In particular, installation of the overhead was slow work, for poor alignment resulted in dewirements and poor insulation in power leakage. The Dayton and Xenia Traction Company's main line, 16 miles long, was built between July 17, 1899, and January 8, 1900, including the electrical installation. The track was laid by the Worcester Construction Company of Massachusetts, and the electrical equipment was installed by the Creaghead Engineering Company of Cincinnati. Similar division of earthwork and electrical equipment among subcontractors was common. Six months for a project of this size was considered relatively good time. Similarly, the section of the main line of the Fort Wayne and Wabash Valley between Logansport and Lafayette (38 miles) was begun June 14, 1906, and put into service June 28, 1907.

So many interurbans encountered shortages of funds, lawsuits, or franchise disputes during construction that average rates of progress are not particularly meaningful. The Toledo Port Clinton and Lakeside, a line that faced no unusual financial problems during its building, was begun at Genoa in April 1903, and by the summer of 1904 had reached Oak Harbor, a distance of 23 miles. The promoters had secured the right to use steam locomotives in construction work for two years, but property owners in Oak Harbor secured an injunction against the use of a locomotive in the streets. The company managed to win the controversy, but its entry into Port Clinton was delayed. Also, of course, delays were caused by the fact that construction on many projects had to be suspended in the winter months.

It was in the construction stage that the interurbans encountered the first major manifestations of the railroads' hostility. Unfortunately for the industry, the two most hostile major railroads were the largest, the Pennsylvania and the New York Central. Both regularly resorted to injunctions to prevent interurbans from crossing their tracks. The Pennsylvania used an injunction to delay completion of the Lake Erie Bowling Green and Napoleon into Woodville for about a year, and the New Paltz Highland and Poughkeepsie Traction Company in New York never did receive permission to cross the New York Central at Highland. The New Paltz line throughout its history operated with an isolated shuttle service in the streets of Highland, separated from the main line by the New York Central's West Shore tracks. The Pennsylvania delayed a crossing by the

Philadelphia and Bristol Passenger Railway long enough to bankrupt the company.

Outright violence between interurban employees and railroad men was not uncommon. When the Ohio Central Traction Company reached Crestline, a fist fight broke out between its construction gang and men of the Pennsylvania and New York Central. When the Petaluma and Santa Rosa approached Santa Rosa, the California Northwestern (a predecessor of the Northwestern Pacific) opposed its entry. Ninety-two local merchants threatened to boycott the railroad unless it permitted the electric line to cross its tracks, but the railroad remained adamant, to the point of spraying the construction crew of the interurban with live steam from two of its locomotives when the crew attempted a crossing. The Petaluma and Santa Rosa managed to move a car across the tracks without making a crossing and proposed to begin a shuttle service in the town's main street. The railroad countered by securing an injunction against the electric line's crossing a railroad spur into a brewery. The injunction was dissolved in May 1905, but in the interim the local merchants provided a free horse-drawn shuttle to meet the electric cars. When the Petaluma and Santa Rosa again tried to install a crossing of the California Northwestern, more violence broke out—an affair known locally as the battle of Sebastopol Avenue—and the crossing was not effected until the interurban secured a restraining order against the railroad crews.[43] Similar incidents occurred on the Maine Central, another railroad known for hostility to electric lines, and elsewhere.

Even if an interurban avoided railroad opposition to its crossing, it was obligated to pay the expenses of installing the diamond and maintaining the crossing in perpetuity, including whatever signaling and interlocking was involved. It is the practice for the junior railroad at a crossing to bear the expenses of maintenance and operation, including the wages of the towermen. Most interurban crossings were simple affairs, but some were interlocked and required attendance. Thus the interurbans had an incentive, even apart from railroad hostility, to install overhead crossings, in spite of the initial expense and the reduction in operating speeds they entailed.

Some railroads scrutinized the behavior of interurban lines to make certain they were adhering to the provisions of their charters. When the Indianapolis Coal Traction Company, a predecessor of the Terre Haute Indianapolis and Eastern, began to build west from Plainfield toward Terre Haute, the Pennsylvania secured an injunction on the ground that the line's charter required it to build west from Danville, a terminus of one of its branches.[44] Once again, the railroad was unsuccessful in making the injunction permanent.

One of the railroads' devices for forestalling interurbans was cutting rates and increasing their own service. The Illinois Central tried to ward off an interurban from Chicago to Kankakee by establishing cheap local service with steam locomotives and orthodox passenger equipment. The

Ann Arbor Railroad, threatened by an interurban from Toledo to Ann Arbor, bought five McKeen cars to institute local service stopping at main highway crossings.[45] A few others did the same, notably the Southern Pacific in Oregon, but there were serious impediments to such a course. The interurbans were largely unorganized, or organized with weaker unions than the railroads,[46] and tended to hire less qualified employees at lower wages. In addition, interurbans were typically free of union full-crew requirements and hours limitations. A railroad local train had a crew of three or four, an interurban car only two. Finally, self-contained gasoline cars were still highly imperfect; their operating cost advantage over steam trains was largely dissipated in heavy maintenance costs and in expenses of breakdowns on the line. Thus, it was unlikely that a railroad could simulate interurban service economically. The Rock Island tried it between Des Moines and Indianola and between Cedar Rapids and Iowa City in 1905, but quickly gave up the effort as hopeless.

Railroad opposition did not, in general, prevent interurbans from being completed, but the enmity of the railroads continued to be manifested in many ways, and became one of the industry's chronic problems. The typical railroad executive was convinced that the interurbans had no ethical right to exist, and was eager to do what he could to eradicate them. The railroads east of the Mississippi, in particular, administered a boycott against which the interurbans fought with only the most meager success. The antipathy of the railroads during the years of construction denied the interurbans use of the railroads' physical plant in many circumstances when it would have been useful. A few exceptions may be noted. The Michigan United bought the old right-of-way of the Michigan Central for about 12 miles west of Kalamazoo after a relocation in 1905, intending to electrify the track, and both the Cleveland Alliance and Mahoning Valley and the East St. Louis and Suburban bought portions of the Baltimore & Ohio's track under the same circumstances. There were a few examples of electric lines' using railroad bridges, including the little Keokuk Electric Company's operation on the Wabash Railroad's Mississippi River crossing, but few interurbans were able to make use of railroad trackage to avoid street running. The Scranton and Binghamton obtained permission to enter Montrose, its terminus, by electrifying a short distance of a Lehigh Valley branch, and a few other interurbans made similar arrangements late in their histories, but they were exceptions.

Some interurbans were able to make use of rights-of-way of abandoned railroads; portions of the Olean Bradford and Salamanca, Pittsburgh Railways, the Utah-Idaho Central, and the Oregon Electric were laid on grades of railroad predecessors. Still other railroad track entered the interurban network when a few railroads, often unsuccessful ones, converted to interurbans. The Cincinnati Georgetown and Portsmouth, the Washington and Old Dominion, the Jamestown Westfield and Northwestern, the Fort Dodge Des Moines and Southern, the Northeast Oklahoma, and several other roads were conversions of steam railroads. Most such roads came to rue the day they had electrified, and ultimately removed their overheads to become diesel freight haulers, once again becoming indistinguishable from the railroads. Finally, some railroads themselves electrified short portions of their trackage and operated with something like interurban technology. Both the New York Central and the Erie had short electrified stretches in New York, and the Southern Pacific had an extensive one in the Willamette Valley of Oregon.

Completion of an interurban was a gala event, frequently celebrated with formal ceremonies at communities along the way. The Cleveland Painesville and Eastern and the Mason City and Clear Lake, among others, chose to open on the Fourth of July for ceremonial reasons; however, it more often happened that an interurban opened late in December to meet franchise requirements for completion within a given calendar year. A few companies gave free rides on opening day as a promotional device. Some interurbans, such as the Indianapolis Crawfordsville and Western, marred their openings by going bankrupt almost simultaneously. But for most roads opening day was an occasion for congratulations and expressions of optimism by corporate and municipal officials alike. The optimism was seldom well founded, and many a town that inaugurated interurban service with the high school band ended it with a *quo warranto* action to get what was left of the tracks out of Main Street.

THE BOOMS IN INTERURBAN BUILDING

It is useful to survey the interurban network about the year 1903, for events of that year combined to bring to an end the first great boom of interurban building. As Table 6 (Chapter 6) indicates, some 2,100 miles of interurban track had been constructed between 1889 and the end of the year 1900, most of it after 1895. Because there is a lag of about a year between the initiation of construction and its completion, the beginning of the building boom in 1900 is reflected in the 1901 figure. Mileage put in service rose from 569 miles in 1900 to 1,015 in 1901, continued upward to 1,488 in 1902, and reached a peak of 1,521 in 1903. The high figure of 1,113 miles in 1904 is a result almost entirely of projects initiated in 1903 or earlier. Thus, during the first building boom promoters had installed or would shortly complete some 5,706 miles of interurban track. About 40 per cent of the country's ultimate interurban mileage had been put in service by the end of 1904.

The mileage of street railways was expanding simultaneously; electric railway track of all types was being built at about ten times the rate of railroad track during this period.[47] This period was also one of considerable consolidation. The formation of the Lake Shore Electric in 1901 out of formerly independent properties was the most notable example, but the Detroit United, the Northern Ohio, and the Mahoning and Shenango, among others, also expanded by consolidation.

By 1903 there were two major networks of interurban lines in Ohio, one across the northern tier of the state covering Toledo, Cleveland, and

Akron, and the other in the southwestern quadrant encompassing Cincinnati, Dayton, Columbus, and Springfield. The two were not connected. Lines that were to become part of the Northern Ohio extended continuously south from Cleveland to Uhrichsville, and Pomeroy and Mandelbaum's Cleveland and Southwestern extended straight south from Cleveland to Wooster. Pomeroy and Mandelbaum also owned the isolated Ohio Central Traction Company, between Bucyrus and Mansfield. In 1902 the Toledo Bowling Green and Southern had opened a continuous line from Toledo to Findlay. In the southern Ohio network most of the suburban lines out of Cincinnati had been completed by this time. Pomeroy and Mandelbaum controlled a major interurban from the outskirts of Cincinnati to Dayton, the Cincinnati Dayton and Toledo. Appleyard's properties ran east and west from Dayton to Columbus and were to arrive in Zanesville on the east in 1904. Appleyard had reached Bellefontaine on the north with track from Springfield in 1903. A direct route from Dayton to Lima via the Dayton and Troy and Pomeroy and Mandelbaum's Western Ohio Railway was established December 1, 1903.

The interurban network had progressed in similar fashion in Indiana. Indianapolis had replaced Detroit as the center of the largest peripheral network, an honor Indianapolis was not to forgo until nearly the end of the industry's history. The interurban had been brought to Indiana by a young Anderson lawyer named Charles L. Henry, who promoted a line between Anderson and Alexandria in 1897. Henry, who was responsible for the popularity of the word "interurban," is often credited with coining it by analogy to the intramural railway at the Chicago World's Fair of 1893, but the word had been used earlier elsewhere: for example, to describe the streetcar line between Minneapolis and St. Paul.

Henry expanded his project into one of the most important interurbans, the Union Traction Company. By 1903, Union Traction had a network out of Indianapolis that reached northeast to Anderson, Marion, and Muncie, and straight north to Kokomo. A year later the company reached the Wabash River at Peru, completing a line to Fort Wayne by connection with the Fort Wayne and Wabash Valley Traction Company. Henry had left the Union Traction in 1902 to promote the Indianapolis and Cincinnati Traction Company and had been replaced in control of the Union Traction by Hugh J. McGowan, president of the Indianapolis Street Railway; W. Kesley Schoepf, head of the Cincinnati Street Railway; and several Philadelphia financiers with whom Schoepf and McGowan were associated: Randal Morgan, Thomas Dolan, George and Peter Widener, William and George Elkins, and J. Levering Jones. These men brought to the industry financial resources much beyond those available to earlier promoters. They were in a position to ride out financial panics that wrecked many other interurban proprietors, and used their financial strength to amass a system that dominated the Ohio-Indiana interurban network until the rise of the big electric power systems in the 1920's.

By 1903 other Indiana interurbans had radiated from Indianapolis to

Lafayette, Martinsville, Richmond, Plainfield, Columbus, and Shelbyville. A large union terminal for the interurbans was nearing completion in downtown Indianapolis. Elsewhere in the state, South Bend had been joined with Elkhart, Goshen, and Michigan City, and Evansville had just been connected with Princeton. Connection between the network around Indianapolis and the southern Ohio trackage was made on August 12, 1903, when an extension of the Dayton and Western Railway was opened between Eaton, Ohio, and Richmond, Indiana. Thus it became possible to make a continuous trip by interurban from Newark, Ohio, to Martinsville, Indiana—a distance of 256 miles.

In Michigan, the radial network from Detroit was nearly complete by 1903. Detroit was connected with Port Huron, Flint, and Jackson, and Everett and Moore were constructing a high-speed route to Toledo to connect with the northern Ohio mileage. In Illinois, Danville and Champaign had been joined by the first line of what was to become William B. McKinley's Illinois Traction system. The New England street railway network was well advanced. West of the Mississippi there were interurbans between Seattle and Tacoma, Spokane and Coeur d'Alene, Portland and Oregon City, and Los Angeles and Pasadena, but most of the Western mileage came later.

The abatement of interurban building toward the end of 1903 was caused in part by the Rich Man's Panic in the fall of that year. Stringency in both the Boston and the Philadelphia money markets made interurban financing difficult well into 1904. An earlier cause of the abatement was the financial difficulty into which the Everett-Moore syndicate was plunged in 1902. At the close of 1901, Everett and Moore were building two major interurbans, the Detroit and Toledo Shore Line and the Scioto Valley Traction Company. By this time they had set their sights on every major electric line—city or interurban—from Wheeling to Port Huron. The syndicate apparently proceeded too rapidly for its liquid resources, and on January 2, 1902, the Reserve Construction Company, the syndicate's subsidiary in charge of building the Shore Line, declared itself bankrupt. Although the reported earnings of the major Everett-Moore properties continued to be favorable, the syndicate found itself unable to meet many of its current obligations. Since Everett-Moore securities were widely held in Cleveland, the failure had severe financial consequences. At least one bank failed and several others experienced runs.

Within a short time, creditors' claims of nearly $12 million were presented to the syndicate. Everett and Moore arranged for their railway and telephone properties to be vested in a committee of Cleveland bankers. Since most of the individual properties continued to be solvent, the creditors agreed to an initial extension until July 1, 1903, and another until April 1, 1905. In February 1902 the syndicate sold 43,000 shares of the Cleveland Electric Railway and 5,000 shares of the Cleveland City Railway, and subsequently sold about 22,000 of its 30,000 shares of the Detroit United as well as 40,000 shares of the Toledo Railway and Light Company.

In the process, the syndicate lost control of the Cleveland Electric Railway, but retained command of the Detroit and Toledo systems. It then reorganized the Northern Ohio Traction Company, one of its most successful properties, as the Northern Ohio Traction and Light Company, at an increased capitalization. It divested itself of its interests in the Aurora Elgin and Chicago and the Scioto Valley Traction Company.

The Detroit and Toledo Shore Line was a particularly difficult problem, since the company owed about $280,000 to the Strang Construction Company, the subcontractor building it. The syndicate made an unsuccessful effort to merge the line into the Detroit United, and finally sold it to the Grand Trunk and the Toledo St. Louis & Western for $1,500,000 in 4 per cent bonds for completion as a steam freight railroad.[48] The Lake Shore Electric, the largest Everett-Moore line, was forced into bankruptcy, but emerged in April 1903 with the syndicate still in control. By means of these various measures, the syndicate had scaled down its obligations drastically by April 1905—the *Street Railway Journal* reported a reduction from $17 million to less than $4 million—and thus was able to emerge from trusteeship.[49]

Not only did the difficulties of Everett and Moore at this time prevent the syndicate from carrying out its own expansion plans, but the stringency they induced in the Cleveland money market killed many of the local independent projects. The syndicate's troubles were almost universally attributed to poor financial management, rather than to innate shortcomings of the interurban. The short depression attendant upon the panic of 1903 further cut into the independent projects. By 1904 it was estimated that two-thirds of the lines in Ohio projected in 1901 had not been built, and that most of them were dead issues.[50]

The Pomeroy-Mandelbaum syndicate suffered losses in the same period. It lost control of the Cincinnati Dayton and Toledo, which was considered a strategic property. The syndicate's line on the towpath of the Miami and Erie Canal proved a complete failure and went bankrupt. It was scrapped in 1905. Pomeroy and Mandelbaum also lost control of two minor lines, the Springfield and Xenia and the Tuscarawas County Traction Company, but their syndicate retained its two most important properties, the Cleveland and Southwestern and the Western Ohio, along with the Ohio Central Traction Company, the interurban between Mansfield and Bucyrus.

The Cincinnati Dayton and Toledo and the canal company passed into the hands of the Widener-Elkins-Schoepf-McGowan syndicate, which had already become dominant among the Indiana interurbans. Schoepf had visions of a north-south line through Ohio, of which the Cincinnati Dayton and Toledo was to be the southernmost line. He was able to realize this ambition, as Pomeroy and Mandelbaum had not, because of the failure of the Appleyard syndicate. Appleyard's principal properties, the Dayton Springfield and Urbana and the Columbus London and Springfield, found their earnings inadequate for their fixed charges and went into receivership in January 1905. The Columbus Grove City and Southwestern, a smaller road, went under less than two weeks later, and in March the Urbana Bellefontaine and Northern, a leased line of the Dayton Springfield and Urbana, followed suit. Appleyard also lost control of his narrow-gauge steam line, the Ohio River & Western. Since he was simultaneously involved in the failure of the German Bank of Buffalo, New York, he was in no position to refinance his properties. His failure was complete, and in February 1906 his interurbans passed into the hands of Schoepf and his associates. They made no effort to acquire the Ohio River & Western or the Dayton Lebanon & Cincinnati Railway, a smaller steam line that the Appleyard syndicate had controlled.

Schoepf immediately began to combine the former Appleyard interurbans into the Indiana Columbus and Eastern Traction Company. Two other properties in the area, the Dayton and Western and the Dayton and Northern, were leased. The IC&E also absorbed for electrification an unsuccessful steam railroad between Lima and Defiance—the Columbus & Lake Michigan—which had been planned as a through line from Columbus to an undetermined port on the east shore of Lake Michigan. Schoepf was interested in the Lima and Toledo Traction Company, which was building from Lima north through Deshler.

The revival of business conditions in 1904, together with the general ease in the money market in 1905 and 1906, brought about the second boom in interurban building, of more or less the same character and magnitude as the first. The revival of building is in some respects more difficult to explain than was the initiation of large-scale construction in 1900 and 1901. The experience of the interurbans during the first building boom had not been particularly satisfactory. One writer inquired among 16 major interurbans in Ohio and found that 9 paid dividends in 1902 and 7 did not. Of 27 companies in Indiana, 2 paid dividends on preferred stock, but none on common stock, and in Michigan only 4 out of 24 companies paid dividends on their common.[51] This poor showing was widely discounted as merely reflecting the interurbans' overcapitalization. Bogart believed that the interurbans' net over costs was 50 per cent above the railroads', but that stock-watering held the nominal return on investment in Ohio interurbans in this period down to about 4.7 per cent.[52]

There were, however, some who turned a jaundiced eye on the performance of the interurbans. Late in 1902, A. A. Lisman of Lisman, Lorge and Co. of New York, a brokerage firm specializing in railroad securities, sent a letter to the *Wall Street Journal* that analyzed the interurbans' prospects in pessimistic terms, but, as it proved, with a high degree of accuracy:

I call your attention to the following striking facts on the continuous flotation of interurban street railways, and the extravagant claims made on behalf of projects of this character.

The average cost per mile of interurban traction, especially when the road proposes to do a freight business, is at least $18,000. Adding thereto the contractor's profit makes the minimum cost per mile of road $20,000. In order to raise this money, roads are generally bonded for $25,000 in 5 per cent bonds. In other words, the fixed charges per mile of road are $1250. To this must be added at least $150 a mile for taxes and legal expenses, not counting damage suits.

Taking the New York street railway report as a guide, it will be seen that the average earnings per mile of interurban traction are $3400, and the average operating expenses are 55 per cent, which is very low. This equals $1870. Add to this maintenance of way and rolling stock, and above all maintenance of electrical equipment, say only $1000 a mile (certainly ultraconservative) for a term of, say, ten years. All projects of this kind for the state of New York show net earnings of not exceeding $530 a mile . . . against fixed charges of minimum $1250.

These figures are taken from official records and the only change made is the addition of very limited charges for maintenance of way, power, and equipment. Only by leaving the latter charge out can interest be earned. As a matter of fact, therefore, the average interurban road from its very inception, when charged with essential expenses for renewal and maintenance, shows a deficit of $800 per mile.

Of course, there can be only one end to this kind of thing. The next reorganization period this country will see will be the reorganization of interurban traction properties, and from all indications this period is apt to come . . . quickly.[53]

Lisman was immediately attacked by Alfred M. Lamar, an investment banker, and by a representative of Tucker, Anthony and Co., a major interurban builder. Both argued that earnings data from Midwestern lines would lead to a more favorable conclusion. Lisman responded with a similar analysis of the Cincinnati Dayton and Toledo that demonstrated an over-all loss of $8,000 for the year ending April 1, 1902, in spite of an operating ratio of 52 per cent. Lisman concluded that "much [of] . . . the capitalization for the last year or two of interurban street railways practically amounted to the issuance of new capital under a pretence of paying for extensions and improvements, but really for the purpose of paying for repairs and maintenance."[54]

The capital market, it appears, agreed with Lamar, who thought that "where conservatively financed, substantially built, and judiciously managed, there is no class of investment today in America that promises a safer and more substantial return";[55] for toward the end of 1904, and particularly in 1905 and 1906, promotion of interurbans again rose to boom proportions. The mileage completed in 1905 (696 miles) reflects the abatement of promotion after the panic of 1903, but the year 1906 saw 1,056 miles put in service, and 1907 a high of 1,478—just short of the peak years of 1902 and 1903. One might expect the capital market to have been more selective in the second boom than the first, but there is little reason to believe that its choice among projects was any more rational. The second boom saw completion alike of the strong Northern

Electric in California and the weak Sandusky Norwalk and Mansfield in Ohio.

The second boom also witnessed the birth of a new trade magazine, the *Interurban Railway Journal,* first published in Indianapolis in 1905. The new organ had none of the restraint of the *Street Railway Journal,* but rather expressed the rampant optimism of the period. From the beginning, it regularly carried a list of suggestions for interurban routes not yet promoted, and some of its writers predicted that eventually interurbans would attract all the passengers from the railroads. After less than two years of unprofitable publication, the *Interurban Railway Journal* became the *Electric Traction Weekly,* and lost its evangelistic character.

The second building boom filled many gaps left by the first. Pomeroy and Mandelbaum connected the networks in northern and southern Ohio in 1905 by extending their Western Ohio from Lima to a connection with the Toledo Bowling Green and Southern at Findlay. Everett and Moore had connected Detroit and Cleveland in 1904 by extending their Detroit Monroe and Toledo, and a series of three short interurbans ran from Cleveland east to Erie, Pennsylvania. Thus, the new connection at Findlay made possible a continuous trip from Erie to Lafayette or from Cincinnati to Flint. Given the low speeds, frequent layovers, and devious routing that a traveler would have encountered, trips of this sort were made, if at all, only as stunts. The industry was doubtless correct, however, in looking upon the new connection as a milestone. The *Street Railway Journal* considered the junction to be as important, in its way, as the completion of the transcontinental railroad in 1869; it sent a golden spike to be driven by President A. E. Akins of the Western Ohio in the main street of Findlay, December 30, 1905.[56] Leading officials of the industry attended the ceremony, including a delegation from the Ohio Interurban Railway Association, which had been founded in the previous year. At the time, it was estimated that the Midwestern interurban network represented an investment of $110 million.

In 1906 the Western Ohio initiated through service between Dayton and Toledo jointly with the Toledo Bowling Green and Southern and the Dayton and Troy Railway. The three lines remained independent, but adopted the name "The Lima Route" together with a rectangular herald to designate the joint service. In the same year, the third connection between Ohio and Indiana was completed, the Fort Wayne Van Wert and Lima Traction Company. The Dayton and Muncie Traction Company had provided a second connection in 1905, but the line was lightly traveled.

Schoepf, by virtue of his control of the Cincinnati Dayton and Toledo and the former Appleyard lines, was now in a position to achieve the Cincinnati–Toledo interurban line that had eluded Pomeroy and Mandelbaum. In 1907 he consolidated his holdings into the Ohio Electric Railway, which became the largest interurban in the state. The Ohio Electric leased the Indiana Columbus and Eastern (which had been formed of the former Appleyard roads), and the Cincinnati Dayton and Toledo, and bought the Lima and Toledo, which was still under construction. The Lima and Toledo had previously leased the Fort Wayne Van Wert and Lima. The lines from Lima to Fort Wayne and Toledo and the railroad from Lima to Defiance that Schoepf was preparing to electrify were separated from the former Appleyard interurbans by a gap between Lima and Bellefontaine. Schoepf closed the gap by building the IC&E north from Bellefontaine in 1908, the same year the Lima and Toledo reached Toledo. Thus, in that year Schoepf completed Ohio Electric's 217-mile main line from Cincinnati to Toledo, by far the longest continuous line of any interurban. The distance between Dayton and Toledo via Bellefontaine and Deshler was 14 miles longer than the Lima Route via Wapakoneta and Findlay, but the Ohio Electric was built to standards that permitted faster running. Ohio Electric limiteds made the trip of 165 miles in five and a half hours, slightly more than an hour faster than the Lima Route. The Toledo Bowling Green and Southern, in particular, was a low-speed operation; its builders had utilized a large number of curves and a great deal of street running in an effort to tap as many towns as possible along the route.

The Ohio Electric was, by any standards, a large undertaking. In the twelve months ending June 30, 1909 (the first full year after completion of the main line), the company carried 23,088,239 people (including city passengers), ran 10,388,950 car-miles, and grossed $2,775,608. The road operated 667 miles of track and owned 430 cars, of which 320 carried motors.

The year 1908 also saw the completion of the Cleveland–Columbus route when the Columbus Delaware and Marion reached Bucyrus from the south with a subsidiary, the Columbus Marion and Bucyrus, and the Pomeroy-Mandelbaum syndicate built 44 miles from Seville to Mansfield to tie the isolated Mansfield–Bucyrus line to the Cleveland Southwestern and Columbus. Through passenger service was never attempted, for the interurban route was 45 miles longer than the Big Four Railroad. In 1907 and 1908, the Youngstown and Southern and the Youngstown and Ohio River were completed to form a north-south route through eastern Ohio. Thus Cleveland and Youngstown were connected in roundabout fashion with the electric lines reaching Wheeling and Pittsburgh via the Ohio River valley.

Many individual interurbans in Ohio were completed during the second building boom. By 1908 the Ohio network was virtually completed; only two important lines were built later, the Fostoria and Fremont Railway in 1911, and the Cleveland Alliance and Mahoning Valley in 1915.

The second boom also brought the Indiana network to substantial completion. The second and more important Indianapolis–Fort Wayne line was completed in 1907 when the Fort Wayne and Wabash Valley (also a

Schoepf-McGowan property) reached Bluffton from the north. Schoepf and McGowan in the same year completed their east-west main line across Indiana, which they organized as the Terre Haute Indianapolis and Eastern Traction Company—invariably known as the THI&E. The Union Traction Company had been hit hard by the panic of 1903 and did almost no building during the second boom. In fact, Union Traction was unable to complete two projects left unfinished at the end of the first boom. In 1903 the company undertook a direct line from Anderson to New Castle, but early in 1904, when the track had been laid as far as Middletown, financial difficulties forced the company to suspend building. The management was able to put the line in service in 1905, but never to complete it to New Castle. Similarly, in the fall of 1903 the company ran out of funds after grading a route from Alexandria to Muncie, installing some bridges, and laying a few miles of rail near Alexandria. The company never continued building, but retained the completed portion intact until World War I, when the rails and bridges were sold for scrap.

During the second boom, however, Union Traction expanded by consolidating. Schoepf and McGowan acquired the Dayton and Muncie in 1906 and split it at the state line, the Ohio portion going to the Indiana Columbus and Eastern (Ohio Electric) as the Dayton and Northern, and the Indiana portion falling to the Union Traction. In 1906 the Union Traction leased the Muncie Hartford and Fort Wayne Railway, which had been built from Muncie to Bluffton by local businessmen in 1903. The Indiana Northern between Marion and Wabash had been absorbed in 1905.

In 1907 the route from Indianapolis to Louisville, composed of three companies, was completed with the construction of the Indianapolis and Louisville Traction Company line between Sellersburg and Seymour. In 1908 the Chicago Lake Shore and South Bend, which was eventually to be the most successful Midwestern interurban, went into service.

Only in Michigan was there relatively little building during the second boom. Elsewhere most of the Milwaukee Electric and the Illinois Traction were built in this period, as were the Des Moines and Central Iowa, the Fort Dodge Des Moines and Southern, the Pittsburgh Harmony Butler and New Castle, the Buffalo Lockport and Rochester, and most of the Louisville and Interurban. The second boom ended with the panic of 1907. The momentum of lines under construction in 1907 produced a mileage of 1,058 in 1908, but this was less than two-thirds of the 1907 total. The two booms together produced about 9,000 miles of line, more than 55 per cent of the ultimate total of about 16,100 miles.

The panic of 1907 produced a credit stringency much more severe than the panic of 1903, and accordingly raised far more havoc with the interurbans. Some projects had to be abandoned midway in construction, and were never completed. Perhaps the most important of these was the Toledo Ann Arbor and Detroit Railroad, which began building from Toledo to Ann Arbor in 1905. The contractor had graded 46 of the 50 miles, had placed the abutments for every bridge save one, and had completed the powerhouse at Petersburg, Michigan, to a point within a few feet of the roof. He had laid about 17 miles of track and placed about 7 miles of poles when the company failed. It was estimated that duplication of the property as it stood would have cost $350,000.[57] Several of the earlier interurbans were completed in spite of bankruptcy during construction, but the panic of 1907 prevented efforts to reorganize the TAA&D. It could not be sold at a receiver's auction on September 16, 1907, and although it changed hands in 1911 and again in 1912, it was never completed. The Toledo Ann Arbor & Jackson Railroad was formed to take control of the property, and in 1913 began operation with a steam locomotive and second-hand railroad equipment between Toledo and the end of track, about two miles south of Petersburg. The company reincorporated as the Toledo–Detroit Railroad in 1915, and extended its track northward eight miles to Dundee. In 1916 and 1917 the Detroit Toledo & Ironton Railroad leased and then purchased the Toledo–Detroit Railroad, and made of it the railroad's present Toledo branch. The line was never operated electrically. The Toledo–Detroit management bought two steel interurban cars from the Niles Car Company, hoping to haul them on the line with steam locomotives, but to operate them under trolley in Toledo. The plan was never executed.

In Indiana, the Huntington Columbia City and Northern Traction Company undertook a line between Huntington and Goshen, but failed in 1907 after grading from Goshen to Lake Wawasee and laying a mile of track. Although about $100,000 had been invested in the project, appraisers valued the property at only $9,640, and in 1908 a court ordered the road sold. The physical assets went for scrap.[58]

Some of the lines cut down by the panic of 1903 had been revived in the second boom but were finally killed in 1907. The Wabash and Rochester Railway, also in Indiana, had graded 35 miles during the first boom, largely by grace of $110,000 in municipal subsidies, but it then exhausted its funds and was unable to lay track or erect an overhead. The local organizers were replaced in 1904 by promoters from Ohio and Pennsylvania, who made some further expenditures before being stopped by the panic of 1907. The Stanley Construction Company sued them for $7,000 for expenses on the grade, and brought the project to a close.[59] Many of the unfinished projects halted with the end of grading because of the heavy expense of track-laying and electrical installation.

Several established lines went bankrupt. The weak Eastern Ohio Traction Company was in bankruptcy even before the panic, and it was joined by the Toledo and Indiana on March 31, 1908, and by the Toledo Urban and Interurban, which owned the northernmost eleven miles of the direct line from Toledo to Findlay, on July 8. The Dayton and Xenia, which reported a loss of $32,842 during 1908, went into receivership on March 11. This company was now proprietor of the two lines running parallel between Dayton and Xenia as a result of absorbing the Dayton and Xenia Rapid Transit, which had built between the two cities to street railway standards. The receiver regarded the Rapid Transit line as redundant, and immediately moved to abandon it.[60] This was the first abandonment in the Ohio-Indiana network, so far as is known. However, in the same year (1908), the Eastern Ohio abandoned a seven-mile branch between Steel Junction (on its Garrettsville line) and Middlefield. It, too, had become redundant, for since 1902 the company had operated a direct line from Cleveland to Middlefield, and had used the branch only for freight and for special movements.

The Columbus Delaware and Marion, which was considered a relatively strong property, had incurred heavy capital expenditures in building the Columbus Marion and Bucyrus as a northern extension, and together with this subsidiary it failed in September 1909. Many of the roads that remained solvent reported heavy deficits in 1908; the little Columbus Magnetic Springs and Northern lost $11,745, and the great Ohio Electric $105,555.[61]

The panic of 1907 left many interurbans too far from completion to be run economically. The northern line of Charles L. Henry's Indianapolis and Cincinnati Traction Company reached Connersville in 1906, and the southern line reached Greensburg in the same year, but the company went into receivership at the same time and never raised funds to build further. Henry, who died in 1927, was still trying to extend the northern line to Cincinnati in the last years of his life. Similarly, the Indianapolis Crawfordsville and Western, which failed upon reaching Crawfordsville—about halfway to its goal of Danville, Illinois—could never be completed. The Northern Electric in California was projected to Red Bluff, but only reached Chico. Every interurban route of the Milwaukee Electric fell short of its target: the Sheboygan line stopped short of Manitowoc and Green Bay, the Watertown line of Madison, the East Troy branch of Janesville and Beloit, the Burlington branch of Lake Geneva, and the Kenosha line of Chicago.

With few exceptions, the interurbans were left with unfulfilled ambitions. Even such roads as the Detroit Monroe and Toledo Short Line, the Boston and Worcester, and the Toledo Port Clinton and Lakeside, all of which were completed in accord with their promoters' intentions, planned branch lines that they never executed. Several companies built two isolated segments in the hope of connecting them but could not do so. The Illinois Traction, the Michigan United, the Pacific Northwest Traction Company, and the Piedmont and Northern, four major interurbans, were each left with a lengthy gap in their proposed main lines. An adverse ruling of the Interstate Commerce Commission prevented the Piedmont and Northern from filling its gap, but the rest were financially unable to complete their systems. The Pacific Northwest endeavored to build from Seattle to Bellingham, and some of the line was constructed as late as 1913. The cost of bridging the many streams along the coast of Puget Sound proved to be prohibitive, however, and the company never closed the void between Everett and Mount Vernon.

William B. McKinley was intent upon having a continuous line from Joliet, where his Illinois Traction had a connection for Chicago, to St. Louis. The general cessation of interurban building in the Midwest in 1908 found him with a reasonably complete network in central Illinois, encompassing Peoria, Bloomington, Springfield, Danville, Champaign-Urbana, and the East St. Louis area. A projected line from Springfield to Jacksonville and some smaller branches were never built. In the Illinois Valley, McKinley controlled the Chicago Ottawa and Peoria from Ottawa west to Princeton and south to Streator. Thus McKinley could complete his system by linking Streator with Mackinaw Junction on his main line, by bridging the Mississippi at St. Louis, and by building east from Ottawa to Joliet. In 1910 McKinley bridged the Mississippi at Venice, Illinois, with a monumental structure—the interurbans' greatest single investment. Beginning in 1909, the Illinois Valley line was built east from Ottawa, and in 1912, McKinley's track reached Joliet. Unhappily, however, McKinley's funds had been so drained by expending $3 million on the McKinley Bridge, and interurban projects had become so difficult to finance, that the company was never able to build the Streator–Mackinaw Junction connection. As a consequence, the company's Illinois Valley line proved much less viable than the rest of the property.

The revival of interurban building after the panic of 1907 had passed away did surprisingly little to correct inadequacies in existing interurbans. The Eastern Ohio never managed to connect the little town of Garrettsville with Leavittsburg, only eleven miles away, to provide a through route from Cleveland to the Mahoning Valley cities of Warren and Youngstown. The Wheeling Traction Company strove for years to close a gap in its projected high-speed line along the west shore of the Ohio between Wheeling and Steubenville, but was never successful. The Winona Interurban in 1910 managed to finish its line between Peru and Goshen, completing the connection between the Chicago area and the central Indiana interurbans. The Winona was a special case, since it enjoyed the backing of several opulent industrialists who were more eager to provide service to the religious camp with which the interurban was affiliated than to receive pecuniary gain. Few other Midwestern interurbans were able to make even short extensions to reach their goals.

Most of the building after 1908 occurred west of the Mississippi, generally in areas of rapid population growth and inadequate transportation. About 5,000 miles of interurban were built after 1908. In 1909, 597 miles were completed, and in 1910, 684; construction continued at the rate of 500 to 675 miles per year until 1914. In 1915 new mileage slipped to 444 and in 1916 to 116; after that it never again reached 100 miles per year. The last interurban was not built until 1927, but all the lines opened after World War I were in some measure special cases.[62]

The modest revival of interurban building after the panic of 1907, as compared with the earlier revival, is not difficult to explain: the industry had simply not proved profitable enough to warrant continued investment except in unusual circumstances. The 2.5 to 3.5 per cent return that the typical interurban of the Ohio–Indiana pattern could earn was not enough to attract investment. The secular increase in traffic that promoters had anticipated proved much too small to make the industry even ordinarily profitable. The Ohio Electric, built to relatively high standards, well equipped, and serving a populous area, earned a net of only $5,073 in 1910 and $1,588 in 1911.[63] The Lake Shore Electric, which served a densely populated area, reported profits throughout this period, but the Toledo and Western, which operated only to small towns, reported a loss of $63,279 in 1910–11.[64] The disparity between the interest rate and the return in the industry became successively greater as the industry declined; it was especially striking in the 1920's, a time of high interest rates. W. H. Sawyer, president of the Alton Granite and St. Louis Traction Company, told the Interstate Commerce Commission in 1924 that the interurbans—by that time looked upon as highly risky enterprises—could borrow only at about 8 per cent.[65] Few could earn even half that rate for more than short periods.

Moreover, by 1908 most of the routes between major population centers in the Midwest, although by no means all, had been built and most new lines would necessarily have been secondary. The costs of interurban building were rising rapidly. The figure of $20,000 per mile so widely cited as typical in the first building boom was obsolete by 1908, and thus new lines would have been even worse off in terms both of traffic potential and of fixed costs. Finally, the statutes limiting steam railroad fares to two cents per mile that were enacted by the Midwestern states beginning in 1906, reduced the fare differential between railroads and interurbans, and so made it difficult for the interurbans to attract long-distance passengers. These laws, which will be discussed at length in Chapters 3 and 5, were a serious impediment to the industry, and contributed to the end of its expansion.

It is noteworthy that motor transport, although it eventually killed the industry, had little or nothing to do with the end of large-scale building in 1908. The automobile was not a serious rival to the industry until after 1911, and did not cause a net loss of passengers until after 1917.

There was no dearth of projects after 1908; proposals good, bad, and indifferent continued to be brought forth just as they had been earlier. As late as 1925, a proposal was made for an interurban of 238 miles to connect St. Louis and Kansas City, to serve 19 intermediate towns without railroad service, and to provide a route between terminals that would be 40 miles shorter than the shortest railroad.[66] The typical interurban of the period 1910–15 was a heavily built line with the prospect of railroad interchange and of carload freight service. The Oakland Antioch and Eastern, the Salt Lake and Utah, the Utah-Idaho Central, the Arkansas Valley Interurban, the Kansas City Kaw Valley and Western, the Waterloo Cedar Falls and Northern, and the Grand Rapids extension of the Michigan Railway are all examples of late interurban building. It became more difficult to finance the purely local style of interurban; but several more came into being after the booms ended, including some of the worst examples: the Kankakee and Urbana, the Lee County Central, the Southern Oregon Traction, and the Sheridan Railway of Wyoming, all of which had histories of the most dismal sort.

Given the two abrupt halts to interurban building, and the high incidence of financial failure at other times, a large number of companies accomplished only a very small amount of what they set out to do. Illinois was particularly characterized by companies of this kind. Promoters of the Bloomington Pontiac and Joliet hoped at least to connect Bloomington and Joliet, and had visions of reaching St. Louis; but they achieved only a 20-mile line between Pontiac and Dwight. The little Central Illinois Traction Company, which operated ten miles between Mattoon and Charleston, was intended to run across the state from a connection with the Indiana interurbans at Paris to some point to the west, possibly Hillsboro on the Illinois Traction.

Several properties never achieved interurban operation at all. The Hutchinson Interurban in Kansas managed only to be a street railway in Hutchinson, and the Omaha Lincoln and Beatrice achieved only a switching line in Lincoln with some suburban operation. The Buffalo Batavia and Rochester Railway endeavored to build a direct third-rail line from Buffalo to Rochester, but finished only a two-mile street railway in Batavia. An affiliate, over which the company proposed to enter Buffalo, operated a suburban line from Buffalo to Williamsville. Three lengthy roads, electrified only for short distances, operated most of their track with gasoline cars and steam locomotives and were shortly abandoned: the St. Joseph Valley Railway in Indiana, the Ocean Shore Railroad in California, and the New York Auburn and Lansing in New York. Many roads projected as interurbans were never electrified at all. The Woodstock and Sycamore Traction Company in Illinois never strung an overhead, but operated with McKeen cars and other self-contained equipment throughout its short history (1911–18). This company always considered itself to be an interurban—part of the northern Illinois network of electric lines—but many properties that failed to electrify became short-line steam railroads, and integrated themselves with the general railroad network. By far the most important of these properties was the Detroit and Toledo Shore Line, already mentioned, but many other small railroads had a similar beginning: among others the Minneapolis Northfield and Southern and the Minnesota Western in Minnesota; the Paris and Mount Pleasant in Texas; the Ferdinand Railroad and the Cincinnati Bluffton and Chicago in Indiana; the Hooppole Yorktown and Tampico and the Macomb Industry and Littleton in Illinois; the Cushing and Oil Fields in Oklahoma; and the Modesto and Empire in California.

The greatest contrast between intention and achievement was the Chicago–New York Electric Air Line Railroad. This company proposed nothing less than a double-track electric railroad in a straight line from

Chicago to New York. It was to have no grade crossings with other railroads, no grades over one-half per cent, and either no curves at all or none that could not be negotiated at 90 miles per hour. The promoters proposed to haul standard passenger trains behind streamlined electric locomotives at an average speed of 75 miles per hour. They would have offered ten-hour service at a flat $10 fare on a route of only 742 miles, more than 150 miles shorter than any existing steam railroad. There is still some question whether the Air Line was a fraudulent scheme or an honest promotion, but it seems probable that it was a sincere but misguided effort to build the project. Its originator and principal promoter was Alexander C. Miller, an experienced railroad man who had spent twenty years as an operating official of the Chicago Burlington & Quincy. Miller had conceived the idea of the Air Line on a train—presumably on the New York Central—which after three hours' fast running out of New York was farther from Chicago, its destination, than it had been when it started.

Had actual construction of the Chicago–New York Electric Air Line never been undertaken, it would be regarded as simply an extreme example of the lunatic fringe of interurban projects. There had been similar schemes earlier. In 1892, for example, the Chicago and St. Louis Electric Railway had been proposed as a straight route between the cities of its name, capable of running up to 100 miles per hour and covering the distance in two and a half to three hours.[67] In 1901, a promoter had proposed an eight-track trolley line between Jersey City and Philadelphia, offering service at 60 miles per hour overall at a flat five-cent fare.[68] Fortunately, neither of these projects was undertaken, but the Air Line was promoted with great energy, and work on it was actually begun. It was first advertised in July 1906, at the height of the second rash of interurban building. It published a periodical, the *Air Line News,* for promotional purposes. Miller wisely decided to finance his project entirely by means of the sale of stock, and by September had sold enough to begin construction. The Air Line planned to build in a direct line, and to tap towns near the right-of-way by short branches served by shuttle trains, an expensive and inconvenient method of providing local service that most interurbans sought to avoid. The Air Line's first route was one of these branches, about three miles from La Porte to South La Porte, Indiana, opened on June 15, 1907. The company bought two standard wooden combines from the Niles Car Company, lettered "New York" on the front and "Chicago" on the rear. The main line was to run east and west through South La Porte. The company began building in 1907, and by 1911 had completed about 15 miles west to Goodrum, a junction named after a major Air Line shareholder.

Even in the flat country of northern Indiana, the Air Line's construction standards proved to be unbearably expensive. One can barely conceive of the expense of the bridges, cuts, fills, and tunnels necessary to drive a straight line through the mountains of northern Pennsylvania. Between South La Porte and Goodrum, the Air Line crossed minor branches of the Monon and Pere Marquette, and the Chicago–Toledo line of the Wabash. For each of these, the company built a heavy girder bridge, and to hold down the gradient to its announced maximum, an earthwork approach of almost a mile. The right-of-way was about 100 feet wide, which the company secured mainly by exchanging stock for land with local farmers. The track was built to steam-road standards with 85-pound rail and white oak ties. Every sixth tie was extended for eventual laying of a third rail for electric power. The orthodox overhead that the company actually installed was considered only temporary. A single track was laid, but space was left throughout for a second.

The downfall of the Air Line came partly from the capital expended on crossing Coffey Creek, a minor stream about 15 miles east of Gary. In order to avoid a grade, the company built a colossal fill, 180 feet wide at the base and two miles long. This fill seriously depleted the company's treasury, and seems to have demonstrated the futility of the Air Line's physical standards. The company had built from Gary to East Gary, and an affiliate, the Valparaiso and Northern, had built from Valparaiso through Goodrum to Chesterton. When the Air Line closed the gap between East Gary and Goodrum, it built a line, which contained a curve, to a point a short distance south of Goodrum, and made use of the Valparaiso and Northern's ordinary elevated crossing of the Baltimore & Ohio. It never attempted a fourth massive grade elevation.

The Air Line survived as long as it did largely because of the irrational support of its stockholders. It was financed almost entirely by the sale of stock to individuals, few of whom seem to have been regular investors in corporate securities. Their enthusiasm was remarkable. An Association known as "The Air Line Stockholders' Association of the World" claimed to have fifty camps throughout the United States, each of which held periodic meetings to rally support for the Air Line. The company, having no fixed charges, weathered the 1907–8 depression, but went bankrupt in 1915. In 1912, when it built its connection to Gary, it violated not only its opposition to curves but its opposition to bonds as well. Default on interest on the bonds of its subsidiary, the Gary Connecting Railway, and other obligations brought its end. What was to have been the Air Line became a part—and a relatively unproductive part—of the suburban lines of the Gary Street Railway.[69] The line from Goodrum to La Porte, which contained the Coffey Creek fill, two vast cuts, and the three major overpasses, lasted less than seven years, and was abandoned in November 1917.

While it operated the Air Line was, as one might expect, utterly uneconomic. In 1909 the management reported an average cost of construction per mile of $334,310—more than triple that of any other Indiana interurban—and gross revenue per mile of $914.54—much the lowest in the state. The little Lebanon-Thorntown Traction Company, a local venture of the poorest sort, was second lowest with $1,412.71 per mile, but it had cost only $12,878 per mile to build.[70] The Air Line in the same year had an operating ratio of 183, although 55 to 60 was common at the time for the major interurbans.

The Air Line was saved from total disaster by the fortuitous circumstance that it had been begun near Gary at the same time that the United States Steel Company's works were established there. The Air Line in its later days invested in what became parts of the Gary Street Railway system, which survived long after the demise of the Air Line proper.

Although wildly improbable schemes were not unusual, there is surprisingly little evidence of outright fraud in interurban promotion. Only two important projects are known to have failed because of embezzlement. In 1908 the Ontario West Shore was projected to run from Goderich, Ontario, north to Kincardine along the shore of Lake Huron. The local promoters arranged with J. W. Moyes of Toronto for his Huron Construction Company to construct the line. Goderich, Kincardine, and the intermediate towns guaranteed $385,000 of the interurban's bonds to bring the line into being. By 1911 the grade had been completed and 16 miles of track laid from Goderich to Kintail, but no funds were left. An engineer from the Ontario Railway and Municipal Board found that only $228,000 had been expended and that $175,000 had disappeared. Moyes refused to cooperate with an investigation, and when a warrant was issued for his arrest, he fled and was never traced. Efforts of the municipalities to have the line completed by the Canadian Pacific Railway or other interests were unsuccessful, and the completed portion was scrapped. About $100,000 was realized and the remaining $285,000 was a pure loss to the city governments.

In 1909 the Covington and South Western Railroad was being promoted as an interurban of forty-five miles from Crawfordsville, Indiana, through the Parke County coalfield to Covington, just across the state line from Danville, Illinois. Most of the grading was finished by 1910, and about four miles of track and overhead were installed in the vicinity of Kingman (pop.: 535). The promoters bought a second-hand streetcar from Fort Wayne and ran an inspection trip for the shareholders, who were chiefly local farmers. One of the promoters then absconded with the project's funds, thus bringing its history to a quick close.

THE PATTERN OF THE INDUSTRY

The geographical pattern of the interurbans is best seen by reference to the accompanying maps in Part II. It is a series of irregular wheels, with their spokes radiating from major cities. Indianapolis had much the largest of these networks: thirteen lines, including a short suburban road to Beech Grove. Five interurban routes radiated from Chicago, nine from Toledo, five from Rochester, and eight from Dayton. Kansas City, Los Angeles, Portland, Seattle, Atlanta, and other cities had major radial networks. Other interurbans were tributary to these networks, and still others —frequently weak roads—were geographically isolated. Every large city in the area bounded by the Mississippi, the Ohio River, the Great Lakes, and the Atlantic was served by an interurban or a rural trolley line with the single exception of Madison, Wisconsin.

Ohio was first in interurban mileage; it had 2,798 miles of line, nearly a thousand more than any other state. Coshocton (1910 population: 9,603) was the largest Ohio town without an interurban. Indiana was second with 1,825 miles, but it was the most thoroughly covered of any state; every town with a population of more than 5,000 was served by an interurban except three—Bloomington, Madison, and Vincennes, and at one time or another various companies made plans to serve these three.[71] Together with Michigan's 981 miles, the interurbans in the eastern Midwest presented a reasonably well integrated network of about 5,050 miles, roughly a third of American mileage in 1914. Pennsylvania had 1,498 miles (much of it on the borderline of interurban technology), Illinois 1,422, California 1,295, and New York 1,129; no other state had more than 500 miles. Canada had 850 miles divided among 25 companies, most of it in Ontario. Only in the Deep South, the Northern Plains states, and the arid West was there little mileage. Low rural population densities, an absence of large cities, and, in the South, low rural incomes made these areas unattractive to interurban promoters.

The longest continuous trip one could take by interurban was, naturally, in the Northeast and Middle West. Between 1910 and 1922 it was possible to travel by interurban from Elkhart Lake, Wisconsin, on the Wisconsin Power and Light Company, to Oneonta, New York, on the Southern New York Railway, a distance of about 1,087 miles. There is no recorded instance of anyone's taking such a trip, but in 1910, as a demonstration of the growth of the interurban, 22 businessmen of Utica, New York, chartered car 502 of the New York Central Railroad's Oneida Railway for a round trip on interurban track to Louisville, Kentucky. Traveling by day and spending nights in hotels, the passengers were royally entertained by interurban executives en route. Although long trips were taken by individual enthusiasts, this was probably the most extensive organized trip ever taken entirely by interurban. The fact that the trip was made in a piece of equipment owned by one of the railroads most hostile to the interurbans is not without irony.

It was never possible to travel by interurban from Chicago to New York; gaps between Little Falls and Fonda and between Hudson and Tarrytown, both in New York, were never filled.

It may be asked how effectively the capital market picked and chose between projects, and thus how rational was the final network. At minimum the capital market brought to fruition most of the obvious lines: Rochester–Syracuse, Cleveland–Toledo, Cincinnati–Dayton, Toledo–Detroit, Chicago–Milwaukee, Seattle–Tacoma. But at the same time, because of the unfounded expectations of the time and the high incidence of amateur promotion and ill-informed investment, and, above all, because of the very short period in which investment was concentrated, many lines were built that were far less attractive than some of the unexecuted projects. An extension of the Milwaukee Electric's Watertown line to Madison would probably have been a reasonably strong part of the interurban network. Similarly, such projected lines as Los Angeles–San Diego, San

Francisco–San Jose, Oakland–San Jose, Toronto–Hamilton, and Omaha–Lincoln would have been more prosperous than perhaps half the mileage that was built. The much promoted Toledo–Defiance line, had it been brought to fruition, probably would have been relatively successful, and certainly would have been more remunerative than the Defiance–Lima line that was put in service. Similarly, if any of the six companies that proposed to build directly from Rochester to Buffalo via Batavia had been able to do so, it would probably have had a stronger line than the Rochester–Lockport interurban.

There was little outright duplication of trackage. Aside from the Dayton–Xenia route, mentioned above, there were parallel services between Milwaukee and Kenosha, Cincinnati and Bethel, Saginaw and Bay City, Lorain and Elyria (Ohio), London and Port Stanley (Ontario), and Evansville and Newburgh (Indiana). Some of this mileage, however, served different tributary local territory. Several pairs of towns were connected by two interurbans running by widely separated intermediate communities, notably Dayton–Piqua, Cleveland–Norwalk, Toledo–Findlay, Cincinnati–Hamilton, Pittsburgh–Butler, Michigan City–South Bend (in part this route was directly parallel), Indianapolis–Fort Wayne, Jamestown–Westfield (New York), and Syracuse–Auburn. It was possible to go from Indianapolis to several towns in Indiana by alternative routes.

Even the Ohio–Indiana network, though it was the most integrated part of the industry, was filled with gaps and anomalies. Some presented a problem immediately—for example, the Eastern Ohio's failure to reach the Mahoning Valley—but others became significant only when the interurbans tried to develop a substantial freight business in the 1920's. The Northern Ohio's line west from Akron ended at Wadsworth, about seven miles short of the Cleveland Southwestern and Columbus' line to Mansfield, Bucyrus, and central Ohio.

A larger and more serious gap separated the Columbus Delaware and Marion from the lines radiating south from Toledo; thus, there was no direct route from Toledo to Columbus. At least 24 companies proposed at one time or another to build from the terminus of one of the Toledo roads (Lima, Findlay, Fostoria, Tiffin, or Fremont) to either Marion or Bucyrus to make the connection. In addition, the Toledo Bowling Green and Southern proposed to build south to meet a northward extension of the Columbus Magnetic Springs and Northern at La Rue. The most important of these projects, the Findlay and Marion Electric Railway, was incorporated in 1901 by a former state senator, John R. Hankey, and was almost brought to fruition. The panic of 1903 halted Hankey's first effort, but he re-formed the project as the Findlay and Marion Railway and Light Company in 1904, and again set about to prepare the way for construction. He acquired all his right-of-way and in 1906 received a franchise at Findlay, but was denied one at Marion. He also failed to get a municipal subsidy at the principal intermediate town, Forest, where he planned to have his car house. Accordingly, Hankey revised his plans to build through Upper Sandusky, but the panic of 1907 rendered the entire project impossible. At the same time, a promoter named Frank M. Ohl was striving to build a line from Fostoria to Marion via Upper Sandusky, but in spite of several incorporations he could never finance the project.

The three connections between Indiana and Ohio were inadequate, since only the route through Richmond directly connected major population centers. Much more useful than either the Fort Wayne–Lima or Dayton–Muncie lines would have been a connection from Portland, Indiana, to Celina, Ohio. Had the Muncie and Portland Traction Company line been extended to Celina—about 26 miles—as the promoters intended, there would have been a relatively direct route from Indianapolis to the northern Ohio interurban centers of Lima, Toledo, and Cleveland. Several other companies proposed to build from various points in Indiana to a connection with the Western Ohio Railway at Celina, and the Western Ohio considered building west, but no such connection was ever made.

The connection between the Ohio–Indiana lines and Chicago via the Winona Interurban was so roundabout that it was more nominal than real. Little through traffic ever developed. There were several proposals for direct lines from Chicago or the Calumet area to towns along the Wabash Valley, but the intermediate population was so small that none was built. In 1915 the St. Joseph Valley and the Toledo and Western came within about 13 miles of providing a direct Chicago–Toledo connection, but their financial condition never allowed them to lay the track —even though the Toledo and Western had previously done some of the grading. Similarly, the lines radiating from Evansville were never connected with the rest of the Indiana network. A predecessor of the THI&E, aiming for Vincennes from the north, halted on reaching Sullivan in 1906, and the Evansville and Princeton Traction Company, building to Vincennes from the south, reached Patoka in 1908 and could build no farther.

The interurban network took shape in an atmosphere of almost unbelievable optimism: the statement of 1903 that interurbans were "the latest harbingers of a higher state of civilization"[72] was in no way exceptional. Today such optimism is difficult to understand. In retrospect, the building of the interurbans must be viewed in opposite fashion. The typical interurban was designed to perform the least profitable kinds of railroad service; it was built with a cheap physical plant and meager provisions for depreciation and maintenance, burdened with heavy fixed charges, and set in a geographical pattern that in great measure was the result of chance. On one side lay the eternal enmity of the major railroads, and on the other loomed the specter of highway transport. By the close of the first act, the interurbans' fate was determined as surely as Lear's, and the ultimate disaster came on as inexorably.

2
The Technology of the Interurbans

The electric interurbans designed their physical plants mainly for single-car passenger trains, running on approximately hourly headway.[1] For such operation to be economic, the interurbans had to be built with smaller capital outlay and operated with lower fuel, labor, and maintenance expenses than the railroads. The low cost at which the interurbans secured their rights-of-way was a great initial help.

The cheapest rights-of-way were on the public highway, where the interurban was often permitted to build without charge, provided it assumed maintenance of the track and of the highway within a short distance of the rails. The great majority of New England rural trolley lines were built in this fashion, as were individual interurbans in other regions. Low initial cost was virtually the only advantage of this form of construction. The railway was forced to follow the gradient and curvature of the highway, both of which were frequently severe. The drainage pattern was commonly poorer than that afforded by private right-of-way, so that ties deteriorated more quickly and track alignment shifted more readily. Even though most such lines were abandoned before the advent of hard-surfaced highways, access to their tracks involved an expense that was avoided on private rights-of-way. Because of highway traffic, electric roads of this type were even more limited in speed than most interurbans, and ran a vastly greater risk of accident. President Theodore Roosevelt was slightly injured in 1902 when a car of the Pittsfield and Lenox Street Railway struck a landau in which he was riding with the governor of Massachusetts. The car, running in the center of the road, nicked the left rear wheel of the carriage, threw the President to the ground, and killed a Secret Service officer. Given the flimsy quality of most horse-drawn vehicles, the danger of personal injury from minor collisions was ever present.

The practice of laying track on the public highway was considered obsolete by most of the Midwestern interurbans by the opening of the building boom of 1901–4, but it continued virtually to the end of construction in New England. When the Norwich and Westerly Railway was opened in 1906, the *Street Railway Journal* called it the first high-speed interurban in Connecticut, and stated that all previous lines had been built to street railway standards.[2] To some extent, the New England lines adhered to this unsatisfactory technology simply out of conservatism, but in part—since joy-riding was a major source of traffic in New England but not in the Midwest—they more or less correctly regarded speed as less important. Eastern highway rights-of-way were narrower, towns tended to be closer together, and a higher percentage of the rural population lived directly on the highway. The greater population density entailed more frequent stops and made the acquisition of a private right-of-way more expensive.

Most of the intercity lines of the Public Service Company of New Jersey and some of the Pennsylvania electric lines were of this kind. The older portion of the Auburn and Syracuse Electric Railroad between Auburn and Skaneateles, New York, was built on the highway, but the Skaneateles–Syracuse mileage was on private right-of-way. These electric lines were more clearly hopeless than the Midwestern interurbans, and were swept away more quickly by abandonment. The Rochester and Sodus Bay Railway in New York, which was almost entirely on the highway, did well to survive until 1929.

The Michigan Traction Company's line between Battle Creek and Kalamazoo, opened in 1900, was the principal Midwestern highway line. The Middletown–Hamilton segment of the interurban between Cincinnati and Dayton had been built on the highway, but the Schoepf-McGowan interests replaced it with a private right-of-way. The Tama and Toledo, an Iowa interurban four miles long, had been built on a country road, but in 1912 was entirely relocated, in some places nearly a mile from the former right-of-way; thereafter it was devoted mainly to interchange freight, although it continued to carry passengers until 1925. Several interurbans made partial relocations: one of the last to do so was the Milwaukee Electric Railway and Light Company, which put its Kenosha line on a new private right-of-way in 1932. Much of the Milwaukee Electric's new track was laid over an abandoned concrete highway.

Considerably better than track on the highway was a right-of-way by the side of the road, upraised by a few inches, and not covered by pavement. Such rights-of-way could also be had cheaply, and in general made for higher speeds and fewer accidents, although cross-traffic from side roads and farm entrances was both hazardous and a deterrent to speed. Moreover, lines beside the highway were under strong pressure to stop at farmers' doors, a practice that curtailed their speed even more. Most of the Pennsylvania electric lines were built by the side of the road, and substantial portions of the Detroit United, the Lake Shore Electric, the THI&E, the Illinois Traction, and many other Midwestern lines were built in this fashion. Some roads, like the New Paltz Highland and Poughkeepsie Traction Company line in New York, managed side-of-the-road operations on rights-of-way of only ten feet, barely a foot and a half wider than the cars. A right-of-way of 15 to 20 feet left room for a ditch between the highway and the track, thereby improving drainage and giving the interurban some freedom from the highway's gradients.

Best of all was a private right-of-way separated from the highway by the farmhouses and barns. Cross-traffic was minimized, and there was less incentive to stop frequently. A right-of-way of this kind was almost a necessity for a third-rail interurban, but location engineers understandably recommended it for others as well. The wider a road's right-of-way, the better its drainage pattern, and the greater its freedom in grading. Heavily built lines, like the Scioto Valley, used rights-of-way of 40 feet and more, occasionally as much as 60 feet. The Chicago North Shore and Milwaukee's main line averaged 100 feet, and the Lackawanna and Wyoming Valley in places was 150 feet wide. Interurbans in the Far West were built primarily on private rights-of-way, but most of the major Midwestern lines were mixtures of side-of-the-road and separate rights-of-way.

When farmers objected to having their farms cut by interurban rights-of-way, many companies—particularly the late builders—escaped from the highway by building next to a railroad. The Scioto Valley, the Buffalo and Lake Erie, the Toledo and Indiana, the Fort Wayne Van Wert and Lima, and many other lines ran for almost their entire lengths at the side of railroads. Many interurbans built away from the country roads in this way, only to see hard-surfaced highways laid alongside them in the 1920's. By 1930 it was common to see a railroad, an interurban, and a concrete highway running parallel across the countryside.

Since the interurbans were not designed for locomotive-and-train operation, they could function with more severe grades and curves than the railroads. Grades of 1, 2, and 3 per cent were no particular handicap. Ernest Gonzenbach, whose standards were higher than most, argued that overpasses at railroad crossings should be built with 2 per cent approaches. He thought that such overpasses could be built for about $32,000 each, the interest on which was less than the maintenance of an interlocking plant.[3] But most overpasses were steeper than 2 per cent, and many interurbans in country that was merely hilly had grades steeper than one finds on any American railroad. The Cincinnati Georgetown and Portsmouth and the Pittsburgh Harmony Butler and New Castle had grades of 8 per cent, and the Northern Ohio had one of 10 to 12.5 per cent, 2,700 feet long. Grades of 6 to 8 per cent were quite common, and the Fonda Johnstown and Gloversville had one of 14 per cent on the streets of Amsterdam, New York, used by city cars equipped with magnetic brakes.

Heavy cut-and-fill work was so expensive that the interurbans avoided it whenever possible. The Ohio Electric had a fill of 110,000 cubic yards between Columbus and Springfield, and the THI&E main line between Greencastle and Brazil had extensive limestone cuts. Tunnels were very rare on interurban lines. There were major ones of about a half-mile on the Oakland Antioch and Eastern in the hills east of Oakland, on the United Railways in Oregon, on the Lackawanna and Wyoming Valley at South Scranton, Pennsylvania, and on the Wilkes-Barre and Hazleton south of Wilkes-Barre. A 400-foot tunnel on the Ohio Electric between Newark and Zanesville was the only one in the Ohio-Indiana network.

The difference between interurban and steam-road construction was most apparent in curve design. Railroads characteristically tried to build long, gentle curves, but the interurbans of the low-speed type tended to maximize the length of their tangents by making their curves sharp. Some interurban engineers argued that, since headway was closer and acceleration more rapid than on railroads, it was desirable to minimize the distance over which speed had to be reduced. Thus a car could brake, negotiate a sharp curve, and accelerate again more quickly than it could negotiate a longer but gentler curve. The equipment had to be able to turn streetcar curves in any case. Heavily built lines, like the Lackawanna and Wyoming Valley, followed orthodox railroad practice in curve design. Most roads used guard rails on curves, and some used restraining rails which bore the weight of the car on very sharp curves.

Interurban track did not differ greatly from railroad roadbed. Ties were laid on the grade at about two-foot intervals, rails laid upon them, and ballast spread about them. Several types of wood were used for ties, but cedar and oak were the most popular. Oak was preferable to cedar, but more expensive. The Detroit United used cedar for interurban track, but oak in cities. Its predecessor, the Detroit Ypsilanti Ann Arbor and Jackson, used white oak on curves and switches, but cedar on tangents. Most interurbans did not use tie plates. The Detroit Monroe and Toledo Short Line used crushed limestone ballast from the beginning, and the Columbus Delaware and Marion, the Western Ohio, and the Toledo Port Clinton and Lakeside also used varieties of crushed rock. The Scioto Valley, the Lake Shore Electric, and the Dayton and Troy used washed gravel, and the Stark Electric and many others used cinders from the company powerhouse. Several companies, including the Arkansas Valley Interurban, were too impoverished when they finished building to ballast the track at all, and by the 1920's all but the strongest interurbans were in various stages of deferred maintenance. Ties lasted longest in rock ballast, least long in earth ballast. On many interurbans in the 1930's, ties and ballast alike had disappeared from sight under a carpet of weeds. Most roads gave up all serious effort to control weeds some time before abandonment, and simply let the cars mow the weeds as they passed. On some lines one could see the outline of the bottoms of the cars cut quite distinctly in the foliage. A few roads, notably the Washington Baltimore and Annapolis, were well maintained to the end.

Since the interurban cars were much lighter than steam locomotives, and were free of the vertical pounding characteristic of reciprocating engines, the interurbans used relatively lightweight rails. Rail weighing 70 pounds per yard was standard throughout much of the Midwest. The Scioto Valley used 72-pound rail and the Union Traction Company 80-pound on its Peru line, which, apart from the Air Line, was the heaviest in Indiana and Ohio. Several of the smaller roads used 60-pound rail, and rail even lighter was laid on some of the lines built to street railway standards. T-rail of the kind used by the railroads was standard, usually in 30- or 33-foot lengths, but occasionally in 60-foot lengths. Opinion was about evenly divided between supported joints (i.e., resting on a tie) and suspended joints (i.e., between ties), but staggered rather than opposite joints were customary. The Illinois Traction Company, the Milwau-

The Technology of the Interurbans

kee Electric lines and the Michigan Railway all had opposite joints in some of their installations, and the South Shore Line in later years laid 115-pound welded rail.

In order to use their rails for power return, the interurbans had to bond them at the joints. Failure to do so led to power leakage, which set up corrosive electrolytic circuits in underground telephone cable sheaths and water pipes, causing static in telephones and leaks in the water system. The earliest bonding device was simply a piece of copper compressed under the fishplate, but soldered or welded bonds were soon found to be more satisfactory. A short length of copper cable was soldered to the rails at each end of the fishplate. Since the high value of copper made it a temptation to thieves, the Cleveland and Southwestern soldered the bond under the rail to make it less accessible. Most roads, however, simply placed one bond on each side of each joint, soldered to the web of the rails. Deterioration of bonds over the years was common, and by the 1930's there was a great deal of sparking as cars passed over rail joints.

Fully 90 per cent of interurban mileage was single-track. Greater or lesser portions of the Lake Shore Electric, the Rochester Syracuse and Eastern, the Chicago North Shore and Milwaukee, the Northern Ohio, and the Scioto Valley, among others, were double-track, and the Pacific Electric had substantial amounts of quadruple track. The Indianapolis and Cincinnati, the Union Traction, and several others were built to one side of the right-of-way in the expectation of eventually double tracking. Much of the Grand Rapids Holland and Chicago, which ran beside the Pere Marquette, was built as a double-track line in the misguided belief that traffic would eventually demand it. This was a rare example of a double-track interurban paralleling a single-track railroad. The Bamberger was originally almost entirely double track, but removed most of its second track when it adopted automatic block signals in the late thirties.

Interurban bridges varied about as much as railroad bridges, although most were of course built to lighter standards. Plate girder spans were customary for overpasses and simple truss spans for small rivers, but other varieties were common. There were relatively few major bridges. The most important was McKinley's great triple-span bridge for the Illinois Traction line at St. Louis, which was about 2,450 feet long (including approaches) and rose to 50 feet over mean high water. The Fort Dodge Des Moines and Southern crossed the Des Moines River valley with an enormous steel viaduct 800 feet long and 156 feet above the river. The main line of the Interstate Public Service Company crossed the Ohio at Louisville by electrifying the Big Four Railroad bridge, and its "Daisy" suburban line crossed the Kentucky & Indiana Terminal bridge—two of the most notable examples of cooperation by steam railroads.

Only two interurbans had recourse to car ferries for river crossings. In 1912 the Evansville Railways opened a line to Henderson, Kentucky, where it had purchased the street railway. The company arranged to lease the Evansville–Henderson branch of the Illinois Central Railroad for most of its right-of-way, but it was forced to arrange its own crossing of the Ohio. Being unable to build a bridge, it ordered a small, single-track, sidewheel car ferry, the *Henderson*. The ship was 130 feet long, just enough for a two-car train, and displaced 88 tons when not loaded. Two gasoline engines propelled it. The Oakland Antioch and Eastern, lacking funds to bridge Suisun Bay, built a wooden car ferry with a six-car capacity, the *Bridgit*. In May 1914, after only a few months of service, the ship was destroyed by fire, and the company replaced it with a similar steel ferry, the *Ramon*. Partly because of the haste with which the *Ramon* had to be built, it contained several remarkable features: notably, a hull built entirely of flat plates, and an eight-cylinder, 600-horsepower distillate-burning engine, 46 feet long, weighing 50 tons. This engine is believed to have been the largest internal combustion engine of the electrical ignition type ever built for marine purposes, and possibly the largest built for any purpose. The *Ramon* operated until it was condemned in 1955. The Toledo Port Clinton and Lakeside, upon completion in 1906, considered building a trestle to Johnson's Island in Sandusky Bay, and a slip at the end for a car ferry to downtown Sandusky, but it never carried out this plan.

STREET RUNNING

The interurbans encountered several right-of-way problems in urban areas. A few of the most heavily built lines, such as the Stark Electric, the Scioto Valley, and the Aurora Elgin and Chicago, built private rights-of-way through towns, but the vast majority resorted to street running. When they were unrestricted, interurbans generally laid standard T-rail in towns, and paved the area of the street for which they were responsible under their franchises—usually between the rails and two feet on either side. Since track maintenance was relatively expensive in paved streets, the interurbans generally used heavier rails and higher-quality ties than usual. Some roads made more substantial arrangements, but most set their ties in sand or gravel ballast and paved them over with bricks or paving stones. A flangeway was cut along the inner sides of the rails by chipping away the edges of the paving blocks. Like so many aspects of the technology of the interurbans, this system of track-laying had little to recommend it except low initial cost. Under the weight of the electric cars and of street traffic, the track settled readily in the sand and became rough and irregular. By the 1920's the street trackage of most interurbans was so badly deteriorated that it was common for wheels to scrape the paving stones, and many streets were scored with flange marks left by derailments. At the end, track of the Toledo and Western had sunk in spots to six inches below the pavement at Blissfield, Michigan. In the twenties and thirties, many towns demanded that the interurbans rebuild their track and repave the streets with concrete or asphalt, a replacement perhaps twice as expensive as the original construction.

In the early years some cities objected to the flangeways between the rails and the paving stones, on the ground that they were a hazard to narrow-wheeled wagons and buggies. Accordingly, some municipal governments demanded that the interurbans lay girder rail of the sort used by street railways, which had a shallow flangeway cast into it. The interurbans usually resisted this requirement, for their cars were normally equipped with larger flanges than streetcars used. If they ground down their flanges, they increased the risk of derailment at high speeds. Alternatively, they could run on girder rail without filing if they were willing to have the weight of the cars supported entirely by the flanges, but this involved a risk of cracked flanges—which were an even greater accident hazard. Some companies compromised on a girder rail with a groove deep enough for railroad flanges, but rail of this type was as difficult for vehicles as T-rail. A few roads—for example, the Fort Wayne and Wabash Valley—secured the right to use T-rail in all their franchises, but Detroit, Cleveland, and several lesser cities required girder rail. T-rail was almost universal in the smaller towns.

The problems of street running were worst when the interurban ran over the tracks of a city company over which it had no direct control. It then had to accept more or less as given the flangeways, curves, and clearances that the street railway had built. Probably the most serious clearance problem was the area between the inside rails on double-track streetcar lines. This distance, known as the "devil strip," varied from one city to another, but was most often four feet. In Cincinnati and Dayton it was only 3.5 feet, which limited car width to about 8.5 feet, less than many interurbans would have preferred. When the Toledo Port Clinton and Lakeside had its first cars built to a width of 9 feet, it found that two of them could not pass one another on the Toledo streets. Other roads were restricted in car length by the curves of 35- to 40-foot radius found on city lines.

Worst of all, not all city systems were built to the standard American and European gauge of 4'-8½". Pittsburgh and most other Pennsylvania cities used 5'-2½", which became known as the Pennsylvania trolley gauge. Cincinnati used 5'-2½", Philadelphia 5'-2¼", Columbus 5'-2", Altoona 5'-3", Louisville and Camden 5'-0", Canton and Pueblo 4'-0", Denver, Tacoma, and Los Angeles 3'-6", Toronto an odd 4'-10⅞", and Baltimore a vast 5'-4½". Most nonstandard gauges arose out of municipal governments' fear that the railroads would buy the street railways and use them for switching freight cars in the city streets. Since the builders of street railways generally intended no interchange, and predicted no large secondhand market, standard gauge offered few outstanding attractions.

Certain interurbans built to the local streetcar gauge. The West Penn, the Conestoga Traction, the Philadelphia and Easton, and many other Pennsylvania interurbans built to the Pennsylvania trolley gauge. The Canton–Massillon interurban was built at 4'-0", but both the interurban and the Canton city system were shortly converted to standard gauge. The Tacoma city lines were converted to standard when the interurban from Seattle arrived, but the Denver–Golden–Leyden interurban (via Arvada) and the Denver Tramway remained 3'-6" to the end. The Toronto and York Radial Railway converted from 4′-10⅞″ to standard and back again. The standard-gauge interurbans in Columbus built their own entries into the center of the city on the streets, but had short stretches of dual-gauge track with the city system; the Pacific Electric had miles of dual-gauge track with the Los Angeles Railway. The Cincinnati Georgetown and Portsmouth had a standard-gauge main line, converted from 3′-0″ at the time of electrification, but it had a 5′-2½″ branch to the Coney Island amusement park. At one time its terminal yard was laid with all three gauges in a remarkable show of complexity. Trenton, New Jersey, had no fewer than four gauges in its streets: 4′-8½″ for the Public Service high-speed line from Newark and for the Trenton-Princeton Traction Company line; 5′-0″ for the Public Service line to Camden; 5′-2″ for the Trenton and Mercer County Traction Company line; and 5′-2½″ for the Bucks County Interurban. There were dual-gauge tracks at two points.

Perhaps the company most seriously afflicted by gauge problems was the Allentown and Reading Traction Company: Allentown used 4′-8½″ and Reading 5′-2½″. The line, 40 miles long, had been built by two predecessor companies, each to the gauge of its terminal city. The road thus required two sets of equipment, and through passengers had to change cars at Kutztown, exactly midway.

Cincinnati was the most difficult terminal city of all, because it had not only a nonstandard gauge but a dual overhead as well. The Cincinnati Street Railway had been enjoined by the local telephone company from using its tracks as a power return, on the ground that this practice interfered with underground telephone circuits. By the time the Street Railway managed to have the injunction lifted, it had equipped so much of its system with a dual trolley that it decided to complete the job. The lines of the Interurban Railway and Terminal Company to Lebanon, New Richmond, and Bethel were built to 5′-2½″, and the cars carried dual trolley poles 18 inches apart. Cars used both poles in Cincinnati, but only the positive pole in the country. In emergencies it was possible to switch polarity and use the negative pole as the positive. Since the trolley wire was centered, the trolley pole was nine inches off center while on the interurban track.

One of the attractions of the Cincinnati subway, a project often promoted but never completed, was a standard-gauge entry for the interurban from Dayton. The last cars of the Cincinnati and Lake Erie had equipment for high-level loading in the subway, but they were never able to use it. In 1922 the Cincinnati Lawrenceburg and Aurora incorporated a subsidiary, the West End Terminal Railway, in order to build a standard-gauge elevated right-of-way from its terminal at Anderson's Ferry to downtown Cincinnati, a distance of nearly seven miles, but the company was much too weak to execute the plan, and never secured an entrance.

Even companies that had no gauge problems had a considerable incentive to build private entrances into cities. The loss in time in street running was always one of the interurbans' worst disadvantages, and it became severe as automobile traffic increased. Simultaneously, however, the proliferation of automobiles had put most of the interurbans in such bad financial condition that they could not afford to build private rights-of-way into their terminals. Exceptions were few. In the 1920's the Columbus Delaware and Marion opened a private right-of-way into Columbus, and the Milwaukee Electric built a high-speed line into Milwaukee from the west. In 1927 the city of Rochester opened a subway entrance for the interurbans that served it, built on the bed of the former Erie Canal, but by 1931 these interurbans had all been abandoned. Electrification of the Illinois Central Railroad suburban service in 1926 gave the Chicago South Shore and South Bend an ideal entrance into Chicago, its first. The interurbans never got off the streets in Cleveland, Toledo, or Indianapolis.

ELECTRIC POWER SYSTEMS

At the outset, the builders of the interurbans had a choice of two possible power systems: low-voltage direct current or high-voltage three-phase alternating current. There was little doubt that the former was preferable. Three-phase electrification required three separate sources of power—two overhead wires and the rails—and the use of an induction motor that could not operate on the low-voltage DC street railway systems. Moreover, the AC equipment had a constant power consumption and could be controlled in speed only by efficiency-loss regulation. Power, however, could be transmitted long distances without significant loss of voltage, and the motors lent themselves well to "regenerative braking," wherein they were converted to generators on downgrades to feed power back into the overhead. For these reasons, three-phase electrification was adapted mainly to mountain electrifications of steam railroads. There were several installations in the Alps, and it was used on the Great Northern's first Cascade Tunnel electrification. It was installed on the ill-conceived Cincinnati–Dayton canal project, but otherwise it was utterly unsuited to the interurbans' conditions.

Street railways had been equipped from the beginning with low-voltage direct current. The difficulty of maintaining voltage over long distances, the principal handicap of DC systems, did not affect most streetcar lines, and DC equipment was well adapted to single-car operation on short headway. The DC motor was relatively simple, and light enough to be carried one-to-an-axle. By the beginning of large-scale interurban building, street railways had almost universally adopted 600-volt DC, about the maximum voltage that could safely be handled in a motor of this type; 550- and 650-volt current were used by some lines, and there were a few other minor deviations, all well within the 50 per cent safety margin customarily provided in the winding of the motors. The interurbans that were built in the boom of 1901–4 adopted DC at or about 600 volts almost automatically because there was no effective alternative. There was a tendency to increase voltage within the safety margin over the years. The Union Traction began with a voltage of 550 and gradually increased it to 650. Such changes usually required no alterations in the rolling stock. The Bamberger adopted 750 volts when it electrified in 1910. The use of DC power at these voltages enabled the interurbans to operate with simple, light motors, and to run on the streetcar lines in their terminal cities.

Most interurbans began by generating their own power, since commercial power was rarely available in large quantities at the appropriate voltage. Many were the first large-scale generators of electricity in the towns they served, and sold power extensively to firms and households. Some gave up power sales when the spread of home appliances created a demand for 60-cycle alternating current that they could not supply. Many converted their powerhouses in the twenties from steam-generating plants to motor-generator arrangements using power from commercial sources, or else arranged to buy commercial power at their transmission voltages. Several roads, such as the Scioto Valley and the Interstate, developed power businesses that dwarfed the rail operations, and survived after the interurbans were abandoned.

Power stations varied in size and equipment depending on the extent and traffic of the lines they served. At first, the 500-horsepower reciprocating engine was quite standard, but 1,000-horsepower, 1,500-horsepower, and larger engines were subsequently used. Steam turbines, which greatly economized space, became common after the Cleveland and Southwestern's pioneer installation in 1903. Water-tube boilers were customary, but the nature of the generators varied with the sort of power system the road employed. Except on very short lines, such as the Dayton and Troy and the Dayton Covington and Piqua, it was impossible to transmit 600-volt DC to the whole railway directly. The losses in power from electrical friction in the feeder lines at the relatively low trolley voltage were so great that additional power feed points were necessary. The Union Traction tried generating at both 600 and 1,200 volts on its earliest line, feeding the 1,200-volt wire into the trolley wire at the distance at which it had lost half its voltage, but this system proved to be unworkable. Almost immediately the interurbans adopted a system of transmitting power at some higher voltage and converting it to the trolley voltage at substations. It is believed that the first substation was installed on the Cripple Creek District Railway in Colorado in 1897, but another was built at almost the same time for the Rapid Railway in Michigan.

Some interurbans, including the Chicago North Shore and Milwaukee, originally used a DC transmission system, in which storage batteries were placed in substations at outlying points. These batteries were connected to the trolley wires through a motor-generator set called a booster. The booster could be arranged to run from the trolley feed to build up the battery during the interval between cars, and it could be rearranged to run

The Technology of the Interurbans

from the battery to feed the trolley wire, boosting the voltage as the cars came within range. This system proved complex and costly, and by the turn of the century had been largely superseded by AC transmission systems.

In the AC system the generating plant produced three-phase alternating current, which was fed into relatively light transmission lines at very high voltage. Some roads built in the late 1890's, such as the Terre Haute Traction and Light Company line, generated at 10,000 to 13,000 volts AC, but a rapid upward trend developed. The Lake Shore Electric transmitted at 16,500 volts between Toledo and Norwalk, the Stark at 22,000, the Cleveland and Southwestern at 24,000, and the Western Ohio at 33,000. The Western Ohio was able to transmit over distances of 80 and 95 miles with this voltage, and its experience led to a general adoption of 33,000-volt transmission. Since power companies also transmitted at this voltage, conversion to commercial power sources later in the interurbans' history was easier than it would have been had the interurbans adopted a unique transmission system.

Three high-tension wires, usually carried at the top of the pole line along the right-of-way, carried power to the substations. A single power station could serve over 200 miles of track. The Western Ohio's station at St. Mary's generated for the entire railway, and the Lake Shore Electric required only two power stations for its whole system. The Union Traction generated power for all its lines except the Indianapolis–New Castle–Portland route from a large power station in Anderson. The company began transmitting at 15,000 volts on the Muncie and Marion lines, but transmitted at 30,000 on the newer Peru division.

The principal piece of equipment in a substation was a rotary converter that acted simultaneously as an AC motor and as a 600-volt DC generator. Output varied according to expected traffic; the Eastern Ohio (a notoriously underpowered line) had converters of only 100 kilowatt output, but the Toledo Port Clinton and Lakeside had some of 500 kilowatts. A substation also included a step-down transformer to reduce the voltage from the transmission line to a safe level for feeding into the rotary converter, one or more blowers, and control equipment. Because the early substations required constant attention, they were typically built adjoining stations, interlocking towers, or the residences of their tenders. Automatic equipment to adjust the DC output to the needs of the line was introduced by Bion J. Arnold on his Elgin and Belvidere Railway in 1915, and became common thereafter.

In addition to their permanent installations, most interurbans owned one or more portable substations. These were cars of about the size and construction of ordinary boxcars, each fitted with transformers and a rotary converter. The car could be spotted on a siding and cut into the transmission line to boost the power in the trolley line whenever there was a heavy concentration of cars at a particular point. Fairs, baseball games, picnics, and outings of various sorts made heavy demands on the trolley line, often quite far from substations. The power distribution of most interurbans was quite spartan, and the loss of power at the extremes between substations was often perceptible.

Distances between permanent substations varied. The heavily traveled, high-speed North Shore Line had substations of 1,000 or 1,500 kilowatts at about three-mile intervals along its double track. Few of the typical low-speed, single-track interurbans approached this frequency. The Toledo Port Clinton and Lakeside and the Scioto Valley, both of which were considered well powered, installed 450-kilowatt substations at 10- to 13-mile intervals. The Western Ohio used 400-kilowatt stations at 12-mile intervals. There was a tendency to increase the distance between substations as the building booms of 1900–1908 progressed. The Union Traction Company placed substations only 7 to 11.5 miles apart on its early trackage, but averaged intervals of 17 miles on its Peru line. The maximum distance between low-voltage DC substations in Ohio and Indiana was reported to be 21 miles on the Interstate Public Service Company.

Most interurbans distributed power to the cars by simple overhead trolley wires, suspended over the center of the track. The Hocking Valley Railroad's subsidiary, the Wellston and Jackson Belt Railway in Ohio, the Pennsylvania Railroad's Cumberland Valley electrification in Pennsylvania, and Paul Smith's Electric Railroad in New York used a trolley line at the side of the right-of-way, but apparently no other interurbans did so. The interurbans at first suspended their trolley wires mainly from what were called "span wires"—insulated wires strung across the track from a double set of poles driven on either side of the right-of-way. Since the second line of poles was a rather needless expense on a single track interurban, this form of construction was soon replaced by suspension from "bracket arms"—simple pipe extensions from a single set of poles. The Union Traction Company used span wires on its early lines between Indianapolis, Muncie, and Marion, but switched to bracket arms on later construction. The typical bracket arm held a horizontal wire at a right angle to the track about six inches beneath the arm. Over the center of the track this wire, through a porcelain insulator, held the trolley wire. Most roads used bracket arm construction on tangents, and span wires on curves, sidings, yards, and over city streets. The Bamberger, the Pacific Electric, the Lake Shore Electric, and many others used span wires on double-track, whereas the Detroit United, the Grand Rapids Holland and Chicago, and a minority of others placed their poles at the center of the right-of-way and hung bracket arms from either side.

The typical pole line carried three wires for the transmission line (or six if for any reason two transmission lines were being run), a pair of telephone wires for dispatching, a second pair of telephone wires for general company business, a feeder wire at the trolley voltage, and sometimes a ground wire to safeguard the lines from lightning. The Newark and Granville's pioneer electrification had little or no lightning protection, and suffered such heavy damage to its motors and powerhouse equipment that it was forced to shut down operations during severe thunderstorms. The ground wire's purpose was to provide an escape for static electricity that would repel lightning. The wire was grounded at approximately every tenth pole, and worked like an ordinary lightning rod.

The feeder line was added in order to reduce the resistance in the trolley line and was cut into the trolley wire at intervals. Some roads achieved the same result by two trolley wires, one for each direction. This also simplified signaling and, since it dispensed with overhead frogs, reduced the risk of dewirements at sidings. (The Cedar Rapids and Iowa City Railway tried to minimize dewirements by a device that threw a switch in the overhead trolley frog simultaneously with the switch in the rails.) The high price of copper scrap during World War I, coupled with the ebb in the interurbans' finances at that time, caused many of these companies to convert to single overhead. The height of the trolley wire from the rail varied from one interurban to another. On the Cincinnati and Columbus it was only 16 feet, but on the Dayton and Troy it was 21, and on the Texas Interurban's electrification of a branch of the MKT Railroad, it was 22. Eighteen feet was the most common distance. Since the height of the wire bore no perceptible relation to the height of the cars, the interurban companies apparently never decided upon an optimum angle between trolley pole and wire.

Overhead suspension had a rival in the form of the outside third rail, which had been used for the intramural railway at the Chicago World's Fair and again for the electrification of the Chicago Elevated, and which most rapid transit lines adopted. It was introduced to the interurbans by the Albany and Hudson in 1900, and adopted by a few lines built subsequently. In the Ohio-Indiana network only the Scioto Valley used it, but it was moderately popular elsewhere among lines that were built for fast running or for heavy traffic.[4] The principal advantage of a third rail was its lower maintenance expense, but it also offered greater conductivity than a copper wire by as much as 750 per cent.

In several ways overhead suspension was superior. Since in any case, the company had to erect a line of poles at about 100-foot intervals for its transmission line, the marginal cost of a set of bracket arms and a line of copper wire was less than the cost of a third rail, together with its insulation and underground connections. It was estimated that overhead could be installed for from $3,500 to $5,000 per mile, but that the third rail would require $5,000–$7,500.[5] The worst disadvantage of the outside third rail was the danger to trespassers on the right-of-way: to touch it was to risk instant death. The problem was particularly serious with children, who could not be warned away by signs, and any sort of protection involved expense to the company. At minimum, it was necessary to fence the right-of-way in populous areas and install railings and cattle guards at intersections.

The Oneida Railway and the Central California Traction Company mounted their third rails upside down from insulators, covered the rail with boards, and made contact from the bottom. Although this arrangement reduced the safety hazard, the alignment of an under-running third rail was difficult to maintain. As the continual upward pressure of the shoes raised the third rail, arcing resulted, burning away the contact surfaces. On the other hand, under-running third rails were well protected from ice formation, one of the principal problems of over-running third-rail systems. Ice, which would almost perfectly insulate a third rail from the pick-up shoe, formed readily in sleet storms and, in particular, during light, cold rains during rising temperatures, when the ground had not yet unfrozen. Ordinary salt was an unsatisfactory melting agent because it was corrosive. The Aurora Elgin and Chicago experimented with painting calcium chloride on the third rail from tanks on the cars, but regularly used mechanical scrapers attached to the trucks.

All third-rail systems had breaks at intersections. Thus car lights went off at every street crossing, and a car that lost momentum in a long crossing had to be connected with the third rail by a portable jumper cable. In order to deal with this problem under one-man operation, the Albany and Hudson equipped its last cars with pantographs and hung short lengths of trolley wire to help them over long intersections. All third-rail lines that had street running had to carry trolley poles, which the conductor put in place at the edge of town. But opposed to these disadvantages were the low maintenance cost of third rail, the high degree of dependability, and a generally good safety record. Third-rail lines were free of dewirements on curves, a serious problem on high-speed lines. Therefore, third rail had its advocates, although they were a minority in the industry.

The distribution of DC power at approximately 600 volts was virtually universal until about 1905. Since most interurbans were tightly budgeted, their promoters looked eagerly for a power system that would reduce the capital expenditure on substations, and promise savings on substation maintenance. (Three-phase AC had by then been discarded by the industry, except for transmission.) In 1904 Charles L. Henry adopted a new type of single-phase AC distribution for the Rushville line of his Indianapolis and Cincinnati Traction Company. Developed by Westinghouse, it required only a single overhead wire and permitted a relatively simple control of the speed of the equipment.[6] Henry later converted the company's Shelbyville division to the same system. Westinghouse and General Electric installed about 21 single-phase AC electrifications on interurbans, including one in Canada and two on American railroads that were adopting interurban-style service on branch lines. The early installations used a voltage of 3,300, but after 1907 Westinghouse also offered a voltage of 6,600. The two installations on railroads, one on the Erie and the other on the Colorado & Southern (under the name Denver and Interurban Railroad), used a voltage of 11,000.

Economy in building and operating substations was the great selling point of single-phase. The Milwaukee Electric's Watertown and East Troy lines were built with a single outlying substation each, and the Fort Wayne and Springfield (22 miles) needed only the powerhouse itself.

Moreover, a single-phase substation was a relatively simple installation, based mainly on a step-down transformer, plus a rotary frequency changer if the frequencies of the transmission line and the trolley wire differed. Such installations could be made for about 60 per cent of the cost of standard DC substations; and because a single-phase substation was simple enough to be operated by remote control from the main powerhouse, maintenance was only about half as expensive as in a DC installation.[7] Henry estimated that the Indianapolis and Cincinnati would save $500,000 on the capital expense of the projected 93-mile line between Indianapolis and Hamilton, Ohio.[8]

Single-phase systems were typically built with a catenary overhead of the type used in railroad electrifications, instead of a simple trolley wire. This more than doubled the first cost of the wire, but since a catenary could be strung from poles 120 to 150 feet apart, or even farther, instead of the usual 100-foot intervals, it reduced the cost of poles, cut power leakage, and improved visibility. The Indianapolis and Cincinnati, however, used a separate set of poles for its transmission line. The Washington Baltimore and Annapolis, the Toledo and Chicago, and the Milwaukee Electric collected power with well-insulated trolley poles, but most AC interurbans used pantographs. The Indianapolis and Cincinnati, the Fort Wayne and Springfield, and the Warren and Jamestown used bow collectors, but the I&C was the only American railway to use them for any long period.

Since it was thought unsafe to use high voltages in urban areas, single-phase lines had to step down voltage for major street running. The Fort Wayne and Springfield stepped down from 6,600 volts on the line to 500 volts in Decatur, its terminus. At the edge of town it had a 200-foot insulated section that could be set for either voltage. The Indianapolis and Cincinnati reduced to 500 volts in Rushville, and the Windsor Essex and Lake Shore to 1,100 in Windsor. The South Shore Line stepped down voltage in Gary, Michigan City, and South Bend. Most single-phase equipment also had to be run on low-voltage DC on street railways, or, as on the Inland Empire, Illinois Traction, and Milwaukee Electric lines, on the DC portions of a company's own lines. This arrangement required at least a dual set of resistances on every car, and demanded a series-wound commutator motor insulated against the inductive effects of AC. Cars also had to carry transformers to step down the AC voltage to a safe level for use in the motors. Because such motors were heavier, more complex, and mechanically less efficient than straight DC motors, and because control and insulation arrangements were also heavier and more complicated, cars with single-phase motors were more expensive to buy, maintain, and operate than DC equipment. The first cars of the Indianapolis and Cincinnati weighed 96,760 pounds each and were possibly the heaviest interurban cars built up to that time. The 55-foot cars of the Denver and Interurban, built in 1908, weighed 125,000 pounds. In 1910 it was estimated that a car weighing 43 tons with DC motors would weigh 54 tons if equipped for AC.

It would have a first cost of $12,000 if fitted for DC, $20,000 if fitted for AC. The writer estimated that maintenance costs would be 2 cents per mile for DC equipment, but 3.5 cents for single-phase.[9] Single-phase equipment depreciated more rapidly, consumed more power, and was more destructive of track. Moreover, it had poor starting torque, it accelerated slowly, and it had the further operating disadvantage that cars usually had to stop in order to switch from the pantograph or other AC pickup to a DC trolley pole at the edge of town. Most roads made the change in wiring automatically with the change in pickup, but a road that used the same pole for both AC and DC risked delay from blown fuses if motormen neglected to switch from low-voltage resistance to high. The Warren and Jamestown switched from its bow collector to a trolley pole in order to pick up 550-volt AC in towns.

The disadvantages of single-phase did not go unnoticed; it was not installed after 1910. At least two roads, the Syracuse Lake Shore and Northern in New York, and the Shore Line Electric in Connecticut, built overheads insulated for 6,600-volts AC, but installed DC instead. The New York road subsequently considered converting to single-phase, but wisely refrained. The solution to the interurbans' power problem would have been a synthesis in which AC was transmitted in the trolley wire at high voltage and then converted to DC in the cars, but only one road—Paul Smith's Electric Railroad, hardly an interurban—had such an arrangement. It carried 5,000-volt AC in its trolley wire but converted to 600-volt DC in the car, first with a rectifier, later with a motor-generator set. Such arrangements are familiar in railroad electrifications.

The fiendish complication of a single-phase power system, together with some of the incidental terminal problems of a major interurban, was admirably exemplified by the Washington Baltimore and Annapolis. Its cars started from Baltimore on the 600-volt DC of the United Railways & Electric Co. Since the local gauge was non-standard, the WB&A laid a third rail on the street at 4'-8½" for somewhat more than a mile to the beginning of its own rails. On its private right-of-way it used a catenary overhead for 6,600 volts AC.

From Seat Pleasant, Maryland, at the District of Columbia line, the WB&A's cars switched to the Benning Road line of the Washington Railway and Electric Company for an entrance into the city. The WR&E used the standard gauge and 600-volt DC, but like the Cincinnati Street Railway, it used an overhead power return that required dual trolley poles. In addition, because the District of Columbia prohibits overhead wires in the central areas of Washington, the WR&E's cars were fitted with removable "plows" for current pickup in a conduit in the middle of each track. The city government in Annapolis also required a double overhead in the streets. Another municipal regulation limited the WB&A to two-car trains in the Washington streets. Finally, the curves on the WR&E were so sharp, and the conduit track so lightly built, that the WB&A's original equipment could get no closer to the heart of the city than 15th and H Streets, N. E. This was a serious handicap, for the line was built mainly to give express passenger service between Washington and Baltimore on schedules approximating those of the Pennsylvania and the Baltimore & Ohio Railroads.

Since street running required 12 to 15 minutes in Baltimore and 18 in Washington, plus about 20 minutes to ride the local car from 15th and H to the center of the city, the company originally scheduled its trains at 66 miles per hour over private right-of-way—some of the fastest running in the history of the interurbans. The first cars were handsome wooden coaches, 62 feet long, equipped for operation of 6,600-volt AC or 600-volt DC, and fitted with four trolley poles each. The high-voltage poles were 15 feet long and the low-voltage 12 feet. The former were used on the company's own line and the latter in Baltimore, but both were used in Washington, with the longer switched to negative. The original cars did not operate on the conduit line.

The WB&A used this system for only two years. In 1910, it re-equipped its trains with rolling stock short enough to run into downtown Washington and the WR&E bolstered its track with I beams to support the new equipment. The interurban sold its original cars to the Rock Island Southern, which was completing the last single-phase road, and to the Bamberger Railroad, a DC line that bought the cars stripped of their motors for use as trailers. Simultaneously, the WB&A converted the overhead on its main line to 1,200-volt DC. It reported that its maintenance expense per car mile fell from .85 cents to .19 cents. The Baltimore–Annapolis line, also AC, was converted in 1914.

Most of the other single-phase lines made similar conversions (see Table 1). The Milwaukee Electric began its conversion to 1,200-volt DC in 1909, the year following completion of its single-phase system. After the development of the automatic substation, single-phase had even less to recommend it. When the Fort Wayne and Decatur Traction Company, formerly the Fort Wayne and Springfield, converted to 1,200 volts in 1917, it installed one substation, bonded one of its rails (only one had been bonded previously), and bought new cars weighing about five-sixths as much as the old. The consumption of current fell to about half.

A few lines, however, retained single-phase for very long periods. The South Shore Line converted to 1,500-volt DC for consistency with the Illinois Central suburban electrification in 1926. The Great Northern retained AC on the Moscow and Colfax lines of its Inland Empire interurban until they were dieselized in 1941. The most tenacious single-phase road was the San Francisco Napa and Calistoga, which was still using AC in 1932 when a fire in its car barn at Napa destroyed most of its equipment and ruined the power plant. That the line was restored to service at all is surprising; that it was rebuilt for single-phase operation is astonishing. The company, unable to replace its cars from the abundant DC rolling stock on the second-hand market, ordered two heavy, steel cars from the St. Louis Car Company, virtually the only interurban equipment installed at the depths of the depression. The company continued to use single-phase until its last remaining line, a switching track into the Mare Island Navy Yard, was converted to diesel power in 1942. The most unfortunate conversion was that of the Windsor Essex and Lake Shore Rapid Railway; the company was converted to 600-volt DC, reequipped, and rebuilt in 1930 by the municipalities along the line in conjunction with Ontario Hydro. The system encountered operating losses almost immediately and was abandoned in 1932. The last interurban to use single-phase was the Visalia Electric in 1945, but this was in freight-only operation.

TABLE 1—SINGLE-PHASE ALTERNATING CURRENT INSTALLATIONS

Company	Voltage	Date of installation	Date of conversion	Type of conversion
Indianapolis & Cincinnati Traction Co.	3,300	1904–7	1924	600 v. DC
Warren & Jamestown Ry.	3,300	1905	1911	600 v. DC
Atlanta Northern Traction Company	3,300	1905	1923	600 v. DC
Bloomington Pontiac & Joliet Electric Ry.	3,300	1905	1915	600 v. DC
Toledo & Chicago	3,300	1907	1913	650 v. DC
Visalia Electric	3,300	1907–8	1945*	Diesel
Fort Wayne & Springfield Ry.	6,600	1907	1917	1,200 v. DC
Pittsburgh & Butler St. Ry.	6,600	1907	1912–13	1,200 v. DC
Illinois Traction Co. (Peoria to Bloomington and Springfield)	3,300	1907	ca. 1910	650 v. DC
Milwaukee Electric Ry. & Light Co. (Waukesha Beach to Watertown, Fruitland to East Troy and Burlington)	3,300	1907–8	1909–10	1,200 v. DC
Washington Baltimore & Annapolis Ry.	6,600	1908	1910	1,200 v. DC
Annapolis Short Line	6,600	1908	1914	1,200 v. DC
York Railways (York–Hanover)	6,600	1907–8	1921	660 v. DC
Richmond & Chesapeake Bay Ry.	6,600	1907	1919	550 v. DC
Chicago Lake Shore & South Bend Ry.	6,600	1908	1926	1,500 v. DC
Rock Island Southern Railroad (Rock Island–Monmouth)	6,600	1910	1926	Steam
Inland Empire	6,600	1906–8	1941	Diesel
Erie Railroad (Rochester–Mt. Morris)	11,000	1906–7	1934	Gas-electric
Denver & Interurban RR	11,000	1908	1926	Abandoned
San Francisco Napa & Calistoga Ry.	3,300	1905–12	1942*	Diesel
Windsor Essex Lake Shore Rapid Ry.	6,600	1907–8	1930	660 v. DC

* Passenger service was abandoned earlier. See the histories of these lines in Part II.

The new DC system of about 1,200 volts to which several of the single-phase lines converted was introduced in 1907 by General Electric on the Indianapolis and Louisville Traction Company between Seymour and Sellersburg, Indiana.[10] The higher voltage increased the cost of building a substation by less than 10 percent and made a negligible difference in maintenance and operating costs. The saving on capital expense was considerable: the entire 41 miles of the Indianapolis and Louisville was operated without a substation. Two ordinary 600-volt generators connected in series in the powerhouse served the whole property, and direct suspension of trolley wire sufficed.* The cars used 600-volt motors, and were wired so that they could operate unchanged on 600-volt trolley wire at half speed or, if a switch were thrown, at full speed in the same manner as a standard 600-volt car. Lighting and other auxiliaries operated at 600 volts, either off the trolley wire on 600-volt line or from a dynamotor on 1,200-volt line. The mechanism for this system added only about a ton to the weight of a car and about $1,500 to the cost.

High-voltage DC was introduced so late in interurban development that few roads converted to it, but it became quite common among roads built after the panic of 1907. The Oakland Antioch and Eastern used it, the Pacific Electric installed it on its San Bernardino line, and the Portland Eugene and Eastern used a similar 1,500-volt DC system. The Oregon Electric converted its Portland–Salem line from 600 volts when it opened its Salem–Eugene extension in 1912, and thereafter operated at 1,200. The Fort Dodge Des Moines and Southern converted from 650 to 1,200 volts when it electrified its Rockwell City branch, but roads that had already invested in DC substations had little or no incentive to change. Low-voltage DC was so standard on the Midwestern interurbans that the Oneida Railway car used in the excursion from Utica to Louisville in 1910 was able to run on its own power throughout, except on the 41 miles of the Indianapolis and Louisville Traction Company. This installation was converted to 600 volts for consistency with the rest of the Indiana network by the Interstate Public Service Company in 1920. Had the 1,200-volt DC system been available in 1901, however, it would doubtless have been adopted almost universally.

Lines that operated their original mileage at 600 volts and later mileage at 1,200 were handicapped to the extent that their low-voltage equipment could not operate on their high-voltage trackage. The Clinton line of the Clinton Davenport and Muscatine Railway was wired for 650 volts, but the Muscatine line for 1,200. The Denison line of the Texas Electric was wired for 650 volts, but both the Waco and Corsicana lines for 1,200. (The Pacific Electric's equipment that was built for the high-voltage San Bernardino line was appropriately numbered in the 1,200 series.)

The Sacramento Northern, after absorbing the former Oakland Antioch and Eastern, was particularly troubled by differences in voltage. Its northern division motorcars, wired for 600 volts, could not operate south of Sacramento under any circumstances, but the southern division equipment, wired for 1,200, could run the length of the railway. Customarily, on through trains from San Francisco or Oakland to Chico only trailers traveled the entire distance, and motorcars were changed in Sacramento. Even so, the operations were a model of complexity. Southern division motor cars were fitted with a trolley pole at each end for operation on

---

* Some roads preferred to use catenary for DC simply because it reduced the risk of dewirements at high speed. It was, for example, installed in the North Shore Line's Skokie Valley route in 1926.

their own line, and a pantograph for use on the Key System, a suburban line that furnished terminal trackage in Oakland. A train bound for Sacramento began its run (after 1939) at the Bridge Terminal in San Francisco, collecting power with the pantographs from a 1,300-volt catenary overhead installed on the Bay Bridge for the Southern Pacific's Interurban Electric Railway suburban trains, which were also wired for high-voltage DC. The Key System on the same track used a 600-volt DC covered top-contact third rail. At the east end of the bridge, the Sacramento Northern trains passed onto the 600-volt DC overhead of the Key System. Before the bridge was opened, the Sacramento Northern had operated on the Key System with motors set for 600 volts, but the company felt it was impractical to reset the motors (which could be done only with the train stopped and the pantograph and trolley poles down) for the short distance between the bridge and the beginning of the company's own right-of-way at 40th and Shafter in Oakland. The Sacramento Northern's cars could operate on 600-volt wire with motors set for 1,200 volts at about 36 miles per hour, only about 4 miles per hour below the top speed of the Key System equipment. This speed, which was about 9 miles per hour above half speed, was made possible by the use of field taps, installed expressly for this operation.

At 40th and Shafter, pantographs were lowered and a single trolley pole put up. On the Key System, each Sacramento Northern car took its own power, but on the company's own tracks, most trains (usually having no more than two motor cars) used only the trolley pole on the first car and distributed power to the rest of the train by a "bus line," for which jumper cables were put in place at 40th and Shafter. The yard at that point was wired for 600-volt DC, and the first two blocks of street running toward Sacramento also carried this voltage. Trains operated at half speed over this trackage, and then began running on high-voltage wire to Sacramento. The company used 1,200 volts until 1936 and 1,500 thereafter. Cars went onto the ferry under their own power, for the wires on the ferry were energized in the slip. Freight locomotives used pantographs on the line, but pole trolleys for going on or off the ferry. At Westgate, just south of Sacramento, a train began running at half speed again on the 600-volt wire in the city.

If the motor equipment was to run north of Sacramento, its motors were set for 600-volt, full-speed operation by throwing a switch under the car, and top-contact third-rail shoes were attached to the trucks at Union Station. Although southern division motor cars had connections for third-rail shoes, they could not carry the shoes on the Bay Bridge, where they would have fouled the Key System's covered third rail. North of Sacramento, open top-contact third-rail operation was standard on the line, but it gave way to pole trolley for street running in Marysville-Yuba City, Live Oak, and Chico.[11]

Only one interurban installed a DC system at a higher voltage than 1,500, and the experiment could hardly have been less successful. The

Michigan Railway equipped its Grand Rapids–Battle Creek–Kalamazoo–Allegan extension, opened in 1915, with a 2,400-volt third-rail system. At this voltage, arcing occurred between the third rail and the journal boxes, causing the undersides of the journal boxes to be eaten away. In sleet storms arcing was so severe that circuit breakers frequently kicked out. When they cut back in, the surge of power at 2,400 volts was enough to burn out the traction motors. When a siege of severe winter weather put 80 per cent of the equipment in bad order, the company gave up the 2,400-volt electrification after only about a year of service and adopted an orthodox 1,200-volt system. During the time that the voltage of 2,400 was used, the danger to passengers was so great that they were loaded from pens called "safety loading platforms," which the conductor unlocked with a switch key when the train arrived.

SIGNALING AND DISPATCHING

Signaling installations on the interurbans ranged from none at all (typical of the smaller lines) to heavy-duty automatic block signals nearly identical to those used by steam railroads. The earliest signaling systems, first installed around 1891, were manual arrangements in which the motorman threw electric switches at sidings to mark his progress. The Washington and Old Dominion, the Philadelphia Suburban Transportation Company, the West Penn, and many other Eastern lines used manual signals to the end. On the West Penn, signaling was done with ordinary 40-watt frosted light bulbs attached to the line poles on either side of the track at sidings and occasionally along the line. The company usually put one at the beginning of a blind curve. The lights were operated by large wooden-handled switches placed in pairs at sidings. Upon entering a siding, the motorman leaned out of his front door to throw both switches. One turned on the bulbs on his right on the section he was about to enter, and the other turned off the bulbs on his right on the section he had just vacated. Consequently, when he arrived at a siding and saw that a bulb was burning on his left, the motorman knew that a car was approaching him on the single track and that he could not safely enter the next section. If the light on his right were burning, he might safely follow a car bound in his own direction. After leaving a siding, the lights on his right should always be lit, whether by the preceding car or by himself. The company posted signs threatening prosecution for murder to anyone who caused a fatal accident by tampering with the switches. Since the West Penn did not operate at high speeds, the signaling system was satisfactory, and the company had an excellent safety record.

The most characteristic interurban signals were trolley-contact signals, introduced about 1895. The most important of these was the Nachod signal, but others were produced under the names United States Electric, Chapman, and Ward. The United States Electric signal was popular in New England. Interurban lines could install contact signals on single track for about $550 per mile, about half the cost of railroad-style continuous block signals. All contact signals were of the type known as intermittent, in which the car triggered the mechanism when entering or leaving a block. The trolley wheel hit a set of electrical contacts placed on each side of the wire and tripped the signal mechanism, which took its power from the trolley line.

Contact signals would have been simple had the interurbans not wanted to use an absolute-permissive system. That is to say, when a car entered a block, it was expected to give two indications, an absolute-stop indication to cars coming from the opposite direction, but a permissive indication to cars following in the same direction, implying that the block was occupied, but might safely be entered. On double track the problem did not arise; and on single track with a wire for movements in each direction, the problem was easily solved. A car entering a block turned on a red light at the far end and a white light at the near end, and upon leaving turned them out again. The difficulty arose on a line with a single trolley wire for both directions. In the Nachod signal, there were two pairs of contacts attached to a quick-acting relay that automatically ascertained the direction in which the car was traveling. The Chapman and the United States signals used pendulums to hold their contacts, which were set off according to the direction in which the trolley wheel struck the pendulum. All contact systems had relays that "counted" cars in and out of blocks so that the signal would not be cleared until as many cars left as had entered. In any installation, a car passing a red signal set by an approaching car in the opposite direction would not turn off the signal. There was a danger that, although the car would not turn off the signal by entering an occupied block, it might do so by backing out, when the crew discovered its mistake. There was no practical way of dealing with this problem on a single trolley wire, but on a line with a wire for each direction, relays could be installed that would reduce the count of cars entering the block when a car backed out. Alternatively, roads that used a single trolley wire for both directions could install their contact signals at sidings.

Intermittent signals involved the risk that a trolley wheel might skip below the wire momentarily at the contact point. In the Ward signal, in which the mechanism was actuated by the rise of the wire from the pressure of the trolley wheel, there was danger that ice might so weigh down the wire that it would not rise sufficiently. These risks were small, but the consequences might be so disastrous that the signal was usually placed a few yards beyond the contact point, rather than some distance behind it, as in railroad practice. Thus, a motorman could see his signal aspect change as a check on hitting his contacts. The Nachod signal gave its aspects with a white light and a red light facing the on-coming motorman, and a metal disk painted white on one side and red on the other, housed between transparent glass roundels. If the block he was approaching was entirely unoccupied, the motorman saw both lights out and the disk horizontal in its housing. As he approached, the white light would be illuminated and the disk would show him its white face. If the sun shone so brightly that he could not see which light was burning, it would also illuminate the disk clearly. At night only the light would be visible. If the block ahead were occupied by a car proceeding in the same direction, the white light and white face of the disk would already be lit, but they would blink as he entered the block. A car approaching would set both light and disk red. Cars from opposite directions entering a block simultaneously would fail to set the signal at all. Motormen had standing instructions to back out and enter again if the signal failed to acknowledge their entrance. The Nachod signal was designed for operation at speeds up to 75 miles per hour—far faster than most interurbans ever operated.

Prior to 1903 the interurbans were unable to use continuous signals such as the railroads used, even apart from their greater cost. Continuous signals were actuated by direct current in the tracks and gave their indications by establishing short circuits between the rails. Since the interurbans already used their rails for a DC power return, they were unable to send another DC circuit through their rails for signaling. Then in 1903 the North Shore Railroad (the suburban electrification of the Northwestern Pacific Railroad in the San Francisco Bay Area), and the New York subway began to use AC circuits for signaling. Thereafter, interurbans that wanted to bear the cost of continuous signals, $1,000 to $2,000 per mile— or were forced to do so by the state regulatory commissions—were able to install them. The Sacramento Northern, the North Shore Line, the South Shore Line, and others used color light indications, but most interurbans used semaphores for continuous systems. These usually differed from railroad semaphores in that the arms moved toward the track rather than away from it to the horizontal stop position. The interurbans feared that a horizontal position away from the track might be obscured by the pole line at long distances.[12]

Automatic train stop and cab signals were rare on the interurbans. The Indianapolis and Cincinnati early in its history used a two-aspect intermittant cab signal, actuated by short third rails at sidings. The Illinois Traction experimented with automatic train stop early in its history, and the Washington Water Power Company used a roof-mounted automatic train stop actuated by a rod working from the signal mast. However, interurban signaling was installed largely in response to orders from state authorities (particularly in Indiana), and thus train-stop devices, which were typically not required, were not widely installed.

Interurban dispatching methods varied about as widely as signaling: they ranged from street railway to railroad practice. The principal distinction of interurban dispatching was the almost exclusive reliance on the telephone rather than the telegraph. The Toledo and Western in its early years sent orders to agents by telegraph in the orthodox railroad fashion of the time, but almost all interurbans relied on the telephone from the beginning. Some interurbans, such as the Lake Shore Electric, the Toledo Port Clinton and Lakeside, and the Dayton and Troy, transmitted written orders through station agents, like the railroads. This was customary on the interurbans in the Far West. As in railroad practice, there were two order forms "31," for which the crew had to sign, and "19," for which they did not.

The most characteristic interurban dispatching system did not use agents as intermediaries, but put the trainmen in direct contact with the dispatcher. The Cincinnati suburban lines in general did not use written train orders, but trusted the trainmen to interpret and retain verbal orders properly. The Stark Electric (like all interurbans) operated by timetable, and when a train ran more than two minutes late, its crew telephoned the dispatcher in Alliance (mid-point of the railway line) for orders. The trainmen took down the orders in triplicate, repeated them to the dispatcher, left one copy in the phone booth, and departed with the other two copies, which were kept by the motorman and conductor. The Union Traction Company originally placed booths at intervals along the track, equipped with semaphores that tripped when the phone rang. Thus, the dispatcher could stop a train for orders on very short notice. In 1910 the company gave up this system on the ground that the semaphore mechanism was unreliable, and began equipping its cars with phones that could be plugged into the dispatching line at jack boxes placed at half-mile intervals along the line. The motorman transcribed his orders on a register similar to devices used for issuing receipts in retail shops; the register issued the original, which the motorman placed on a nail before him, and retained the carbon for comparison in case of accident. The Detroit United pursued the opposite course, first using phones in the cab and then converting to booths along the right-of-way.

Most of the larger interurbans established register points, where crews reported either to the agent or directly to the dispatcher before leaving. They were then given any orders waiting for them together with a clearance card, notifying them that all opposing trains had arrived and permitting them to proceed. The Stark had a register point at Alliance, and larger roads had several. Most roads (the Dayton and Troy is an exception) did not have agents report the passing of trains to the dispatcher, a virtually universal practice on the railroads. Surprisingly, the Scioto Valley Traction Company, the most railroadlike of the Ohio and Indiana interurbans, divorced its agents from the dispatching process.

Interurbans carried on their dispatching apart from their agents partly because many of the agents were not full-time employees, and partly because in many cases the stations were poorly suited to the purpose. The Utah-Idaho Central was known for handsome brick stations in its major towns, and the Scioto Valley, as usual, built to railroad specifications. The THI&E and the Illinois Traction systems also had many stations of the railroad type. However, unheated, unattended shelters large enough for half a dozen people were common at rural stops. In the smaller towns, where interurbans did street running, they typically used local stores as agencies. Drug stores were the most common, but the St. Joseph Valley road used a bank at one point, and hotels, restaurants, hay-grain-and-feed stores, and establishments of other sorts were used by various lines. Interurbans, like the Springfield Terminal of Vermont, that were mainly feeders to steam railroads, typically used the railroad station. The Illinois Terminal used the Wabash Railroad stations in Champaign and Urbana after eliminating street running, and after 1932 the Arkansas Valley Interurban used the Rock Island station in Hutchinson. In larger towns, the interurbans often rented single stores and fitted them out with ticket offices, waiting rooms, and baggage facilities, and loaded passengers and freight on the street in front of them. The Lake Shore Electric station in Sandusky and the Northern Texas Traction terminal in Fort Worth were of this sort; and the main station of the North Shore Line on the Chicago Elevated was a somewhat elaborate example of it. In cities, the interurbans usually tried to arrange off-the-street loading, often in connection with a loop for turning cars. To conserve space, the West Penn, the THI&E, Union Traction, and many others placed stations in the middle of loops.

Rarely did an interurban have a major terminal of the kind the railroads had built in cities. Even in Cleveland the interurbans terminated in the Public Square. Provision was made for them to run into the Cleveland Union Terminal, but they never did so. The Arkansas Valley had an excellent brick station in Wichita, and there were large union interurban stations in Salt Lake City and Sacramento. The Pacific Electric's elevated terminal in Los Angeles was a major station in the railroad style.

The greatest of interurban stations was the Indianapolis Traction Terminal, built in 1904 by Schoepf's associate Hugh J. McGowan. It consisted of a trainshed covering nine tracks with a span of 175 feet, as well as a nine-story office building, designed in a restrained Romanesque style by D. H. Burnham and Company, architects of the Union Stations in Chicago and Washington. The office building housed the ticket offices, the waiting room, and retail shops on its ground floor, and the general offices of several major interurbans in its upper stories. The Schoepf-McGowan Indiana lines had their headquarters there, and after its formation in 1906, the Central Electric Railway Association kept its offices in the building. McGowan himself used an office on the top floor. The Terminal became, in a real sense, the physical center of the interurban industry. Its traffic concentration was far heavier than that of any other interurban station. In 1918, it handled 128,145 trains, which carried 7,519,634 passengers in or out of the city. All Indianapolis interurbans except the small Beech Grove Traction Company (essentially a suburban line) used the Traction Terminal, but it was more than ample for the traffic. Like many lesser parts of the interurbans' physical plant, it was built in the expectation of traffic increases that never came. It was built and operated by the Indianapolis Traction and Terminal Company, which until 1919 controlled the Indianapolis Street Railway. During a reorganization, it became a subsidiary of the street railway and remained one until the end of the interurban in Indiana. For many years the terminal company and the street railway were controlled by the THI&E, but after 1932 they were independent. The street railway charged the interurban companies one cent per passenger for every car using the terminal, plus a fee for using the tracks in the streets from the city limits.

Although no other interurban station compared to the Indianapolis Traction Terminal, the Union Traction Company had a major station with a four-track trainshed at Muncie, and the Indiana Service Corporation had a substantial station in Fort Wayne. The Indianapolis Traction Terminal, the Salt Lake Terminal, and most other interurban stations became bus terminals after abandonment, but some were razed, and others were converted to other purposes. A few became residences; the Arkansas Valley Interurban's depot in Wichita became a radio station, and the interurbans' Union Station in Sacramento a market.

PASSENGER EQUIPMENT

Interurban car design varied between regions, and developed considerably during the history of the industry. The New England electric lines began service with equipment much like streetcars. The typical car was wooden, about 35 to 40 feet long, seated some 32 to 50 people, and was geared for maximum speeds of about 25 to 35 miles per hour. The New England lines were equipped about 55 per cent with open cars and 45 per cent with closed, reflecting the importance of joy-riding in the summer months. The basic summer car was the "cross-bench open," fitted with wooden benches running the width of the car without a center aisle. They were entered directly from the open sides by one or two steps running the length of the car. The conductor walked along the steps to collect fares while the car was in motion. On double-track lines, the left side was often barred as a safety precaution. Some of the earliest of these cars had only a single truck, mounted rigidly on the frame, but the majority carried double trucks in the usual fashion. On equipment of this sort, it was quite common to install what were called maximum traction trucks, which had a single motor mounted on the axle of a pair of large-diameter wheels, followed by a pair of unpowered smaller wheels. Some roads differentiated rural from urban equipment with front windows to protect the motormen from wind and rain. Almost all lines left the motormen exposed to the elements on open cars designed for city service. Canvas curtains could be lowered to protect the passengers from summer rain. Convertible and semiconvertible cars were used in city service, but not widely on rural lines.

Winter equipment of the New England lines also followed the streetcar pattern closely. Since the speed of loading was less significant, rural cars often had smaller vestibules than city equipment and sometimes had more ample seating arrangements, but otherwise they were quite similar. The New England rural trolley lines declined so much more rapidly than the Midwestern interurbans that almost all of them operated with this style of equipment to the end. With the decline of joyriding about the time of World War I, open equipment was increasingly retired from service.

The Technology of the Interurbans

Some California electric lines, operating in a mild climate, bought cars with open seating sections. The "California type" car, which had a third or half its seats in an enclosed portion in the center and the rest in open sections front and back, was used by the Peninsular Railway and by many streetcar lines. The Pacific Electric's characteristic early car was divided about equally between an open platform at one end and an enclosed saloon at the other. Most California interurbans operated with closed equipment, however.

Some Midwestern interurbans at first used rolling stock of the New England model. The Sandusky Milan and Norwalk opened with enclosed cars of the general New England style, and the earliest cars of the Cleveland and Chagrin Falls and the Akron Bedford and Cleveland were similar. Few Midwestern interurbans used open cars, although the Dayton Covington and Piqua and the Tiffin Fostoria and Eastern did so early in their histories. From the outset, beginning with the Newark and Granville Street Railway, most Midwestern interurbans developed a distinctive type of heavy wooden car, patterned more nearly on the railroad coaches of the day than on street railway equipment. The cars varied from one company to another, but most of them had certain features in common: wooden construction, railroad-style clerestory roofs, railroad-style trap doors at the rear, windows placed in pairs surmounted by small fanlights of art glass, and truss-rod-and-turnbuckle strengthening under the floor. Most interurban cars were combines, if only because they had to be able to handle salesmen's cases without advance notice. The baggage compartments were usually limited to about ten feet at the front of the car, but roads such as the Sacramento Northern and the Salt Lake and Utah that did a heavy express or package freight business had combines that were mainly devoted to their baggage compartments. Most large roads had some straight coaches as well. Lines with heavy passenger traffic usually had trailer coaches that could be hauled by the motor cars. It was customary to provide smoking compartments behind the baggage sections of interurban combines. Seats were covered with various materials—plush and leather were most common in the general passenger compartment and rattan in the smoking compartment. Car interiors were finished in mahogany, cherry, oak, or other hard woods.

Exteriors were finished in a variety of colors. The Union Traction Company and the Schoepf-McGowan lines generally used Pullman green in their early operations, and the color was also adopted by the Sacramento Northern and the electric lines of the Great Northern. The Southern Pacific's electric lines used a red livery, and in the 1920's the Union Traction Company also adopted red. For many years the Milwaukee Electric Company used dark green with a canary yellow letterboard, and the Lehigh Valley Transit used scarlet and cream. The Lake Shore Electric used the orange long identified with the Big Four Railroad, finding that it offered maximum visibility—an important safety consideration—and was quite durable. This color was adopted so widely that it came to be known as "traction orange," and by the 1930's it had become a trademark of the industry. The Indiana Railroad, the great consolidation of Indiana interurbans in 1930, adopted it, as did the Illinois Terminal. The South Shore Line still uses tasteful livery of traction orange with a maroon letterboard. Many lines chose unique color schemes for identification. The Cleveland and Southwestern used a light green until about 1927 (when it too adopted traction orange), and for many years advertised itself as "The Green Line." The Cincinnati and Lake Erie used a handsome red.

The standard wooden interurban car was a thing of beauty that has been all too little appreciated. In the truest sense, it exemplified functional design. Most of the interurbans, when they ordered their initial rolling stock, were short enough of capital funds that they could waste no money on embellishment. Given the engineering knowledge of the time, the cars were built in straightforward style to provide the service at a minimum original cost. Front ends were gently rounded to reduce clearance problems in street running; the stained glass in the window frames served as a sunshade; clerestory roofs were adopted for ventilation. With all of this, the interurban cars acquired an unconscious and unintentional streamlining that was very effective.*

Although a good many of the original wooden interurban cars were replaced during the twenties, most companies continued to use this type until the end. Even companies that bought enough modern cars to provide base service, such as the Cedar Rapids and Iowa City and the Ohio Public Service, retained heavy wooden equipment for emergencies. The ability of these cars to go on in spite of meager maintenance was, in many cases, remarkable. Almost all the wooden interurbans have now been destroyed. Most were burned for their metal, but a few became summer cottages, roadside stands, or farm buildings; barely a dozen have been preserved as museum pieces. It is a pity that so few of these cars were preserved, for the best of them were exemplary pieces of American design.

The variations in car designs were caused by clearance restrictions, local ordinances, the character of the traffic, the specialties of the car builder, and, in considerable measure, simply by local tradition. Lines with light passenger traffic, such as the Cincinnati Georgetown and Portsmouth and the Toledo and Western, tended to buy short cars from the beginning. Most

---

* In 1904, Union Traction made a series of tests in an effort to develop a car design that would minimize wind resistance, and concluded that a rounded front end and a parabolic rear would be the optimum combination. It never built any cars to this design, apparently believing that the marginal saving in operating costs would be trivial. Two lines, the Stark Electric and the Indianapolis New Castle and Toledo, ordered cars built to the opposite of this plan, fitted with a parabolic front and a rounded rear. This arrangement served no functional purpose, but was expected to give the impression of great speed. Two of the cars ordered for the INC&T were diverted to the Winona Railroad before delivery, where they were used in joint Indianapolis–Goshen service with the Union Traction. They were called "windsplitters," but they were not considered particularly speedy. The six cars of this design, delivered to the INC&T, became Union Traction property after a merger in 1912.

of the roads around Toledo began service with relatively short equipment, 40 to 50 feet long over-all, preferring to operate small cars frequently. In contrast, the lines in central Ohio, even though they served a less populous area, tended to use longer cars, but to operate on less frequent schedules. Early standard equipment of the Lake Shore Electric and the Cleveland and Southwestern was 51 feet long, but the Ohio Electric, the Columbus Delaware and Marion, and their neighbors operated cars of 50 to 61 feet. In Indiana there was considerable variety. The Union Traction Company and the Fort Wayne and Wabash Valley used 61-foot cars, but the lightly traveled Kokomo Marion and Western used 45-foot equipment. There was a marked tendency in Indiana to buy longer cars, and 61.5 feet became a very standard length. The Columbus Delaware and Marion and the Ohio Electric experimented, apparently without much success, with extra-long excursion cars for low-rate summer outings. The CD&M had excursion cars 67 feet long, closely fitted out with rattan seats and equipped with extra large windows. In 1906 the CD&M bought a pair of standard passenger cars of the same length, fitted for baggage-chair car service, but after only three years sold them to the Illinois Traction, where they had a long career. Width was dictated mainly by clearances in street running, but most roads used a width of eight to nine feet. Eight feet six inches was probably the most common car width. Roads built to steam-road standards could sometimes use cars wider than 9 feet; the Fort Dodge Des Moines and Southern had one car, No. 62, famous for a width of 9 feet 10 inches. When running on the Chicago Elevated, the North Shore Line and the Chicago Aurora and Elgin encountered curves of only 90-foot radius, not so severe as most on street railways, but they were limited to car widths of 8 feet 8 inches by high-level station platforms.

Electric-car builders primarily built streetcars. In 1909 the interurbans' orders for 1,245 passenger cars amounted to nearly 50 per cent of all street and interurban electric cars, but the percentage fell away rapidly to less than 10 per cent by 1920. (A list of major builders of interurban cars is appended to this study.) Niles and Jewett came closest to being specialists in interurban equipment. Since interurbans tended to buy from nearby suppliers to reduce transportation expense, the principal concentration of car builders was in Ohio. Niles, Jewett, Barney and Smith, Kuhlman, and the Cincinnati Car Company were all located there. The Schoepf-McGowan lines bought heavily from the Cincinnati Car Company, in which Schoepf had an interest. The Lake Shore Electric bought its early equipment from Barney and Smith, and later bought from Niles and Jewett.

Most of the interurbans bought from a variety of builders, and none became so closely identified with a single car builder as, for example, the Pennsylvania Railroad with the Baldwin Locomotive Works, or the New York Central with the American Locomotive Company. The Illinois Traction used equipment from nearly every major Midwestern car builder, but its master mechanic, J. M. Bosenbury, developed an elegant car design that was evident in almost all its main-line rolling stock. Several builders, when left to their own discretion, developed individual characteristics of car design. Barney and Smith used an angular front end, and Kuhlman specialized in center-entrance equipment. Niles designed particularly graceful wooden equipment; the cars it built in 1906 for the Northern Electric Railway, predecessor of the Sacramento Northern, were among the most handsome in the history of the industry. They were in regular service for 34 years.

In terms of its electrical equipment, the interurban car was quite a simple device. Four-motor cars were almost universal, but the Lake Shore Electric, the Lake Erie Bowling Green and Napoleon, and a few others originally used two-motor equipment. Motors ranged from 50 to 100 horsepower, depending on the size of the car and the speed for which it was intended. The principal engineering problem in the car's electrical equipment was developing a device that would transmit power from the wire to the motors in variable rates at the control of the motorman. The controller was developed in the 1880's as the equivalent of a throttle for electric cars. Several types were built, but the basic DC controller provided the motorman with a set of resistances that he could cut out successively by revolving a cylinder against a series of electrical connections. The cylinder was designed to make a variable number of contacts, depending on the position of the controller handle. The number of controller positions, or points, varied depending on the range of speeds for which the car was intended.[13]

On a standard 600-volt car, the four motors were usually wired so that motors one and four (numbered from the front of the car) were permanently connected in parallel. Numbers two and three were connected in the same fashion. (This practice varied, however. Some roads put the two motors in a truck in permanent parallel.) At the first four or five points, resistances were cut out until the two pairs of motors were operating in series at the trolley voltage. This brought the car to about half-speed. Series connection was particularly effective for starting and acceleration. The next point put the two pairs of motors in parallel and introduced resistances once more. These resistances were cut out at successive points until at the last point the motors operated in parallel at the trolley voltage, producing the highest speed of which the car was capable.

On a 1,200-volt DC car, motors one and four were permanently connected in series, as were two and three. At the first four or five points, all motors were operated in series, but at the next point the two pairs of motors were put in parallel. Resistances were cut out in the same way as on a 600-volt car. Since 600-volt motors were used, the car could also be wired in the same fashion as a 600-volt car, and choice between the two wirings could be made by throwing a switch. It was in this fashion that 1,200-volt cars, such as those of the Sacramento Northern described earlier, were able to travel on 600-volt line at full speed.

On the earlier cars, the motorman was depended on to open the controller according to the capacity of the motor at each speed. Opening the controller too quickly would overload the motor and cause a circuit breaker to kick out, and opening it too slowly would waste power and damage the resistors. Therefore, later equipment was fitted with automatic controllers, in which relays limited the current, regardless of how fast the motorman advanced his handle. A single-ended car—one designed for operation in one direction only—had a single controller on the front platform equipped with a reversing mechanism. Some single-ended cars carried small backing controllers on the rear platform for low-speed movements in reverse. Double-ended cars carried controllers at each end and were equipped with trolley poles front and back. Double-ended cars were popular in New England, California, and Utah, but the Midwestern companies leaned strongly to single-ended cars, and only lines that had to operate out of stub-end terminals, such as the North Shore Line, the Aurora Elgin and Chicago, and the Dayton Covington and Piqua adopted double-ended equipment.

In 1897 Frank Sprague installed a device called multiple unit control on the South Side Elevated in Chicago; this device permitted motors in any number of electric cars to be operated from a single controller. It was a great invention; without it rapid transit in the modern sense would have been impossible. Although its principal applications were to subways and elevated railways and to railroad electrifications, it was also important for the most heavily traveled interurbans. For most of the smaller roads, there was no problem, since single-car operation was adequate for their traffic, but the Union Traction, the Lake Shore Electric, and other major lines in the early years often scheduled trains in two or three sections. Because the marginal expenditure on installing multiple unit control on new equipment was not very great, and because Sprague's MU controllers were superior for large motors even in single-car operation, after 1905 the major interurban companies tended to equip all new cars in this fashion. The Lake Shore Electric, the Northern Ohio, the Illinois Terminal, the three principal lines out of Chicago, and the two big California interurbans were all operators of multiple-unit trains, but the central Indiana lines, although largely equipped with MU controllers, operated mainly with single cars and motor-trailer sets. The Milwaukee Electric ran three-car MU trains, the Pacific Electric five-car, the Sacramento Northern six-car, the North Shore Line, the South Shore Line, and the Chicago Aurora and Elgin eight-car. In exceptional circumstances, even longer trains were operated; the Pacific Electric's boat trains for the Catalina Island steamer contained six cars, and the South Shore Line operated excursion trains as long as fifteen cars. The three Chicago lines were limited by platform lengths, the Sacramento Northern by its car ferry, and many interurbans by municipal regulations for street running.

The brake systems of the interurbans presented a similar choice between single-car and multiple-unit operation. If a company intended to use only single-car trains or motor-trailer sets, it could install straight air brakes, in which application released compressed air directly from a reservoir into the brake cylinder, where it actuated a piston rod connected by levers to the brake shoes. Since there was no way of controlling this simple operation for more than a very short train, the companies that planned multiple-unit operation usually had to install automatic air brakes of the sort used by the railroads. In automatic installations, the air compressors charged an air line, which filled a reservoir in each car. The motorman applied his brakes by releasing air from the line, which opened a triple valve, sending air from the reservoir into the brake cylinder. Automatic installations were more expensive than straight air, and involved higher maintenance expenditures. In particular, there was a tendency for triple valves to stick in their open positions, making it difficult to release brakes. For multiple-unit equipment, however, there was no effective alternative to automatic air brakes.[14]

There were a few examples of electric cars without air brakes, although they were more common in Britain than in America. The West Penn Railways, in this as in other respects, was unorthodox. Its main-line cars carried no air compressors, but used a combination of a Westinghouse electro-magnetic track brake and a goose-neck hand brake. The track brake consisted of four bars of iron that hung loosely from the trucks on springs between the wheels immediately over the rails. When a motorman wanted to stop, he pushed his controller handle into a position that converted the traction motors into generators and fed the resulting current into the track brakes. The iron bars themselves gripped the rails and, as they went down, actuated a series of levers to tighten a set of wheel brakes. Thus, the faster the car was traveling, the more electric braking power it generated, but as soon as it stopped, it lost all braking power, and the track brake released completely. For this reason, motormen used the handbrake to hold the cars when stopped, and differed individually in the relative reliance they put on the electric and hand brakes while moving.

Multiple-unit operation also presented the problem of coupling. The interurbans developed after the railroads had abandoned link-and-pin coupling in favor of the Master Car Builders', or MCB coupler, invented by the Virginia dry goods clerk, Eli Janney. Since the interurbans originally had no intention of interchanging equipment with the railroads or, in general, with one another, they had no immediate reason to adopt MCB couplers, and few of the early lines did so. Many adopted the Van Dorn coupler, which was almost as simple as a link-and-pin, but less likely to cost a switchman his fingers. The Van Dorn was housed in pockets similar to a link-and-pin, but instead of the link it used a notched piece of metal that was fitted into one car's coupler with a pin and then pushed into the other by moving the two cars together. It engaged a like pin on the other car, and remained engaged until either pin was drawn.

The other principal interurban coupler was the Tomlinson, a simple arrangement in which a latch engaged with a counterpart on the other car. Since neither a Tomlinson nor a Van Dorn could mate with an MCB coupler, both proved troublesome when interchange was undertaken. Therefore most roads eventually adopted an MCB coupler, modified for interurban use. The standard railroad draft gear gives the coupler a play of less than a foot in either direction, and was thus completely unsuited to typical interurban use. The interurban lines, therefore, installed their couplers, of whatever type, at the end of shanks of as much as a five-foot radius, moving in an arc of nearly ninety degrees. In this fashion it was possible to maneuver a train of several cars around streetcar curves. Since interurban track was much more irregular than railroad, there was an additional problem that cars with MCB couplers might come apart through vertical movement. For this reason, J. M. Bosenbury, the most prominent engineer in the industry, developed an extra-height coupler knuckle that became a characteristic of the Illinois Traction. The Ohio Brass Company added the "sliding lock" working in a groove on the face of the knuckle to prevent vertical uncoupling.

Almost all the interurbans that used an MCB coupler used a slotted knuckle and drilled a hole vertically through it to permit motor cars to tow non-MCB equipment by means of shackle bars in emergencies. This kind of coupler was adopted as standard for interchange equipment by the Central Electric Railway Association. The Association, originally formed by the major Ohio and Indiana lines to deal with interline passenger traffic problems, began about 1907 to issue standard designs for couplers, wheels, brakes, multiple-unit connections, and other equipment used in interchange. The designs were drawn by its Master Mechanics' Association.

The Tomlinson and the later Van Dorn couplers had the advantage that multiple-unit contacts could be mounted on the coupler face, permitting electric connections to be made without the customary jumpers between cars. The Indiana Railroad, which used MCB couplers on its standard equipment, ordered Tomlinsons for its last set of cars because of this advantage. Only the Washington Baltimore and Annapolis mounted MU connections on MCB couplers, but it equipped them with tight-lockpin-and-pocket fittings to prevent vertical movements of the faces. The movement away from Van Dorn, Tomlinson, and other non-standard couplers to MCB predominated, and the Northern Ohio, the Spokane Coeur d'Alene and Palouse and many others made the transition. The Scioto Valley used a Van Dorn on its passenger cars but an MCB on freight. For a time, cars of the Fort Dodge Des Moines and Southern and the Inter-Urban Railway carried both a Van Dorn and an MCB at each end. The Pacific Electric used an MCB on its freight equipment, but after 1914 it equipped its passenger cars with a Westinghouse automatic coupler that made both electric and air connections on impact, and could be uncoupled by controls in the cab. The Portland–Lewiston Interurban, completed in 1914, also used this coupler. It found its principal market, however, among rapid-transit lines, and became standard on the New York subway.

Other equipment of the interurban cars varied according to statutory requirements and local custom. Iowa interurban cars were distinguished by a locomotive bell mounted on the roof, since this was required of most of the Iowa roads. The Interstate Public Service Company in Indiana adopted the locomotive bell voluntarily. The Sacramento Northern and other California lines used a power-operated gong mounted on the cab. Most roads used wooden or steel pilots, mounted below the floor at each operating end, but a few cities, notably Los Angeles and Toledo, required a fender—a loose conglomeration of steel strap designed to gather up a pedestrian who was struck by a moving car. Since Lima required a pilot, cars between Toledo and Lima had to be equipped with a portable fender at the Toledo city limits, or fitted with a fender at one end and a pilot at the other, and turned in the proper direction before street running. A few of the early cars used oil headlights, but arc lights replaced them, and in turn were replaced by standard bulb lamps.

Truck design underwent two improvements: the wheel base was lengthened from about six to about seven feet, and toward the end of the interurban era castings were adopted in preference to bolted connections.[15] Interurban cars required four-wheel trucks to negotiate streetcar curves, although the firm of John Stephenson in 1904 built an experimental car with six-wheel trucks. The South Shore Line equipped two parlor and two dining cars in the 1920's with six-wheel trucks, but by that time the line had gone beyond the interurban style of equipment and was becoming an electrified standard railroad.

Although the trolley pole was a simple device, several changes were made in it over the years. On some of the last equipment, the springs were mounted on the pole, rather than on the base, and a few cars, particularly in California, used pneumatic rather than spring pressure. Twelve feet was the most common pole length. Almost all roads initially used a wheel about six inches in diameter, somewhat larger than in street railway practice, but there was never agreement on what was the proper pressure against the wire. The higher the pressure, the less the prospect of dewirement at curves and switches, but the greater the wear on the wheel and the damage to the overhead when dewirements occurred. The Cincinnati Milford and Loveland, which had a top speed of only 45 miles per hour, used 18 pounds of pressure and got 7,500 miles out of a single wheel; the Fort Wayne Van Wert and Lima used 45 pounds and had to replace wheels at 2,500 miles. The Dayton and Troy used 28 pounds on local cars and 34 on limiteds. Trolley wheels tended to wear out of a round shape into hexagons because of friction as the car started, resulting not only in dewirements but in arcing that damaged the trolley wire and set up interference in radio sets.

The trolley wheel itself was so simple that little could be done to improve it. In 1916 the Portland–Lewiston Interurban installed a device called the Miller trolley shoe that rapidly came to replace the trolley wheel on high-speed lines. It needed about ten pounds less pressure against the wire, reduced arcing and dewirements, and had a long life expectancy. It also increased the life expectancy of the overhead by about threefold. A

The Technology of the Interurbans

trolley shoe could be lubricated with a graphite solution to reduce friction without significant loss of conductivity.

The principal technological development in the industry was in car design itself. The heavy wooden car was more or less universal during the main periods of interurban building—the steel car was then barely in its infancy. Steel equipment received its greatest impetus from the Pennsylvania Railroad's heavy purchases of steel coaches beginning around 1906 for operation through the Hudson River tubes into Pennsylvania Station in New York. Steel cars had been purchased by the Interborough Rapid Transit Company for the New York subway in 1904, and had proved a great success.

Around 1912, the price of wood rose to the point where steel construction became economic for interurbans in general. The Seattle Renton and Southern bought a series of steel suburban cars in 1909. The Lehigh Valley Traction Company bought composite wood and steel cars in 1912 for its new limited service between Philadelphia and Allentown via Norristown, and in 1913 Union Traction bought a series of ten heavy steel cars for main-line service. Union Traction officials believed that steel construction would reduce maintenance expenditures and depreciation, and increase passenger protection in case of accident. The cars were 61 feet long and equipped with arch roofs, free of clerestories. Steel equipment was ordered within the next few years by the Toledo Fostoria and Findlay, the Toledo Bowling Green and Southern, the Lake Shore Electric, the Detroit United, and several other companies.

Between 1913 and about 1922, equipment of this sort was essentially standard in orders by the interurbans. The new cars differed from their predecessors mainly in construction material; the division between baggage space, the smoker, and the general passenger compartment was maintained, and a two-man crew was still required. The stained window-glass that was characteristic of the interurbans appeared in the first steel cars, but after 1914, translucent white glass replaced it in most new car construction, and after 1917 most new cars were built without upper window sashes of any kind. The first steel cars carried the familiar truss-rods and turnbuckles of the wooden cars, but these, too, were omitted from later equipment. Construction of heavy steel cars continued virtually to the end of the interurban era—the Chicago Aurora and Elgin put ten of them in service in 1945 and the Grand River Railway one in 1948—but after the early twenties the building of this type of equipment greatly declined. It probably reached its zenith aesthetically with a pair of 60-foot cars fitted out with parlor chairs that were built for the Columbus Delaware and Marion in 1926.

During this period, several of the major roads rebuilt their wooden equipment to simulate steel. Metal sheathing was screwed to the wooden sides, stained glass was covered with steel plate, and in some cases clerestories were enclosed or cut away to make arch roofs. The Illinois Traction and its successor, the Illinois Terminal, remodeled most of its equipment in this fashion in the twenties and thirties. It was common in Indiana, Wisconsin, and Iowa, but most of the Ohio interurbans were abandoned without any large-scale reconstruction of their wooden equipment.

Whatever the structural advantages of heavy steel cars may have been, they were notorious power consumers, and were hard on track. The Columbus Delaware and Marion's parlor cars weighed 47½ tons, and the South Shore Line's 60-foot coaches of 1926 weighed 57 tons, among the heaviest passenger equipment of its length ever built. In addition, since this kind of equipment required standard two-man crews for passenger operation, it made no saving in labor costs. As the decline of the industry became severe after World War I, the interurbans were forced to reduce their costs, for they could do little to increase their revenues. Thus, they turned simultaneously to lighter equipment and to one-man crews. The first interurbans to install lightweight steel cars were the Cincinnati Lawrenceburg and Aurora and the Cincinnati Milford and Blanchester, which ordered similar 40-foot cars from the Cincinnati Car Company in 1918 and 1920, respectively. The cars were equipped with railroad roofs, but were otherwise built to street railway standards. The motorman, seated on the front platform, collected fares or tickets in the fashion becoming popular in streetcars.

Most of the car builders produced lightweight equipment in the mid-twenties, but the Cincinnati Car Company was preeminent. In 1921, it received an order for interurban cars for the Kentucky Traction and Terminal Company, and produced ten 40-foot cars, light in weight and distinguished by graceful curved sides. These cars were so successful that they were duplicated in 1924 for the Buffalo and Erie Railway, which had a community of ownership with the Kentucky Traction, and which ordered fourteen cars. The new cars weighed only 18½ tons. In their first ten months of service on the Buffalo and Erie, they reduced power consumption 31.3 per cent and all operating costs, including maintenance, by 20.2 per cent. They were not fast, but, being able to brake and accelerate quickly, they were better adapted to local service than the older equipment.

The Cincinnati Car Company concentrated on the production and sale of cars of this general design, which became so standard in the 1920's that such cars were popularly known in later years as the "Cincinnati rubber stamp lightweights." Large models were built for the Indianapolis and Southeastern, the Dayton and Troy, and the Cleveland Southwestern, and small ones for the Cincinnati Georgetown and Portsmouth and the Toledo and Western. Many other interurban lines bought them, and several companies, notably the Cincinnati Street Railway and the Dayton City Railway, bought similar cars for city service. The standard design of the cars made it easy for them to be transferred to other companies as their original owners abandoned. Thus, even when the Cincinnati Car Company ceased operation in 1931 and was liquidated in 1938, the interurbans were not seriously affected. The Dayton and Troy's lightweights served on the Lehigh Valley Traction, and the Indianapolis and Southeastern's on lines of the Nashville–Franklin, the Georgia Power Company, the Inter-City Rapid Transit, the Beech Grove Traction Corporation, and the Shaker Heights Rapid Transit. Cars of both companies saw service on the Milwaukee-Waukesha interurban line in its last days.

Acceptance of lightweight cars followed no particular pattern. Both the Cleveland Southwestern and the Stark Electric used them extensively, whereas the Lake Shore Electric and the Northern Ohio in the same territory never did so. Smaller roads, such as the Toledo and Indiana, the Toledo and Western, and the Kankakee and Urbana, adopted them readily, and several of the companies were doubtless able to stave off abandonment for nearly a decade because of the economies these cars provided. The Shore Line Electric, which had operated between New Haven and New London in Connecticut, suspended its operations in 1919, but reopened between New Haven and Saybrook with lightweight equipment in 1923, and operated until 1929, when it was finally abandoned. The Illinois Traction adopted lightweight equipment only for its Illinois Valley division and for local and suburban services at St. Louis, Danville, and Litchfield. The Sacramento Northern showed no interest in lightweight cars.

Several roads, even though they did not buy lightweight equipment, turned to one-man operation of standard equipment. The usual system was to reverse the seats, place the controller on what had been the rear platform, and mount the trolley pole over the baggage compartment. Folding, air-operated doors were often installed at the right front. The Indiana Railroad made such changes on most of its heavy equipment, as did the Bamberger and the Cincinnati and Lake Erie. The Texas Electric engaged in similar rebuilding without reversing ends of the equipment.

The lightweight cars of the 1920's had little to recommend them beyond economy. Their riding quality was generally inferior to heavy equipment (particularly in view of the track deterioration of the time), and their interior arrangements were usually no more comfortable. They were no faster. In all, they represented a reversion from equipment of the steam railroad sort to equipment similar to streetcars. The lightweight cars bought by the Northern Indiana Railway in 1930 were very similar in body style to contemporary streetcars of the Des Moines Railway, and the Cincinnati Car Company's lightweight cars furnished to street railways and interurbans were very much alike. In the course of some thirty years, the industry had come full circle.

Around the year 1930, several interurbans began to experiment with lightweight, high-speed cars of radically new design, intended not only to cut costs, but to provide speed and comfort that would lure the public back from the highways. Early in 1929, Dr. Thomas Conway, Jr., president of the Cincinnati and Lake Erie, initiated an effort to design such cars for service from Cincinnati to Dayton, Columbus, and Toledo. Conway had assembled the C&LE out of the former main lines of the Ohio Electric, and was seriously trying to modernize the property. He felt it was necessary to retain local service, but he believed that the interurbans had a possible area for expansion in limited service over distances of 70 to 220 miles. The Cincinnati and Lake Erie, consequently, ordered twenty lightweight cars from the Cincinnati Car Company, half of them fitted out as coaches, half as coach-observation cars. They were only 43 feet 9 inches long and 11 feet 4 inches high, but they were geared for speeds in excess of 80 miles per hour, and designed to provide a comfortable ride even on deteriorated track. They were the first cars in which there was a large-scale, successful use of aluminum. Conway called the cars "The Red Devils," fitted them with electric tail signs, and advertised them extensively. One was shown in a famous newsreel winning a race with an airplane. Needless to say, the aircraft was a biplane of the slowest sort. The Toledo Bowling Green and Southern planned similar cars shortly before its abandonment in 1930.

When the Indiana Railroad was formed in 1930, its management made an attempt to modernize similar to Conway's on the C&LE. It ordered lightweight, high-speed equipment from American Car and Foundry and from Pullman similar in size and character to Conway's cars, but incorporating considerably more aluminum, as well as multiple unit control. The 21 coach-baggage cars built by Pullman and the 14 coach-observation cars built by AFC provided the core of the Indiana's passenger service to Fort Wayne and Louisville until the end of the railroad in 1941. The Indiana lightweights were clean-lined, free of embellishment, very much in the interurbans' tradition of functional design, but they were designed so close to the end of the interurban era that no other cars were built on their model. In 1932, the Fonda Johnstown and Gloversville installed five high-speed cars built by Brill, closely following the design of some recent suburban equipment of Conway's Philadelphia and Western Railway. The C&LE's lightweights later served on the Cedar Rapids and Iowa City and on the Lehigh Valley Transit, and the Fonda Johnstown and Gloversville cars ended their careers on the Bamberger Railroad. Although the Indiana Railroad's design was the most advanced of the three, only two of its thirty-five cars survived, one on the Cedar Rapids and Iowa City and the other on the Lehigh Valley Transit.

Only two interurbans used equipment that was built to the standards the railroads have used since the streamlined train was introduced about 1934. In 1941, the North Shore Line placed two streamlined air-conditioned, four-car articulated units called "Electroliners" in Chicago–Milwaukee service. The units were 156 feet long, and rode on five trucks each; they were a clever effort to design a full train, internally connected yet able to negotiate the curves of the Chicago Elevated. Finally, in 1946, during the brief postwar burst of optimism concerning railroad passenger traffic, the Illinois Terminal ordered three stainless steel combines, two coaches, and three parlor cars, which were used as three trains in St. Louis–Peoria and St. Louis–Decatur service. When they arrived, the company discovered that they were too long to make the curves into the Peoria station. Believing it uneconomic to modify the station, the railroad cut back its passenger service to East Peoria. The new equipment, working under this handicap, proved unable to halt the secular decline in traffic, and in 1956, after only eight years of service, it made the Illinois Terminal's final main-line passenger runs. By this time the market for second-hand equipment, which had been brisk in the thirties and during the war, had disappeared. The Illinois Terminal cars were unsuited to service on the South Shore Line, and no other electric line was looking for equipment.

Apart from the main course of development in car architecture, there were numerous experiments. The Stark Electric experimented unsuccessfully with cars that were entered from a folding door running the width of the car across its rear end. Center-entrance cars, built primarily by Kuhlman in Cleveland, met with limited acceptance around World War I. The high-speed line of the International Railway between Buffalo and Niagara Falls was the principal user of these cars, but several of the Ohio lines and the Toronto Suburban bought a few.

Parlor, observation, and sleeping cars, which were usually found only on the most heavily traveled interurbans, followed the lines of orthodox equipment except in interior fittings. A few interurbans used open platform observation cars, long considered a *sine qua non* for luxury on the railroads.[16] Relatively few interurbans used second-hand railroad passenger equipment, but the Oakland Antioch and Eastern electrified an ancient Southern Pacific combine for service on its Danville branch, and the London and Port Stanley owned some former Pennsylvania Railroad coaches dating from the nineteenth century. The Washington Baltimore and Annapolis, the Dayton and Troy, the Stark Electric, the Bamberger, the Rockford and Interurban, and several other lines used cars from the New York City Elevated as passenger or express trailers, particularly during the two World Wars. The Milwaukee Electric was fond of articulated units, and the WB&A also bought some.

FREIGHT EQUIPMENT

Interurban freight equipment was divided between self-propelled freight or express cars and various locomotive-and-trailer combinations. Most interurbans originally bought one or more cars called box motors, wired in the same fashion as passenger equipment, but fitted with bodies for carrying less-than-carload freight or express. In the 1920's, when the interurbans made a concerted effort to increase their freight traffic, many of the standard passenger cars that were being replaced by lightweight equipment or being made idle by the decline in passenger business were converted to box motors. The conversion consisted primarily in replacing the windows with solid sides, and cutting one or two wide doors in each side. Many cars were regeared for lower speeds. The Cincinnati Hamilton and Dayton bought new box motors, but the majority resorted to conversion. Line cars, snow plows, and other work equipment were fashioned in the same way. Consequently, the freight and work equipment of the interurbans was typically heterogeneous, usually dilapidated, and frequently jerrybuilt. The Indiana Railroad's freight and work motors, which were almost all inherited from predecessors or converted from the passenger equipment of the four main constituent companies, demonstrated a variety that would have been virtually beyond human ingenuity to devise intentionally. Out of some 100 cars, there was no series greater than three with substantially similar design, and fully 90 per cent were unique.

Most box motors could pull one or more trailers, which were usually of similar design but without cabs, motors, or trolleys. The Midwestern lines widely adopted a standard trailer designed by the Central Electric Railway Master Mechanics' Association in 1926. It had rounded ends with radial couplers and could be interchanged freely in Indiana and Ohio. Cattle cars were fairly common in Indiana, and some interurbans had flatcars and gondolas. Except on such roads as the Toledo and Western, the Illinois Traction, and the Wilkes-Barre and Hazleton, which had significant railroad interchange, cabooses were uncommon; the crew on the typical interurban freight rode in the box motor.

Only a few interurbans used refrigerator cars. The Illinois Traction had ice-cooled refrigerator cars with radial couplers and railroad roofs, as well as orthodox models for railroad interchange. The three major Utah interurbans owned refrigerator cars, which operated in interchange on the Utah interurban network. The North Shore Line was a pioneer in using mechanically actuated refrigerator cars, and the Northern Ohio converted several interurban boxcars into electrical refrigerator cars.

Interurbans that interchanged with railroads could typically handle one or two boxcars or hoppers with a box motor, but any longer train usually required a genuine locomotive. The two chief types of interurban locomotives were box cabs and steeple cabs; both had the usual two trucks of four wheels each. Box cabs were similar in outline to box motors, but they did not carry freight themselves, using their interior space for electrical equipment instead. Steeple cabs had their controls toward the center of the locomotive, separated from the draw-bars by sloping hoods. Compressors and other noisy equipment were put under the hoods. Steeple cabs were built in various sizes and shapes by most of the major car builders, but the Baldwin Locomotive Works, in conjunction with Westinghouse, produced a standard line, mainly of about 50 to 60 tons, that was the interurbans' most common locomotive. General Electric also built steeple cabs for interurban use. The major Iowa interurbans, all of which interchanged freight with the railroads, used steeple cabs almost exclusively, and they were popular in Indiana and Ohio as well. The Illinois Traction had some, but operated mainly with box-cab locomotives. The Illinois Traction, the Piedmont and Northern, and the Oakland Antioch and Eastern at times hauled passenger trains with locomotives, but this practice was rare.

The Technology of the Interurbans

In the later days, when a few of the interurbans had made the conversion to heavy freight-haulers, some multiple-truck locomotives were put in service. The Illinois Terminal rebuilt several of its box cabs into articulated, four-truck locomotives that had as much tractive power as some Mikado steam locomotives. The Oregon Electric's four-truck power, built with traction trucks taken from scrapped passenger equipment, later served on the Fort Dodge Des Moines and Southern and on the North Shore Line. The largest locomotives ever to serve on an interurban are three 89-foot 2—D+D—2 locomotives of 6,000 horsepower each, placed in service on the South Shore Line in 1949. A series of twenty of these engines had been built for the Soviet Union, but were not shipped because of American controls on strategic exports. Three were rewired from 3,300 to 1,500 volts and converted to standard gauge for the South Shore Line, twelve were sold to the Milwaukee Road for its Rocky Mountain electrification and the rest were sold to the Paulista Railway of Brazil. In 1955, after the New York Central removed the electrification of the Cleveland Union Terminal and shifted some of its locomotives to its New York electrification, the South Shore Line bought ten of the displaced locomotives (nine from New York and one from the former electrification of the Detroit River tunnel), and so completed the conversion from interurban to railroad standards in both its passenger and its freight equipment.

In addition to standard locomotives, various cut-down passenger cars, regeared box motors, work motors, and other unorthodox equipment were used for pulling freight cars. A work motor was usually a motorized flatcar with a single cab at the center with visibility front and rear, but other motorized flatcars served the same purpose. The Galesburg–Monmouth line of the Rock Island Southern, which became incredibly dilapidated in its last days, was reduced to hauling its box cars with a former street railway Differential dump car from Kansas City. The Charles City Western, the Des Moines and Central Iowa, the Bamberger, the Salt Lake and Utah, and a few other roads, mainly in the West, hauled freight cars with passenger equipment, but this was never a common practice. The Indiana Railroad operated a fast freight trailer on passenger trains on the Terre Haute line.

Since many interurbans that hauled carload freight had nonelectrified sidings, they faced the problem of providing motive power that could operate away from the trolley wire. The North Shore Line had steeple-cab locomotives that could operate on batteries for short periods, and the Illinois Terminal had triple-powered locomotives that could operate from the wire, on batteries, or with diesel engines. The Pacific Electric operated several former Southern Pacific steam locomotives, one of them a large 4-8-2, and several diesel-electric switchers. The Bamberger, the South Shore Line, and the Illinois Terminal had diesels for the same purpose. Self-contained locomotives presented a serious safety problem to roads that used trolley-contact signals, since they failed to trip the mechanism on entering a block; the Pacific Electric and Bamberger put trolley poles on some of their self-contained power for this purpose.

CITY EQUIPMENT

The interurbans, as we have mentioned, characteristically provided city service in the important towns along the line. This varied from major streetcar systems that actually overshadowed the interurban lines, such as the Detroit United or the Northern Indiana's big city operation in South Bend, to very minor operations of a single car, such as the Aurora Plainfield and Joliet's city line in Joliet. The Northern Ohio's Akron operation and the Lake Shore Electric's Lorain Street Railroad were simply major street railways, operated with equipment strongly influenced by the design of cars in Cleveland. Accordingly, city equipment on the interurbans had about the same range as on independent street railways. The earliest equipment was typically single-truck wooden cars, some of which were open for summer use. Double-truck wooden cars became common in the first decade of the century, and double-truck steel cars in the second.

By the time of World War I, the unsatisfactory earnings of the street railway industry impelled a search for a lightweight car for lightly traveled lines. The effort to design one was carried on with particular vigor by the firm of Stone and Webster, which managed street railways in Texas, the state of Washington, and elsewhere. In 1916 Charles O. Birney, the firm's engineer in charge of car design, produced plans for a short, single-truck car about 28 feet long, weighing 6.5 to 9 tons—about a third of the weight of a standard car. It was to be a one-man car, then a novelty on street railways, equipped with a "dead man control," whereby the circuit breaker was automatically cut out when the motorman's hand left the controller handle. The trade at first called them "safety cars," but over the years they became unambiguously known as Birney cars.

Orders for Birney cars increased from 187 in 1916 to 280 in 1917, 644 in 1918, 1,383 in 1919, and reached a peak of 1,699 in 1920. Most of these orders came from street railways, but the Birney car at this time became preeminently the city car of the interurbans. The THI&E completely equipped Terre Haute with Birneys, making it the first major city to be all-Birney. The North Shore Line used them for local service on its entry into Milwaukee along 5th and 6th streets, and the Illinois Traction used them in Decatur, Peoria, Champaign-Urbana, and Danville. The Sacramento Northern, which claimed to be the first interurban to adopt Birneys, used them in street service in Sacramento and Chico and between Marysville and Yuba City. Union Traction, Lake Shore Electric, Stark, and many other lines in the Ohio–Indiana network used them. The Detroit United operated about 250 in city service.

By 1916 the interurbans' city operations were on the verge of such a decline that in the long run the operation of the Birney cars could not have proved profitable. At best, they permitted the interurbans to carry on their declining city services as economically as possible. After 1920 the purchase of Birney cars fell drastically. In 1921 565 were produced; thereafter the number never approached 500. The cars had poor riding qualities, were easily derailed, and were underpowered (they usually had only 50 horsepower) even for the light service they operated. By the mid-twenties, the bus was widely demonstrating its superior economy for this sort of traffic.

Birney also designed a double-truck car of similar construction which, although widely adopted, was never so common as the single-truck Birney. The double-truck Birney, however, was long enough and versatile enough to serve in interurban service itself. The American Car Company sold double-truck Birneys as rivals to Cincinnati and Kuhlman lightweights. The Texas Interurban used double-truck Birneys geared for interurban speeds, and the Union Electric in Kansas and the Sand Springs Railway in Oklahoma were operated mainly with them in later days. The Springfield Terminal in Vermont had a pair of double-truck Birneys built as combines by Wason, and it used them as its regular equipment for about 20 years.

Few interurbans survived long enough to use Presidents' Conference Committee cars in city service. These cars, universally known as PCC's, were the product of research by a staff of engineers retained by a committee of presidents of major transit companies in an effort to devise a fast, high-capacity streetcar for heavy urban routes. Dr. Thomas Conway, Jr., was also instrumental in initiating this design. The effort was very successful, and after the pilot model was produced in 1934, the PCC design was almost universal in car orders until the end of streetcar building in the 1950's. They could accelerate quickly, run quietly on rubber-centered wheels, and stop instantly with a combination of wheel and track brakes. Features of the PCC design have been incorporated into rapid-transit equipment in Chicago, and modified PCC equipment has been built for the Netherlands and other countries. Pittsburgh Railways, a heavy user of PCC cars, equipped several for service on its interurbans to Charleroi and Washington; and the Pacific Electric used double-ended PCC's on its Glendale–Burbank line. In 1949, the Illinois Terminal put eight double-ended PCC's in its St. Louis–Granite City suburban service—probably the last order of passenger equipment by an American interurban.

SAFETY

The technology of the interurbans permitted them to offer passenger and freight service on schedules similar to those of the buses and trucks that replaced them, but the question necessarily arises how safely they did so. Since no one seems to have computed the accident rate per passenger mile, one cannot generalize accurately; but certainly, if compared to the automobile, which took over most of the passengers, the interurbans were a model of safety. The interurbans were subject to crossing accidents and involvements with pedestrians in the same fashion as the railroads. The worst of these is believed to have been an accident near Bellevue, Ohio, in 1929, in which a car of the Lake Shore Electric struck a bus, killing 19 people. Given the interurbans' deteriorated physical condition in their last years, it is remarkable that more accidents were not caused by equipment failures. However, the simplicity of interurban equipment and low schedule speeds reduced the hazards in this respect.

The interurbans' serious accidents were quite uniformly of a single type: collisions resulting from misinterpretation or violation of train orders, from sloppy dispatching techniques, or from faulty signaling. A collision in 1916 on the Southern Cambria Railway, a line with a notorious safety reputation, near Brookdale, Pennsylvania, killed 28 people. A head-on collision between two special trains on the Hales Corners line of the former Milwaukee Electric in 1950 killed 10 people and injured 47 others, precipitating receivership of the property and hastening its abandonment a year later. One of the smallest interurbans had one of the worst wrecks: the Central Illinois Traction Company, a ten-mile line between Mattoon and Charleston, in 1907 suffered a head-on collision that killed 18 and injured 50. This line was one of the first interurbans to be forced into receivership by damage claims.

In 1909 and 1910, the interurbans suffered a series of collisions that gave the industry unwelcome notoriety in its safety practices. On October 4, 1910, a head-on collision on the Illinois Traction at Staunton killed thirty-seven people when a northbound local train failed to wait for the second section of a scheduled train.[17] On June 19, 1909, a train of the Chicago Lake Shore and South Bend ran beyond the siding where it was to meet a train approaching in the opposite direction and crashed into it, killing the motorman and ten passengers.

The worst of all interurban wrecks occurred at Kingsland, Indiana, at 12:15 P.M. on September 21, 1910, on the Bluffton branch of the Fort Wayne and Wabash Valley. An extra car southbound from Fort Wayne to Bluffton struck a northbound scheduled car at full speed, killing 41 passengers. The principal danger in head-on collisions was that the heavier or faster moving car would rise at the moment of impact, shearing off the body of the lighter or slower car and telescoping it. In the Kingsland accident, conditions could hardly have been worse: the northbound car was the lighter of the two, and was crammed with passengers, most of them bound for a fair in Fort Wayne. The loss of life would have been even greater had not the conductor of the scheduled train, himself injured, flagged down its second section before it reached the scene of the accident. Damage claims forced the company into bankruptcy.

In the course of the same week as the Kingsland disaster, the Union Traction Company suffered two fatal head-on collisions. On September 17, a motorman and one passenger were killed on the Union City line, and on September 24, an extra freight train collided with a scheduled passenger train a mile north of Tipton on the Peru division, killing a motorman and six passengers.

The Indiana Railroad Commission investigated the Indiana wrecks in some detail and its conclusions were hardly flattering to the industry. Violation of train orders had been responsible for all four accidents, and in all cases there was reason to believe that the train crews were incompetent. In the Union City line collision of Union Traction, one crew had overrun a meeting point, and in the Tipton crash the crew of the freight had ignored the schedule for the on-coming passenger train. The surviving motorman in the earlier crash had fled, and the conductors proved to be former farmers with little experience in interurban service, and largely ignorant of the rules of operation.

The death of the motorman of the train at fault in the Chicago Lake Shore and South Bend accident left certain facts obscure, but it appeared that both members of the crew were casual about taking train orders; neither had a copy of the order about him after the wreck. Moreover, Conductor Kinney, who survived, proved to be something of a railroad ne'er-do-well who had been discharged from the Wabash for drinking on duty. There was some evidence he had been drinking before the collision. The Indiana Commission severely criticized the company for failing to discover the man's poor record on the railroads, and stated that "to have employed him was the worst railroading we have ever known, and it may be compared to shooting a gun into a crowd of people."[18]

Circumstances surrounding the Kingsland disaster were considerably worse. The southbound extra train had been ordered to proceed to Bluffton, clearing scheduled trains by five minutes. Its motorman, B. T. Corkwell, and its conductor, Del Wilson, tried to reach siding 107 at Kingsland, two sidings beyond the point where they had been ordered to meet the train with which they collided. Corkwell had been discharged by the Union Traction Company in 1908 for losing his temper and had been hired by the Fort Wayne and Wabash Valley for city service in 1909. He had been promoted to interurban service in April 1910, and received two warnings and 90 demerits in six months of service. On July 30, less than two months before the Kingsland accident, Corkwell had been given 50 demerits for meeting a car at the wrong siding. Wilson had gone to work in interurban service the day before the accident, in spite of a poor written examination. In the course of less than seven months, Wilson earned 190 demerits, and was discharged in March 1911.[19]

The commission criticized the Fort Wayne and Wabash Valley strongly for hiring poorly qualified personnel. In the two years from September 21, 1908, to the date of the collision, 72 motormen and conductors left the company's service, about half resigning, and half discharged for drunkenness, incompetence, insubordination, overrunning meeting places, and other failures to follow train orders. Since the Bluffton branch had 38 trains per day and no block signals, safety depended on adequate dispatching procedures and crews competent to execute orders. Yet because the interurbans paid lower wages, they attracted the least able employees away from the railroads, and many of the men promoted from street railway service were not well qualified for interurban duty.

The commission recommended higher standards for interurban personnel, and urged the introduction of block signaling. The commission at this time did not have power to demand signaling devices, but in response to its appeal, the legislature authorized it in 1912 to require signaling on the interurbans where, in its judgment, safety demanded it. Since the safety record of Union Traction on its signaled lines had been good, the commission proceeded to require automatic signals on the state's most heavily traveled track. By 1913, about 18 per cent of Indiana's interurban mileage was protected by signals, and most of the main lines were eventually covered. The later history of the Indiana interurbans was much more satisfactory; the safety record of the Indiana Railroad in particular was one any common carrier might envy. The THI&E prided itself on having never caused the death of a passenger.

Even without the pressures of public regulation the interurbans had ample incentive to adopt safety devices. Early in their history, interurbans in large numbers adopted a device called an anti-climber, a horizontal, corrugated steel plate riveted to the end sill of each car. In collisions, the anti-climbers meshed and caused a considerable dissipation of energy at the moment of impact. In low-speed collisions, they prevented one car's overriding the floor of the other, but even in high-speed collisions they were of some benefit. Interurbans varied in the extent to which they relied on anti-climbers, but almost all used them from about the time that steel cars were introduced. The Lake Shore Electric had used them since early in the century, and the Interstate Public Service Company was so attached to them that it used double-height anti-climbers on some of its suburban equipment.

The anti-climber was one of several pieces of interurban equipment to be adopted in the diesel-electric locomotive. The typical diesel-electric locomotive is operated from a controller based on the same principle as the controller on an electric car; the engineer has no direct control over his diesel engines, which vary their revolutions automatically according to his admission of electric power to the traction motors. The air horn, a universal piece of equipment on diesel locomotives, was developed to replace the whistle in order to economize on the meager supplies of compressed air on the interurban car. Telephonic dispatching has become customary on the railroads. The revival of interest in urban rapid transit stimulated by traffic congestion, and by the decline of the central business districts of major cities, may cause engineers to draw further on the experience of the interurbans. Although by the test of financial gain the interurban ranks very low among technological developments, it has made a modest contribution to the growth of knowledge in society.

3
Passenger Traffic

From the beginning of interurban operation to the general dissolution of the industry in the 1930's, the principal source of income was local passenger traffic. Dr. Thomas Conway, Jr., estimated that in 1902, during the first building boom, 94.4 per cent of the revenues of electric lines, apparently including some city operations, were created by passenger traffic, as compared with only 22 per cent for the railroads.[1] As late as 1931, the Midwestern interurban lines were still deriving about 60 per cent of their revenue from passenger service.[2]

Passenger traffic fell largely into two classes: farmers and members of their families making short trips into towns and cities for shopping or social visits, and commercial travelers or villagers going from one town to another. To both, the interurban proved a boon that is difficult to appreciate from the perspective of a society centered about the automobile. For the first time, a farmer's wife was able to go into town, shop for an hour or two, and return to the farm by dinner time. A resident of a country town could spend part of a day in the city and return home at his leisure. The salesman who had been able to visit one or two towns in a day could now visit four or five. Even on the busiest railroad lines in the Midwest locals rarely ran more often than twice a day, but an interurban might schedule 16 cars a day. By 1909, the Illinois Traction was scheduling 106 trains a day in or out of Springfield, more than all the railroads combined, and in 1911, the interurbans regularly ran 140 trains a day in or out of Columbus.

At the beginning, hourly service was the goal of most of the major interurbans. The Union Traction Company had on-the-hour departures out of Indianapolis on each of its main lines, and the Lake Shore Electric offered approximately hourly service between Cleveland and Toledo. Even such minor lines as the Evansville Suburban and Newburgh, the Dayton Covington and Piqua, and the Dayton Springfield and Xenia ran cars hourly. The Fort Wayne and Decatur operated at 90-minute intervals and the Toledo Bowling Green and Southern throughout its history ran locals every two hours. Regular scheduling offered the public (to whom timetables were notoriously unpleasant) a convenience of some magnitude, but a fixed schedule often conflicted with technological considerations, particularly with the need to minimize layovers at terminals. Because the Fort Wayne and Northwestern's run was just barely too long for an hourly schedule with four cars, it ran at intervals of 1 hour and 10 minutes. Lightly traveled lines, such as the Toledo and Western, the Aroostook

Valley, and the Salt Lake and Utah, operated a few times a day at irregular intervals, like the railroads. In general only lines serving major metropolitan areas operated trains much after midnight, but the little Bridgeton and Millville Traction Company in New Jersey had a departure for Bivalve about 3:00 A.M. for the benefit of oyster fishermen who wanted to be on their boats by dawn.

The interurbans depended so heavily on frequent service as an advantage over the railroads that they had a considerable incentive to offer frequent, regular schedules, even though individual runs might lose money. As traffic declined in the twenties, the problem of losses on individual runs became successively more severe. Cutting the schedule, the obvious solution further reduced the attractiveness of the interurban car over the automobile for short trips. Like fare increases in the later years, cutting the schedule intensified the loss of traffic so greatly that to some extent it was self-defeating. Accordingly, many interurbans retained heavy scheduling to the end. The Inter-City Rapid Transit between Canton and Massillon, Ohio, operated half-hourly until the end of rail service.

Nonetheless most roads were forced to cut schedules, some drastically. The Utah-Idaho Central operated only two trains a day in each direction by 1940, although it added a third during World War II. The Fort Wayne–Lima Railroad ultimately sank to seven round trips per day, and the Columbus Delaware and Marion to only three, with an additional trip over its Bucyrus extension. A few interurbans, notably the Fort Dodge Des Moines and Southern and the Illinois Traction, reduced service to a single run per day before abandoning passenger service. The THI&E in 1930 ran one trip per day on its weakest line, the Lebanon–Crawfordsville branch, one of the few examples of once-a-day operation on the Ohio-Indiana network.

To some extent, the two principal kinds of interurban passenger traffic rivaled rather than complemented each other. If a line tried to maximize its farm-to-town traffic, it did so at the cost of increasing its competitive disadvantage to the railroads in running time, and thus it made the line less attractive to town-to-town riders. Since most of the early lines were built by men with backgrounds in street railways rather than in railroads, there was a tendency to put a stop at every crossroad and almost at every farm. On the lines built on highways in the New England fashion, the average speed was so low that the marginal loss of time in stopping at a farmhouse was insignificant, but for the Midwestern interurban built on a private right-of-way, the delay in stopping at a farm became significant, and the expense of braking and accelerating was worth considering. Since many of the passengers who boarded at rural stops rode only a mile or two, and paid fares of only a nickel or a dime, this traffic was not particularly profitable, but a line that served no major towns (such as the Bluffton Geneva and Celina) had no alternative to concentrating on it. The Cincinnati Georgetown and Portsmouth and the Dayton Covington and Piqua tried to maximize this traffic by placing five stops to the mile, but the Lake

Shore Electric used just two and the Scioto Valley only one. The Detroit Ypsilanti Ann Arbor and Jackson was cursed with a franchise that required its local cars to stop wherever signaled.[3]

The speed of local trains varied according to the number of stops per mile, the terrain, and the relative difficulty of street running, but 20 miles per hour was initially the center of a narrow range typical of most Midwestern interurbans and others as well. The Lake Shore Electric's locals spent exactly 6 hours running the 120 miles between Cleveland and Toledo, including about an hour of street running in the terminal cities. The Fort Wayne and Decatur needed 1 hour and 5 minutes for its 22 miles, and the Dayton and Xenia 55 minutes for its 16 miles. The Toledo Bowling Green and Southern required 2 hours and 30 minutes for a trip of 51 miles. The Northern Ohio's locals, which were hampered by lengthy street running in both Cleveland and Akron, spent 1 hour and 50 minutes on the trip of 34 miles. The Union Traction's locals on the direct line between Indianapolis and Muncie covered the 57 miles in 2 hours and 40 minutes. Schedule speeds increased somewhat over the years under the pressure of highway competition. The New England electric cars did only a little better than half as well as the Midwestern interurbans. From New York it was a trip of 8 hours and 30 minutes to New Haven and 19 hours and 12 minutes to Boston, an average of less than 12 miles per hour. To go from New York to Camden, New Jersey, on cars of the New England style in 1904 would have taken 9 hours, with but a single change of cars in the entire 104 miles. In 1903 the Massachusetts Railway Commission limited single-truck cars on the public highway to 15 miles per hour.

At the opposite extreme, the interurbans west of the Mississippi frequently averaged well over 20 miles per hour on their local services. Standard time for Bamberger Railroad locals over the 36 miles between Salt Lake City and Ogden was 1 hour and 20 minutes, and the connecting Utah-Idaho Central, taking advantage of a good physical plant and a low tributary population, covered the 95 miles from Ogden to Preston in 3 hours flat. The Salt Lake and Utah's local trains ran the 67 miles of the main line in 2 hours and 30 minutes. The Cedar Rapids and Iowa City covered a main line of 27 miles in 55 minutes, and the Waterloo Cedar Falls and Northern scheduled its locals at 30 miles per hour. Sacramento Northern locals on the southern division averaged nearly 30 miles per hour, in spite of being handicapped by stiff grades just east of Oakland and by the ferry crossing of Suisun Bay.

One of the principal determinants of the interurbans' speed was the length and difficulty of their street running. Only a few interurbans escaped street running entirely—for example, the Cincinnati Georgetown and Portsmouth, an electrified steam railroad. Others, such as the Aurora Elgin and Chicago and the Stark Electric, had very little; the Stark had only about half a mile in Canton, some in Alliance, but none in the lesser towns on the line. The Stark was particularly remarkable in this respect, since it had no pretensions to being a general freight hauler. The Lackawanna and Wyoming Valley had no street running whatever, but it was built to interchange carload freight with the railroads.

At the opposite extreme, the Cleveland Painesville and Eastern had nine miles of street running, mainly in Cleveland, most of it barren and unproductive. The major interurbans spent as much as 45 minutes reaching their terminals in Cleveland and Detroit, 20 in Toledo, 25 in Indianapolis, and 30 in Buffalo.[4] Detroit–Cleveland expresses spent more than 2 of their 5 hours and 40 minutes elapsed time in street running. Cars of the Public Service Fast Line leaving Newark spent 35 minutes in the streets before they reached a private right-of-way, and then spent 30 in Trenton. They also had extensive street running in New Brunswick. Cincinnati–Toledo cars on the Ohio Electric and its successors spent 40 minutes in the streets of Dayton. The Sacramento Northern spent 11 or 12 minutes on the Key System between the ferry terminal and its yard in Oakland.

A few interurbans minimized their running time in cities by building down back streets. The Interstate, troubled with a gauge difference in Louisville, built its private entrance down secondary avenues and took only about ten minutes to reach its terminal. Similarly, the Washington Baltimore and Annapolis entered Baltimore on streets not heavily traveled. The Bamberger achieved its admirable schedule speeds by approaching both its Salt Lake City and Ogden terminals through a mixture of private rights-of-way and running on back streets.

Many of the interurbans were required by franchise to stop at every corner in major cities when hailed, but the proximity of stops to residences was an advantage over the railroads in intercity service, and on the whole (particularly if the interurban cars had to follow streetcars for long distances) there was little or no loss of time involved in stopping. The Washington Baltimore and Annapolis stopped at any platform on the Benning Road car line in Washington; but the street was so long and so heavily traveled that the interurban cars could not maintain higher average speeds than the streetcars under any circumstances.

Some franchises required interurban cars to carry intracity passengers at the local fare, and cars serving Indianapolis carried special registers for this purpose. Prior to World War I, when the Indianapolis Street Railway sold tickets at six for 25 cents, few passengers preferred to pay 5 cents on the interurban cars, but thereafter, when there was no fare differential, local riders became a nuisance. The fare division with the street railway for intracity passengers was frequently unfavorable. The division adopted in Dayton, where the city line took three cents and the interurban retained two cents, was imitated in other cities, and became the most common arrangement in the industry. Interurban officials widely felt that local passengers were unremunerative at this division. The Cincinnati Milford and Loveland Traction Company paid the street railway in Cincinnati three cents out of every five collected from a local passenger, plus a rental of $3,000 per year for use of the track, $1,000 for use of the overhead, $900 for the reading of fare meters, 75 per cent of expense for track maintenance (amounting to $1,200–$1,500 per year), and 21.3 per cent of gross revenue on freight hauled through the streets. The expense of this arrangement was so prohibitive that the interurban stopped running into the city in 1915, forgoing the advantage that a common gauge with the street railway had given it.

Although street running was slow and unprofitable, few interurbans gave it up. Some (mentioned in the previous chapter) managed to acquire private rights-of-way into cities, and the Detroit United in 1924, after its separation from the street railway in Detroit, began to transfer passengers to buses on the outskirts of the city. The inconvenience of the transfer largely canceled out the saving in time, since one of the interurbans' principal advantages was their direct entry into downtown areas, and the Detroit United shortly restored its entrances into downtown Detroit. Whatever the disadvantages of the Washington Baltimore and Annapolis's half-hour of street running in Washington, it brought the interurban to a terminal at 11th Street and New York Avenue, about a mile closer to the central business district than was the Union Station, which both of its railroad rivals used. In addition, an interurban received some advertising value from having its cars in major streets.

Given the interurbans' physical limitations, in cities and out, their ordinary running times were markedly inferior to the local trains of the railroads, which could usually average at least 25 miles per hour even with rather frequent stops. Consequently, the interurbans had more difficulty attracting town-to-town passengers than some of the promoters had anticipated, and the industry found itself with an alarmingly short average haul. In 1909, the average revenue per passenger of all Ohio interurbans was only 8.3 cents. The strong Scioto Valley had the highest average revenue, 29 cents, and the Dayton and Troy was second with 26.8 cents, but the big Ohio Electric, which had substantial numbers of urban riders, averaged only 10.9 cents.[5] The average for all Ohio interurbans remained at eight-odd cents per passenger until about the time of World War I, after which it moved upward slowly. By 1926, the average passenger paid 11.4 cents and by 1932, 12.7 cents. Many individual interurbans had much worse records: for example, the Alton Jacksonville and Peoria in Illinois in 1910, when it had completed only five miles of line, averaged about 5 cents per passenger.

The low average receipts per passenger were reflected in earnings per car mile so small that they boded ill for the future. Revenue per car mile for all Ohio interurbans in 1909 was 25.8 cents, and individual figures ranged from the Dayton and Troy's 40.2 cents to the Sharon and New Castle's 11.7 cents. Since operating expenses averaged only 15.1 cents for all Ohio roads in the same year, the operating ratios of most roads were quite favorable, but as will be shown in Chapter 6, the rise in operating costs relative to receipts caused this ratio to move steadily against the interurbans throughout their history. By 1920, average revenue per car mile in Ohio had risen to 45.7 cents, but at the same time operating costs had reached 36.1 cents.

LIMITED SERVICES

In an effort to attract passengers for longer distances, several of the Midwestern interurbans by 1905 were running expresses, which stopped only in towns. The Lake Shore Electric's Cleveland–Toledo expresses made the trip in 4 hours and 20 minutes, a saving of 1 hour and 40 minutes over the local trains, even though they stopped in every major town. The Northern Ohio's expresses saved about 25 minutes between Cleveland and Akron. Several roads—among them the Aurora Elgin and Chicago—alternated locals and expresses throughout the day. Most of the New England lines, owing to their technology, were unable to offer anything but local service, but the Boston and Worcester took advantage of its private right-of-way to run hourly expresses, interspersed with locals on the half hour. In the West, the Bamberger Railroad took advantage of inadequate railroad service to offer relatively frequent trains between Salt Lake City and Ogden, with several expresses saving 10 to 20 minutes over the local times. Although two railroads paralleled the Bamberger, their passenger service was almost entirely incidental to transcontinental movements.

A few lines went a step further, adopting limited service with stops only in major towns, often only in county seats. There were two major periods of interest in limited operation, one about 1905–6 and the other beginning about 1922. The first was an effort to lure long-distance passengers from the railroads, the second to draw them from automobiles; neither was successful. The Union Traction Company was particularly interested in limited service because it operated several routes that had relatively insignificant steam railroad competition. The Big Four in 1905 connected Indianapolis and Marion, 72 miles apart, with two direct trains a day in either direction, and made connections at Anderson for two more. The fastest train made the trip in 1 hour and 38 minutes, but the rest all required more than 2 hours. The Union Traction Company which offered approximately hourly local service, operated two fast cars, called the Marion Flyers, that gave two-hour-and-40-minute service morning and evening from each terminal. Between Indianapolis and Muncie, via New Castle, it operated an even faster car, the Muncie Meteor, that made the 63-mile trip in 1 hour and 50 minutes. It left Muncie at eight in the morning and Indianapolis at five in the afternoon. It stopped only in New Castle, and took 50 minutes less time than the local cars.

The most important of the Midwestern intercity limited services was Union Traction's joint operation between Indianapolis and Fort Wayne with the Indiana Service Corporation and its predecessors. There was never really adequate railroad service between Indianapolis and Fort Wayne, the two largest cities in Indiana. The most direct route was on the Big Four from Indianapolis to Muncie, and thence on the Lake Erie & Western to Fort Wayne. As long as both roads were controlled by the

New York Central, they ran through coaches, but when the Lake Erie & Western passed into the hands of the Nickel Plate Road in 1922, through service was discontinued, and in 1929 passenger service on the Muncie–Fort Wayne segment was abandoned entirely. No other route offered even reasonably close connections.

To fill this void, the Union Traction operated Indianapolis–Fort Wayne trains via Peru and via Bluffton, both in connection with the Fort Wayne and Wabash Valley and its successors. The Peru route was the longer by 12 miles—136 miles to 124—and the Bluffton route passed through somewhat larger towns, including Anderson and Muncie. Running time was about 4 hours and 45 minutes by either route. About the time of World War I, there were 12 trains a day in either direction, eight via Bluffton and four via Peru. Particularly after 1922, service on these lines was brought to a very high standard. The two companies had pooled their equipment for these trains almost from the beginning, and had offered buffet service as early as 1906, although they appear to have discontinued it not long afterward.[6] The companies installed two parlor-buffet cars on the Bluffton line in 1923, and two on the Peru line in 1926. The limiteds via Bluffton were known as the "Hoosierlands," and their counterparts on the Peru line as the "Wabash Valley Flyers." In December 1930, upon delivery of the high-speed lightweight cars, some of which had lounge seats available free to all passengers, the parlor cars became redundant and were discontinued. Dining service was abandoned simultaneously.

Until 1926 Union Traction participated jointly with the Winona Railroad in a similar interline operation between Indianapolis and Goshen. Since railroad service from Indianapolis to the South Bend–Elkhart area was never more than meager, here the interurbans were able to compete on relatively favorable terms. Each company contributed a car, and provided a round trip from each terminal every day. Running time was about five hours and thirty minutes in each direction. The arrangement was discontinued when Union Traction objected to the Winona's introduction of lightweight cars into the equipment pool.

The Interstate Public Service Company took advantage of the heavy population at both its termini, Indianapolis and Louisville, to offer a limited service similar to the Indianapolis–Fort Wayne interline operation. Despite adequate passenger service on the parallel Pennsylvania Railroad, the president of the company, Harry Reid, inaugurated eight limited trains per day, equipped with parlor-dining service. Reid ordered five motorized parlor cars from American Car and Foundry in 1923 to establish this service, and in 1925 had the company shops convert a former Winona Railroad car into a sixth parlor-diner. The six cars—an exceptionally large number for a road the size of the Interstate—characteristically ran in multiple unit with heavy steel combines. The limiteds, known as the Dixie Flyers (southbound) and the Hoosier Flyers (northbound), covered the 117 miles in 3 hours and 45 minutes.

In California, the Oakland Antioch and Eastern and its successors, the

San Francisco–Sacramento Railroad and the Sacramento Northern, offered de luxe limited service in spite of fast and frequent service on the Southern Pacific. The fastest trains, the Comet and the Meteor, made the 93-mile trip between San Francisco and Sacramento in 3 hours and 15 minutes, including a 15-minute trip on a Key System passenger ferry between San Francisco and Oakland and a ten-minute crossing of Suisun Bay by car ferry. Since the Southern Pacific was also burdened with a ferry crossing of San Francisco Bay and a car-ferry crossing of the Carquinez Strait, the interurban was not severely handicapped in its schedules. Some of its motor cars assigned to limited service were specially geared for 73 miles per hour, and were capable of high speeds even when hauling unpowered open-platform parlor trailers. The northbound Meteor covered the 47 miles from the ferry to Sacramento in 1 hour and 5 minutes—relatively fast time for an interurban. Because the intermediate territory was flat and almost unpopulated, there was no impediment to fast running. When the Southern Pacific opened its bridge across the Carquinez Strait in 1930, the Sacramento Northern suffered a competitive disadvantage from which it never recovered. To be sure, its traffic to points north of Sacramento, which the limiteds also served, was sustained for a time, but the traffic from San Francisco to Sacramento declined considerably. The company hoped that its entrance into San Francisco over the Bay Bridge beginning in 1939 would improve its competitive position, but its hopes were in vain, and all but local commutation service out of San Francisco was abandoned in 1940.

Usually, however, limited service was offered by interurbans that had no important railroad competition. Between Peoria and St. Louis, the Chicago & Alton Railroad offered only a slow local service, and in 1933 abandoned even that. Consequently, the Illinois Traction Company operated two or three limited trains a day on its main line, fitted out with parlor and dining service. It owned six open-platform observation cars, the largest number of any interurban. In 1936, its successor, the Illinois Terminal Company, enclosed the rear platforms and air-conditioned the cars. Aside from the North Shore Line's parlor-buffet service on the Electroliners, the Illinois Terminal was the last interurban to operate parlor cars; the parlor trailers built with its lightweight equipment of 1948 remained in service until 1951.

In Ohio, the Cleveland–Lima service was in several respects parallel to the Indianapolis–Fort Wayne operations. Until the Nickel Plate Road inaugurated its Cleveland–St. Louis passenger train in 1928, there was no direct railroad service from Cleveland to Lima. It was mainly to set up a direct Cleveland–Lima interurban route that the Lake Shore Electric and the Western Ohio built the Fostoria and Fremont Railway in 1911, and arranged trackage rights on the Toledo Fostoria and Findlay between the new line and the Western Ohio at Findlay. The Lake Shore Electric and the Western Ohio bought four virtually identical heavy wooden combine cars from Jewett in 1912, and offered early morning and mid-afternoon departures in each direction. When the Toledo Fostoria and Findlay was abandoned in 1930, the Western Ohio acquired the portion over which it had trackage rights and operated it under the name of the Fostoria Arcadia and Findlay Railway until January 16, 1932, when the entire Fremont–Lima trackage was abandoned. Cleveland–Lima limiteds had been abandoned earlier. The same year saw the Lake Shore Electric lose its connection for Detroit, the Eastern Michigan–Toledo Railroad, with which it had also operated interline expresses.

For many years the THI&E and the Dayton and Western operated a through service between Indianapolis and Dayton, three times a day in the peak years. In 1916 the THI&E, together with the Ohio Electric (which was then in control of the Dayton and Western), instituted a through car called "The Columbian" between Indianapolis and Zanesville —a distance of about 250 miles. The service required 8 hours and 50 minutes, and was so much slower than the Pennsylvania Railroad, the Big Four, and the Baltimore & Ohio, which it paralleled in various areas, that it was soon discontinued. The Dayton and Troy, the Western Ohio, and the Toledo Bowling Green and Southern operated their coordinated schedules between Toledo and Dayton under the name of "The Lima Route" until 1930, often with pooled equipment. In 1905 their average speed between Dayton and Lima of 33 miles per hour was considered to be the best in the area.[7]

Only a few interurbans were built primarily for limited service. The most important was the Washington Baltimore and Annapolis, which ran an express train on its main line every half-hour and a local every two hours. The Buffalo–Niagara Falls high-speed line of 1917 was designed for quick service from terminal to terminal. The interurbans between Houston and Galveston and between Beaumont and Port Arthur were also chiefly interested in express business. The Puget Sound Electric was built principally for Seattle–Tacoma direct service, although it operated local trains that were essentially suburban in character. Similarly, at its height, the Lackawanna and Wyoming Valley ran an hourly express between Scranton and Wilkes-Barre, with locals at 20-minute intervals.

In so far as any really fast running could be found on the interurbans, it was almost entirely on lines of this sort. The WB&A's famous scheduled speed of 66 miles per hour on its private right-of-way has already been mentioned. In 1925, the magazine *Electric Traction* instituted an annual trophy to be awarded to the interurban with the best over-all speed performance. It was won in the first two years by the Galveston–Houston Electric Railway, which averaged just over 40 miles per hour over-all with standard wooden equipment built about 1910 but geared for high speeds. After 1927, the trophy was won annually by the North Shore Line or the South Shore Line, both of which had been heavily rebuilt for high-speed operation. Both lines regularly scheduled trains for operation between intermediate stations at more than 60 miles per hour after the mid-twenties, and even in the late 1950's the North Shore Line was regularly turning in more than two thousand miles of 60-mile-per-hour running every day. The North Shore Line's performance was particularly remarkable since the company did it with orthodox pole trolleys and partly with directly suspended trolley wire. The South Shore Line always used pantograph and catenary.

Since any express or limited service depended to some extent on freedom from the delays of frequent stops in rural areas, express trains alienated the rural population, who saw the home-to-market service as the principal function of the interurban. Since the farmer and his wife adopted the automobile later than the commercial traveler, the express and limited trains proved less viable than the locals.

The interurbans that operated high-speed intercity service frequently handled heavy commuter traffic, which also required a large terminal population. A combination of the two, together with carload freight traffic, enabled the South Shore Line to outlive the rest of the industry, and supported the neighboring North Shore Line for a very long period. The Chicago Aurora and Elgin derived most of its revenue from commuters. The Sacramento Northern operated commuter trains between San Francisco and Pittsburg, and commuters made up a large part of the traffic of the Bamberger Railroad. The Pacific Electric in its later days carried mostly commuters and other suburban passengers. Most of the communities in the Midwestern interurban network were too small to have dormitory suburbs, but the Cleveland lines carried some commuters, and the Indiana Railroad ran a frequent suburban service to Fort Harrison on its main line to Muncie. Both the Detroit United and the Milwaukee Electric operated extensive suburban service.

In most cases, suburban service was a late development. During the interurban era the great majority of the urban labor force lived within city limits, and by the time American cities began to degenerate into industrial cores surrounded by residential suburbs, most of the interurbans had been abandoned. One occasionally hears speculation that one or another of the interurbans might have survived, had it lasted until its tributary areas became residential suburbs—e.g., that the Eastern Ohio Traction Company, an exceptionally weak interurban in its lifetime, might have survived as a rapid-transit line (like the City of Shaker Heights Rapid Transit) serving Cleveland's present-day dormitory suburbs. Given the unprofitability of rail suburban services in general, such interurbans could have been preserved only by public subsidy, first to get the track off the streets and then to cover operating deficits. Although traffic congestion may drive municipalities to subsidize suburban rapid transit in the future, the interurbans had virtually entirely disappeared before serious consideration was first given to such plans.

Sleeping cars were operated by three of the interurbans that were most interested in limited service: the Illinois Traction, the Interstate, and the Oregon Electric. No other interurbans ever operated them in regular service, although during the second building boom, when limited services were being widely established, there was some expectation that overnight travel would develop on the longest lines. About 1903, Harris F. Holland of Indianapolis formed the Holland Palace Car Company, which he hoped would serve the interurbans in much the same fashion as the Pullman Company served the railroads. From the shipbuilding and car manufacturing firm of Harlan and Hollingsworth he bought a pair of cars capable of being fitted either as sleeping cars or as parlor cars. Late in 1904 he put them into daylight service between Columbus and Zanesville, and later they operated on the Western Ohio between Dayton and Lima and on the Dayton and Western–THI&E joint line between Dayton and Indianapolis.

In 1906, the Holland Palace Car Company was reported to be bankrupt. In 1907, Holland's cars, named "Theodore" and "Francis," passed into the hands of the Illinois Traction where they were put into night operation between East St. Louis, Springfield, and Decatur. A car was opened in East St. Louis at 9:30 P.M., departed at midnight, arrived in Springfield at 4:00 A.M., then laid over until 8:00, and arrived in Decatur at 9:30. One dollar was charged for a berth to either city. Within a few months the service was cut back to Springfield. Sleeping-car traffic over such a short distance could at best be limited, however; the Illinois Traction's real interest was in offering cheap berths on night trains between Chicago and St. Louis. It hoped to charge $1.50 for a lower berth, undercutting the Pullman rate by 50 cents. The company never completed its line from St. Louis to the Chicago area, but beginning in 1910 it ordered five sleeping cars built to its own specifications, and it operated them on its main lines in central Illinois for many years. A pair ran between St. Louis and Springfield, a second pair ran between St. Louis and Peoria, and beginning in 1925, the fifth ran alternate nights between St. Louis and Champaign. Later the Champaign and Springfield services were consolidated and operated nightly.

These cars were built as trailers in the expectation that they would be more quiet than the Holland motor cars. The Illinois Traction reduced one of the Holland cars to maintenance-of-way activity, and scrapped the other. The new sleeping cars were regularly hauled by combines geared for heavy duty, but several in a train required a separate locomotive. Sleeping cars were discontinued on the Danville line in 1929, but they ran to Peoria until 1940. The last cars used in this service were a former parlor car and a former coach, both converted to bedroom sleepers in 1930 and later air-conditioned. By the end patronage had fallen to an average of 1.8 passengers per car, and the future was hopeless.

The Interstate Public Service Company opened sleeping car service between Indianapolis and Louisville in 1924 with three steel sleepers similar to the Illinois Traction equipment. The distance was so short (only 117 miles) that the trip took under four hours by the Interstate's daylight expresses. The sleeping car left Indianapolis at 11:30 P.M., and about 2:00 A.M. was set on a siding at Scottsburg, Indiana, for most of the night. It was pulled out at 6:10 and brought into Louisville at 7:05. Similar service was operated northbound with a layover at Greenwood, just south of Indianapolis. The space charge was $2.75 for a lower berth and $2.00 for an upper. Although the Interstate advertised the service extensively, it was a financial failure, and the Indiana Railroad, after succeeding to the property, abandoned the sleeping cars in 1932.

The Oregon Electric in 1912 bought a pair of sleeping cars from the Barney and Smith Car Company, again modeled closely on the Illinois Traction's equipment. The distance between Portland and Eugene was only 143 miles, but was scheduled for six hours. The tributary population was only a fraction of what either the Interstate or the Illinois Traction served, and the sleeping cars survived only until 1928. The cars, together with those of the Interstate, were sold to the Pacific Great Eastern Railway, a steam railroad in British Columbia which was then so poor and so lightly traveled that the cars' small capacities—ten sections each—and low second-hand prices were both most attractive. Most of the Illinois Traction's sleeping cars were reduced to bunk cars for maintenance-of-way crews, and the cars on the Pacific Great Eastern met the same fate in the 1950's.

The Schoepf-McGowan management and its successors manifested little or no interest in sleeping cars, even though several runs on the Schoepf-McGowan lines were as likely prospects as any of the three runs on which such cars were actually put into service. The Ohio Electric's line from Cincinnati to Toledo, for which Schoepf is reported to have considered sleeping cars, was longer than any of them, but most of its passengers rode to intermediate points. Because of the inferior rival railroad service, and because they were longer, the two Indianapolis–Fort Wayne lines were more promising than the Indianapolis–Louisville interurban, but no sleeping cars were ever installed. In 1917 the North Shore Line announced that it intended to institute sleeping car service between Chicago and Milwaukee, but it never did so.

Almost all the interurbans that instituted parlor or dining services in the 1920's gave them up some time before abandonment. The low seating capacity of a parlor car made it a relatively unprofitable piece of equipment, and most interurban dining service was a simple à la carte buffet, such as the Pullman Company offered in parlor cars, in which the porter prepared the food. The North Shore Line offered full meals in dining cars until 1949, when it cut back to buffet service in its Electroliners. Dining cars on the Sacramento Northern, the South Shore Line, the Milwaukee Electric, and the Chicago Aurora and Elgin had been abandoned by the early 1930's. Such services were probably never really profitable, but were carried on in a belief that they were necessary adjuncts of limited operation. As parlor and dining services were discontinued, there was a tendency to increase the number of stops of expresses and limiteds, and to increase their running times. Track deterioration contributed to the same end. The Indiana Railroad blurred the distinction between limited and local, and finally operated its major schedules with lightweight cars at about a 35-mile-per-hour average.

INTERURBAN PASSENGER FARES

Except in such special operations as the Indianapolis–Fort Wayne and Cleveland–Lima runs, the interurbans' service was sufficiently inferior to the railroads' that they had to depend on greater frequency, greater willingness to stop near one's home, and lower fares. A few long-distance travelers may have been attracted by the absence of soot and cinders, or by the novelty, or in the later years, by a hobbyist's interest in the industry, but in the main only a desire to economize accounted for riding interurbans for long distances. The New England lines characteristically used a zone system, whereby the passenger paid five cents every time the car passed a zone boundary. Some permitted the passenger to buy a multi-zone ticket before boarding, but most simply had the conductor collect nickels at specified points. This kind of travel was usually extremely cheap, with fares ranging between 0.4 cents and 1.5 cents per mile. The most common fare in New England was about 1 cent per mile, and in New Jersey average fares were less than 1.25 cents per mile.[8] One could travel from New York to Boston for only $3.05. Several lines in New York and most in Pennsylvania used zone systems, notably the West Penn Railways, but in the Midwest almost all of the interurbans issued tickets in the fashion of the steam railroads. At first, nearly all Midwestern interurbans charged fares between 1.5 cents and 2 cents per mile. The Union Traction regularly charged about 1.5 cents and the THI&E about 1.7 cents. The Ohio roads tended to have slightly higher fares: the Lake Shore Electric averaged 1.8 cents, and the Scioto Valley, the Fort Wayne Van Wert and Lima, and the Western Ohio all about 2 cents. In the Far West, fares were considerably higher; the Spokane and Inland Empire, for example, charged 2 cents to 2.5 cents per mile.[9] Most companies gave reductions of about 10 per cent for round-trip tickets.

A few roads charged a penalty for paying a cash fare on the car, but the number of passengers who boarded at nonagency stations was so great that most roads did not do so. In 1907, about 60 per cent of Midwestern fares were paid at ticket offices, 40 per cent in cash on trains. Conductors on the larger lines were equipped with an official-distance table for computing cash fares on a mileage basis between points en route. Such tables showed the distance not only between stations but between intermediate halts too small to be listed in tariffs. Since in Indiana a premium could not be charged for a cash fare unless a ticket office had been open for 30 minutes before train time, the interurbans in the state made no effort to differentiate between tickets and cash fares.

Lines that served major cities generally offered commutation rates and a few roads, particularly those out of Lima, issued individual mileage-coupon books. Most roads issued school tickets at low rates, 1 cent per mile and less. The structure of fares in Ohio and Indiana in 1905 is shown in Table 2.

Interurbans differed on the problem whether to charge an extra fare on limited trains. The Union Traction and some of the other Indiana companies in the early years instituted fees of 5 cents to 30 cents, depending on the distance traveled, to discourage local passengers on fast trains, and most roads charged fees for parlor seats. The Scioto Valley charged 25 cents; the THI&E and the Dayton and Western charged 50 cents for a parlor seat on their joint service between Indianapolis and Dayton, and other roads made similar charges. While they operated parlor-buffets, the Chicago Aurora and Elgin and the North Shore Line (after giving up full parlor cars in 1933) charged nominal fees refundable if the passenger purchased anything from the buffets. The Oneonta–Herkimer interurban in New York charged only 15 cents for a parlor seat. The differential between coach and parlor car was never so great as on the railroads, since the interurbans never used a separate first-class tariff. The premium on the Indianapolis-Fort Wayne parlor cars was only about 0.5 cents per mile.

TABLE 2—AVERAGE (MEAN) INTERURBAN PASSENGER RATES IN OHIO AND INDIANA, 1905

	Ohio		Indiana	
	Cents per mile	Number of companies reporting	Cents per mile	Number of companies reporting
Cash fare	1.84	23	1.68	8
Single-trip ticket	1.77	17	1.68	6
Round-trip ticket	1.63	20	1.45	6
Commutation (family)	1.45	12	1.23	3
Commutation (individual)	1.09	17	1.20	5
Mileage book	1.37	6	1.22	2
Interline coupon	1.48	10	1.67	1
School ticket	1.03	12	0.94	4

SOURCE: *Street Railway Journal*, XXX (1907), 869.

Since most of the railroads charged individual fares of about 3 cents per mile, interurban fares at the outset were about half to two-thirds of railroad rates. In 1901 the Lake Shore Electric charged only $1.75 for a Cleveland–Toledo ticket — the comparable railroad fare was $3.25.[10] Lake steamers, operating between Cleveland and Toledo, charged an even lower fare. Differentials of this magnitude, combined with the more frequent service, were enough to attract much of the local traffic. Several railroads acted quickly to retain passengers by cutting fares. The Hocking Valley Railway cut its rate between Columbus and Lancaster to 75 cents (a cut of about 1.19 cents per mile) when the Scioto Valley was opened, and the Minneapolis and St. Louis met the rates of the Inter-Urban Railway between Des Moines and Perry with a cheap thirty-day-excursion round trip. In both cases, legal actions were taken against the railroads for discrimination. The Wabash in 1903 staged a full-scale rate war against the new interurbans in the Wabash Valley, matching their fares between all points.

Railroad rate cutting was no more than a harassment, but beginning in

1906, the interurbans began to suffer seriously from railroad competition as a consequence of state laws restricting railroads to coach fares no higher than 2 cents per mile. Ohio passed such a law in 1906, and Indiana and Illinois followed suit in 1907. Among the states with significant interurban mileage, Iowa, Michigan, Wisconsin, and Pennsylvania also passed two-cent-fare laws. There was initial confusion over whether the interurbans were covered by the acts, but in both Ohio and Indiana the laws were finally construed to apply only to steam railroads. The Michigan statute, however, was held to apply to interurbans. But the point of law was not particularly significant; the interurbans could not charge higher fares than the railroads without losing most of their long-distance travelers. Because most of the interurbans were already charging fares at or just below the legal maximum for the railroads, the immediate effect of the laws was to reduce the railroad-interurban fare differential drastically, and in many cases to eliminate it entirely. At once it became more difficult to attract long-distance passengers away from the railroads. This was the major reason for canceling many of the parlor-buffet services that had been instituted around 1905, and it contributed to the slackening of interurban building in the Middle West in 1908. The interurbans' disadvantage was not so great as it might appear, for many railroads immediately gave up round-trip reductions and curtailed excursions. For one-way travel, the differential between steam and electric rates was reduced to about 10 to 15 per cent, but for round trips it amounted to 20 or 25 per cent.

Ohio began to grant relief from its two-cent-fare law in 1918 and Indiana repealed its statute in 1919, when both had become obsolete because of the inflation following World War I. While these laws were in effect, they constituted a depressing influence on the industry and contributed to the poor financial showing of the interurbans during the war. In 1917, the Electric Railway War Board, which had been set up by the industry, estimated that the net income of 127 interurbans was only $9,816,180, compared with $21,228,006 in 1913. In 1918, William G. McAdoo, Director General of the United States Railroad Administration, issued an order increasing the basic steam railroad coach fare to 3 cents per mile. Since the railroads were nationalized, McAdoo's order took precedence over the state two-cent-fare laws. The interurbans, with a few exceptions, were not nationalized, but they benefited from the increase in the steam-electric fare differential. Many of them immediately sought rate increases from the regulatory commissions, but since wages and other costs were rising rapidly, the fare relief did not prevent 1918 from being a very bad year for the industry. (For a picture of the growth and decline of revenue passengers on the Ohio interurbans see Table 3; for the Indiana interurbans see Fig. 4, p. 216.)

The kind of traffic the interurbans carried was not likely to be increased by war conditions, and only a few interurbans experienced anything in the nature of a war boom. The Washington Baltimore and Annapolis carried a great number of naval personnel to and from Annapolis, and it provided land to the Federal government for construction of Camp Meade, a major army post about half-way between Baltimore and Washington. The Baltimore and Ohio and the Pennsylvania Railroad also served the camp, but nevertheless the WB&A was provided with a steady stream of organized troop movements and individual travel throughout the war. The North Shore Line did a heavy business to Great Lakes Naval Training Station and to Fort Sheridan, and the Inter-Urban Railway thrived on traffic to Camp Dodge, Iowa.

TABLE 3—TOTAL REVENUE PASSENGERS CARRIED BY OHIO INTERURBANS, 1907–33

Fiscal year (ending June 30)	Revenue passengers	Fiscal year (ending June 30)	Revenue passengers
1907	74,090,750	1921	245,330,709
1908	97,076,387	1922	226,294,810
1909	154,251,425	1923	196,616,679
1910	157,851,752	1924	210,125,773
1911	168,998,448	1925	193,134,819
1912	188,159,788	1926	179,418,298
1913	180,995,437	1927	166,106,891
1914	193,273,618	1928	156,075,916
1915	181,563,665	1929	126,755,878
1916	190,987,015	1930	110,940,104
1917	211,123,417	1931	84,872,813
1918	234,285,911	1932	56,192,527
1919	256,963,473	1933	39,544,202
1920	234,885,075		

SOURCE: *Annual Reports of the Railroad Commission of Ohio,* 1907–11; *Annual Report of the Public Service Commission of Ohio,* 1912; *Annual Reports of the Public Utilities Commission of Ohio,* 1913–33.

The Southern New York Railway, which did not parallel a railroad, increased its fares to 5 cents per mile—possibly the highest rate in the interurbans' history. Rates on the Midwestern lines rose to about 2.5 cents per mile in January 1918, and to about 2.75 cents in February 1919, a level at which most of them remained during the 1920's.[11] Since railroad fares increased during the war to about 3 cents per mile and rose to 3.6 cents in 1920, the interurbans during the twenties had a perceptible differential in their favor. In the same period, however, they found themselves faced for the first time with competition from an even cheaper carrier, the motor bus. Bus fares during the twenties averaged about 2.25 cents per mile, but some were as low as 1.8 cents. Because the interurbans were generally unable to compete with the railroads in service, they were particularly vulnerable to a new carrier that also offered inferior speed and comfort, but did so at an even lower fare.

In retrospect, it is fairly clear that the most effective course would have been to cut fares in an effort to compete with the bus lines. By the late twenties, the alternatives to the industry's services were so abundant that the demand for interurban transportation was elastic; that is, a rise in fares would cause so many riders to use other forms of transportation that the gross receipts would be lower after a fare increase than before it, and conversely, a reduction in fares would increase gross revenue. Few interurban managers seem to have recognized this, and there was little general rate cutting until after 1932, when half the industry had already disappeared. Since the interurbans were a regulated industry, they were able to maintain their level of rates in the face of declining demand and, after 1929, of a rapidly falling price level. Regulatory commissions almost invariably assume inelastic demand conditions, and rarely propose lower rates as a means to higher earnings. Professor Albert S. Richey, who computed an annual index of fares in the electric railway industry (based mainly on street railway fares) demonstrated that fares rose from an index of 157.1 in 1929 (1913 = 100) to 162.3 in 1932, while costs of operating materials fell from 148.9 to 116.1 and wages fell from 230.6 to 217.5.[12] Although this circumstance was essentially the reverse of the condition that had hampered the interurbans during World War I, they now received no benefit from it, since traffic was declining so rapidly that the industry was being annihilated.

Rate cutting in the late 1920's mainly took the form of cheap excursion fares, especially on Sundays, more liberal round-trip fares, and more extensive commutation arrangements. Around 1926, the Stark, the Northern Ohio, and the Youngstown and Ohio River each issued passes for unlimited Sunday travel at 50 cents. In the same period, the Detroit United and the Washington Baltimore and Annapolis cut commutation rates, and both the North Shore Line and the South Shore Line established cheap Sunday round-trip fares. The Kansas City Kaw Valley and Western in 1925 cut its maximum round-trip fare to 75 cents, but did not change its one-way tariffs. In 1927 the Pittsburgh Harmony Butler and New Castle cut its maximum one-way rate to $1, except for trips into Pittsburgh. The Indianapolis and Cincinnati in 1925 cut its basic fare from 3 cents to 2 cents per mile for a month as an experiment. In the same year, the Chicago South Bend and Northern Indiana cut its mileage rate from 3 cents to 2 cents, but in 1926 raised it again to 2.5 cents. Several interurbans in the same period raised their fares. The Warren and Jamestown, which used a zone system, increased the number of 5-cent zones from 11 to 14 in 1928, increasing its mileage rate from about 2.5 cents to 3 cents. The Gary Railways, the Northern Ohio, and several others had minor upward fare revisions in this period. By the onset of the depression, most interurbans were still charging between 2.4 cents and 3 cents per mile, with reductions for round-trip and multiride tickets. A few of the Western lines that had achieved greatest integration with the railroads charged the railroads' standard rate of 3.6 cents per mile.

The first interurban to make a drastic fare cut was the Piedmont and Northern; it could hardly have been more successful. In September 1932, the company cut fares from 3 cents per mile to 1 cent and experienced about a tenfold increase in traffic. Its passenger volume rose from 5,332 passengers per month in 1931 to 49,939 in 1933. When the company's own equipment proved inadequate for the crowds, it bought steel coaches from the Pennsylvania Railroad to haul with electric locomotives. This experience was unique; no rational interurban operator could have expected to duplicate it. Nonetheless, it demonstrated that there was still hope in fare reduction.

General fare reductions were to a great extent responses to the railroads' own reductions, which began about 1933. In that year the Illinois Terminal cut its basic fare to 2 cents per mile, equaling the typical railroad reduction. The Indiana Railroad in 1933 cut one-way fares from 3 cents per mile to 2 cents, and round-trips from 2.7 cents to 1.5 cents. The Cincinnati and Lake Erie adopted a 2-cent scale in 1936, but since 1932 it had offered a special fare of $4.00 on its overnight car between Cincinnati and Toledo, or $7.20 round trip. The Midwestern interurbans that were in operation after 1933 generally offered 2-cent fares throughout the 1930's, or for as long as most of them survived. The Indiana Railroad did not vary from a 2-cent rate, but it increased its round-trip to 1.8 cents in 1938. The company had a mid-week excursion fare of even less than 1.5 cents, however.

It is easy to overestimate the importance of fare reduction in the 1930's. Managements that tried to continue electric operations had no alternatives to rate cutting, and doubtless it helped them survive a short while longer than they would have otherwise. The fundamental problem was that fares could not be economically reduced to the level of the marginal cost of driving an automobile. Neither could the interurbans offer door-to-door service. Had the automobile not reduced the interurbans' traffic volume so greatly, the most heavily traveled interurbans could probably have competed successfully with buses until well after World War II. But the problem was essentially hopeless; no fare policy could have saved the industry from extinction.

INTERLINE ARRANGEMENTS

Given the local nature of the interurbans' traffic, interline passenger-accounting was much less significant for the interurbans than for the railroads, but quite early in their history the Ohio, Indiana, and Michigan interurbans discovered they must make some arrangement for interline ticketing and baggage checking. Elsewhere in the Midwest, interurbans were sufficiently isolated from one another that these problems did not arise. In the East, where zone fares prevailed and where baggage was not checked, the electric lines also avoided interline problems. The three major Utah interurbans had little difficulty making out interline tariffs and setting up accounting arrangements, and in the Far West the interurbans were so largely controlled by the railroads that they participated in railroad interline organizations.

By 1906, when the Ohio-Indiana network was taking virtually its final form, interurban managements recognized the need for interline arrangements of two sorts: first, a joint ticketing arrangement that would permit a passenger to make a long, continuous trip over several lines, and second, a coupon book that would permit a passenger to make short trips in various directions at a standard mileage rate on any interurban. The second arrangement was much the more important; few people took extended interurban trips, but commercial travelers were constantly making short trips with little or no advance preparation. The railroads had a distinct advantage over the interurbans in this respect, for their passenger traffic body for the area, the Central Passenger Association, issued a book of mileage coupons valid for 1,000 miles of travel on member railroads. Commercial travelers bought these books widely, finding that they cut travel costs, reduced the necessity of carrying a large amount of cash, and permitted the holder to change his itinerary freely. The Schoepf-McGowan lines issued similar books for travel at a flat rate of 1.5 cents per mile, but the coupons were not accepted on most independent interurbans.

It was principally a desire to issue a universal mileage book that caused 38 major Ohio and Indiana interurbans to organize the Central Electric Railway Association. The Ohio interurbans had organized the Ohio Interurban Railway Association early in 1904, and the Indiana lines had established the Indiana Electric Railway Association later in the same year. Representatives of both bodies met in Dayton in January 1906, to unite the two into a joint organization. Edward C. Spring, superintendent of the Dayton Covington and Piqua Traction Company, was chosen president, and Charles L. Henry vice-president. The organization had two executive boards, one representing the Ohio lines, the other the Indiana lines.[13] The C.E.R.A. provided some of the usual functions of a trade association for the Midwestern interurbans, meeting periodically for camaraderie and discussion of problems of mutual interest to the interurbans. However, the American Street and Interurban Railway Association (after 1910 the American Electric Railway Association), to which the Midwestern lines also belonged, was the industry's principal trade association.

The C.E.R.A.'s first effort to issue a mileage book was a failure. The Association considered issuing a general book of the type sold by the Schoepf-McGowan lines, but decided against it on the ground that fares of individual roads differed too greatly to make it possible. The Ohio roads would have had to reduce their rates about 25 per cent to the Indiana level, a step most of them were unwilling to take. For this reason, the C.E.R.A. initially issued a book of 240 coupons, each worth 5 cents, amounting to $12 worth of transportation for $10. The Schoepf-McGowan lines, considering such a book inferior to their own, continued to issue their book of 1,000 miles of travel for $15. Since the C.E.R.A. book was less popular than the Schoepf-McGowan book, the Association began efforts in 1908 to issue a general 1,000-mile book for travel on member lines. To do so it needed the right to adjust fares of individual roads, as well as their power of attorney for the deposit of interline tariffs with the Interstate Commerce Commission and the state railroad commissions. Several of the lesser roads, already beset by the business depression and the new two-cent-fare laws, were quite reluctant to delegate their rate-making powers to a body in which they had small voice. Nonetheless, the Association went ahead and in 1908 established a subsidiary, the Central Electric Traffic Association, to draw up interline tariffs and to submit them to the regulatory authorities. Two years of experience under the two-cent-fare laws gave the issuance of the 1,000-mile book an urgency it had not had in 1906. The legislation made it especially difficult to attract the commercial traveler away from the railroads.

The Central Electric Traffic Association had induced 24 of the 38 roads belonging to the C.E.R.A. to begin honoring a 1,000-mile book by the fall of 1908, and it began to issue one in October. Other interurbans joined subsequently, and 35 companies, aggregating about 3,550 miles, were participating by 1916. By the end of 1917, about 43,500 books had been sold, and the venture was regarded as successful. With the realization or at least the prospect of increases in fares during World War I, the problem of differences in mileage rates between companies again became serious. Consequently, in November 1917 the Traffic Association voted to abandon the mileage book and to begin issuing a book of 2,000 coupons of one-cent tickets for $17.50. The Association continued to issue this book throughout the 1920's. In the West, the Utah interurbans banded together in similar fashion to issue a 1,000-mile book, which they sold for most of their history.

The Central Electric Traffic Association was also entrusted with administering a tariff of interline one-way and round-trip fares. Like the mileage book, the interline tariff was to some extent a response of the industry to the difficulty of attracting long-distance passengers from the railroads following the two-cent-fare laws. The tariff set out rates, beginning in 1909, on 30 interurbans between the 32 most important junctions in the Ohio-Indiana network. Any given fare was computed between two junctions, plus the local fares for travel on either side of the base points. Most of the early tariffs of individual interurbans provided for a charge of 25 cents per trunk handled, but both the coupon book and the standard interline ticket provided for baggage checking in the fashion of the steam railroads. The usual provision for free transportation of children under the age of five and half-fare for children under twelve was also made.

The C.E.R.A. also attempted to deal with the relative obscurity of the interurbans. In the early years the companies relied heavily on newspaper advertising of their departures, and except for the largest lines—particularly the Illinois Traction—interurbans made little effort to circulate their timetables beyond their local areas. Consequently, a traveler found it more difficult to schedule an interurban trip than a railroad trip in a distant area. In 1910 the Association decided to issue a map of the system, and two years later, after considerable expense and difficulty, published one showing in great detail the interurbans, member and non-member alike, in the area bounded roughly by Milwaukee, Evansville, Pittsburgh, and Buffalo. The Association revised the map at intervals and issued it continually until 1931.[14]

The Association also undertook an even more ambitious project, a consolidated timetable of member lines on the order of the *Official Guide of the Railways*. Although the timetable was proposed at the same time as the map, it was not actually issued until 1917. It was about the size of a major steam railroad timetable, and was distributed in the same fashion. It was imperfect in that it included only the schedules of member interurbans, but it was nonetheless a major accomplishment. Unfortunately, the project was not pursued, and only a few revised issues were produced. The C.E.R.A. also designated as an official publication the *Central States Guide,* issued by the Guide Publishing Company of Norwalk, Ohio. This periodical, which was sold for 25 cents, contained timetables of transportation companies of all sorts, and included detailed interurban schedules for the entire Midwest. The major interurbans published schedules in the *Official Guide of the Railways*.

The C.E.R.A.'s membership eventually embraced every major interurban from the South Shore Line and the roads out of Evansville to the Cleveland Painesville and Eastern and the Wheeling Traction Company, including almost all the trackage in Michigan. Several street railways that had no pretensions to being interurbans joined, including the Cleveland Railway Company and the Muskegon Traction and Lighting Company. The Association explicitly opened membership to railroads and steamship lines; no railroad is reported to have joined, but both major Lake Erie steamer lines, the Detroit and Cleveland Navigation Company and the Cleveland and Buffalo Transit Company, did so. In September 1924, when membership was quite inclusive, the Association encompassed 536 miles of street railway and 5,433 miles of interurban line,[15] about a third of the interurban mileage in the United States. Apart from its functions in passenger traffic, the Association performed similar operations for freight—issuing tariffs and supervising interline relations. The Central Electric Railway Accountants' Association endeavored to standardize accounting practices, particularly in connection with interline accounting, and the Central Electric Railway Master Mechanics' Association did particularly valuable work in standardizing car dimensions and fittings. The C.E.R.A. survived about as long as the Ohio-Indiana lines presented a unified network, and disbanded when the industry was in the throes of disintegration, late in 1931. The remaining mileage had been reported earlier that year to be 3,737 miles—about two-thirds of the network's greatest extent. President Conway of the Cincinnati and Lake Erie did not lament the Association's passing, feeling that it had devoted itself excessively to good fellowship and insufficiently to the problems of the industry. The Master Mechanics' Association became the Central Transit Equipment Association, and both the Accountants' Association and the Traffic Association announced their intention to continue independently.[16] Officials of the Indiana Railroad deposited tariffs with the Interstate

Commerce Commission in the name of the Central Electric Traffic Association as late as 1938. These tariffs were all canceled by April 1941, following abandonment of the Indiana's Indianapolis–Muncie–Fort Wayne line.

JOINT TRAFFIC ARRANGEMENTS WITH THE RAILROADS

However much success the Midwestern interurbans had in joint traffic relations with one another, they had precious little with the railroads. The Central Passenger Association voted in July 1901 that a joint ticketing agreement between the Nickel Plate Road and the Sandusky Norwalk and Southern (which was soon after incorporated into the Lake Shore Electric) should be abrogated and similar arrangements avoided. The Association codified this policy by enacting its Rule 19, which prohibited members from establishing joint tariffs with electric lines. This decision, though it could hardly have been unexpected in light of the railroads' attitude toward the interurbans during construction, was a blow to the electric lines, which fancied themselves valuable feeders to the railroad network.

Although most of the railroads participated in the boycott with enthusiasm, several of them decided it was to their interest to violate Rule 19. In particular, the Toledo St. Louis & Western, known as the Clover Leaf (now the St. Louis line of the Nickel Plate Road), widely entered into interline rates with the Ohio interurbans, notably with the Lake Shore Electric for through tickets from Cleveland to St. Louis. Since its own railroad line from Toledo to the Indiana state line served no major towns, the interurbans in the Lima area were valuable connections for traffic to and from the west. In 1904, when the Central Passenger Association requested it to end the agreement, the Clover Leaf refused. In the same year, the Erie declined to abrogate a joint tariff with the Chautauqua Traction Company, and the Nickel Plate Road, when accused of a violation of Rule 19, replied with almost Gilbertian ambiguity that it would "observe the resolution except where it is found in [our] interest to do otherwise."[17]

Probably the most important of the early arrangements between a railroad and an interurban was the joint tariff of the Chicago Cincinnati & Louisville Railroad and the Union Traction Company for Chicago–Indianapolis service via Peru. Although running time was markedly inferior to any of the three direct routes—the Monon, the Pennsylvania, and the Big Four—the fares were very cheap. The railroad and the interurban offered an excursion fare of $2.50 round trip, less than a half-cent per mile, but even regular fares undercut those of the standard railroad routes considerably. The Chicago Cincinnati & Louisville is the best example of a railroad driven by desperation to deal with the interurbans. It was itself built during the interurban building booms, having been begun in 1900 and completed in 1907. The existing railroads looked upon it as an interloper, and subjected it to discrimination similar to the treatment they accorded the interurbans. Although the road had the shortest route from Chicago to Cincinnati, it found it to be almost impossible to develop enough interchange freight traffic to survive. It frequently failed to cover its operating costs and was financially much worse off than the large interurbans in this period. It went bankrupt in 1908, and after the Chesapeake & Ohio bought it at a receiver's sale in 1910, the joint traffic arrangements with the Union Traction Company were discontinued.

There were other examples of arrangements by interurbans with individual railroads—the Wheeling & Lake Erie Railroad engaged in some —but the interurbans' general efforts to be admitted to tariffs of Central Passenger Association members were almost entirely unsuccessful. In 1906 when D. G. Edwards, president of the Union Traction Company, wrote to the Association to suggest that the steam and electric lines should cooperate, the Association established a committee of three to confer with him. In the following year this committee recommended the repeal of Rule 19, but the Association took no action. In 1908 the Association again declared its policy to deny electric lines "interchange of travel." However, in 1909 it agreed to an exchange of printed tariffs and rate circulars proposed by the Central Electric Traffic Association, so that each body could disseminate information about the other among its own members.

The Central Electric Traffic Association generally followed Central Passenger Association policy in connection with excursions and group rates, but it did so without recognition from the C.P.A. In 1911 the Grand Rapids Holland and Chicago applied to be put on the C.P.A. mailing list for tariffs of summer excursions and convention fares, but it was told that it could receive them only on payment of the usual subscription charge. In the same year the International Railway petitioned that coupons for round trips between Buffalo and Niagara Falls on its electric cars be included in interline tickets of railroads terminating in Buffalo, but not themselves serving Niagara Falls. The Association responded that such an arrangement was not expedient. In 1912 the Illinois Traction, one of the most successful interurbans in arranging integration with the railroad system, was denied free copies of Association tariffs. In this period the only electric line given general admission to joint tariffs by the C.P.A. was the Oregon Electric, presumably admitted because of its affiliation with the Hill railroads.[18]

The attitude of railroads west of the Mississippi toward the interurbans was characteristically less adamant than its eastern counterpart. One railroad, the Chicago Great Western, was particularly sympathetic to the interurbans, entering widely into joint tariffs, showing interurban lines on its timetable maps, and even arranging for the Waterloo Cedar Falls and Northern to haul passenger trailers behind steam locomotives on its track between Waverly and Sumner as part of a through route between Waterloo and Sumner. The Cedar Rapids and Iowa City was admitted to interline passenger tariffs in 1909, and the Fort Dodge Des Moines and Southern in 1910. In 1912 the Missouri-Kansas-Texas Railroad agreed to joint tariffs with the Illinois Traction. In the Far West railroad control of the interurbans was pervasive enough that the problem usually did not arise. The Pacific Electric regularly honored Southern Pacific tickets in local service.

With the decline of the interurbans, it became successively easier for the remaining lines to be admitted to the railroads' traffic associations. By the mid-twenties the major railroads recognized that highway vehicles, not interurban cars, were the chief threat to their intercity passenger traffic. The North Shore Line began participating in interline ticketing with the railroads in 1927 and the South Shore Line in 1937. However, one should note that the Lehigh Valley Transit (which survived until 1951) never participated in railroad passenger tariffs, nor did the Bamberger Railroad, even though the latter participated extensively in railroad interline freight arrangements.

Many interurbans coordinated their service closely with the railroads, even though they had no through ticketing arrangements. The Dowagiac line of the Benton Harbor–St. Joe Railway and Light Company was built mainly to give the two cities a quick access to the main line of the Michigan Central. The Springfield Troy and Piqua regularly connected with trains of the Erie Railroad at Maitland, about three miles northwest of Springfield, Ohio. The Thurmont branch of the Hagerstown and Frederick provided a connection between Frederick and the main line of the Western Maryland Railway, and train-meeting was an important part of the operations of the New England electric lines. The Toledo Bowling Green and Southern and its affiliate, the Findlay Street Railway, connected Findlay with trains on the Nickel Plate Road at Mortimer, five miles to the north. The North Shore Line in the late twenties scheduled its crack train, the Eastern Limited, to connect closely with the Twentieth Century Limited of the New York Central at La Salle Street Station, which it served via the Chicago Elevated.

In later days, several railroads took advantage of connections by electric lines to replace their own abandoned passenger service. When the Monon gave up carrying passengers into Michigan City in 1928, it arranged for through ticketing from points south of Monon to Michigan City via Hammond and the South Shore Line. Similarly, when the Chesapeake & Ohio cut its passenger trains back from Chicago to Hammond in June 1933, it arranged for through ticket holders to use the South Shore Line into the city. After July 31, 1938, when the Soo Line discontinued passenger service into Milwaukee, it used the Milwaukee Electric as a connection from Waukesha. The Soo Line made the Milwaukee Electric party to its tariffs, and included a coupon for the Milwaukee Electric in its tickets to or from Milwaukee. The electric line thereafter sold interline tickets furnished by the Soo Line.

Joint traffic arrangements between interurbans and steamship lines were fairly common, since each provided a low-priced alternative to railroad service. The Grand Rapids Holland and Chicago had a through tariff between Grand Rapids and Chicago with the Graham and Morton Line, and the Grand Rapids Grand Haven and Muskegon had similar arrangements with the Goodrich and Crosby lines for Chicago and Milwaukee, respectively. To meet the Goodrich ships, the interurban operated a limited that covered the 34 miles between Grand Haven and Grand Rapids in 1 hour and 20 minutes, and in the early years the company served breakfast on the eastbound car. The Benton Harbor–St. Joe Railway and Light Company's Watervliet interurbans met Graham and Morton Line steamers at the wharf at Benton Harbor to load passengers for the resorts at Paw Paw Lake. Several of the interurbans in Ohio and Ontario coordinated their service with Lake Erie steamer lines. During the navigation season the Toledo Port Clinton and Lakeside and its successors regularly connected at Bay Point with small steamers to Sandusky until 1925. The Lake Shore Electric ran to the wharf in Sandusky to connect with steamers for Cedar Point and the Lake Erie islands. The San Francisco Napa and Calistoga arranged its schedules to connect with the steamers of the Monticello Steamship Company at Vallejo, providing a direct route from the Napa Valley to San Francisco. The Northern Electric had joint tariffs with Sacramento–San Francisco steamers.

The Niagara St. Catharines and Toronto Railway indirectly owned two steamships, *Northumberland* and *Dalhousie City,* which plied between Toronto and Port Dalhousie, providing a through route to Niagara Falls in conjunction with the interurban. Evansville Railways owned a subsidiary, the Crescent Navigation Company, which connected with its interurban line, the Evansville and Ohio Valley, to provide motor launch service on the Ohio River. Launches met interurbans at Rockport two or three times daily, and ran to Owensboro, Kentucky (10 miles downstream) in 51 minutes. A similar service was operated twice daily upstream 25 miles from the end of the line at Grandview to Cannelton, Indiana.

SPECIAL SERVICES

Apart from standard passenger service, the interurbans ran a variety of excursions and special services. Sunday excursions were very common, usually at fares from 1 cent to 1.35 cents per mile. The automobile cut into the excursion traffic heavily, but in the 1930's the Sacramento Northern began to offer special Sunday rates from San Francisco and Oakland to Sacramento, with fares of about a half-cent per mile. This effort was quite successful, and throughout the summer the road was able to run Sunday trains of the full six cars permitted by the ferry. The interurbans usually took advantage of special events to operate excursions. The Indiana Columbus and Eastern ran special trains to the Dayton air races in the 1920's, and most of the lines out of Indianapolis ran specials to the Memorial Day automobile races. The Interstate ran extra trains to the Kentucky Derby, and both the South Shore Line and the Northern Indiana operated specials to South Bend for football games at Notre Dame University each year. The South Shore Line throughout its history has done a heavy excursion business to the Indiana Dunes State Park. The largest single special movement in the industry's history was probably the North Shore Line's transport of over 225,000 people to Mundelein, Illinois, in connection with the Twenty-eighth Eucharistic Congress of the Catholic Church on June 24, 1926. In its own cars and equipment leased from the Chicago Rapid Transit, the company moved this enormous crowd in perfect safety and with relatively little delay.

Most of the major interurbans operated special trains to state and county fairs, and the Eastern Ohio's branch from Steel Junction to Middlefield had no passenger service except for operations to an annual fair at Burton. The Toledo Port Clinton and Lakeside depended heavily on resort traffic and ran a large number of specials each summer to the encampment of the Ohio Methodist Conference at Lakeside. The Winona Interurban operated special cars to the religious assembly at Winona Lake with which it was affiliated.

Even as the excursion business was being wiped out by the automobile, the interurbans found a new source of revenue in inspection trips for railway enthusiasts. Interest in the interurbans as a hobby arose in the years of the most rapid decline of the industry; indeed, much of the documentary record of the interurbans has survived only because of the photographs and collections of ephemera by hobbyists who recognized that the industry would shortly be extinct. When the Washington Baltimore and Annapolis was to be abandoned, enthusiasts in its area organized a farewell excursion, and thereafter the last profitable act of many an interurban was a special trip for a club of railroad fans.

Aside from excursions, the interurbans' chief promotional device for joy-riding was the amusement park. A great many interurbans operated amusement parks at some distance from major cities, and a frequent if somewhat anomalous subject for articles in the *Electric Railway Journal* was choice of games, rides, and exhibitions for these enterprises. Lagoon, the park of the Bamberger Railroad, was a great success, attracting over a quarter-million customers per year. Amusement parks declined simultaneously with the interurbans, but some, including Lagoon, developed a trade by automobile and managed to outlive the electric lines that built them. Ravinia Park, built by the North Shore Line, became the summer home of the Chicago Symphony Orchestra.

Something of a special case in interurban passenger service was the school train. Apart from special reduced fares for school children, which most interurbans provided, several lines contracted with school boards to operate trains exclusively for school children. This activity was mainly identified with Western interurbans, which served areas of low population density and, accordingly, of very large school districts. The Utah-Idaho Central, which had possibly the lowest population density of any big interurban—under 400 people per mile—in its later years derived over 80 per cent of its passenger revenue from transporting school children, mainly under contract with school districts. Indeed, the only regular passenger train the company ever operated on its Quinney branch was a two-car school train, provided at cost under contract to the local school district. Both the Bamberger and the Salt Lake and Utah operated similar trains, and the Sacramento Northern scheduled morning and afternoon school trains between Oakland and Concord that regularly required five cars. These services helped to initiate the movement toward consolidated schools, in which Utah was a pioneer. The Utah-Idaho Central and the Salt Lake and Utah kept up this traffic until they were abandoned.

The history of the interurbans is so dominated by their financial failure that it is difficult to consider seriously their positive contribution to American transportation development. Their principal influence was, clearly, in conditioning the rural population to a greatly increased mobility that was fully realized only with the general acceptance of the automobile. The farmer's wife going to market and the commercial traveler going from town to town, the twin supports of the interurban, became standard rural automobile drivers in later years. Since the interurbans typically radiated from major cities (the customary Canadian name for them was radial railways) they made a contribution to urban development. In northern Ohio, where the dominant railroad pattern is one of main lines running east and west, connecting Chicago and the seaboard, the interurbans contributed to the commercial growth of Cleveland. Indianapolis, Toledo, and Columbus also benefited from their interurban networks. The distinction between urban and rural was never again so sharp as it had been before the interurbans were built. The words of W. E. Balch, manager of the Merchants' Association of Detroit, may have been hyperbolic when he said that, "Generally speaking, the interurbans are the greatest asset that a retail center can have,"[19] but the interurbans were assuredly a considerable force in the development of urban retail districts.

At the same time, the interurban justified the fears of some of the local merchants in that it did initiate the commercial decline of many small towns. The automobile was a much greater force in this decline, but the relative importance of the small Midwestern town as a retailing center was never again what it had been before the interurban came.

Both the rise and the decline of the interurban were harbingers of the decline of the railroads. Their rise was the first real threat to railroad domination of passenger traffic. At the time the first interurbans were built, the railroads carried over 95 per cent of the intercity passengers; most of the rest traveled on steamboat lines that were drastically limited in the areas they could serve. The railroads had generally vanquished the steamboats on the Western rivers, although substantial numbers remained, mainly in overnight and other short-run services. On the Great Lakes, Long Island Sound, the Hudson River, Chesapeake Bay, and the Puget Sound, the steamboat remained in service by offering greater comfort, lower rates, and somewhat greater safety than the railroads; however, many of these steamers were railroad-controlled.

On land, the interurban was the first major challenge to the railroad passenger train. In 1926, when the interurbans had already passed their peak, they accounted for 11.7 per cent of American passenger miles by common carriers, and the railroads 75.2 per cent.[20] The rise of the interurban demonstrated that there was a substantial amount of local traffic that could readily be taken away from the railroads.

Because the passenger traffic the interurbans carried was the kind most vulnerable to automobile competition, the interurbans' own decline relative to highway transport foreshadowed the decline of the passenger train. The interurbans' percentage of passenger miles as common carrier fell to 6.3 by 1929, 2.7 by 1939, 1.0 by 1950, and 0.3 by 1956.[21] The railroads' percentage by 1956 was 34.9, but all common carriers were being dwarfed by the automobile, which was rapidly approaching a figure of 90 per cent of all intercity passenger miles. Examiner Howard Hosmer of the Interstate Commerce Commission, in a widely cited report, suggested that at the average rate of withdrawal of railroad passenger service trains in the postwar era, passenger service other than commutation would be non-existent by 1970.[22] Many of the railroads' responses to the decline of passenger traffic have been similar to the course pursued by the interurbans somewhat earlier: development of lightweight equipment, greater reliance on auxiliary bus service, reduction in schedules, and outright abandonment of passenger operations.

4
Freight Traffic

THE INTERURBAN INDUSTRY as a whole was so heavily dependent upon passenger traffic that, for most companies, baggage, mail, express, and freight were peripheral activities. A notion of the relative importance of nonpassenger revenues on the Midwestern interurbans may be had from Table 4. As late as 1920, interurbans that carried freight were estimated to be deriving only 9 per cent of their gross revenue from freight service.[1] In 1926, when interurban freight traffic was near its peak, electric railways accounted for only 0.3 per cent of all freight ton miles.

TABLE 4—GROSS RECEIPTS OF INDIANA INTERURBANS BY SOURCE, 1911

Passengers	$12,266,376.07
Baggage and special car service	81,357.33
Mail	9,859.10
Express	272,505.79
Milk	91,833.65
Freight	1,028,607.00
Switching and miscellaneous	49,914.50
Total transportation revenue	$13,800,453.44
Nontransportation revenue	311,825.60
Total operating revenue	$14,112,279.04

SOURCE: *Annual Report of the Railroad Commission of Indiana*, 1911, p. 470 (corrected for error in addition).

For various reasons, these figures understate the importance of freight to the industry. First, there were certain companies that derived most of their revenue from it: the Kaydeross Railroad at Ballston Spa, New York, received over 85 per cent of its gross from freight operations from the beginning. Many of the Far Western interurbans were built primarily as freight haulers: Visalia Electric, Inland Empire, Tidewater Southern, Yakima Valley, and to a great extent, Oregon Electric. Second, freight hauling proved to be more profitable than the interurbans' promoters had expected. Since almost the entire plant had to be in existence for passenger service in any case, the additional cost of moving freight was usually fairly modest. Finally, freight traffic increased in volume quite steadily throughout the history of the interurbans until the late twenties, and was responsible for whatever was salvaged from the extinction of the industry. In so far as the interurbans ever found an unexpected success, they found it in freight hauling.

BAGGAGE AND MAIL

As we have seen, baggage was originally a significant source of revenue for the interurbans. Prior to the enacting of the two-cent-fare laws of 1906–8, the differential between steam and electric passenger fares was enough so that the interurbans could charge a fee, usually 25 cents, for each piece of checked baggage. After this fee was dropped by members of the C.E.R.A., excess-weight charges continued to be a revenue item. On a full-fare ticket, 150 pounds were typically checked free, and most roads put an absolute limit of 250 pounds on any single checked item. The Schoepf-McGowan lines charged a fee for baggage checked on tickets costing under 25 cents.

Most of the large interurbans, and many of lesser lines as well, carried U.S. mail, usually in closed pouches but occasionally in railway post office cars (RPO's), where the mail was sorted in transit. The closed-pouch service was mainly restricted to short distances, for which interurban service was well suited. Inadequate compensation for mail handling was a standing complaint in the industry. At the beginning, the interurbans received 3 cents per mile for handling closed pouches and 7.5 cents for providing RPO compartments. They considered neither compensation adequate, and felt that the postal authorities discriminated against them in favor of the railroads. The Benton Harbor–St. Joe Railway and Light Company complained in 1917 that its mail payments just covered the cost of handling the pouches.

Railway post office cars, like limited trains, were provided mainly where railroad service was inadequate or absent. In all likelihood, the first intercity electric RPO car is one that ran on the Knox County Electric between Rockland and Camden (Maine) in 1893. There were several others in New England, notably in the Connecticut Valley of Massachusetts and in the Old Colony area south of Boston. The Philadelphia and Easton operated an RPO between Doylestown and Easton about 1904–8, compensating for lack of direct railroad service between Easton and Philadelphia. The connecting Bucks County Electric ran an RPO between Doylestown and Bristol. The Annapolis Short Line operated an RPO between Baltimore and Annapolis until about 1910, and the Washington and Old Dominion operated one in Virginia until about 1940, the last in the East to be abandoned.

On the whole, RPO's were rather rare in the Ohio-Indiana interurban network; however, the Toledo and Western, the Eastern Ohio, and the Cincinnati Georgetown and Portsmouth, none of which paralleled a railroad, operated them, as did the Cleveland and Southwestern and the Cleveland Painesville and Eastern. The RPO came late to Indiana; in 1935, after the Nickel Plate Road gave up passenger service on the former Lake Erie & Western branches between Indianapolis and Michigan City and between Fort Wayne and Rushville, the Indiana Railroad equipped three of its heaviest cars with mail compartments and initiated RPO service between Indianapolis and Peru and between Waterloo and Dunreith. The Indianapolis–Peru service was abandoned in 1938. The Waterloo–Dunreith line was cut back to Fort Wayne and New Castle in 1937, and abandoned on January 18, 1941, when the Indiana Railroad gave up its last major passenger route, the Indianapolis–Fort Wayne line via Bluffton.

The Illinois Traction early in its history operated an RPO between Peoria and Springfield, and mail was frequently sorted on interurbans farther west. The Fort Dodge Des Moines and Southern, the Texas Electric, the Inland Empire, and the Pacific Electric at various times ran RPO cars. The San Francisco Napa and Calistoga participated in a joint RPO with the Monticello Steamship Company, with most of the sorting done on shipboard between San Francisco and Vallejo. The Los Angeles–San Bernardino RPO of the Pacific Electric, abandoned on May 6, 1950, was the last on any American electric line, but it was something of a special case, since it had been established only in 1947.[2] The Denison–Dallas RPO of the Texas Electric operated from 1908 to 1948.

EXPRESS

Express operations on the interurbans were mixed with less-than-carload (LCL) freight service to so great an extent that no clear division between the two is possible. Many of the lines in New England and New York made no explicit differentiation, but simply charged different rates for two or three classes of service. The Utica and Mohawk Valley and the Oneida Railway, for example, provided both pick-up and delivery under class A rates, either pickup or delivery under class B, and neither under class C. Class A rates were about equal to railroad express, class B about 5 cents per hundredweight below A, and class C about ten cents below A. The New York State Railways' interurbans out of Rochester had two classes: A, with drayage on both ends, and B, with drayage at neither. Class A was offered at express rates and class B at three to five cents above railroad LCL rates; class A cargo was generally carried on passenger cars, class B on box motors. Under the New England three-rate system, class A shipments commonly were guaranteed to go out on the first available car, class B shipments on the day of receipt, and class C shipments only "with reasonable dispatch."

In the early years, there was even less consistency in the Midwest in interurban freight and express practice. In 1906 the Dayton Covington and Piqua was offering wagon service for both express and freight, but the Indiana interurbans typically offered it for neither. As time passed, there was a tendency to provide drayage for expedited service at rates approximating railroad express; but it was not provided for standard service at charges comparable to railroad LCL rates. Most interurbans eventually came to haul both express and LCL, but at the outset many aimed at one or the other. The lines radiating from Cleveland generally set their sights on railroad express rates because at the outset express was permitted in the streets of Cleveland and freight was not. In 1898, the principal Cleveland interurbans, predecessors of the Lake Shore Electric, the Northern Ohio, the Cleveland Painesville and Eastern, and the Cleveland Southwestern and Columbus, formed a joint body called the Electric Package Company to operate their baggage and express services and to provide drayage in Cleveland and in several major cities in northern Ohio. It operated until 1937. There were similar organizations in Dallas and in Albany, New York.

In 1906, the Electric Package Company had 40 wagons and 53 agents in cities and towns, as well as 14 express messengers who rode cars of the member companies. Each company operated its own cars and periodically received its share of the Package Company's earnings. The Package Company charged rates by the hundredweight, depending on the distance. The highest rate, 75 cents per hundredweight, applied to shipments on the Lake Shore Electric between Cleveland and Toledo, the longest distance (120 miles) on any of the member lines, and covered by a box motor in about seven hours. The Package Company had a simple tariff consisting of a standard set of rates and another set (at a 10 per cent differential) for fruit, poultry, eggs, and produce. Milk in cans was handled by the member roads individually, but usually in the same cars that carried express for the Package Company. The Company used railroad express rates as bench marks, and made no effort to attract the heavier sort of package freight from the railroads.

The Eastern Ohio, alone among the Cleveland interurbans, did not participate in the Electric Package Company. Wishing to take advantage of its freedom from direct railroad competition, it was eager to develop a general freight business at approximately railroad LCL rates. The Western Ohio and the Dayton and Troy, which worked closely together as parts of the Lima Route, began by emulating railroad express service, but changed to a policy of rates approximating LCL about 1906. Simultaneously, they withdrew from the Southern Ohio Express Company, an organization similar to the Electric Package Company which operated over the Lima Route and the Cincinnati–Dayton interurban. The Dayton and Troy and the Western Ohio began developing joint tariffs with other Ohio and Indiana interurbans, and before long had agreements with all their major connections. The Lake Shore Electric and the Cleveland Southwestern and Columbus, both of which began by hauling express only, initiated tariffs at LCL levels in 1911. The other members of the Electric Package Company began hauling LCL in the same period.

An additional incentive for concentrating on LCL rather than express was the generally harmonious relations between the interurbans and the four major old-line express companies: Adams, United States, Wells-Fargo, and American. Most of the major interurbans early in their histories were affiliated with one or more of the four. The Ohio Electric disbanded the Southern Ohio Express Company in 1909 and contracted with United States. The Albany and Southern contracted with American; the

Toledo and Indiana and the Toledo Port Clinton and Lakeside with Wells-Fargo; the Fort Wayne and Wabash Valley with both Wells-Fargo and Adams; and the Detroit United with United States, Adams, and Wells-Fargo. The Columbus Delaware and Marion used Wells-Fargo because its principal railroad connection, the Erie, used it.

The interurbans held a variety of contracts with the express companies, of which the most common—and the most favorable for the interurbans—was a rate division. The interurban's share was almost invariably either 40 or 45 per cent, subject to a minimum for a haul below a stipulated distance. Since many of the interurbans' hauls were quite short, the minimum provision worked in their favor. A minority of the interurbans were paid on a strict basis of tonnage hauled, and a few small lines received a flat sum per month. The express companies, in the main, treated the interurbans in nondiscriminatory fashion, since the relationship was mutually beneficial. The express companies benefited from the electric lines' frequent schedules, and the interurbans in return received access to wagon service in towns where they had none of their own. Moreover, the express companies frequently retained the interurbans' agents as their own in towns where they had none. The remuneration—10 per cent of the business originating through the agent—was a small sum, but interurban agents were paid so poorly that the marginal increment was significant. Since most interurban agents did not need to know telegraphy, they were paid at lower rates than their counterparts on the railroads.

Most interurbans (17 out of the 25 polled by the American Electric Railway Association in 1916) handled their own express in addition to the express of the old-line companies. This was usually handled at the same rate, if there was pickup and delivery, or at a rate above LCL by some premium for expedited service if there was not. The interurbans' own express movements were handled on the same cars as the shipments of the express companies, and there was little to choose between the two in overall speed.

Following World War I, the interurbans were driven to greater reliance on their own express operations. In 1918, the four major express companies were consolidated into the American Railway Express Company, which arranged an exclusive contract with the United States Railroad Administration for handling express on the railroads. Since the new company was heavily dominated by railroad interests, it began immediately to discriminate against the interurbans. Because the interurbans terminated far more express traffic than they originated, there was little they could do. The Indianapolis and Cincinnati, which had been handling express for Adams for a 40 per cent division of the rate, was earning about $400 per month from the traffic. Although its contract continued with American Railway Express, the amount of traffic routed to it fell to little more than one-tenth of the previous level. In May 1918, the last full month before the merger, the I&C received $456.72 from Adams, but in July, just after the merger, it received only $58.26 from American Railway Express. In August the sum rose to $130.47, but in September it fell to exactly $.04. For the entire second half of 1918, the I&C received only $275.80. Charles L. Henry, the president of the company, retained the September check and brought it to the attention of the C.E.R.A.[3]

The Association was so worried by the decline in express revenues that it polled its members. It found that of the thirty-four interurbans responding, nine had never had contracts with the old-line express companies, twenty had previously had contracts but had had them canceled by American Railway Express, and five were still handling American Railway Express shipments but in greatly reduced amounts.[4] For the twenty companies that reported their earnings, express revenues had totaled $127,796 for the first six months of 1918, but only $17,938 for the same period in 1919. Given the secular decline in passenger traffic that began around 1918, and the rise in operating costs caused by the war, the blow came when the interurbans were least able to bear it. Twenty-four of the companies responding to the C.E.R.A.'s poll carried express of their own, but they did it mainly on a station-to-station basis. This traffic increased somewhat after the formation of American Railway Express, but it was handicapped by the lack of interline agreements and was restricted to such short distances that most interurbans found it uneconomic to establish pickup and delivery service for it. The Illinois Traction immediately set up its own express service on a station-to-station arrangement at tariffs about 25 per cent under railroad express to compensate for lack of drayage. Since it had relatively long hauls to a number of destinations, it was better able than most interurbans to set up local pickup and delivery service, and did so in its major cities in 1926. The Indiana and Ohio lines were generally too poor to follow suit.

The Electric Package Company—or Agency, as it had become—continued to provide pickup and delivery in Cleveland throughout the twenties and to charge rates about equal to railroad express. It differentiated express from LCL not only by drayage, but by superior insurance, more lax packaging requirements, and cash-on-delivery collection. Its rates were above LCL by approximately the amount of drayage. Because of Cleveland's large population and its extensive interurban network, the Electric Package Agency was a relatively successful undertaking; for most interurbans, however, the loss of the express companies' traffic was a calamity for which there was no remedy.

LCL FREIGHT

The interurbans were driven by their technology, even more than by the loss of their express traffic, to rely principally on LCL in their freight operations. In this they were, like Captain Ahab, doomed ere they set sail, for LCL became a most unprofitable part of railroad service. In freight as in passenger traffic, the interurbans were best suited to do what was least remunerative.

Since most interurbans radiated from a major metropolitan area, they typically centered their freight operations about an LCL freight house in their principal terminal city. This was usually no different from railroad freight houses; it was a shed with bays for wagons or trucks on one side and for cars on the other. Freight was hand-carried or moved from wagon to car by hand truck or dolly. Baggage compartments of passenger cars were sometimes loaded at freight houses before the car moved to the passenger terminal. Although most interurbans never gave up carrying packages on passenger cars, greater reliance was put on box motors and trailers as the years went on. Even small roads such as the Northern Indiana Power Company line operated one round trip each day with a box motor, and such major interurbans as the Detroit United and the Union Traction regularly operated two or three trips on main lines, and occasionally even more. The crew consisted of a motorman and a conductor, and often a third man who served as express messenger, freight handler, or brakeman. Partly because of the weakness of union organization on the interurbans, the division of responsibility was never so narrow as on the railroads. In small towns, the interurbans commonly had no facilities for storing freight, and thus had no alternative to delivering it. Usually the crew carried it by hand to the sidewalk in front of the consignee's store, but in some towns arrangements for delivery were made with local drayage firms.

The principal shippers by interurban freight were wholesalers in cities. Foodstuffs, dry goods, small machinery, pipe, hardware, and the like were all shipped in substantial volume. The radial pattern of the interurbans and their frequent service made them ideal for shipments to local retailers. For the first time, a retailer could call an order into the city in the morning and receive it in the afternoon. Service was fast enough so that perishables could be shipped without refrigeration. W. E. Willingson, secretary of the Detroit Wholesale Merchants' Bureau, estimated that 70 per cent of shipments by wholesale houses in Detroit went out by interurban as late as 1919.[5] In 1905 the Toledo and Indiana handled 3,800,000 pounds of LCL outbound, but only 800,000 pounds inbound.

Because of the dominant outbound LCL movement, the interurbans commonly scheduled a box motor out of the major freight house in the late morning to make deliveries before the close of the business day. The Salt Lake and Utah Railroad scheduled all its trains as nominally mixed, but regularly arranged for its express and LCL to be handled mainly on its noon departure from Salt Lake City. To this service, which it called its "Red Arrow Fast Freight," the company assigned its car 603, a combine that seated only 26, but held as much freight as a small box motor. The car ran in multiple unit with full-length box motors when freight traffic was heavy. The Columbus Delaware and Marion dispatched its local freight out of Columbus at 10:00 A.M., and similar schedules were arranged by other Midwestern interurbans.

Speed was the interurbans' one great advantage in freight service. A box motor could run at 30 miles per hour in the country and maintain a schedule that was not much inferior to a local passenger train. An interurban could do in a matter of hours what might take the railroads days. For this reason, the interurbans had little incentive to undercut railroad rates; most of them followed railroad LCL tariffs slavishly. A few tried charging higher rates because of their greater speed, but this policy made it difficult to attract traffic. The Kansas City Western, which charged about 8 per cent above railroad LCL until 1916, found that its receipts expanded greatly when it cut its rate to the railroad level. The phrase "Express service at freight rates" was used by so many interurbans in advertising that it became a cliché of the industry. In 1915 the Lewiston Augusta and Waterville Street Railway in Maine took over its express traffic from an express company and initiated LCL service at railroad rates under railroad classification.

The interurbans' principal disadvantage as freight carriers—the lack of pickup service—was initially no great handicap, since most of the wholesalers who shipped by interurban had their own wagons or trucks. Several interurbans arranged with drayage firms to pick up LCL at the shipper's expense if he had no team. Most of the interurbans that provided free pickup for LCL at the outset shortly gave it up. The Hudson Valley Railway, the United Traction Company, and the Schenectady Railway, which operated the joint service called "Electric Express" in the Albany area, gave up drayage of LCL in 1909. There was little free drayage in the Midwest by 1911.

The factors that suited the interurbans for LCL traffic also enabled them to carry milk. Their radial pattern coincided with the milksheds of large cities, and their frequent schedules avoided the need for refrigeration. Many interurbans hauled milk on their passenger cars, but the more heavily traveled lines picked it up on inbound box motors. Since the dominant LCL movement was outward and the milk movement inward, the two nicely complemented each other. Outbound box motors were the more heavily loaded, for the empty milk cans had to be returned to the shippers; however, because there was no time limit for returning them, the empty cans could be carried aboard any box motor that was not fully loaded. Milk was always carried under a separate tariff that provided for return movements of empty cans. In the Cleveland area about 1906, the interurbans uniformly charged a rate of 1.5 cents per gallon for any distance under 100 miles.

Given the notorious political power of the dairy farmers, milk rates frequently became a hot political issue. In 1913 and 1914, the Detroit United had a lengthy controversy with the Michigan Railroad Commission on milk rates. The Interstate Commerce Commission had set a railroad rate for ten-gallon cans of twenty cents for distances under twenty-five miles, twenty-one cents for distances up to thirty miles, and so forth. Since this was a traffic the interurbans had no difficulty attracting from the railroads at competitive rates, the Detroit United immediately increased its rates to the ICC level. The company previously had had various lower rates that were inconsistent between areas. The new rate was soon appealed to the Michigan Railroad Commission, which ruled that the interurban might charge no more than twelve cents per can for distances under twenty miles and fifteen cents for distances up to thirty miles, both with free return. When the Detroit United protested, the Commission adopted a scale of fifteen cents for all movements up to thirty miles, twenty-two cents up to thirty-five miles, and successively higher rates for longer distances.[6] This question of rates was a vital matter to the company, which carried about 2,000 cans per day into Detroit, mainly from points within thirty miles. It had through rates and interchange of milk with the Michigan United for longer hauls. Since transportation charges were only a small fraction of the total cost of milk to the consumer, the company was convinced that the demand for its milk hauling was inelastic.

The Indiana interurbans covered virtually the whole Indianapolis milkshed, and rapidly came to dominate transportation of milk into the city. In 1919 they were reported to be bringing in milk at the rate of 191,000 cans per year, as compared with 186,000 for all railroads.[7] The Louisville and Interurban hauled about 200,000 gallons of milk and cream per month. Its average haul was 15 miles and monthly revenue about $3,000. Milk was picked up at roadside crossings, in front of farm houses, and at passenger stations. Clusters of milk cans on small platforms three to four feet high were conspicuous along interurban rights-of-way. The interurban industry had a standing complaint over the fact that milk rates also applied to cream, even though the companies were liable to damage claims for the full value of the cream.

In hauling LCL freight, the interurbans labored under several handicaps analogous to their passenger problems, but in some ways even more severe. First, franchise requirements were frequently restrictive. Rochester, New York, and many smaller cities demanded that freight move through the streets only by night. Indianapolis limited freight trains to four cars, but other cities limited them to two. Detroit prohibited trailers in the streets and levied a tax of one dollar per round trip for movements of box motors.

Second, the interurbans' facilities for freight solicitation were limited. Responsibility was usually centered in a general passenger-and-freight agent who was necessarily concerned principally with passenger traffic. Only the largest interurbans, such as the Illinois Traction and the Iowa lines, had separate freight-traffic staffs. Local agents had little opportunity to solicit freight, particularly if their duties included tending a substation— as they often did. The typical lack of freight houses in outlying towns prevented any serious effort at building up inbound LCL traffic.

Third, traffic arrangements for interline LCL movements were limited. Not until the interurban network in Ohio and Indiana had almost disappeared were there consolidated classifications and tariffs. Individual lines published rates for interline movements from their own properties, but these tariffs were limited and often inconsistent. Prior to World War I, this was only a minor problem, but during the effort to stimulate interurban freight traffic in the 1920's it became serious. With the great expansion in automobile ownership early in the decade, the leaders of the industry faced the fact that passenger revenues could no longer be relied upon so heavily. Charles L. Henry told the convention of the C.E.R.A. in 1923 that the success of the industry depended on freight, since passenger revenues were unlikely to expand enough to support it.

Most of the major interurbans made a serious effort to expand their freight hauling during the twenties. The Central Electric Traffic Association, which was principally engaged in issuing passenger tariffs, began to draw up a consolidated freight tariff about 1924, and published it under the title of the *Joint Class Rate Tariff*, effective January 1, 1926. Within the next two years it issued the *Joint Exception Tariff*, the *Prepay Class Rate Tariff*, and the *Joint Dispatch Freight Tariff*. The last of these covered package shipments on passenger cars—essentially express—and provided rates about 150 per cent of the Central Freight Association first-class LCL rates. Since these tariffs appeared within two years of the mass abandonments in the Midwestern network, they were much less useful than they would have been a decade earlier. The rates provided only for station-to-station service. Railroad classifications were observed.

Fourth, physical facilities for interline movements were inadequate. Box motors usually operated only on their own lines, and the process of transshipment was expensive. It became increasingly expensive over time, in fact, because in freight handling, as in most of their other operations, the interurbans achieved no significant increase in productivity by modernizing or improving equipment.

In an effort to economize on this expense and to expedite service, several lines cooperated on interline freight schedules. The most important of these was a joint service between Indianapolis and Benton Harbor, Michigan, called "The Cannonball," inaugurated in 1914 by the Union Traction, the Winona, and the Northern Indiana. This train made the overnight trip in about thirteen hours. In the summer there was a heavy southbound movement of perishables from the fruit farms of southern Michigan, and the Northern Indiana Railway interchanged LCL extensively with steamships of the Graham and Morton Line at Benton Harbor. The other principal interline freight service in the Midwest was an overnight run between Indianapolis and Detroit via Fort Wayne called "The Airplane." There were regularly scheduled interline movements between Chicago and Rockford, between Boston and Springfield, between Cleveland and Columbus, and between various other points in Ohio. Services of this kind were almost always overnight, partly because of franchise limitations and partly in order to offer early morning delivery. Depending on the traffic, these runs were made by box motors moving between companies or, preferably, by trailers hauled by box motors of the individual companies, which was clearly the easier way of providing the service.

The C.E.R.A. had been issuing standards for the dimensions of interchange equipment and standard designs for trucks, couplers, and brake equipment since 1907, and it published a periodical, the *Official Interurban Equipment Register,* which offered data on cars of member lines, including equipment used in interchange. During the 1920's the interurbans were chronically short of trailers, but were too badly off financially to buy sufficient new ones. There had been a period of fairly heavy trailer building about 1910 to 1914, but by the twenties many of these cars were in poor condition from inadequate maintenance and habitual overloading. In 1925 F. W. Brown, general superintendent of the Michigan Railroad, estimated that freight traffic on the Midwestern network had increased fourfold in the past ten years, but that freight rolling stock had scarcely doubled in amount.[8] New box motors were being built out of old passenger equipment on most Midwestern lines, but trailers generally had to be built new. In 1923, T. H. Stoffel of Westinghouse Electric estimated that the members of the C.E.R.A. needed 500 box cars immediately.[9] When the Interstate, which was making a strong effort to increase its freight revenue, bought twenty boxcars in 1921, the order was considered noteworthy. These cars were essentially built to the current specifications of the Pennsylvania Railroad, modified with rounded ends, fitted with radial couplers, and otherwise adjusted to C.E.R.A. standards.

Beginning about 1921 and continuing until about 1926, there was a second period of concentrated trailer building. In 1924 it was estimated there were 275 box motors, 700 trailers, and 100 stock cars on the Ohio–Indiana–Michigan network.

There was widespread feeling that the C.E.R.A. ought to develop a standard boxcar of its own design for purchase by member roads. In 1925 nine C.E.R.A. members—the Northern Ohio, the Michigan Railroad, the Western Ohio, the Toledo Bowling Green and Southern, the Penn-Ohio, the Lake Shore Electric, the THI&E, Union Traction, and the Detroit United—agreed to buy boxcars of a standard design from Kuhlman, the Cleveland car builder, and requested the Central Electric Railway Master Mechanics' Association to develop a set of plans. The Master Mechanics' Association designed a radial-coupler car 49 feet, 8 inches long between the coupler faces, 9 feet wide and 12 feet, 7 inches high, able to negotiate a curve of a 35-foot radius. It had a capacity of 40 tons and rode on arch-bar trucks, which were archaic, if not obsolete, on the railroads. Since they were bolted together instead of cast, such trucks were lighter and cheaper than modern railroad trucks, but for the light loadings and low speeds of the interurbans they were still adequate.

When the new standard cars appeared in 1926, only five of the nine lines that had initiated the design (the first five mentioned) could afford to buy any, but several other Midwestern lines later did so. The Northern Ohio made the largest initial purchase (25 cars) since it was one of the leaders in the effort to build up interline freight service in this period. It converted from a Tomlinson to an MCB coupler to facilitate interchange of freight equipment, and negotiated agreements with several lines in northern Ohio. In 1922, it arranged interchange with the Mahoning Valley, the Stark, and the Penn-Ohio, and adopted a joint tariff for LCL at railroad rates. By 1925 these lines had expanded their arrangements to include the Lake Shore Electric, the Cleveland Southwestern, the Lima Route interurbans, the Detroit United, and the two major steamship lines out of Cleveland—the Detroit and Cleveland Navigation Company and the Cleveland and Buffalo Transit Company. They also initiated through rates to Pittsburgh with the Pittsburgh Harmony Butler and New Castle, which was doing its best to build up freight service in spite of a broad gauge, 5'-2½", which prevented it from interchanging equipment with its Western connections.

In 1928 the Northern Ohio, the Penn-Ohio, and the Lake Shore Electric formed a joint agency called the Electric Railways Freight Company to operate their LCL and other freight business in much the same fashion as the Electric Package Agency had been carrying express for some 30 years. The Toledo and Indiana and the Ohio Public Service joined shortly, although both were mainly handlers of carload freight. The new company provided joint billing, solicitation, and freight handling, but left car operation to the separate companies. A subsidiary, Elway Transit, provided pickup and delivery service. In 1927, eighteen Midwestern interurbans, including these roads, established an interline dispatch service to cut delivery times. Little came of either the Freight Company or the interline dispatch service, for both were developed too near the end of the Midwestern network to be successful. Both were abandoned about 1931.

It was in interline arrangements of this sort that gaps in the interurban network became most significant. Particularly difficult was the gap between the Illinois Traction, which was successful in building up freight traffic, and the THI&E, which was not. As late as 1928, the general managers of the two companies met in Danville to discuss a physical connection. The Illinois Traction Company favored a direct line from Danville to Crawfordsville along the Peoria and Eastern Railroad. The projected line was about 41 miles long and would have permitted direct movement of freight in interurban or railroad equipment from the Illinois Traction at Danville to Indianapolis via the THI&E's Crawfordsville branch. Because such a line required bridging the Vermillion River twice and the Wabash once, it would have cost between $4 and $5 million. To invest such sums was inconceivable for the feeble THI&E, and was probably uneconomic for the Illinois Traction, which would have been better advised to invest in a connection between its isolated Illinois Valley division and its lines south of Peoria. The two roads also considered building a connection between Ridge Farm on the Illinois Traction and Paris on the THI&E. Since this distance was only 20 miles and there was no major river crossing, the line could have been built for about $800,000. The city of Terre Haute, however, prohibited heavy freight movements on its streets, and thus if the line via Paris was to carry railroad freight cars, a belt line would have had to have been built around Terre Haute at a cost of about a million dollars. This, too, would have been far beyond the financial resources of the THI&E. The THI&E was so weak that physical connection could not have saved it; at best, interchange could only have staved off abandonment of the Crawfordsville or Paris lines for a few years after 1930 and 1932, when, respectively, they were abandoned.

Bridging gaps by transshipment to motor trucks was no solution, for the expense of freight handling became unbearable. Moving LCL freight successively by local truck, interurban car, intercity truck, interurban car, and local truck meant handling it six times at minimum, compared to twice by truck alone. Nonetheless, there were two principal examples of such arrangements: the Michigan Railroad contracted with a truck line to bridge its gap between Owosso and Flint, and the Buffalo and Erie made a similar arrangement to connect with the interurbans in northern Ohio. In the mid-twenties the B&E was making an aggressive effort to survive, and was eager to participate in the interline freight movements of the Northern Ohio and its connections. After 1922 it was isolated from the Ohio lines by the abandonment of the Cleveland and Erie Traction Company between Conneaut and Erie. The Pennsylvania and Ohio Electric Railway between Ashtabula and Conneaut was abandoned in 1924. In 1925 the B&E established a through tariff for Buffalo–Cleveland freight with the Cleveland Painesville and Eastern, and arranged truck transport between Erie and Ashtabula. Freight handling was so expensive that the service would doubtless have failed even if the Cleveland Painesville and Eastern had not been abandoned in 1926.

Even where there were not total gaps, interurban routings were often roundabout. The Indianapolis–Detroit service was indirect, compared with what would have been possible if the Portland–Celina segment had been built. The railroads had always been characterized by many indirect freight routings, but they never relied so much on speed to attract freight traffic.

In spite of all the impediments, the efforts of the interurbans to establish freight service were generally successful as long as their task was to attract LCL from the railroads. After World War I, LCL freight houses were virtually the only major structures being built by the interurbans. In 1920, the Cleveland and Erie and the Northwestern Pennsylvania opened one in Erie, and the THI&E one in Terre Haute. The largest interurban freight house was built in Indianapolis in 1924, late in the history of the industry. The Indiana interurbans had established a joint freight terminal on the grounds of the Indianapolis Traction Terminal in 1905, and enlarged it in 1911. The THI&E established a freight terminal of its own at Kentucky and Oliver Avenues in 1918. In 1924 the THI&E's terminal was expanded greatly at a cost of about a million dollars, and thereafter was used by all the Indianapolis interurbans. The new terminal could handle more than 80 cars at platforms and had yard space for another 30. The Penn-Ohio opened a freight house in Youngstown in 1925, and the Northern Ohio one in Akron in 1926. The joint freight station in Columbus, built in 1911, was expanded to serve 30 cars in 1927, and the Interstate built a freight house in Louisville in 1929.

In an address to the American Electric Railway Association in 1929, Dr. Thomas Conway, Jr., pointed out that freight traffic had been almost the only bright spot in the industry's dismal history in the 1920's. For the companies reporting to the Interstate Commerce Commission between 1921 and 1927, operating revenues had fallen by 23 per cent, passenger revenues by 34 per cent, number of passengers carried by 43 per cent, investment by 16 per cent, and mileage by 15 per cent. Freight traffic in the same period increased absolutely by 41 per cent.[10] Freight revenue as a fraction of operating revenue rose in the same years from about 12 per

TABLE 5—SELECTED OPERATING DATA OF ELECTRIC RAILWAYS REPORTING TO THE INTERSTATE COMMERCE COMMISSION, 1921–1932

Year	No. of carriers	Miles of road	Investment (in millions)	Operating revenue (in millions)	Passenger revenue* (in millions)	Freight revenue (in millions)	Net (in income millions)
1921	303	14,438	$1,529	$235	—	$29	$2.5
1922	294	14,439	1,566	235	—	31	10.4
1923	271	14,165	1,566	236	—	37	13.6
1924	273	14,234	1,578	211	—	36	9.2
1925	260	14,074	1,477	207	$153	39	14.0
1926	252	13,221	1,373	192	138	39	12.2
1927	235	12,277	1,273	181	126	40	14.2
1928	223	11,591	1,265	167	116	38	13.0
1929	211	10,076	1,133	153	103	38	16.4
1930	195	8,958	977	128	86	31	10.7
1931	176	8,276	904	101	68	24	—1.5
1932	157	7,391	802	71	47	17	—9.5

SOURCE: *Statistics of Railways in the United States*, Interstate Commerce Commission, 1921–32. The I.C.C., it should be remembered, used a category of electric lines broader than the interurbans, including such roads as the Hudson and Manhattan Tubes. On the other hand, the I.C.C. did not gather data on some of the smaller roads we have included. Accordingly, mileage and investment figures shown here are different from our own estimates for the interurbans.
* Data on passenger revenue are not available for the years preceding 1925.

cent to about 22 per cent. Freight revenue on the Interstate, of which about two-thirds was LCL, represented 6 per cent of gross earnings in 1916, 8 per cent in 1917, 16 per cent in 1920, and 45 per cent in 1922.[11] These figures in part reflect the decline of passenger revenues in the period, but the industry as a whole had an absolute increase in freight revenues up to 1925. A committee of the C.E.R.A. reported in 1929 that freight earnings of members rose from $13,637,000 in 1918 to $24,085,000 in 1925, but thereafter showed no appreciable rise. The committee pointed out that railroad freight receipts had shown much the same pattern, which it attributed quite properly to the growth of highway transport. In 1917 there were 326,000 trucks registered in the United States; in 1926 there were 2,766,222.

Trucks took from the interurbans chiefly the high-rate traffic and the short-haul traffic. The interurbans had previously done particularly well at short movements, since the mileage rate was relatively high, especially in interline rate divisions. The interurbans found themselves increasingly limited to carrying pipe, castings, and machinery, which were bulky, cumbersome, and expensive to handle.[12] Conway estimated that in 1927, 84.5 per cent of all freight moving distances less than 20 miles moved by truck, although for distances above 100 miles trucks carried only 2.3 per cent of all tonnage. For distances of 20 to 39 miles, 54.7 per cent moved by truck; for those of 40 to 59 miles, 32 per cent; and for those of 60 to 99 miles, 24 per cent.[13]

Thus by the mid-twenties, almost all interurban LCL was vulnerable to truck competition. The New England rural trolley lines, limited in speed and restricted to short hauls, were the hardest hit. As early as 1917, the Connecticut Company reported that it had lost 75 per cent of its short-haul freight business to trucks. About half its freight cars returned to New Haven empty after being sent out loaded. The New England Electric Freight Association, a promotional body, was organized in 1918 under the stimulus of the electric lines' deteriorating competitive position. The Eastern Massachusetts Street Railway gave up carrying freight in 1920, before many of the Midwestern lines began their serious effort to attract it. Most Midwestern lines experienced a decline in traffic as soon as a hard-surfaced highway was completed between their termini.

Several courses were open to the interurbans. First, they could join the truck lines by means of joint tariffs. The Southern Ohio Public Service Company, which operated the former Ohio Electric line between Columbus and Zanesville in the 1920's, had joint rates to several points along the highways east of Zanesville. The West Penn interchanged at Greensburg with Alko Express Lines, a trucking firm that served south central Pennsylvania. Such arrangements were also handicapped by the high cost of transshipment, and were never particularly successful. Since by the mid-twenties trucks could operate almost anywhere an interurban went, there was little point in restricting LCL to the rails for the limited distances the interurbans served.

Second, the interurbans could begin pickup and delivery. The truck lines' advantage over the interurbans was mainly in door-to-door service rather than in speed or economy. The electric lines had generally concluded from their early experience that free drayage of LCL was uneconomic, but by about 1925 the loss of traffic to trucks was heavy enough that they began to reconsider. In 1924 the Boston and Worcester began pickup and delivery, as did the Illinois Traction in 1926. By that time, 515.1 of the Illinois Traction's 555 miles of main line were paralleled by hard-surfaced highways, and the company felt it had no alternative to offering free drayage. The Bamberger followed suit in 1927, after a hard-surfaced highway was completed between Salt Lake City and Ogden. The Pacific Electric began truck service in 1929.

The member lines of the C.E.R.A. in general did not follow suit and made no provision in their joint tariffs for prorating expenses of free drayage. In 1927 the Association established a committee on pickup and delivery which, two years later, reported strongly in favor of establishing it at the interurbans' expense. By 1929 most of the member lines were in such desperate straits that they were almost uniformly unable to assume a new expense of this magnitude. Several were providing drayage by arranging with trucking firms for 25 per cent additional charge, or for 15 cents per hundredweight, but this was a poor substitute for all-truck service. In 1926 the major lines at Indianapolis began making pickups of LCL by truck, just as railroads did by trap cars. In January 1931, the THI&E established free pickup and delivery of LCL of class four and higher. The Indiana Railroad inaugurated free drayage of LCL in its major cities in 1934 and 1935.

Third, the interurbans could begin handling highway equipment by rail. Typically this was done by using containers for LCL that could be loaded at the shipper's warehouse and trucked to the interurban car, carried to another city by rail, and then trucked to the destination. During the 1920's the interurbans and the railroads simultaneously adopted this arrangement. It was particularly attractive to interurbans with a gauge problem; the standard-gauge Cincinnati Lawrenceburg and Aurora adopted container cars in 1921 as a means of reaching a downtown freight house. Thereafter, the Detroit United, the Boston and Worcester, the Rockford and Interurban, the Cincinnati and Lake Erie, and several other lines adopted container systems. The C&LE contracted with a freight forwarder, Cargo Transport, Inc., to haul containers at a flat rate of 15 cents per mile per container. Regularly three containers were moved per flat car, but the interurban charged a minimum rate of 30 cents per car per mile. Container arrangements were limited to major points on the interurbans, since transloading facilities were too expensive to be installed at small towns.

The alternative to container cars was loading an entire highway semitrailer on a flat car and moving it bodily from one city to another. This activity, only recently adopted by the railroads on any large scale, was pioneered by the interurbans. It can be traced back as early as 1894–95, when the Oakland San Leandro and Haywards Electric Railway handled express wagons on flat cars between on-line points and Oakland, where the wagons were transshipped by ferry to and from San Francisco.[14] A similar arrangement was used on the Toledo and Maumee Valley in the late 1890's.

Hauling of semitrailers was inaugurated in 1926 by the Chicago North Shore and Milwaukee to compensate for its inability to bring freight into downtown Chicago over the Chicago Elevated. Its freight station at Montrose Avenue was in a residential neighborhood more than six miles from the railroad LCL houses. Prior to 1920, it arranged with a private truck firm for pickup and delivery at an expense to the shipper of 18 cents per hundredweight. In 1920, it discontinued this arrangement and established a downtown freight house at Franklin and Austin streets. It began to transship LCL to trucks at Montrose Avenue, and for about six months charged shippers 10 cents a hundredweight for shipments on the truck service. In 1921, it began to include the downtown freight station in its tariffs at a rate of about 1.5 cents per hundredweight above Montrose Avenue. Since the company was losing about 15.6 cents per hundredweight on the truck movements, it had a very real incentive to cut the cost of transshipment. In 1926, it ordered 22 new semitrailers and converted 26 of its old semitrailers to be carried on specially designed flatcars between Milwaukee and Chicago.[15]

At the outset, service was provided only between the Franklin Street freight station and Milwaukee, but in April 1927, the North Shore Line inaugurated tariffs for picking up freight at the shipper's door with a semitrailer for delivery to any on-line point. Live stock and perishables were excluded, a minimum tender of 6,000 pounds was required and a minimum charge of $21.00 was made. The company felt this arrangement was a substitute for railroad trap-car service. Similar pickups were initiated in Milwaukee in November 1927. In 1928, tariffs were provided for shipments too large for a single semitrailer. In 1930, pickup service was extended to Racine.

With the coming of the depression, the North Shore Line's LCL traffic, including the piggy-back operation, declined drastically relative to truck lines in the area. Seeing no way of arresting the trend, in April 1932 the company began to haul common carrier or privately owned semitrailers on its flat cars between Chicago and Racine or Milwaukee. The company charged from $12.00 to $18.00 for a loaded trailer, depending on its length, and half-rate for an empty movement. The road handled 2,967 units in 1932 and 6,504 in 1933, but in 1934 the Wisconsin regulatory authorities prohibited the truck lines using the service from delivering in Milwaukee on the ground that the rail haul was being used to avoid a state highway-user tax levied on the basis of ton miles operated. The order was disastrous to the interurban, which hauled only 75 semitrailers in 1935. In 1936, when the order was lifted, traffic rose to 733 units. Piggy-backing increased steadily until a peak of 18,314 units was reached in 1943. After the war the combination of opposition by the Brotherhood of Teamsters, highway improvement, release from wartime restrictions, and an increased supply of truck drivers caused the traffic to fall drastically. By 1947 the North Shore Line was hauling mainly semitrailers loaded too heavily to pass inspection, and found it could not generate enough traffic to make the arrangement profitable. Accordingly, on April 28, 1947, the company canceled its tariffs and gave up the operation.[16]

Although the North Shore Line's experience with piggy-backing was much the most important of any interurban's, other roads also engaged in the operation. In the late twenties, the lines participating in the Electric Railways Freight Company in the Cleveland area experimented with a four-wheel full trailer hauled on a specially built flatcar. The Lake Shore Electric put this device, called a Bonner Railwagon, into service between Cleveland and Toledo, largely to avoid lengthy street running in both cities. The west loading ramp was just outside the Toledo city limits, but the east ramp was 19 miles west of downtown Cleveland.[17]

Efforts of the interurbans to overcome truck competition by opposing certification of motor carriers before the regulatory bodies were generally unsuccessful (see Chapter 5, below). A great deal of truck transport was unregulated, and in states where entry was restricted, truck lines were usually able to get certificates of public convenience and necessity by demonstrating an ability to provide some service beyond the interurban's scope. Usually expansion of door-to-door operation was ground enough for certification.

Not one of the interurbans' efforts to deal with the trucks' comparative advantage for LCL hauling was a success. Nothing could simulate economically the trucks' ability to move freight from door to door. None of the interurbans that survived the general annihilation of the industry did so on revenues from LCL freight; indeed, several interurbans gave up carrying freight before they abandoned passenger service. The Georgia Railway and Power Company, which survived until 1947 as a passenger carrier, gave up freight service in 1926. The Springfield Street Railway and the Worcester Consolidated Street Railway, two affiliated lines, abandoned freight in 1927—only a year after they established an interline container-car movement with the Boston and Worcester. In 1931 the Stark Electric and the Wheeling Traction, both of which continued passenger service for several years, abandoned their freight operations.[18] The West Penn gave up freight service in 1941, but carried passengers until 1952.

INTERURBAN CARLOAD FREIGHT

By the late 1920's it was clear that if anything was to save the interurbans, it would be hauling carload freight. The interurbans had done some of this in their own equipment since their earliest days. Typically, their tariffs provided for carload movements at a percentage reduction below the LCL class rate. Commodity rates were provided for certain bulk cargoes, notably coal, stone, gravel, sand, hay, grain, livestock, and lumber. As early as 1907, the Illinois Traction served seven coal mines exclusively (parallel railroads served over 100) and had 365 cars for coal service.[19] The Pittsburgh Harmony Butler and New Castle handled coal from an on-line mine in broad-gauge side-dump gondolas. The Leyden line of the Denver and Intermountain was built mainly to haul coal. Interurbans began serving coal mines chiefly to supply their own power houses, but expanded their shipments to include on-line purchasers.

Stone, sand, gravel, and other aggregates were hauled by many interurbans, for they were quarried widely in the United States and were low enough in value for it to be uneconomic to ship them any great distance. In addition, since the interurbans' declining years coincided with the building of the hard-surfaced highways, the demand for aggregates in the interurbans' territory—indeed, often only a few feet from their rights-of-way—was heavy throughout their later history. This traffic was, in a sense, self-destructive, but while it lasted it was profitable. The Tiffin Fostoria and Eastern served a quarry at Bascomb, Ohio, from which it hauled gravel and crushed stone for road building along its own line and along that of its affiliate, the Toledo Fostoria and Findlay. It used a differential dump car to haul the aggregates, and also to pull gondola cars loaded with stone. It charged a rate of 32 cents per ton for an average haul of eight miles. There was a similar charge for the movement on the TF&F. The TF&E reported in 1922 that it was earning a net income of 86 cents per car mile from this traffic, compared with 14 cents from LCL freight and 0.4 cents from passenger operations. The Toledo and Western in 1916 earned about $10 per car for hauling stone, and carried over 2,000 cars, mainly for road-building. A washed gravel plant at Mackinaw was the first major on-line industrial customer of the Illinois Traction. It produced an average of 20 cars per day in 1916, but as many as 40 in the peak season. The Illinois Traction also served nine brick works at that time, and in the 1920's hauled a substantial traffic in paving bricks. The Denver and Intermountain hauled a large amount of clay to brick works in Denver.

Several interurbans had regional specialties. The Utah interurbans, the Sacramento Northern, and the lines around Toledo carried large quantities of sugar beets in carload lots from rural areas to processing plants. The local nature of the traffic lent itself well to interurban conditions. In 1915 the Toledo and Western handled 1,995 carloads, primarily in October. When the Toledo Bowling Green and Southern was abandoned in 1930, the Ohio Public Utilities Commission required it to retain freight service from sidings north of Bowling Green to Toledo until the end of the sugar beet harvest. The Maine roads carried large amounts of potatoes.

The interurban that made the greatest effort to develop carload freight traffic without railroad interchange was unquestionably the Interstate Public Service Company. Its president, Harry Reid, believed that the short-haul passenger traffic that had brought the interurbans into being was lost forever by the early 1920's, and that the industry would have to rely on intermediate-range passenger traffic, such as the Indianapolis–Louisville service of his company, and on freight traffic. For this reason, he initiated the limited passenger service described in Chapter 3, and developed extensive carload freight operations. Before World War I, the company had been handicapped by a prohibition against hauling livestock in the streets of Indianapolis, but the restriction was lifted for the duration of the war and later removed permanently. The company proceeded to build livestock pens along the line and terminal facilities in Indianapolis. Since the company served a generally flat terrain, it was able to operate trains of ten to twenty stock cars. The other Indiana interurbans also developed this traffic, and in 1923 the Indiana lines hauled in all 11,596 carloads of livestock into Indianapolis, about 30 per cent of all freight brought by interurban into the city. In 1927 the Union Traction Company appointed special agents for livestock traffic between the principal cities on its lines and Indianapolis.

The Interstate, in addition to its livestock traffic, arranged through rates with the Monon Railroad and with the Southeastern Express Company for LCL and express. The company endeavored to develop bulk movements from barges on the Ohio River to on-line points, but was handicapped by lack of loading facilities. It developed enough freight traffic for about four trains a day. It followed the classification and tariffs of the parallel Pennsylvania Railroad closely.

Carload freight on the interurbans was subject to all the limitations by franchise and physical condition that impeded LCL, and more. Franchise limitations on train length were particularly troublesome in this connection. Like most of the major interurban lines, the Cincinnati and Lake Erie was endeavoring to build up its freight service, and by the onset of the depression had succeeded fairly well. In 1930 it received 15 box motors from the Cincinnati Car Company, built of new steel bodies on trucks of scrapped passenger equipment. These cars could handle up to 12 standard C.E.R.A. trailers in flat country, but the company usually handled only five through city streets. The city of Springfield objected to this practice and sought to limit the company to two trailers.

The legal rights of the municipal government and the C&LE were nothing if not confused, since the company was operating without a franchise. The Indiana Columbus and Eastern in 1907 had been granted a 25-year franchise to run in the streets, but had operated without franchise since being put in receivership in 1921. When the C&LE succeeded to the IC&E's properties in 1929, it continued to operate without a franchise in Springfield. Unsuccessful in its efforts to restrict the length of freight trains, the city government in 1931 voted to expel the company from the streets entirely. It wanted the interurban to electrify the tracks of the Erie Railroad to the west of the city, and to bypass it as the Illinois Traction had done at several points. This the company was unwilling and probably unable to do.

Springfield was the C&LE's principal junction town, and therefore the question was vital to the interurban's survival. The company contested the city's action in the courts and in 1934 secured a favorable verdict from the Supreme Court of Ohio. The court held that ejection of the company would constitute abandonment apart from the procedures established by law.[20] This case and several like it did much to free the remaining Ohio electric lines from the threat of expulsion by local communities, many of which had long since lost interest in the interurbans and were eager to see the tracks removed from their streets. The lines that had been built with 25-year franchises were frequently operating without a renewal, and under this judgment of the court, they gained a considerable measure of freedom from municipal governments.

Similarly, it was in carload freight operations that the physical handicaps of the interurbans became the most damaging. The Cincinnati and Lake Erie's grade out of Cincinnati was so steep—5 per cent—that its standard box motors could handle only two trailers each when on it. In 1927 the predecessor Cincinnati Hamilton and Dayton had bought a box motor as powerful as a standard Baldwin-Westinghouse 50-ton steeple cab locomotive, but nonetheless it could take only five trailers up the grade.

Even on flat terrain the power supplies of many interurbans were so meager that train operation was a problem. The Sacramento Northern, which was heavily built, required freight trains to remain in sidings for five minutes after passenger trains passed to maintain voltage. In addition, train operation was so slow (about 15 miles per hour on most roads) that it interfered with dispatching passenger movements. Moreover, a line such as the Fort Dodge Des Moines and Southern that had little passenger service might prefer to conserve its electric power output in the daytime for sale to industrial buyers. For all these reasons, many lines that had no franchise restrictions on moving freight in city streets in the daytime chose to move all their carload freight at night. With the decline of passenger traffic, the technological incentives for night scheduling of freight decreased, but so much of interurban freight traffic, even of carload freight, was aimed at first morning delivery that night operation remained the norm.

One of the interurbans' principal problems in operating carload freight was the lack of on-line industrial spurs. Their rights-of-way were so narrow that the companies were unable to sell parts of them for industrial purposes. Indeed, a line with a 10- or 15-foot right-of-way at the side of the road had no room even to put in a passing siding unless it acquired some additional land. Some roads had to unload trailers on the main track and charged an hourly fee to the consignee for tying up the line. A less satisfactory arrangement would be hard to conceive. The Benton Harbor–St. Joe Railway and Light Company had no on-line industry, but did a substantial carload traffic in fruit—some 400 cars per year—much of it for interchange with the Graham and Morton Line at Benton Harbor. Having no on-line loading facilities, the interurban relied on direct loading from farmers' wagons at sidings or at crossroads. Inbound traffic, mainly fertilizer, was unloaded in the same fashion. In urban areas, the interurbans were typically built through residential neighborhoods in which there were few industrial plants. Even where interurbans served industrial areas, running a spur into a plant was a more expensive matter than it was for a railroad, for it usually entailed tearing up a pavement, laying a track, and repaving the street. For the carload traffic an interurban could reasonably expect from an on-line firm, the investment in track-laying was frequently uneconomic.

The most common on-line plants were, as one would expect, grain elevators. Some companies, notably the Illinois Traction, were active in building them or in acquiring land for cooperatives to build them. Quarries and small coal mines, as we have mentioned, were often served by electric lines. Petroleum bulk storage depots were common because organized gasoline-retailing postdated the building of almost all the interurbans. The electric lines served relatively few factories, because lack of railroad interchange was a severe handicap for traffic in heavy manufactured goods.

It is a nice irony, when one considers how greatly its products contributed to the demise of the interurbans, that General Motors was a relatively frequent shipper by electric freight. The Union Traction Company served its Delco-Remy plant in Anderson, the Cincinnati and Lake Erie its Frigidaire plant at Dayton, and the Detroit United several of its plants in Michigan. General Motors regularly shipped motors from Delco-Remy to its plants in Michigan. Once, in 1927, it required a carload to be sent very quickly, and early in the day requested a car from the Union Traction. The car was delivered in Anderson at 2:00 P.M., picked up loaded at 4:37, and set out for unloading in Flint at 7:00 A.M. the following day. This was service the railroads could not easily match, but it presented no particular problems for truck operators.

Clearly, much of the interurbans' carload freight was as vulnerable to highway competition as LCL. The gasoline business, in particular, deserted them quickly, and even stone and sand could be hauled economically on the highways for the short distances the interurbans carried them. Long-distance movements of carload freight became increasingly difficult over time, since each interurban abandonment limited the destinations available to the remaining lines.

RAILROAD INTERCHANGE

During the 1920's it became successively more apparent that the interurbans' own carload freight operations were inadequate, and that only participation in railroad interchange and rate division would save the industry. The impediments to the interurbans' entry into general railroad freight operations were greater than to almost any of their other operations. In addition to their other franchise restrictions, the interurbans in some cities were absolutely prohibited from hauling steam railroad freight equipment. The Hudson Valley, which handled paper and pulp wood to and from local firms, was prohibited by franchise from hauling railroad cars in Saratoga Springs and Glens Falls. Hauling railroad equipment through city streets was frequently physically impossible, in any case. Railroad flanges were too deep for standard girder rail, and were often too deep for flangeways cut into paving stones. The play of railroad couplers was inadequate for the 35- and 40-foot radius curves that were common in street running, and many interurban clearances were too restrictive for railroad cars. Where interurbans used off-standard gauges, the problem was clearly insoluble. In western Pennsylvania, several of the 5'-2½" gauge lines served industrial areas in which they might have been able to develop interchange freight traffic for short distances. Portions of the West Penn and of the Harmony Route, in particular, might have been used for industrial switching if they had been of standard gauge.

Even apart from franchise restrictions and physical limitations, the adamancy of the railroads was enough to prevent any widespread participation of the interurbans in railroad freight operations. Railroad hostility manifested itself in several ways. First, the railroads widely refused to interchange equipment with the electric lines. Almost all the interurbans had initial physical connections with railroads during their construction periods, because the railroads, as common carriers, could not avoid hauling their construction materials. The contracts with the railroads typically provided that the interchanges were only for freight designed for the interurban company's own use, and the connecting tracks were often removed as soon as construction was completed.

This form of railroad opposition was somewhat easier to overcome than other forms, since several of the state public utility commissions, which were vested with power to enforce interchange among railroads, interpreted the provision to include the interurbans. In 1907 the Indiana State legislature enacted a statute making it the duty of all carriers to provide reasonable and proper facilities for interchange at junctions. The law provided that the state railroad commission might order physical interchange between railroads and interurban lines where it could be accomplished without damage to tracks or equipment. The Farmland Stone Company, which owned a stone quarry and crusher at Maxville, Indiana, on the Union Traction, brought an action under the new statute to compel the Big Four to deliver coal to the Union Traction at Winchester for delivery to Maxville, about six miles distant. When the commission ordered interchange, the railroad protested to the courts, but without success.[21]

Second, even when physical interchange was established, the interurbans usually failed to gain admission to rate division with the railroads and to membership in the per diem agreement. These were both very serious handicaps. If an interurban picked up or set out a car in interchange with a railroad, typically it had to bill the shipper or consignee separately for a switching movement. The Chicago Harvard and Geneva Lake, which interchanged but was not a party to rate division, charged shippers a flat fee of $5 for hauling a box car to or from an on-line siding.[22] A shipper could avoid the additional fee and the bother of making out a second check by putting in a railroad siding instead of an interurban siding. Since most interurbans were within a short distance of railroad tracks, the great majority of their potential shippers had such an option. The Central Freight Association, like its counterpart, the Central Passenger Association, denied the interurbans membership, and endeavored to prevent individual railroads from making joint rates with electric lines. When the Ohio Electric took over the Columbus & Lake Michigan to electrify it and operate it as a branch, the Central Freight Association considered revoking the joint tariffs in which the C&LM had participated as a short-line steam railroad. Because the Association questioned the legality of a refusal to continue acting as agent for the deposit of the C&LM's tariffs with the Interstate Commerce Commission, it decided to continue, but it specifically directed its members not to extend tariffs and rate divisions to other parts of the Ohio Electric.[23]

The Indiana statute that required physical interchange at the discretion of the railroad commission also required joint rates, but only between carriers that derived more than a third of their revenue from freight. In Indiana, therefore, almost all the interurbans were denied effective relief, and in many other states the electric lines had no legal recourse against the railroads' exclusion. The Michigan Railroad Commission was empowered to compel interchange and through rates only to points not served directly by railroad. Under this statute, the Detroit United was able to establish interchange service at a few points—notably with the Michigan Central at Oxford for the towns of Ortonville, Goodrich, and Atlas on its Flint division—but in general the company continued to suffer from a boycott by the railroads.

Failure to be admitted to the per diem agreement was equally serious. The railroads have participated since 1902 in an agreement to pay a standard fee, called per diem, for the use of one another's equipment in interchange. The fee has varied over time, and the variations have had economic significance, since increases give railroads an incentive to purchase more rolling stock and reductions do the reverse. In the years when the interurbans were being built, the per diem charge was a flat 50 cents. Failing to be admitted to the agreement, the interurbans were charged demurrage on railroad equipment, just as industrial firms were. Demurrage at this time was a dollar per day, beginning 48 hours after the car was delivered to the property, but the differential between per diem and demurrage became increasingly greater in later years. Since the spread between the two rates provided a significant source of revenue for a short line, failure to be accorded per diem rates was ruinous to the freight revenues of lines that did only a short distance switching business.[24]

The industry was acutely aware of its handicaps in these respects. In 1916, Ernest Gonzenbach, who was then general manager of the Empire United Railways, stated that the industry had found it almost impossible to secure physical interchange with the railroads and participation in their tariffs.[25] As late as October 1928, the Indiana Chamber of Commerce, in response to interurban pressure, passed a resolution in favor of greater interchange and more through rates between the steam and electric lines. Even in 1958, a factor in the decision of the Bamberger Railroad to abandon was the road's inability to gain admission to interline tariff agreements providing for the milling of products in transit.

Integration with railroad freight-hauling was least difficult in the west, and steadily became more difficult as one moved eastward. On the Pacific Coast, the interurbans had little or no trouble securing interchange and rate division. They had no serious physical impediments to interchange. The largest interurbans were controlled by the railroads, and the rest presented no significant threat to railroad traffic. The Pacific Electric served as a vast switching network for the Southern Pacific, and did a heavy carload business between Los Angeles and the port facilities at San Pedro. In Texas, the interurbans were built to Midwestern physical standards, but the Texas Electric, alone among the major lines, was able to make enough modifications in its plant to develop a sustaining freight business. The road amended its charter to do so. Beginning in 1928, it developed a railroad interchange business, largely in baled cotton, and survived as a freight and passenger carrier until 1948.

In the Midwest, success in carrying railroad freight depended on an interurban's physical standards, on the cooperation of its railroad connections, and on its freedom from direct railroad competition. The Iowa lines were well established from all three points of view. The major interurbans had no physical barriers to interchange, and with the exception of the Clinton Davenport and Muscatine, they generally cut across the main railroad lines instead of paralleling them. With the same exception, all of the large Iowa interurbans were connected directly or through other interurbans with the Chicago Great Western, the most cooperative major railroad. As early as 1907, it had been the only railroad in Chicago willing to enter into joint tariffs with the Grand Rapids Holland and Chicago and the Graham and Morton Line. It established LCL and CL tariffs with its interurban connections, interchanged with them freely, and granted them favorable car service facilities. In 1917, when the Kansas City Clay County and St. Joseph was unable to gain admittance to the per diem agreement, the Chicago Great Western furnished it box cars free for a three-day period. Since no other railroad was willing to interchange with the interurban, the Chicago Great Western could make any arrangement it wished. By this time, per diem was 60 cents per day, but demurrage had risen to $2 per day for the first five days and $5 per day thereafter. Demurrage at these rates was almost prohibitive to the electric lines.

Partly because of their relations with the Chicago Great Western, and partly because the Western railroads in general were not so adamant as the Eastern, all the major Iowa interurbans had been admitted to the per diem agreement and to joint tariffs by World War I. The most successful of these was the Waterloo Cedar Falls and Northern, which had operated as a standard railroad in its traffic arrangements ever since its completion in 1915. The Cass family, who owned it, were indefatigable spokesmen for railroad interchange in the interurban industry, and their company was living proof that they were right. By the mid-twenties, the WCF&N was performing 70 per cent of the industrial switching in Waterloo, and had reciprocal switching agreements with every railroad in the city. It hauled meat, livestock, building materials, farm equipment, and a great deal of grain. It engaged in solicitation throughout the country, participated completely in railroad tariffs, and belonged to every major railroad organization in its area: the American Railroad Association, the Railway Accounting Officers' Association, the Western Weighing and Inspection Bureau, the Association of Railway Executives, the Chicago Claims Conference, and the Freight Claims Association. Consequently, whereas the industry as a whole was on its death bed in the late 1920's, the WCF&N was gaining new strength. Its net operating income rose from $28,288 in

1925 to $203,734 in 1928. In that year, the contribution of the John Deere agricultural implement factory in Waterloo alone was $238,409 to the line's gross receipts.[26] Net income rose simultaneously with a marked decline in passenger receipts.

The Fort Dodge Des Moines and Southern was a less spectacular success, but it too built up a self-sustaining freight traffic. It was so thoroughly a part of the railroad network that it was one of the few electric lines to be operated by the United States Railroad Administration during World War I. The Mason City and Clear Lake was, for a small company, remarkably successful in freight hauling. Of the major Iowa interurbans, only the Clinton Davenport and Muscatine failed to develop enough freight traffic to survive more or less intact, but even this road made a serious effort and was preserved in part. Its predecessor company, the Iowa and Illinois Railway, began in 1912 to haul carload freight between Clinton and Davenport with a steam locomotive, but abandoned the service as unprofitable in 1915. When the Clinton Davenport and Muscatine was formed by consolidation a year later, it began electric carload service over the entire line. In 1916, it handled 30,432 tons of freight; in 1926 it handled 194,586 tons. In the 1930's it handled about 10,000 carloads per year; however, this traffic was concentrated heavily on fourteen miles between Davenport and Le Claire. When the company ceased operation in 1940, this trackage was taken over by the Burlington and Milwaukee railroads and operated jointly as the Davenport Rock Island & Northwestern, a switching road.

The Illinois Traction also made the transition to a freight-hauling railroad, but its path was much harder than that of the Iowa roads. W. B. McKinley recognized about the time the property was taking its final shape that it would have to be modified physically to permit handling of railroad cars. Many of the curves in cities were of the usual 40-foot radius, and most of the major cities on his system restricted the road to hauling freight in the streets between midnight and 6:00 A.M. In 1907, McKinley began construction of a five-mile bypass around Decatur, which he finished four years later after spending some $275,000. The company built a similar but slightly longer belt line around Springfield, where it had the additional incentive of avoiding charges levied by the local street railway for moving freight cars over its tracks. Belt lines were also built at Edwardsville and Granite City in the same period, and the company arranged to use property of the Illinois Central and the Chicago & Alton in Lincoln to ease its curvature.

These changes not only facilitated the physical handling of freight, but opened promising industrial sites on the edges of cities. Because it was unlikely these sites would be developed unless the company could interchange with the railroads, the very existence of the belt lines gave rise to pressure for interchange from the local chambers of commerce. The company was generally unsuccessful in compelling interchange through the Illinois Railroad and Warehouse Commission, but in 1910 the Chicago & Eastern Illinois agreed to a physical connection at Glover, between Danville and Urbana, and entered into extensive joint tariffs with the interurban. In the same year, the Illinois Traction arranged joint rates for LCL movements with the Chicago Rock Island & Pacific, and established through movements via drayage in Peoria. Similar arrangements were soon after made with the Minneapolis & St. Louis, and by 1916, physical interchange had been established with the Southern Railway, the Chicago & Alton, the Wabash, the Chicago Peoria & St. Louis, and the two major terminal roads, the Terminal Railroad Association of St. Louis and the Peoria & Pekin Union. The latter had been particularly hostile to the company and had admitted it to interchange only on order of the Interstate Commerce Commission.[27] By 1919, McKinley had negotiated agreements with every railroad in his area except the New York Central and the Pennsylvania, both of which remained implacable toward the interurbans.

Compared to the accomplishments of most interurbans, the success with which the Illinois Traction participated in railroad freight operations was remarkable. But its progress in this period by no means solved its problems. In particular, it found that it needed two sets of equipment, one for movements through city streets, where most of its LCL houses were still located, and another for interchange. Radial coupler equipment was universally prohibited in railroad interchange throughout the interurbans' history. The Central Electric Railway Master Mechanics' Association in the late 1920's considered developing a dual-purpose box car, fitted with a coupler that could meet interchange requirements on the railroads and move radially on the interurbans, but nothing came of the proposal.

The Illinois Traction was admitted to the per diem agreement in 1912, but rapidly discovered it to be almost impossible to retrieve its box cars when they left the line. In part the problem arose because there was no inbound movement to match the heavy outward movement of grain from elevators on the line, but in part it was a product of railroad hostility. The company could expect little cooperation in efforts to regain cars from its connections. This was one reason for the company's building an elevator at Glover and transshipping from its own radial coupler box cars to standard equipment on the Chicago & Eastern Illinois. The company also found this a way to circumvent the physical problem of street running in Champaign and Urbana, where curves precluded railroad equipment. The problem of street running became acute in the mid-twenties when the city of Champaign prohibited freight movements in the streets. The company, finding all except the Danville–Urbana segment about to be cut off from its most friendly connection, arranged to electrify about six miles of the Wabash and the Illinois Central in Urbana and Champaign. After the bypass was opened in 1926, railroad equipment was handled freely over the system, except for the city of Bloomington, where the company never escaped from the streets. In spite of special jointed-coupler shanks, its locomotives could never haul interchange freight through Bloomington; through freights from Decatur to Peoria set out their railroad cars at the south end of the city and picked up others at the west. Largely because of this disability, the line through Bloomington failed to survive as a diesel freight operation, unlike most of the rest of the property.

The three major Chicago interurbans made sufficient physical modifications to build up an interchange carload freight traffic. The South Shore Line was a special case: it served an area that began a colossal industrial development as the interurban was being completed; moreover, the company had few physical impediments to interchange. As its president, Jay Samuel Hartt, remarked, the builders had been wise enough not to wrap it around every court house en route. Its street running, though lengthy, was on the whole quite straight. The North Shore Line was always heavily dependent on passenger service, but it developed a terminal business for coal and lumber yards, and occasionally hauled manufactured goods to and from plants in Milwaukee, Racine, and Kenosha. One of its incentives to build the Skokie Valley line in 1926 was its inability to handle carload freight south of Highland Park on its shore line. The neighboring Chicago Aurora and Elgin developed a similar terminal traffic in coal, lumber, and the like, and both gained full admission to railroad interchange and interline traffic arrangements; however, neither had the on-line industrial development to support the property.

Aside from the South Shore Line, only one company in the C.E.R.A.'s network — the Youngstown and Suburban — developed enough carload freight traffic to survive. There were, however, several lines that for a time carried freight in interchange with the railroads in substantial volume. For some years the most successful freight hauler in the network was the Toledo and Western. Since its main line served a drained swamp that had previously been without railroad service it was able to gain admission quickly to the per diem agreement and to rate divisions. The Toledo Railway and Terminal Company was willing to interchange with the Toledo interurbans, and the Wabash treated the line like a railroad. As early as 1903 the T&W was hauling railroad cars and it developed an extensive interchange business in agricultural products. By 1917 over half its revenues came from freight. In the 1920's it hauled a heavy traffic of automobiles from the Willys-Overland plant at Toledo for interchange with the Wabash at Adrian. Between 1924 and 1933, the interurban was controlled jointly by the Wabash and Willys-Overland. About a half-mile has survived as a diesel switching line. Both the Toledo and Indiana and the Toledo Port Clinton and Lakeside handled railroad equipment from the outset. The latter developed a sizeable traffic in coal and quarry products; parts of the property remained in freight service until 1958.

The other main Ohio freight hauler in interchange was the Cincinnati Georgetown and Portsmouth, which continued the freight traffic it had operated before it was converted to standard gauge and electrified. The Youngstown and Suburban took advantage of an industrial tributary area to carry on a freight traffic—largely in coal—that enabled it to continue. The C.E.R.A. lines in general lacked the financial strength to undertake physical changes of the sort that saved the Illinois Traction. In so far as they carried railroad equipment they did so only as a special case. The Union Traction hauled stone from a quarry at Orestes to an interchange with the Nickel Plate Road nearby and performed similar short hauls elsewhere. The THI&E connected several coal mines with railroad interchanges. The track between the Binkley mine and Terre Haute outlasted the Indianapolis–Fort Wayne line of the successor Indiana Railroad, and apart from short segments preserved by other firms, was the Indiana's last rail operation. It was abandoned in 1942. The Indianapolis–Fort Wayne line could probably have been preserved as a freight line in the same fashion as the Illinois Traction if the company had been able to bypass Anderson, Muncie, and perhaps some of the lesser towns. The Insull interests, mindful of their success with the South Shore Line, had long-range plans to convert parts of the Indiana Railroad to freight hauling, but the company was far too weak ever to undertake them.

The Springfield Troy and Piqua took advantage of the Erie Railroad's failure to build through Springfield, Ohio, to develop a freight traffic from an interchange at Maitland to plants along its entrance into the city. The three miles from Maitland to Springfield became a freight terminal operation called the Springfield Suburban Railway in 1923, after the rest of the interurban had been abandoned.

But the lines that survived are atypical. The meagerness of freight hauling on most of the Ohio-Indiana network is exemplified by the Marion and Bluffton Traction Company and its affiliate, the Bluffton Geneva and Celina Traction Company. The two companies served two grain elevators, a milk condensor, and a quarry, the Erie Stone Company of Bluffton. The two lines had a direct connection with the Toledo St. Louis & Western and with a poverty-stricken steam short-line, the Cincinnati Bluffton & Chicago. The CB&C linked them with the Lake Erie & Western, which, in spite of an affiliation with the New York Central, was reasonably cooperative with the interurbans. The Toledo St. Louis & Western, much the most cooperative railroad in Ohio or Indiana, made cars available to the two interurbans at the per diem rate. The interurbans each owned a box motor, and used the pair in a pool, one to carry LCL and the other to haul carload freight in interchange.

Stone for on-line delivery was the principal cargo; it was brought out of the quarry at Bluffton by a railroad locomotive and delivered to the interurbans at a switching fee of 10 cents per ton. A box motor could handle about 750 tons on level ground, or 300 tons anywhere on the line. Interchange principally involved moving coal from the connections to on-line points. Except in the case of the switching movements for stone, the interurbans had to bill separately from the railroads. These two companies found this arrangement more profitable than a division of rates, but reported it was unpopular with shippers. In 1914 the two companies carried 816 carloads of stone, 240 of coal, 226 of hay, 121 of corn, 51 of tomatoes, and lesser quantities of other commodities, mainly agricultural products and building materials.[28] It is not surprising that operations of this sort were quickly swept away.

In the east, successful freight interchange was very rare. There was no significant volume of interchanging among Pennsylvania lines. In New York, the Southern New York Railway and the Jamestown Westfield and Northwestern both handled standard equipment in interchange, since neither paralleled a railroad. For most New England lines, interchange was physically impossible. To be sure, there were some exceptions. The Springfield Terminal, the only railroad serving Springfield, Vermont, built up a heavy traffic between the machine tool plants in Springfield and the Boston & Maine Railroad at Charlestown. The Claremont Railway operated a similar business at Claremont, New Hampshire. The Atlantic Shore Railway in southern Maine operated a passenger service of the orthodox New England style, but hauled interchange freight from the beginning. The Aroostook Valley was from the outset an integral part of the railroad network, and derived most of its revenues from hauling potatoes. The Lewiston Augusta and Waterville Street Railway and the Cumberland County Power and Light Company did some hauling of box cars.

The Bangor Railway and Electric Company on its Charlestown line developed a heavy freight business in interchange with the Maine Central. By 1914, the Bangor line was grossing $65,000 per year and handling over 50 per cent of the freight on Maine electric lines. It was 25 miles long and served a population of only about 2,500, but it hauled such a heavy traffic in potatoes that the company participated with the University of Maine in an experimental farm near Bangor. The line surmounted considerable physical obstacles. It had an 8 per cent grade at one point and a curve of 72 feet radius on a 5 per cent grade in a Bangor street. Since box cars could maneuver this curve only when uncoupled, box motors pulled them around with a shackle bar attached, link-and-pin fashion, to the slotted knuckle of a typical MCB outline interurban coupler. Elsewhere on the line, a box motor could handle about four box cars at fifteen miles per hour. The heavily built Portland–Lewiston Interurban was designed for handling railroad equipment, but the management was never able to induce the Maine Central to engage in interchange.

In the South, the Washington and Old Dominion and the Piedmont and Northern were freight haulers from the beginning, and the Hagerstown and Frederick had a light carload traffic on its Thurmont branch. The Monogahela West Penn developed an outbound interchange traffic in coal, but it was never enough to preserve the company. In all, some 14 per cent of American interurban mileage developed enough carload freight traffic to survive as part of the railroad network. This is a pitifully small figure, but when compared to anything else in the interurbans' history, freight hauling must be considered a success.

COLLECTION GEORGE KRAMBLES

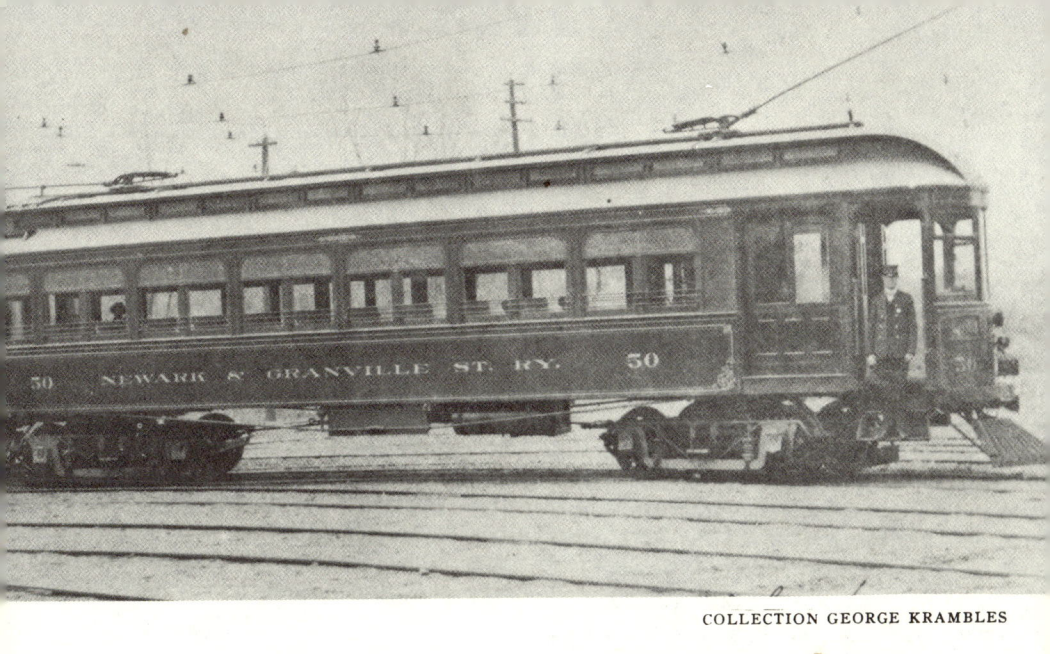

Above. A Jewett car built for the first interurban, the Newark and Granville Street Railway, photographed about 1902. Equipment built in the 1890's for this small line in Ohio greatly influenced the design of Midwestern interurban cars during the building booms of 1900–1908.

Below. A Niles combine, No. 21, delivered in 1905 to the Toledo Port Clinton and Lakeside Railway; it is shown in the orange livery of the successor, the Ohio Public Service Company, in 1938. Cars of this style were built by the hundred for the Ohio-Indiana interurbans, but this car alone has survived. Repainted and restored, it operates at the Ohio Railway Museum in Worthington.

COLLECTION GEORGE KRAMBLES

W. H. BASS PHOTO

Above. The Indianapolis Traction Terminal, the largest and most impressive interurban edifice, erected by Hugh J. McGowan in 1904. The Central Electric Railway Association and several individual interurbans had their offices in the building; the insignia of the THI&E is visible on the second-story window. In 1914 seven million passengers used the terminal.

Below. An early scene on the Shore Line Electric Railway in Connecticut. Grading, track, and overhead are all more substantial than was usual in New England. Car No. 2, a Jewett wooden center-entrance car, represents an unusual design.

COLLECTION GEORGE KRAMB

Left. A cross-bench open car of the Union Street Railway, used on the intercity line between New Bedford and Fall River, Massachusetts. Equipment of this style was almost universally used on the New England rural trolley lines in the summer months.

STEPHEN D. MAGUIRE

Right. Springfield Terminal Railway combine No. 10 (1900), at the barn in Springfield, Vermont, in 1945. The railway is still in existence as a diesel freight hauler, and No. 10 is a museum piece at the Connecticut Electric Railway Museum at Warehouse Point.

Below. A small wooden car with a railroad roof, a typical New England closed car. No. 1199 of the Connecticut Company was serving out its last days in New Haven in 1940.

GEORGE W. HILTON

COLLECTION GEORGE KRAMBLES

Right. The interior of car No. 302 of the Chicago South Bend and Northern Indiana Railway, photographed at South Bend about 1920. The smoking compartment was beyond the first door, the baggage compartment beyond the second. The fare register is an Ohmer, one of the makes most commonly used on the interurbans.

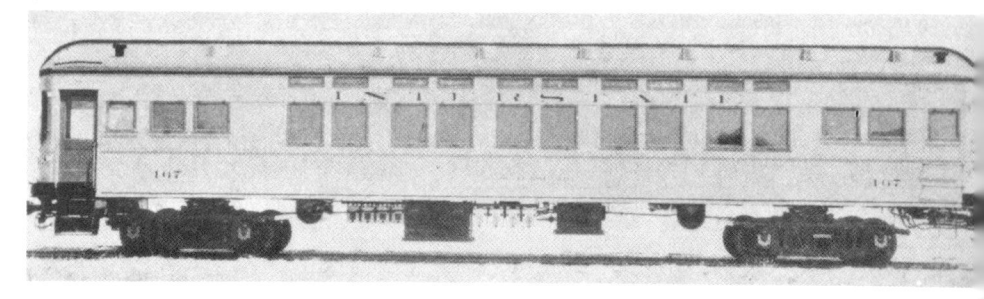

COLLECTION GEORGE KRAMBLE

COLLECTION GEORGE KRAMBLE

Above. One of the three sleeping cars of the Interstate Public Service Company, photographed by the builder, American Car and Foundry Company, in 1924. An economic failure, the cars operated in service between Louisville and Indianapolis for eight years. Upper-berth windows were characteristic of interurban sleeping cars.

Right. A builders' photograph of the interior of an Interstate sleeping car.

COLLECTION GEORGE KRAMBLE

COLLECTION GEORGE KRAMBLES

Above. The St. Louis Car Company built No. 304 in 1905 for the Indianapolis and Cincinnati Traction Company, the pioneer single-phase AC interurban. The car is taking 3,300-volt current from a bow collector; the trolley pole in the rear took low-voltage current in cities. Cars of this series were reduced to trailers in 1924, when the company converted to DC. The coupler is a Van Dorn.

Below. A Brill combine of the Hagerstown and Frederick Railway in Maryland. Equipment of this style was typical of the Pennsylvania rural electric lines. Passenger service on this road survived until 1954.

W. E. JOHNS

THI&E PHOTO, COLLECTION GEORGE KRAMBLES

Above. The THI&E, one of the weakest of the big interurbans, was too poor to buy new equipment in the 1920's, and rebuilt its original equipment extensively. Here, in 1927, a Jewett car of 1907 emerges from the company shop with the stained-glass window sashes blocked off, leather bucket seats installed, and a new sheet-metal pilot fitted in place. As cars were upgraded they were named for former company officials, Indiana colleges, historic sites, and the like—in this case, Wiley High School in Terre Haute. No. 122 ran mainly on branches out of Terre Haute.

Below. On the day of the West Penn Railways' abandonment, August 9, 1952, car No. 709 ascends the hill on Main Street in Connellsville. A few hours later this car made the last run of this long-lived, broad-gauge interurban. On the lamppost at the right may be seen one of the 40-watt light bulbs used in the West Penn's manual signaling system, protected by a characteristic slope-roof wooden housing.

RUSSEL N. SCHRAM

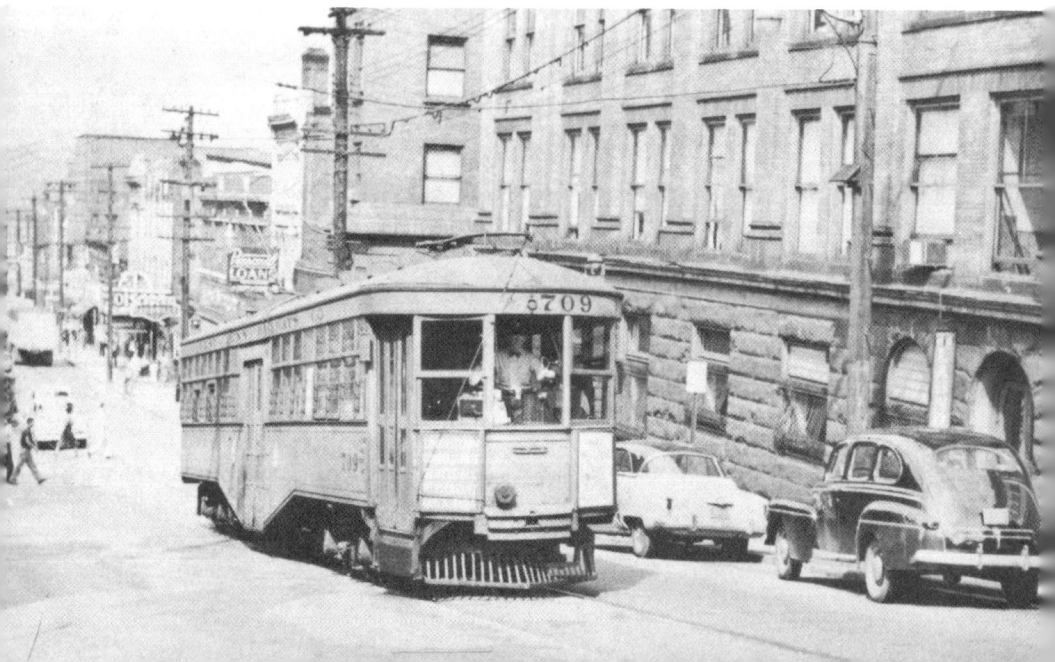

Top. Texas Electric Railway freight trailer No. 620 unloading LCL freight at Hillsboro, Texas, in 1938. Trailers built before World War I usually had inside-mounted doors, like baggage cars, but trailers built in the 1920's typically had outside doors, like railroad boxcars. This trailer is a converted passenger car.

Middle. A standard Baldwin-Westinghouse steeple-cab locomotive, running on the Cedar Rapids and Iowa City Railway in 1948. This was the locomotive the interurbans used most commonly for hauling railroad freight cars. Because of the importance of railroad interchange to the last interurban survivors, these locomotives circulated widely through the second-hand equipment market. CR&IC No. 58 had previously served on the Washington and Old Dominion Railway.

Bottom. Box motor No. 709 of the Indiana Railroad at Indianapolis in 1936. The car was formerly No. 150 of the THI&E, a wooden passenger car built by Jewett for the Indianapolis Crawfordsville and Western in 1906. Similar rebuilt passenger equipment hauled most of the Indiana Railroad's freight.

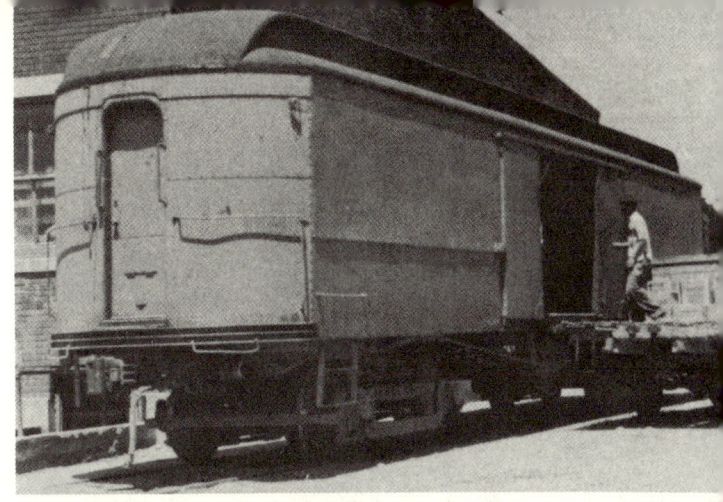

PHOTOGRAPHS—COLLECTION GEORGE KRAMBLES

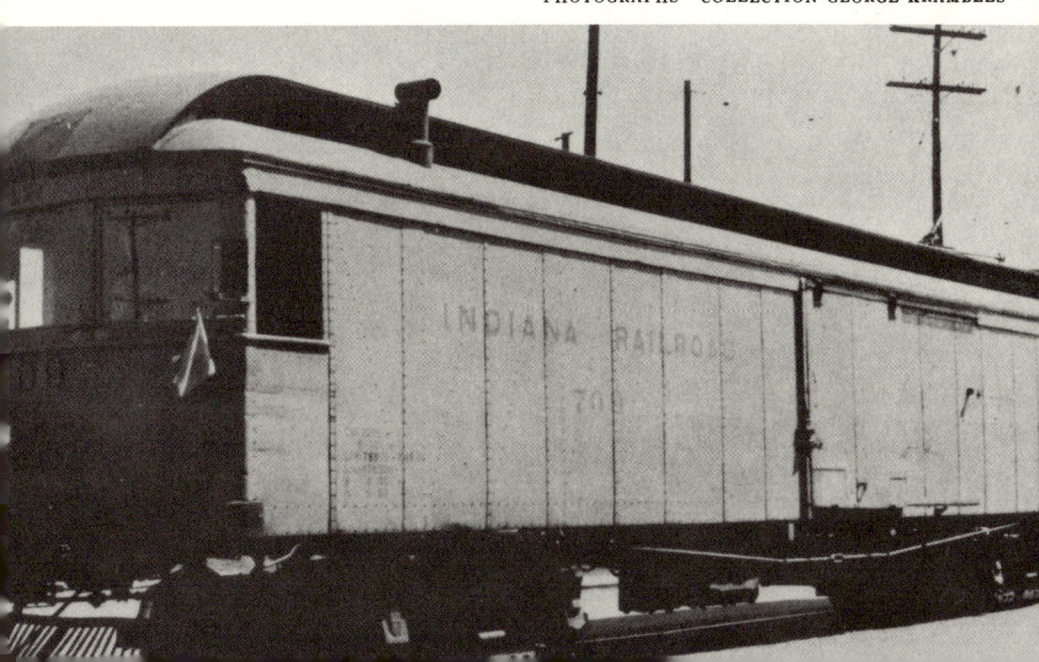

W. E. JOHNS

Above. A two-car train on the largest Canadian interurban, the British Columbia Electric Railway. Its cars of this style ran until 1958.

Below. One of the four motor cars built by the Ottawa Car Company for the ill-fated modernization of the Windsor Essex and Lake Shore Rapid Railway in 1930. When the railway was abandoned only two years later, the new equipment was sent to the Montreal and Southern Counties; car No. 623 is shown pulling the trailer built along with the four cars away from Marieville in 1947. Three of the motor cars were active until 1959 on the Niagara St. Catharines and Toronto.

COLLECTION GEORGE KRAMBLES

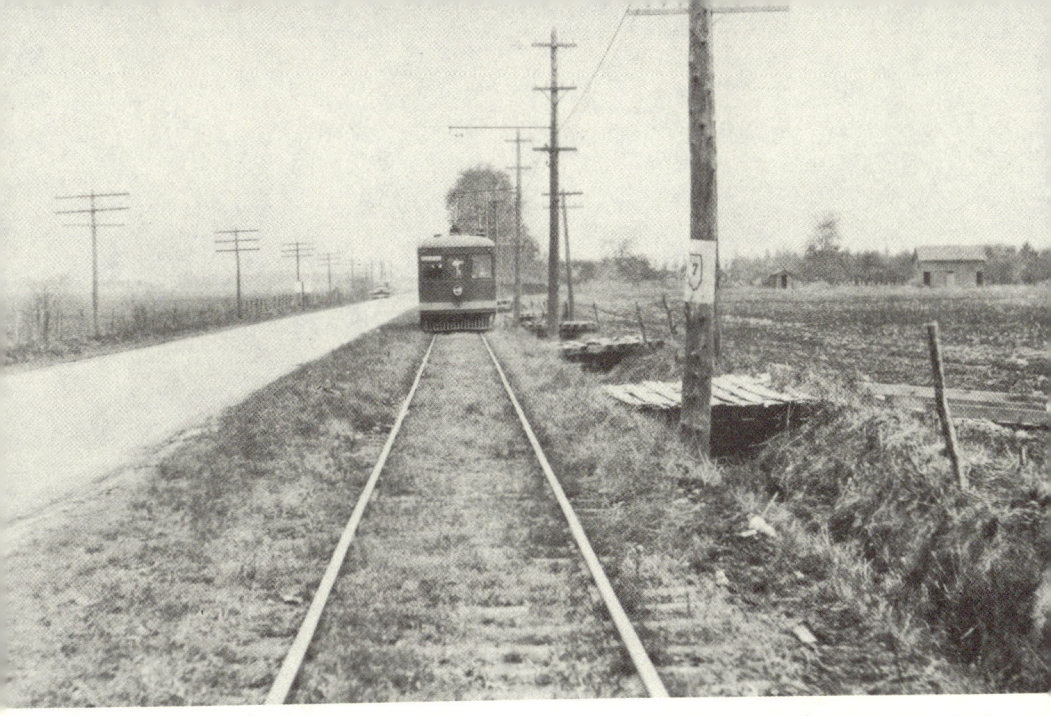

COLLECTION GEORGE KRAMBLES

Above. Lightweight car No. 61 of the Chicago and Illinois Valley Railway on a side-of-the-road right-of-way in 1927. Note that a dual overhead (a line for each direction) had been removed. The condition of the track is typical of the interurbans' declining years.

Below. One of 12 lightweight cars built by the Cincinnati Car Company for the Cleveland Southwestern Railway in 1924. Cincinnati lightweights, distinguished by gracefully curved sides, were the cars most often ordered by the interurbans in the 1920's. Economies resulting from the use of one-man equipment such as this enabled several interurbans to survive well into the 1930's or 1940's, but the Southwestern gave up in 1931.

COLLECTION GEORGE KRAMBLES

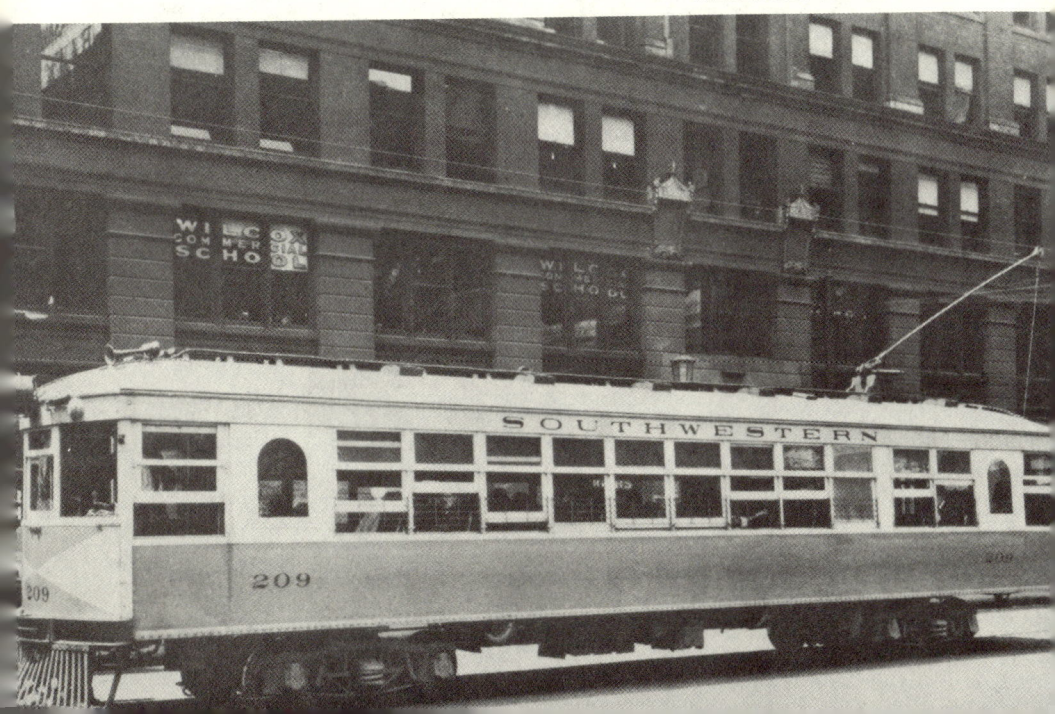

Right. A single-truck Birney car, the interurbans' favorite city equipment. This car was used by the Cedar Rapids and Iowa City Railway on its local service in Cedar Rapids. It is shown at the car house (c. 1925), just in from a run.

PHOTOGRAPHS—COLLECTION GEORGE KRAMBLES

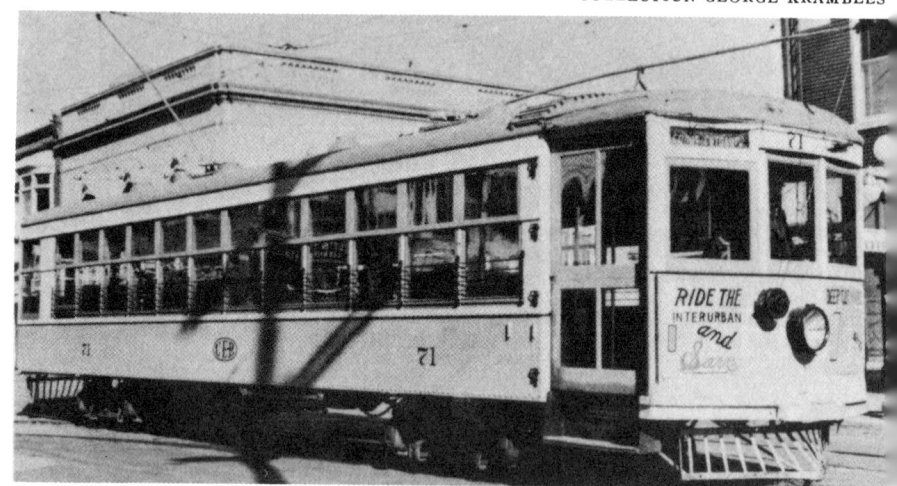

Above. The Union Electric Railway of Kansas cut fares drastically in the depression in an effort to draw traffic back from the highways. Here dash signs on car No. 71, shown at Coffeyville (1938), advertise cent-a-mile fares. The car is an American Car Company double-truck Birney, built for the Oklahoma Union Railway. It was to end its days on the Sand Springs Railway at Tulsa.

Left. An articulated unit of the Milwaukee Electric Railway and Light Company at Racine in 1934. This equipment was rebuilt from steel cars built in 1924 for the Indianapolis and Cincinnati Traction Company.

COLLECTION GEORGE KRAMBLES

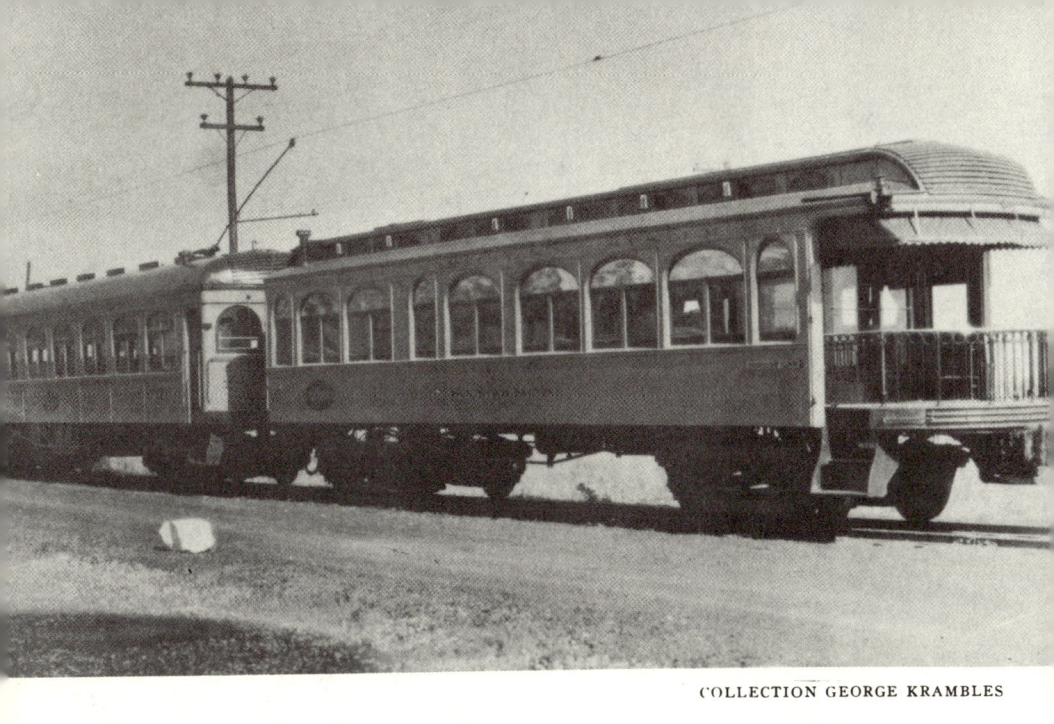

Above. Heavy combine No. 284 and the parlor car "Sangamon," photographed at the Illinois Traction system's Decatur shops in 1926, typical of the company's limited trains at that time. Both cars are examples of the design of the Illinois Traction's distinguished master mechanic, J. M. Bosenbury.

Below. Line car No. 78 of the Cedar Rapids and Iowa City Railway, at work on the overhead (1948). The car was formerly a passenger car of the Southern New York Railway.

COLLECTION GEORGE KRAMBLES

W. E. JOH[N]

Above. Car No. 302 of the Bamberger Railroad, running as train 18, leaving Ogden, Utah, for Salt Lake City (1938).

Below. Two heavy, steel multiple-unit cars of the Pacific Electric, shown descending the approach to the elevated Main Street Station in Los Angeles (1950). The coupler is a Westinghouse automatic.

COLLECTION GEORGE KRAMBL[E]

ARTHUR ALTER

Above. Sacramento Northern train No. 3 at Robla, California, September 2, 1940. Heavy wooden equipment and open third-rail running were characteristic of the northern division of this interurban. This is one of a series of photographs taken during the last two years of the company's operation by the brilliant photographer, the late Arthur Alter.

ARTHUR ALTER

Above. A three-car train of southern division equipment crosses Suisun Bay on the SN's car ferry *Ramon*.

A. J. HARLAN, COLLECTION R. H. KINDIG

Left. A scene on the highest interurban, the Cripple Creek District Railway in Colorado (c. 1902). The road served gold mines in the Cripple Creek - Victor area; some small mines may be seen in the background. The car is a design of the late 1890's.

WILLIAM S. BILLIN[?]

Above. Utah-Idaho Central No. 513, built by the American Car Company in 1915, stands at the Ogden station beside Bamberger Railroad's car No. 126, a lightweight car built by Brill for the Fonda Johnstown and Gloversville in 1932. Both are good examples of the car architecture of their day. The UIC adopted its garish livery for maximum visibility rather than for aesthetic effect.

Below. Des Moines and Central Iowa Railroad's car No. 1714 at Perry, Iowa, in 1940. The big Jewett combine, built in 1918, had come to Iowa from the abandoned Lake Shore Electric in 1939. The roof-mounted bell was characteristic of Iowa cars.

COLLECTION GEORGE KRAMBL[?]

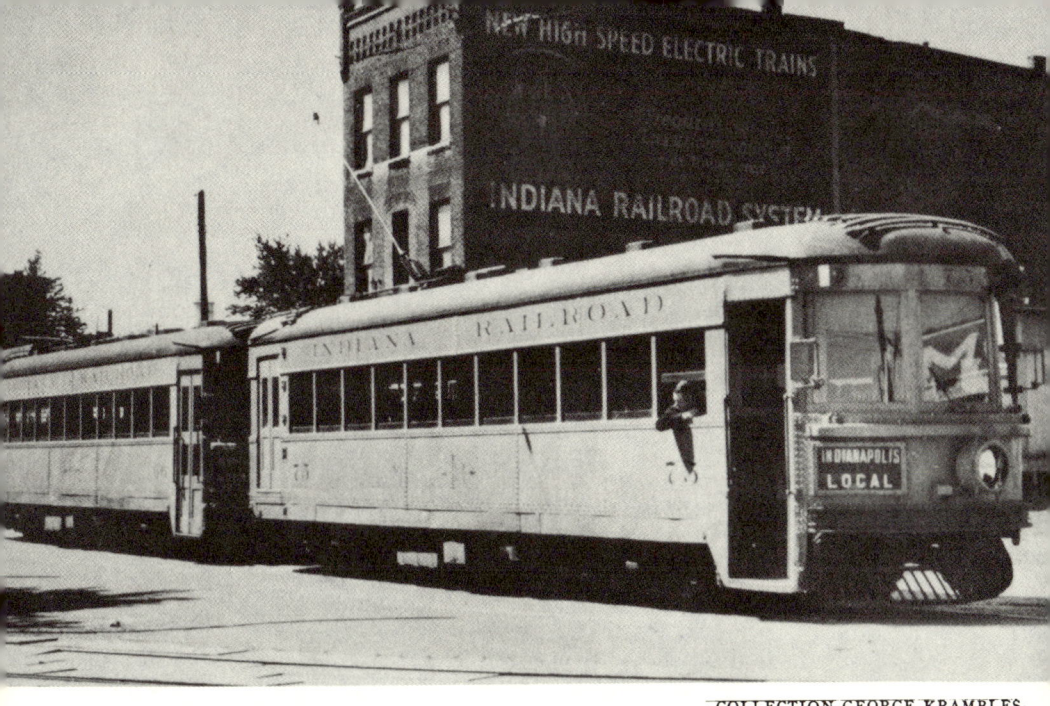

COLLECTION GEORGE KRAMBLES

Above. Two lightweight, high-speed cars of the Indiana Railroad, running in multiple unit, stopped on Main Street in Anderson (1934). The Anderson station, a typical store-front structure, is in the background. The cars, built by Pullman in 1931, served the Indiana for just ten years.

Below. The Baltimore terminal of the Washington Baltimore and Annapolis Electric Railway. The station, less changed than most, now serves buses.

COLLECTION JOHN E. MERRIKEN, JR.

COLLECTION GEORGE KRAMBLE

Above. An Electroliner, one of the pair of four-car articulated units bought by the Chicago North Shore and Milwaukee in 1941. The train is shown on the Chicago Elevated during its first year of service.

Below. A combine and parlor car of the Illinois Terminal Railroad's postwar order of passenger equipment—the last interurban cars built. Placed in service in 1948, they served only until 1956.

COLLECTION GEORGE KRAMBLE

5
The Interurbans and Government Regulation

As a common carrier, serving the general public by transporting freight and passengers, the interurban was subject under common law to potential government control over all phases of its operations, including service and rates. In the early days of the industry, the control actually exercised over the interurban was nominal in most states, except for franchise requirements imposed by local governments. Effective state control over public utilities generally did not develop until after the industry was well established, and for as long as the lines were primarily passenger carriers, they were subject to little control by the Interstate Commerce Commission. State and Federal control over the industry gradually increased after 1907. The relative importance of local, state, and Federal control varied, depending on the nature of a line's operations and the passage of time, but on the whole state control was the most significant.

LOCAL AND STATE JURISDICTION

The interurbans became subject to the control of local governments primarily because they needed franchises in order to lay track on public property, particularly on city streets and, in the East, on rural highways. The terms of these franchises varied widely, but almost all of them placed some restrictions on the lines in return for the use of public property. Restrictions fell into three major categories: paving requirements, restrictions on freight operation, and restrictions on fares.

As we have seen in Chapter 1, when the interurbans operated on city streets, like the street railways, they were customarily required to pave between the rails and for a certain distance, often two feet, on each side. This became a serious burden when automobiles increased the costs of street paving, and the companies complained bitterly about the added expenses imposed on them by the development of a type of transportation that took business from them. They charged, quite correctly, that their costs of paving greatly exceeded the added costs of street construction and maintenance for which they were responsible. Various attempts were made to induce state commissions to take action to relieve them of this burden, but with little success. To be sure, as the financial position of the industry deteriorated after 1918, some states finally took action; Maine, for example, gave its Public Utilities Commission the power to reduce paving obligations. But for the most part the obligations remained until the end of interurban operation, and were in some instances a factor leading to abandonment.

Especially in the states east of Illinois, franchises also placed serious restrictions upon freight operation on city streets. Some prohibited any freight operations, but more commonly the handling of standard railway freight-car equipment, or of more than a specified number of cars was prohibited. Other cities restricted the hours for freight operation (1:00 to 6:00 A.M., for example) or the type of freight that could be handled. The interurbans initially agreed to these requirements with little hesitation, since they were not interested in doing a general freight business, but when freight ultimately became of critical importance, they found the restrictions to be serious obstacles, and the cities to be reluctant to lift the barriers. In a few cases the companies were able to obtain state legislation to override the franchise rules (the Indiana legislature, for example, authorized the handling of cattle); more often they failed.

Although the urban municipalities were not able to exercise any general control over intercity fares, they were enabled by franchise terms to gain limited control over them and to exercise extensive control over fares charged to intracity passengers on the interurban cars. The rural and rural-urban townships of New England often exercised very complete franchise control over fares on the intercity trolley lines.

Local franchise fare control usually took the form of the requirement that the fare could not exceed five cents per zone and five cents within the city limits—the same rule that was applied to street railways. These figures were not unreasonable in the early days of the industry, but ultimately they became intolerably low, and strenuous efforts were made to obtain increases—particularly by the city systems, which were most affected. In some instances, the local governments recognized the inevitable and permitted adjustments, but in many cases they stuck doggedly to the terms of the franchise.

As a consequence, the interurbans turned for relief to the states, and in a few instances, to the Federal government.[1] State action was sought on the grounds that state public utility control legislation took precedence over franchise requirements, and this view was widely accepted by the state railway commissions and the state courts. For example, in Massachusetts, where the franchise control over intercity trolley lines was particularly extensive, in a number of cases (beginning with the Bay State case in 1916, which involved fares from Arlington to Winchester [1]*) the state commission authorized fare increases contravening the franchise figures and this decision was upheld by the courts. The Pennsylvania commission took the same position in the *Borough of Wilkinsburg v. Pittsburgh Railways* case in 1918 [2], pointing out that since the control over rates was a basic state function (derived from police powers), the franchises were not controlling, even though agreed upon by the companies. This rule was applied to interurbans in 1918 in a case involving the Buffalo and Lake Erie [3]; fares above the franchise limits were

---
* Citation references are given in brackets and will be found at the end of the chapter.

authorized because of higher costs and inadequate earnings. The Illinois Supreme Court took this position in *Chicago and So. Traction v. I.C.RR* [4], and the Wisconsin court in *Manitowoc v. Manitowoc and Northern* [5]. Other state courts typically took similar positions. The argument that the franchise rates were binding because they had been accepted by the companies was rejected on the ground that the municipality and the company were both aware of the reserve power of the state to control rates when the agreement was made. In New York State a long and bitter controversy raged over the question. The two public service commissions at first hesitated to take jurisdiction; when one attempted to do so, it was overruled in the Quinby case in 1918 [6]. In 1919, however, the court partially reversed itself, and the commissions gradually gained control.

In a bitterly fought case in Oregon in 1914, the state's Railroad Commission authorized United Railways to raise its Portland–Linnton fare from five cents to ten cents, despite a clause in the franchise limiting the fare to five cents. Consequently, the Multnomah County Court revoked the franchise, and the company was forced to discontinue operations on this portion of its line [7].

In a very limited number of cases (see below), primarily involving the Wheeling Traction and its affiliated companies and the Penn-Ohio, the Interstate Commerce Commission authorized rate increases contravening franchise requirements.

The franchises to use the streets were frequently given for limited periods, and some municipalities were reluctant to renew them, especially after the development of the automobile led to an increased desire to rid the streets of rails. In a number of cases lines were forced to cut their operations back to the city limits or to build expensive off-street facilities. Since the cost of such building was often prohibitive, the net result was to force some lines out of business, or out of passenger service. The United Railways, the Oregon Electric, and the Portland Traction were all forced off the streets in Portland, and the Arkansas Valley was forced to build a new entrance into Hutchinson a few years before the road was abandoned. In Ohio, however, the attempts of Springfield and other cities to force lines off the streets failed because of the court's interpretation of the laws relating to abandonment. In Indiana and other states there was specific legislation barring municipalities from forcing companies to remove track.

In contrast, some cities tried to employ the franchise requirements to prevent companies from abandoning lines or passenger service. For example, in 1932 Escalon tried to use its franchise grant to prevent the Tidewater Southern from discontinuing passenger trains. But in these cases the courts typically overruled the municipalities.

State control over the interurbans took three forms—charter control, direct statutory requirements, and administrative control by the state regulatory commissions. The charters granted by the states for the incorporation of interurban enterprises contained some general restrictions on their activities, but these were usually unimportant. More significant were the statutes that required the lines to fulfill certain conditions. Some of these related to matters of service, such as that washrooms be provided on all interurban cars, or that there be separate facilities for colored and white passengers. The most important statutes were the ones that established maximum railway passenger fares. The interurbans were often interpreted to be railways for the purposes of these provisions, and thus were subject to them. And even when they were not subject, it was difficult for them to charge fares higher than those of competing steam roads.

Primarily, however, state control of the interurbans took the form of regulation by the commissions that had jurisdiction over railroads and public utilities. State railway legislation dates back to the 1870's; it was applied to the street railroads, as to other public utilities, to a limited extent before 1900, but in general it did not become effective until the period between 1907 and 1917. Significant state control thus came after a large part of the interurban system had been built. The legislation usually mentioned interurbans by name (or as a part of the class of electric railways). In some states the interurbans were subject to the same kind of control applied to all steam and street railways and to public utilities, but often with some specific provisions added that applied only to the industry. Other states provided substantially different treatment for steam and street railroads, interurbans either being given special treatment as a third class (Indiana and Ohio), or being included by provision of the law in the class with steam roads (California). New England intercity trolley lines were typically subjected to street railway rather than to steam-road provisions of the laws.

State regulatory laws set up certain standards of regulation, and gave the commission established to enforce the act substantial discretion in interpreting the general provisions, such as that rates be reasonable and nondiscriminatory. These decisions were subject to appeal to the courts, of course, but rarely would the courts overrule the commissions on questions of fact.

JURISDICTION OF THE INTERSTATE COMMERCE COMMISSION

The original Interstate Commerce Act of 1887 gave the Commission control over railroads, without defining what was meant by a railroad. As the interurbans developed, questions arose about their status, and the I.C.C. at first took the position that they were railroads within the meaning of the Act and thus fully subject to control if they did an interstate business. This interpretation was first employed in the 1897 case of *Willson v. Rock Creek Ry. Co.* [8] involving a suburban street railway operating from the District of Columbia to Chevy Chase Lake in Maryland. The Commission adopted the position that such lines were not specifically excluded by the Act and were therefore necessarily subject to its control, provided that they did an interstate business. In the Chicago and Milwaukee case in 1907 [9] the Commission maintained that the Act made no distinction among railroads on the basis of type of power employed.

Applying this doctrine in 1909, the Commission ordered a reduction in the fares of the Omaha and Council Bluffs Street Railway between Omaha and Council Bluffs. The company appealed, ultimately to the United States Supreme Court (*Omaha Street Ry. v. I.C.C.* [10]), which overruled the Commission, on the ground that the company was purely a street railroad that did not haul freight, and that therefore did not fall within the scope of the legislative intent. Congress had taken much the same point of view when it had dealt with the issue three years earlier in enacting the Mann-Elkins Act, which prohibited the I.C.C. from requiring the establishment of through routes or joint rates "between electric passenger railways not engaged in the general business of transporting freight" and other railroads.

Since the Omaha decision and the Mann-Elkins Act applied only to suburban street railways, the I.C.C. continued to exercise full jurisdiction over interurban electric lines operating between cities and doing an interstate business in any form. For example, in the 1921 case of *Beall v. Wheeling Traction* [11], the I.C.C. reaffirmed its right to control the interurbans, even to the extent of their intrastate rates when they affected interstate commerce; the Commission noted that the Wheeling Traction line used high-speed interurban cars, handled freight, and participated in interstate freight and passenger rates.

The Transportation Act of 1920 provided for the specific exclusion of interurbans from certain aspects of I.C.C. control; but because the exclusions were limited in scope, the Commission successfully maintained that their presence in the Act reaffirmed its control over the interurbans in all other respects.

The principal exclusion of "street, suburban or interurban electric railways not operated as a part of a general steam railroad system of transportation," applied to the sections of the Act giving the I.C.C. the authority to issue certificates of convenience and necessity for construction or abandonment, and control over security issues and interurban finance. Two basic problems arose in the interpretation of this exclusion: (1) how was an electric interurban railway to be defined, and (2) what was meant by the term "operated as a part of a general steam railroad system"?

Two years elapsed before the I.C.C. attempted to clarify the meaning of these phrases in any detail. In the first electric railway abandonment case that came before it (January 1921), involving the United Railways [12], the question of jurisdiction was not raised. Later in the year, however, the Michigan United Railways was held to be excluded from control [13]. In 1922, in a case involving control of the Sacramento Northern by the Western Pacific [14], the jurisdictional question was raised, for the Sacramento Northern claimed exemption as an electric interurban. The Commission dealt with the problem at some length, laying down general rules that were applied in subsequent cases. The basic statement was as follows:

The service of such [interurban electric] railways, however, is distinguished by its local and limited character and by the fact that the bulk of their revenues are derived from the transportation of passengers. Their facilities for handling freight are usually inadequate or lacking so as to disable them from engaging in its general transportation. The amount of business interchanged by them with connecting carriers is ordinarily very small. [15]

The Commission went on to point out that the use of electricity as a source of power was not in itself a controlling consideration, and that the nature of the business of the company as a whole, not of particular segments, determined its classification.

On this basis the Commission concluded that the Sacramento Northern was not an interurban and thus was subject to its jurisdiction; a substantial portion of its revenue came from freight handled in standard freight cars interchanged with the steam roads; it participated in many joint rates; and it had a very high ratio of sidings to line mileage. The Commission also noted that even if it ruled the SN to be an interurban, it would still be subject to its jurisdiction because of its close affiliation with the Western Pacific.

However, in 1923 the I.C.C. held the Boise Valley to be excluded [16], despite the fact that it handled standard freight equipment, because the bulk of the revenue was derived from passenger service. The ratio of freight to passenger revenue was at this time regarded as a controlling consideration.*

As a result of the Sacramento Northern and the Boise Valley cases, there were relatively few disputes over the meaning of the certificate and security-issuance clause exemptions over the next several years. For example, in cases involving the Central California Traction, the Spokane Coeur d'Alene and Palouse, the Oregon Electric, and the Illinois Traction no objection to the Commission's jurisdiction was raised, and the I.C.C.

* In 1924 the Commission dealt at some length with the classification of electric lines with respect to the excess-earnings recapture clause, for which the exclusion applied to the same group; however, lines "engaged in the general transportation of freight" were not subject to the exclusion, even though meeting the other requirement, and therefore the coverage of the exclusion was somewhat less broad. The Hudson Valley was ruled to be covered by this exemption (despite its ownership by the Delaware & Hudson) because its freight business was negligible, and the Interstate because it did not engage in general interchange of freight with steam roads, even though 23% of its revenue was from freight. On the other hand, in 1926 the Lackawanna and Wyoming Valley was held to be engaged in the general transportation of freight and thus not covered by the exclusion, since it conducted a general interchange of freight with steam roads, even though freight revenues accounted for only 20% of its total revenues. This road, in view of the Boise Valley case, was subject to the exclusion relating to certificates for construction or abandonment.

made no effort to control the typical Indiana-Ohio type of interurban in so far as these questions were concerned.*

In 1928 the Commission carefully restated its interpretation of the provisions in the Piedmont and Northern case [17], which involved the effort of the road to build two extensions. The line claimed that as an electric interurban it was not subject to I.C.C. jurisdiction. The Commission held that it was not an electric interurban because it gained most of its revenue (92 per cent) from freight, which it handled in standard equipment interchanged with steam roads, and because it participated in joint rates. The United States Supreme Court specifically upheld this interpretation of the Act [18]).

In the next several years a number of cases arose, and in general the decisions followed the pattern of earlier years. The Cincinnati Hamilton and Dayton [19] and the Glendale and Montrose [20] were held to be exempt on the basis of limited freight operation; and this rule was also applied in the Eastern New York Utilities case [21], which involved the abandonment of the Albany–Hudson line. Conversely, the Pacific Electric [22] was held to be subject to I.C.C. control as an integral part of the Southern Pacific system; the Minneapolis Anoka and Cuyuna Range [23] was held subject because of its extensive interstate freight business and interchange with steam lines; and this rule was also applied to the Northeast Oklahoma, which gained 80 per cent of its revenue from freight, and which the Commission emphasized was a commercial railroad and not an interurban. In the NO decision, and in many others after 1928 (the James-

---

* In 1927 the Commission reviewed the question in some detail relative to the Locomotive Inspection Act, which contained the same exclusion as the sections relating to certificates and securities. In its report entitled *Rules for Testing other than Steam Power Locomotives* (122 ICC 414), the Commission noted the general basis for its interpretation of the phrase. Among the criteria given were whether the company engaged in the general transportation of freight or merely handled it incidentally; whether it used standard railway equipment and interchanged this with steam roads; and whether it participated in through routes and joint rates with steam roads. In conformity with these rules it grouped the electric lines on which it had information into three classes: those exempt (including such roads as the Berkshire, the Hudson Valley, the Massachusetts Northeastern, the Southern Indiana, the Wilkes-Barre and Hazleton, the Worcester Consolidated, the Springfield, and surprisingly, the San Francisco Napa and Calistoga); those subject (including such roads as the Arkansas Valley, the Bamberger, the Chicago area roads, the Detroit United, the Interstate, the Northeast Oklahoma, the Pacific Electric, the THI&E, most of the Iowa lines, the Petaluma and Santa Rosa); and those having no electric locomotives (including most of the Ohio roads, Union Traction of Indiana, and other lines). This third class included most of the borderline cases.

The ruling that the Interstate, the Detroit United, and the THI&E were not covered by the exclusion clearly marked a departure from the previous patterns; the Interstate had been specifically ruled to be excluded from certificate control several years before. These three roads were primarily passenger carriers; although they did some interchange business with steam lines, it was very limited in scope. The listing was apparently drawn up without adequate investigation, and did not invariably serve as a precedent for subsequent action.

town Westfield and Northwestern case in 1935, for example) the Commission referred to the Piedmont and Northern decision as a precedent.

As late as 1930 the Commission still regarded the percentage of freight revenue as a primary determinant; the Youngstown and Suburban was ruled exempt in a trackage-rights case in 1931 [24], even though it engaged in substantial freight business involving interchange, essentially because the bulk of its revenue was from passenger service. In this instance the road was seeking to become subject to I.C.C. jurisdiction and changed its charter to permit steam operation in an effort to do so. However, in 1933 the Peninsular was held subject [25] despite the predominance of passenger revenue because it was regarded as an integral part of the Southern Pacific system. A year later, in a strongly contested case, the Grand River Valley was ruled subject [26] because it had discontinued all passenger service two years before.

In the twenties and early thirties, a number of questions of interpretation arose concerning the Railway Labor Act. This act (1926) contained a similar exclusion provision, which had been interpreted very narrowly by the labor board, which ruled exempt a number of lines, such as the North Shore, that interchanged standard freight equipment. The I.C.C. began to interpret this rule in the same fashion as it had the certificate and security clauses, and held the Chicago North Shore and Milwaukee Railroad [27] to be exempt from the Labor Act on the grounds that the road gained less than half of its revenue from freight and did not interchange freight cars at either of its major terminals. The Commission, however, was beginning to realize that it was on shaky ground on its percentage-of-freight-revenue rule, and was forced to reconsider the issue in detail in the Texas Electric case in 1934 [28]; in the previous year this road had gained 54 per cent of its revenue from freight. The Commission centered its decision around the meaning of the term "interurban," holding that the Texas Electric was not an interurban at all but a commercial railroad, since its freight business involved the interchange of standard equipment, even if less than half of its revenue was gained from freight service. In 1939 the I.C.C. reversed itself on the North Shore [29] on the basis of a more careful investigation of the issues. The Texas Electric rule was also applied to the Utah-Idaho Central, which appealed to the United States Supreme Court. The Court sustained the Commission in *Shields v. Utah Idaho Central RR* [30].

In 1938 the Commission shifted its basic policy materially, ruling the Indiana Railroad subject to the Railroad Retirement Act and the Railway Labor Act [31]. This line, a typical Midwestern interurban, received only about 25 per cent of its revenue from freight, and 75 per cent of this was from LCL shipments. Its own freight equipment was not interchangeable with the steam roads, but it did handle standard freight cars on limited portions of its line, and participated in some joint rates; consequently, the I.C.C. held that it was not an interurban. This decision materially narrowed the scope of the exclusion, and almost all remaining interurban lines were brought under I.C.C. control in matters relating to abandonment and construction, finance, and labor relations. The Commission reaffirmed this action in two abandonment cases involving the Indiana Railroad in 1939 [32] and 1940 [33]. By this time, of course, most of the typical interurban network had gone; had the I.C.C. changed its policy a decade before, the significance of the change would have been far greater.

From 1940 on relatively few disputes arose. In 1940 the Commission ruled [34] that all of Pacific Electric's operations, even purely local car lines, were subject to control since the financial results of their operation affected interstate commerce. In 1940 the Trenton–Princeton Traction was held subject as a subsidiary of the Reading [35], and in 1941 the Texas Electric was held subject in an abandonment case, the I.C.C. reaffirming its earlier decision. The Kansas City Kaw Valley and Western was held subject in 1949 [36] since it provided no passenger service at all. In 1946 the Holt–Tuscaloosa line of the Alabama Power Company, a streetcar line handling some freight, was held subject.

The last case arose in 1955, when the Chicago North Shore and Milwaukee sought to abandon its shore line; in its decision the I.C.C. reviewed the history of the issue in some detail [37]. It reaffirmed its jurisdiction over the North Shore on the ground that it was not an interurban within the terms of the Interstate Commerce Act because of its extensive freight interchange with steam roads (although much less than half of its revenue came from freight service). The Commission likewise pointed out that even though the shore line itself, viewed as a separate entity, might be considered as a suburban electric railway not subject to certificate control, the jurisdiction depended on the nature of the property as a whole, not on that of a particular segment. The Commission pointed out that although in certain cases in the past the North Shore had been ruled to be an interurban exempt from this portion of the act (in fact the United States Supreme Court had essentially said as much), these cases were not valid precedents for the present one.

Certain phases of I.C.C. control were not subject to exclusions. Consolidation clauses did not provide for the exclusion of interurbans, and thus, for example, the Commission assumed jurisdiction in the case of the Monongahela West Penn, although its freight revenue was negligible and it had no joint rates with steam roads.

Similarly, power over joint rates was unlimited except for the rule that the Commission could not compel the establishment of through routes with electric passenger railroads not engaged in the general transport of freight. In a number of cases the Commission compelled steam roads to establish through routes with electric lines, and in the Louisville case (see p. 163 below) compelled several electric lines to establish joint rates among themselves. In one case [46] it compelled continuation of a joint rate between a water carrier and an electric line.

In the field of rate regulation, the Commission was subject to no restrictions except those arising out of the Omaha case relating to street railroads. Following the pattern of the Steubenville case [38], interstate rates of electric lines were often subjected to individual control or made subject to *ex parte* general changes, in some instances over the objections of states and cities. But the Commission pressed its right of control, even when this meant overriding franchise requirements (unless travel was wholly within a city), and on the whole its policy was upheld by the courts. The Commission also subjected purely intrastate rates to its control when it could be demonstrated that low intrastate rates were prejudicial against interstate commerce. One of the most significant cases involved the Penn-Ohio, which was prevented by franchise restrictions from raising its rates on its intrastate service to a level comparable to its interstate rates. The I.C.C. authorized an increase on the intrastate portion; the Ohio Supreme Court overruled it, but the Commission was sustained upon appeal to the United States Supreme Court (*Village of Hubbard v. U.S.* [39]). In this case the Supreme Court specifically stated that the various restrictions in the Interstate Commerce Act relating to control over interurbans applied only to the specific sections involved, not to the entire Act.

Thus, as a result of a long series of Commission decisions and court cases, the picture of I.C.C. jurisdiction evolved as follows: (1) Strictly streetcar operation, including electric suburban lines, were subject to no I.C.C. control of any type. (2) Interurban operations of all usual types were subject to Commission control over rates, through routes, filing of reports, and the like, and to the other sections of the Interstate Commerce Act that contained no restrictions on interurban control. (3) Control over certificates of convenience and necessity (for construction, abandonment, etc.), security issue, and locomotive inspection, plus operation of the Railroad Retirement Act and the Railway Labor Act, applied to those lines (1) held not to be "interurbans" within the meaning of the term in the Act, and (2) operated as a part of a steam-road system. Until 1939 this rule in practice excluded from I.C.C. control a road using typical interurban equipment and concentrating on passenger business, with its freight business either negligible, or confined primarily to special equipment not interchangeable with the railroads. The type of interurban that most frequently survived down into the thirties—one that conducted extensive interchange with steam roads, used standard freight equipment, and participated in through rates—was subject to I.C.C. control over these categories even though less than half of its gross revenue came from freight operation.

The Commission's policies in applying the Act to interurbans gave rise to relatively little complaint; despite the lack of a precise definition, the rules established by the Commission worked comparatively well. Partly for this reason, the Commission's frequent requests for a more precise legislative definition of its powers relating to electric lines were never heeded by Congress.

It should be noted that the interurbans were not necessarily opposed to I.C.C. control; in some instances they even favored it because it freed them from oppressive state or local action. For example, the I.C.C. gained the power (as a result of court decision) to require increases in intrastate rates regardless of state maximum fare laws in cases in which there was discrimination between intrastate and interstate commerce or a burden on the latter. I.C.C. control was also beneficial in certain abandonment cases. The aspect of control to which the interurbans most strongly objected was their inclusion under the provisions of the Railway Labor Act and the Railroad Retirement Act.

STATE AND FEDERAL REGULATORY POLICIES

The most significant aspects of state and federal regulation were the policies concerning passenger and freight rates, service, abandonments, and motor-carrier competition.

Rates

To the typical interurban, the most important rate was its passenger fare. Passenger fares were usually established on a mileage basis, following the pattern of the railways, although the New England intercity trolley lines and some shorter lines in the East generally used the zone fare characteristic of suburban street railways. The strict mileage basis gave rise to very few disputes, since questions of discrimination and rate relationships did not arise. Some state commissions (Indiana's, for example) prescribed a maximum mileage rate for all interurbans. The only major issue was that of the general rate level; and to the extent to which a particular line used the rate-per-mile figure typical of other roads, individual rate cases were very rare indeed. However, some controversies and commission action did arise. For example, in Wisconsin in 1912 the Milwaukee-Waukesha rate was held to be reasonable in terms of the earnings on the investment. In a 1916 Pennsylvania case involving the Mahoning and Shenango, the company was permitted to charge a higher per-mile fare on one of its lines, which had higher operating costs than its other lines.

The problems of reasonable return on investment and valuation of the properties, which have been so vexatious with power companies, rarely arose because in most instances when fare increases were sought, or fare reductions opposed, it was obvious that the company's earnings were so inadequate that no precise determination of return was required. However, in the period from 1912 to 1920 several cases of this type did arise involving New England intercity trolley lines. The basic case involved the Middlesex and Boston [40]: the Massachusetts commission held that the company was entitled to a reasonable return on prudently invested capital, not on present value of property. Questions of return also arose in the Concord Maynard and Hudson case in 1917, in which the company was allowed to shift from a zone to a mileage basis.

One of the most complete investigations of required return was made in 1910, when the Puget Sound Electric Railway sought to increase fares for its suburban service. This action led to complaints and to an investigation by the Washington commission (*RR Com. Washington v. Puget Sound Electric Ry.*). A careful valuation of the company's property was made, and rates were determined on the basis of the two principles of allowing the company an over-all 7 per cent rate of return on investment, and of charging each user "no more than the service was worth." On the latter basis, a reduction in suburban fares was ordered.

As noted previously, the fares of many interurbans in time became at least partly subject to I.C.C. control, although relatively few interurban fare cases ever came before the Commission. The most significant were those involving the Wheeling Traction and the Penn-Ohio, in which increases were permitted on the grounds of increased cost and the relationship of intrastate and interstate rates. The few interurbans that still operated passenger service after 1945 participated in general postwar rate level increases.

The policies of control of interurban freight rates by the state commissions and the I.C.C. did not differ in any significant way from those of control of steam-road rates. Purely local rates in no way related to interstate commerce were controlled by the states,[2] whereas the I.C.C. controlled all interstate rates, and the intrastate rates that affected the relationship between interstate and intrastate business. In practice, relatively few cases directly affecting electric roads arose, apart from joint-rate issues.

The matter of joint rates was of fundamental importance to the interurbans in the period after 1910. As we noted in Chapter 4, the steam roads, especially in the Midwest, were very reluctant to establish through routes and joint rates with the interurbans, which they regarded not as railroads but as some inferior species. Some interurbans were not interested in freight hauling, but many (largely west of Indiana) felt that the development of interchange, the use of standard freight equipment, and the establishment of joint rates were essential for their prosperity (and ultimately, their survival). Failure to establish interchange prevented any through movement of cars, and even with interchange, the lack of joint rates often made through shipments prohibitively expensive.

Some cases involving interchange and joint rates arose before the state commissions or courts. One of the major cases involved the Hudson Valley line, which, unlike most Eastern lines, sought to handle standard freight equipment from the earliest years. The steam roads refused to turn over to it cars routed to destinations on the line; but in 1905, after a series of court cases, the New York Supreme Court upheld lower court decisions requiring the steam lines to interchange with the road. A later case (1915) involved a Michigan commission order requiring the Michigan Central to install an interchange track with the Detroit United at Oxford; the commission was upheld by the United States Supreme Court. Generally, however, the interurbans had only limited success in obtaining state commission action, in part because of the wording of state legislation relating to interchange and joint rates.[3]

Because a large portion of the potential through-freight business was interstate in nature, most interurbans turned to the I.C.C. for assistance. In the first major case—the "cabbage" case in 1907 (*Chicago and Milwaukee Electric Ry. v. Illinois Central, et al.* [41])—the predecessor of the Chicago North Shore and Milwaukee requested the I.C.C. to establish joint rates from points on its line to points on the Illinois Central and connecting roads. Most of the shipments in question were of cabbages, which southern Wisconsin growers sought to move from the line's sidings. The Illinois Central had established joint rates, and then had canceled them upon the protest of the Chicago & Northwestern. The Commission rejected the electric road's request because the territory was already adequately served by the older carriers. The sidings in question were less than a mile from ones on the Northwestern's tracks. The Commission pointed out that a new road built into an area should not be allowed to divide the business of existing carriers when the service of the latter is adequate.

The second major case (*Cedar Rapids and Iowa City v. Chicago and Northwestern* [42]) came a year later. The Cedar Rapids line had joint rates with the Milwaukee through Cedar Rapids, but sought to compel the Northwestern to establish them as well. The Northwestern refused, on the grounds that the interurban was not a railroad, and that the road's policy was to refuse to establish through routes with electric lines because they lacked adequate cars and could not reciprocate with equipment. The Commission sustained the Cedar Rapids line, on the ground that the towns it served did not have adequate service by other roads (being several miles from these roads), and it compelled the Northwestern to establish joint rates. However, the Commission would not order the establishment of joint rates from Iowa City on the grounds that this point had adequate service via the Rock Island.

The third case (*Cincinnati and Columbus Traction Co. v. Baltimore and Ohio Southwestern RR Co.* [43]) differed from the first two in that the steam roads centered their objections on other factors and no previous physical interchange existed. The case involved the attempt of the C&C to compel the B&O and the Norfolk & Western to establish interchanges and joint rates at various points. The interchanges had once existed but had been removed when the interurban was completed. The steam roads argued that under Ohio law interurbans were separately classified from steam roads and had no right to obtain interchanges with the latter, but the Commission rejected their argument as being irrelevant in cases involving interstate commerce. The steam roads concentrated their opposition on the contention that the C&C should not have been built and should not be allowed to milk their revenues. They added that its physical shape was so poor that it could not safely handle steam-road cars—its own freight cars had been retired by a steam road as unfit for use. The Commission, however, also rejected these arguments, on the ground that the road could probably operate safely. It ordered the establishment of interchanges and joint rates (although not to towns also served by the steam roads) on the grounds that some of the towns were located at substantial distances from the steam roads—five to ten miles—and thus that existing service was inadequate. This decision was appealed to the Supreme Court [44] and was reversed, so far as the requirement to install interchanges was concerned, on the grounds that in terms of the act this could be required only with lateral branch lines, not with a line that essentially paralleled the major road involved.

However, it was generally established by 1911 that the electric roads had the right to demand joint rates, providing that the requirements of the Act relating to need, and to the avoidance of short-hauling the other carrier were met. In 1913, in a far-reaching decision (*St. Louis Springfield and Peoria RR v. Peoria and Pekin Union* [45]) the Peoria & Pekin Union was required to establish through routes with the Illinois Traction Company to points on its line and beyond. The P&PU had done so for all steam roads entering Peoria, but had refused to do so for Illinois Traction except under prohibitive terms. The I.C.C. insisted on equal treatment of the interurban. In *Milwaukee Produce and Fruit Exchange v. Crosby* [46], the Crosby Transportation Company, a Great Lakes water carrier, was required to reestablish joint rates with the Grand Rapids Grand Haven and Muskegon for shipment of fruit and vegetables from Michigan points to Milwaukee; it had canceled them because of the complaints of the Grand Trunk, with which it had a similar arrangement. In 1920 various Eastern roads were denied the right to cancel joint rates with the Toledo and Western, which, they claimed, had been established by error in a tariff revision [47]. In *Michigan Railway Co. v. Pere Marquette* [48], the Pere Marquette was required to establish through routes with Michigan Railway Company from certain points that lacked adequate service from steam lines. In both the Crosby and the Michigan Railway cases, however, as in others, the Commission would not order through routes from points that already had adequate service from steam lines.

In several cases the electric lines were unable to get favorable Commission action because the circumstances did not seem to justify it. For example, the application (1914) of the Chicago Ottawa and Peoria was denied because the shippers already had adequate service, and that of the Michigan Railway because it could not give adequate evidence of need.

By 1920 Commission action had made it clear that the steam roads could not refuse to establish joint rates from interurban points not adequately served by the steam lines, and that terminal companies must not discriminate between interurban and steam roads. But the steam roads could not be compelled to short-haul themselves, and the Commission would not order joint rates from points adequately served by steam roads. The Commission's orders did lead to voluntary establishment of many additional joint rates, and after 1920 the steam roads' general opposition on principle to the establishment of joint rates with electric lines tended to diminish. Joint passenger rates between steam and interurban lines were not widely established (see Chapter 3).

As a rule the interurbans voluntarily established joint rates among themselves, but in one major case the I.C.C. required such action. In 1913 the Louisville Board of Trade requested that joint rates be established from Louisville to Indianapolis and points beyond over the four interurban lines which at that time comprised the through route. Three of these were lines owned by Samuel Insull; the fourth, the Indianapolis and Louisville (extending from Sellersburg to Seymour), was independent. The I&L was willing to establish the through routes, and charged that the Insull roads refused to do so in order to embarrass it and facilitate purchase of it at a low price. The Insull roads stated that their opposition was based on the congested condition of the lines resulting from heavy passenger traffic. The Commission ordered the establishment of the joint rates, and prescribed rate divisions [49].

Service

Control over service requirements rested primarily in the hands of the state commissions, except for limited municipal franchise control. A large number of cases, most of them of little significance, arose over the years concerning the quality and nature of passenger service. On rare occasions state commissions required an increase in the frequency of trains or, conversely, prevented a reduction. For example, as late as 1950, the Illinois commission permitted the Illinois Terminal Railroad to reduce service on the Bloomington line, but required the operation of four trains per day instead of the three the company sought.

Other action arose from the demands of passengers. Complaints were frequently made that too few cars were provided to meet rush-hour traffic peaks (particularly on suburban runs), and in some instances lines were ordered to add cars, as in a 1917 Pennsylvania decision involving the Reading Transit's Lebanon–Palmyra line [50]. Passengers frequently requested more stops than the company thought desirable, in terms of maintaining speed. In a 1913 case, for example, the Wisconsin commission required the Chicago and Milwaukee to provide additional stops in Racine, but laid down a basic rule that interurbans should not be required to provide an excessive number of stops in view of the importance of speed.

Complaints were also frequently made about the quality of track and equipment. In a few instances commissions ordered track improvements (for example in the case of the Lebanon–Palmyra line); but typically so long as a company could afford to keep its track and equipment in adequate shape it would do so, and if it could not, commission orders were not likely to prove very effective. Occasionally, however, a commission ordered a line to make improvements or to cease operation because of the unsafe condition of its track. Examples of this included the Kaydeross line in New York in 1929 and the Rochester–Clear Lake line in Illinois. A commission might restrict the speed on a line because of unsafe track, as happened in 1920 on the Caldwell Traction Company's McNeil line, in Idaho.

Many state commissions laid down general rules relating to safety, such as the use of nonelectric rear lights, railway crossing protection, and the like. The most far-reaching action of this sort was the attempt of the Indiana commission, following the disastrous wreck at Kingsland in 1910, to require the installation of block signals on all interurban lines where the traffic justified it. This action was based on authorization given by law in 1912. The California commission stepped up its safety requirements after the two serious accidents in the summer of 1913.

In the years of declining business, many interurbans sought to use one-man cars. In a number of states the legislation permitted them to do so only upon approval of the state commission. Approval was usually given (for example, in California, in the case of the Petaluma and Santa Rosa in 1928), but sometimes denied.

Building and Extension of Lines

Most of the interurban network of the country was built before either the state commissions or the I.C.C. were given the power to require certificates of convenience and necessity to build or extend lines; a company had only to obtain its charter and necessary local franchises before building. To be sure, in some New England states and in New York the commissions gained this power at an early date, but they very rarely used it to prevent the construction of a line. In Connecticut the power (in the hands of the courts) was limited to control over the construction of lines that competed with existing roads.[4] New lines were typically sought by the municipalities involved, and construction rarely involved competition with other interurbans.

The New York commission rendered several decisions in construction cases shortly after 1900. In 1902 [51] the Rochester Syracuse and Eastern was granted permission to build from Rochester to Syracuse despite the opposition of the steam roads because it demonstrated that there was a need for better service than the steam roads could provide. In 1905 the Buffalo Lockport and Rochester was authorized to build from Rochester to Lockport despite strong steam-road protests, again because better service would be offered, although substantial steam-road service already existed. Steam-road opposition rarely succeeded in blocking construction; however, in 1905 an application to build an interurban from Rochester to Elmira was denied by the New York commission because the existing service was felt to be adequate.

In 1920 the I.C.C. was given power over new construction, but only over lines to be used in interstate commerce and not subject to other exclusions. This power came too late to have much effect. There was little construction after 1920, and much of it was built without I.C.C. approval because of the interpretation that the lines were interurbans and thus not under the Commission's jurisdiction. Of the lines whose construction was approved, most were freight feeder lines of certain electric roads clearly subject to Commission control: the Sacramento Northern, the Oregon Electric, and the Illinois Terminal.

In at least four cases, however, permission to build was denied. In 1931, the East Texas Electric Company's application to make extensions in the Beaumont area in order to provide additional access to the area for various steam lines was denied on the ground that undesirable duplication would result. In 1942 the Northeast Oklahoma was denied permission to build a line to connect with the Santa Fe because it would create unnecessary additional competition [52]. In 1925 the I.C.C. refused to grant a petition of the Aroostook Valley (approved by the Maine commission) to build an extension from New Sweden to St. Agatha, on the ground of insufficient traffic.

The most celebrated case was that of Piedmont and Northern [53]. After the Supreme Court upheld I.C.C. jurisdiction over this road, the company applied for permission to build two new lines, one to join its existing lines, the other to connect its northern line to the Norfolk & Western at Durham. If these lines had been built, a new main north-south route would have been created, in conjunction with the N&W and the Georgia & Florida. The I.C.C. denied the application on the grounds that the existing lines provided adequate service and that the new route would merely divert business from them, contrary to the intent of the legislation. As of 1960 the proposed lines were still shown as projected on the Piedmont and Northern's map in the Railway Guide.

Abandonment

That a large portion of regulatory action was concerned with the abandonment of lines is not surprising, given the typical history of the interurbans. Prior to 1920, public control over abandonment rested entirely in the hands of state and local governments. The control that affected railroads and public utilities generally dates back to the period before state commission control. Courts frequently held that any public utility was obligated to continue to supply service once it had begun operations, on the basis of charter grants of such privileges as eminent domain. Although the courts were reluctant to permit abandonment, they universally ruled that a company clearly demonstrating losses from its over-all operations must be permitted to abandon.

Actually, very few cases of abandonment arose before the states were given control, so few in fact that the acts providing for state control of railways and utilities originally made no reference to abandonment at all except to provide for forfeiture of charter for companies that did not complete and operate their lines. As abandonments increased, either the state commissions assumed control over them by interpreting the provisions giving them power over facilities and service to include interurban abandonments, or the laws were amended to give the commissions this specific authority.[5] However, because of this varied statutory background, the exact powers granted the commissions and the policies they have followed have differed to some extent.

In 1920 the Interstate Commerce Commission was given power over railroad abandonment; consequently, interurban control since then has been divided between the I.C.C. and state authorities. In brief summary, the pattern of jurisdiction may be divided into four categories.

Street railway lines (even if interstate), and interurbans of an intrastate character not engaged in a general interchange freight business on any scale, nor operated as a portion of a steam railroad system, were subject only to state jurisdiction. As noted above, after 1939 the I.C.C. broadened its jurisdiction to include lines carrying on even limited interchange business.

Intrastate lines not a portion of a steam-road system, but subject to I.C.C. control because of their interchange joint-rate freight business, required I.C.C. approval of abandonment with respect to interstate business only, and state approval with respect to intrastate business, and thus for actual abandonment of the track. If the interstate business was a substantial portion of the total, its abandonment would virtually force approval of the abandonment of the intrastate operation.

Interurbans operating in more than one state and those operating as a portion of a steam road (e.g., the Trenton–Princeton Traction Company [242 ICC 45] which was a subsidiary of the Reading) were exclusively subject to I.C.C. control.

Discontinuance of passenger service only was subject to exclusive state control regardless of the nature of the operations, for until 1958 the I.C.C. had no power over passenger service.

State Commission Policy. The right of a state commission to prevent the abandonment of part of a utility's lines had long been recognized, and was upheld by the United States Supreme Court in 1925 in the *Fort Smith Traction v. Bourland* case, which involved a street railway [54]. An interurban, as a public utility, had an obligation to continue to supply all the services it offered to the public unless the Commission sanctioned it to do otherwise, and thus it could be prevented from discontinuing particular services. In practice, however, permission was seldom denied because the companies usually did not file application until conditions became hopelessly bad. One of the few denials on record involved the application of the Charleston Interurban to abandon one of its lines; permission was refused on the grounds that over-all operations were profitable and that the line was needed by the public [55]. In 1955 the California commission denied the Metropolitan Coach Lines (the successor to the Pacific Electric in the passenger field) the right to abandon service on its lines from Los Angeles to San Pedro and Long Beach. Several factors were involved, including the greater speed of the electric line, the growing highway congestion, and the aggravating effect of bus operation on smog.

In literally hundreds of cases, applications for permission to abandon portions of the carrier's line were granted. One of the earliest cases (1917) dealt with the application of the Oakland Antioch and Eastern to discontinue operations over the track owned by the Sacramento Valley from Dixon Junction to Dixon [56]; the California commission authorized abandonment upon the company's demonstration that substantial operating deficits were being incurred. The first major contested case in California arose in 1924, when the OA&E sought permission to abandon its San Ramon Valley branch [57]. The commission pointed out that it believed it had power to prevent partial abandonments if it saw fit, but in this case it granted the application in view of the continued operating deficits, the failure of the area to grow as anticipated,* the effects of auto use, and the limited possibilities for financial improvement and the company's general unprofitability.

Several other early cases occurred in Pennsylvania. In 1917 the state commission ruled that operation of a particular line could be discontinued if it was demonstrably constituting a drain upon the system as a whole and thus endangering it. The commission restated the doctrine in 1932 in the Pennsylvania-New Jersey Railways case, involving that road's Bristol–Morrisville line whose revenues did not cover costs. Various other arguments for abandonment were accepted in particular cases. East Penn Traction was permitted to abandon its Pottsville–Glen Carbon line in 1928, and Lehigh Traction its Hazleton–McAdoo line in 1929, because the settling of the ground surface caused by mining operations had rendered operation unsafe. In 1936 the Shamokin–Mt. Carmel line abandonment was granted on the ground that the right-of-way was required for highway widening. Typically the emphasis in the granting of the application was upon public convenience and necessity, and failure of the line's revenue to cover costs was interpreted as a demonstration of lack of public necessity for the line.

Other states followed the same basic rule as Pennsylvania in allowing partial abandonment, although they differed somewhat in details. On the grounds of declining traffic and inadequate earnings the Wisconsin commission in 1924 permitted the abandonment of Wisconsin Public Service's Omro line, and the Maine commission the abandonment of the Androscoggin and Kennebec's Augusta–Winthrop line [58].

The great majority of the interurban abandonment cases to come before state commissions involved total abandonment. At first, some state commissions simply held that they had no legal power to prevent such action, particularly if the charter was surrendered. This view was taken by the Ohio commission in the abandonment of the Lake Erie Bowling

---

* Ironically, two decades later, this became one of the most rapidly growing areas in California.

Green and Napoleon in 1916, and by the Pennsylvania commission in several early cases. Ultimately, however, in most states formal approval of total abandonment requests was required either by law or by commission interpretation. It was universally agreed that a commission could not require continued operation at a loss, since this would amount to deprivation of property without due process. This rule was affirmed by the United States Supreme Court in the Brooks-Scanlan case in 1920 [59], which involved the abandonment of a steam railroad. The commissions' rulings, however, usually were couched in terms of convenience and necessity: the decline in traffic and inadequate revenues were cited as evidence of lack of necessity for continued operation. The fact that a petitioning company could not raise capital for essential repairs of the line constituted an additional argument for abandonment.

The number of cases of total abandonment is tremendous, and only a few will be noted as examples. In 1933 the Pennsylvania commission permitted the Wilkes-Barre and Hazleton [60] to abandon because its revenue had fallen hopelessly below its operating costs. In 1926 the Wisconsin commission, in granting the Northern States Power Company's application to abandon its Eau Claire–Chippewa Falls line, noted that the public clearly preferred a competing bus service [61]; in permitting the Wisconsin Public Service Company to abandon its Green Bay–Kaukauna line in 1938 [62], the commission noted the adverse effects of cars and buses on revenues, and its own inability to compel any utility to continue operations at a loss. The Maine commission, in the Rockland South Thomaston and St. George case in 1918 [63], stated emphatically that it could not prevent the scrapping of a line that had discontinued service under court order, and that could be operated only at a loss. In 1919 the New Hampshire commission, in the case of the Exeter Hampton and Amesbury [64], indicated that it had no choice but to permit the abandonment of an electric line that could not cover costs and a reasonable return, and needed funds for rehabilitation. The Virginia commission, in authorizing abandonment of the Richmond–Ashland line in 1936, noted that it could not require continued operation of a line whose revenues did not cover its expenses, and which was completely insolvent.

Closely related to the due-process rule was the rule that a profitable affiliated company could not be required to meet the losses of an unprofitable electric railway. This was noted as early as 1919 by the New Hampshire commission in the Exeter case, and was reaffirmed by the Illinois Supreme Court in the Northern Illinois Light and Traction case in 1922 [65].

The commissions in some instances imposed conditions, such as the requirement of substitution of bus service, or a delay in abandonment during which any party willing to operate the line had the right to buy it at salvage value. The first delay of this sort was imposed in 1919 in the New Hampshire case involving the Exeter line.

Two types of jurisdictional disputes over abandonment arose. In some instances the claim was made that a firm's obligations under local franchises prevented it from discontinuing service; this claim was frequently overruled. The other type of dispute involved the courts and the commissions. Occasionally a Federal court having jurisdiction in an interurban's bankruptcy proceedings ordered discontinuance of operations prior to commission action (for example, in the Salt Lake and Utah case in 1946). The commissions and the courts have now taken the position that such action takes precedence over commission action in the case of entire abandonments (as, for example, the 1918 case of the Bluffton Geneva and Celina) but not partial abandonments.

I.C.C. Policy. The basic policies of the I.C.C. on interurban abandonment were similar to those of the states, and identical to its policies for the steam roads. Actually, of course, the I.C.C. acted on a relatively small proportion of total interurban abandonments. Before 1920 the Commission had no control; from 1920 to 1938, the period in which the great interurban network vanished, the Commission's interpretation of its jurisdiction excluded the typical interurban from the need of obtaining permission.

Between 1920 and 1950, only 38 interurban abandonment applications came before the Commission; four cases (involving the Boise Western, the Eastern New York Utilities Company, the Lewiston and Youngstown Frontier, and the Glendale and Montrose) were dismissed for lack of jurisdiction, and all the other applications were granted. Twelve involved complete abandonment, 26 partial abandonment. The first case, involving the United Railways (Oregon), was an uncontested one which actually involved only the transfer of operations to another road. The second was also uncontested, involving the Deadwood Central line from Lead to Deadwood, South Dakota; permission to abandon was granted because of operating losses. Most of the early cases were noncontroversial, and by the time any significant cases came to the Commission, the principles to be followed had been well established in steam-road cases.

The I.C.C. authorized partial abandonments whenever there was evidence of substantial loss, which there was in all the cases that came before it; owing to the generally depressed condition of the industry the controversial type of case common with steam lines, in which a profitable system was seeking to abandon a minor branch, did not arise. In ruling on one of the few questionable applications, that of the Toledo and Western to abandon its Pioneer line [66], the Commission concluded that despite the injury to the users, abandonment must be permitted because of the line's losses and the unprofitability of the company as a whole. Other contested cases involved the Pacific Electric [67], in which the recommendations of the California commission were accepted, and the later abandonments of Indiana Railroad. In several instances, notably in a 1950 Pacific Electric case [68], the Commission ruled that when lines were subsidiaries of steam roads, the parent could not be expected to meet the deficits.

Total abandonment cases, when contested, were usually decided in terms of the rule that an enterprise, as a whole, cannot be required to operate at a loss. The Kaydeross line in New York was permitted to abandon in 1930 [69] because of its continued deficits and its inability to make necessary repairs; the Commission maintained that despite injury to shippers, the line's continued operation would constitute a burden on interstate commerce. Despite strong opposition, the Grand River Valley [70] and the Jamestown Westfield and Northwestern [71] were permitted to abandon because of deficits; the JW&NW, however, was bought at salvage value during a 60-day delay imposed on these terms, and operated 20 years longer before it was finally abandoned.

Abandonment of Passenger Service Only. Applications to discontinue passenger service only aroused the bitterest protests. In the first such case, the California commission in 1924 [72] approved the Visalia Electric's application to discontinue passenger service on the ground that since revenues had fallen far below costs, the services were clearly not required by the public. This rule was restated several times by the California commission, which was the one primarily involved in this type of case. For example, in the contested Sacramento Northern case in 1940 [73], the commission pointed out that it must base its decision on public convenience and necessity, but in doing so must consider the financial position of the company, the loss of revenue, and the consequent operating losses demonstrating the absence of public need for service. The commission noted that there was no chance of improvement in earnings, and that although improved service might increase revenues, a company cannot be expected to make such improvements when the service is unprofitable.

The state commissions generally accepted the position that passenger service must "stand on its own," that companies could not be expected to cover out-of-pocket passenger deficits from freight service profits. If a passenger deficit could be clearly demonstrated, permission to abandon was usually granted. It was not necessary, however, that the passenger service cover its allocated share of common costs, since these would continue even if the service were abandoned.

Some of the most difficult cases in the field involved the Pacific Electric, whose lines carried substantial numbers of passengers. Most of the PE's abandonments were strongly opposed, yet the company was able to demonstrate substantial losses on the lines in question and unprofitable operation in general. In 1939, when the first major abandonments were made, the State commission conducted one of the most complete inquiries ever made into the operation of an interurban system.[6] The general conclusion was reached that bus transportation was superior, and the right to abandon was granted—a decision that may prove to have been undesirable from the long-range standpoint of traffic control in the Los Angeles area. The company was permitted to abandon most of its passenger service, and in 1953 to dispose of all remaining passenger operations to the Metropolitan Coach Lines, a company organized for the purpose of providing bus service in lieu of rail. This company was permitted to abandon some of its lines, but finally, for reasons noted above, further abandonment was stopped; in 1958 the property was acquired by the Los Angeles Metropolitan Transit Authority.

One of the few applications to abandon passenger service to be rejected was that of the Portland Traction Company in Oregon in 1955. The state commission ruled that although the company incurred a small deficit from passenger service, the combined service was profitable, and the passenger service was essential to the communities served. In 1958 the company abandoned its passenger service in defiance of the commission's orders; after considerable legal action the commission gave up the struggle.

Motor-Carrier Competition

Another matter of primary concern to the interurbans was government regulation of motor carriers, particularly buses. The policies of different states greatly influenced the life spans of particular interurban lines, although the ultimate fate of the industry was probably not significantly affected.

The right of governments to control the establishment of new firms in competition with existing public utilities, including common carriers, was firmly established in the courts long before the days of state commission regulation; the basic case in American jurisprudence is the 1837 Charles River Bridge case [74]. But few states attempted to exercise any control over the building of new railroads or interurbans; competing interurban lines were seldom built, and the desire for lines in new areas was so great that the question of control did not arise.

With the development of motor transportation, however, the question of control of entry became a significant issue. A bus line required little capital investment, and new lines frequently started up in competition with electric lines and with other bus lines. Much of the agitation for motor-carrier control arose out of this situation, rather than out of the desire to control rates.

The states followed two patterns in developing motor-carrier control, largely by the accident of the exact wording of laws relating to transportation companies. In several states, these laws gave the state commissions power over all common carriers, or all companies engaged in the transportation of freight and passengers for hire, and thus by interpretation the commissions assumed power over commercial bus and truck operations without a change in the law. These states included Arizona (1915), Arkansas (1929), California (1916), Georgia (1915), Illinois (1914), Nebraska (1925), and Pennsylvania (1914). Actual regulation was in some cases instituted a year or so later than the date given. Only three of these states had any significant interurban mileage. In several states, after the commissions had assumed control, legislation was enacted to clarify their powers over motor carriers (in California in 1917, for example).

In the other states the original laws applied only to railroads, and thus the commissions lacked power over motor carriers until new legislation was enacted. Some states acted quickly as motor transport developed—New York and Colorado, for example, passed laws in 1915—but most states did not enact legislation until after 1920. Ohio did not provide for control of motor carriers until 1921, Michigan until 1923, Indiana, Kansas, Massachusetts, Oregon, and Wisconsin until 1925, and New Jersey and Kentucky until 1926.

In all cases, the legislation specified that common-carrier motor operation could not be undertaken until the firm had obtained a certificate of convenience and necessity, which was issued at the discretion of the commission upon the showing of public need for the service. In a number of states[7] the law required the commission to take into consideration the adequacy of existing steam and electric railway service in determining the necessity for the motor carrier service; in one state (Texas) the law specifically prohibited the commission from considering such service. In most states, however, no such restrictions were placed on the commissions' determination of public convenience and necessity.

With a very few exceptions the state legislation contained grandfather-clause provisions,[8] under which motor carriers operating as of a certain date, usually set near the time of the law's enactment, were automatically entitled to certificates of convenience and necessity. The same policy was typically followed in the states in which the commissions assumed control under existing legislation. In states in which a law of this sort was not enacted until after 1920, effective motor competition with the interurbans was usually already established, although in some instances the interurbans had protected themselves by establishing or purchasing bus lines parallel to their rail lines prior to the enactment of legislation.[9]

Most state commissions were hesitant to permit bus competition with interurban lines because they recognized that such competition would in some cases make it impossible for an interurban to continue operation, and (particularly in the early years) they typically took the position that interurban service was superior to bus service. Their decisions, however, were based on their evaluation of the adequacies of existing service, the importance of ensuring its continuation, and the advantages offered by bus service. Only rarely was a denial of a bus application based on the argument that the electric lines should be "protected."

To be sure, policies differed somewhat from state to state, but the majority followed the lead of California, Pennsylvania, Illinois, and New York and restricted bus competition severely. In contrast, the Michigan commission and a few others took the opposite position and granted bus certificates without regard to electric railway service.

In 1916–17 the right of the California Railroad Commission to regulate motor transport was established in the courts and by legislation. In October 1917, in the Blue Star Auto Stages case, the commission denied the right of this company to operate buses between Oakland and Danville, arguing that existing railway service was entirely adequate [75]; it thus extended the doctrine laid down in September in the Santa Clara Valley

Auto Line case [76] that a certificate would not be granted a bus operator if existing bus service was adequate. In November of 1919 a certificate was denied for bus service from Los Angeles to San Pedro on the ground that existing electric railway and bus service was adequate. In 1919, not only was an application of a bus line to compete with the Visalia Electric between Visalia and Lemon Cove denied, but the company was forced to begin its line at the Lemon Cove terminus of the Visalia Electric; it was not permitted to overlap even for through business beyond the electric line's territory [77].

The doctrine thus established before 1920 was in general followed throughout the subsequent years. In 1922, in denying an application for bus service competing with the Pacific Electric line in the San Bernardino area [78], the commission stated that there must be clear evidence that existing facilities were inadequate or unsatisfactory before competition would be allowed. A bus line was denied permission to compete with the San Francisco Napa and Calistoga in 1924 [79] and again in 1927, both times because the existing service was considered adequate. In 1928 bus competition with the Pacific Electric line between Hollywood and Ocean Park was denied on this basis, as well as on the ground that the Pacific Electric service was essential and would be endangered by bus competition. In a 1930 case, bus competition against the Petaluma and Santa Rosa was similarly denied, the commission pointing out that the ability of the electric line to continue service would be impaired. Once again, the commission stressed the rule developed years before: as long as an existing rail line provides adequate transportation service, it is entitled to protection from the competition of motor transport.

In the light of this general philosophy, not only in California but in other states with similar legislation, the burden of proof was placed on the applying motor carrier to demonstrate the necessity of the service. The service had to be more than convenient; it had to be necessary in terms of the interests of large numbers of users. Necessity did not mean indispensability, but to prove necessity meant to prove that the existing service was inadequate. In hearings on this question, commissions frequently looked into the frequency, speed, and quality of rail service; they also listened to witnesses for both sides and gave attention to petitions on behalf of bus companies. Sometimes applicants were able to demonstrate the inadequacy of existing service; more often they were not, even when they went to the trouble of presenting witnesses in their favor. The California commission, among others, recognized that users of the service would often favor the impossible: the establishment of the new service and the retention of the old as well.

All this should not imply, of course, that the California interurbans lacked bus competition. On routes between larger cities, such as the Central California Traction Company's Stockton–Sacramento line and the Sacramento Northern's Oakland–Sacramento run, bus service had been initiated before 1917, and such carriers had received certificates on the basis of grandfather-clause rights. Only rarely was new bus competition permitted by the commission.

Pennsylvania also took a strict stand on motor transport at an early date, and stuck to it throughout the life of its electric lines. The basic policy was laid down in 1917 in the case of *Alleghany Valley Street Ry. Co. v. Greco* [80] : a bus line would not be given a certificate so long as electric railway service was adequate. This was reaffirmed and extended in a number of succeeding cases. In 1921 the commission denied an application to establish bus service between Chester and Darby on the grounds of the importance of retaining street railway service and the adequacy of existing service. This ruling was repeated in the Southern Pennsylvania Traction Case in 1921, in which the commission took a very extreme position, namely that even the inadequacy of existing rail service was not sufficient justification for a bus permit—the rail carrier must first be given an opportunity to improve its service. In 1924, in the case *Re Gray* [81], permission to establish bus service competing with West Penn Railways was denied on the grounds that the existing service was adequate and that competition under the circumstances would be wasteful.

In permitting the abandonment of the Bristol–Doylestown line in 1923, the Pennsylvania commission referred to the low incidence of electric line abandonments in that state, which it attributed in large part to the policy of preventing bus competition.

The third major state in which bus competition was severely restricted was Illinois. The Illinois commission assumed control over motor carriers in 1914. It later held that it had no power over carriers doing an intercity business, but this interpretation was overruled by the state Supreme Court in 1919 in *P.U.C. v. Bartonville Bus Line* [82]. The commission had already established the rule of denying permission to establish bus competition with street railways, and following the Bartonville decision, this rule was extended to interurban operations. In 1921 bus competition with the Chicago and Joliet was denied on the grounds that it would result in reduced electric railway service and higher over-all cost; the commission stated specifically that it would not permit bus service paralleling electric railway lines so long as the service of the latter was adequate [83]. Both points were reaffirmed in 1923 and upheld by the state Supreme Court in the Chicago and West Towns case [84]. In 1923, in *Re T. L. Clark Truck Company* [85], the commission also denied a certificate to a bus line seeking to operate between Danville and Georgetown in competition with Illinois Traction.[10] In later years, however, the Illinois commission liberalized its policy with court sanction and allowed the development of extensive bus competition with the passenger service of the Illinois Traction system and other lines.

The New York commission gained power over motor carriers at an early date (1915), lost some of it by legislation in 1916, and regained general control in 1919. New York's policy was on the whole substantially less restrictive than that of Pennsylvania, California, or Illinois; the commission held that the requirement of convenience and necessity did not involve absolute necessity. Sometimes the commission accepted the interurban argument; in 1915, for example, in the Gray's Petition case [86], an application for a bus line on Long Island was denied on the ground that electric railways needed protection against bus competition to survive. More often, however, bus applications were judged in terms of relative service. Thus in 1927 a bus line was permitted to compete with the New York State Railways between Sherrill and Oneida in order to bring to an end rush-hour crowding of cars. In 1917 bus competition with the electric lines in Troy was permitted so long as the lines were well removed from car lines [87]. In 1924, in the case *Re Jamestown-Fredonia Transit,* bus competition with an interurban was permitted because it eliminated the need for transfer of cars. In the *Re Bee Line* case in 1925, bus competition with an electric line was permitted, after previously being denied, because the railway had not improved its service.

The Ohio commission did not gain control over motor carriers until 1921, and thus many bus lines benefited from grandfather-clause rights. But the law gave the commission power to grant motor-vehicle certificates only if existing transportation facilities failed to meet or could not be made to meet the needs of public convenience; the motor service must be *necessary*—not merely convenient. The courts interpreted the law to mean that rail carriers whose service was adjudged inadequate must be given a chance to improve it before bus competition was allowed; and the Ohio Supreme Court increased the commission's tendency to deny applications by its decision in the Cincinnati Traction case [88], in which it held that the commission had granted a permit without properly weighing the evidence.

In a major case in 1924, *Re J. B. McLain* [89], the request to establish a bus line between Columbus, Chillicothe, and Portsmouth in competition with both the Scioto Valley and an independent bus line between Chillicothe and Portsmouth was denied. The commission rejected the applicant's contention that only the evidence of existing motor transport could be considered, observing that it was obliged to consider all existing transportation facilities to ensure their conservation. The commission noted the adequate service of the Scioto Valley, its extensive unused capacity, the danger of abandonment if the decline in traffic continued, and the lack of assurance that the bus line could provide adequate service if the electric line was abandoned.

In 1929 the commission did permit the Cannonball bus line to extend its service from Chillicothe to Columbus instead of connecting with the Scioto Valley at the former city, on the grounds that the gains to the public outweighed the loss to the company, but it denied the bus company the right to pick up and carry local passengers within the territory of the Scioto Valley. This principle became generally recognized by most states.

In 1928 the Ohio commission, contrary to its general policy, permitted the establishment of a bus line in direct competition with a portion of the Stark Electric. The Stark appealed to the Ohio Supreme Court, which reversed the commission's decision, pointing out its failure to consider the effects of the bus line upon existing carriers; upon further appeal, the United States Supreme Court upheld the Ohio Supreme Court. Such court decisions would have been impossible in states in which the law made no reference to existing carriers.

In Indiana motor-carrier regulation was not introduced until 1925, by which time the state's interurban lines were virtually all paralleled by bus lines. The commission, therefore, was not able to alter the situation materially. In the relatively few cases that did arise, however, it took a position similar to Ohio's. In 1928, for example, the right to establish bus competition with a portion of the THI&E was denied on the ground that increased competition with existing carriers was unsound. In a similar case in 1926, bus competition against the Union Traction line between Union City and Winchester was denied. In the same year, however, in the case *Re Gary Railways* [90], a bus line was granted a certificate for operation between Gary and Crown Point despite competition with a rail line that was suffering serious financial difficulties. Two considerations led to this decision: first, there appeared to be little chance that the rail line could adequately provide all the service needed in a rapidly growing area, and, second, in large measure the rail and bus routes were not adjacent.

In 1927 the Wisconsin commission gained the right to deny bus line applications if rail service was adequate. By this time, however, the Wisconsin interurbans were already suffering severely from bus competition; the Milwaukee lines survived for a long period largely because of superior service. The West Virginia commission, which gained control of motor carriers in 1923, took an extremely severe stand against bus competition, a major factor in the relatively long survival of some interurbans in that state. Maryland (*Re W. L. Dean* [91]), Colorado (*Re Paradox Land and Transport Co.* [92]), and Washington (*Re N. H. Stedman* [93]) all indicated that they would not permit bus competition if existing service was adequate. Iowa followed the same policy, which prolonged the life of many of its interurbans.[11]

A basically different policy was followed in Michigan. In 1923 the Michigan commission granted permission to the Wolverine Transportation Co. to operate buses between Detroit and Mt. Clemens, a route served by the Rapid Railway. When the interurban appealed the decision (*Rapid Railway Co. v. Michigan P.U.C.* [94]), the commission took the position that since the state motor-carriers act specified merely that certificates should be granted on the basis of public convenience and necessity, it could not consider the effects of proposed bus lines on existing rail carriers. The Michigan Supreme Court upheld this position, pointing out that the act in no way indicated that a policy of protecting railroad interests was intended, the aim of the legislation being merely to control highway usage. One member of the Court vigorously dissented.

The consequences of the Rapid Railway decision were far-reaching; the policy it affirmed was without question a major reason why the Michigan interurban network—physically one of the best in the country—collapsed before those of neighboring states. Virtually the entire network was gone by the end of 1930.

Many interurbans themselves set up bus lines in time to receive grandfather-clause rights, to which they as well as independent carriers were entitled. In other instances they sought bus certificates at the same time as independent operators, and most state commissions (notably Pennsylvania's) gave them preference, indicating the advantages of coordinated service and the disadvantages of competition. This policy, it may be noted, was directly contrary to the Interstate Commerce Commission's policy relating to truck lines.

Some interurbans did not seek to install bus service (as a supplement to or in lieu of rail service) until after independent operators had entered the field. State commissions differed in their handling of such applications. For example, the International Railway was authorized to replace Buffalo–Tonawanda service in 1937 by buses even though an independent bus line served the route, and the East Bay Street Railways of Oakland was permitted to do the same with its suburban Hayward line in 1933, but the California commission restricted the bus-operating rights of the Sacramento Northern to prevent competition with established lines of the River Auto Stages.

In their early decisions the commissions were often influenced by the limited finances and inadequate equipment of the bus operators, and by the fact that some had operated unlawfully before seeking a certificate. The applicants for bus permits argued that bus service was "modern" and interurban service "outmoded," and that by ruling against buses the commissions would be checking progress. The analogy of the canal boat and the railroad was often put forth, but the commissions typically disregarded this line of reasoning, basing their decisions on the specific nature of the services in a particular area. As time passed, interurban service deteriorated and lines were abandoned, whereas the general quality of bus service and the financial stability of the industry continued to improve. Consequently, some commissions (Illinois, for example) became increasingly liberal in granting bus certificates, feeling that the interurban was ultimately doomed. Other commissions, however, maintained their protection so long as the interurbans wished to continue passenger service. And in some cases, as we have seen, interurbans whose service was demonstrably inadequate were given the chance to improve it before bus competition was authorized.

In contrast, the protection of interurban freight service from truck competition was generally limited from the outset, partly because of the greater advantages that trucks offered over rail carriers, and partly because of the difficulties in controlling private trucking. The decision in the Utah case *Re Wedgwood* in 1921 [95] is typical: trucks were permitted to operate between Salt Lake City and Ogden in competition with the Bamberger and with steam roads on the ground of superior service. The commission stressed that it must not bar progress. It reaffirmed this position in 1924, when it allowed the establishment of truck service from Ogden to Garland.

In Ohio, in 1932, the Lake Shore Electric sought to prevent the Norwalk Truck Line from receiving a certificate to operate between Bellevue and Elyria, parallel to its tracks, by arguing that its own LCL service adequately served the territory. In rebuttal the truck line pointed out that although the electric line operated through the town of Berlinville (pop.: about 100), it had no freight facilities closer than Berlin Heights, more than a mile away; and the traffic manager of a Toledo textile wholesaler testified on Norwalk's behalf that direct service to Berlinville would be to his interest. This and similar evidence that expanded door-to-door service would be useful won the franchise for Norwalk.[12] The Lake Shore had attempted in 1927 to prevent Norwalk from increasing the size of its fleet of trucks under its original certificate, but failed to do so.[13]

The Pennsylvania commission, in several early cases, did attempt to prevent truck competition. In a 1921 case it denied a certificate to a truck line to operate from Pittsburgh to Butler because it would result in losses for the interurban line between these two points; in 1923, in *Re Endicott*, it took a similar position in denying truck competition with electric lines in the Erie area, on the grounds that although the trucks would serve some persons better, the decision must be based upon the over-all need for electric railway service. After about 1925, however, there was little or no restriction of truck competition in Pennsylvania or elsewhere.

On the whole, the interurbans had no reason to criticize the motor-carrier policies of the various state commissions. If anything, these policies protected the interurbans to a surprising degree, although in practice the significance of this protection was often greatly lessened by the grandfather clauses. In the period in which interurban service was clearly superior to bus service, and it was obvious that traffic would not support both, the commissions with substantial justification resisted popular demands for competing bus service. On the other hand, the charge of impeding progress was largely groundless: most commissions clearly did not preserve interurban passenger service after it had become economically obsolete. Had state regulation of motor carriers been established earlier, some of the best interurban lines would have lasted longer—perhaps a decade longer in some instances—but their ultimate abandonment would not have been prevented.

FINANCIAL CONTROL

In most states, commissions did not exercise any significant control over the interurbans' security issues, consolidation arrangements, and other matters of the industry's finance until the interurban network was well established. The only exception was Massachusetts; after 1893 the state commission exercised detailed control over interurban security issues, and prevented stock watering by requiring that stock be issued only for cash, and for sums not less than par value. The amount of bonded indebtedness was subject to control after 1909. These measures prevented the overcapitalization so common in other states, although control over short-term borrowing was inadequate; but they interfered in some cases with adequate financing. Above all, they made it difficult to rehabilitate weak roads, and thus encouraged the consolidation of weak and strong trolley lines, to the ultimate detriment of the latter. The Massachusetts commission made no effort to check this consolidation.

In other states financial control came so late, if at all, that it was not highly effective. Consolidation was typically permitted, and usually meant the strengthening of the roads. In one major case, however, the Indiana commission in 1929 temporarily prevented the merger of the THI&E with the Insull properties, primarily on the ground that the electric railways would not carry their share, as they were essentially being supported by the power companies involved in the merger.

After 1920 the I.C.C. gained power over the finances of the interurbans subject to its control, as was noted above in the case involving Western Pacific control of the Sacramento Northern. Typically the I.C.C. approved requested security issues and the financial arrangements of the interurbans, but in at least one case it compelled a change in plans; when the Southern Pacific sought control of Central California Traction, the objections of the other carriers led to the development of a plan whereby the Western Pacific, Southern Pacific, and the Santa Fe shared jointly in ownership [96]. The Northwestern Pacific's purchase of the Petaluma and Santa Rosa was initially denied but ultimately realized, as President Maggard of the NWP reportedly purchased personally the controlling stock in the P&SR.

In 1935 Congress enacted the Public Utility Holding Company Act; the Securities and Exchange Commission interpreted the provisions concerning the elimination of holding-company systems to require that the power companies divest themselves of their electric railway affiliates and dissolve the pyramided holding company structures. As a consequence, the interurbans that were elements in the holding company systems were separated, usually by public sale of the stock. This was the fate of Illinois Terminal, originally owned by Illinois Power Company, the West Penn, the Ohio Public Service, the Portland Traction lines, the Milwaukee system, the Monongahela West Penn, and others. Most interurbans had been abandoned before the act became effective.

OTHER ASPECTS OF GOVERNMENT RELATIONS WITH THE INTERURBANS

A few of the interurbans, chiefly the first lines to be built, received government grants of money and land, but in general such assistance was rare. Canadian roads were aided much more liberally. As the industry began to decline and the abandonment of many lines became imminent, several states acted to provide aid via property tax relief. The Maryland legislature provided exemption for the Washington Baltimore and Annapolis in 1934 but failed to extend it in 1935, and the result was the immediate abandonment of the road. Much more widespread action was taken in Ohio in 1933, when all interurbans were temporarily freed from property taxes, so long as they were not paying dividends. This measure, however, did not prevent wholesale abandonments. In other states, although no formal relief from taxes was usually provided, assessments of interurban property were often drastically scaled down in conformity with the principle, commonly accepted in state valuation of utility property for tax purposes, that the assessed value figure should primarily reflect the earnings of the company.

In the United States local governments very rarely undertook the operation of an interurban line, and such action was confined to intercity trolley lines rather than interurbans in the strict sense. In Massachusetts, when the weak Northern Massachusetts was abandoned in 1924, two local transportation districts were formed to take over segments of the line. The towns of Athol and Orange operated the line of that name, and the Greenfield and Montague was formed in the Greenfield–Turners Falls area. The former had seven miles of line, the latter nine. Both operated with considerable success for several years, finally replacing the electric lines by buses. The Greenfield and Montague outlasted most of the New England rural trolley lines.

Another instance was the San Mateo (California) line of the United (later the Market Street) Railways. This line originally had many characteristics of an interurban, but in later years was essentially a suburban streetcar line, although operated with interurban-type cars. It passed into the ownership of the city of San Francisco in 1944 and was abandoned in 1949. In 1958 the remaining passenger service of the Pacific Electric (by then operated by the Metropolitan Coach Lines) was acquired by the Los Angeles Metropolitan Transit Authority. When the Chicago Aurora and Elgin discontinued passenger service in 1958, efforts were made to sell the line to the state of Illinois or the Chicago Transit Authority, but without success. When the Milwaukee Electric abandoned its East Troy line in 1939, the village of East Troy acquired a seven-mile segment connecting the town with the Soo Line, and has continued to operate it for freight service.

In Canada (as will be noted in Part II) extensive plans for publicly owned lines were developed in the period between 1912 and 1922 in the province of Ontario, but these were never carried out.[14] However, three lines in that province passed into the hands of municipalities, and were operated for a time by the Ontario Hydroelectric Power System. The Sandwich Windsor and Amherstburg was purchased by the municipalities in the Windsor area from Detroit United Railways in 1920, operated until 1934 by the Ontario Hydro, and after that by the municipalities themselves. The neighboring Windsor Essex and Lake Shore was purchased in 1929 by the municipalities it served in order to forestall its abandonment, and was operated under contract by Ontario Hydro until abandonment in 1932. The Toronto and York Radial system, with an interurban line from Toronto to Sutton, on Lake Simcoe, and suburban lines to Port Credit and West Hill, was purchased by the city of Toronto in 1921. Ontario Hydro operated the system for the city until 1927, and thereafter the city operated it until abandonment. A portion of the Port Credit line was incorporated into the city system and is still operated as a streetcar line. The London and Port Stanley was owned by the city of London and the Nipissing Central by the Province of Ontario.

When the Canadian National Railway system was formed, it inherited several electric lines from its predecessors, including the Toronto Suburban, the Niagara St. Catharines and Toronto, and the unfinished (and never finished) Toronto and Eastern. The NStC&T was retained, the other two lines abandoned. The CNR also inherited the Montreal and Southern Counties, which it operated until 1957. In 1951 it bought the Quebec–St. Joachim line from the Quebec Railway Light and Power Company, and obtained ownership of a good entrance into Quebec City for its main line to Murray Bay. The Quebec–St. Joachim service, essentially suburban, was abandoned in March 1959—one of the last electric passenger operations in either Canada or the United States. The last true interurban operation in either country was the Thorold–Port Colborne run of the NStC&T; it, too, was discontinued in March 1959. Government ownership was clearly a factor contributing to the long life of many of the Canadian interurbans.

CITATIONS

1. Mass. PSC, 1916; 38. 244 Mass. 462
2. 3 Penn. PSC 552
3. 3 Penn. PSC 609
4. 92 NW Rep. 583
5. 145 Wisc. 13
6. 223 NY 244
7. Ore. RR Com. Report, 1914, 99
8. 7 ICC 83, 1897
9. 13 ICC 20, 1907
10. 230 US 324, 1913
11. 60 ICC 600, 1921
12. 65 ICC 728
13. 67 ICC 452
14. 71 ICC 653
15. *Ibid.*, pp. 656–57
16. 79 ICC 167
17. 138 ICC 363
18. 286 US 299
19. 154 ICC 603
20. 166 ICC 625
21. 158 ICC 101
22. 150 ICC 649
23. 162 ICC 673
24. 175 ICC 699
25. 189 ICC 395
26. 202 ICC 359
27. 219 ICC 135
28. 208 ICC 193
29. 234 ICC 13
30. 305 US 179, 1938
31. 229 ICC 48
32. 233 ICC 612 and 619
33. 240 ICC 359
34. 242 ICC 9
35. 242 ICC 45
36. 271 ICC 705
37. 290 ICC 765
38. 38 ICC 281, 1916
39. 226 US 474, 1925
40. Mass. PSC, 1914; 107
41. 13 ICC 20, 1907
42. 13 ICC 250, 1908
43. 20 ICC 486, 1911
44. US v. Baltimore and Ohio Southwestern, 226 US 14

45. 26 ICC 226, 1913
46. 30 ICC 653, 1915
47. 59 ICC 122
48. 59 ICC 496, 1922
49. 27 ICC 499
50. 3 Penn. PSC 458
51. NY RR COM. 1902; 255
52. 252 ICC 273
53. 138 ICC 363, 1928
54. 267 US 330, 1925
55. PUR 1916F 338
56. 13 CRC 545, 1917
57. 24 CRC 57
58. PUR 1928E, 347
59. 251 US 396, 1921
60. 12 Penn. PSC 291
61. 30 Wisc. RR Com. 435
62. 31 Wisc. RR Com. 617
63. PUR 1918E 877
64. PUR 1919B 251
65. PUR 1922E 690
66. 193 ICC 239
67. 242 ICC 9, 573, and 275 ICC 649
68. 275 ICC 649
69. 162 ICC 594
70. 202 ICC 359
71. 207 ICC 603
72. 25 CRC 457
73. 42 CRC 598
74. 11 Pet. 420
75. 14 CRC 198
76. 14 CRC 112
77. 16 CRC 874
78. PUR 1922D 495
79. 25 CRC 65
80. PUR 1917A 723
81. 7 Penn. PSC 1
82. 290 Ill. 574
83. 1 Ill. CC 131
84. 309 Ill. 87
85. PUR 1923A 325
86. PUR 1916A 33
87. PUR 1917A 700
88. 122 Ohio St. 699
89. PUR 1924B 188
90. Ind. Dec. 587M
91. PUR 1920C 972
92. PUR 1924E 572
93. PUR 1925D 812
94. PUR 1924B 585
95. PUR 1921D 262
96. 131 ICC 125, 1927

6

Finance

A complete picture of the financing, financial control, and financial successes and failures of the interurbans would depend on more information than is available. Nevertheless, the data are more adequate than for most industries, and permit a fairly detailed outline of the interurbans' finances. We have relied chiefly upon data published by the various state commissions, the Interstate Commerce Commission (after 1920), Poor's and Moody's Manuals for the various years, and company reports.

The pattern of initiation and development of interurban companies varied substantially. Some of the roads, particularly the earlier ones, were the offspring, directly or through a subsidiary, of the street railways. For example, the Illinois Traction Company came into being when William B. McKinley, a Champaign investment broker, acquired the local street railways in Champaign and Danville, and expanded them into what was to become one of the largest interurban systems. Union Traction of Indiana was the creation of Charles L. Henry, an Anderson lawyer, who, like McKinley, first entered the traction field by purchasing the local car lines. Other interurbans were promoted by local businessmen unaffiliated with the street railways: the Bamberger was developed by a pioneer Utah coal-mine operator, Simon Bamberger, and the Arkansas Valley by a group of Wichita businessmen. The Kankakee and Urbana was the project of Dr. C. A. Van Doren, an Urbana dentist, who was aided by several prominent Urbana businessmen. In some instances families primarily involved in other fields became interested in interurbans; the Balls of Muncie owned the Muncie and Portland and owned stock in the Union Traction Company; the Krogers of Cincinnati owned the Cincinnati Milford and Loveland; and H. J. Heinz was a backer of the Winona.

A number of lines, mostly in the Midwest, were promoted by syndicates formed by large urban financial interests, which frequently controlled other utility and industrial empires as well. Many of the leaders of these syndicates had little first-hand experience with the transportation business. They sought out potential routes, established separate companies, had the lines built, and retained control over them, often with very little financial investment on their own part. Chapter 1 discusses the chief syndicates of Ohio and Indiana; other syndicates operated two or more interurban networks in widely separated areas. One of the Ohio groups, for example, started the Washington Baltimore and Annapolis, and the Fisher group developed lines not only in Pennsylvania but in Illinois as well—the Illinois projects were intended as part of a through line from Chicago to St. Louis. The Siggins brothers, after developing interurbans around Warren, Pennsylvania, turned their attention to southeastern Kansas and built the Union of Kansas and the Southwestern Interurban. The Von Echa syndicate of Harrisburg concentrated on several small lines in Ontario, including the Grand Valley, the Woodstock Thames Valley and Ingersoll, and the Hamilton–Brantford line (which was finally completed by other interests).

The capital structure of the early companies typically showed total par value of stock and maturity value of bonds of about the same magnitude; a 1914 sample of 146 companies operating 9,300 miles of track (about 60 per cent of the industry) indicated total debt outstanding of $382 million and stock of total par value of $443 million. About one-fourth of the stock was preferred. The total reported cost of road and equipment for these companies was $794 million. Most of the funds, however, came from the sale of bonds, the stock often being issued to the promoters without equivalent dollar investment in the enterprise. The net result was substantial overcapitalization and reported figures of cost of road and equipment in excess of the actual cost. The amount of water in the stock varied from line to line, but for the roads as a whole it was probably at least 25 per cent of the total capitalization. Some companies sold stock to the public (Arkansas Valley, for example), and their issues were freely quoted on the exchanges, but often the stock was closely held and not regularly traded. A few companies, among them the Dayton and Troy, departed from the usual pattern and were free of debt from the beginning. On the other hand, some roads—such as the Northern Electric and the Indianapolis and Louisville—were plagued by debt in excess of any reasonable cost figure. A few, such as the Visalia Electric, were financed almost entirely by advances from the parent company (in this case the Southern Pacific).

The bonds were sold to a variety of interests. Sometimes the contracting firms took them in payment, as happened with the Chicago and Joliet. Some bonds, such as those of the Grand Valley, were acquired by General Electric, which in the early years of electric traction sought by this means to aid the development of the industry. In rare cases the promoters put up all the funds and acquired the bonds as well as the stock, but most commonly the bonds were sold to banks or investment banking firms, and either held by them or sold to their clients. Boston, Cleveland, and later Philadelphia were major centers for interurban bond financing.

COSTS OF CONSTRUCTION

It is difficult to obtain accurate data for construction costs, since the figures reported in the statements of the companies reflect some watering. When construction was financed almost entirely by the issuing of bonds (stock being issued to the promoters for little or no cash investment), the cost of road and equipment was written up to approximate the total capitalization. In the sample covering 6,400 miles for 1909, the reported average cost of road and equipment (including power facilities) was about $60,000 a mile. Variation among roads was substantial, however. For some of the earliest lines, built on highway rights-of-way and with minimum standards, the cost probably averaged about $10,000 a mile. For example, the 22-mile line of the Hamilton Grimsby and Beamsville was built in 1896 for a reported $271,707. Lines built around 1900 to low standards, with limited terminal costs but on private rights-of-way, cost around $20,000 a mile. In 1909, for example, the Mason City and Clear Lake showed a book investment of only $21,000 a mile, the Springfield and Washington $15,000, and the Bloomington Pontiac and Joliet $20,000.

As costs and construction standards increased, and the quality of equipment improved, the total cost rose markedly. The Washington Baltimore and Annapolis, primarily double-track, reportedly cost $175,000 a mile, the Detroit Monroe and Toledo Short Line $132,000, the 1917 high-speed Buffalo–Niagara Falls line $225,000, and the North Shore's Skokie Valley line $271,000. The Skokie Valley line was by no means typical, however, because of its unusually heavy and expensive construction. A careful study of construction costs was made by the Ontario Hydroelectric Power Commission when it was planning a network of electric railways just after World War I; the proposed system as a whole was estimated at $140,000 a mile, and the most expensive segment, from Toronto to St. Catharines, at $280,000 a mile.

As improvements were made and new equipment was added, the average reported book cost of existing line reached $80,000 in 1914 and about $85,000 in 1924. By 1924 the reproduction cost was undoubtedly at least this high, since the water in the earlier figures had been largely squeezed out by rising price levels. But this did the interurbans little good, except to hold the rate of decline in the return on investment down to less than the rate of the rise in the operating ratio.

On the basis of these cost data, some estimate of the total investment in the industry can be made. The 1914 figure of $794 million total investment for 9,300 miles of line comes to $85,400 per mile; if this figure is applied to the total interurban mileage of about 16,000 miles, the over-all investment in road and equipment would have been about $1.36 billion. In view of the initial tendency to overstate actual cost and equipment, this 1914 figure was undoubtedly excessive, the actual figure being nearer $1 billion. Considerable amounts, however, were spent for modernization after 1914, to bring the total sum, up to the period of disintegration of the industry, to perhaps $1.2 billion. Had the industry been built in the 1920's, the cost would have been in excess of $1.6 billion and perhaps as much as $2 billion, considering increased land values.

FINANCIAL RESULTS IN THE PEAK YEARS

The financial history of the interurban industry was a very unhappy one, characterized by only moderate profits in its best years, and a less than typical return during most of the seven decades of operation. In the years of rapid expansion, investment in interurbans was based primarily on expectations of greater earnings in the future rather than of a high current return. When these expectations did not materialize, further expansion was largely out of the question, and within a short period of time the development of the motor vehicle initiated the secular decline.

Several terms used in the subsequent analysis must be explained. The *rate of return* is the ratio of earnings, after taxes and depreciation but before interest payments, to the reported figure of capital investment in road and equipment. *Operating ratio* refers to the ratio of operating expenses to operating revenues. Thus if the expenses are one-half the revenue, the ratio is 50 per cent; other things being equal, the lower the ratio, the better the earnings position. Taxes have been included with operating ex-

TABLE 6—STATISTICS OF ELECTRIC INTERURBAN RAILWAYS, 1889–1959

Year	Miles built*	Miles abandoned†	Miles in service‡	Operating ratio, %	Rate of return, %	Car orders
1889	7	0	7	—	—	—
1890	0	0	7	—	—	—
1891	66	0	73	—	—	—
1892	54	0	127	—	—	—
1893	146	11	262	—	—	—
1894	52	0	314	—	—	—
1895	225	0	539	—	—	—
1896	224	0	763	—	—	—
1897	214	0	977	—	—	—
1898	338	0	1,315	—	—	—
1899	223	0	1,538	—	—	—
1900	569	0	2,107	—	—	—
1901	1,015	0	3,122	—	2.1	—
1902	1,488	0	4,610	—	2.6	—
1903	1,521	0	6,131	—	2.9	—
1904	1,113	0	7,244	—	2.7	—
1905	696	0	7,940	—	2.7	—
1906	1,056	0	8,996	—	2.9	1,204
1907	1,478	0	10,474	59	2.7	927
1908	1,074	23	11,525	60	2.8	727
1909	597	0	12,122	59	2.8	1,245
1910	684	0	12,806	58	3.1	990
1911	500	0	13,306	59	3.2	626
1912	556	10	13,852	63	3.1	783
1913	668	16	14,504	63	3.2	547
1914	611	20	15,095	68	2.8	384
1915	444	36	15,503	67	2.7	336
1916	116	39	15,580	67	2.8	374
1917	85	103	15,562	67	3.0	185

Finance

TABLE 6 (*Concluded*)

Year	Miles built*	Miles abandoned†	Miles in service‡	Operating ratio, %	Rate of return, %	Car orders
1918	52	144	15,470	75	2.7	255
1919	29	70	15,429	76	3.0	128
1920	0	92	15,337	79	3.0	227
1921	13	102	15,248	84	2.1	107
1922	15	237	15,026	81	2.3	128
1923	51	220	14,857	83	2.3	253
1924	51	264	14,644	85	2.2	170
1925	0	302	14,342	87	1.8	177
1926	45	689	13,698	91	1.1	139
1927	34	510	13,222	91	1.1	116
1928	0	914	12,308	90	0.9	53
1929	0	869	11,439	93	0.5	69
1930	0	1,017	10,422	101	—0.5	35
1931	0	1,219	9,203	101	—0.9	40
1932	0	1,303	7,900	115	—1.3	2
1933	0	1,029	6,871	110	—0.8	0
1934	0	548	6,323	106	—0.6	0
1935	0	294	6,029	104	—0.3	0
1936	0	124	5,905	100	0.0	0
1937	0	494	5,411	105	—0.6	0
1938	0	798	4,613	105	—0.7	0
1939	3	902	3,711	101	—0.1	8
1940	0	514	3,197	100	0.0	0
1941	0	505	2,692	97	0.6	10
1942	0	5	2,687	87	3.1	0
1943	0	7	2,680	88	3.0	0
1944	0	0	2,680	87	3.7	0
1945	0	16	2,664	89	3.5	0
1946	0	214	2,450	96	1.1	8
1947	0	316	2,134	99	0.3	0
1948	0	296	1,838	—	—	0
1949	0	83	1,755	—	—	0
1950	0	236	1,519	—	—	0
1951	0	262	1,257	—	—	0
1952	0	240	1,017	—	—	0
1953	0	167	850	—	—	0
1954	0	59	791	—	—	0
1955	0	393	398	—	—	0
1956	0	64	334	—	—	0
1957	0	52	282	—	—	0
1958	0	73	209	—	—	0
1959	0	0	209§	—	—	0

SOURCE: See Fig. 7, p. 190.
The sign — means that figures are not available. After 1947 there is no suitable base for comparison with earlier years.
* This figure does not include line relocations.
† Abandonments consist of discontinuance of all service, or of passenger service only, if the latter occured first.
‡ Miles in service figures consist only of miles in passenger service.
§ Applications to abandon 99 miles of the remaining trackage were before the I.C.C. or state regulatory commissions as of March 1960.

penses in calculating these ratios, partly because the principal taxes paid were local property levies, and partly because the tax data were not segregated in many of the profit and loss statement summaries.

The data are imperfect in several ways. First, as we have seen, the investment figures were frequently exaggerated, with the value of road and equipment written up to equal the inflated total capitalization figures. Not until later decades, after most roads were built, were such practices effectively prevented by regulation. As a consequence, the actual rates of return were somewhat better than the reported figures; the reported figures, however, give some indication of the general level of return, and a good measure of trends in earnings. Second, in the expense figures of the earlier years depreciation charges were often absent or inadequate, a feature that tended to offset the overvaluation of assets in so far as the rate-of-return figure is concerned. Third, there are no data at all for some companies, especially in the pre-1912 period, when many did not issue profit statements and figures are not available from state regulatory agencies. Finally, many companies were closely affiliated with transit and power enterprises, and the financial results were not always broken down by type of activity. Thus the choice of firms for the sample studies had to be made in part on the basis of availability of data.

Two procedures were used in building up the data of return on investment. First, six years, roughly at five-year intervals (1902, 1909, 1914, 1920, 1924, and 1929), were selected, and data collected for all companies for which information was available, typically about half of the companies, and well over half of the mileage. For 1902 data of the Bureau of the Census were employed. Second, a smaller sample of firms whose earnings reflected the general trend in the key years was selected, and earnings data were calculated for each year. The primary sample, carried through the period from 1906 through 1930, consisted of fourteen typical companies* whose earnings fitted the general pattern in the key years very closely except for 1920; World War I and its aftermath affected various companies so differently that a sample suitable for other years does not fit precisely. A separate sample was required for the period prior to 1906, since so few of the primary sample firms were in operation in this period. Likewise, it was necessary to select a different sample to carry the figure beyond 1930, since the typical road was abandoned in the period between 1927 and 1933.

On the basis of this data, Figure 1 shows the typical rate of return for

---

* The companies were the Auburn and Syracuse; the Rochester Lockport and Buffalo; the Bamberger; the Indianapolis and Southeastern; the Olean Bradford and Salamanca; the Cleveland Southwestern; the Lake Shore; the Scioto Valley; the Toledo Fostoria and Findlay; the Pittsburgh Harmony Butler and New Castle; the Wilkes-Barre and Hazleton; the Central California Traction; the Warren and Jamestown; and the San Francisco Napa and Calistoga. Not all of these were in operation for all the years covered.

the industry for the period from 1900 to 1914; the data for the subsequent years are presented in Chapter 7 in the analysis of the decline of the industry. One of the most surprising features is the very high stability of the rate of return over the entire period from 1901 to 1914 (and on to 1920), the range being between 2.6 per cent and 3.2 per cent. The rate increased very noticeably from 1901 to 1903, remained almost stable at a figure slightly under 3 per cent to 1909, and then rose to a high of 3.2 per cent in 1913. The comparatively low rate of return is also surprising, considering the rapid expansion of the industry. Although the actual return on invested capital was clearly somewhat better than the 3 per cent indicated, it could not have exceeded 4.5 to 5 per cent at best. Expansion was clearly taking place on the basis of expectations of improved earnings from population growth, and not because of a high current profit. Very few companies paid dividends in this period.

For the year 1902, financial results of a sample of forty larger interurban systems, with total mileage of 1,870, were included in the Bureau of the Census volume, *Electrical Industries, 1902*; subsequent Census studies did not segregate interurbans in such a way as to make the data usable. For these firms the operating ratio was 60, and the rate of return approximately 3 per cent. Fifteen per cent of the companies had ratios better than 50 per cent, nearly two-thirds had ratios between 50 and 70 per cent, and 6 per cent had operating deficits. The rate of return figure was based upon reported capitalization, which clearly overstated actual investment. Interest consumed $2.1 million out of $2.8 million net after taxes, and only $200,000 was paid in dividends, on stock of a total par value of about $150 million. Seven of the companies paid dividends on preferred stock (of the eleven that had this type of stock), and eight of the forty paid on common stock. Only 13 per cent of the stock outstanding received dividends.

The 1909 sample, compiled from reported data for the companies, is a much larger one, which shows results basically similar to those for 1902. In all, 111 companies, with 6,441 miles of line, about 56 per cent of the total in that year, were included. The gross revenue was $38 million, and the operating expenses $23 million, yielding a net of $14 million. But this constituted only a 2.8 per cent return on reported investment, and interest consumed $12 million of the $14 million profit. Only 24 lines showed a return of better than 5 per cent, and two (the Mattoon–Charleston and the Morris County) showed operating deficits. Operating ratios averaged 61, with a range from 40 for the Chippewa Valley and 44 for the Olean Bradford and Salamanca to over 100 for the deficit roads. Of the large systems, the Lake Shore showed an operating ratio of 54 and a return of 3.1 per cent; the Northern Ohio 54 and 4.8 per cent; the Union of Indiana 57 and 5.5 per cent; and the THI&E 56 and 3.7 per cent.

From 1909 to 1914, the gross revenues of the roads in the sample study

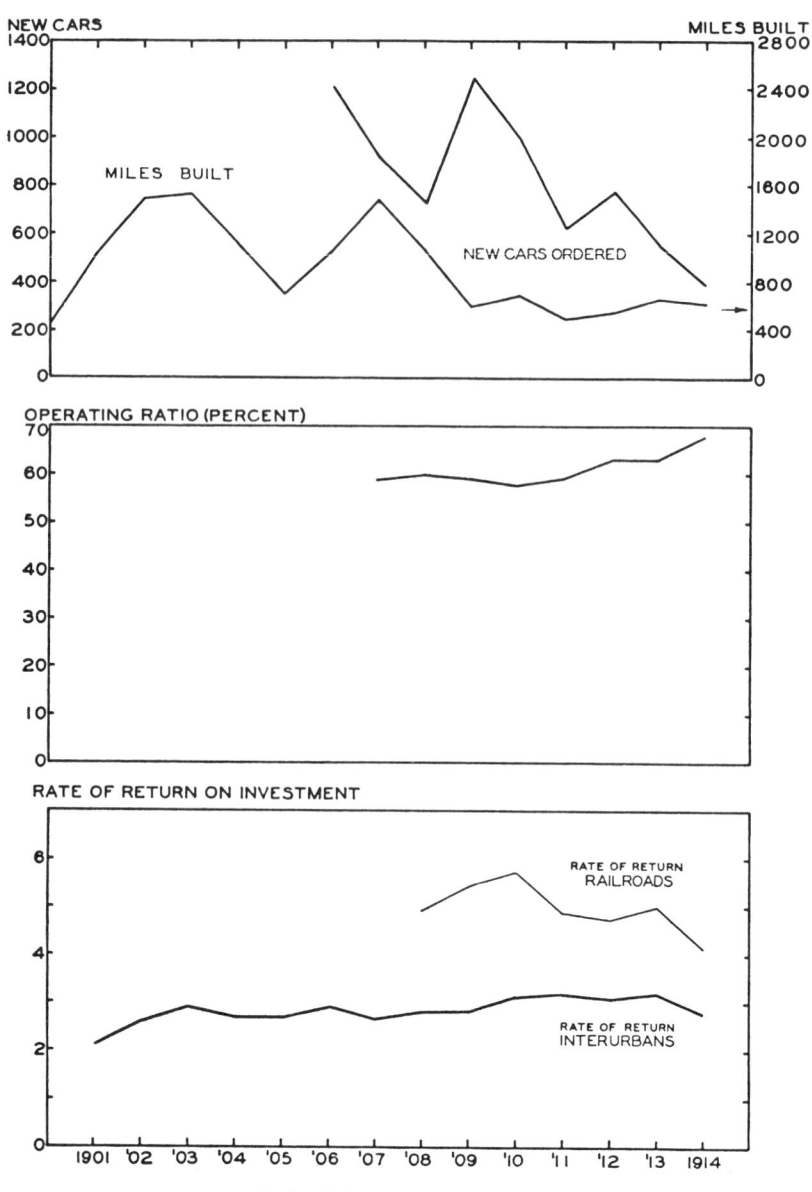

FIGURE 1. Statistics of Interurbans, 1900–1914

Figures of car orders were obtained from lists of new equipment reported in the *Electric Railway Journal*. Figures of miles built were obtained from data for individual roads. Rate of return and operating ratios were calculated from the data for the sample firms. Figures of railroad rate of return (offered for comparison) were obtained from *Annual Reports*, Interstate Commerce Commission.

rose steadily, but operating expenses grew still faster; thus the operating ratio rose gradually from 59 to 68, but net revenues increased enough in dollar terms to increase the rate of return slightly, from 2.8 to 3.2 per cent in 1913, one of the best financial years in the history of the industry; it then fell back to 2.8 in 1914. The number of new interurban cars purchased fell very drastically in this period, from the high of 1,245 in 1909 to 384 in 1914. With minor exceptions, this trend was destined to continue unbroken down until 1933, when no new cars were ordered.

The large sample for 1914 consisted of 143 roads, with 9,312 miles of line; it showed a substantial increase in revenue per mile over 1909, as well as higher revenue and profits totals, and approximately the same rate of return on investment (2.7 per cent). This sample was larger than the one for 1909; if the identical roads are used in the two samples, the 1914 rate of return is slightly better, the newcomers of the period being on the whole somewhat less profitable than the older lines. Three roads (The Albany Southern, the United of Oregon, and the Grand River Valley) showed deficits; three others (the Toledo Fostoria and Findlay, the Nashville–Franklin, and the Sand Springs) showed returns in excess of 10 per cent on reported invested capital. But the percentage of companies with returns in excess of 5 per cent had fallen sharply, from 22 to 11 per cent of the total. Perhaps the most significant indicator that all was not well was the substantial rise in the operating ratio to 66 per cent; although the volume of business was continuing to rise, the firms had to face an even faster rise in total expenses. The earnings picture after 1914 will be presented in the following chapter.

ELEMENTS IN OPERATING EXPENSES

The exact breakdown of operating expenses varied with time and the circumstances of a given road. In earlier years, direct car-operation expenses accounted for about 34% of the total, on the average; power, 23%; maintenance of way and maintenance of equipment, each 11%; general expenses, 19%; and miscellaneous, 3%.[1] In 1907, operating expenses constituted 56% of revenue, rentals 10%, and taxes 3%, to give a combined figure of 69%; interest accounted for 22%, 4% was added to surplus, and 4% was paid out in dividends. As time passed, power expenses fell substantially and transportation expenses increased; an estimate of costs for the proposed Hydro Radial lines in Ontario in 1920, based on experience of other roads, suggested power costs of from 13% to 14% of the total, and transportation costs as high as 39%. By 1924, maintenance-of-way costs had risen to 18% of the total, exceeding power (16%); transportation costs were about 35%, maintenance of equipment 12%, and general, 15%.

Typical costs per car mile (including all operating expenses) were about 12 cents in 1902, 15 cents in 1907, and 35 cents in 1924, most of the increase occurring after 1914. The costs obviously varied among lines; for example, in the 1919–20 period, the THI&E reported costs per car mile of 45 cents; the Detroit United, 42 cents; the Lake Shore, 41 cents; the North Shore, 39 cents; and the WB&A, 32 cents. The small systems typically had lower figures.

The actual direct out-of-pocket costs per car mile were about 10 cents in 1907 and 20 cents in 1924. At the customary fare of 2 cents a mile, only five passengers per car mile were necessary to cover out-of-pocket cost in 1907, or eight passengers to cover all operating expenses. Wage rates roughly doubled between 1910 and 1920, but this was offset in part by the shift of many lines to one-man operation. Materials costs increased about 50 per cent over the period.

As with railroads, a portion of interurban costs were fixed and could not be adjusted in light of changes in traffic. But the extent to which operating expenses could be adjusted was much greater than might be expected, as is shown in Figure 6 (p. 223). For the Indiana interurbans, for example, when revenue fell from $14 million in 1928 to $11.4 million in 1930, expenses fell from $13.4 to $11.2 million. In succeeding years, as traffic fell, expenses continued to fall sharply, in part because of the abandonment of lines. Figure 4 (p. 216) shows a similar pattern for the sample study. The reductions in expense were attributable to reduction of car mileage, which lessened all expenses relating directly to transportation, and to a decrease in maintenance expenditures.

However, there were in practice definite limits to the adjustability of expenses. When changes in traffic were too small to permit a reduction in car mileage, virtually no expense adjustment was possible. The maintenance-expense reductions were often only temporary; if service was to be continued, higher expenditures would become necessary. Finally, there were certain levels below which expenses could not be reduced; there were minimum maintenance figures, and if service was cut back too sharply, its usefulness was almost completely destroyed. Once traffic fell below a certain figure, therefore, further declines could not be accompanied by expense reductions.

The one type of cost that could not be reduced by a company was interest. Consequently, a company with the typical heavy debt compared to total capitalization could be thrown into bankruptcy by even a slight loss in traffic.

A significant question, in terms not only of the history of the industry, but of economic analysis in general, is that of the relationship of cost per passenger mile to traffic density. We cannot determine this relationship precisely, but it can be approximated by a study of the relation between revenue per mile and the operating ratio: given the high degree of uniformity of fares per mile, the operating ratio is a fair reflection of the relative cost per passenger mile. Figures 2a and 2b present scatter diagrams for the sample of roads included in the 1914 and 1924 studies.

The charts show a definite inverse relationship, up to a certain point, between the revenue per mile and the operating ratio, indicating that greater traffic volume did not bring proportional increases in total operating expenses. The data, of course, reflect both short-run and long-run economies of large-scale production. The chart also suggests that when a certain level of business is reached, further increases do not reduce direct expenses per unit of business. The roads having the heaviest traffic density were the suburban area roads, which on the whole had less favorable operating ratios than other firms with lesser but substantial density. This can be attributed partly to higher wage levels, partly to greater peak load problems.

The charts show a substantial dispersion due in part to the following limitations of the data: (1) fares per mile were not entirely uniform; (2) the volume of freight traffic varied somewhat among the roads, and freight costs may not have followed the same patterns as those of passenger traffic; and (3) other elements in the picture, such as the average length of trip and the extent of purely streetcar operation, varied, as did wage rates and other expenses.

The analysis includes only direct costs, since costs arising out of the fixed investment (interest, for example) are not reflected in the operating ratio. If these other costs were taken into consideration, the tendency for average cost to fall as revenue increased would be strengthened.

It is also obvious from the data that a road simply could not operate with revenue per mile less than a certain figure in a given year. The data suggest that in 1914, for instance, a road could not cover operating expenses with revenue of less than about $1,500 a mile, whereas in 1924 the figure was about $3,000. But even with revenue of $1,500 a mile there was no chance of earning a reasonable return on investment; with this figure and an 80 per cent operating ratio, a 5 per cent return could be obtained only if the investment were no more than $6,000 a mile. And even in 1914 it was virtually impossible to build a line for less than $20,000 a mile. With an operating ratio of 70 per cent (about the best that could be expected in 1914 for light-density roads), to earn 5 per cent on a typical cost figure of $30,000 a mile would have required a gross revenue of $5,000 per mile.

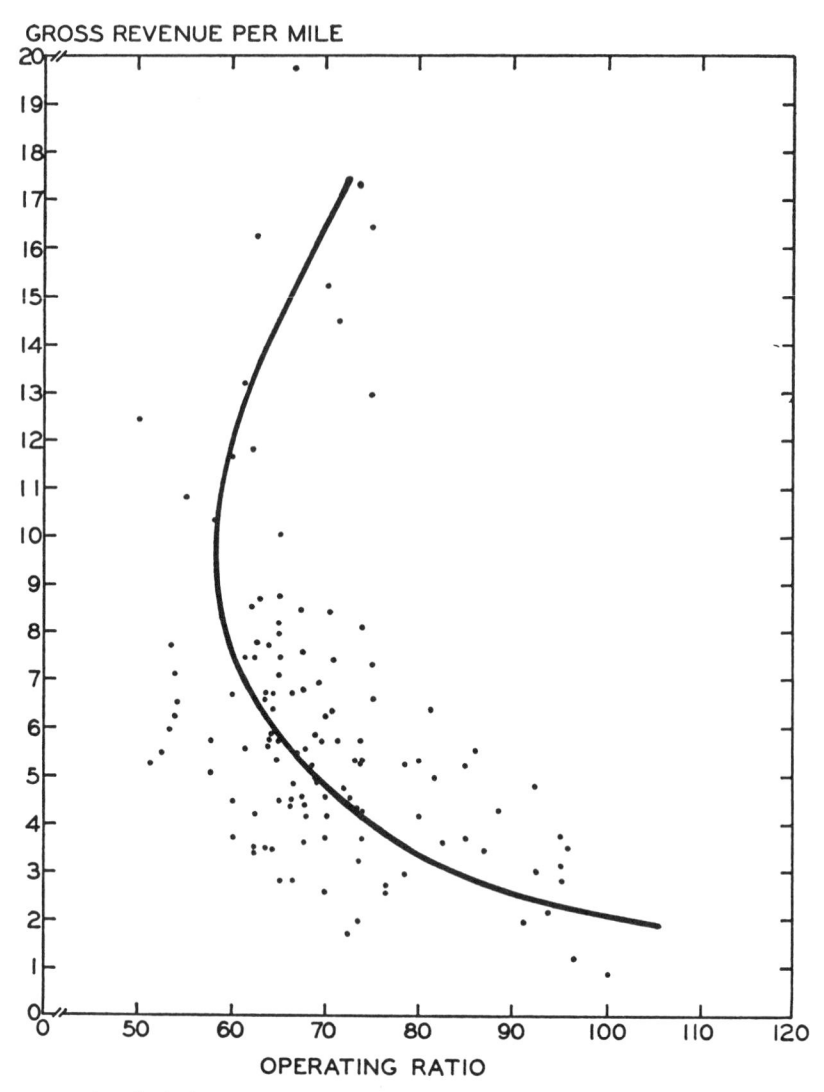

FIGURE 2a. Relationship Between Operating Ratio and Gross Revenue Per Mile in Thousands of Dollars (118 Interurbans, 1914)

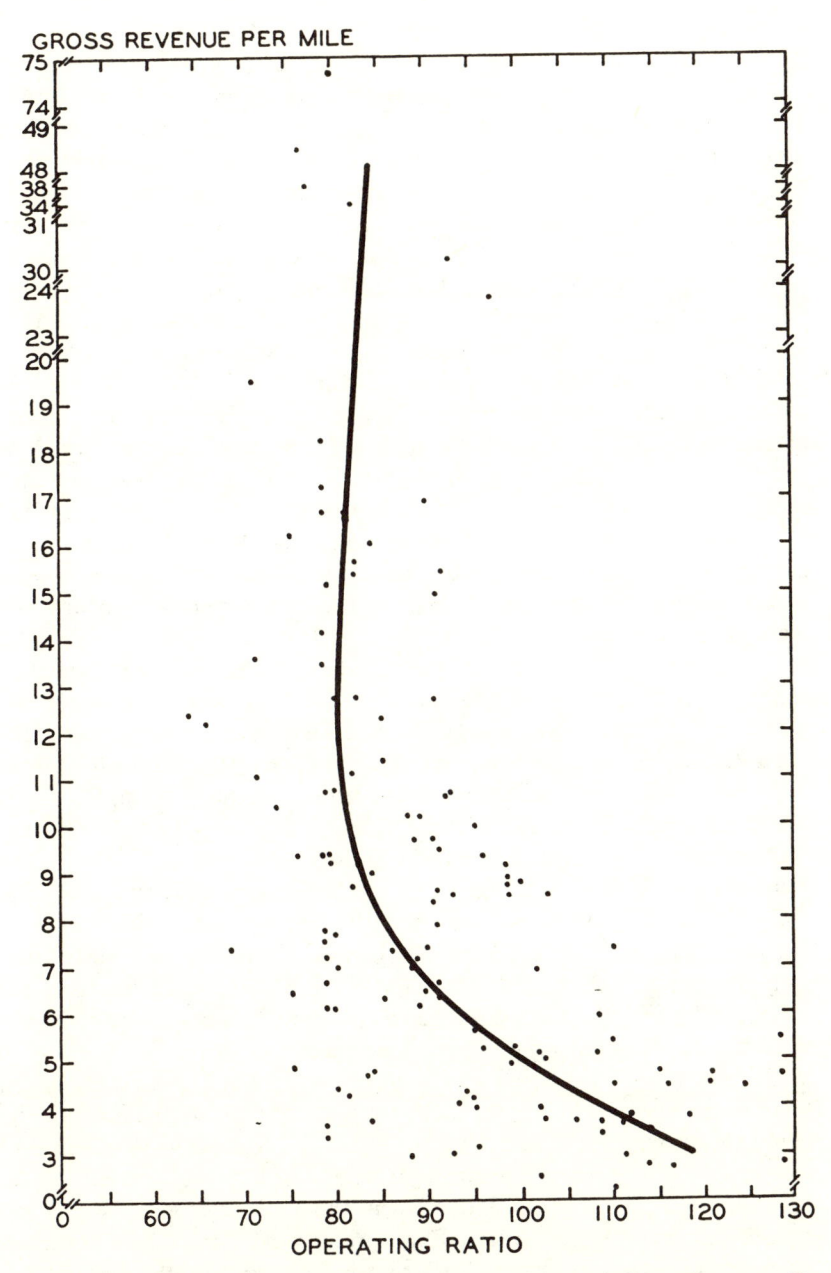

FIGURE 2b. Relationship Between Operating Ratio and Gross Revenue Per Mile in Thousands of Dollars (124 Interurbans, 1924)

BANKRUPTCY AND REORGANIZATION

The typical interurban line, financed largely by debt, and at best capable of earning only a relatively low return, quickly fell into bankruptcy. Except for captive roads held above water by their railroad or power company owners (such as the Peninsular and the Oregon Electric), and for a very few others enjoying particularly favorable earnings positions or an exceptional freedom from debt, all the interurbans went bankrupt at one time or another, and often several times. Some lines, such as the Buffalo Lockport and Rochester, were in bankruptcy before they even got fully under way, being unable to meet obligations in the period of building. The very long period that frequently elapsed between initial construction and final completion was an inherent source of difficulty.

Typically, however, the roads survived their early lean years, and encountered difficulties only as their traffic began to decrease, or as costs rose sharply, for example, during the World War I period. The net profit margin of the typical road was so slight that any adverse condition could bring on a financial crisis, and few roads were able to build up any significant cash reserve. During the late twenties, bankruptcy became increasingly common; a few roads avoided it by abandoning operations before they were obliged to default.

Usually at least 10 per cent of the mileage of the industry was owned by companies in bankruptcy. For example, in 1909, 23 companies, with 1,187 miles, were operated by receivers. The total included not only small roads but such larger ones as the Indianapolis and Cincinnati, the Eastern Ohio Traction, the Buffalo Lockport and Rochester, and the Washington Baltimore and Annapolis. In 1920, 36 roads, with 1,398 miles, were in receivership, including the Aurora Elgin and Chicago, the Western New York and Pennsylvania, Buffalo and Lake Erie, and the Denver and Interurban. The 1924 figures show 30 companies with 1,981 miles bankrupt, including the Northern Electric, the Michigan, the Union of Indiana, and the Indiana Columbus and Eastern; the Cleveland Southwestern emerged from receivership during the year. There were, of course, numerous steam railroad bankruptcies during this period as well.

Except when conditions were hopeless, receivership eventually led to foreclosure sale and reorganization, the control typically passing to the bondholders, with the old stockholders (many of whom in the earlier years had invested little money) being squeezed out. Many of the earlier reorganizations brought little reduction in the total debt outstanding, and thus did not solve the difficulties. For example, the Chicago and Interurban went into receivership for the fourth time in 1922; none of the previous reorganizations had reduced the debt, yet the road had never been able to earn interest on its bonds except in the most favorable years. After 1920 reorganizations were often much more drastic, resulting in a sharp scaling down of debt; this was true to some extent of the various companies that became the Cincinnati and Lake Erie. The Bamberger and the Salt Lake and Utah reorganizations in the late thirties likewise greatly reduced debt outstanding.

By the twenties the roads were encountering considerable difficulty in obtaining funds for modernization, yet it was evident to the management of many companies that new equipment offered the only possibility for survival. In some instances limited funds were obtained from bondholders upon reorganization, but primarily the roads turned to the equipment trust technique, just as the railroads did in this period. The Cincinnati and Lake Erie, the Indiana Railroad, and other roads were able to dispose of equipment trust certificates (which were essentially agreements whereby they rented the equipment from the trustees, and thus the payments gained priority over existing interest claims). Most of the funds invested in these certificates were, of course, ultimately lost.

FINANCIAL CONTROL

With respect to financial control the interurbans fell into several patterns, whose relative importance varied over time: complete independence, absorption into larger interurban networks, affiliation with electric power companies, and control by holding companies, steam roads, or city transit systems. Some 162 companies, with a total of about 35 per cent of all interurban mileage, remained independent throughout their operations. About 6 per cent of the total mileage became part of such large interurban systems as the Cincinnati and Lake Erie, the Lake Shore system, and (earlier) the Ohio Electric Railway. About 3,700 miles of interurban properties were affiliated with electric power companies; of this, all but 250 miles eventually became subject to holding company domination. The holding companies also gained control over some 1,832 miles of interurban properties not directly affiliated with power companies (such as the North and South Shore lines and the Indiana Railroad), and 480 miles affiliated with city transit systems. In all, about 5,800 miles (36 per cent) eventually passed into the holding company network. Steam railroads controlled 28 companies (2,170 miles); city transit systems not subject to the control of holding companies had direct control over 16 companies, operating 1,059 miles. In many instances, steam railroad or holding company control came only after many years of local independent or local power company control, and in some cases holding company domination lasted for only a few years.

Independent Companies

The Bamberger is a good example of the many interurbans that remained independent enterprises, promoted, owned, and managed by local interests. Such lines were financed by bonds sold both locally and to more distant interests. First as a steam road, and ultimately as an interurban, the Bamberger was promoted, financed, and developed by the Bamberger family of Salt Lake City, who also had investments in coal mines and other interests, but were primarily concerned with the railway. Not until 1956 was the road sold to outside investors. Other good examples of local control include the Kankakee and Urbana, the Waterloo Cedar Falls and Northern, the Arkansas Valley Interurban, the Evansville Suburban and Newburgh, the Olean Bradford and Salamanca, the Dayton Covington and Piqua, the Rock Island Southern, the Illinois Central Electric, and the Utah-Idaho Central. Many other roads that began as locally promoted enterprises eventually passed into the hands of other enterprises—for example, the Petaluma and Santa Rosa.

Closely related to this form, but on a larger scale, were the independent interurban systems of substantial magnitude, formed by extending early lines and building or acquiring additional lines. Several examples, including the Union Traction of Indiana, the Everett-Moore properties, the Illinois Traction, and the Ohio Electric, were noted in Chapter 1. The Ohio Electric collapsed in 1921, and out of its constituents was developed, in the late twenties, the Cincinnati and Lake Erie.

In a few instances, lines that were independent of other utilities were controlled by industrial firms. Thus the Hershey Transit was owned by the Hershey Chocolate Company, the Kaydeross by paper mills and later by a bank, and the Northeast Oklahoma by Eagle-Picher, a lead-producing company.

Power Company Affiliates

The interurban developed in the same period as the electric power industry, and the same firms often controlled both enterprises. In some instances an interurban company entered the power field simply as a means of selling electricity generated in excess of what it required for its cars. In other cases, the power companies built the interurbans, in part to increase the use of power. The exact relationships varied widely. Sometimes, especially in later years, the operation of an interurban was a very incidental part of the operation of a large power system; the Mattoon–Charleston and Southern Illinois lines of Central Illinois Power are examples, and the tiny Roby and Northern (in Texas) is an even more extreme case. In other cases both types of activity were important, as with the interurban lines operated by Puget Sound Power and Light, the Illinois

Traction line (Illinois Power), the lines operated by Northern Indiana Power and Indiana Service, and others. In some cases one corporation provided both electric power and interurban service (Southern Indiana, Potomac Edison, and Virginia Electric Power, for example); in others the rail enterprise was a separate, subsidiary company (e.g., Pacific Northwest Traction and Boise Valley Traction).

In the long run most of the utility-affiliated interurbans became elements in holding company systems. But a few, including the Iowa Southern Utilities line and the Cedar Rapids and Iowa City, did not. In some instances holding company control came at only a very late date, as with the Northern Ohio Traction and Light line and the Portland Electric Power Company.

City System Affiliates

Several interurbans were directly affiliated with large urban transit systems, either as integral parts of the city operations or as subsidiary companies. Among the city systems that directly operated important interurban lines were International (Buffalo), Detroit United (an Everett-Moore property for many years), Pittsburgh Railways (although originally the interurbans were separate companies), Oklahoma Railways, York Railways, and Conestoga Traction. Interurbans directly affiliated with large city companies included the Louisville and Interurban, the Des Moines and Central Iowa, the various affiliates of Reading Traction, the Denver and Intermountain, the Toronto and York Radial, and the THI&E. Networks integrating large city and interurban lines together with electric power distribution included the Milwaukee Electric Railway and Light system and the Portland (Oregon) Electric Power Company system. Apart from these cases, of course, many city systems operated long suburban car lines that could scarcely be classed as interurbans (the Market Street Railway of San Francisco, East Bay Street Railways of Oakland, Baltimore Transit, the Washington, D.C., systems, Utah Light and Traction, and St. Louis Public Service, as well as the extensive New England operations). On the other hand, many interurbans operated city service incidental to the main-line operations.

The Holding Company Empires

By the 1930's successive mergers and expansions of holding companies had brought most of the electric power companies under the control of a few large systems. About half the total electric power output was provided by three systems—Electric Bond and Share, United Corporation, and the Insull group. These holding companies were, with a few exceptions, primarily interested in electric power, gas, and, in some instances, water systems, but as they acquired control of these utilities, they fell heir to a number of interurban lines. The exceptions, in which the holding companies deliberately acquired extensive interurban properties, were the Insull and the American Waterworks systems.

The Insull Empire. The Midland United-Midwest Utilities system was by far the most important of the holding companies in which the interurbans played a major role. This system was developed primarily by Samuel Insull, aided by the investment banking firm of Halsey, Stuart and Co. With headquarters in Chicago, the company centered its attention on the Midwest, although it included properties in New England and elsewhere. Originally the company was primarily concerned with power companies and confined its interurban properties largely to a few power company affiliates, notably:

1. The Central Illinois Public Service properties, including the Chicago and Joliet, the Southern Illinois, and the Mattoon–Charleston line.
2. The Chicago and Interurban Traction Company.
3. The Illinois Northern Utilities line—the Sterling Dixon and Eastern.
4. The Wisconsin Power and Light interurban lines.
5. The Interstate Public Service line, representing the consolidation of the roads from Indianapolis to Louisville.
6. The tiny Roby and Northern, in Texas.
7. The Pittsburg County, in Oklahoma.
8. The Portland–Lewiston Interurban.
9. A group of upper New England intercity trolley lines, including those of the Central Maine Power Company, the Manchester and Nashua, and the Portland Railroad.

In the 1920's, by gaining control over National Electric Power Company, the Insull interests also acquired a group of Pennsylvania companies, including the interurban lines of the Scranton Railway, the York Railways, the Altoona and Logan Valley, and the Lewistown and Reedsville. (National had also controlled the Youngstown and Suburban, but sold it to independent interests.) The Kentucky Traction Company (Lexington) and the Columbus Delaware and Marion also came under Insull control.

In addition, the Insull group acquired control of three Chicago area roads, the North Shore, the South Shore, and the Chicago Aurora and Elgin. The CA&E had been modernized under the direction of Dr. Thomas Conway, Jr., who had originally been sent to represent the interests of the bondholders. Insull proceeded to modernize the North Shore and the South Shore and to provide high-speed entrances for them into downtown Chicago. He then began to acquire additional Indiana interurbans, including those in the Gary area, the Indiana Service Corporation, the Northern Indiana Power Company, the Fort Wayne and Northwestern, and in 1930, the big Union Traction system, purchased at a foreclosure sale. Out of these lines in central and southern Indiana, together with the Interstate, he formed the Indiana Railroad, which he partially modernized. A year later he acquired the bankrupt THI&E, originally a Schoepf-McGowan property, which had been in financial difficulties for several years. Control was gained over the Winona, but it was never merged into the Indiana Railroad. The interurban losses, together with the general financial mismanagement of the system, caused the whole empire to collapse in 1932. The interurbans that survived (the North Shore and the South Shore) were reorganized and gained independent status. The Indiana Railroad was operated by a receiver for several years prior to abandonment.

The North American Company. The North American Company was one of the pioneer holding companies; it developed in Milwaukee out of the Milwaukee Electric Railway and Light Company and then spread into other areas. The most important of its interurban properties were those of the original Milwaukee company; in addition, it owned the Wisconsin Traction Company, with its interurban from Neenah to Kaukauna (but not the Wisconsin Power and Light lines); the important East St. Louis and Suburban system; and the tiny Keokuk-Warsaw line. It also controlled the Washington Railway and Electric Company, which operated several suburban lines.

In 1926 both the North American Company and the Insull interests sought control of the North American Light and Power Company, which owned the vast Illinois Traction system, including the Chicago Ottawa and Peoria and the Cairo and St. Louis. As we have noted, this system had been built up by William B. McKinley with the aid of Canadian capital; as McKinley's interests turned to politics, the control of the system passed into the hands of Clement Studebaker of the South Bend automobile family. An agreement was reached between the North American Company and the Insull group to divide equal minority control of North American Light and Power (including Illinois Traction) between them, leaving direct management control in the hands of Studebaker. When the Insull system failed in 1932, North American acquired full control of Illinois Traction, which it retained until it was broken up under the terms of Federal legislation in the late 1930's.

The American Waterworks and Electric Company. One of the most extensive networks of interurbans, including several lines that lasted until a very late date, was developed by the American Waterworks system, which controlled a far-flung empire of water systems and a network of electric power companies fanning out from the Pittsburgh area. The interurban properties consisted of:

1. The West Penn Railways (including the Alleghany Valley), an extensive system of suburban-interurban lines forming an arc around Pittsburgh on the north, east, and southeast. There was no financial connection with Pittsburgh Railways.

2. The Monongahela West Penn Railways, a system of interurbans in the Fairmont-Clarksburg area in West Virginia, and in the vicinity of Marietta, Ohio.

3. The Wheeling Traction lines, connecting Wheeling with Steubenville and other nearby cities. There were several underlying companies, which at times operated independently, including the Steubenville Wellsburg and Weirton.

4. The Potomac Edison (Hagerstown and Frederick) lines in central Maryland, together with the connecting Chambersburg Greencastle and Waynesboro.

Stone and Webster Properties. The Stone and Webster system differed somewhat from many holding companies in the greater emphasis placed on management supervision and engineering development as opposed to purely financial control; for example, a Stone and Webster engineer developed the Birney car. The system was primarily interested in large urban power systems, and gained control over only those interurbans that were affiliated with the power systems. The properties were very widely scattered, as the following list of interurban holdings suggests, but there was some concentration in Texas and the Pacific Northwest.

1. The Northern Texas Traction Company, including its subsidiary the Tarrant County Traction Company. This company also operated the Fort Worth city lines.

2. The Galveston–Houston Electric Railway, one of the most profitable interurbans over many years.

3. The East Texas Electric Railway, in the Beaumont-Port Arthur area.

4. The important Puget Sound properties, including the Pacific Northwest Traction line—ultimately the North Coast Lines—and the Puget Sound Electric Railway.

5. The Virginia Electric Power Company's Richmond–Petersburg line.

6. The Houghton County Traction Company, in upper Michigan (later disposed of to Central Public Service).

The General Electric Affiliates: Electric Bond and Share and the American Gas and Electric Company. In the early days of the power and traction industry, the General Electric Company and its predecessors, in order to develop the market for its products, aided in the financing of many utility enterprises by purchasing their bonds and stock. In 1905, Electric Bond and Share was incorporated to take over these holdings and to extend General Electric's efforts to build up the utilities. The emphasis on power companies increased and that on electric railways decreased, but nevertheless Electric Bond and Share and its affiliates maintained control over several interurban properties, among them:

1. Boise Valley Traction, an affiliate of Idaho Power Company.
2. The Texas Interurban, an affiliate of Dallas Railways.
3. Lehigh Valley Transit.
4. Conestoga Traction.
5. Valley Railways (in the Harrisburg area).
6. Ohio Service Company (Cambridge).
7. Ohio Valley Electric Railway (Ironton), later disposed of to Central Public Service.
8. Southern Pennsylvania Traction and affiliated companies in southeastern Pennsylvania.
9. Benton Harbor–St. Joe Power and Light.
10. The Walla Walla Valley, before its acquisition by Northern Pacific.

United Corporation, including Commonwealth and Southern. In the late 1920's, under the auspices of the Morgan and Bonbright investment banking firms, the United Corporation was formed to bring together a number of subsidiary holding companies. The most important of these, from the standpoint of interurbans, was the Commonwealth and Southern Corporation, which had been formed from various companies, primarily in Michigan and in the South.

The interurban properties of Commonwealth included:

1. A large portion of the Michigan interurban network, including the Michigan Railway, the Michigan Electric Railway, and the Grand Rapids Holland and Chicago.
2. Two Illinois lines, the Rockford and Interurban (disposed of in the mid-twenties), and the De Kalb Sycamore and Interurban (abandoned in 1923).
3. Southern Indiana Power (Evansville–Patoka).
4. Interurban lines in the Atlanta area affiliated with Georgia Power, plus the Gulfport and Mississippi Coast and the Laurel–Ellisville line in Mississippi.
5. Northern Ohio Traction and Light and the Penn-Ohio system, control over which was obtained in the late twenties.

Associated Gas and Electric. The Associated Gas and Electric Company, the Mange-Hopson system, was in some respects the largest of all the holding companies. But its interurban properties were not of primary importance, and most were not obtained until the 1930's, many being grouped together under a subsidiary holding company called Railway and Bus Associates. These included two former General Gas and Electric properties: (1) The Reading Traction Company and its affiliates, including the Oley Valley, Schuylkill Valley, and Lebanon Valley lines; and (2) the Salisbury and Spencer, in North Carolina, hardly an interurban. Associated's other properties were:

1. The Southern New York Railways, long an independent company.
2. The New York State Railways, Schenectady Railways, and United (Albany), acquired when these properties were allowed to go into receivership by the New York Central and the Delaware & Hudson. They were soon abandoned.
3. The Massachusetts Northeastern.

Cities Service Properties. Henry L. Doherty's Cities Service system was a combination of oil- and gasoline-producing companies and public utilities; although the former aspect was dominant, the utility holdings, including those of interurbans, were significant. The major lines were:

1. The Toledo and Indiana.
2. The Toledo Ottawa Beach and Northern, an affiliate of the Toledo city system.
3. The Ohio Public Service Company's lines, including its Mansfield and Port Clinton lines.
4. The Cumberland and Westernport.
5. The Bartlesville Interurban, in Oklahoma.
6. The St. Joseph and Savanna, an affiliate of the St. Joseph transit and power system.
7. The Grays Harbor Railway and Light (Washington).
8. The Grand River Valley, in Colorado, originally owned by the Penrose-Carlton interests.
9. In earlier years, the Toledo and Western. This property was later sold to Willys interests and the Wabash Railroad.

Others. The other holding companies had only limited interurban properties. Standard Gas and Electric owned the Pittsburgh Railways (by virtue of its control of the Philadelphia Company) and the Wisconsin Public Service Company; it also controlled the Market Street Railway in San Francisco. The United Light and Power Company owned the Mason City and Clear Lake and the Clinton Davenport and Muscatine. The Central Public Service Company owned five lines: (1) the Ohio Valley

Electric Railway (in later years); (2) the Portland Electric Power Company line; (3) the Willamette Valley Southern; (4) the Houghton County in Michigan (a Stone and Webster line before 1926); and (5) the Wheeling Public Service Company line (but not Wheeling Traction, an American Waterworks property).

On the whole, the holding company movement probably strengthened rather than weakened the interurbans, by providing greater access to capital for modernization. The money that the Insull interests poured into rebuilding the South Shore and North Shore lines in all likelihood could not have been obtained by independent interests. The affiliated power companies often bore most of the general administrative expenses of the interurbans. On the other hand, absentee control lessened community sympathy for the companies. When the holding companies were broken up by the Federal government, most of the power companies were required to divest themselves of their interurban (and city transit) affiliates, a rule followed because of the belief that the power users were subsidizing the traction properties. By this time the interurbans were near extinction anyway; the stronger properties, such as the South Shore and the Illinois Terminal, were able to survive despite separation from the power interests, and the weaker lines were doomed in any case. Some might have lasted for a slightly longer period, however, had the long-standing affiliations with the power companies been retained.

Railroad Subsidiaries

Far fewer interurbans were affiliated with railroads than with the power companies. The roads that became railroad properties were for the most part developed by independent interests, and then acquired by the railroads at a later date—in many cases not until after 1920. Railroad companies acquired interurbans for one of two reasons: to develop a unified electric and steam railroad passenger service in the territory they served (this motive was found primarily in the East, and usually before 1910); and to obtain additional freight feeder lines (a common concern of steam roads entering new territory in competition with established lines). Occasionally both motives were involved. In a very few instances the interurban was owned and operated directly by the railroad, using track also employed for steam freight trains. The principal examples, which we have noted previously, were the Erie's line from Rochester to Mt. Morris, the New York Central's Oneida Railway between Utica and Syracuse, and the Southern Pacific's lines in Oregon.

For convenience, we shall summarize here the experience in railroad ownership, classified by area and by owner. Histories of the interurbans individually may be found in Part II. We also include here important rural trolley lines owned by railroads.

NEW ENGLAND

Canadian Pacific. The Aroostook Valley Railroad was acquired by the CPR in 1931 from the Arthur Gould interests. This road, which used some CPR track from the outset, was a freight feeder for the railroad.

New York New Haven & Hartford. Under the Mellen regime, the NH acquired a vast network of New England urban and rural trolley lines, including the Berkshire Street Railway, the New York and Stamford, the Connecticut Company, the Rhode Island Company, the Springfield Street Railroad, and the Worcester Consolidated Street Railway. The high prices paid for these properties during the early years of the century, combined with the decline of the electric lines, imposed a severe drain on the NH and weakened it greatly.

Boston & Maine Railroad. The B&M owned the Springfield Terminal Railway of Vermont and formerly owned a small network of trolley lines in the vicinity of Concord, Nashua, and Manchester, New Hampshire.

THE MIDDLE ATLANTIC STATES

Baltimore & Ohio Railroad. After the end of the WB&A, the B&O operated the Baltimore & Annapolis Railroad.

Delaware & Hudson Railroad. Influenced by the same motives as the New Haven, the D&H acquired a network of lines in eastern New York, consisting of the United Traction Company (which operated an extensive streetcar system in Albany and Troy plus an intercity connection), the Hudson Valley Railway, and a half interest in the Schenectady Railway.

New York Central Railroad. In addition to sharing ownership of the Schenectady Railway with the D&H, the NYC owned the Empire State Railways, which had a large interurban and street railway network in upstate New York. The New York State Railways comprised the Oneida Railway, the Rochester and Eastern, the Rochester and Sodus Bay, and the Utica and Mohawk Valley.

Pennsylvania Railroad. The PRR's subsidiary, the Cumberland Valley Railroad, controlled the Chambersburg and Gettysburg and electrified a short portion of its own line for interurban-style service.

Erie Railroad. In addition to its electrified line at Rochester, the Erie owned three lines in the southern tier of New York and northern Pennsylvania: the Elmira Corning and Waverly, the Waverly Sayre and Athens, and the Corning and Painted Post.

Reading Company. After 1929, the Reading owned the Trenton–Princeton Traction Company.

MIDWEST

Wabash Railway. In 1924 the Wabash, jointly with the automobile manufacturer, Willys-Overland, came into control of the Toledo and Western.

Pennsylvania Railroad-Pittsburgh & Lake Erie Railroad. In 1946 these two railroads, through their jointly owned subsidiary, the Montour Railroad, came into possession of the Youngstown and Suburban.

Hocking Valley Railroad. This road, now a part of the Chesapeake & Ohio, owned the Wellston and Jackson Belt in Ohio.

Missouri Pacific. The Coal Belt Electric of Illinois was a Missouri Pacific Railroad subsidiary.

A group of eleven railroads bought the Illinois Terminal in 1956, at the time of elimination of passenger service and electrification.

Illinois Central–Chicago Rock Island & Pacific. In 1956, these two roads purchased the Waterloo Cedar Falls and Northern, and now operate it as the Waterloo Railroad.

SOUTHWEST AND ROCKY MOUNTAINS

Missouri Pacific. The MP in 1927 opened the Houston North Shore, the last interurban built.

Chicago Burlington & Quincy. Through its subsidiary, the Colorado & Southern, the Burlington controlled the former Cripple Creek District Transit, which had passed into the hands of the Colorado Springs & Cripple Creek District Railway. The latter was controlled by the Colorado & Southern from 1904 until its abandonment. The Burlington also owned the Deadwood Central in the Black Hills of South Dakota.

FAR WEST

Great Northern–Northern Pacific. The GN acquired the Spokane Coeur d'Alene and Palouse in 1927. The NP purchased the Walla Walla Valley from Pacific Power and Light in 1921. The Spokane Portland & Seattle, a railroad jointly owned by the GN and the NP, acquired both the Oregon Electric and the United Railways of Oregon.

Union Pacific. The UP owned the Yakima Valley Transportation Company in the Washington apple country.

Southern Pacific. In the San Jose area, the SP owned the Peninsular Railway. The Pacific Electric, the largest firm in the interurban industry, was promoted by Henry E. Huntington, former president of the SP, and was an SP subsidiary from 1911. Huntington personally owned the Los Angeles Railways, the local city system. The Visalia Electric served the SP as a freight feeder in the fruit-growing area around Visalia.

The Petaluma and Santa Rosa, although promoted locally, was controlled by the SP's subsidiary, the Northwestern Pacific, after 1932.

Western Pacific. The Sacramento Northern came into the hands of the WP in 1921. The San Francisco–Sacramento Railroad was later acquired and made part of the SN. The Tidewater Southern was acquired by the WP shortly after its development.

The Central California Traction Company was owned one-third each by the WP, SP, and Santa Fe after its sale by the Fleishhacker interests in 1928.

Railroad ownership resulted in the continuation of a number of lines for freight operation long after they would have been abandoned by independent operators; it was profitable for the parent railroad to continue to operate a line at a loss if its indirect contribution to the revenues of the railroad system were adequate to offset the loss. This has clearly been the case with such lines as the Oregon Electric, the Spokane Coeur d'Alene and Palouse, and the Sacramento Northern. On the other hand, the steam roads (except in New England and New York in the early days) had little or no interest in interurban passenger service, and often allowed it to deteriorate, in some instances discontinuing it at a somewhat earlier date than independent lines might have. Railroad ownership often led to higher expenses of operation, primarily because of increased union insistence on steam-road wage and service agreements.

7
The Decline of the Industry

FEW MAJOR INDUSTRIES have ever disappeared so quickly and completely as the interurban. A relatively stable if not particularly profitable industry as late as 1917, it had been decimated by the early thirties, and the lines that did survive beyond that period were able to do so only because of freight; they were no longer the typical interurban passenger carrier. By 1960 the last remnants of the interurban passenger operations had disappeared, except for a few suburban carriers, which have some interurban characteristics but are far removed from the typical interurban. A portion of the original mileage is still used for freight operation. The last truly interurban operation in America, as we have seen, was the Thorold–Port Colborne run in Canada.[1] Today, the only remaining vestiges of the typical line, particularly in the Midwest, are occasional grades and bridge abutments marking a right-of-way, scattered sections of rail working up through the asphalt covering on a town's main street, a service station or store that was once an interurban station, an old passenger car serving as a hen coop. Even these traces are rapidly disappearing.

WEAKNESSES MANIFEST IN THE PEAK YEARS

In a sense the industry never reached a high level of continued prosperity. The seeds of the decline were sown in the years of expansion, and were ripening even before the expansion was completed. Accordingly, as noted earlier, many lines never reached their planned destinations, major gaps remained between systems, and projected lines that were potentially stronger than some in operation were never built. Several major weaknesses, which indicated potential dangers and in some instances aggravated the decline, were apparent as early as 1910.

The primary indicator that all was not healthy in the industry was the relatively limited rate of return on investment in the best years. As we saw in Chapter 6, even in 1902, as well as in 1909, the average return on reported investment was no better than 3 per cent (although some individual roads did much better), and even if the most liberal allowance is made for overcapitalization, the figure did not exceed 5 per cent. In 1910, as in 1960, this was not a sufficient figure to lure additional capital into an industry, even though it might permit retention of existing investment for a long period. The industry raised as much capital as it did only because of the strong and largely unfounded optimism of investors; fairly moderate returns were expected to improve as population and the volume of business grew.

A closely related problem was the large amount of capitalization represented by debt. The over-all debt figure was nearly 50 per cent, although much greater for many companies, and the significance of the figure was increased by the general overcapitalization. As a consequence, interest ate up a large proportion of total net operating revenue, and few companies were able to pay dividends for any substantial period. Furthermore, most companies faced the constant danger of bankruptcy; and the draining of earnings for interest seriously impeded the ability of the companies to modernize by reinvesting their earnings.

Underlying these financial problems were the basic physical limitations of the interurbans. As we have pointed out, although they were superior to other modes of travel for short distances, they suffered from various disabilities that made them potentially far more vulnerable than longdistance railroad passenger service to the competition of new forms of transportation. These disabilities included lack of high-speed entrances to downtown areas, poor track construction, excessive grades and curvature, poor signal systems, and inadequate ballast. As the roads began to emphasize longer-distance travel, such limitations became more serious, yet by then the funds for major improvements were often lacking.

A final disability was the hostile attitude of many local governments to street running, which had become increasingly unpopular as time went on, with complaints out of all proportion to any real hazards to traffic—compared, for example, with the hazards presented by the large transport trucks of later decades.

The interurbans also suffered from the hostility against utility companies that was prevalent after 1900; although they were occasionally hailed as saviors from railroad monopoly, more often they were regarded with disfavor as monopolists themselves. This was particularly true when they were affiliated with city streetcar systems, which were typically unpopular in this period. One consequence, in many states, was the tendency to place excessive burdens on the companies for the use of public property.

THE PATH OF THE DECLINE

The decline of the industry began very slowly in the period immediately preceding World War I, gained momentum during the war despite the good record of many lines in this period, continued at a steady pace until 1924, and then burst forth in full strength in the late twenties, culminating in complete collapse in the early thirties. There followed the gradual disappearance of the remnants (a process interrupted by World War II), which culminated in the years between 1947 and 1953. But the typical interurban, as such, had disappeared by 1933.

Several measures of the decline are available. One is the fall in the rate of return on investment, and the ultimate development of operating deficits. Another is the cessation of construction, and the gradual increase in abandonments, as well as the decline in new equipment purchases. The financial series introduced in Chapter 6 will be carried through the years of the decline in this chapter, with detailed data for the selected years 1920,

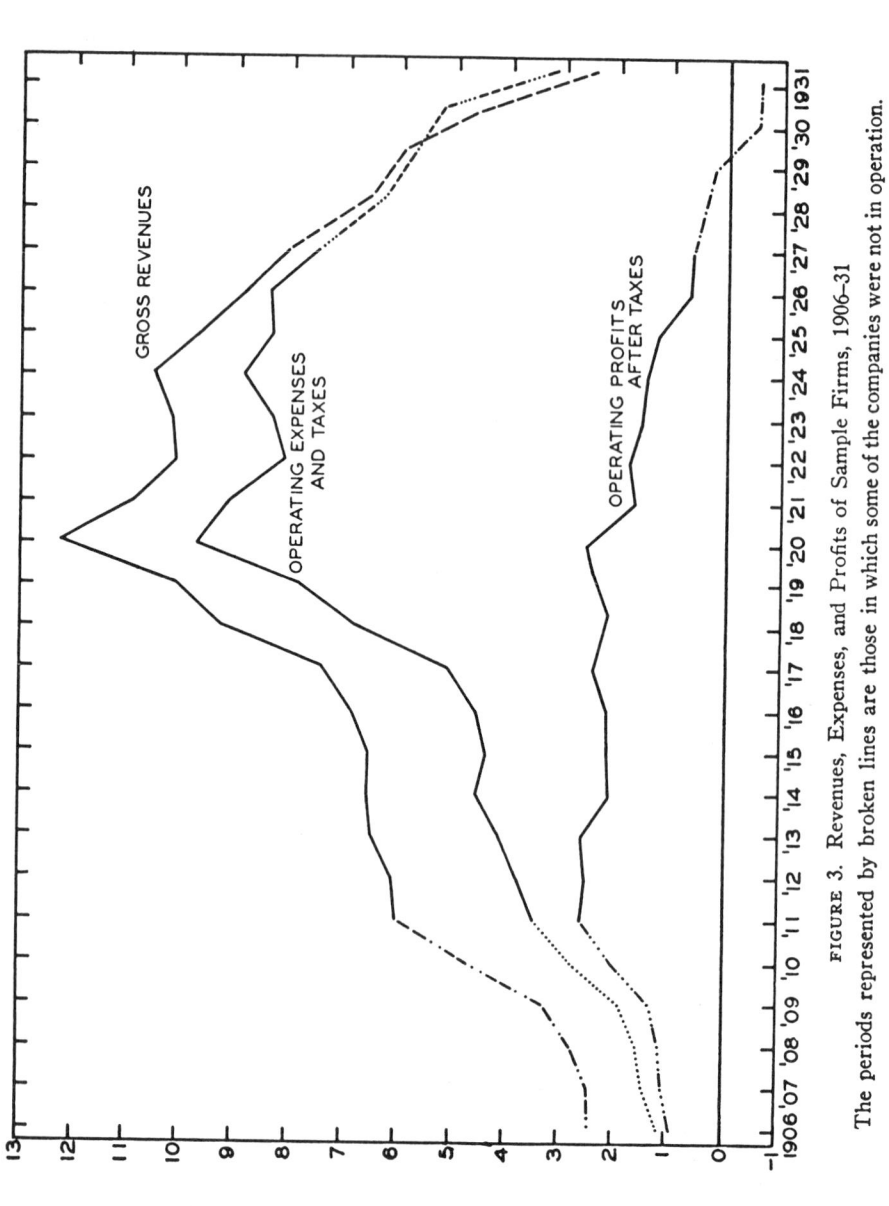

FIGURE 3. Revenues, Expenses, and Profits of Sample Firms, 1906-31

The periods represented by broken lines are those in which some of the companies were not in operation.

1924, 1929, and 1934, and with data based on the sample group of firms for the intervening and subsequent years (see Fig. 6, p. 223).

The six-year period from 1915 through 1920 was the one in which the downward trend definitely began, its course obscured somewhat by the war, which brought temporary prosperity for some roads and served to hold up the rate of return. The sample-study firms (Figure 3) showed a steady rise in gross revenue from 1913 (except for a drop in 1915) to 1920, the figure for 1920 being almost twice that for 1914. This increase in large part merely reflected higher price levels, and operating expenses increased at a more rapid rate; thus, although the net operating profit rose somewhat (from $2.2 to $2.4 million, for the sample companies), it did not keep pace with total revenue, and the operating ratio rose very sharply from 67 to 79. For the sample, however, the rate of return rose slightly between 1914 and 1920, since investment remained almost unchanged, while net profit increased slightly. By 1920 the rise in the price level had squeezed out much of the water in the capitalization. The rise in operating profit in this period was broken by a sharp drop in 1918 as expenses climbed rapidly; considerable recovery was evidenced by 1920, however.

Many companies, especially smaller ones, were not only adversely affected by the rise in expenses, but did not experience a gain in traffic from war conditions, and were affected by the growth of the motor vehicle much more than the sample firms. Thus the large sample study for 1920 shows a much more dismal picture than that of the small sample. Twenty-six firms, or nearly one-fifth of the 145 firms in the group, showed operating deficits; the median return on investment was only 1.5 per cent, and the average 2.6 per cent. The average operating ratio was 85. Among the 26 showing a deficit were such lines as the Cleveland and Erie, the Dayton and Western, the Inter-Urban Railway of Iowa, the Coal Belt, the Kankakee and Urbana, the Grand River Valley, and the Oregon Electric. Compared to 1914 a higher percentage showed returns in excess of 5 per cent; this group includes such lines as the Interstate, the Detroit Monroe and Toledo Short Line, the Detroit Jackson and Chicago, the Petaluma and Santa Rosa, and the Napa Valley line.

The steady financial deterioration of many firms and the unimpressive rate of return for the industry as a whole led to a cessation of construction on the one hand and to the abandonment of some roads on the other. The year 1915 was the last one in which any significant new mileage was built, a total of 444 miles—the lowest figure since 1900. The figure fell to 52 miles in 1918, and in 1920 (for the first time since 1890) no new lines were built. Building in 1915 included the Arlington–Corona line of Pacific Electric, and the completion of the Ogden Logan and Idaho, much of Salt Lake and Utah's main line, the Arkansas Valley, and the last lines of Michigan United. In 1916 and 1917 the Portsmouth–Ironton line was finally completed, as was the Guthrie line of the Oklahoma Railway, and the Kankakee and Urbana's line to Paxton. In 1918 the International

Railway completed its high-speed line from Buffalo to Niagara Falls to replace a slow local route, and in the same year the Sapulpa–Tulsa route was built.

Late in 1914 the long series of abandonments began when the Cleveland and Eastern cut back its hilly, light-traffic Garrettsville route 24 miles to Chagrin Falls.[2] The process gained momentum slowly; 1915 saw the abandonment of the Portland–Linnton segment of the United Railways (Oregon) and of passenger service on the Lee County Central (Illinois). In 1916 the weak Lake Erie Bowling Green and Napoleon, and in 1917 the Bluffton Geneva and Celina, and the Sacramento Valley, among others, were abandoned. In this year the number of miles abandoned exceeded the number built for the first time. Total mileage passed its peak during 1916, and began its long and steady fall. The abandonments of 1918, like those before, were of weak roads that were squeezed by rising costs and that benefited little from the war: among them were the Alton Jacksonville and Peoria, the St. Joseph Valley, the Lebanon and Franklin, and the Bethel line of the Interurban Traction and Terminal in southern Ohio. This was the year in which the New England trolley routes began to disappear rapidly, as the Bay State abandoned 31 miles and made plans to abandon 350 more. Canada's first major abandonment, the London and Lake Erie, also occurred in 1918, and in 1919 the important and ill-fated Shore Line in Connecticut went out (although part was later revived). These were all marginal roads, most of which should clearly never have been built. Some served only small towns with limited traffic; others duplicated the lines of stronger roads.

The period from 1920 to 1924 showed a sharp drop in revenues and profits from 1920 to 1921, and then a leveling off, the decline becoming very gradual. However, by 1924 the operating ratio for the sample firms had risen from 79 to 85. to continue the fifteen-year trend, and the rate of return had fallen to 2.2 (although it was almost exactly stable for the years 1921–24). The large sample study for 1924, covering 147 companies and 9,092 miles of line, showed an average operating ratio of 85, but a median figure of 90; the small companies were hit particularly hard in this period. Gross revenues for the entire group were almost identical to those of 1920. Texas Electric had the lowest operating ratio (64), Chautauqua the highest (133). Pacific Electric, with a tremendous growth in business, had improved its return to 4 per cent and Lake Shore was up to 4.3, but the Union of Indiana, which had been one of the best systems, was down to 2 per cent, the Detroit United (interurban only) had dropped to 1.3 per cent, and the Indiana Columbus and Eastern to 0.8 per cent. Thirty-four roads showed operating deficits, including the Oregon Electric, the Peninsular, the Chicago and Interurban, the Lima–Toledo, the Indianapolis and Cincinnati, the Boise Valley, the Inland Empire, the Hudson Valley, the Union of Kansas, the Southern New York, the Toledo and Western, and the Denver and Interurban.

The number of miles abandoned, still confined to small systems, steadily rose in this period, from 102 miles in 1921 to 264 in 1924. Typical examples of abandonments included the Victor–Cripple Creek line high in the Rockies, after a fire destroyed its equipment; the Springfield Troy and Piqua, the first of the relatively important Ohio roads to go; the Cleveland and Erie (thus breaking the connection from the Midwest to New York State); the Washington Water Power Company's lines out of Spokane, the first significant West Coast abandonment; and the weak Sandusky Norwalk and Mansfield. The Joliet and Eastern, the Springfield and Washington, and the Jersey Central Traction were other examples. The United of Oregon discontinued electric passenger service in 1923 but replaced it by steam-powered trains operating through to Vernonia on the nonelectrified portion. The Pennsylvania and Ohio Traction went out in 1924, and the Visalia Electric discontinued passenger service but retained its track for freight operations, the first of many West Coast roads to take this step. As a matter of fact, VE had discontinued gas-electric passenger service on its line to Strathmore in 1920.

It is surprising that any construction at all took place in this period, and the amount was in fact negligible. Virtually all construction occurred in the Southwest. The steam-operated Northeast Oklahoma was electrified and extended, and in 1923 and 1924 the Texas Interurban built its lines to Terrell and Denton, to fulfill obligations made in order to secure the renewal of Dallas city-line franchises. After 1925 only two new passenger lines were built. In 1926 the North Shore's Skokie Valley cut-off was completed and placed in operation, to replace the slow Shore Line route for main-line trains. In 1927 the Houston North Shore, a Missouri Pacific subsidiary, was completed between Houston and Baytown, largely to provide freight service to an area lacking other rail lines. Apart from the building of some freight-only trackage, largely by the Sacramento Northern (to Clarksburg and Oxford, and to connect its Vaca Valley line with the main line), construction was at an end. The Sacramento Northern, however, extended passenger service over the San Francisco Bay Bridge in 1939, only to discontinue it two years later. In 1956 the South Shore Line placed in service a six-mile bypass around East Chicago to eliminate street running, but this merely replaced existing track.

The 1925–29 period saw a rapid deterioration in the financial position of the industry, and extensive abandonments, despite a high level of prosperity in the nation's economy. The gross revenue of the sample firms fell steadily, to the point that the 1929 figure was only half the 1920 figure. Expenses also fell, but net operating income was squeezed badly; the rate of return fell to 0.5 per cent as the operating ratio for the sample firms rose to 93. The downward trend could not go much further without disaster, and disaster was not long in coming.

The larger sample group for 1929 is much smaller than the others because of abandonments; 96 firms, with 7,966 miles, accounted for 65 per cent of the industry. The average rate of return was 1.57 with a median of 0.5, but 45 per cent of the companies were operating at a deficit, and only four companies showed a return of better than 5 per cent. The situation was as dismal for many of the big companies: the Lake Shore and the THI&E had operating deficits, and the Union Traction a negligible operating profit. The Pacific Electric held up better, with a 1.8 per cent return, and some of the roads specializing in freight were showing good returns—the Visalia Electric and the Petaluma and Santa Rosa, for example. The typical nonsuburban type of interurban, however, could barely keep its head above water in the last year of prosperity.

The year 1925 marked the beginning of the great surge of abandonments that was destined within a seven-year period to sweep out most of the industry. In that year 302 miles of line were abandoned. In 1926 the figure more than doubled; 689 miles were abandoned, including such relatively large roads as the Cleveland Painesville and Eastern and the Grand Rapids Holland and Chicago, as well as the Denver–Boulder line. Five hundred and ten miles went out in 1927, including the Olean Bradford and Salamanca on the New York–Pennsylvania border, the Chicago–Kankakee line, the Mesaba, and the Fond du Lac–Neenah line—the first of the major Wisconsin roads to go. But the 1927 picture merely foreshadowed what was to follow; the figures reached 914 miles in 1928 and 869 in 1929. The most spectacular collapse was that of the extensive Michigan Railways system, one of the most modern high-speed routes, completely abandoned during 1928 and 1929, together with a large portion of the adjacent Detroit United System, and the Grand Rapids Grand Haven and Muskegon. Apart from these, significant 1928 abandonments included the Northwest Pennsylvania south from Erie, the extensive Hudson Valley in the Saratoga area, and the Neenah–Green Bay line in Wisconsin. The trend toward eliminating passenger service became noticeable; it included the Grand River Valley in Colorado and branches of the Fort Dodge Des Moines and Southern. Abandonments in 1929 included the Columbus–Zanesville line, the Southern Pacific electrified lines in Oregon (returned to steam operation), the Boise Valley, the Allentown and Reading, and other Eastern lines. This same five-year period saw the almost complete disappearance of the New England intercity trolley routes (Table 7), which vanished at a much faster pace than the interurbans themselves. Not only did they have little or no freight service, but they were more vulnerable to motor competition.

In its weakened condition the industry was in no position to withstand the impact of the depression, and its collapse was dramatic. Of the basic sample group, only six of the fourteen firms remained by 1931, and these firms showed a net operating deficit equal to about one-sixth of operating revenues. A study of 56 companies for 1934 showed a total net operating deficit of over $1 million, with 63 per cent of the firms showing operating deficits, and only three having a return of 2 per cent or better—the Piedmont and Northern, the Charles City Western, and the Northeast Oklahoma, all primarily freight carriers.

The Decline of the Industry

TABLE 7.—ABANDONMENT OF MAJOR NEW ENGLAND INTERCITY TROLLEY ROUTES, BY YEAR

Year	Miles abandoned	Year	Miles abandoned	Year	Miles abandoned
1917	60	1925	200	1933	164
1918	25	1926	135	1934	9
1919	200	1927	302	1935	33
1920	99	1928	186	1936	5
1921	35	1929	137	1937	142
1922	32	1930	228	1938	0
1923	40	1931	182	1939	8
1924	101	1932	78		

A detailed study of the statistical measures of the Indiana interurbans' decline has been made by Dr. George T. Oborn for the years 1921–41; major items are shown in Figures 4 and 5. The data cover the interurban operations of all Indiana lines. Passenger revenue fell steadily from 1921 to 1929 (although revenue was relatively stable from 1924 to 1928), but the decline was offset in large measure by increasing freight revenue. After 1929 both revenues fell drastically. Although sharp reductions were made in expenses, operating deficits appeared by 1930. Revenues increased from 1932 to 1936, and then began to fall again, a decline that continued until the industry disappeared.

To provide a rough index of the behavior of the industry after 1931 a new sample was selected (the basic sample was so decimated as to be useless); it included some sixteen firms* for which data were obtained through World War II. With a few exceptions, these were the strongest companies financially, and most of them depended heavily on freight business. For 1929 the rate of return for this group was 2.34, compared to the 0.5 figure for the whole industry. Even so, five companies showed an operating deficit. By 1931 the group as a whole showed a deficit, and in 1932 this reached much larger proportions; in that year, only four companies in the sample showed an operating profit—the South Shore, the Lackawanna and Wyoming Valley, the Utah Idaho Central, and the Texas Electric. Up through 1940 the sample continued to show an over-all deficit, although less than the 1932 figure.

The total abandonment figures swelled to 1,017 miles in 1930, 1,219 in 1931, and 1,303 in 1932, and then fell to 1,029 in 1933. The six years 1928–33 accounted for a total of 6,351 miles abandoned (including the mileage on which passenger service was discontinued), or 48 per cent of

---

* The sample included the Jamestown Westfield and Northwestern, the Lackawanna and Wyoming Valley, the Indiana, the Cincinnati and Lake Erie, the Bamberger, the three Chicago area roads, the Lake Shore, the Pittsburg County, the Salt Lake and Utah, the Utah-Idaho Central, the Sacramento Northern, the San Francisco Napa and Calistoga, the Union of Kansas, the Waterloo Cedar Falls and Northern, and the Southwest Missouri. Some of the largest, including the Lake Shore, Indiana, and Cincinnati and Lake Erie, were abandoned before the period was over.

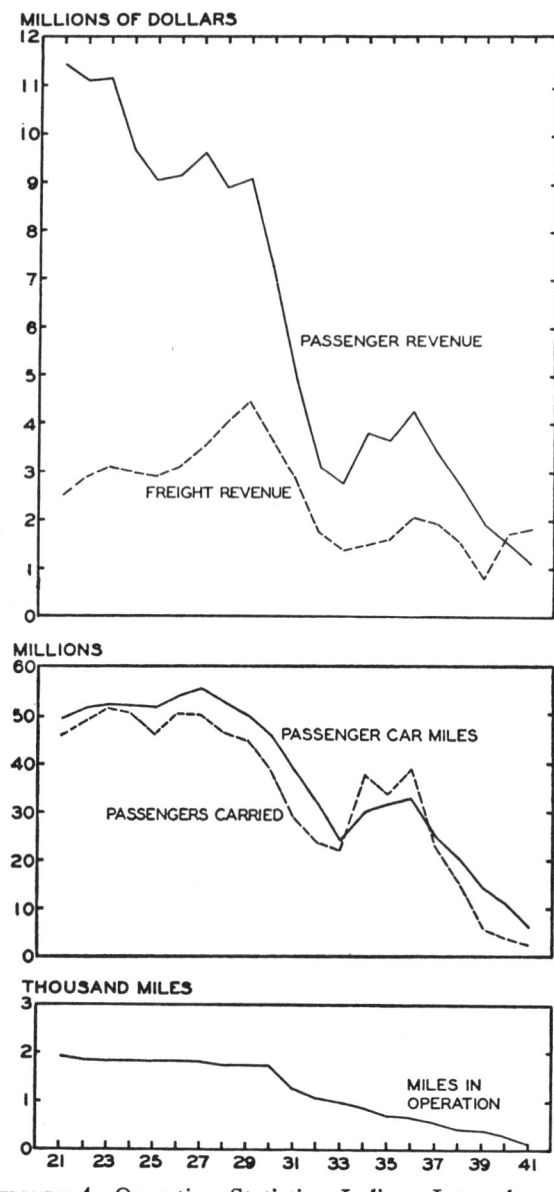

FIGURE 4. Operating Statistics, Indiana Interurbans, 1921–41

Based on data compiled by Dr. George T. Oborn from annual reports of the Indiana companies filed with the Public Service Commission of Indiana. Reproduced by permission.

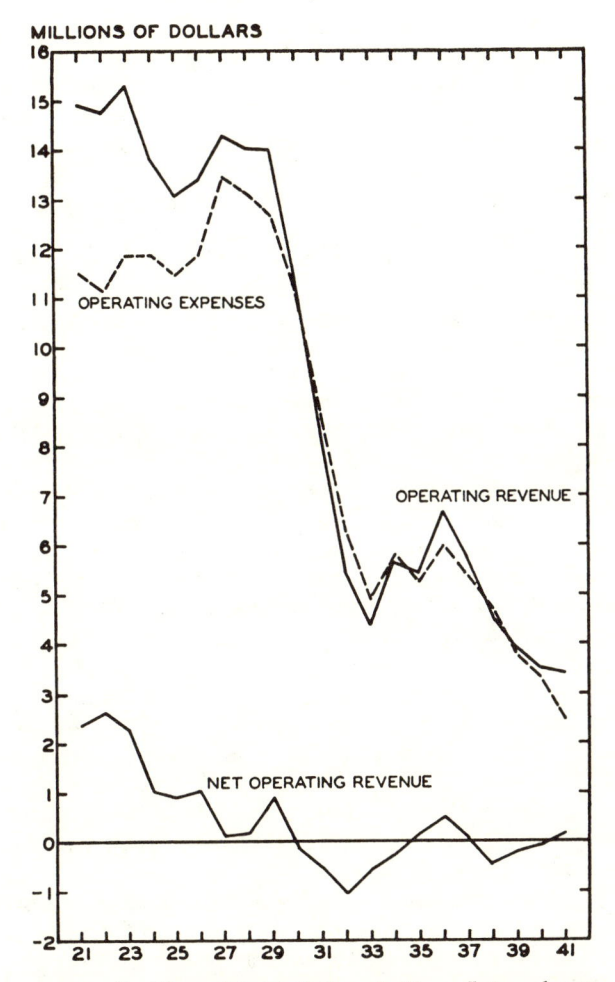

FIGURE 5. Financial Statistics, Indiana Interurbans, 1921–41

Based on data compiled by Dr. George T. Oborn from annual reports of the Indiana companies filed with the Public Service Commission of Indiana. Reproduced by permission.

the total mileage remaining in 1928. Abandonment was particularly severe in the Ohio Valley states. A few major abandonments in this period should be noted. The year 1930 saw the following service discontinued: the Elgin and Belvedere and other shorter Illinois lines, a few weaker routes of the Union Traction, much of the extensive THI&E system, and the third-rail Scioto Valley in Ohio. In the next year came the first big abandonments in Texas (Texas Interurban and Tarrant County Traction) and the end of the big Cleveland Southwestern and Columbus, the remainder of the Eastern Michigan (Detroit United), the major routes out of Pittsburgh to New Castle and Butler, the Eastern Pennsylvania, some very extensive mileage of the heavy-duty interurbans of upper New York State, and the interurban New Brunswick–Trenton–Camden line of the Public Service of New Jersey. In 1932, the greatest collapse occurred in Ohio, with the abandonment of the extensive Western Ohio system and its affiliates, as well as of the Northern Ohio Traction and Light, and the Fort Wayne–Lima line. The Indiana Railroad's lines eastward from Frankfort were discontinued, as was the important Lafayette–Peru route of Indiana Service. Several Pennsylvania lines, including much of the big Conestoga Traction system, and the Boston and Worcester—one of the few true interurbans in New England—ceased operation. Two California interurbans, the Tidewater Southern and the Petaluma and Santa Rosa, eliminated passenger service.

In 1933 the gloomy toll continued. The Peninsular in California abandoned most of its lines; the Central California Traction and the Oregon Electric eliminated passenger service, and, farther east, so did the Southern Iowa. The Kansas City Clay County and St. Joseph, the Chicago and Joliet, the Toledo and Western (despite substantial freight service), parts of the Monongahela West Penn, and another New England interurban, the Portland–Lewiston, were among the casualties, together with the remainder of the Berkshire Street Railway, one of the last of the New England trolley routes. To be sure, as business conditions improved in 1934, the abandonment rate slackened to 548 miles. Nonetheless, the Northern Indiana and the connecting portion of the Winona were abandoned, to break the Chicago–Indianapolis link, and the Wilkes-Barre and Hazleton and the Northern Texas Traction (Fort Worth–Dallas) were among the other major routes discontinued.

New equipment purchases continued for a time on a small scale as some roads continued their modernization programs despite the depression. In 1930, for example, the North Shore and the Northern Indiana ordered a total of 35 new cars; and in 1931 the Indiana acquired 35 new lightweight cars, the Fonda Johnstown and Gloversville 5, and the Philadelphia suburban routes 15. The figure fell to 2 in 1932 (along with 5 for the Philadelphia suburban lines) for the San Francisco Napa and Calistoga to replace cars burned in a fire. In 1933 and 1934, not a single interurban passenger car was ordered.

With the bulk of the mileage gone and business conditions improving, the rate of collapse slackened after 1934, and the financial position of the remaining companies improved slightly; the magnitude of the deficits fell steadily from 1932 to 1936 and in the latter year the sample firms, as a whole, just covered operating expenses. But deficits recurred, and reached a peak in 1938. By 1940 once again the firms taken as a group just covered expenses. By 1936 abandonments had fallen to 124 miles, the lowest since 1921, in part because so much of the network was already gone. When the upward trend did not continue, firms began to give up hope, and the 1939–41 period experienced the elimination of most of the remaining passenger service and much of the track mileage. The figure reached 798 in 1938 and 902 in 1939. The Lake Shore Electric (Toledo–Cleveland) went out in 1938, after a long period of deficits, and the Cincinnati and Lake Erie, modernized a decade before, in 1939. This year also saw the beginning of the collapse of the Pacific Electric, which until then had made no significant abandonments. In 1940 the Indiana eliminated virtually all its mileage, the remainder going in 1941. The entire Ohio-Indiana-Michigan system was now gone except for a few scattered miles of track. Finally, in 1940 and 1941, the Sacramento Northern, which was still operating much the same service as it had three decades before, discontinued all intercity passenger operations. No new cars were built during the 1935–38 period, but the cars acquired in the late twenties and early thirties in the modernization programs were transferred around the country to the remaining lines as their original roads were abandoned.

By the outbreak of World War II, therefore, only some 2,700 miles of the interurban system were left. Remaining roads included:

1. The three Chicago area roads, and the inner portions of the suburban lines of the Milwaukee Electric, no longer typical interurbans.
2. The Illinois Terminal (formerly the Illinois Traction) connecting St. Louis with Peoria, Springfield, Danville, and intermediate cities. This road, originally a typical interurban, had early begun to develop its carload freight business with substantial success.
3. The four Utah lines, all of which depended primarily on carload freight interchange with the steam roads. Passenger business was still important, however, particularly for the Bamberger.
4. The remainder of the Pacific Electric System, hardly an interurban at all since the urbanization of the area served had transformed it into a metropolitan-area, rapid-transit type of operation. Its freight terminal operations were of substantial importance, yet were yielding only about one-fourth of total revenue.
5. The seven Iowa lines, most of which operated passenger service, but depended primarily upon freight revenue.
6. Lines in the Southwest, including the 168-mile Texas Electric, the Houston North Shore, the Oklahoma Railway, the Union (in Kansas and Oklahoma), and a few smaller ones.
7. The Piedmont and Northern, primarily a freight carrier, in the Carolinas.
8. The West Penn system, with over a hundred miles of track in the area east and south of Pittsburgh, solely a passenger carrier, and resembling the New England trolley type of operation.
9. A small number of isolated roads, which for various reasons had survived, including, for example, the Potomac Edison, in the Hagerstown and Frederick areas, and the Lehigh Valley Transit in Pennsylvania.

Most of these lines, however, had lost their typical interurban character, either because the passenger service had become incidental to standard freight operation or because their operations had become suburban in character. Apart from the lines noted, there were a number of former interurbans still operating for freight service only. Most of these survived down to 1960 and will be listed below.

The war years brought prosperity to some of the remaining lines, as both freight and passenger business increased. Some roads were hard pressed to provide adequate equipment, and for the first time in years funds were available to improve track and to paint equipment. The rate of return for the sample firms was 3.66 in 1944, the highest in the history of the industry, although still low by comparison with other fields of business. However, even in 1944, five of the remaining eleven firms in the sample showed an operating deficit, and the North Shore, which had greatly benefited from the war activity, earned half the profit of the entire sample group. Abandonments totaled only 28 miles for the four war years.

There was some feeling at the end of the war that most of the companies that had been able to survive so long had stabilized their position, and would operate more or less indefinitely. The Illinois Terminal, for example, ordered new passenger equipment for its main lines. Some passenger lines on the point of abandonment in 1942 were of course expected to go. But the war had been over less than a year when it became apparent that the downward trend was to include a much wider group. By 1947 the rate of return for the sample group had fallen to 0.3. Slowly and steadily, from 1947 to 1956, the remaining lines, excepting only a few, either were abandoned or discontinued passenger service. The peak years were 1947 and 1955, and by January 1, 1960, only 209 miles remained in operation, with applications filed to abandon nearly half of this.

The major abandonments in the period can be summarized briefly. In 1946 came the expected abandonment of the Oklahoma and the unexpected one of the Salt Lake and Utah; 1947, the Utah-Idaho Central, the Pittsburg County, and others. In 1948 the big Texas Electric system, hard hit by damages from a wreck, ceased operations. In 1950 came the end of the heavily traveled Baltimore and Annapolis passenger service and the Denver suburban lines, and drastic cuts in service on the Illinois Terminal. In 1951 the last of the Milwaukee interurban lines, also weakened by a wreck, ceased operations, as did the Lehigh Valley Transit, one of the last of the eastern Pennsylvania routes. In 1952 the Bamberger, the Salt Lake Garfield and Western, and the Charles City Western all eliminated electric passenger service, and in 1953 the Cedar Rapids and Iowa City did the same. The West Penn discontinued the last of its lines, and Illinois Terminal its Bloomington line. In 1955 service ceased on the shore line of the North Shore, and in Canada, passenger service ceased on the Lake Erie and Northern and the Grand River. This year and 1956 brought the end of the now very limited passenger service on the two big Iowa lines, the Fort Dodge and Waterloo roads, and the Illinois Terminal.

The Pacific Electric gradually cut service, and in 1953 sold its remaining lines (excluding track) to the Metropolitan Coach Lines. In 1958 the Portland Traction ended its interurban service after 65 years, the longest-lived interurban passenger operation in the country. British Columbia Electric also ended the last of its service in the same period. In March 1959 the last two Canadian passenger operations (Thorold–Port Colborne and Quebec City–St. Joachim) were discontinued.

A substantial percentage of the postwar abandonments involved only the elimination of passenger service, since it was this that had been most affected by the sharp increase in automobile usage after World War II. However, some of the lines lacked sufficient freight service to continue operation, especially in view of the increased competition from trucks.

A final trend was the almost complete replacement of electric power by diesel operation as soon as passenger service was discontinued. In such cases, diesel operation usually became more economical because of the costs of maintaining the electric distribution systems. In some instances roads first introduced diesel equipment because of inadequate power, and then made the shift completely. Companies that used a third rail for power distribution had the additional incentive of eliminating an accident hazard, and the California Railroad Commission essentially forced the northern lines of the Sacramento Northern to convert to diesel operation when it banned further use of open-running third rail in 1945. The conversion sometimes brought passenger service to an end earlier than otherwise, but it had no significance from a long-range standpoint. Only two roads have continued to operate passenger service by self-propelled equipment after electric power was abandoned. One is the Houston North Shore, which operates one round trip a day; the other is the Salt Lake Garfield and Western, which operates summer-only service to the resort Saltair. A few other lines, such as the Washington and Old Dominion, operated diesel passenger service for a time, and then discontinued it.

Regional Differences

Table 8 shows the abandonment by region by five-year intervals. The Pacific Coast, North Central, Southwest, and Southern regions were more resistant to abandonment than the great Ohio Valley network and the Middle Atlantic states. For example, by 1939, 94 per cent of the mileage in the Ohio Valley was gone and 86 per cent in the Middle Atlantic states, but only 55 per cent in the North Central states, 54 per cent in the South, and 60 per cent on the Pacific Coast and in the Southwestern states. The peak abandonment year on the Pacific Coast was 1940, in the Southwest 1948, and in the North Central states 1955, in contrast to 1930 in the Ohio Valley and 1931 in the Middle Atlantic states. The differences almost entirely reflect variations in the importance of carload freight service, which enabled the Southern and Western roads to continue to operate and to provide passenger service.

Figure 6 presents a summary of the life history of the industry from 1906 to 1958. The rate-of-return figure is based upon the data of the

The Industry

TABLE 8.—INTERURBAN MILEAGES ABANDONED,* BY REGION, BY FIVE-YEAR PERIODS

Region	1893–1913	1914–19	1920–24	1925–29	1930–34	1935–39	1940–44	1945–49	1950–54	1955–59	Operating
Pacific Coast	21	97	181	411	491	400	453	198	337	77	20
Southwest	0	26	49	98	329	245	90	380	0	10	0
North Central	10	34	108	604	389	164	124	100	226	495	117
Ohio Valley	29	200	382	1,202	2,478	1,356	223	94	0	0	72
Middle Atlantic	0	0	165	831	1,275	354	62	88	281	0	0
New England	0	33	30	71	75	0	0	33	7	0	0
South	0	22	0	68	79	93	79	32	113	0	0
Total	60	412	915	3,285	5,116	2,612	1,031	925	964	582	209

* Including the discontinuation of passenger service only.

various samples, and must of course be regarded as an approximation, with the figures understating somewhat the actual level of the return in earlier years because of the water in the reported figures of capital investment. The miles built and abandoned and car-order series show actual figures. Several relations between the various series should be noted. In the first place, construction fell very sharply and virtually ceased before the rate of return declined substantially. In part this behavior reflected the completion of many of the major routes, and in part the recognition that the over-all rate of return in the industry was inadequate and was unlikely to improve. Secondly, as would be expected, after the rate of return fell drastically, new construction and car orders came to a complete end and abandonment increased rapidly. When recovery from the depression started, however, a number of companies optimistically continued to operate despite a very low return.

New car orders followed much the same pattern as new construction, the decline in part reflecting the reduction in new mileage built. However, between 1915 and 1925 car orders stabilized at a level somewhat higher, compared to the peak years, than did construction in the 1911–14 period, and car ordering continued at a moderate level for a decade after construction virtually ceased, the final decline closely following the downward trend in the rate of return after 1925.

THE SITUATION IN 1960

By January 1960, there were no typical interurban passenger lines operating in the United States. The closest approximation was the Chicago South Shore and South Bend, which operated frequent service between downtown Chicago and South Bend, Indiana. This line had become primarily a suburban operation, with substantial carload freight

The Decline of the Industry 223

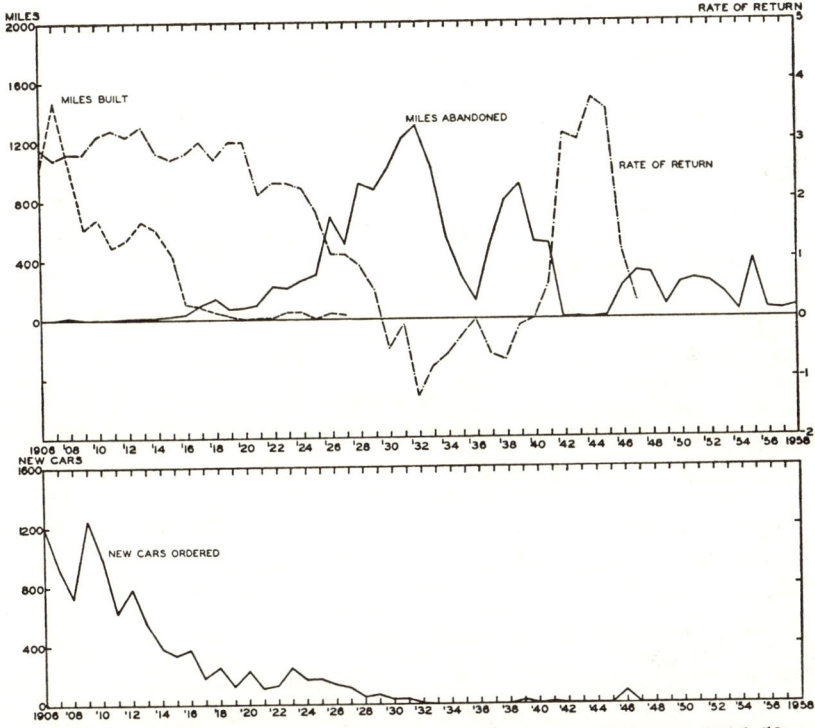

FIGURE 6. Statistics of the Decline of the Interurban Industry, 1906–58

Rate-of-return figures were based upon the sample studies. Mileage figures were compiled from data for individual companies. Car-order figures were obtained from lists of equipment purchases reported in the *Electric Railway Journal*.

service, but the portion east of Michigan City still bore some of the interurbans' characteristics. The Chicago North Shore and Milwaukee still operated its essentially suburban 78-mile line from Chicago to Milwaukee, plus the branch to Mundelein. In the autumn of 1958 the road requested permission for complete abandonment, and the I.C.C. examiner recommended approval in November 1959. Abandonment in 1960 is likely. The Los Angeles Metropolitan Transit Authority still operated the essentially urban, rapid-transit, Long Beach line of Pacific Electric. The Philadelphia and Western's line to Norristown was also a suburban operation.*

The total U.S. mileage still in operation for freight service in 1960 was 2,151 miles, or about 14 per cent of mileage once in use (see Table 9).

---

* In Cuba, a 70-mile interurban still operated in 1959 from Casa Blanca (across the Bay from Havana) through the Hershey plantation area and eastward to Matanzas. The equipment consisted of 30- to 40-year-old interurban cars, mostly wooden. Operations were still carried on in the same interurban fashion typical of its opening days, forty years earlier. In Canada, as we have seen, the last typically interurban lines were abandoned in March 1959.

TABLE 9.—MAJOR SEGMENTS OF FORMER INTERURBAN TRACKAGE OPERATED FOR FREIGHT SERVICE ONLY, JANUARY 1, 1960

Company	Owner	Miles	Year abandoned passenger service*	Present source of power
PACIFIC COAST:				
Spokane Coeur d'Alene & Palouse (Great Northern)	GN	159	1939–40	D
Walla Walla Valley	NP	14	1931	D
Yakima Valley Transportation Co.	UP	21	1935	E
Portland Traction	indep.	40	1935, 1951, 1958	D
Oregon Electric	SP&S	154	1932	D
United (now part of SP&S)	SP&S	20	1934**	D
Petaluma and Santa Rosa	SP	22	1932	D
Sacramento Northern	WP	178	1941	D‡
Central California Traction	WP-SP-ATSF	55	1933	D
Tidewater Southern	WP	39	1932	D
Visalia Electric	SP	19	1924	D
Pacific Electric	SP†	370§	various years	D‡
Salt Lake Garfield & Western	indep.	17	1952¶	D
Total Pacific Coast		1,108		
SOUTHWEST:				
Kansas City Kaw Valley	indep.	13	1935	E
Northeast Oklahoma	indep.	42	1933–40	D
Tulsa and Sapulpa Union	indep.	14	1933	E
Sand Springs	indep.	10	1955	D
Houston North Shore	MoP	34	1949¶	D
Total Southwest		113		
WEST CENTRAL:				
(Chicago Aurora & Elgin‖	indep.	52	1957	E)
Cedar Rapids and Iowa City	indep.	27	1953	D
Waterloo (W CF & N)	IC, RI	64	1956	D
Charles City Western	indep.	19	1952	E
Mason City and Clear Lake	indep.	11	1936	E
Southern Iowa	indep.	18	1933	E
Des Moines & Central Iowa	indep.	18	1949	D
Fort Dodge Des Moines & So.	indep.	144	1956	D
Illinois Terminal	11 RR's	277	1956	D
Lee County Central	indep.	3	1915	Gasoline
Total West Central		633		

* Year given is that of major passenger service abandonment; in some cases partial abandonment took place in other years.

† Additional trackage operated for passenger service, in the case of the Pacific Electric, by the Los Angeles Metropolitan Transit Authority.

‡ Limited use of electricity.

§ Approximate figure. Six hundred eighty-seven miles of track (as distinguished from line) were operated; the terminal-switching nature of part of operations makes it difficult to ascertain an accurate line-mile figure comparable to those used for other roads.

¶ Limited diesel-powered passenger service operated since discontinuance of electric operation.

‖ Operations suspended in 1959, but the line is still intact.

** Electric passenger service discontinued 1923.

The Decline of the Industry

TABLE 9 (Concluded)

Company	Owner	Miles	Year abandoned passenger service*	Present source of power
OHIO VALLEY:				
Southern Indiana (Interstate) ..	indep.	5	1939	D
Youngstown and So.	Penn-NYC	19	1948	D
Total Ohio Valley		24		
MIDDLE ATLANTIC AND NEW ENGLAND:				
Aroostook Valley	CP	33	1946	D
Springfield Terminal	B&M	6	1949	D
Washington & Old Dominion ..	C&O	52	1941	D
Grafton & Upton	indep.	10	1928	D
Southern New York	indep.	3	1933	D
Lackawanna & Wyoming Valley	indep.	19	1952	D
Baltimore & Annapolis	B&O	22	1950	D
Total Middle Atlantic and New England		145		
SOUTH:				
Piedmont & Northern	indep.	128	1951	D
Total Mileage		2,151		

Of this, 1,108 miles are on the Pacific Coast, representing almost half of the mileage once in operation in these states. Most of the remainder is in the Plains states, Iowa and Illinois; only a negligible portion of the Ohio Valley and Middle Atlantic mileage remains. The survival of the Western lines can easily be explained. These roads were built at an earlier stage of economic development than the Midwestern and Eastern roads (although typically at a later date), and thus complemented the steam roads rather than merely paralleled them. The managements recognized the importance of freight service from the beginning, and the steam roads were willing to cooperate with them instead of fighting them as competitors. Many quickly passed into the control of steam roads, and were deliberately developed as freight feeder lines. They were typically built to handle standard equipment. Since they handled primarily the long-haul freight business, they were much less subject to truck competition than the short-haul-traffic roads of the Midwest and East. It should be noted, however, that many of these roads, like most branch lines of main-line railroad systems, are not self-supporting (with traffic, freight rates, and divisions of through rates). Their deficits are covered by the parent companies, and they could not stand on their own feet as independent roads unless they received more favorable rate divisions. This is true, for example, of such major lines as the Oregon Electric and the Sacramento Northern. The deficits, of course, do not demonstrate that the parent companies should abandon them, since their contributions to system revenue usually offset their own deficits. Some of the smaller lines have fared better, as, for example, the Tidewater Southern. The 1957 earnings picture of a number of former interurban companies, including ones still operating passenger service, is shown in Table 10.

TABLE 10.—EARNINGS STATISTICS, FORMER INTERURBAN LINES, 1957

Company	Railway operating revenue	Railway operating expenses	Operating income (after taxes)
Baltimore & Annapolis	$ 1,199,534	$ 1,069,786	$ 29,765
Bamberger	714,919	748,939	—79,527
Charles City Western	219,695	167,131	14,191
Chicago Aurora & Elgin	992,435	1,653,112	—760,876
Chicago North Shore & Milwaukee	5,652,978	5,916,455	—603,414
Chicago South Shore & South Bend	7,698,700	6,923,455	422,056
Fort Dodge, Des Moines & So.	2,548,340	2,338,305	107,367
Kansas City & Kaw Valley	135,856	140,564	—19,690
Mason City & Clear Lake	187,756	179,024	—2,647
Municipality of East Troy	16,084	12,468	3,015
Pacific Electric	14,885,456	13,807,219	—188,364
Portland Traction	948,490	915,493	—61,978
Salt Lake Garfield & Western	215,841	148,152	44,156
Sand Springs	711,516	662,136	8,488
Southern Iowa	43,445	55,914	—19,268
Tulsa & Sapulpa Union	104,974	84,002	4,355
Yakima Valley	260,965	231,019	9,664
Illinois Terminal	12,768,150	9,869,680	988,591
Piedmont & Northern	5,333,054	2,689,774	797,463
Sacramento Northern	2,067,322	1,872,799	—168,651
Aroostook Valley	269,352	174,161	35,275
Springfield Terminal	71,302	94,904	—67,619
Washington & Old Dominion	476,405	347,934	11,637
Cedar Rapids & Iowa City	982,694	504,407	153,058
Walla Walla Valley	317,838	170,870	68,681
Waterloo	1,598,029	1,172,095	4,934
Central California Traction	565,591	481,227	—13,306
Petaluma & Santa Rosa	220,473	265,490	—113,876
Tidewater Southern	881,754	582,663	33,370
Visalia Electric	180,061	150,582	3,838

SOURCE: Interstate Commerce Commission, *Transport Statistics in the United States, 1957*, Part IV, *Electric Railways*, and Part I, *Railroads*. Roads listed through the Yakima Valley are classified as electric railroads, and those below as railroads.

THE CAUSES OF THE DECLINE

The interurban industry thrived for a time because it met a need for short-distance intercity travel more satisfactorily than existing facilities; in turn, it collapsed as other and more suitable forms of transport developed. The two primary factors in its decline were the development of the motor vehicle and a lag in the productivity per worker relative to that in industry.

Although the electric streetcar (from which the interurban was developed) and the automobile were invented at roughly the same time, the electric railway developed much more rapidly, for it was basically a much simpler mechanism and more easily brought to a high level of performance. Widespread use of the motor vehicle depended not only upon the invention of the internal combustion engine, but also on the perfecting of pneumatic tires, starters, and the like, which took more time. Moreover, it was easier and cheaper to provide track for interurbans than to build year-round highways suitable for motor traffic.

It seems clear that had the automobile been developed earlier, the interurban would _never_ have existed! Gradually (particularly after 1912) the engineering problems were solved, the motor car reached a stage of development comparable to the interurban of fifteen years before, and the number of cars in use made it politically necessary and economically feasible to provide highways. Until a reasonably satisfactory highway system was completed, the interurban held its own fairly well, but after the mid-twenties, when the car came into common use, the interurban network began its serious decline. The automobile, not the bus, was the primary threat to the interurban, since it was far more convenient for the type of trip to which the interurban had been particularly suited—the short-distance trip to a nearby city. The car depended on no schedule; it was more adaptable to the carrying of parcels; and, if several persons were traveling, its direct out-of-pocket cost was less than interurban fares. As cars and highways improved, the relative advantages of the car, and the distances over which it was suited to travel, increased. The volume of business was rarely sufficient to allow interurban operation at less than hourly intervals, and thus substantial time was often wasted, even though for a long time speeds exceeded those feasible for cars.

The automobile alone destroyed many interurbans because the remaining business was insufficient to justify the operation of any public carrier. There are many areas in the United States that today have either no public transportation or only one or two bus runs per day, areas that once had extensive interurban service. In other areas a substantial volume of traffic remained, but a new menace—the bus—appeared and diluted the remaining business still more. The effect of the bus on interurban operations was not merely one of competition. As we have seen, the interurbans themselves often operated buses, largely to protect themselves against independent bus lines; but this operation cut into the business available for the interurban cars, and ultimately encouraged further abandonments.

The relative merits of interurban and bus operation shifted over the years as buses were improved. With good equipment and track, the interurbans could give service far superior to that of the typical bus of the twenties, and equal if not superior to the service of today. But as track and equipment deteriorated and bus service improved, the advantages were often lost. Speeds were comparable; the interurbans had the advantage if they had private rights-of-way into the larger cities, whereas buses were superior if the interurban cars were slowed down by street running and impeded by streetcars. Interurbans that were unable to reach downtown areas were typically less convenient than buses. In some instances, as with cars, people preferred bus service because it was "modern," even if by any objective standards the interurbans were superior.

But the primary advantage of the bus was its relative economy. Although operating costs were not necessarily lower, the license and gasoline taxes were much less, per mile, than the cost of maintaining interurban track and trolley wire; thus the over-all cost was definitely lower, unless sufficient freight service was available to bear the track costs. A number of interurbans that continued passenger service until a relatively late date were able to do so only because the track costs were borne entirely by freight. But higher maintenance standards were required for passenger than for freight service, so that even with substantial freight business the point was often reached at which abandonment of rail passenger service became desirable. As time went on and buses were improved, even the direct costs often became less, especially if two-man operation was necessary for the interurbans.

Just as private cars—and, in some instances, buses—cut into interurban passenger service, at a later date trucks began to take interurban freight traffic. The type of freight service that the interurbans had stressed—the short-haul, high-rate merchandise service—was the type for which trucks had the greatest advantage, in terms of both speed and cost, largely because rehandling was avoided. The least vulnerable type of interurban freight business was the main-line-feeder carload business, and in general the interurban trackage in use today is that over which this type of business was most successfully developed.

The development of the motor vehicle seriously affected the interurban in another way, namely, by requiring improved street paving, by slowing down street operation, and by leading to demands for removal of tracks from the streets. Substantial expenditures were also often required for crossing-protection signals.

It should be noted that the rise of the motor vehicle did generate some freight business for the interurban, in the handling of gasoline and materials for paving. Unfortunately, by 1950 most of this business had been lost to trucks or pipelines.

The second basic factor in the decline of the interurbans is one common to most service industries in a period of rapid industrial growth: namely, the lag in the increase in productivity per worker compared to the increase in manufacturing, which typically benefits most from technological change. Some developments in the interurban field increased productivity, particularly the introduction of the one-man car, but on the whole it is obvious that the increase was less than that typical in manufacturing over the same period. The Barger study for the National Bureau of Economic Research showed an actual decline in output per interurban worker between 1902 and 1922, from an index of 118 to one of 104 (1929 = 100). The failure to increase productivity was aggravated by the decline in the industry, and in turn it intensified the decline; the index dropped from 104 in 1922 to 92 in 1931 and 78 in 1938.[8] Declining industries generally experience falling output per worker, as the reduced volume of business makes it more difficult fully to utilize personnel.

The net result of the decline in productivity per worker was an increase in the relative cost of interurban service compared to that of providing other goods. Thus, increases in rates greater than price increases in other fields would have been required to maintain a given profit position, but for the most part this was impossible because of the loss of business that would have resulted. This problem existed even before the automobile, whose development, however, greatly intensified it by making the demand for interurban service at higher rates even more elastic. Hourly wage rates in the interurban field in the early fifties were roughly 10 times what they had been in 1912, and the general price level 2.5 times as high, yet interurban fares were only about twice as high. Thus, to allow the same profit position with a given volume of business, a sixfold increase in output per man would have been required, or, in other words, one-sixth as many man hours should have been sufficient to move a given volume of traffic. No such change occurred, of course, and thus firms could not operate profitably with the same volume of traffic as in 1912.

This phenomenon is well illustrated in the case of the one type of service in which electric railways continued to have an advantage—the handling of suburban traffic into large cities where a private right-of-way was available and street traffic congestion could be avoided. Under such circumstances, bus service or the automobile is definitely inferior to rail service, especially for commuting to work and for routine shopping trips. As traffic congestion has grown, the relative service advantages of this type of rail operation have increased, and despite obsolete equipment the volume of business has remained almost stable, or even increased. In the early fifties most of these lines had far greater traffic per mile than the typical interurban of 1912. Yet at tolerable fares (or perhaps at any fares) they could not operate profitably, with one or two exceptions, and thus abandonment became inevitable. The lines were simply squeezed by their inability to increase their own productivity to match the increases taking place in manufacturing; thus their wage costs continued to rise relative to revenue until finally the lines were forced out of business. They were further injured by the rise in the ratio of peak-load to off-peak business, which lessened the utilization of equipment and manpower.

In some instances efforts to increase productivity were blocked by union insistence on minimum crews in excess of the amounts required for safety; this was a factor in the abandonment of the North Shore's Shore Line route, and the electric service of the Southern Pacific in Oregon and in the San Francisco Bay Area. It is difficult to see why union policy should be so suicidal, yet occasionally it was. To be sure, such policy was not typical. In most instances the unions of interurban employees did not block productivity improvements, partly because the financial position of the companies and the workers' jobs both were so obviously precarious.

AGGRAVATING FACTORS

In addition to the two basic difficulties, the decline of the interurbans was aggravated by other circumstances, frequently overlooked, some of which are virtually inevitable in a declining industry.

The general price level rose sharply during and immediately after World War I. It was in practice difficult for the interurbans to make rate adjustments comparable to price increases in other industries, quite apart from the factors mentioned above, because of regulation, the slow adjustment of steam road fares, and a considerable element of "tradition" in interurban fares that created opposition to increases and that the typical industry did not encounter. These difficulties were largely transitional, but they helped to weaken the industry at the time the decline was starting. The rise in the price level was advantageous in one respect; the interurban investment in right-of-way and capital equipment had been made largely at the old price level, and thus the return-on-investment figure looked somewhat better than it would have in terms of cost levels of subsequent years.

Furthermore, the limited profitability of the industry, coupled with the relatively small size of the average company, prevented any extensive research from being carried on in the industry. Some work was undertaken by the equipment firms, and a limited amount by universities, especially Illinois and Purdue, but the total was not at all comparable to that in other fields. Once the industry began its rapid decline, the equipment firms lost all interest.

When mass purchasing ceased, the cost of new equipment reached prohibitive levels because of loss of economies in manufacturing, especially compared to the mass-produced buses. In time, the task of maintenance became increasingly difficult because parts were no longer produced, a situation aggravated for many companies by the use of widely diverse second-hand cars. Cannibalization of some cars to keep others going—a common practice—came to an inevitable end. The car and parts problems reflect the loss of external economies of large-scale production.

Another contributing factor, as we have seen, was the unfriendly attitude of some of the city governments, which occasionally reached the point of forcing the interurbans off the streets. This could easily result in the interurban's abandonment (as it did in the Portland Traction case), for business fell off sharply once the convenience of downtown service was lost. In a few cases the states forced abandonment by requisitioning an interurban's right-of-way for highway widening, but usually such a policy was avoided.

Some abandonments were accelerated by the Federal public utility holding-company legislation of the 1930's, which typically divorced transport companies from power companies. This had several effects. It removed the financial support of the more profitable power systems from the interurbans, and the interests of the managements in continued use of electric power. The virtually forced sale of some companies resulted in their purchase by groups solely interested, for one reason or another, in bus operation. Actually, however, this occurred in only a few instances in the interurban field; it was far more common with city transit.

A final factor, which undoubtedly played its part in the interurban's decline, might be termed the psychology of obsolescence. After the decline was well under way, many people (outside the industry itself) came to regard the industry as doomed, and the interurban car as obsolete. The car and the bus were "modern" modes of transport; the interurban was as "outmoded as the horse and buggy." It ceased to be "the thing to do" to ride the interurban; the fashionable way to travel was by car or bus. Although this attitude was more damaging to some companies than to others, it inevitably played a part in the decline, even with the suburban high-speed carriers that were clearly more efficient passenger carriers than any type of motor vehicle. As equipment and track deteriorated, the tendency to avoid the interurban increased. Many companies made little effort to attract the public in the later years, even when they had funds to do so; advertising was regarded as an unattainable luxury, and schedules were often left as they had been several decades before. This attitude was not universal, but it was widespread. Shippers likewise became reluctant to locate plants on interurban lines that might soon be abandoned.

ATTEMPTS TO FIGHT THE DECLINE

What does an industry do to attempt to check a downward secular trend? The interurbans experimented with various solutions, most of which have been noted in previous chapters, and will be merely summarized here.

The first was the attempt to develop freight business. Virtually all the early interurbans started life as almost exclusively passenger carriers, and the freight business developed very incidentally and often reluctantly, in the form of carrying packages on the passenger cars as a service to merchants. As we explained in Chapter 4, after 1914 the interurbans made an effort to build up their freight traffic, with considerable temporary success, despite major obstacles.

A second reaction, especially after 1920, was the establishment of bus routes, after the initial hostility to the motor vehicle on the part of interurban management was overcome. Several motives were involved. One was to secure grandfather-clause rights, and thus to block out independent operators. Another, particularly in later years, was to replace rail service on light-traffic runs. This was true of the Bamberger, the Chicago and Joliet, the Penn-Ohio, and the Utah-Idaho Central. A third motive was to provide additional feeder lines in lieu of branches, a policy followed by the Milwaukee Electric, for example. Unfortunately in most cases there was insufficient business to continue this type of operation. Finally, a few interurbans went wholeheartedly into general bus operation in territory far beyond that served by their rail lines. The North Coast Lines, an outgrowth of the Pacific Northwest Traction, and the Blue Ridge Lines, an offspring of the Hagerstown and Frederick, are examples. However, many interurbans—including most of the Ohio lines and Illinois Terminal—never made any extensive use of buses at all; and a number of roads that did operate them later sold out their rights—for example, the Salt Lake and Utah and the Sacramento Northern.

As the interurbans were abandoned in their entirety, some companies converted to complete bus operation, in some instances by expanding their own bus subsidiaries. This was true of the Indiana Railroad and the Cincinnati and Lake Erie. There are extremely few such operations still in existence; however, the Mason City and Clear Lake and the Harmony Route, both of which converted to bus operation for passenger service, continued to operate for a long period, as did a few other roads. Most roads sold out to bus firms: the C&LE sold out to Greyhound, and the Indiana Railroad lines became part of the Trailways System.

As we have noted in earlier chapters, some of the stronger roads sought to meet their problems by modernization. One step was the introduction of lightweight one-man cars, especially after 1920. The Chicago and Joliet and the Kentucky Traction were highly successful with this type of equipment in the twenties, and their efforts were widely publicized. Many companies, however, never replaced their old heavy equipment, either because they lacked funds or because they were not willing to risk the investment.

Later in the 1920's came the consolidation of several Midwestern roads into two large systems, accompanied by substantial modernization. The first such system was the Cincinnati and Lake Erie, which by consolidation established a through route from Cincinnati to Columbus and Toledo, with connections to Detroit and Cleveland. This system developed as an outgrowth of the Cincinnati Hamilton and Dayton electric line, which was reorganized and modernized in 1926 for the bondholders under the direction of Dr. Thomas Conway, Jr., who had just completed similar work on the Chicago Aurora and Elgin. To ensure continued through service, the C&LE absorbed the Indiana Columbus and Eastern and the Lima–Toledo. New lightweight, one-man, high-speed equipment was obtained, track was rebuilt, and freight service was emphasized. For several years the road did fairly well, until the depression and continued motor-vehicle development forced it to abandon between 1937 and 1939.

The other major consolidation involved the creation in 1930 of the Insull-controlled Indiana Railroad. The system centered around the Union Traction of Indiana, but also included the former Interstate, the Indiana Service lines out of Fort Wayne, the Northern Indiana Power lines around Kokomo, and ultimately what remained of the THI&E. Some modernization was carried out during the depression, and new high-speed equipment was purchased. But the changes had come too late; the system gradually disintegrated, and the last segments were abandoned in 1941.

Other forms of physical modernization included freight bypasses of business areas (such as those of Illinois Terminal), improved entrances to large cities (such as the work of South and North Shore lines in the late twenties, and of the Milwaukee Electric), a type of project that few roads could afford, and roadbed improvements. The Arlington and Fairfax experimented unsuccessfully with cars that could run either on rails or on road surfaces.

Modernization of any kind was impeded by lack of funds and by difficulties in raising additional capital. Profit figures were so low that additional securities could not be sold, at least not at tolerable cost, especially in view of the prospective increased motor competition—a danger that investors took more seriously than management. Actually, no degree of modernization could have saved the typical interurban; all that was achieved at best was the prolongation of life by a few years.

ATTITUDES IN THE INDUSTRY DURING THE YEARS OF DECLINE

From the vantage point of 1960 it is easy to present the picture of the decline and its causes. But to what extent did officials of the firms in the industry foresee the decline and its continuation? The answer can be obtained only from papers presented at conventions, from editorials and articles in trade journals, from annual reports of the companies, and from corporate records. The following discussion is based on these sources, which are so numerous that no effort has been made to document the statements extensively.

Through 1910 optimism prevailed in the industry, and there was no thought of future difficulties—a state of euphoria quite common in a rapidly growing industry. And given the circumstances that produced the industry and the rate of national economic growth, such optimism was not unfounded; but people became overoptimistic. Lines were built that proved unprofitable from the start; traffic was overestimated or the anticipated growth of the area was not realized. No one should logically have expected the Lee County Central (Illinois), a line from Amboy (pop.: 1,900) through Lee Center (pop.: 250) to an electric pole at a crossroads labeled Middlebury, to have earned a profit. But mistakes are not unusual in the early years of an industry, and some of the early lines proved unprofitable because they were not completed to intended destinations. Moreover, most of the larger lines were sufficiently profitable in their earlier years to warrant the investment.

The year 1911 was the first one in which interurban officials began to call attention to an unsatisfactory over-all rate of profit in the industry. It was attributed to two major factors: first, to the fact that many lines had been built in anticipation of traffic increases that had not materialized; and, second, to the fact that fares were set too low in relation to costs, which were tending to rise. Commonly, the promoters of the roads seem to have overestimated revenues and underestimated costs, perhaps in part deliberately in order to raise capital. From the earliest days the fares had been set from 1.5 to 2 cents a mile, substantially less than the steam-road fares of the period, which were between 2 and 3 cents. The steam-road fares tended to fall around 1908, partly because of interurban competition, partly owing to the enactment of two-cent-fare laws. As the interurbans came to realize that a 1.5-cent-fare level was too low, they found it increasingly difficult to raise, at least where they were subject to steam-road competition. The general level of costs was rising gradually; equipment costs were increasing as standards were raised; more money was being spent on signal systems and other line improvements, on stations, and on additional services, such as baggage-checking.

But in 1911 and 1912 there was no thought given, at least not publicly, and one suspects not privately either, to the potential threat of the automobile. In this sense the expectations in the industry began to go seriously astray. Nonetheless, it should be remembered that the number of cars had increased very slowly, and that the bus had not yet become of any consequence, especially in intercity service (even though as early as 1896 a bus system had been proposed for Cleveland, and bus operation had become extensive in London and Paris). In 1912 there were only two intercity bus routes in operation in Indiana, charging a five-cent-per-mile fare, and able to operate only in the summer months.

The year 1913 was the first in which interurban officials took any discernible notice of the automobile; by then there had begun to be some perceptible effect on the volume of business, especially business of a suburban character. Sales of cars were increasing very rapidly in this period, from 63,000 in 1908 to 356,000 in 1912, and almost 900,000 in 1915. In 1914 the potential threat of motor transport to the electric railways was abruptly brought to the attention of the companies by the phenomenal spread of the "jitney." In the fall of that year, a number of persons in Los Angeles, many of them unemployed, began to operate old touring cars on the main streets during rush hours, carrying passengers for fares less than the streetcars. The movement spread like wildfire across the country, and caused drastic losses in street railway business, as the jitneys which picked up persons waiting for streetcars took the cream of the traffic, and left the transit companies with the less profitable business. The jitney was largely an urban phenomenon, one which was eventually legislated out of existence, but it carried a warning to the interurbans.

Despite these trends, and occasional forebodings, the industry as a whole did not take the motor vehicle seriously before 1915. Between 1912 and 1915, several major interurban systems were completed, including the western portion of Michigan Railways, and the two large Utah lines. There was no recognition whatsoever of the real dangers; interurban officials simply could not foresee the expansion of motor vehicle use. In any field, it is difficult at a particular time to envisage future developments, and there is a great tendency to project present conditions into the future. By 1914 few people thought that the interurban industry was going to continue to expand rapidly; for one thing, most of the major routes had already been built. Still, there was no anticipation of the decline. So long as highways were barely passable, cars hand-cranked and highly unreliable, and buses unable to operate for less than five cents a passenger mile, interurban management could not take them very seriously; similarly, today we find it hard to imagine the average family having two helicopters for everyday travel.

The 1915–19 period was characterized by a growing recognition of the threat from the motor vehicle and by demands for the regulation of bus lines. Only the short-haul business and the weaker lines seemed threatened; there was as yet no thought that the industry as a whole was in any danger. At the same time, it was clearly recognized that expansion of any magnitude was at an end, and by 1920 there were fewer miles of track in operation than in 1915, despite the construction of some new projects.

In 1915 interurban officials expressed serious concern about the automobile, as opposed to the 1914 attitude that it was a minor nuisance. Many indicated that the increasing popularity of the car was "discouraging," and was causing a loss of traffic. However, although a few expressed fears about potentially serious losses, most held to the belief that the auto's appeal was merely that of a novelty. Typical is the following excerpt from a 1916 speech by C. L. Henry, pioneer Indiana interurban developer: "The fad feature of automobile riding will gradually wear off, and the time will soon be here when a very large part of the people will cease to think of automobile rides, and the interurbans will carry their old time allotment of passengers."[4]

By the next year the problem had become worse. Even so, the eternal optimist Henry went so far as to state in 1917 that the automobile menace was actually less, that the fad was over. The following statement from the 1917 Annual Report of the Spokane and Inland Empire Railroad Company is typical of management attitudes:

Automobile competition obtains to about the same extent as stated in the last annual report. The slight decrease this year in interurban passenger earnings, of only 1.6%, as compared to large decreases in previous years, may be taken as a favorable sign and as indicating that the desire for private ownership of automobiles throughout our territory for pleasure purposes has been substantially met and possibly that the peak of their use in competition with electric lines has been reached. While we do not anticipate further loss of any considerable revenue from this cause, it cannot be expected that there will be any such decrease in automobile use as to increase our passenger revenue (p. 5).

Other people in the industry were less optimistic, but very few if any foresaw the actual trends. Bus operation expanded rapidly after 1915; two years later, when motor carriers were brought under regulation in California, 500 companies, mostly intercity, filed their tariffs with the commission. President Paul Shoup of the Pacific Electric complained bitterly of jitney, bus, and auto competition, and constantly sought stricter regulation. The PE was one of the first major companies to feel the effects of the motor vehicle, although these effects were obscured in large measure by the very rapid growth of population in the Los Angeles area.

By 1920 there was a general acceptance of the view that the auto and bus were here to stay, and that the effects on traffic were permanent and significant, but there was still little recognition of the real dangers. The fad doctrine gave way to the belief that the loss of traffic to the motor vehicle was significant, but that the situation had stabilized, and that many riders could be lured back from the auto as soon as people realized how costly the latter was. One of the last adherents of the fad doctrine was Sir Adam Beck, developer of the Ontario Hydroelectric Power system, who was urging during this period the construction of a network of electric railways in Ontario.

The truck likewise was regarded as a growing menace after 1918, and the interurban industry strongly protested the government's encouragement of the "ship by truck" campaign during the war, designed to lessen the pressure on the railroads, which were hard pressed to carry all available business. As late as 1918 a few officials still thought that the truck would not last as an element in the transport picture, but by 1919 most realized that it would, and sought regulation. However, the interurban industry was still convinced that the truck was limited to very short hauls (twenty miles was a commonly stated figure), that the business beyond this "belonged to the electric railways," and that they could get it if they sought it. At the same time, it was frequently argued that the interurban freight rates were too low, that express service was being provided at freight rates and that increases were desirable.

Both the situation and the attitudes in the industry remained much the same in the 1920-24 period, and consequently the notion that the industry had stabilized gained strength. There was the slight revival of construction that we have noted (the building of the Texas Interurban, the Houston North Shore, and the Northeast Oklahoma). Abandonments continued apace, but these involved the small, weak roads, whose disappearance had largely come to be taken for granted. The general attitude was firmly intrenched that the long-distance and suburban lines could survive, while light-traffic lines between small towns could not, in much the same way as around 1947, when, although it was generally recognized that railroad branch-line passenger service was doomed, long-distance main-line service was regarded as permanent.

In the early 1920's, use of the automobile expanded rapidly, and with the greatly improved mechanical qualities and the rapid extension of highway networks, it became a standard household item rather than a rich man's toy. Truck service likewise expanded, but a widely publicized statement by Pierce Arrow President Graham in 1920 that the truck was superior to the interurban for freight and would ultimately replace it was roundly criticized by the interurbans. In some areas bus service was also growing (although the jitney had largely disappeared), and many interurbans were protecting themselves in the bus field by operating their own lines. When the interurbans introduced bus service, they usually regarded it merely as a supplement to the rail operations; however, when Indiana

Columbus and Eastern established bus lines in 1922 it frankly stated that if it found buses to be cheaper and equally satisfactory it would ultimately abandon its rail lines. The company pointed to the lack of rate control and the free roadbed as the primary advantages of bus operation.

Some of the most complete statements on attitudes toward the industry around 1920 are to be found in the testimony presented to the Sutherland Commission investigating the plans for a network of electric railways in Ontario.[5] An expert of the J. G. White Engineering Co. testified that "the idea of any one suggesting financing of an electric interurban road would not be given very serious consideration. Of recent years that feeling has been accentuated because they have all been in such a bad way" (p. 27). A number of interurban officials from the United States mentioned the effect of motor competition; the statement of vice-president Coen of the Lake Shore is typical: "I think the auto passenger car and auto truck are real methods of transportation that have to be considered with any method of transportation, electric or otherwise. They are here to stay as I see it" (p. 54). The Commission concluded: "It will be quite clear that the competition with the electric railways of traffic on highways and good roads, particularly that of motors and motor trucks, has grown to be so extensive as to be a factor of great financial importance in considering the projection of a system of (electric) railways" (p. 55). The Commission recommended against the proposed system largely on this basis. Its conclusions were condemned by Sir Adam Beck, who argued that the dangers of motor competition were greatly exaggerated by the Commission, and that trucks could not continue to operate once they were made to pay a share of highway costs.

By the mid-twenties such optimism as remained was noticeably shaken. Even Dr. Thomas Conway, Jr., like Henry an eternal optimist, admitted that the situation was critical, and that substantial mileage would be scrapped. But he, and others, argued that the demise of the industry was not inevitable, that with public cooperation, modernization, new equipment, greater speed, better terminals and city entrances, consolidation, and concentration on hauls over 50 miles, the industry could get back on its feet.

After 1925 the business and profits of the interurbans fell so rapidly and abandonments spread so quickly that there could be little reasonable doubt about the future of most roads. L. F. Loree, president of the Delaware and Hudson Railroad, an important operator of electric lines in New York, told the St. Louis Chamber of Commerce in 1926 that he believed the investment in street and interurban railways would have to be "wiped off the books" because of the growth of highway transport. The collapse of the Michigan Railways, one of the best systems, must have raised doubts in the minds of the most optimistic, and indeed, the pessimistic statements began to multiply. T. C. Fraser, president of the Winona, indicated in a letter written to Dr. George T. Oborn, that soon after he joined the company in 1926 he realized that the passenger business would be short-lived, and eventually totally lost to the private automobile.

But officials of some of the larger systems still believed that they could survive if they modernized, and poured considerable amounts of money into improvements. Even the president of the Eastern Michigan, successor to the Detroit United, indicated in 1929 that his system was surmounting its problems, but three years later it was completely abandoned. The position of the automobile and the truck was unquestioned, yet there persisted the belief that substantial business yet remained for the interurban. The notion that trucks could not operate effectively beyond 50 miles continued. The rule also came to be accepted in this period that an interurban could not survive on passenger traffic alone, but the old obstacles to freight operation had by no means been overcome.

The depression destroyed most of the remaining hope, although some modernization programs were carried forward, and a few people felt that if the industry could survive the depression, it would prosper again; the Lake Shore, for example, was sustained by this hope for several years, despite severe operating deficits. Conway was willing to state in 1933 that the interurbans were standing on the threshold of a new era—that those which survived and readjusted their service could look to a promising future. By 1934 even the greatest optimists recognized that the interurban system was dead, and that only a few lines operating under the most favorable circumstances could survive, even in prosperity.

Throughout the period from 1915 to 1925 the expectations of most people in the industry were clearly wrong, and even after that date some erred seriously in their views on the future of the industry. There was a constant tendency to believe that conditions had stabilized, a failure to see the basic nature of the secular trend downward. The errors of 1914 are relatively easy to explain; those of 1924 much less so. Some of the public statements clearly involved wishful thinking, whereas others may have been made mainly to influence potential investors. But many undoubtedly reflected sincere beliefs. The errors resulted in the pouring of additional money into modernization in the late twenties (much of which was completely lost); other roads would have spent more if they could have gotten it. Some roads, such as the Indianapolis and Cincinnati, continued to plan for extensions even as late as the mid-twenties, when the trends should have been perfectly obvious. Some roads abandoned passenger service only two or three years after they had spent substantial sums on new equipment and track improvements; this was true, for example, of the Fonda Johnstown and Gloversville, the Indianapolis and Cincinnati, the Washington Baltimore and Annapolis, and the Napa Valley line. But in most of these instances it was not only the secular decline in the industry that was not foreseen, but the depression as well; some of the investments of the late twenties would not have been so disastrous had prosperity continued.

In the postwar years, there was little overoptimism on the part of the remaining companies. Many officials were convinced that the lines were doomed as passenger carriers, and they merely ran their equipment until it wore out. The only major mistake was that of the Illinois Terminal, which, not foreseeing the last final burst of auto popularity that was to destroy most of its remaining business, acquired several new cars in 1948, only to retire them in 1956.

The most significant lesson that can be learned from the story of mistaken expectations in the interurban field is how difficult it is for an industry which is declining to realize it is actually experiencing a secular decline that will eventually destroy it. The basic fault lies in the failure to project trends, and in the constant tendency instead to expect existing conditions to continue in the future. Even after the trend has gone on for a substantial period of time, the belief persists that the readjustments have been completed—that equilibrium has again been restored.

8

The Decision to Abandon

A REVIEW of the circumstances, financial and otherwise, at the time of abandonment, and of the effects of passenger service abandonment, is interesting not only from the standpoint of the history of the industry, but also in terms of the broader scope of business policy relating to abandonment, which has seldom been studied.[1]

THE PERIOD OF OPERATION AT A LOSS

Most interurbans operated at a loss for a number of years before discontinuing service. The available data do not permit us to give figures for the entire industry, but are adequate for a sample covering a substantial portion of the industry, consisting of 119 companies, which operated nearly half the total interurban mileage. Information for the other companies either is completely unobtainable, or cannot be separated from data on affiliated enterprises, particularly city transit and power.

Table 11 below shows the distribution of these companies by the num-

TABLE 11.—DISTRIBUTION OF INTERURBAN COMPANIES BY NUMBERS OF YEARS OF OPERATING LOSSES* IMMEDIATELY PRECEDING ABANDONMENT

Years of operation at a loss	Number of companies	Mileage
15 and over	3	129
10–14	3	139
7–9	13	612
6	11	1,443
5	11	495
4	12	780
3	16	812
2	25	1,455
1	16†	722
0	9‡	549

* After taxes.

† Of these 16 companies, 7 had experienced losses only in the final year during the last 5 years; 5 had experienced losses in 2 out of the last 5 years; 2 in 3 out of the last 5 years, and 2 in 4 out of the last 5 years.

‡ Of these 9 companies, 2 experienced losses in none of the last 5 years, 4 in 1 of the last 5 years, 2 in 3 of the last 5 years, and 1 in 4 of the last 5 years.

ber of years they ran at an operating loss before abandonment. The final year is included only if the company was in operation for over six months of the year. In only nine cases did liquidation occur without the company's running at a direct operating loss for at least one year, and of the nine only two had covered their operating expenses in the five preceding years.

As the table shows, the greatest number of companies operated at a loss for two years; the median figure was three years. Nearly a third of the companies operated at a loss for five years or more. The sample includes large companies as well as small, and, as the mileage figures indicate, there is no significant correlation between size of the company and length of time of operation at a loss. The high mileage figure at the six-year interval is due to the abandonment of the Indiana Railroad. Of the other large systems, the Lake Shore operated at a loss for eight years, accumulating a total of operating losses of nearly $3 million. The Cincinnati and Lake Erie operated at a loss for four years; greatly increased losses in 1937 precipitated abandonment. The Northern Ohio and the Michigan Railroad both suffered losses for four years, the Cleveland Southwestern and Eastern Michigan for two, the Texas Electric for only one year (with high profits only a few years before). In the year of abandonment the TE actually showed a profit because it had virtually eliminated maintenance.

The period of deficit operation for some companies was little short of fantastic. The prize must be awarded to the Southern New York, which, after a profit of $16,000 in 1922, operated at a deficit for every one of the 19 years preceding its almost total abandonment in 1942. In several of these years, the operating expenses were more than twice as great as the revenues; the relatively small road built up an accumulated deficit of $1.7 million over this interval. The Grand River Valley, in Colorado, was a very close rival, with 15 consecutive years of losses (1918–33). The Peninsular, in the San Jose area in California, totaled 16 years, the Southwest Missouri reached 12, the Union of Kansas 11, and Springfield and Xenia 12—and over these 12 years the annual gross revenues of this road fell from $106,000 to $16,000. The Indiana Railroad, although operating only 6 successive years at a loss, suffered losses during 10 of the 11 years of its existence. If the Indiana's record is broken down into its constituent parts, the THI&E portion showed losses for 14 out of its last 15 years. Two of the three roads that exceeded 12 years of operating losses gained a large portion of their revenues from carload freight business.

As a rule, companies that operated with losses for very long periods were abandoned at a relatively late date. There was a tendency for roads that slowly sank into a long period of losses without a drastic decline in business (such as the Union of Kansas, and the Grand River Valley) to continue longer than those that experienced within a briefer period—say, five years—a very sharp drop in business from a good rate of profit to a rate of substantial losses. A slow decline typically encouraged a stronger belief that conditions would improve; when the decline was rapid, the trend became so obvious that the management realized abandonment was inevitable. This was particularly true when the decline occurred during the prosperity years of the 1920's, as was common with many of the lines: roads that were still prosperous in 1929 but suffered losses in the early thirties in some instances regarded the loss situation as purely the product of the depression and thus temporary. Consequently, they operated as long as they could, or until a return of better economic conditions at the end of the decade failed to restore their profits. This was clearly the case with the Lake Shore, the Cincinnati and Lake Erie, and the Indiana Railroad.

This phenomenon is further illustrated by a review of those roads that were abandoned before the point of operating at a loss was reached. For example, the Galveston–Houston abandoned in 1936; although it had never suffered operating losses, its gross had fallen from $640,000 in 1928 to $208,000 in 1935, and its net operating profit from $213,000 to $24,000. Moreover, the decline had continued on through the depression years as business activity recovered. The Scioto Valley abandoned in 1931, despite a fairly substantial earnings figure for 1930, after a steady drop in business from the mid-twenties had cut its gross in half. The Stark Electric likewise survived the worst years of the depression without losses; revenues had increased slowly from the low years until 1936, but when they began to fall again in the next two years, the management concluded that the old trend was continuing, and abandoned without waiting for losses. The Texas Electric reacted similarly in the postwar years; it had experienced very high profits during World War II, but after seeing its gross fall by half between 1944 and 1947 in the face of rising costs that squeezed profits drastically, it abandoned after only one year of losses.

The available figures, of course, do not give an entirely accurate picture. To begin with, as business declined, maintenance was often deferred; consequently, losses were understated, in the sense that with the actual level of maintenance, operations could not have continued indefinitely. Likewise, the depreciation charges were without question often inadequate, relative to actual decline in the value of assets.

How did the companies that operated for long periods at a loss finance the deficits? In the first place the operating expense figures include depreciation charges, and thus to some extent the losses represented failure to accumulate depreciation reserves. However, careful examination of the expense data suggests that this was only a minor factor in most instances (partly because the depreciation charges were often so low). The actual cash deficits were made up in two principal ways—by exhausting cash reserves, and by incurring current liabilities in the form of unpaid bills, unpaid taxes, or advances by the owners. By 1937, for example, the Southwest Missouri reported current liabilities of $4 million, equal to the book value of the entire property (which was, of course, greatly in excess of any realizable value). The Southern New York piled up $800,000 of such liabilities before the property was sold to salvage dealers in the late 1930's.

Theoretically, a company should liquidate when it reaches the stage at which an average return on salvage value exceeds the present and projected return made on the property, and thus before reaching the point of actual losses, provided that there is no expectation of improved profits.

Operation for several years at a direct operating loss indicates a failure to follow this rule.* except when there was hope of improvement; in some instances such hope was held, even though there was no logical justification for it. In other instances salvage value was very low, sometimes no more than $1,000 a mile, and thus the interval between the optimum abandonment point and the point of incurring an operating loss was very slight. But clearly many companies operated far too long in light of the circumstances; management was either too optimistic, or too reluctant to see the enterprise dissolve. A study of these cases also suggests that the actual time of abandonment was greatly influenced by the particular points of view of the various officials who made the decisions, points of view that varied widely even when objective circumstances were much the same. However, the discretion rarely created a range of more than five years.

Regulatory policies appear to have had little effect on the timing of total abandonments. Many were made without the sanction of the commissions, and when requests were made they were usually granted quickly. As we have seen, partial abandonments were often delayed much more.

THE FINAL BLOW

A review of specific abandonments reveals a surprisingly high number of cases in which abandonment was directly and immediately prompted by accidents, damages, and other factors that forced either liquidation or a large capital investment that was impossible or clearly undesirable from a profit standpoint.

Several lines were so badly weakened by damage claims growing out of wrecks and loss of business resulting from them that they were forced out of business. The Southern Cambria, the Texas Electric and the Indianapolis–Seymour† lines are examples, together with the Milwaukee Rapid Transit and Speedrail Company, whose heroic efforts to operate successfully several interurban lines of the Milwaukee Electric Railway and Transport were cut short by a collision between two special trains (the motorman of one was the president of the company) in September 1950. Damages to the line itself were often a cause: the end of the Dayton and Troy, for example, occurred when a bridge collapsed under the weight of a train in 1932. Two Pennsylvania lines suspended operation when shifting ground resulting from coal-mining operations rendered the track unsafe. Many other lines abandoned when track and equipment generally deteriorated beyond safe use.

The interurbans had a long history of destruction of car barns by fire, and in several cases these caused the elimination of passenger service. The Bamberger, for example, lost its car repair shops and its equipment and parts in a fire in 1952, and a few months later abandoned passenger service

---

* After making adjustments for the receipt of depreciation charges, which represent return of capital.

† In this case the accident brought an end to the line by enabling the company to cancel a long-term lease.

since it was unable to keep equipment repaired; it had given no indication of abandoning service prior to this time. The Waterloo Cedar Falls and Northern lost all its passenger equipment except one car in a fire in 1954, and after attempting to keep service going with this car for a time, was forced to suspend later in the year.

Another major factor in abandonment decisions was the loss of connections or access to downtown areas. The San Francisco Napa and Calistoga was virtually forced to suspend operation when the independently operated ferry service from Vallejo to San Francisco ceased operations in 1937, cutting off a large part of the company's passenger business. In the Midwest, abandonments affected the remaining roads because of the serious losses of business from connections, so they in turn were forced to abandon. Companies that reached downtown areas on streetcar tracks were sometimes forced to abandon when the city companies abandoned their lines; this was true, for example, of the Seattle–Everett interurban line, and the Nashville–Franklin. The end of the passenger service of the Portland Traction was assured when its cars were barred from the bridge over the Willamette River by which they reached the downtown area.

Other special circumstances militated against the interurbans. The London and Port Stanley in Ontario was forced to suspend when Ontario Hydro changed from 15- to 60-cycle power, and the railroad lacked funds to convert its power-plant equipment to the new cycle. The obsolescence of the 25-cycle powerhouse at Anderson was cited as a reason for the abandonment of the Indiana's Indianapolis–Richmond–Dayton line. Highway-widening caused abandonment of portions of the United (Oregon), the Peninsular, the Hagerstown and Frederick, and several others. These are merely examples; the list could be multiplied indefinitely.

It is obvious, of course, that in virtually all such cases, the particular circumstance was not the basic cause of abandonment; had operations been profitable, capital could have been obtained and the replacements or repairs made. But the numerous cases of this type suggest, as does the profit and loss data above, either that unprofitable firms tend to operate too long, frequently until some event occurs that forces them to suspend, or that the nature of capital replacement in some fields is such that liquidation of the business is not advantageous until some major capital replacement becomes necessary.

GENERAL DETERIORATION

The physical condition of the lines in their later years differed markedly. Some roads that conducted profitable freight operations maintained their track and passenger equipment in good condition down to the time passenger service was abandoned. This was true, for example, of the Sacramento Northern, the Bamberger, and the Lake Erie and Northern. But more commonly the service gradually deteriorated, until the last months of operation showed an unbelievable state of equipment and track. This process of decline went on gradually over a period of several years. In some instances it was in a sense deliberate; the roads were earning operating expenses and covering a portion of depreciation charges, and they drew out as much as they could in the way of earned depreciation charges before they abandoned, in the meantime neglecting all maintenance except what was needed to keep the cars running. In other cases it was unintended; revenues were inadequate to permit maintenance, yet the company kept operating in the hope that conditions would improve.

The process of decline was of course a cumulative one, as the track and the cars engaged in a life and death struggle to see which could keep going longer. As maintenance declined, the cars caused progressively more damage to the track, and the rougher the track became, the greater the extent to which the cars were pulled apart. The heavy steel cars were capable of withstanding worse track than either the old wooden cars or the new lightweight ones, but in turn were much harder on the track.

A ride on some of the lines in the last days was an experience never to be forgotten. Particularly on the wooden cars the bodies jerked back and forth and threatened to fly off the trucks every time the cars started or stopped quickly. Windows rattled in their rotting sashes, and interior doors that would no longer close banged against their frames. The gentle rolling motion of earlier years gave way to a violent rocking that made it impossible to keep parcels in the luggage racks, and the rocking in turn was intensified by twisting lurches as one set of wheels passed over a dip in the rails where the ties had rotted. Track in city streets—more expensive to repair—was often in the worst shape, and the rocking sometimes became so bad that the car steps grated on the pavement. The wheels bumped endlessly on every worn rail joint, and the bumps were transmitted in full force to such passengers as were brave enough to ride. Power was often inadequate, because equipment failed to function to the optimum, and at night the lights commonly went completely out when a car started or pulled up a heavy grade. Sometimes it was possible to get up a hill only if the car shot down the previous hill and over a quivering trestle at top speed. Cars broke down and had to be towed in, and some were cannibalized to keep others running. Some cars developed permanent lists to one side as springs weakened. Occasionally a car would leave the rails completely to turn over in the ditch, although wrecks in the later years were very rarely caused by worn tracks (most of the interurban accidents, other than some in earlier years on poorly laid track, were head-on collisions).

How these cars kept running, month after month, at speeds of 50 miles an hour or so, on track on which main-line railroad officials would be reluctant to run a handcar, was little short of phenomenal. But the day of reckoning came at last. Either the equipment became so badly worn that operation was impossible, or the company simply ran out of money with which to pay bills. The last car (sometimes the same car, with the same motorman, that had made the first run some thirty years before) pulled into the barns, and the power was shut off. Equipment was scrapped, stations were sold, right-of-way usually reverted to the farmers, and cars that showed any possibilities for further use often were loaded on flat cars and shipped away to some other line with a few hundred dollars to spend to replace cars of its own that were beyond repair.[2]

FINANCIAL EFFECTS OF THE ABANDONMENT OF PASSENGER SERVICE

The financial effects of eliminating passenger service is of substantial interest, particularly in light of conflicting claims about losses from rail passenger service generally. An exact estimate is impossible, because of the changes in nonpassenger revenues and expenditure levels over the years in which the discontinuance occurred, but in most cases these changes were sufficiently small that a reasonably accurate estimate can be made.

We have chosen a sample of 30 companies, most of the cases in which such discontinuance occurred. In seven of the cases, an estimate is impossible. In five, passenger revenues and costs were such small percentages of totals that it was impossible to trace the effects; this is true of the Piedmont and Northern (only 0.5 per cent of its revenues being from passenger service in later years), the Waterloo, the Fort Dodge Des Moines and Southern, the Yakima Valley, and the Charles City Western; in none of these cases was the gain at all significant. In the case of the Oregon Electric and the Spokane Coeur d'Alene and Palouse, sharp changes in freight business during the period of discontinuance of passenger service made estimates impossible.

In two cases there was no evidence of any direct gain, the decline in expenses being equivalent to the loss in passenger revenue. One was the Denver and Intermountain; if anything, a slight loss resulted from the abandonment. The other was the Pacific Electric. When this line disposed of its remaining passenger service to the Metropolitan Coach Lines in 1954, the fall in expenditures was a little less than the lost passenger revenue. In other words the passenger service had just been paying its way. This is not to imply that PE made a bad bargain; the equipment had badly deteriorated, and the company was paid well by Metropolitan for the service.

There were seven cases in which definite savings resulted, but shifts in freight business were so great that it is impossible to estimate the exact amount of savings. These were (the figure in parenthesis indicating the percentage of total revenues obtained from passenger service in the year preceding discontinuance): the Walla Walla Valley (7%), the Sand Springs (15%), the Illinois Terminal (6%), the Washington and Old Dominion (12%), the Grand River Valley (18%), the San Francisco and Napa Valley (15%), and the Willamette Valley Southern.

The other cases are listed in Table 12.

In all these cases, significant improvement in earnings resulted from

TABLE 12.—APPROXIMATE SAVINGS FROM ELIMINATION OF PASSENGER SERVICE

Company	Passenger revenue as percentage of total revenue*	Approximate savings	Net operating profit (after taxes)*
Visalia Electric	8	$ 20,000	$ 64,812
Cedar Rapids & Iowa City	7	150,000	148,896
Tidewater Southern	4	70,000	—2,723
Petaluma & Santa Rosa	5	10,000	68,000
Central California Traction†	25	80,000	95,591
Southern Iowa	20	30,000	38,000
Southern New York	45	40,000	—126,000
East St. Louis Columbia & Waterloo	30	20,000	—31,442
Arkansas Valley Interurban	15	70,000	63,808
Baltimore & Annapolis	70	100,000	1,951
Sacramento Northern†	30	100,000	—465,595
Aroostook Valley	2	35,000	71,040
Bamberger	8	145,000	187,244
Lackawanna & Wyoming Valley	60	30,000	—109,116

* Figures are for the year preceding the elimination of passenger service.
† Limited amount of streetcar service operated after interurban service was discontinued.

elimination of passenger service;* in general most of the lines operated the service several years longer than was justified by financial gains. In most instances service was discontinued following a long period of declining passenger revenue; for example, Tidewater Southern's 1931 passenger revenue was only 22% of that of 1920; that of Visalia Electric had fallen continuously from a high of $54,000 in 1912 to $15,000 in 1923. The number of passengers carried by San Francisco and Napa Valley had fallen from 310,000 in 1925 to 66,000 in 1935.

An examination of the changes in expenses following the abandonment of passenger service reveals that most of the saving occurred in maintenance of equipment (the decline ranging from one-third to five-sixths of the previous year's figures), and in power and transportation, in which the dollar savings was usually the greatest. Maintenance-of-way expenditures decreased in most cases, frequently by as much as one-third, but increased in a few. This reflects the improved earnings position, and the interurbans' policy, like the railroads', of determining expenditures for way-maintenance (above an absolute necessary minimum) in terms of the current profit situation, rather than in terms of any objective measure of needs. Likewise, in most instances, general expenses rose. Thus only a small proportion of the costs common to freight and passenger service was eliminated.

In several cases, the companies estimated the loss from passenger

* For companies earning a substantial total profit and paying corporate income tax rates approaching 52%, the net gain was only about half the indicated figure, since tax liability increased. The government was essentially bearing half of passenger service losses in such cases.

service in their applications to discontinue this service, and in general these estimates were fairly accurate, in terms of the actual experience. Thus Tidewater Southern claimed out-of-pocket losses of $28,000, Petaluma and Santa Rosa of $11,000, Central California Traction of $40,000, and Sacramento Northern of $88,000. These losses all approximated the actual savings. Visalia Electric claimed a loss figure of $54,000, which included an allocated share of common costs; the actual savings were of course far less.

The experience shows clearly that the lines made the decision to abandon passenger service strictly on the basis of marginal cash return considerations, without any allocation of common costs to the service, and thus on the basis appropriate in terms of economic analysis. But it is also clear that most of the roads operated passenger service several years beyond the point at which the service was breaking even. Several factors were responsible: belief in possible improvement (despite the long downward trend), possible fear of rejection of the application by regulatory authorities, and personal reluctance to give up a service for which the lines had first been built. The officials of many lines took pride in their passenger service, and regarded the freight activity as a sort of drudge work.

A reluctance to abandon passenger service may have destroyed a few roads that could have continued as freight carriers—the Salt Lake and Utah is a prime example—but the typical Midwestern interurban had so little carload-freight business that it could not possibly have subsisted on freight operations alone. The Winona, which had somewhat more freight than other lines, managed to eke out a hand-to-mouth existence on this basis for a decade.

THE AVERAGE LENGTH OF LIFE

The interurbans' average length of life as a passenger carrier was 28.8 years (weighted arithmetic average); the median (on a mileage basis) was 28 years. The average ranged from a high of 33 years in the North Central states to a low of 24 years in the New England states, as is shown in Table 13.

Table 13 also shows the distribution of miles abandoned by years of operation, in ten-year groups. The longest life, 65 years, was that of the Portland Traction's line from Portland to Oregon City, opened in 1893 and abandoned (passenger service only) in 1958. Relatively few companies lasted beyond 50 years; these included several lines of the Pacific Electric and the Illinois Terminal Company, portions of the Chicago North Shore and Milwaukee, the Chicago South Shore and South Bend, a small part of the West Penn, and a few others. Virtually all the mileage over 50 years was in the Pacific Coast and North Central states, plus the South Shore line. In Canada, the Vancouver–New Westminister line of British Columbia Electric rivaled the Portland line, with 62 years of service.

At the other extreme, 78 miles were operated less than 5 years. It is difficult to pinpoint the company with the shortest life; the Fidalgo City and Anacortes lasted a reported two years, but some residents of the area say that it actually ran only a few trips. The Lee–Huntington line of the Berkshire (scarcely an interurban) ran only two summers. In Canada, the Vineland extension of the Hamilton Grimsby and Beamsville lasted only one year. The Caldwell Traction (Idaho) line to Wilder was operated electrically only two years. The Sand Point line in Idaho, the Emigration Canyon line in Utah, the Texas Interurban, and parts of the Shore Line in Connecticut lasted less than ten years. Most of these were roads built at relatively late dates, but some of the roads lasting for only short periods, such as the Anacortes line, were among the first built.

TABLE 13.—LENGTH OF LIFE OF INTERURBAN LINES, BY REGION

Region*	0–9	10–19	20–29	30–39	40–49	50–59	60 and over
MILES ABANDONED†							
Pacific (28.2)	97	611	793	651	417	103	14
Southwest (26.4)	78	147	513	332	157	0	0
North Central (33.2)	22	371	714	372	579	302	11
Ohio Valley (27.8)	76	683	2,656	2,333	218	72	0
Middle Atlantic (28.9)	0	313	1,565	803	356	16	3
New England (24.4)	33	67	91	51	0	7	0
South (30.6)	22	62	142	210	50	0	0
Total (28.8)	328	2,254	6,474	4,752	1,777	500	28
PERCENTAGE DISTRIBUTION							
Pacific (28.2)	4	23	29	24	15	4	1
Southwest (26.4)	6	12	42	27	13	0	0
North Central (33.2)	1	16	30	16	24	13	–‡
Ohio Valley (27.8)	1	11	44	38	4	2	0
Middle Atlantic (28.9)	0	10	51	26	12	1	–‡
New England (24.4)	13	27	37	20	0	3	0
South (30.6)	5	13	29	43	10	0	0
Total (28.8)	2	14	40	30	11	3	–‡

* Figures in parentheses indicate the average length of life (years).
† In the case of lines abandoning passenger service only, the length of life is calculated to the date of this abandonment.
‡ Less than one per cent.

An examination of the earnings records over the years makes one fact obvious: there were virtually no lines that maintained a high level of earnings consistently throughout the history of the industry. The most successful of all the roads was the Piedmont and Northern—not as a typical interurban but as a carload freight hauler. The Detroit Monroe and Toledo Short Line and its neighbor, the Detroit Jackson and Chicago portion of the Detroit United, were successful for a number of years, and the Lake Shore consistently did better than most large Midwest roads. Interstate did extremely well for two decades. The Southwest Missouri, the Stark, and the Galveston–Houston earned profits consistently for a long period of time. Few Western roads did as well; as interurbans they were, almost without exception, not overly profitable, and some that survived as freight haulers were extremely unprofitable—the Oregon Electric and the Spokane and Inland Empire were among the worst examples. The most successful lines were in general the ones that connected larger cities in the Midwest. The heavy density suburban carriers, such as the Chicago area roads and the Pacific Electric, were not particularly successful in earlier years, but typically grew in strength in the twenties, the era of decline in the usual intercity type of operation.

The most unsuccessful—the complete failures—were roads connecting small towns, with inadequate traffic potential under the best circumstances. These included such lines as the Kankakee and Urbana, the Alton Jacksonville and Peoria, and the Lake Erie Bowling Green and Napoleon. The Chicago and Interurban had about as dismal a record as any, and the Fort Wayne Van Wert and Lima was in constant difficulties. The United of Oregon showed an operating loss for every year of its operation as an interurban, beyond the first.

THE PERSONAL TRAGEDY OF ABANDONMENT

The collapse of the industry has been described above in terms of facts and figures. But these cannot convey the personal losses and the tragedy that the decline of an industry creates, that are inevitable in a dynamic economy. Little sympathy need be lost on the owners of the large syndicates which promoted a number of the roads, who, with little investment of their own, hoped to reap high rewards, and ended up with worthless stock. Although they performed an important function in the growth of the industry, they usually suffered little in terms of a loss of their own funds. But many lines were promoted by local businessmen who persuaded their friends and neighbors to purchase stock, and much of their money was ultimately lost. The tragedy often involved the employees. When the companies were established, younger men were typically employed, and many of them stayed with the roads. As they reached the age at which transfer to other jobs was almost impossible, the roads curtailed service, and then were abandoned. The employees were often left without pensions and with little in the way of accumulated savings. The effects were particularly severe when roads were abandoned in the thirties, when even younger persons found it difficult to acquire jobs.

One of the best statements of the personal significance of the decline is to be found in the recently published autobiography of Carl Van Doren, whose father promoted the Kankakee and Urbana:

My father at that time was deeply troubled. The last of his enterprises, an electric railroad that would run north and south through Urbana, was still in its earliest stage; yet even then he may have had more qualms about it than he was ever to confess. The line would compete not only with the Illinois Central railroad, which it paralleled, but with automobiles and trucks—more

The Decision to Abandon 251

numerous every year, and destined in the end to bankrupt this little Kankakee and Urbana Traction Company of which he was president. People put money into it because he asked them to; they believed in him as he believed in it, for his initial faith in it was very strong; and thoughts of these people were to rob him of much sleep before he died. The railroad never did prosper, though it ran for years: not so far as Kankakee whose name it bore but at least as far as Paxton, which scarcely qualified as a terminal point. We all witnessed the dismal, slow disaster without any power to stop it on our part. It was eventually, in combination with the agricultural depression of the 1920's, to take away from him whatever wealth he had; my mother, by buying a few houses and renting them, and by renting rooms in her own house to university people, saved them both in so far as they could be saved. All of this was a heart-rending spectacle, and I am ahead of my story once more through mentioning it now.[8]

Part II

THE INDIVIDUAL INTERURBANS

PART II presents a brief history of each interurban, by state. The choice of the companies to include has been necessarily somewhat arbitrary, since, as we have noted, a rigorous definition of the term "interurban" is impossible. In general we have preferred to err by inclusion rather than by omission. An attempt has been made, however, to exclude both suburban operations of a strictly streetcar type and the rural trolleys of the New England type, except for brief mentions at the conclusion of the sections dealing with particular states. Main-line railroad electrifications, including main-line suburban operations, have also been omitted, except when they took on basically interurban characteristics, as have metropolitan-area rapid-transit lines, including such roads as the Key System and the New York Westchester and Boston.

Lines that have been extensively discussed in Part I, particularly the major roads of the Central Electric Railway Association network, have been treated somewhat more briefly than other lines. However, since Part II has been designed primarily as a reference work, we have not hesitated to duplicate relevant information also found in Part I.

Every effort has been made to ensure accuracy of dates; we have cross checked against various sources, and made local enquiries when necessary, but the paucity of reliable information on some roads creates the danger of some error.

On the maps, heavy solid lines indicate interurban routes, light lines indicate rural trolley routes and surburban operations, and broken lines indicate non-electrified lines, primarily those which planned to electrify but did not. No effort was made to include all suburban lines.

Ohio

No state approached within a thousand miles of Ohio's interurban mileage of 2,798. No Ohio town of 10,000 was without interurban service, and the territories along the shore of Lake Erie and from Toledo south to Cincinnati had highly developed networks. Almost the entire system had taken shape by 1908, and virtually all of it had vanished by 1939. About half the state's mileage had been abandoned by 1932. The geographical conditions that had brought forth the Ohio interurbans—well-populated farm areas devoted to diversified agriculture, numerous medium-sized cities and towns, and a very large number of rural villages—did not generate the carload traffic that saved much of the interurban mileage west of the Mississippi. In addition, by the 1920's most of the Ohio interurbans could not afford the physical modifications that would have enabled them to interchange freight with the railroads. Only the Youngstown and Southern has survived as a freight carrier, along with short segments of other lines that are used in local switching.

The Ohio interurbans were particularly homogeneous physically. With a single exception (the Scioto Valley Traction Company) all used an overhead pole trolley, and with another exception (the Hocking-Sunday Creek Traction Company) all used low-voltage DC power. Except for some of the Cincinnati, Columbus, and Wheeling suburban lines, all were standard gauge.

CINCINNATI LAWRENCEBURG AND AURORA ELECTRIC STREET RAILROAD COMPANY

This interurban was a standard-gauge line along the Ohio River from Anderson's Ferry, at the west end of Cincinnati, to Aurora, Indiana (25 miles), with a branch from Valley Junction to Harrison, Ohio (8 miles). It was completed in 1900. Plans for extension west to Rising Sun, Madison, and Louisville were never implemented. In 1913 flood damage forced the road into receivership, from which it did not emerge for 15 years, one of the longest receivership periods in the industry's history. The line is principally noteworthy for its pioneer purchase of lightweight, one-man equipment in 1918. The company was severely handicapped by its remote terminal, but like the rest of Cincinnati's standard-gauge interurbans, it never achieved entry into the center of the city. After reorganization as the Cincinnati Lawrenceburg and Aurora Electric Railway Company in 1928, the line survived for only two years, and was abandoned in 1930 after a year of operating losses. Six miles from Anderson's Ferry to Fernbank were converted to 5'-2½" gauge and operated by the Cincinnati Street Railway until 1941. The lightweight cars were sold to the Sand Springs Railway at Tulsa, Oklahoma.

CINCINNATI GEORGETOWN AND PORTSMOUTH RAILROAD

This company completed a 3-foot-gauge steam railroad between Cincinnati and Georgetown (41 miles) in 1886, and in 1902 both converted it to standard gauge and electrified it. A branch from Lake Allyn to Batavia was opened at the same time. The company also operated a 5'-2½" line to Coney Island that entered Cincinnati over the street railway. The standard-gauge line was extended from Georgetown to Russellville (8 miles) in 1904. An affiliate, the Felicity and Bethel Railroad (9 miles), was opened in 1906. The CG&P hoped to build east to Portsmouth, but although it did some grading between Russellville and West Union, it lacked the funds for completion. The road always retained much of the character of a shortline railroad, in spite of its electric operation. It interchanged railroad freight, operated a railway post office, and even interchanged a passenger car with a steam shortline, the Ohio River and Columbus Railway to serve Ripley, Ohio. The Felicity and Bethel used a steam locomotive for freight service.

The company failed in 1927 and was reorganized in 1928 as the Cincinnati Georgetown Railroad Company. The new corporation abandoned the Georgetown-Russellville extension in 1933, and in 1935 abandoned the outer 20 miles of the remaining main line, as well as the Batavia branch. It gave up passenger service at the same time. In 1936, it abandoned the rest of the property.

CINCINNATI AND COLUMBUS TRACTION COMPANY

This was a standard-gauge interurban, 53 miles long, between Norwood, at the edge of Cincinnati, and Hillsboro. It was chartered in 1901 and opened on April 22, 1906. It was promoted locally and early in its history was known as "The Swing

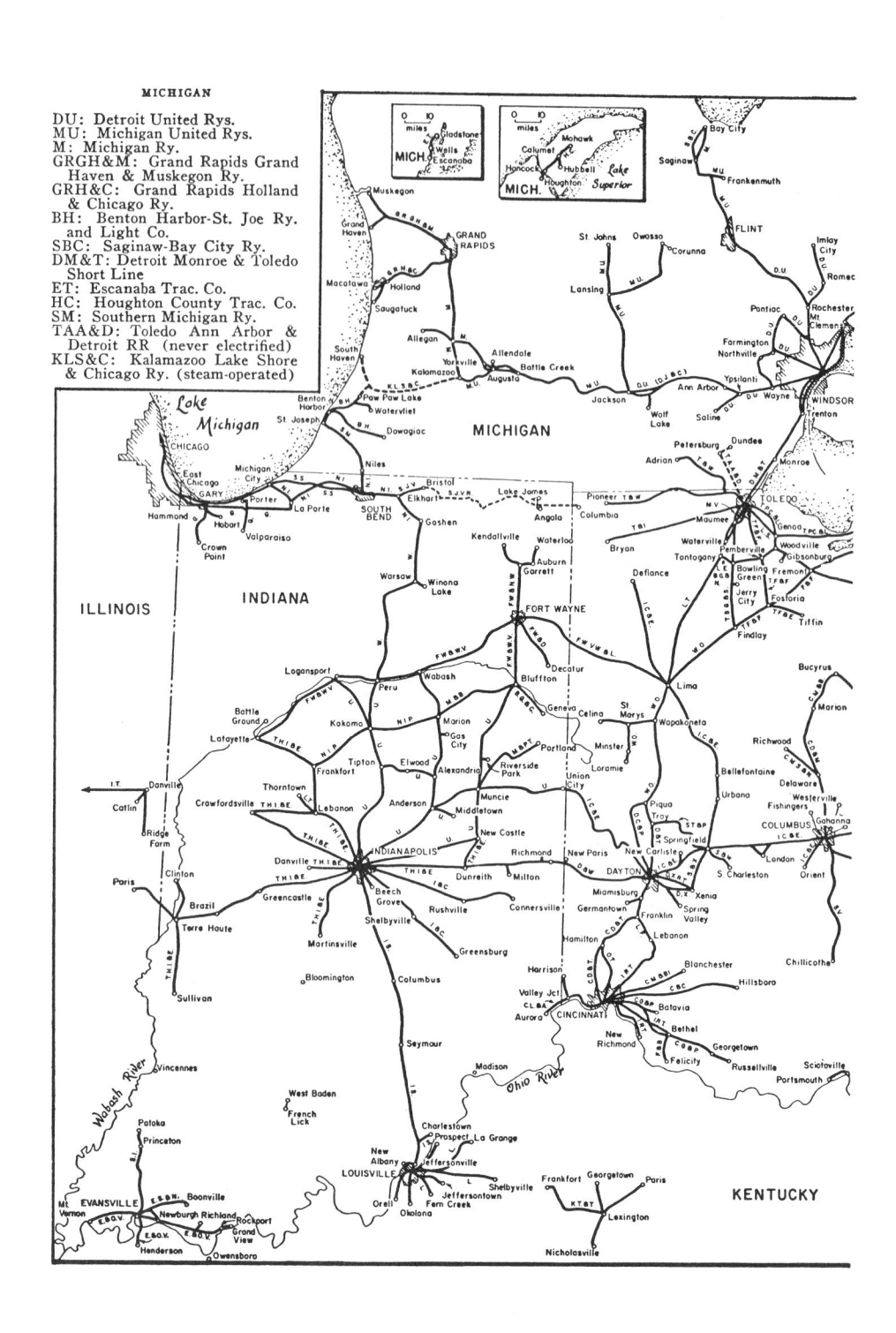

MICHIGAN

DU: Detroit United Rys.
MU: Michigan United Rys.
M: Michigan Ry.
GRGH&M: Grand Rapids Grand Haven & Muskegon Ry.
GRH&C: Grand Rapids Holland & Chicago Ry.
BH: Benton Harbor-St. Joe Ry. and Light Co.
SBC: Saginaw-Bay City Ry.
DM&T: Detroit Monroe & Toledo Short Line
ET: Escanaba Trac. Co.
HC: Houghton County Trac. Co.
SM: Southern Michigan Ry.
TAA&D: Toledo Ann Arbor & Detroit RR (never electrified)
KLS&C: Kalamazoo Lake Shore & Chicago Ry. (steam-operated)

INDIANA

SS: Chicago South Shore & South Bend RR
G: Gary Rys.
NI: Northern Indiana Ry.
W: Winona Interurban Ry.
SJV: St. Joseph Valley Trac. Co.
SJVR: St. Joseph Valley Ry. (never electrified)
THI&E: Terre Haute Indianapolis & Eastern Trac. Co.
IS: Interstate Public Service Co.
U: Union Trac. Co. of Indiana
FW&D: Fort Wayne & Decatur Trac. Co.
FW&NW: Fort Wayne & Northwestern Ry.
FW&WV: Fort Wayne & Wabash Valley Trac. Co.
NIP: Northern Indiana Power Co.
M&B: Marion & Bluffton Trac. Co.
BG&C: Bluffton Geneva & Celina Trac. Co.
I&C: Indianapolis & Cincinnati Trac. Co.
SI: Southern Indiana Gas & Elec. Co.
E&OV: Evansville & Ohio Valley Ry.
ES&N: Evansville Suburban & Newburgh Ry.
A: Angola Ry. & Power Co.
LT: Lebanon-Thorntown Trac. Co.
M&PT: Muncie & Portland Trac. Co.

OHIO

Northeast

P&O: Pennsylvania & Ohio Ry.
CP&A: Cleveland Painesville & Ashtabula RR
CP&E: Cleveland Painesville & Eastern RR
EOT: Eastern Ohio Trac. Co.
NO: Northern Ohio Trac. & Light Co.
S: Stark Electric RR
CA&MV: Cleveland Alliance & Mahoning Valley Ry.
M&S: Mahoning & Shenango Ry. and Light Co.
YS: Youngstown & Southern Ry.
Y&OR: Youngstown & Ohio River RR

OHIO (CONTINUED)

SEL&BV: Steubenville East Liverpool & Beaver Valley Trac. Co.
WT: Wheeling Trac. Co.
CSW&C: Cleveland Southwestern & Columbus Ry.
LS: Lake Shore Elec. Ry.
SN&M: Sandusky Norwalk & Mansfield Elec. Ry.
MRy: Mansfield Ry. Light & Power Co.

Northwest

F&F: Fostoria & Fremont Ry.
TF&E: Tiffin Fostoria & Eastern Elec. Ry.
TF&F: Toledo Fostoria & Findlay Ry.
TPC&L: Toledo Port Clinton & Lakeside Ry.
T&W: Toledo & Western Ry.
T&I: Toledo & Indiana RR
MV: Maumee Valley Rys. and Light Co.
LT: Lima & Toledo Trac. Co.
LEBG&N: Lake Erie Bowling Green & Napoleon Ry.
WO: Western Ohio Ry.
TBG&S: Toledo Bowling Green & Southern Trac. Co.

Central

IC&E: Indiana Columbus & Eastern Trac. Co.
FWVW&L: Fort Wayne Van Wert & Lima Trac. Co.
ST&P: Springfield Troy & Piqua Ry.
D&T: Dayton & Troy Elec. Ry.
DC&P: Dayton Covington & Piqua Trac. Co.
D&W: Dayton & Western Trac. Co.
DX: Dayton & Xenia Transit Co.
D&XRT: Dayton & Xenia Rapid Transit Co.
S&X: Springfield & Xenia Ry.
S&W: Springfield & Washington Ry.
CN&Z: Columbus Newark & Zanesville Elec. Ry.
SEO: Southeast Ohio Ry. & Light Co.
CP&L: Cambridge Power Light & Trac. Co.
CD&M: Columbus Delaware & Marion Ry.
CM&B: Columbus Marion & Bucyrus Ry.
CMS&N: Columbus Magnetic Springs & Northern Ry.
SV: Scioto Valley Trac. Co.

South

CD&T: Cincinnati Dayton & Toledo Trac. Co.
OT: Ohio Trac. Co.
LF: Lebanon & Franklin Trac. Co.
IRT: Interurban Ry. & Terminal Co.
CM&Bl: Cincinnati Milford & Blanchester Trac. Co.
C&C: Cincinnati & Columbus Trac. Co.
CG&P: Cincinnati Georgetown & Portsmouth RR
CL&A: Cincinnati Lawrenceburg & Aurora Elec. St. RR
PSt.: Portsmouth Street RR & Light Co.
OV: Ohio Valley Elec. Ry.
W&JB: Wellston & Jackson Belt Ry.
H-SC: Hocking-Sunday Creek Trac. Co.
G&N: Gallipolis & Northern Trac. Co.
OR: Ohio River Elec. Ry. & Power Co.
MWP: Monongahela West Penn Trac. Co.
F&B: Felicity & Bethel RR

KENTUCKY

L: Louisville & Interurban RR
KT&T: Kentucky Trac. & Terminal Co.

Line," after its principal promoter. The company's ambitions to build east to Chillicothe or Columbus were never realized. It paralleled no railroad, although the Baltimore & Ohio had a branch into Hillsboro. The company was never profitable enough to pay a dividend. The property was so badly damaged in the flood of 1913 (which injured all the lines in the area) that the company applied for voluntary receivership, from which it never emerged. In common with most interurbans, it had a very bad year in 1918, when it lost $21,036. The receiver concluded the property was hopeless and in 1919 applied for abandonment. Permission was granted, but an unsuccessful effort on the part of local residents to refinance the road and to continue it in service delayed sale for scrap until 1920. Its power business outlasted the rail operation, but was also sold to local interests in 1920. Its cars, heavy Jewett combines, were sold to the THI&E, the Joplin and Pittsburg, and the Northeast Oklahoma, which was about to electrify.

CINCINNATI MILFORD AND BLANCHESTER TRACTION COMPANY

A predecessor company, the Cincinnati Milford and Loveland Traction Company opened a 5'-2½" line from Madisonville, on the outskirts of Cincinnati, to Milford (17 miles) in 1903. The road built an additional 12 miles to Blanchester in 1906. The company never operated to Loveland, and never carried out its plans to build to Columbus. Cars were equipped with a double trolley for running on the 8 miles of the Cincinnati Street Railway between Madisonville and a downtown terminal at 5th and Sycamore. The company found its trackage rights too expensive and after 1915 no longer came into the center of the city.

The road was put in receivership in 1917 and in the following year was reorganized as the Cincinnati Milford and Blanchester Traction Company. The Kroger family, which controlled the company, abandoned the segment from Newtonsville to Blanchester in 1922, and sold the rest to interests connected with the Cincinnati Georgetown and Portsmouth Railroad in 1926. The company was hopelessly uneconomic, and was abandoned in the same year, save for the Madisonville–Milford line, which was incorporated into the Cincinnati Street Railway. The CM&B's lightweight cars, very similar to the last cars of the Cincinnati Lawrenceburg and Aurora, were also sold to the Street Railway. The surviving Milford line was cut back to Mariemont in 1936 and abandoned entirely in 1942.

INTERURBAN RAILWAY AND TERMINAL COMPANY

Three 5'-2½" lines out of Cincinnati comprised this company. The first was built along the Ohio River to New Richmond (19 miles) in 1902 by the Cincinnati and Eastern Electric Railway. The second, the Suburban Traction Company, opened a line to Bethel (32 miles) in June 1903, and the third, the Rapid Railway, finished a line northeast to Lebanon (33 miles) in October of the same year. The three companies were consolidated in 1902. This company was also badly damaged by the flood of 1913, and in 1914 went into a receivership from which it was never removed. The Bethel line was particularly weak, since most of it was within sight of the Cincinnati Georgetown and Portsmouth, a somewhat stronger company. The IR&T Bethel line had the advantage of entry into the downtown area over the Cincinnati Street Railway, but this was not enough to save it, and it was abandoned in 1918. The remaining lines to Lebanon and New Richmond were abandoned in 1923.

OHIO TRACTION COMPANY (MILL CREEK VALLEY LINE)

The lesser of the two interurbans connecting Cincinnati and Hamilton was this 5'-2½" line through Wyoming and Glendale. It was built by predecessor companies between 1897 and 1901, and brought together by merger as the Cincinnati and Hamilton Traction Company in 1902. This road had great difficulty securing a franchise in Hamilton in 1901, but did so after threatening to run motor vehicles from the city limits to the business district as train connections. In 1902 the property was leased to the Cincinnati Interurban Company, which in 1905 became a wholly owned subsidiary of the Ohio Traction Company, a Schoepf-McGowan corporation that controlled the street railway in Cincinnati. It operated as the Mill Creek Valley Line of the Ohio Traction Company until 1926, when it became part of the Cincinnati Street Railway itself. The Street Railway cut the line back to Glendale in 1926, and discontinued it in 1932.

LEBANON AND FRANKLIN TRACTION COMPANY

This interurban was opened on May 28, 1904, between the towns of its name, which were 11 miles apart. It connected at Lebanon with the broad-gauge Interurban Railway and Terminal Company and at Franklin with the Ohio Electric's Cincinnati-

Dayton line, from which it purchased power. It carried its passengers in a coach and combine. Short interurbans that served no important center of population were the weakest in the industry, and thus it is not surprising that this company was among the first to be abandoned. On December 11, 1918, the Ohio Public Utilities Commission granted it permission to abandon, effective January 1, 1919.

DAYTON AND WESTERN TRACTION COMPANY

This road began service from Dayton to Eaton, Ohio, on June 26, 1898, and completed its line to Richmond, Indiana, in 1903. Although its main line was only 38 miles long, and it had only a single branch (New Westville–New Paris: 3 miles, built in 1903), the company was significant because of its strategic location. It had the most direct connection between the Indiana and Ohio networks, and formed part of a continuous line from Terre Haute to Zanesville. As a result, it had a much larger roster of equipment than most roads of its size, and throughout its history was either sought or controlled by the major interurbans with which it connected. It was built by interests affiliated with the Dayton and Troy Electric Railway and the city lines in Dayton, but in 1906 it was leased in perpetuity to the newly formed Indiana Columbus and Eastern Traction Company (q.v.). In the following year, the lease, along with the properties of the IC&E, passed into the hands of the Ohio Electric Railway.

As a consequence of the financial difficulties that caused the Ohio Electric to go bankrupt in 1921, the Dayton and Western was returned to its owners in April 1920. It had eleven years of independence, during which it made a serious effort to develop interline limited traffic with the THI&E, but in 1931 the company went bankrupt. The road became one of the few interurbans to default on an equipment trust (except at abandonment), and surrendered its best cars, which the Cincinnati Car Company had lengthened and modernized in the 1920's. The Dayton and Western then acquired five Cincinnati lightweight cars from the Cleveland Southwestern, which had recently been abandoned. Also in 1931, the Dayton and Western came under supervision of the Cincinnati and Lake Erie Railroad, which operated it until 1936. Traffic was declining drastically during this period—gross revenue fell from $293,000 in 1929 to $74,000 in 1933—but the line was kept as the last connection (after 1932) between the Indiana Railroad and the Ohio interurbans. In 1936 the receiver sold the property to the Fidelity Trust Company of Indianapolis, as trustee, and it in turn leased the physical plant and a single piece of equipment, a freight motor, to the Indiana Railroad. The Indiana Railroad operated the property with its own equipment for nine months, and terminated its lease effective May 9, 1937. The trustee then dismantled the road.

SPRINGFIELD AND XENIA RAILWAY

The Springfield and Xenia Traction Company was built between the cities of its name (20 miles) in 1902, but failed and was sold under foreclosure to the Springfield and Xenia Railway Company in 1904. A second company of this name succeeded to the property in 1906. The interurban provided hourly service, serving Antioch College at Yellow Springs en route.

In 1928 the company applied to the regulatory authorities to abandon, and received permission, subject to the usual condition that the property be sold within 60 days at scrap value to any buyer who proposed to continue operation. The Springfield and Xenia Railroad was formed locally to buy the property. The line was continued in operation until July 1934, when it was abandoned. Gross revenue had fallen from $106,000 in 1923 to $16,000 in 1933, and the road had failed to cover operating costs for twelve consecutive years.

DAYTON AND XENIA TRANSIT COMPANY

In addition to city service in Dayton, this company operated three interurban lines, two between Dayton and Xenia (each 16 miles long), and a branch from Belmont to Spring Valley (14 miles). The two lines to Xenia were built simultaneously in 1899. The Dayton and Xenia Rapid Transit Company laid its track on the main highway between the two cities and opened it in December 1899. In January 1900, the Dayton and Xenia Traction Company opened a parallel line on a private right-of-way only a short distance away. In 1899 the latter company had absorbed the Dayton Spring Valley and Wilmington Transit Company, whose line to Spring Valley had been completed earlier that year.

In 1901 the Traction Company absorbed the Rapid Transit Company and operated it for seven years as a secondary line. The Traction Company (which after 1901 was known as the Dayton and Xenia Transit Company) was badly hurt by the depression of 1907, and was put in receivership. The receiver immediately sought to abandon the Rapid Transit line, which had been neglected to the point that an open car had been used on it in the winter. It was abandoned in March 1908—the first significant abandonment of a Midwestern interurban. The rest of the property was sold to the Dayton Springfield and Xenia Southern Railway under foreclosure in 1909. In 1926 this company was in turn reorganized as the Dayton and Xenia Railway Company. The outer 12 miles of the Spring Valley branch (Spring Valley–Beaverton) had been abandoned in December 1917, and the remainder in 1923, but the main line covered its operating costs throughout the worst years of the depression and survived until September 30, 1937.

SPRINGFIELD AND WASHINGTON RAILWAY

On December 24, 1904, the Springfield South Charleston Washington Court House and Chillicothe Traction Company opened an interurban of 15 miles from Springfield to South Charleston. Ambitions to build along the Detroit Toledo and Ironton and the Cincinnati Hamilton and Dayton railroads to Chillicothe were never realized. If completed, the interurban would probably have been a weak one; but the portion that was put in service was hopeless and failed almost immediately. The original corporation was succeeded at a foreclosure sale by the Washington Traction Company in December 1905, but in 1907 the new company also went bankrupt. The Springfield and Washington Railway was organized in 1908, and managed to operate until 1922. On December 31 the line was abandoned, except for a three-mile segment retained for industrial switching by the Baker Wood Preserving Company.

SPRINGFIELD TROY AND PIQUA RAILWAY

General Asa S. Bushnell, a former governor of Ohio, organized this interurban as a direct line between Springfield and Troy; a projected branch to Piqua was never built. The interurban was about 30 miles long, lightly graded, and poorly patronized, since the tributary territory was not heavily populated. The company shared a powerhouse in Springfield with two other small lines, the Springfield and Xenia and the Springfield and Washington. Four 50-foot wooden passenger cars purchased from John Stephenson provided service from the opening in 1904. The company was relatively unsuccessful and had a short life. It was reorganized in 1917 as the Springfield Terminal Railway and Power Company but failed again and was abandoned in 1923, except for a segment of 3.3 miles between Springfield and Maitland, which was maintained for freight-terminal operations under the name the Springfield Suburban Railroad.

The company had interchanges with the Erie and the Detroit Toledo & Ironton at Maitland, and had several sidings to industrial plants along its entry into the city. The company had a private right-of-way parallel to the Detroit Toledo & Ironton almost into the heart of Springfield, but even so, had some curves into industrial sidings so sharp that trainmen had to insert special drawing links in place of standard coupler knuckles on box cars. This practice ended only in 1946, when alignment in Springfield was eased. The line was dieselized about a year later. The demise of *Collier's* magazine cut shipments into the Crowell Collier Publishing Co., the largest firm on the road, and rendered operations unprofitable. The line applied for abandonment in 1959, and part of the switching track passed into the hands of the DT&I.

DAYTON AND TROY ELECTRIC RAILWAY

This company opened an interurban between Dayton and Troy (20 miles) in December 1901, and in the following year acquired under perpetual lease the Miami Valley Railway between Troy and Piqua (11 miles), which had been in operation since 1893. The Dayton and Troy was entirely built on private right-of-way except in towns, and was partly double-tracked. The company was conservatively financed and more railroad-like in its dispatching and operating procedures than most interurbans.

Throughout the Dayton and Troy's history, it worked closely with the Western Ohio and the Toledo Bowling Green and Southern as "The Lima Route." Beginning in 1906, the D&T participated in an equipment pool with the other two lines, but in 1916 it withdrew. It continued to offer closely coordinated schedules, however.

In the 1920's the company offered cheap excursions and made other attempts to reverse the decline of passenger traffic; and in 1929 it bought a series of well-equipped Cincinnati lightweight cars. The road was put in receivership in March 1932, but was making an effort to continue in the face of losses. Abandonment of the Western Ohio in January 1932, had reduced its traffic greatly. At noon on Wednesday, August 3, 1932, the Dayton and Troy's bridge over the Miami River at Dayton collapsed under the weight of a box motor and trailer, whereupon the receiver, having insufficient funds to repair the damage, moved to abandon the railway immediately. On August 10, motorman Peter Sprecher, who had brought the company's first car into Dayton in 1901, took its last one from the north end of the bridge to the car house at Tippecanoe City.

DAYTON COVINGTON AND PIQUA TRACTION COMPANY

This interurban was founded as the Dayton and Troy Traction Company, but in 1901, as a result of the completion of the Dayton and Troy Electric Railway, it changed its name and its intended destination. The line was built north from Dayton along a branch of the Cincinnati Hamilton & Dayton Railroad to Covington and then east to Piqua, where it arrived on May 12, 1903. Its termini were thus the same as those of the Dayton and Troy, but its route was longer (34 miles) and its territory less productive. It also lacked the close cooperation of the Western Ohio that the Dayton and Troy enjoyed. It was very much the weaker of the two companies and went bankrupt in 1922. Although the company had never shown an operating loss, there were no purchasers at a receiver's sale, and the property was abandoned on November 6, 1926. At the beginning, the company used short wooden equipment, but after 1918 performed most of its service with a pair of steel center-door cars built by the Cincinnati Car Company.

The DC&P is remembered for one notable accomplishment: it was one of the few interurbans to outlast the railroad it paralleled; the branch of the CH&D was abandoned in 1923.

WESTERN OHIO RAILWAY

The Western Ohio Railway was a major interurban of about 115 miles of line, with its center around Lima, Ohio. It was incorporated in 1900, and its first line, Lima to Wapakoneta and Minster (36 miles), was opened in 1902. By 1903 the company had additional lines from Wapakoneta to Piqua (32 miles) and from St. Mary's to Celina (10 miles). The company intended to lay track at once from Lima to Findlay (33 miles) to close the gap between the interurbans of northern and central Ohio, but it was unable to do so because of the financial stringencies of 1903-4. The line was built in 1905, and the company began to participate in the "Lima Route" interline service between Toledo and Dayton in the following year. The company had plans for further building, in particular a line from Celina to Portland, Indiana, but the general cessation of interurban building after 1908 allowed only one to be executed. In 1910 and 1911, the company's subsidiary, the Minster and Loramie Railway, built a 3-mile extension to Fort Loramie. From 1911 to 1920 this extension was separately operated, but thereafter was integrated with the rest of the Western Ohio. The company also participated with the Lake Shore Electric in building the Fostoria and Fremont Railway (q.v.) in 1911, and obtained trackage rights on the Toledo Fostoria and Findlay to connect with it. The new line permitted establishment of the Cleveland–Lima interline service described in Chapter 3.

The Western Ohio was in relatively weak condition after World War I. In 1921 the Union Trust Company of Cleveland, one of its creditors, petitioned for receivership, but none was established. In 1927 the company defaulted on interest payments on its first mortgage, and in 1928 was foreclosed and reorganized as the Western Ohio Railway and Power Company. In 1930 the new company sold its power operations to the Central Ohio Light and Power Company, but actually expanded its railway holdings. Upon abandonment of the Toledo Fostoria and Findlay in 1930, the WO arranged to continue the Fostoria-Findlay segment, over which it had trackage rights, so that the Cleveland–Lima route could be maintained. It organized the Fostoria Arcadia and Findlay Railway for this purpose. At this time, interline service to Fremont was provided with Kuhlman lightweight cars of the WO and the F&F, built in 1922.

Since the WO had always depended more than most interurbans on interline traffic, the abandonments of its connections, especially the Toledo Bowling Green and Southern in 1930, hurt it seriously. The company suffered its first operating loss in 1930. It continued to operate despite declining traffic and mounting losses until January 16, 1932, when the Western Ohio, the Fostoria Arcadia and Findlay, and the Fostoria and Fremont were all entirely abandoned.

TOLEDO BOWLING GREEN AND SOUTHERN TRACTION COMPANY

This interurban was throughout its history an affiliate of the Findlay Street Railway. In 1900 the Street Railway opened a 5-mile extension north to Mortimer to connect with the Nickel Plate Road main line. In 1901 the Street Railway merged with the Toledo Bowling Green and Fremont Railway, which had connected Toledo and Bowling Green in 1896, and built south to Trombley and Jerry City in 1900. The new company, the Toledo Bowling Green and Southern Traction Company, was completed by building 12 miles of track between Trombley and Mortimer. The company was leased to the Toledo Urban and Interurban Railway, which owned about two miles of track at Perrysburg, and had trackage rights over the Toledo and Maumee Valley between Toledo and Perrysburg. A through route of 51 miles from Toledo to Findlay was completed in 1902. The TU&I defaulted on its lease in 1908, and was sold the following year to a company called the Toledo and Findlay Railway, which was in turn purchased by the TBG&S. At this time, the TBG&S came into control of the west side line of the Toledo and Maumee Valley, which it used for entrance into Toledo.

As a consequence of being built in large part early in interurban development, the road had a poor physical plant that was always a handicap to it. Originally the company operated with short wooden equipment, but in 1918 it bought four well-designed steel combines from the Cincinnati Car Company. About this time, it withdrew from the equipment pool with the Western Ohio, but continued to make close connections with WO cars in the Lima Route service. Its only branch, Trombley-Jerry City (2 miles) was abandoned in 1920. The company incurred deficits after 1926, but never went bankrupt. It was abandoned, together with the nearby Toledo Fostoria and Findlay, with which it had worked closely, on October 1, 1930.

MAUMEE VALLEY RAILWAYS AND LIGHT COMPANY

On August 1, 1894, the Toledo and Maumee Valley Railway opened two lines, one on each side of the Maumee River, between Toledo and Maumee—a total of 22 miles. A subsidiary, the Toledo Waterville and Southern Railway, one of the numerous companies that tried to build from Toledo to Napoleon and Defiance, built a line from Maumee to Waterville (6 miles) in 1901. In December 1902 the two companies were merged into the Maumee Valley Railways and Light Company, controlled by the Everett-Moore interests. About 1908 the west line passed into the hands of the Toledo Bowling Green and Southern Traction Company (*q.v.*), which thereafter leased trackage rights on it to the Maumee Valley. The Waterville extension was unprofitable, mainly because it was so close to the Maumee River that it suffered almost annual flood damage. It was so badly damaged by the flood of 1913 that it was not rebuilt. The builders of the Lima and Toledo (Ohio Electric), who had originally planned to enter Toledo over this branch, changed their mind and built their own entrance into Toledo via Waterville in 1908.

The Maumee Valley's operation was integrated with the Toledo Railways and Light Company, which owned it and furnished most of its equipment. In 1921 the Maumee Valley went into bankruptcy, and in 1924 was abandoned. Its gross revenues no longer covered operating costs, and the trackage rights over the TBG&S were proving prohibitively expensive.

TOLEDO FOSTORIA AND FINDLAY RAILWAY

This project was conceived and financed by five local Ohio businessmen. The road was opened between Findlay and Fostoria (15 miles) in August 1901. There was no further construction during the first interurban building boom, but during the second (in August 1905), the company built north from Fostoria to Pemberville (18 miles), creating a junction with the Lake Erie Bowling Green and Napoleon. The company built north from Pemberville to Toledo (19 miles), and so completed the interurban on June 20, 1908. The company was relatively successful. It operated hourly service between Findlay and Fostoria, and service every two hours between Fostoria and Toledo.

On two occasions the company acquired other interurban properties. In 1916 it purchased the bankrupt Lake Erie Bowling Green and Napoleon, retained the Pemberville–Bowling Green segment as a branch (11.5 miles), and scrapped the rest. On January 1, 1925, the company purchased the Tiffin and Fostoria Railway (14 miles), which until two years earlier had been the Tiffin Fostoria and Eastern Electric Railway (*q.v.*).

The company on May 15, 1925, abandoned the former LEBG&N line into Bowling Green, apparently because the track and overhead had deteriorated badly. The company was unprofitable in the late 1920's, and applied for abandonment shortly after the onset of the depression. The Toledo–Fostoria line and the Tiffin branch were abandoned October 1, 1930, but the Findlay–Fostoria line was sold to men affiliated with the Western Ohio Railway and Power Company (*q.v.*).

FOSTORIA AND FREMONT RAILWAY

In 1909 the Lake Shore Electric and the Western Ohio Railway (*q.v.*) organized this company to permit them to offer a joint service between Cleveland and Lima. It was completed in 1911, the last but one of the major interurbans built in Ohio. The line was dispatched by the Lake Shore dispatcher at Fremont and originally operated with two second-hand LSE cars, plus equipment of the parent companies. After 1922, two new Kuhlman lightweight cars, built to plans of the Western Ohio, provided local service. After 1929, the two cars participated in an equipment pool with cars of the Western Ohio and the Dayton and Troy in Dayton–Fremont through service. The Lake Shore and the Western Ohio were represented equally on the board of directors. The Fostoria and Fremont survived as long as the Western Ohio—until January 16, 1932. A single box motor and about two miles of track between Fremont and Ballville were retained in service to switch coal from the Nickel Plate Road to a generating plant of the Ohio Power Company. This operation ended in 1953, and the track was removed in 1957.

TIFFIN FOSTORIA AND EASTERN ELECTRIC RAILWAY

The Tiffin and Interurban Consolidated Railway Company, one of the earliest projects in Ohio, was trying to build between Tiffin and Fostoria (14 miles) in 1896 when it failed and was sold under foreclosure to the Tiffin and Fostoria Electric Railway Company. In 1898 D. H. Kimberley and his associates, who were connected with the Cleveland Exchange Banking Company, purchased the property and reorganized it under the name of the Tiffin Fostoria and Eastern Electric Railway Company. The Tiffin and Fostoria Railway Company acquired the property without change in ownership in 1923, and on January 1, 1925, the entire line was sold to the Toledo Fostoria and Findlay (q.v.), which operated it until 1930. The TF&E operated the street railway in Tiffin until 1919.

LAKE ERIE BOWLING GREEN AND NAPOLEON RAILWAY

This company is a major example of the ill-conceived projects of the first interurban building boom. Its largest community, Bowling Green, had only 5,067 residents (1900), and the tributary territory was lightly populated. Fortunately, most such projects were stillborn. The line was opened on Thanksgiving Day in 1902, between Bowling Green and Pemberville (11.5 miles), which was to become a junction with the Toledo Fostoria and Findlay. The company's principal purpose was to provide Bowling Green with a connection to the Lake Shore Electric at Woodville. It built east from Pemberville in 1903–5, but encountered the Pennsylvania Railroad's usual adamancy when it sought to make a crossing at Woodville. An overhead crossing was put in service in 1906 and the extension (6 miles) to Woodville was completed. Plans to build farther east toward the Marblehead Peninsula were never executed, but the company received a franchise for street running in Port Clinton in 1903.

The company also sought to build west to Grand Rapids and thence along the east bank of the Maumee River to Napoleon and Defiance. In 1910, after stronger companies had ceased building in Ohio, the LEBG&N built the first segment of this projected line, 6 miles from Bowling Green to Tontogany, a junction with the Ohio Electric. Almost immediately afterward the company went into bankruptcy. In 1911, when the company was unable to pay a debt of only $325, the road was put in the hands of a receiver. At a sale in 1916 it was purchased for $225,000 by the Toledo Fostoria and Findlay (q.v.).

TOLEDO AND INDIANA RAILROAD

The Toledo and Indiana Railway built an interurban line from Toledo to Wauseon (34 miles) in 1903, and in 1905 extended it from Wauseon to Bryan (22 miles). Although the company was profitable, it was placed in receivership in 1907 as a result of a dispute concerning stock ownership; it was reorganized in 1910 as the Toledo and Indiana Traction Company. In the following year the road was sold to Henry L. Doherty of New York and reconstituted as the Toledo and Indiana Railroad, the name it retained for the rest of its history. The line ran along the north side of the Lake Shore and Michigan Southern (New York Central) main line through flat terrain, and handled carload freight in interchange with the railroads. Although the volume of carload freight was never great, the company depended heavily on it for revenue.

The company had at least four plans for reaching Indiana, none of which it could execute. About 1906 it planned to build along the LS&MS to Butler and Waterloo for a connection with the Toledo and Chicago (Fort Wayne and Northwestern). Later, it considered building directly from Bryan to Fort Wayne via Hicksville, or northwest from Bryan to a connection with the St. Joseph Valley near the state line.

Finally, it proposed a branch from Delta to Napoleon and Defiance, with an extension along the Wabash Railroad to Fort Wayne.

In 1935 the T&I's entry into Toledo on the Dorr Street city line was abandoned. The company was forced to cut its service back to Vulcan at the edge of the city, but continued service for another four years, until October 25, 1939. The road had operating losses for 13 of its last 16 years, and ultimately passenger service was reduced to only four trips per day to Bryan.

TOLEDO AND WESTERN RAILWAY

The Toledo and Western was probably the first electric line intended to be a general carrier of passengers and carload freight on the order of a short-line railroad, but operated with orthodox interurban equipment. Frank E. Seagrave of Toledo conceived of the project in the mid-1890's but was unable to secure financing and to begin construction until 1900. In March 1901, the line reached Sylvania and in December reached Adrian, Michigan (36 miles). An underpass beneath the Wabash Railway was not completed and the track could not be joined with the street railway in Adrian until 1903. From Allen Junction track was pushed west to Fayette (31 miles) in 1902 and to Pioneer (12 miles) in 1903. The company graded toward the Indiana state line, but never was able to build to a connection with the Indiana interurbans.

Because the road's main line did not parallel a railroad, it was successful in establishing freight interchange with the railroads, and developed a modest traffic in agricultural products, particularly in sugar beets. But owing to the sparse population along the line, the road was financially unsuccessful; it failed, and was sold in 1906 to Cleveland owners affiliated with Everett and Moore. The new company, the Toledo and Western Railroad, passed into the hands of Henry L. Doherty in 1913, along with several other Everett-Moore properties.

The property went bankrupt again in 1921, was reorganized as the Toledo and Western Railway, and sold to the Willys-Overland Company and the Wabash Railway in 1924. Thereafter, the road was principally engaged in hauling Willys-Overland automobiles from Fitch yard at Toledo to an interchange with the Wabash at Adrian. This traffic reached about 13,000 cars per year in the late 1920's and amounted to about five-sixths of the road's traffic. Since the new management was indifferent to passenger service, cars ceased to run into downtown Toledo in 1925, and passenger service was entirely abandoned in 1933. LCL freight operations were dropped in the same year. Meanwhile, the traffic in automobiles declined rapidly in the 1930's and ceased in 1933. Much of the agricultural traffic had already been lost to trucks and beginning in 1931 the company failed to cover operating expenses.

Accordingly, the T&W sought and received permission to abandon the main line from Allen Junction to Pioneer in 1933, but most of it was retained in freight service with gasoline or diesel locomotives by two small companies, the Ohio and Morenci Railroad, and the Pioneer and Fayette Railroad. The O&M, organized by the Joseph Schonthal Company, a firm of scrap dealers, bought the line from Allen Junction to Morenci, Michigan, and the P&F, a local project, bought the line between Fayette and Pioneer. The T&W operated the Adrian branch only until 1935, when it applied for abandonment. The segment between Adrian and Riga, Michigan (12.5 miles), was preserved by the Blissfield Railroad, also a Schonthal subsidiary, which operated it electrically for nine months, beginning on January 1, 1936. In September the village of Blissfield ordered the company either to repair its tracks in the main street, which had deteriorated badly, or to remove them. Unable to afford improvement, the company abandoned the line. The O&M acquired about 1.7 miles of track in Blissfield for switching with a gasoline locomotive on track too light for the steam engines of the connecting New York Central.

After the abandonment of the T&W's Adrian branch, the O&M cut back from Allen Junction to Berkey, but operated the Berkey–Morenci segment (20 miles) until 1950. It operated the isolated Blissfield trackage until 1954. The Pioneer and Fayette secured permission to abandon its line late in 1942, with the exception of a half mile at Franklin Junction used for switching in connection with the Wabash. This trackage is still in service.

FORT WAYNE VAN WERT AND LIMA TRACTION COMPANY

This interurban connecting Lima and Fort Wayne (62 miles) was opened on November 1, 1905. The right-of-way closely paralleled the Pennsylvania Railroad's main line. In 1906 the company was leased by the Lima and Toledo Traction Company, and in 1907 became a part of the Ohio Electric Railway. After the bankruptcy and dissolution of the Ohio Electric in 1921, the company returned to operation in receivership under its own name. In 1926 it was reorganized as the Fort Wayne-Lima Railroad under the control of officials of the Indiana Service Corporation, which equipped it with six semi-lightweight cars of ISC design. From 1930 to 1932, the road was supervised by the Indiana Railroad, but operated independently. It went into receivership again in 1931, and was abandoned June 30, 1932. The lightweight cars were sold to the Oklahoma Railway.

INDIANA COLUMBUS AND EASTERN TRACTION COMPANY

The Indiana Columbus and Eastern Traction Company was formed in 1906 by Randal Morgan of Philadelphia, W. Kesley Schoepf of Cincinnati, and Hugh J. McGowan of Indianapolis to bring together under a single management several properties that were in varying stages of financial distress. The panic of 1903 had caused the syndicate of interurbans organized by A. E. Appleyard of Boston to dissolve, and had caused the syndicate of F. J. Pomeroy and M. J. Mandelbaum to lose some of its most important mileage. Morgan, Schoepf, and McGowan bought the following Appleyard properties, all of which had gone into bankruptcy in 1905: the Dayton Springfield and Urbana Railway (40 miles, opened 1900); the Columbus Grove City and Southwestern Railway (15 miles, opened 1898–1901); and the Urbana Bellefontaine and Northern Railway (18 miles, opened 1903). The IC&E then leased two properties running west from Dayton, the Dayton and Western (*q.v.*) and the Dayton and Northern (Dayton–Greenville, 42 miles, opened 1901). The IC&E also leased the portion of the Dayton and Muncie Traction Company, an affiliate of the D&N, between Union City and Greenville (12 miles, opened 1904), and the Columbus Newark and Zanesville Electric Railway, which had completed a line from Newark to Zanesville (30 miles) in 1904. In the same year the IC&E purchased the first interurban built, the 7-mile Newark and Granville Street Railway (1889). In 1906 the CN&Z acquired the Columbus Buckeye Lake and Newark Traction Company (34 miles, completed 1902), with which it had been closely associated.

In 1907 the IC&E was leased to the Ohio Electric Railway, which operated it until the OE's dissolution in 1921. The Schoepf-McGowan interests acquired in the name of the IC&E an unsuccessful steam railroad, the Columbus and Lake Michigan (Lima–Defiance, 40 miles), which they electrified in 1909. The gap in the IC&E between Bellefontaine and Lima was closed by the Ohio Electric in 1908.

From 1921 until 1929, the IC&E operated independently, but in receivership. In 1922 it abandoned its short branch into New Carlisle (7 miles, built about 1901), and the Columbus–Orient branch (formerly the CGC&SW). In 1923 it divested itself of the Lima–Defiance line, which operated as an independent gas-car road until 1929. In 1925 the long Union City branch was discontinued. A cutoff north of the town of London had been built about 1907, and in 1928 the trackage through London was abandoned. What was left of the IC&E in 1929 was incorporated into the Cincinnati and Lake Erie Railroad (*q.v.*), which operated it until 1939.

The Columbus Newark and Zanesville was not operated as part of the IC&E after the dissolution of the Ohio Electric. It was sold at an auction in 1925 and reorganized as the Southern Ohio Public Service Company; in 1929 it was abandoned entirely. The pioneer Newark and Granville line had been discontinued in 1923.

OHIO ELECTRIC RAILWAY

The Ohio Electric Railway, the largest interurban in Ohio, was organized by Randal Morgan, W. Kesley Schoepf, Hugh J. McGowan, and their associates on May 16, 1907. The company had originated two years earlier, when the same men formed the Ohio Syndicate, and organized the Cincinnati Northern Traction Company to lease the Cincinnati Dayton and Toledo Traction Company, proprietor of the important road between Cincinnati and Dayton. The line had been built by two companies, both affiliated with the Pomeroy-Mandelbaum syndicate, the Cincinnati and Miami Valley Traction Company (Hamilton–Dayton, 36 miles, opened 1897), and the Cincinnati and Hamilton Electric Street Railway (College Hill–Hamilton, 14 miles, opened 1898). The Pomeroy-Mandelbaum interests consolidated the two companies into the Southern Ohio Traction Company in 1900. The new company was in turn consolidated with the Miamisburg and Germantown Traction Company (5 miles, completed 1901), and two street railway properties into the Cincinnati Dayton and Toledo Traction Company in 1902. The Pomeroy-Mandelbaum interests were financially distressed by the panic of 1903, and so lost control of the property to the Schoepf-McGowan syndicate.

The Ohio Electric assumed the lease of the CD&T, and leased the Indiana Columbus and Eastern Traction Company that the Schoepf-McGowan syndicate had organized out of former Appleyard properties in 1906. It also leased the Lima and Toledo Traction Company (73 miles when completed), which, although unfinished, had itself leased the Fort Wayne Van Wert and Lima Traction Company in 1906. When the gap between Lima and Bellefontaine was closed and the line from Lima to Toledo was completed (both in 1908), and when the Defiance branch was electrified in 1909, the Ohio Electric consisted of about 617 miles of line. It operated city service in Lima, Dayton, Hamilton, Newark, and Zanesville.

Size did not mean strength, however, for the Ohio Electric never paid a dividend, and was never free of financial problems. It suffered from the two-cent fare laws after 1906, and suffered about $1.5 million damage in the 1913 flood. Increasing costs, especially for paving and for street maintenance, relatively rigid fare structures, and rising highway competition all contributed to the company's disintegration. In 1918 it surrendered the Dayton–Cincinnati line to new owners, the Cincinnati and Dayton Traction Company, and in 1920 it turned the Dayton and Western back to its owners. In January 1921, the company went bankrupt, and was dissolved. The IC&E, the Columbus Newark and Zanesville, the Lima and Toledo, and the Fort Wayne Van Wert and Lima all went bankrupt at the same time, but resumed independent operation.

The CN&Z and the FWVW&L were reorganized independently in 1925 and 1926, respectively, and never again operated jointly with the IC&E and the L&T. The L&T was reorganized in 1924 as the Lima–Toledo Railroad. In 1929, both the Lima–Toledo and the IC&E were reunited with the Cincinnati–Dayton line as the Cincinnati and Lake Erie Railroad (*q.v.*).

CINCINNATI AND LAKE ERIE RAILROAD

As the first event in the disintegration of the Ohio Electric Railway (*q.v.*) the line between Dayton and Cincinnati was transferred to an independent company, the Cincinnati and Dayton Traction Company, organized on April 26, 1918. This company itself failed and was reorganized into the Cincinnati Hamilton and Dayton Railway Company in 1926. The new company, which had no connection with the railroad of the same name, was headed by a former professor of finance, Dr. Thomas Conway, Jr., who had already been successful in reviving the Chicago Aurora and Elgin Railroad. He ordered new equipment that the property badly needed, and increased the maintenance of its roadbed. He did well at building up freight service in interurban equipment, and by virtue of his wide contacts in the railroad industry was more than ordinarily successful in establishing through rates for LCL with the railroads. Conway believed that there was still a place for the interurban in the medium distance range of passenger traffic, and thus conceived of regrouping the main lines of the former Ohio Electric.

In 1929 Conway brought together (effective January 1, 1930) under the ownership of his company, the Indiana Columbus and Eastern and the Lima–Toledo Railroad. The CH&D changed its name simultaneously to the Cincinnati and Lake Erie Railroad. The new company consisted of the old Ohio Electric main line from College Hill (Cincinnati) to Toledo (216 miles) and a single branch from Springfield to Columbus (44.5 miles). Since both were relatively strong lines, by the standards of the industry, they were considered good prospects for survival. Between 1931 and 1936, the C&LE operated the Dayton and Western (*q.v.*), also a relatively important line. Conway ordered 20 new cars capable of high speeds and offering considerable comfort, and inaugurated limited service between Cincinnati, Columbus, Toledo, and Detroit. It was too late, however, for such efforts to be successful. In 1932, the company was put in receivership under Conway, and a retrenchment of its operations began. Abandonment of the Eastern Michigan Toledo Railroad in 1932 ended through service to Detroit. The C&LE's Springfield–Toledo line was abandoned on November 19, 1937, and the rest of the interurban lines were discontinued by May 31, 1939. The company's bus subsidiary took over passenger service along the same routes. Rail service from Dayton to Southern Hills (3 miles), mainly on Dayton city streets, was not replaced by buses until September 28, 1941.

Conway's endeavor to make a success of the C&LE was the most concentrated effort at survival of any of the Ohio interurban lines, and in most respects paralleled the experience of the Insull interests with the Indiana Railroad.

SOUTHEAST OHIO RAILWAY AND LIGHT COMPANY

This small and unsuccessful interurban was built between Zanesville and Crooksville (14 miles) about 1906. After several years of unprofitable operation it was succeeded by the Southeastern Ohio Railway Company on January 1, 1916. It operated under this name until 1924, when it was abandoned.

TOLEDO PORT CLINTON AND LAKESIDE RAILWAY

The first line of the Toledo Port Clinton and Marblehead was opened from Genoa to Port Clinton (23 miles) in 1904, and extended to Marblehead (12 miles) in 1905. At the outset the company's cars entered Toledo by trackage rights over the Lake Shore Electric, but in 1906 the company built its own line to the city from Genoa through Curtice to Ryan, terminus of the Starr Avenue city line, over which the interurban cars entered the business district. In 1911 the company built an extension of about 3 miles from Marblehead to a pier at Bay Point, from which steamer service was provided by an independent operator to Cedar Point and Sandusky during the navigation season.

The line passed into the hands of the Northwestern Ohio Railway and Power Company in 1912, and operated under that name until 1924 when it was purchased by the Ohio Public Service Company, an affiliate of the Cities Service Corporation. The Bay Point extension and the steamer connection were abandoned in 1925. The rest of the OPS line continued in passenger service until July 11, 1939, and parts of the line survived for almost 20 years longer in freight service. The easternmost 4 miles were abandoned in 1940. In 1945 the Ohio Public Service Company, in compliance with its obligations under the Public Utility Holding Company Act, sold the property to the Toledo and Eastern Railroad after scrapping the line east of Clay Center, 11 miles east of Ryan. The remainder survived until 1958 on traffic hauled from a dolomite quarry at Clay Center for interchange with the Wheeling & Lake Erie at Curtice, and on coal hauled from Curtice to Ryan, destined for a plant of the Toledo Edison Company. When the coal freight was shifted to water transport, the company was abandoned.

By the test of survival, this was one of the most successful interurbans in Ohio, both in passenger and freight service. Although tributary population was only about 15,000, the Marblehead Peninsula was an important resort area, and produced large amounts of fruit. The TPC&L had been built to higher physical standards than most interurbans, could handle railroad cars from the outset, and had relatively abundant power. One of its cars (No. 21), a Niles combine, is preserved as a museum piece at Worthington, Ohio; it is the best extant example of wooden interurban car design.

LAKE SHORE ELECTRIC RAILWAY[1]

One of the largest and most important interurbans, the Lake Shore Electric was organized by the Everett-Moore syndicate in 1901 out of several predecessor companies.

Cleveland–Toledo service was inaugurated on December 7, 1901. Completion of the Sandusky–Fremont direct line in 1907 shortened the run by 5 miles and reduced running time by about 30 minutes. In 1926 the company built a cutoff around Sandusky, mainly for freight. The road had participated in Cleveland–Lima joint service with the Western Ohio since 1911 and in Cleveland–Detroit service with the Detroit Monroe and Toledo Short Line since 1916.

The Lake Shore Electric was initially one of the strongest interurbans in the Ohio–Indiana network. Serving a dense population, its earnings as late as the 1920's

PREDECESSOR COMPANIES OF THE LAKE SHORE ELECTRIC

Route	Mileage	Builder	Opening date
Sandusky–Norwalk	17	Sandusky Milan & Norwalk Ry.	1893
Cleveland–Lorain	28	Lorain & Cleveland Electric Ry.	1897
Toledo–Norwalk (including a 3.5-mile branch to Gibsonburg)	65	Toledo Fremont & Norwalk Ry.	1901
Sandusky–Lorain (including 13-mile branch, Ceylon Jct.–Norwalk)	45	Sandusky & Interurban Electric Ry.	1901
Lorain–Elyria	9	East Lorain Street Ry.	1894
Sandusky–Fremont	23	Lake Shore Electric Ry.	1907

were favorable, but in the depression the company ran up operating losses such as few other interurbans even approached. The company failed to cover operating costs by $500,000 per year in 1932 and 1933. Receivership was established in 1933, but the company persisted in operating, apparently in the hope that improvement would follow the end of depression. The company began to have serious labor disputes in 1935, and a strike of its freight employees in 1937 led to the abandonment of freight service. The road had been unable to interchange with the railroads, but had been aggressive in developing LCL and CL freight movements in interurban equipment. However, nearly all its important interurban connections had been lost by 1937.

As of 1937 the Lake Shore continued to provide its local service interspersed with Toledo-Cleveland limiteds, all operated with traditional heavy equipment. Only the Sandusky-Norwalk line had been abandoned (1928), apart from a short branch between South Lorain and Beach Park (1926). By the end, the line had run up operating losses of some $3 million over a period of about eight years. At a receiver's auction on January 4, 1938, no purchasers appeared except a finance company to which the Lake Shore owed over $800,000. This firm operated the road until May 14, 1938, when it was abandoned. Even then an effort was made to establish cooperative ownership by the employees, but without success. An LSE affiliate, the Lake Shore Coach Company, established bus service as a replacement.

SANDUSKY NORWALK AND MANSFIELD
ELECTRIC RAILWAY

This company was chartered in 1904, and in the following year opened an interurban south from a connection with the Lake Shore Electric at Norwalk to Plymouth (17 miles), with a short branch from Newmans to Chicago Junction (now known as Willard). The company had difficulty financing its last 8 miles from Plymouth to Shelby, but finally did so through its subsidiary, the Plymouth and Shelby Traction Company, in 1907.

The Sandusky Norwalk and Mansfield paralleled no railroad for most of its distance, but served too small a population to be successful. Receivers were appointed in 1912 for the SN&M and the subsidiary Plymouth and Shelby. The P&S was taken out of receivership in 1914, but returned in 1917. The lines shared a receiver with the Lake Erie Bowling Green and Napoleon, with which the SN&M was a strong contender for the title of weakest Ohio interurban. In 1921 when the enterprise was unable to pay its power bill, operation came to a halt. The property was reformed as the Norwalk and Shelby Railroad and operated with gasoline-powered equipment until 1924, when it was abandoned.

In spite of the dismal history of the SN&M, two of its cars were among the last to be active; converted to line car and snow plow as Nos. 50 and 90 of the Toledo and Eastern, they remained in service until 1958.

MANSFIELD RAILWAY LIGHT AND
POWER COMPANY

In 1901 the street railway company in Mansfield, then known as the Citizens Electric Light and Power Company, built an interurban line of 12 miles to Shelby. In April 1903, the company was succeeded by the Mansfield Railway Light and Power Company, which was for a short period affiliated with the Cleveland and Southwestern. The MRL&P operated the interurban and street railway until 1915, when a group of preferred-stock holders brought suit successfully to have the company dissolved. It was replaced by the Mansfield Public Utility and Service Company, which was in turn replaced in 1918 by the Richland Public Service Company. The property was sold in 1922 to the Ohio Public Service Company, which operated it until its abandonment on March 1, 1934. The Kuhlman lightweight car bought for the interurban line by the OPS in 1924 is preserved at the Ohio Railway Museum in Worthington.

CLEVELAND SOUTHWESTERN AND
COLUMBUS RAILWAY

This company was the principal interurban property of the Pomeroy-Mandelbaum syndicate, and with the exception of the Ohio Electric, was the largest interurban in the state. It consisted of two main lines, one west from Cleveland to Norwalk and the other southwest to Bucyrus, plus several branch lines. Pomeroy and Mandelbaum built the road through a series of subsidiaries, which upon completion were merged into other Pomeroy-Mandelbaum properties. For this reason a detailed corporate history would be tedious and of little value. The line west to Norwalk reached Elyria in 1895, Oberlin in 1897, Wellington (terminus of a branch) in 1899, and Norwalk in 1902. A line between Elyria and Lorain, lying slightly to the west of the Lake Shore Electric's route between the same cities, was finished in 1900.

Between 1899 and 1902 the syndicate built an isolated line, the Ohio Central Traction Company, between Bucyrus and Mansfield. The syndicate also owned a line straight south from Cleveland to Medina (reached in 1897) and Wooster (1901). With the exception of the Ohio Central, the various properties were merged to form the Cleveland and Southwestern Traction Company in 1903. The syndicate had various plans for joining the Ohio Central to the rest of the property, but finally decided to build a 45-mile interurban from Seville on the Wooster line to Mansfield, largely parallel to the main line of the Erie Railroad. This project was completed in 1908, but in 1907 the Ohio Central was merged into the rest of the property to form the Cleveland Southwestern and Columbus Railway. Connection for Columbus was made via the Columbus Marion and Bucyrus and its parent, the Columbus Delaware and Marion.

The CSW&C encountered the problems common to the interurbans during and after World War I, and failed in 1922. In 1924 the road abandoned its western line beyond Oberlin, since Norwalk was not large enough to support two interurbans to Cleveland. The rival Lake Shore Electric was somewhat the faster road, and carried most of the traffic. The property was reorganized in 1924 as the Cleveland Southwestern Railway and Light Company, but the attrition of mileage continued. Branches to Grafton and North Amherst were abandoned in 1926. The company entered receivership again in July, 1930, and in November applied for abandonment. The remaining lines were discontinued on February 28, 1931.

In the last years of the Southwestern's operation, main-line service on the southern division was provided chiefly by a series of six steel cars built by Kuhlman in 1919, and on the western division by 12 Cincinnati Car Company lightweight cars built in 1924. Five of the latter were sold to the Dayton and Western, where they operated until 1936.

COLUMBUS MARION AND BUCYRUS RAILROAD

This interurban (18 miles) was built by the Columbus Delaware and Marion Railway (*q.v.*) to form a connection to the Cleveland Southwestern and Columbus Railway, which completed its track from Cleveland to Bucyrus in 1908. The CM&B was itself opened in August 1908. The expense of building the CM&B forced both the CD&M and the CM&B into bankruptcy in 1909. The company emerged in 1914 as the Columbus Marion and Bucyrus Railway. The line's principal importance was as a connection for the CD&M, and it was in itself rarely profitable. It operated passenger trains every two hours, half as frequently as the CD&M. It did not engage in through Cleveland–Columbus passenger service, but it handled a nightly through freight train. After four years of increasing deficits, the company went bankrupt for the second time in 1930. In 1931 it was absorbed by the CD&M, but operated for less than two years. On September 9, 1932, the Public Utilities Commission gave the CD&M permission to abandon it on ten days' notice, but it was not abandoned until 1933.

COLUMBUS DELAWARE AND MARION RAILWAY

In 1901 James Holcomb and J. E. Lattimer of Cleveland purchased the Columbus Clintonville and Worthington Street Railway at Columbus and arranged a right-of-way to Marion, buying out a rival promoter who controlled the street railway in Delaware. When it was opened in 1903, the road was a moderately heavily built interurban of 50 miles, located mainly on a private right-of-way 20 feet wide, separated from the highway by a ditch and the pole line. Plans for building north were curtailed by the panic of 1903, but in 1908 the line opened a subsidiary, the Columbus Marion and Bucyrus Railroad (*q.v.*), a project that put both roads into bankruptcy in 1909. The company emerged in 1917 as the Columbus Delaware and Marion Electric Company. It sold power extensively in its area, and was part of the Middle West Utilities System.

During the 1920's the company was aggressive, but to little avail. In 1923 it relocated about 6.5 miles of its entrance into Columbus onto private right-of-way, and in 1926 it bought two excellent heavy-steel parlor cars, similar to new equipment of the Interstate Public Service Company. The two new cars provided limited service under the names "The Capitol" and "The Northern" six times daily in each direction. The company operated hourly until the beginning of the depression.

The abandonment of the Cleveland Southwestern caused the CD&M to lose about $76,000 per year in freight revenues, and made further operation very difficult. The CD&M, together with the CM&B, which it had absorbed in 1931, went bankrupt on March 7, 1933, after four years of operating deficits. The receivers immediately applied for abandonment, and received permission on April 5, 1933, but kept the line in service until the fall. A segment of 5.3 miles survived at Owens to switch coal into a power station of the Marion Reserve Power Company. This trackage was dieselized in 1952, but is still in service.

COLUMBUS MAGNETIC SPRINGS AND NORTHERN RAILWAY

This small interurban (18 miles) connected the Columbus Delaware and Marion Railway at Delaware with Magnetic Springs, a minor resort town, and Richwood, a station on the Erie Railroad. The Delaware–Magnetic Springs segment (11 miles) was opened by the Delaware and Magnetic Springs Railway in 1904, and the remainder by a subsidiary, the Richwood and Magnetic Springs Railway, in 1906. In the same year both companies, which were controlled by W. M. Galbraith of Pittsburgh, were consolidated into the Columbus Magnetic Springs and Northern Railway. The company owned Magnetic Park in Magnetic Springs and had hopes for the development of the town as a resort that were never fulfilled. Galbraith also had plans for expansion, both north and south. He hoped to build north from Richwood to La Rue (12 miles) to a junction with the Toledo Bowling Green and Southern, which around 1906 had plans to build south from Findlay. About 1907 he bought the Columbus Urbana and Western in expectation of using it as an independent entrance to Columbus, but neither plan was executed.

Lacking these extensions, the interurban was impossible and it had a short life. On December 14, 1918, the Ohio Public Utility Commission permitted it to be abandoned, effective January 1, 1919.

YOUNGSTOWN AND SOUTHERN RAILWAY (YOUNGSTOWN AND SUBURBAN)

The Y&S laid track from Youngstown to Columbiana (16 miles) in 1904, but operated with steam power until 1907, when it electrified and extended its line to a junction with the Youngstown and Ohio River Railroad at Leetonia (3 miles). The interurban was projected as a third-rail line, but it was electrified with an orthodox overhead. From the outset the company was able to handle railroad equipment, and it built up a sizeable traffic in inbound coal for on-line delivery, mainly in interchange with the Youngstown and Ohio River Railroad (an interurban) and the Pittsburgh Lisbon & Western (a steam railroad). The company went into receivership in 1915, and was reorganized in 1916 as the Youngstown and Suburban Railway, a name it used until 1944 when it reverted to the Youngstown and Southern Railway Company. In 1945, the road absorbed the Pittsburgh Lisbon & Western, with which it had operated closely for several years; both were controlled by the Montour Railroad. The Montour, itself controlled jointly by the Pennsylvania and the Pittsburgh & Lake Erie (New York Central), had secured control of the Y&S in 1928 in order to gain entrance into Youngstown. The Montour's efforts to build its own extension into Youngstown had previously been denied ICC permission.

In 1948, the Y&S abandoned passenger service; it was the last Ohio interurban to do so. The Columbiana-Leetonia extension was abandoned later in the same year, but the remainder of the property continued in freight service. In 1960 it was still in service, operated with diesel power.

YOUNGSTOWN AND OHIO RIVER RAILROAD

This company built its interurban from Salem to East Liverpool (36 miles) from 1906 to 1909. In connection with the Youngstown and Southern at Leetonia, the line provided a relatively direct route between Youngstown and the Ohio River at East Liverpool. The company was relatively well situated, since its two major interurban connections, the Youngstown and Southern and the Stark, were strong firms, and it had a friendly steam connection in the Pittsburgh Lisbon & Western. In fact, it had 7 miles of trackage rights on the PL&W between Salem and Washingtonville—one of the few Midwestern examples of an interurban electrifying a short stretch of a railroad. The company served several coal mines, which were initially a source of carload traffic. The decline of the on-line coal mines in the late twenties hastened the interurban's end. The company went into receivership in 1930 and was abandoned in 1931.

STEUBENVILLE EAST LIVERPOOL AND BEAVER VALLEY TRACTION COMPANY

This company was formed in 1917 out of several predecessors, all of which had been controlled since 1911 by the Tri-State Railway and Electric Company. The earliest was the East Liverpool and Wellsville Street Railway Company, chartered in 1892. The line of the SEL&BVT was completed about 1906 between Steubenville and Beaver, Pennsylvania (43 miles), although portions had been in service for some years. The interurban was mainly double-track, and was integrated with extensive street railway operations in Steubenville, East Liverpool, and smaller communities. Because of the dense population along the Ohio River, which the interurban paralleled, the company was long-lived, and was not abandoned until 1939.

SCIOTO VALLEY TRACTION COMPANY

The Scioto Valley Traction Company was the most heavily built interurban in Ohio, and the only third-rail line in either Ohio or Indiana. It was opened between Columbus and Circleville (27 miles) in 1904, together with a branch from Obetz Junction to Lancaster (24 miles). In 1905 the Circleville line was pushed on 20 miles to Chillicothe. The two routes were intended to be built on from Chillicothe to Portsmouth and from Lancaster to Athens, but the extensions were never undertaken.

The company proved quite successful. It operated hourly passenger service on both lines, and ran three additional limiteds to Chillicothe. It found its principal success in the power business, which eventually came to overshadow the rail operations. By the late 1920's, the road was furnishing power to some fifty communities, mainly in the suburbs of Columbus, and by 1941 the company served 106 communities. The company recognized the changing character of its operations by changing its name to the Scioto Valley Railway and Power Company in 1923, and to the Ohio Midland Light and Power Company in 1932. Passenger and general freight service were abandoned September 30, 1930, and the tracks removed except for about 13 miles in the vicinity of Obetz Junction, which were retained to switch coal from the Chesapeake and Ohio Railway at Groveport and the Norfolk and Western Railway at Obetz to the company's power station near Lockbourne. This trackage was dieselized in 1956 and abandoned in 1957 and 1958, except for a 2-mile segment between Lockbourne and the powerhouse.

Revenues from the power business account for the unusual circumstance that general rail operations were abandoned without the company's showing a single annual deficit.

WELLSTON AND JACKSON BELT RAILWAY

This property was built in 1895 and 1896 between Jackson and Wellston (18 miles) through a coal-mining area. The line was unique among Ohio interurbans in two respects: it was controlled by a steam railroad, the Columbus Hocking Valley & Toledo Railway (now part of the Chesapeake & Ohio), and it operated with side-mounted rather than center-mounted trolley poles. It was a highly unsuccessful operation, and was one of the first Midwestern interurbans to be abandoned completely; the railroad scrapped it in 1915.

GALLIPOLIS AND NORTHERN TRACTION COMPANY

This obscure railway is first reported when the Gallipolis and Point Pleasant Railway (5 miles) succeeded the Gallipolis Street Railway Company at a foreclosure sale in 1895. Record of the company disappears in 1902-7. In 1907, a company called the Kanauga and Gallipolis Traction Company was reported to be building between Gallipolis and Point Pleasant. The Kanauga Traction Company was reported to have been completed between these termini on February 6, 1908, and to have been operated with gas cars. It was purchased at a receiver's sale in 1913 by the Gallipolis and Northern Traction Company, which was reported to be electrically operated. The G&N was sold for scrap at a sheriff's sale in May 1923.

PORTSMOUTH STREET RAILROAD AND LIGHT COMPANY

The street railway in Portsmouth operated an interurban to Ironton (29 miles) along the north bank of the Ohio River, parts of which were among the first and the last track to be laid in Ohio. The first 12 miles from Portsmouth to Sciotoville were opened November 16, 1893, but the remainder was not built until 1916-17. After 1923, the company was known as the Portsmouth Public Service Company. The interurban line was abandoned in 1929.

OHIO RIVER ELECTRIC RAILWAY AND POWER COMPANY

This property was opened in November 1900, to serve an area of very limited population. It was an electric line 13 miles long between Racine, Pomeroy, and Gravel Hill, built largely to street railway standards. It was reorganized in 1925 as the Ohio River Railway and Power Company, and abandoned in 1929.

HOCKING-SUNDAY CREEK TRACTION COMPANY

This company was chartered in 1909 and opened in short stretches between Nelsonville and Athens (15 miles) between 1910 and 1915. It was first operated with a McKeen car, but then electrified with low-voltage DC in 1911. In the following year, to avoid building a substation for the last 6 miles to Athens, the electrification was changed to 1,200-volt DC, the only such installation in Ohio. The company always used cars of the street railway type. Since traffic consisted largely of coal miners and their families, the company was hard hit by the local decline of the coal industry after 1923, and in 1925 it went bankrupt. It was reorganized in 1926 as the Nelsonville–Athens Electric Railway Company. The company continued to offer hourly service well into the depression, but its financial situation became hopeless, and it was abandoned on November 14, 1932. The road had applied for an R.F.C. loan of $115,000 to continue, but it was abandoned before a decision on the loan was made. Around 1915 the company had made plans for extension from Nelsonville to Lancaster to connect with the Scioto Valley Traction Company, but construction was never undertaken.

CAMBRIDGE POWER LIGHT AND TRACTION COMPANY

This company opened an interurban from Cambridge to Byesville (7 miles) about 1903 and initiated hourly service with two cars. In September 1910, the property was purchased by the Midland Power and Traction Company, which in 1912 became the New Midland Power and Traction Company. In this same year, the line was extended from Byesville to Pleasant City (5 miles). On January 1, 1915, the road was acquired by the Ohio Service Company, which operated it for the rest of its history. Since Pleasant City is a village of only about 500, and Byesville a town of less than 2,500, the line served a very small tributary population and did well to survive until January 31, 1927.

EASTERN OHIO TRACTION COMPANY

This property consisted of two short lines running east from Cleveland to Middlefield and Garrettsville, which were at various times operated jointly and separately. The southern line was undertaken by the Cleveland and Chagrin Falls Electric Railway, and opened to Chagrin Falls on May 1, 1897. A subsidiary, the Chagrin Falls and Eastern Electric Railway was completed to Hiram in 1902 and to Garrettsville (39 miles) in 1903. A branch from Steel Junction to Middlefield (7 miles) was used only for freight and special passenger movements. The northern line was built directly to Middlefield (33 miles) in 1900 and 1901, and a single branch to Chardon (8 miles) was built simultaneously. In 1902 the two properties were consolidated into the Eastern Ohio Traction Company, which went bankrupt in 1904.

The company was unfortunately situated in almost every respect. It served a sparsely settled, hilly territory with a weak physical plant. It had stiff grades and a power supply so meager that cars on the Garrettsville line were limited to 10 or 15 miles per hour. The company had several wooden trestles that were expensive to maintain, and it had lengthy street running in Cleveland, the northern line on Mayfield Road and the southern on Kinsman Road. If the company had been able to build an extension from Garrettsville to Leavittsburg on the Mahoning and Shenango Railway, it would have been able to offer direct service from Cleveland to Warren and Youngstown. This would probably have given the road as long a life as most interurbans, but as it was the company began to wither more rapidly than any other company of its size. In 1908 the company abandoned the Steel Junction–Middlefield branch, which duplicated the main line of the northern division.

In 1910, the northern division was reorganized as the Cleveland and Eastern Traction Company and the southern as the Cleveland Youngstown and Eastern Railway. Joint management was continued. The Chagrin Falls–Garrettsville extension was abandoned on December 27, 1914, and the remainder of the southern division was renamed the Cleveland and Chagrin Falls Railway in the following year. Both lines lasted only another decade, and were abandoned simultaneously on March 31, and April 1, 1925.

CLEVELAND ALLIANCE AND MAHONING VALLEY RAILWAY

This was the last interurban opened in Ohio. It was projected during the second building boom as a high-speed line from Cleveland via the Randall race track to Ravenna, where it was to divide into lines south to Alliance and east to Warren. In 1907 the company acquired a segment of the former main line of the Baltimore & Ohio Railroad between Ravenna and Newton Falls and was reported to be about to electrify it.

The panic of 1907 caused postponement of all the company's plans without a mile of track being placed in service. Five years later it built the line from Ravenna to

Alliance (17 miles), which it opened January 2, 1913. The management then proceeded to electrify the Ravenna–Newton Falls railroad line and to build east 9 miles to Warren. Service began in 1915. The company was at this time an affiliate of the Stark Electric. Since 1915 was a poor year for the industry, and the secular decline began within three years, the company never built the projected main line from Cleveland to Ravenna. It connected at Ravenna with a branch of the Northern Ohio, by means of which it gained roundabout access to Cleveland.

The company was not viable in its final form, and failed in 1920. The receiver announced that he would apply for abandonment in 1924, but reconsidered and permitted the property to be sold at auction in 1925. The Northern Ohio bought the road and operated it as part of its own system until 1931.

NORTHERN OHIO TRACTION AND LIGHT COMPANY

The Northern Ohio Traction Company, one of the oldest, largest, and most important interurbans, was formed by the merger of the pioneer Akron Bedford and Cleveland Railroad (1895) with the street railway in Akron, the Akron Traction and Electric Company. The urban system in Akron and the interurban to Cleveland were the twin supports of the company, and made it one of the strongest Everett-Moore properties.

In 1900 and 1906, the company made two important acquisitions. In 1900, it purchased the Akron and Cuyahoga Falls Rapid Transit Company, which had built a line from Akron to Kent about 1897. This line was shortly extended east to Ravenna. In 1906 the Northern Ohio Traction and Light Company (as it had become in 1902) acquired the Canton–Akron Consolidated Railway, which ran south from Akron to Canton, Massillon, New Philadelphia, and Uhrichsville. This line had been built by predecessor companies between 1892 and 1903. Everett and Moore had high hopes of building south to Wheeling (about 46 miles) but never did so. Branches from Massillon to East Greenville and from Akron to Wadsworth were built in 1907 and cut short by the panic.

Although the line south of Massillon was weak, the Northern Ohio proved to be relatively prosperous, largely because its interurban operations were combined with extensive urban transport and electric power holdings. The company operated the street railways in Akron, Canton, and Massillon, and produced electric power for the area. The power production of the company became so important relative to the rail operations that in 1926 the name was changed to the Northern Ohio Power and Light Company. In the late 1920's, the road was a property of the Commonwealth and Southern public-utility system.

Interurban operations expanded through acquisition of the Cleveland Alliance and Mahoning Valley Railway (*q.v.*) in 1925, but shortly began to decline. The Akron–Canton line was abandoned in 1928 and the Massillon–Uhrichsville line in 1929. In the interim, freight connection between Akron and Canton–Massillon was maintained over the Alliance branch and the Stark Electric; passengers were carried by bus. The old Canton–Massillon line, built in 1892 and now isolated, was sold to the Inter-City Rapid Transit Company in 1930, and was operated with former Indianapolis and Southeastern lightweight cars until December 17, 1940. The lines from Ravenna Junction to Ravenna, Alliance, and Warren were abandoned in 1931. All that was left was the original Cleveland–Akron line. Although this route had been re-equipped with 30 fine heavy steel cars built by Kuhlman in 1920 and 1921, it was handicapped by excessive street running, and was weaker than its heavy tributary population would indicate. It was abandoned in 1932.

STARK ELECTRIC RAILROAD

The Stark Electric Railway, named for the county it served, opened an interurban in 1902 from Canton to Sebring (24 miles), via Alliance, where it controlled the Alliance Electric Railway Company. The two companies were combined into the Stark Electric Railroad in 1903, and the track was extended east to Salem (9 miles) in 1904. The property was notable for its eagerness to avoid street running. It built around every minor town, and had plans which it was unable to execute to build around Alliance, its principal intermediate city. The company held its street running in Canton to about half a mile as it entered the center of the city over the Northern Ohio, after a stretch of private right-of-way parallel to the Wheeling & Lake Erie.

The interurban, which paralleled the main line of the Pennsylvania Railroad, had a tributary population of about 2,000 per mile. The company sold electricity extensively in Alliance until 1927, when its power business was sold to the Alliance Power Company, a subsidiary. The Stark was a relatively strong interurban, and avoided receivership until 1932. Even then it covered its operating expenses during the worst of the depression and survived until 1939. The Stark used a remarkable variety of equipment in its history: orthodox wooden interurbans, wooden cars with parabolic front ends and folding doors across the rear end, center-door, heavy steel cars, and finally Cincinnati lightweight cars.

MAHONING AND SHENANGO RAILWAY AND LIGHT COMPANY

This corporation was formed in 1905 out of about 16 predecessor street railway and power companies in the Youngstown-Niles-Warren area. Interurban lines comprising about 53 miles of a system of combined street and interurban railways totaling 173 miles. The principal interurban lines from Youngstown ran to Warren (1895), New Castle (1900 and 1902), and Sharon (1901). Other interurban routes connected Warren and Leavittsburg (1901), Niles and Mineral Ridge (1899), and Hubbard and New Castle (1902).

After 1911, the electric railways were part of the Republic Railway and Light Company, a holding company that operated the gas and electric utilities in the area. In 1920 the company changed its name to the Pennsylvania-Ohio Electric Company, and embarked on a modernization program that was widely hailed in the trade journals. The company was particularly successful in defeating jitney competition. In 1926 the company was granted the Coffin Award as the outstanding electric railway of the year, mainly for the high quality of its urban service in Youngstown.

In the same year that the company received the Coffin Award, it turned its electric railway operations over to a subsidiary, the Penn-Ohio Public Service Company, which in turn was succeeded in 1930 by the Transportation Securities Corporation. The TSC operated the transit properties through a variety of subsidiaries, and pursued a policy of conversion to buses. The Warren–Leavittsburg branch had been dropped in 1924, Hubbard–New Castle in 1925, and Niles–Mineral Ridge in 1927. The Youngstown–Warren main line was converted to bus operation January 1, 1932, and the Youngstown–New Castle branch in 1933. The Youngstown–Sharon line survived until 1939.

CLEVELAND PAINESVILLE AND EASTERN RAILROAD

This interurban was chartered in 1895 and opened between Cleveland and Painesville (30 miles) on July 4, 1896. In 1898, the company opened an alternative main line, called the shore line, between Cleveland and Willoughby (20 miles). About this time, the company acquired the Painesville Fairport and Richmond Street Railway (6 miles) which had operated street railway service in Painesville since 1893, and had a line from Painesville to Fairport on Lake Erie. In 1900 the Everett-Moore syndicate, which controlled the CP&E, organized a subsidiary, the Cleveland Painesville and Ashtabula, to build east 27 miles to Ashtabula. The extension was completed in 1904, but in the course of the financial difficulties of 1902-3 the Everett-Moore syndicate had lost control of it. They regained the CP&A in 1906 and merged it into the CP&E.

The CP&E labored under several handicaps, particularly its excessive street running in the east side of Cleveland. The eastern connection, the Pennsylvania and Ohio Railway, was a very weak company, and the next line east, the Cleveland and Erie, was weaker still. As a result, no through passenger service between Cleveland and Buffalo was attempted, and there were no serious efforts at through freight service until after the P&O and C&E were abandoned and truck service substituted. The CP&E itself was abandoned in 1926 after two years of operating deficits. Although the company had an undistinguished record, it never went bankrupt, and remained under control of the Everett-Moore interests throughout its history. Part of the right-of-way is now used by the Fairport Painesville & Eastern Railroad.

PENNSYLVANIA AND OHIO ELECTRIC RAILWAY

The Pennsylvania and Ohio Electric, which operated entirely in Ohio, was chartered in 1898 and opened in 1901 between Conneaut and Ashtabula (14 miles). In 1902 a branch was built from Ashtabula to Jefferson (10 miles). The road connected at Ashtabula with the Cleveland Painesville and Eastern and at Conneaut with the Cleveland and Erie, and it was thus part of a direct line of interurbans between Cleveland and Buffalo. The Jefferson branch was the beginning of a line that was never completed, intended to run south through Middlefield on the Eastern Ohio Traction Company to the Warren-Niles-Youngstown area. The interurban in its final form was very weak, and after a poor year in 1918 was sold at a receiver's sale in 1919. It was reorganized in 1919 as the Pennsylvania and Ohio Traction Company. The new company never earned a profit and was abandoned on March 1, 1924.

*

There were three short lines at Columbus which when completed were suburban lines rather than interurbans:

COLUMBUS URBANA AND WESTERN RAILWAY

The Urbana Mechanicsburg and Columbus Electric Railway was chartered in 1900 and built in 1903. Its name was changed to the Columbus Urbana and Western Railway in 1904. Although the promoters hoped to reach Urbana (47 miles), the line was never built beyond Fishinger's Bridge (9 miles). It was coveted as a possible entrance into Columbus by several lines, but it never had a northern connection. Its principal traffic consisted of pleasure seekers going to the dam near Fishinger's Bridge, celebrated in James Thurber's short story, "The Day the Dam Broke." The electric line was replaced by bus service in 1925.

OHIO AND SOUTHERN TRACTION COMPANY

S. B. Hartman built this short electric line (5 miles) between Columbus and the Hartman Stock Farm, of which he was proprietor. In spite of its short length, the road used interurban-style equipment. Since it was strictly an adjunct to the stock farm, it operated at deficits that would have soon killed an independent interurban. In 1926 the line had an operating ratio of 294.81 per cent. In 1929 it was abandoned.

COLUMBUS NEW ALBANY AND JOHNSTOWN TRACTION COMPANY

The promoters of this company intended to build a line from Columbus northeast to Johnstown (23 miles), but reached only Gahanna, a country village about 6 miles from the edge of Columbus, in 1901. The line was built to 5'-2" gauge, and thus cars could enter the city over the broad gauge streetcar system. The road was sold in 1923 to the Columbus Railway Power and Light Company and incorporated into the streetcar system. The CRP&L had a similar line of its own to Westerville.

Indiana

INDIANA, with 1,825 miles of interurban, was second only to Ohio in the absolute size of its interurban network.[2] Lines radiated from Indianapolis to every major town in central Indiana except Bloomington (see map, pp. 256–57). Only the areas about Bloomington, Vincennes, and Madison, and the lightly populated territory between the Wabash River and the Calumet region had no interurban service. Although the history of the Indiana interurbans generally parallels the experience in Ohio, the industry in Indiana was, from the first, more highly concentrated. The Schoepf-McGowan interests early in the twentieth century came to dominate the Union Traction Company, the Terre Haute Indianapolis and Eastern, and the Fort Wayne and Wabash Valley. Later, Samuel Insull acquired control of every major interurban in northern and central Indiana except the Northern Indiana Railway and the Indianapolis and Southeastern. Whereas the principal Ohio interurbans, except the Lake Shore Electric and the Cincinnati and Lake Erie, were quickly affected by adverse circumstances and gave up in the early 1930's, the Insull interests made a serious effort to modernize and perpetuate the main lines of the Indiana system. Only in the case of the Chicago South Shore and South Bend (treated in the section on Illinois) were they successful.

GARY RAILWAYS[3]

The street railway in Gary had an extensive network of suburban lines which it considered to be its interurban divisions. The company was a member of the Central Electric Railway Association, but except that private right-of-way and side-of-the-road running were customary, operations were similar to the rural trolley lines of the east. There was little differentiation of street and interurban lines.

Most of the property was built relatively late, during the great growth of population in Gary after 1909. The earliest component of the system was the grandiose Chicago–New York Electric Air Line, described in Chapter 1. This enterprise, built between 1906 and 1912, became the lines east to La Porte, Chesterton, and Valparaiso. More orthodox projects connected Gary with Hammond in 1910, Crown Point in 1912, Indiana Harbor in 1913, and Hobart in 1913. The failure of the Air Line in 1915 broke the property into several firms, but all were reassembled in 1924 by Samuel Insull's Midland United Corporation. The Hobart and Crown Point lines had been independent, but were absorbed in 1924 and 1928, respectively.

The company suffered heavily from the depression, which created severe unemployment in the Gary steel mills. The La Porte line (the original Air Line) had been dropped in 1917 and the Chesterton branch in 1922. The Crown Point line went in 1933, the Valparaiso route in 1938, and the Indiana Harbor and Hobart lines in 1939. The war postponed the abandonment of the Hammond line until 1946; the last of the street railway trackage was converted to buses in 1947.

ST. JOSEPH VALLEY TRACTION COMPANY[4]

This company operated two interurban cars on 9 miles of line from Elkhart to Bristol, opened in 1910. The company also owned a line from Bristol to La Grange (24 miles), and an affiliate, the St. Joseph Valley Railway, had a further line from La Grange to Columbia, Ohio (37 miles). The two companies were promoted by H. E. Bucklen, a patent-medicine manufacturer of Elkhart, who financed them without public issue of securities. They were operated integrally, but the line east of Bristol operated with a variety of steam and internal combustion power. The company intended in time to electrify the entire property, but never did so. Bucklen hoped to extend the line to a connection with the Toledo and Western Railway and thus to form part of a direct interurban route from Chicago to Toledo, but neither he nor the Toledo and Western's management was able to close the gap of about 13 miles between Columbia and T&W's terminus at Pioneer.

Bristol (pop.: 568) was too small to support interurban service, and the nonelectrified portions of the line never developed enough freight traffic to be economic. In addition, the road had a bad safety record. When Bucklen died in 1917, only two years after the track had reached Columbia, his heirs found it impossible to continue the property. The Northern Indiana Railway, which had leased the electrified line between 1910 and 1912, agreed to operate it again during the terminal receivership, but refused to buy it. The interurban was abandoned on April 17, 1918, and the nonelectrified line the following day.

NORTHERN INDIANA RAILWAY[5]

This company, which operated the city streetcars in South Bend, Elkhart, Goshen, La Porte and Michigan City, connected these communities by interurban lines, and also operated an interurban from South Bend north to Niles and St. Joseph, Michigan. The Michigan City line between South Bend and New Carlisle was parallel to the Chicago South Shore and South Bend.

The Northern Indiana Railway was formed in 1905 out of its predecessor companies, and in 1907 it passed into the hands of James Murdock and Sons, who controlled the major traction properties at Evansville and Lafayette, and were allied with the Schoepf-McGowan interests. The Murdocks renamed the company the Chicago South Bend and Northern Indiana Railway, but it was always generally known by its first and shorter title. The Murdocks gained control of the St. Joseph line in 1910, but operated it independently under the name of the Southern Michigan Railway.

The interurban was initially a relatively strong one because of the heavy population of the South Bend-Elkhart area. The company developed through passenger and freight service with the Winona Interurban to connect with the Union Traction in central Indiana, and it worked closely with Lake Michigan steamer lines at St. Joseph and Michigan City. The St. Joseph line hauled large quantities of fruit in the summer months. The company participated in the C.E.R.A. interline freight traffic arrangements, but did not engage in general interchange with the railroads.

The company was profitable through the early twenties, but its revenues declined so rapidly after 1923 that it went bankrupt in 1927. The subsidiary Southern Michigan Railway soon followed suit. In 1930 the Northern Indiana Railways was formed to take over the assets of both companies. The new firm made an aggressive effort to continue, buying ten new lightweight cars from the Cummings Car and Coach Company (Cummings' last order), inaugurating pickup and delivery of LCL, and building a new entry into South Bend along Bendix Drive for the Michigan City interurban.

ELEMENTS OF THE NORTHERN INDIANA RAILWAY

Route	Mileage	Builder	Opening Date
Elkhart–Goshen	11	Indiana Electric Ry.	1898
Elkhart–South Bend	15	Indiana Railway Co.	1899
La Porte–Michigan City	14	Chicago & South Shore Ry.	1903
South Bend–La Porte	28	Northern Indiana Ry.	1908
South Bend–Niles	11	South Bend Northern Ry.	1903
Niles–St. Joseph	24	Southern Michigan Ry.	1906

The effort was hopeless and the company again went into receivership on December 31, 1931. The receiver began to retrench in 1932 by abandoning the Michigan City streetcar service, and on May 30, 1934, he abandoned the Elkhart city service and all the interurban lines. Local operations in La Porte and Goshen had been abandoned in 1918 and 1920, respectively, but the South Bend–Mishawaka city lines were not replaced by buses until 1940.

Following abandonment of the interurban lines, the company returned the lightweight cars to Cummings, declining Cummings' offer to rebuild them for city service. The cars, still nearly new, went to the Indiana Railroad, where they were used in various suburban and interurban services.

WINONA INTERURBAN RAILWAY[6]

In 1902 the Winona and Warsaw Railway Company was organized to build a street railway from Warsaw to Winona Lake (3 miles), the site of the Winona Assembly, a religious camp associated with Billy Sunday and other fundamentalist leaders. In 1904 the Winona Interurban Railway Company was incorporated to build an interurban from Goshen to Warsaw and south to some point on the Wabash River. Both companies were controlled by the Winona Assembly, and both were intended mainly to carry passengers to religious meetings. The Goshen–Warsaw segment (26 miles) was opened in 1906, and in the following year the company established joint service with the Northern Indiana between Winona Lake and the steamers at Michigan City. The interurban chose Peru as the southern terminus, and in 1907 leased and electrified an unsuccessful steam railroad, the Eel River Railroad, between Peru and Chili (9 miles). In 1910 it finished the line from Warsaw to Chili (33 miles), and thereby had a continuous interurban line from Goshen to Peru. In the same year, the Winona Interurban leased the Winona and Warsaw for 99 years. Suburban service was provided between Peru and Oakdale with city-style equipment.

During construction the Winona encountered a bizarre problem, unique in the history of the industry. Prospective traffic to the Winona Assembly was, of course, greatest on Sundays, but the organizers of the Assembly and of the Interurban, who included H. J. Heinz of Pittsburgh (the president) and J. M. Studebaker of South Bend, were strong sabbatarians, and were willing to operate the interurban only on weekdays. Since the territory was lightly populated, the railway proved so unprofitable that it could not earn the interest on its debt. Its principal creditor, the Electrical Installation Company of Chicago, which had accepted $425,000 of bonds in part payment of construction costs, brought suit to compel the company to operate on Sunday. Being faced with the prospect of receivership if it did not agree, the line began to carry passengers on Sundays in March 1909. The general manager, Sol S. Dickey, was so violently opposed to this course that he resigned.

The Winona was significant as the connection between the interurbans of northern Indiana and the general Indiana-Ohio network. Although it developed interline passenger and freight service with the Northern Indiana and the Union Traction, described in Chapters 3 and 4, the on-line territory did not generate much local traffic. The company failed in 1916 and was reorganized as the Winona Service Company, an identity it held for ten years. In 1926 the line became the Winona Railroad and was operated under this name until its abandonment. Officers and directors were largely shared with Insull's Interstate Public Service Company. After 1926, when interline passenger trains between Goshen and Indianapolis were discontinued, the Winona's passenger operations were unsuccessful, in spite of three new lightweight cars. In 1934 when the Northern Indiana was abandoned, the Winona lost its access to the streets of Goshen, gave up its mainline passenger service, and cut its line back to an interchange with the Wabash at New Paris. Birney cars continued to carry passengers on the Winona Lake branch till 1938.

The Winona had been successful in establishing railroad freight interchange, and had a traffic mainly in coal that enabled it to survive for 18 years. The road was de-electrified in 1938, and abandoned south of Warsaw in 1947. The New Paris–Warsaw segment continued to operate with diesel, gasoline, and propane locomotives in spite of extreme deterioration, but in 1951 the company received permission of the I.C.C. for total abandonment. In 1952 operations were discontinued, and the track removed.

FORT WAYNE AND DECATUR TRACTION COMPANY

In 1903 the Fort Wayne and Springfield Railway was incorporated, but owing to the financial panic in the fall of the year, was unable to accomplish its financing. In 1905-6 the line was financed and construction begun. The promoters opened the line to Decatur (22 miles) on February 1, 1907, hoping it would be the first leg of a line to Springfield, Ohio. They had decided to install single-phase AC at 6,600 volts on the ground that it would eliminate the need for a substation. This was a serious mistake, which had to be rectified in 1917 by conversion to DC at 1,200 volts.

The projected extension to Springfield (via Celina) was never built, but the company did some grading between Decatur and Berne. The management also considered building straight south along the Grand Rapids and Indiana Railroad to Richmond, but never did so. The company failed in 1912 and was replaced by the Fort Wayne and Decatur Traction Company in 1916. The new company lasted only 11 years and was abandoned in 1927. After 1920, the Indiana Service Corporation controlled the company, but never incorporated it into its own system. A local effort to refinance the line and to save the portion in the suburbs of Fort Wayne failed.

TERRE HAUTE INDIANAPOLIS AND EASTERN TRACTION COMPANY

The THI&E, the second largest interurban in Indiana, operated 402 miles of line, only some 8 miles fewer than the Union Traction Company. The THI&E was formed by Randal Morgan, W. Kelsey Schoepf, and Hugh J. McGowan on March 1, 1907, out of four main predecessor companies: the Indianapolis and Western Railway, the Indianapolis and Eastern Railway, the Richmond Street and Interurban Railway, and the Indianapolis Coal Traction Company. On March 25, 1907, the THI&E acquired the Terre Haute Traction and Light Company, and in the following month Schoepf and McGowan leased the Indianapolis and Northwestern Traction Company for 999 years. Simultaneously, the THI&E acquired the Indianapolis and Martinsville Rapid Transit Company, and in 1912 it acquired the Indianapolis Crawfordsville and Danville Electric Railway, named the "Ben Hur Route" in honor of Crawfordsville's most distinguished citizen, General Lew Wallace, author of the novel *Ben Hur*.

The THI&E served possibly a wider range of territory than any other Midwestern interurban: farm lands in central Indiana, an important coal-mining region around Brazil, and urban areas at Indianapolis, Terre Haute, Lafayette, and Richmond. The company controlled the Indianapolis Street Railway. Its physical plant ranged from side-of-the-road construction in flat terrain to some heavy cut-and-fill work between Greencastle and Brazil. The company operated throughout its history with long wooden combines built by a variety of car builders. The road was never prosperous enough to buy more modern equipment (it owned only one double-truck steel car in its history), but in the 1920's it rebuilt most of its main-line cars,

ELEMENTS OF THE THI&E

Route	Mileage	Builder	Opening date
Indianapolis–Danville	20	Indianapolis and Western Ry.	1906
Indianapolis–Dublin	52	Indianapolis & Eastern Ry.	1900
Dunreith–New Castle	11	Indianapolis & Eastern Ry.	1903
Dublin–Richmond	17	Richmond Street & Interurban Ry.	1903
Indianapolis–Plainfield	14	Indianapolis & Plainfield Electric R.R.	1902
Plainfield–Greencastle	26	THI&E	1907
Greencastle–Brazil	17	THI&E	1908
Brazil–Terre Haute	15	Terre Haute Electric Co.	1900
Terre Haute–Clinton	16	Terre Haute Electric Co.	1903
Terre Haute–Sullivan	26	Terre Haute Traction & Light Co.	1906
Terre Haute–Paris	21	THI&E	1907
Indianapolis–Lafayette	68	Indianapolis & Northwestern Traction Co.	1903
Lebanon–Crawfordsville	23	Indianapolis & Northwestern Traction Co.	1904
Indianapolis–Martinsville	30	Indianapolis & Martinsville Rapid Transit Co.	1903
Indianapolis–Crawfordsville	45	Indianapolis Crawfordsville & Western Traction Co.	1907

producing a variety of equipment that few roads could equal.

The THI&E operated local cars hourly, or less frequently, but typically ran one or more expresses on major routes on schedules of about 35 miles per hour, stopping only in large towns. The "Highlander" ran to Terre Haute, the "Ben Hur Special" to Crawfordsville, and the "Tecumseh Arrow" to Lafayette. The THI&E used orthodox equipment on its expresses, except on the "Hoosier" and "Buckeye Specials," three daily runs to and from Dayton, on which parlor cars were operated jointly with the Dayton and Western for several years after 1922.

The THI&E proved to be one of the weakest of the big interurbans. In 1921 the company carried about 22,800,000 passengers, grossed about $4,099,000 from operations, and reported assets of about $30,519,000. During most of the twenties, the interurban showed operating deficits, but auxiliary income from the sale of power and from earnings of the Indianapolis Street Railway kept the company from showing net losses. Thus, although interurban operations had been carried on at a loss for most of the decade, the THI&E was able to avoid receivership until April 2, 1930. Randal Morgan had retained his interest in the company until his death in 1926. Samuel Insull was planning to incorporate the THI&E main line into his Indiana Railroad, but had no interest in the THI&E's extensive branch-line operations. Accordingly, the Danville, Martinsville, and Lafayette lines, together with both Crawfordsville branches, were abandoned on October 31, 1930, and the Sullivan and Clinton lines were both abandoned in the spring of 1931. Until then the company had had no abandonments except the short Cambridge City–Milton branch (2 miles, built about 1902) in 1925.

The company was sold at auction June 23, 1931, to Insull's Midland United Corporation, the only bidder, for $2.5 million, the minimum bid set by the court. The acquisition was an unwise move, for the company reported an operating loss of about $282,000 for the first six months of 1931, even though most of the weakest lines had been abandoned. Insull's effort to acquire the THI&E in 1929, before the bankruptcy, had been forestalled by the regulatory authorities.

What was left of the THI&E was incorporated into the Indiana Railroad system on June 30, 1931. The decision had already been made to abandon the Terre Haute–Paris branch and the Indianapolis–Dunreith segment of the main line to Richmond, but regulatory proceedings delayed abandonment until January 1932. The Terre Haute–Indianapolis and Dunreith–New Castle–Richmond lines became part of the main-line operations of the Indiana Railroad (q.v.).

INTERSTATE PUBLIC SERVICE COMPANY

This company operated a major line of interurban from Indianapolis to Louisville, parallel to the Pennsylvania Railroad. Grading south from Indianapolis was begun very early, in the winter of 1895–96, by the Indianapolis Greenwood and Franklin Railroad, but the company was unable to open its line (21 miles) until 1901. The road was extended from Franklin to Columbus in 1902, and the name was changed to the Indianapolis Columbus and Southern Traction Company in January 1903. In 1905–6 construction was pushed south to Seymour, but the Pennsylvania Railroad's refusal to permit a grade-crossing just south of Columbus prevented service on the extension until 1907, when the Indiana Supreme Court sustained a circuit court's order for the crossing.

The remainder of the interurban was built north from Louisville. In 1903 Samuel Insull and his associates formed the Louisville and Southern Indiana Traction Company, one of their earliest ventures, which acquired the street railways in New Albany and Jeffersonville and arranged to run over the Big Four Railroad bridge into Louisville. The company laid some standard-gauge track in Louisville to reach a joint terminal with the Louisville and Interurban Railway. In 1905 the property passed into the hands of the Louisville and Northern Railway and Lighting Company, a newly organized Insull corporation that began to extend the trackage northward. It reached Charlestown in 1906 and Sellersburg (14 miles from Louisville) in 1907.

The gap between Sellersburg and Seymour was closed by an independent line, the Indianapolis and Louisville Traction Company, incorporated in 1905 and finished in 1907. Through service with limited trains called the Dixie Flyers (southbound) and the Hoosier Flyers (northbound) was initiated in 1908. Since the Seymour–Sellersburg line was electrified with the General Electric 1,200-volt DC system—the first such installation — only cars of the I&L could be used in the through service. Relations between the I&L and its connections were not harmonious, for the I&L management believed that the Insull interests were trying to drive down the value of the I&L in hopes of purchase by denying it joint rates and by otherwise discriminating against it. In 1912 Insull secured control of the entire route (acquiring the IC&S under 999-year lease) and organized the Interstate Public Service Company to operate it. The property included a main line of 117 miles, a short branch to Charlestown, and a 5'-0" suburban line over the Kentucky and Indiana Terminal bridge to New Albany. Suburban service was also provided over the Big Four bridge to Jeffersonville and New Albany. The company had extensive street railways in Jefferson and New Albany, and a smaller local operation in Columbus.

In 1920 and 1921 the entire road was extensively rehabilitated and converted to a uniform DC voltage of 650. At the same time, eight heavy steel cars were purchased from the Cincinnati Car company for limited service. The parlor-diners that were regularly used in this service were bought in 1923 from American Car and Foundry, which had a plant at Jeffersonville. The company offered five parlor-diner trips per day in each direction, plus an overnight sleeping car.

Harry Reid, president of the Interstate, also developed freight operations vigorously (see Chapter 4), but the road was handicapped by an inability to handle railroad equipment on the main line. The company considered two plans for by-passing Franklin, where it had three consecutive right-angle curves, but it executed neither. The main line was marked by severe curves in Jeffersonville and Columbus as well.

In spite of its limitations, the Interstate was among the most successful interurbans. It developed an extensive power business that proved more profitable than the rail operations. In 1931 it was reorganized as the Public Service Company of Indiana, and its rail lines were thereafter operated by the Indiana Railroad (*q.v.*).

FORT WAYNE AND WABASH VALLEY TRACTION COMPANY

This company operated the street railways in Fort Wayne, Wabash, Peru, Logansport, and Lafayette, the principal cities in the Wabash Valley, and connected them with a major interurban line. The company was organized under the name Fort Wayne and Wabash Valley Traction Company in 1904 by the Schoepf-McGowan interests. Predecessor companies had connected Peru and Wabash in 1901, Fort Wayne and Wabash in 1902, and Peru and Logansport in the next year. The FW&WV, through subsidiaries, built west from Logansport to Lafayette in 1907, and south from Fort Wayne to Bluffton to complete the Indianapolis–Muncie–Fort Wayne line in the same year. The company's only other route was an 8-mile line from Lafayette to the Tippecanoe Battle Ground, built in 1905.

The FW&WV's main line ran through the Wabash River Valley for most of its length, and thus served an area atypical of the flat farm lands of the other major Indiana interurbans. The company maintained a high standard of passenger service, particularly in connection with the Union Traction Company in Fort Wayne–Indianapolis limited service.

Mainly as a consequence of the Kingsland disaster of 1910 (described in Chapter 2), the company went into voluntary bankruptcy in February 1911, emerging as the Fort Wayne and Northern Indiana Traction Company. The new corporation in turn failed and was sold at a receiver's auction to the Indiana Service Corporation on December 28, 1919. During the 1920's, the road operated under this name and made two important acquisitions: in 1924 it bought the Fort Wayne and Northwestern Railway (*q.v.*) and in 1926 the Marion and Bluffton Traction Company (*q.v.*). Samuel Insull acquired the Indiana Service Corporation in 1925 and re-equipped the interurban with excellent steel equipment, but the road suffered the usual loss of traffic in the late 1920's. Aside from the Battle Ground branch, which had been cut back in 1922, the road was absorbed intact into the Indiana Railroad System in 1930.

UNION TRACTION COMPANY OF INDIANA

The largest interurban in Indiana, the Union Traction Company had 410 miles of interurban line and about 44 miles of street railway in Anderson, Marion, Muncie, and Elwood. The company had a particularly complicated corporate history, and the origin of its several lines is summarized below.

The company was established by Charles L. Henry of Anderson, who was replaced in control by the Schoepf-McGowan interests in 1902. The road had purchased the Marion Electric Street Railway in 1899, and in 1903 it bought the Elwood and Alexandria Railway. The Indiana Northern was absorbed in 1905 and the Muncie Hartford and Fort Wayne was leased from local businessmen in 1906. In the same year the company bought the Indiana mileage of the Dayton and Muncie Traction Company.

In 1912, Union Traction leased the direct line between Indianapolis and New

Castle that had been built by the Indianapolis New Castle and Toledo Electric Railway. This road, which adopted the bucolic name, "The Honey Bee Route," had been begun in 1906 as a long line from Indianapolis to New Castle, Celina, and Toledo, but it had failed in the panic of 1907. It was completed to New Castle by the receivers in 1910 and reorganized on the eve of its lease to the Union Traction. In the name of the successor Indianapolis New Castle and Eastern Traction Company, the Union Traction built north from New Castle to Muncie in 1913, and in 1916 leased the Muncie and Portland Traction Company for the INC&E. The Union Traction also hoped to build from Portland to Celina, as so many had wished to do before, but it was unable to do so.

The Union Traction Company operated the usual local services, and had extensive limited operations, described in Chapter 3. The road's decline in passenger traffic matched that of the industry as a whole after 1917, and the company went bankrupt in 1925. Receiver Arthur Brady, former president of the company, pursued the unusual course of expanding the physical equipment of the property. He bought a series of 15 steel cars that together with the road's earlier steel equipment virtually eliminated wooden motor cars from the main-line expresses. The secular decline in traffic continued, however. The road carried 19,683,276 passengers in 1917, but only 14,225,836 in 1928. Freight traffic increased rather steadily to 1926, but thereafter declined slightly.

The company's net deficit rose from $419,633 in 1924, immediately before the receivership, to $786,410 in 1929. Despite this dismal showing, Samuel Insull prepared to acquire the property to make of it the principal component of his projected Indiana Railroad (*q.v.*). The Union Traction had no abandonments whatever until 1930, although it had secured permission to abandon the Anderson–Middletown branch in 1925. This line was abandoned in 1930, on the eve of sale of the property to Insull's Midland United Corporation, along with the weak Muncie–Union City branch. The rest of the interurban passed into the hands of Midland United on July 2, 1930.

FORT WAYNE AND NORTHWESTERN
RAILWAY (TOLEDO AND CHICAGO)

Beginning in 1899 there were several proposals to connect Waterloo, Kendallville, and Garrett with Fort Wayne, but none was executed until 1907, when the Toledo and Chicago Interurban Railway built a Y-shaped line of 42 miles between the towns. Alternate cars leaving Fort Wayne ran to Kendallville and Waterloo. At first a car going to one of the northern termini ran to the other before returning to Fort Wayne, but later a shuttle car ran all day between Kendallville and Waterloo. Under either arrangement one could go from one of the three terminals to either

ELEMENTS OF THE UNION TRACTION

Route	Mileage	Builder	Opening date
Marion–Jonesboro–Gas City	6	Marion Electric Street Ry.	1893
Marion–Summitville	17	Marion Electric Street Ry.	ca. 1898
Anderson–Alexandria	11	Union Traction Co.	1897
Summitville–Alexandria	6	Union Traction Co.	1898
Elwood–Alexandria	9	Elwood & Alexandria Ry.	1899
Indianapolis–Muncie	57	Union Traction Co.	1901
Elwood–Tipton	11	Union Traction Co.	1902
Indianapolis–Kokomo	56	Union Traction Co.	1903
Marion–Wabash	20	Indiana Northern Traction Co.	1904
Kokomo–Peru	20	Union Traction Co.	1904
Kokomo–Logansport	24	Union Traction Co.	1904
Muncie–Bluffton	41	Muncie Hartford & Fort Wayne Ry.	1903
Anderson–Middletown	10	Union Traction Co.	1905
Muncie–Union City	32	Dayton & Muncie Traction Co.	1905
Indianapolis–New Castle	45	Indianapolis New Castle & Toledo Electric Ry.	1910
New Castle–Muncie	18	Union Traction Co., lessee, for Indianapolis New Castle & Eastern Traction Co.	1913
Muncie–Portland	32	Muncie & Portland Traction Co.	1906

of the other two on virtually every trip, either directly or by changing at Garrett. There was little parallel railroad passenger service, and the interurban served as an outlet for Fort Wayne to the main lines of the Baltimore & Ohio and the New York Central.

Like its neighbor, the Fort Wayne and Springfield, the Toledo and Chicago electrified with single-phase AC, an error its successor corrected by converting to 650-volt DC in 1913. The company intended to build east to Bryan to a connection with the Toledo and Indiana Railway, with which some of its promoters were affiliated, and west to Goshen on the Northern Indiana Railway, thus providing a fairly direct line between Toledo and Chicago, but neither extension was undertaken. Earlier, consideration had been given to building east to Alvordton, Ohio, to meet the Toledo and Western, since Frank Seagrave of the T&W had been interested in the Toledo and Chicago when it was first promoted about 1903.

The Toledo and Chicago was completed with an indebtedness of $540,000, which it was unable to bear. It went into receivership in 1908, and in 1913 was reorganized as the Fort Wayne and Northwestern Railway Company. It continued under this name until 1924, when it was sold for $20,000 per mile to the Indiana Service Corporation, which continued to operate it after 1930 within the Indiana Railroad (q.v.).

NORTHERN INDIANA POWER COMPANY

The Kokomo Marion and Western Traction Company was incorporated in 1902 to build from Marion west along the Toledo St. Louis and Western Railroad. It built from Kokomo to Greentown (9 miles) in 1903, but like many interurbans, was unable to make further progress until the second building boom. In 1905 it reached Marion (18 additional miles). In 1911 it organized a subsidiary, the Kokomo Frankfort and Western Traction Company to build to Frankfort. This extension (26 miles) was opened in 1912, but the company was never able to build west to Crawfordsville and Terre Haute, as it had hoped. In 1912 the two interurbans were merged into the Indiana Railways and Light Company, which in 1922 became the Northern Indiana Power Company, an Insull property. As such it became one of the original components of the Indiana Railroad System (q.v.), but being a lightly traveled part of the system, it survived only a brief period.

The line was handicapped by running at right angles to the dominant pattern of interurbans radiating from Indianapolis.

MARION AND BLUFFTON TRACTION COMPANY

The Marion Bluffton and Eastern Traction Company was incorporated in 1905 to build an interurban from Marion to Bluffton, Decatur, and points in western Ohio. It was opened December 1, 1905, between Marion and Bluffton (32 miles), but never built farther east. Its officers were interested in the Bluffton Geneva and Celina Traction Company (q.v.), built in 1910, and the two interurbans pooled their equipment for through service. The MB&E also operated through service with the Kokomo Marion and Western Traction Company for a short period about 1908.

In 1912, as a consequence of a serious wreck and a long-standing dispute with the Moore-Mansfield Construction Company (which had built the line), the MB&E went into bankruptcy. Two years later it emerged as the Marion and Bluffton Traction Company. In 1926 it was absorbed by the Indiana Service Corporation, and was incorporated into the Indiana Railroad System (q.v.) on formation of the latter in 1930. It was one of the most short-lived lines of the Indiana Railroad and the first to be operated with one-man equipment.

BLUFFTON GENEVA AND CELINA TRACTION COMPANY

During the interurban building booms, several promoters had proposed to close the gap in a direct line from central Indiana to northwestern Ohio by building from Bluffton, junction of the Union Traction and the Fort Wayne and Wabash Valley, to Celina, end of the branch of the Western Ohio Railway. None did so, but in 1909 L. C. Justus, who was interested in the Marion and Bluffton Traction Company (q.v.), undertook construction. The earlier promoters who had proposed this connection had envisioned a line through Berne, Indiana, but when the Berne town government refused a subsidy, Justus decided to build through the small town of Geneva (pop. about 900), 5 miles to the south, where the local bank aided him in financing. The road was opened to Geneva (19 miles) in February 1910, and some grading was done east toward Celina. When Justus was killed in the Kingsland disaster of the same year, the line lost its leader. It was never extended east of Geneva, and was unable to survive in its completed form. In 1917 the line was abandoned and the rails shipped to France for wartime use. This road was the most short-lived in the Ohio-Indiana network.

INDIANA RAILROAD SYSTEM

By 1930 Samuel Insull and his Midland United Corporation controlled all the major interurbans in central Indiana, except the Indianapolis and Southeastern, which was within two years of abandonment. Since the companies were proving unprofitable, Midland United was confronted with a choice of abandoning them or consolidating them into a single system for modernization and improvement. In retrospect, there is little doubt that the interurbans should have been abandoned forthwith, but the Insull interests, apparently on the basis of their success with the Chicago South Shore and South Bend Railroad and the Chicago North Shore and Milwaukee, decided to consolidate their holdings and to abandon the lines that were hopeless, but to retain and improve the rest. The two Indianapolis-Fort Wayne lines were particularly good prospects for rebuilding, since they served several major towns and were free from railroad passenger competition between terminals. The entire interurban was troubled with severe curves in cities that prevented railroad interchange except for very short distances. The depression, together with the collapse of Insull's utility empire in 1932, made any large-scale modernization impossible, and the new organization (the Indiana Railroad System), in spite of a brave effort to carry on, liquidated the entire central Indiana interurban network in the course of about 11 years.

Because the Indiana Railroad's traffic arrangements and equipment policy have been described in the text, this description will be limited to a chronology of the company's history.

On July 2, 1930, the Indiana Railroad succeeded to the properties of the Union Traction Company, which was in receivership but substantially intact. At the same time the Indiana Railroad assumed management of the interurban rail lines of the Indiana Service Corporation and the Northern Indiana Power Company, even though these firms retained their corporate identities. The Public Service Company of Indiana was formed to take over the former Interstate Public Service Company, but its rail properties were also operated by the Indiana Railroad System. When these properties were brought together, application had already been made for abandonment of the Union Traction's Muncie-Portland, Kokomo-Logansport, and Marion-Wabash branches, which were discontinued, September 15, 1930. Since the Indiana Railroad had acquired the Union Traction on condition that these lines be dropped, they never appeared in the Indiana's timetables or maps.

On June 30, 1931, the Indiana Railroad abandoned the Alexandria-Tipton branch, but added the main line of the THI&E from Richmond to Terre Haute and Paris and a branch from Dunreith to New Castle. The segment from Brazil through Terre Haute to Paris was purchased in the name of the Public Service Company of Indiana, but the rest was bought by the Indiana Railroad itself. In January 1932, the Indiana abandoned the Terre Haute-Paris branch and the Indianapolis-Dunreith segment of the main line to Richmond. Thereafter, Richmond trains ran via the Indianapolis-New Castle line and the former THI&E New Castle-Dunreith branch.

About this time, negotiations were under way for absorption of the Winona Railroad into the Indiana Railroad, but the failure of Insull's system ended this prospect.

On May 22, 1932, the Indiana abandoned the Peru-Lafayette line of the Indiana Service Corporation, and on July 1, 1932, all of the Northern Indiana Power Company's interurban between Marion and Frankfort. The connecting Marion-Bluffton branch of the Indiana Service Corporation had been dropped on August 16, 1931. Also on July 1, 1932, the Indiana abandoned the Anderson-Marion line, which included the pioneer Anderson-Alexandria interurban. The affiliated Fort Wayne-Lima Railroad was also scrapped in 1932. In 1933 the Charlestown branch of the Public Service Company of Indiana was cut off, and in 1934 the local operations in New Albany and Jeffersonville were discontinued, although local groups perpetuated the New Albany city lines and the former Interstate's broad-gauge New Albany-Louisville bridge crossing.

On July 28, 1933, the Indiana Railroad failed and was placed in the hands of Bowman Elder, receiver. Elder was able and aggressive, and managed to keep the property substantially intact until 1937. In 1936, as a result of improvement in business conditions, the company showed an operating profit—the only one in its history—but it did so only because of the earnings of its bus lines. Elder, in fact, expanded the road in 1936, when the Indiana leased the Dayton and Western for two years. In 1937 a combination of the recession, the secular forces operating against the interurbans, and an order of the Securities and Exchange Commission for the dissolution of the Midland United initiated further abandonments that annihilated the Indiana Railroad in the course of about four years. The operating loss on rail services in 1937 was $224,800, and in 1938, $273,000. Rail operations were so uneconomic that Midland United could hope to divest itself of the company (except as scrap) only by conversion of the remaining rail lines to bus operations.

The Indiana Service Corporation's lines from Fort Wayne north to Waterloo, Garrett, and Kendallville were discontinued March 15, 1937, and on May 9 the long Indianapolis–New Castle–Richmond–Dayton line, including the Dayton and Western, was abandoned. There was no longer a connection with the Ohio interurbans. On September 11, 1938, the lesser of the two Indianapolis–Fort Wayne lines (via Peru) was dropped. November 1, 1939, the Louisville line was cut back to Seymour, and January 11, 1940, the long Terre Haute line was abandoned. The principal remaining routes, the Indianapolis–Fort Wayne line via Bluffton and the Muncie–New Castle branch were abandoned effective midnight January 18, 1941.

With the end of the second Fort Wayne line, the Indiana Railroad as an interurban was essentially dead. For a time the Public Service Company of Indiana continued passenger service under its own name with a single car per day between Indianapolis and Seymour in fulfillment of a franchise obligation, but on September 8, 1941, a head-on collision between one of the two remaining passenger cars, lightweight No. 78, and a line car, No. 772, brought passenger service to an abrupt end. Proposals to restore this line to handle war-time traffic came to naught. Three segments of the Indiana Railroad remained in freight service: until 1942 the Indiana itself retained 8 miles east from an interchange with the Milwaukee Road in Terre Haute to haul coal from Binkley Mine; the Indiana Service Corporation retained the Garrett–Fort Wayne line to carry coal from the New York Central and Pennsylvania railroads to its powerhouse until 1945 (a short segment in Fort Wayne survived in switching service until 1952); and the Southern Indiana Railway was formed to operate a small portion of the former Interstate line between Speeds and Watson Junction. The last of these is still in service using diesel locomotives, but the rest of the Indiana Railroad, which totaled about 600 miles at its peak, is now abandoned. The company continued as a major motor bus operator in Indiana, and with the last of the interurban lines removed, emerged from receivership on June 22, 1941. The bus line, still known as the Indiana Railroad, was sold for $650,000 to the Wesson Company in 1942, and the truck operations of the Indiana Railroad were sold in 1943 to the Interstate Motor Freight System.

INDIANAPOLIS AND CINCINNATI TRACTION COMPANY

After Charles L. Henry left the Union Traction Company, he began promoting an interurban intended to be a double-tracked, high-speed line from Indianapolis to Hamilton, Ohio, where it would connect for Cincinnati. He projected the road about 1902, and by 1905 was able to open 41 miles of single track to Rushville. This interurban was the first installation of Westinghouse single-phase AC electrification, described in Chapter 2. The road was extended to Connersville (17 miles) in 1906.

Henry, apparently in an effort to protect himself from a rival interurban to Cincinnati, in 1904 purchased the Indianapolis Shelbyville and Southeastern Traction Company, which had built an orthodox low-voltage DC road from Indianapolis to Shelbyville (28 miles) in 1902. The company was building an extension to Greensburg (21 miles) when Henry bought it. He had the extension equipped with single-phase AC for uniformity with his Connersville line, and had the Indianapolis–Shelbyville segment converted to single phase when the extension was opened on January 25, 1907.

In 1906, before either extension had been completed, the company encountered financial difficulties and went into voluntary receivership with Henry as receiver. The road emerged in 1910 without change of name, but its financial problems had prevented it from building east. Henry had acquired a right-of-way from Connersville to Hamilton along the Cincinnati Hamilton & Dayton Railroad, but was never able to build on it. One of the industry's most optimistic executives, Henry conceived a new plan for building to Cincinnati about 1922, this time from Rushville through Brookville to College Hill in the north suburbs of Cincinnati and to a connection with the stillborn Cincinnati subway. The cost of the extension was estimated at $4 million, but it would probably have been higher. It had long since become impossible to finance major interurban projects, and nothing was done to implement the plan.

In 1904 Henry had announced that he was considering extending the Shelbyville–Greensburg line to a connection with a line to be built north from Madison by local businessmen, but nothing came of this proposal.

The Indianapolis and Cincinnati suffered more from misguided equipment policy than any other major interurban. The single-phase electrification had proved expensive and unwieldy and was replaced in 1923 and 1924, at the time the new extension to Cincinnati was proposed, by an orthodox 600-volt DC system. The passenger rolling stock was replaced with twelve heavy-steel combines purchased from the Cincinnati Car Company. This type of equipment was already archaic for medium-density lines when the I&C bought it, and only six years later (1929) was replaced by 13 Cincinnati Car Company curved-side lightweight cars. Four of the 1923 cars were sold to the Union Traction, and eight to the Milwaukee Electric, where they were rebuilt into articulated units. The company was reorganized after bankruptcy in 1929 as the Indianapolis and Southeastern Railroad Company, but it survived only three years. On January 14, 1932, at the depth of the depression, it was abandoned. Buses assumed the service and the lightweight cars were sold to the Beech Grove Traction Company, the Nashville–Franklin Railway, and the Inter-City Rapid Transit of Canton, Ohio.

SOUTHERN INDIANA GAS AND ELECTRIC COMPANY

On December 8, 1903, the Evansville and Princeton Traction Company opened a 28-mile interurban between the cities of its corporate title. The company proposed to build north to Vincennes, and then either northeast toward Indianapolis or straight north toward Terre Haute. Branches to Owensville, Poseyville, New Harmony, Washington, and Petersburg were also projected. In 1906 the line passed into the hands of the Evansville Princeton and Vincennes Interurban Railway, and in 1908 to the Evansville and Southern Indiana Traction Company, which also controlled the street railway in Evansville. The Princeton interurban was always operated separately from the three lines of the Evansville and Ohio Valley Railway, the interurban subsidiary of the Evansville Railways.

Expansion northward from Princeton was cut off by the decline of interurban building in 1903, but began again in 1907. In 1908 the line was extended straight north 4 miles to Patoka, along the projected route to Vincennes and Sullivan, which had been reached from Terre Haute in 1906. The directors voted to build on northward in the following spring, but encountered the general difficulty of financing interurban projects after 1907, and were never able to extend the line. Extension to Sullivan was proposed as late as 1915, however.

The line passed into the hands of the newly organized Public Service Company of Evansville in 1912, which in 1921 changed its name to the Southern Indiana Gas and Electric Company, the name under which the property operated for the rest of its history. The interurban operated until 1933, when it was abandoned. Four lightweight cars, the road's only modern equipment, were transferred to Evansville street railway service.

EVANSVILLE AND OHIO VALLEY RAILWAY

The street railway in Evansville operated interurbans east to Grandview, west to Mount Vernon, and south to Henderson under the name of the Evansville and Ohio Valley Railway. The first of the three lines to be built was the one to the east, opened in 1907 between a connection near Newburgh with the Evansville Suburban and Newburgh to Rockport (21 miles), a town on the Ohio River. The builder, the Evansville and Eastern Electric Railway, almost immediately had a dispute on fare divisions with the ES&N, over which its cars entered Evansville, and as a consequence built its own line from Newburgh to Evansville (10 miles) in 1908. A 3-mile branch from Richland Junction to Richland City had been opened in 1907, and in 1911 the main line was extended east 6 miles from Rockport to Grandview. Like the ES&N, the Evansville and Eastern was heavily built, and enjoyed a carload-freight traffic, mainly in coal and in foundry moulding sand. Its passenger service was orthodox, except for river-launch connections from Rockport to Owensboro, Kentucky, and from Grandview to Cannelton (described in Chapter 3).

The Evansville and Mount Vernon Electric Railway (22 miles) was opened in 1906. Proposals to build west into southern Illinois were never executed. Evansville Railways consolidated the two interurbans with the city system in 1907, and in 1912 built a third interurban, the Evansville Henderson and Owensboro Railway, to Henderson. This interurban included the car-ferry operation mentioned in Chapter 2.

The system was reorganized in 1918, and the three interurban lines became the Evansville and Ohio Valley Railway in 1919. In 1927 a car bound for Henderson hit an open switch and was wrecked, killing 4 persons and injuring 50. The damage claims bankrupted the company and precipitated the abandonment of the Henderson line in the following year. The two launch services of the subsidiary Crescent Navigation Company and the interurban to Mount Vernon were also abandoned in 1928, but the line to Grandview survived in passenger service until 1938. In 1941 the line was abandoned except for 13 miles between Rockport, Posey, and Richland, which served several sand pits. This segment was itself abandoned in 1946.

EVANSVILLE SUBURBAN AND NEWBURGH RAILWAY

In 1889 the ES&N opened a steam railroad, primarily for transporting coal, from Evansville to Newburgh, 10 miles up the Ohio River. The railroad was quite successful, and in 1904 the management decided to electrify it. Electric operation began in 1905, and in 1906 an electrified branch from Stockwell to Boonville (4 miles), parallel to the Southern Railway, was opened. In the same period, the small steam "dummy" engines previously used for freight service were replaced by mogul-type steam locomotives, which thereafter hauled the coal trains. The LCL freight was handled on a box motor in orthodox interurban fashion.

Because of the coal traffic, the ES&N was one of the most successful interurbans. Passenger service was discontinued in 1930 on both lines, but probably would have continued longer had fire not destroyed the Boonville substation. Freight service was discontinued on the Newburgh line in the same year, but the track was not removed until 1941. The Boonville line remained in freight service until 1947, and was dismantled in the following year. A box motor and a former Evansville and Ohio Valley Railway steeple cab remained in switching operation on a remnant of the interurban until 1956 under the name Cook Transit Company, serving the brewery of F. W. Cook and Sons in Evansville.

LEBANON-THORNTOWN TRACTION COMPANY

This small company connected Thorntown with Lebanon (10 miles), an important junction on the Indianapolis and Northwestern division of the THI&E. The line was opened in July 1905, and throughout most of its history two small Cincinnati Car Company combines provided service on two-hour headway. The road survived until July 6, 1926. One of its cars was sold to the THI&E, and the right-of-way passed into the hands of the parallel Big Four Railroad.

*

There were two short electric lines in Indiana, each of which had some interurban characteristics.

BEECH GROVE TRACTION CORPORATION

Indianapolis was connected with Beech Grove (6 miles) in 1911. Although Beech Grove was barely beyond the southeast city limits of the capital, the company joined the Central Electric Railway Association, used interurban technology, and in its later years bought second-hand lightweight cars from the Cincinnati Georgetown and Portsmouth and the Indianapolis and Southeastern. Its initial cars are believed to have been second-hand from the Winona Interurban. Beech Grove cars did not use the Traction Terminal, but looped south of the business district.

This little company made one of the most heroic efforts to survive. It held to a 10¢ fare to the end, and was reduced to such dire circumstances that it paid its employees partly in fare tokens. It did not abandon until 1937, when its electricity bill was so far in arrears that the Indianapolis Railways cut off its power supply.

ANGOLA RAILWAY AND POWER COMPANY

Angola was connected with a resort at Paltytown on Lake James (3 miles) by this short electric railway. It operated in the summer months only from 1904 to 1918, when it was abandoned. Although in its finished form the line was hardly an interurban, the original owner hoped to extend it from Angola to Bryan, Pioneer, or Celina for connection with the Ohio interurbans.

Michigan

Michigan's 981 miles of interurban rounded out the network of the Central Electric Railway Association (see map, pp. 256–57).[7] In terms of both opening and closing dates, the Michigan lines were pioneers. The suburban lines out of Detroit were among the earliest interurbans, but because of the rapid rise of highway transport in Michigan, public and private alike, the state's interurban mileage was among the first to be swept away completely. The state's last interurban car ran on the Northern Indiana Railway's St. Joseph line in 1934.

DETROIT UNITED RAILWAY

In the late 1890's Detroit was the principal center of interurban building in the United States; not until 1903 was its radial network surpassed by Indianapolis'. The entire network was amalgamated into the Detroit United Railway system in 1901 by the Everett-Moore syndicate, which had previously controlled most of the individual lines. The Detroit United also operated the extensive street railway in Detroit. The financial problems of the Everett-Moore syndicate in 1902 and 1903 drastically limited any expansion of the system. After 1903 only two major lines were built, one to Monroe in 1904 completing the line to Toledo, and a long projected branch from Romeo to Almont and Imlay City in 1915.

Each of the four major lines of the Detroit United was operated with some degree of autonomy. The system's most profitable interurban route was operated under the name Detroit Monroe and Toledo Short Line Railway. This was one of the most heavily built Midwestern interurbans, laid with 70-pound rail on crushed-rock ballast, and free of grade crossings with railroads. About half the line was double-tracked. Running time of locals for the 57-mile trip was 2 hours and 50 minutes at the outset, but was later reduced by about 25 minutes. Limiteds made the trip in about

ELEMENTS IN THE DETROIT UNITED RAILWAY

Route	Mileage	Builder	Opening date
Detroit–Mt. Clemens (west line)	22	Rapid Railway	1895
Detroit–Mt. Clemens (east line)	27	Detroit Lake Shore & Mt. Clemens Ry.	1898
Mt. Clemens–Port Huron	45	Rapid Railway System	1900
Ypsilanti–Ann Arbor	9	Ann Arbor & Ypsilanti Street Ry.	1890; 1896*
Detroit–Ypsilanti	30	Detroit Ypsilanti & Ann Arbor Ry.	1898
Ypsilanti–Saline	10	Detroit Ypsilanti & Ann Arbor Ry.	1899
Ann Arbor–Jackson	37	Detroit Ypsilanti Ann Arbor & Jackson Ry.	1901
Northville–Wayne	16	Detroit Plymouth & Northville Ry.	1898
Detroit–Northville	27	Detroit & Northwestern Ry.	1899
Farmington Jct.–Pontiac	16	Detroit & Northwestern Ry.	1899
Detroit–Pontiac	26	Detroit & Pontiac Ry.	1897
Royal Oak–Romeo	27	Detroit Rochester Romeo & Lake Orion Ry.	1900
Lake Orion Jct.–Flint	40	Detroit Lake Orion & Flint Ry.	1902
Detroit–Wyandotte	13	Wyandotte & Detroit River Ry.	1893
Wyandotte–Trenton	4	Wyandotte & Detroit River Ry.	1900
Monroe–Toledo	21	Toledo & Monroe Ry.	1901
Detroit–Monroe	26	Detroit Monroe & Toledo Short Line Ry.	1904
Romeo–Imlay City	17	Detroit Almont & Northern Ry.	1915

* Date of electrification.

2 hours and 5 minutes. Six limiteds a day were run to Cleveland in connection with the Lake Shore Electric. Short-distance traffic north of Trenton was handled mainly by the parallel Trenton suburban line of the DUR. After 1930, three Cincinnati–Detroit trains per day were operated with lightweight cars of the Cincinnati and Lake Erie.

The Jackson line operated under the name of the Detroit Jackson and Chicago Railway. The DUR assumed its funded debt in 1907 and operated it thereafter, although it never acquired title to the road. Through service to Kalamazoo and Lansing was provided jointly with the Michigan United. Traffic, particularly to and from Ann Arbor, was heavy in the early years, and the line was relatively profitable until the mid-twenties.

The Port Huron route, known as the Rapid Railway, benefited from the comparative lack of railroad competition. The Flint line had the only significant railroad freight interchange on the system, in addition to substantial passenger traffic. Interline limiteds were run to Saginaw and Bay City jointly with the Michigan United. Parlor cars were operated to Pontiac beginning in 1923 and to Flint in 1924. Much of the Port Huron and Flint divisions, being built early, was lightly graded, side-of-the-road trackage. The company operated the street railways in Port Huron, Flint and Pontiac.

Since the automobile became common in Michigan relatively early and the state regulatory authorities gave the interurbans no protection against highway transport, the Detroit United was one of the first big systems to disintegrate. In 1920 it sold its Canadian affiliate, the Sandwich Windsor and Amherstburg (*q.v.*), and in 1922, after decades of public hostility and bickering with the municipal government, the company sold its Detroit street railway to the city. The interurbans quickly proved unprofitable as an independent operation, and the company went bankrupt in 1925. The Farmington–Northville and Ypsilanti–Saline lines were abandoned in 1925, the Farmington–Orchard Lake branch, the Wyandotte suburban line, and the Imlay City branch followed in 1927. The Plymouth–Northville branch was discontinued in 1928.

In 1928, the company was reorganized as the Eastern Michigan Railways. Simultaneously, the Detroit Monroe and Toledo was reconstituted as the Eastern Michigan–Toledo Railroad. The Jackson line was not included in the new organization, but was transferred to the Michigan Electric, which operated it only until 1929. The Detroit Street Railway took over the Farmington suburban line. The interurbans were so unprofitable that the new company wound them up quickly. The Port Huron line was abandoned in January 1930, and the Flint–Pontiac lines in April 1931. Abandonment of the Toledo line was delayed by the regulatory commission, but it took place on October 4, 1932. No other major city's interurban network was abandoned so early.

An 8-mile segment of the Port Huron line between Algonac and Marine City was purchased by the Chris-Craft Corporation to serve its plant at Algonac, and until 1957 was operated with a pair of gasoline locomotives under the name of the Algonac Transit Company.

ELEMENTS IN THE MICHIGAN UNITED RAILWAY

Route	Mileage	Builder	Opening date
Jackson–Battle Creek	44*	Jackson & Battle Creek Tr. Co.	1903
Battle Creek–Kalamazoo	24	Michigan Tr. Co.	1900
Jackson–Lansing	37*	Lansing & Jackson Railway Co.	1909
Lansing–St. Johns	21	Lansing & Suburban Tr. Co.	1901 ; 1904‡
Lansing–Owosso	32*	Michigan United Railways	1911
Jackson–Wolf Lake	12	Jackson Consolidated Tr. Co.	1901
Saginaw–Frankenmuth	14	Detroit Flint & Saginaw Ry.	1905
Flint–Frankenmuth Jct.	24	Saginaw & Flint Ry.	1909
Battle Creek–Gull Lake	3	Michigan Tr. Co.	1900
Kalamazoo–Grand Rapids†	50*	Michigan Ry.	1915
Battle Creek–Allegan†	43*	Michigan Ry.	1915‡
Saginaw–Bay City†	14*	Michigan Ry.	1914

* Third-rail lines; others used overhead.
† Lines of the Michigan Railway; the preceding lines were operated by MUR.
‡ Date of electrification.

MICHIGAN UNITED RAILWAY

This company operated city lines in Lansing, Kalamazoo, Battle Creek, and Jackson, and had two isolated interurbans, one from Kalamazoo to Owosso, via Jackson and Lansing, and the other from Flint to Saginaw. A subsidiary, the Michigan Railway, operated interurbans between Grand Rapids and Kalamazoo, Battle Creek and Allegan, and Saginaw and Bay City.

The Michigan United was formed of predecessor companies in 1906. The Michigan Railway was distinguished by exceptionally high physical standards; the Grand Rapids–Kalamazoo–Battle Creek line was equipped with 67'-6" steel cars weighing 142,600 pounds each. Cars fitted as coach-parlor combinations provided limited service between Grand Rapids and Kalamazoo at an over-all speed of 39.8 miles per hour. The Battle Creek–Allegan line was an electrification of a Michigan Central Railroad branch, and this entire division was operated to railroad standards.

In 1905 the Michigan United acquired the former main line of the Michigan Central between Kalamazoo and Mattawan when the railroad was relocated and double-tracked. The Michigan United hoped to electrify the line as part of a westward extension, but instead it was arranged that the track should be used by the Kalamazoo Lake Shore and Chicago Traction Company, a road being promoted by the proprietors of the Chicago and South Haven Steamship Company. The KLS&C connected the former Michigan Central track with the Pere Marquette's Lawton–South Haven branch, which it leased, to form a direct line from Kalamazoo to the steamer connection at South Haven. The KLS&C was steam-operated. In 1911 the Michigan United leased the KLS&C for a five-year period in hopes of electrifying it with a third rail to complete a route across the state, but the project was never executed. In 1925 the KLS&C was sold for scrap; the line of the Pere Marquette reverted to its owner.

Between 1916 and 1924 the Michigan Railway leased the Grand Rapids Holland and Chicago Railway as its northwestern division.

Through services with the Detroit United west from Jackson and north from Flint compensated to a great extent for the company's failure to close its gap between Owosso and Flint.

In spite of a physical plant that was superior to most other interurbans—indeed, partly because of the heavy fixed charges incurred in building it—the system was generally unprofitable after World War I. The Michigan Railway was reorganized as the Michigan Railroad in 1919, and the Michigan United as the Michigan Electric Railway in 1923. The Michigan Railroad failed again in 1924. Both companies suffered heavy deficits after 1924, and were abandoned between 1927 and 1929. The short Frankenmuth and Wolf Lake lines were cut off in 1927, and the Grand Rapids–Kalamazoo–Battle Creek–Jackson trackage was abandoned in 1928. The lines from Jackson north to Lansing, St. Johns, and Owosso and the isolated Flint–Saginaw–Bay City line were discontinued in 1929. The important Detroit Jackson and Chicago, acquired from the bankrupt Detroit United only in 1928, was also abandoned in 1929.

GRAND RAPIDS GRAND HAVEN AND MUSKEGON RAILWAY

One of two interurbans connecting Grand Rapids with ports on Lake Michigan, the Grand Rapids Grand Haven and Muskegon was opened in 1902. The Grand Rapids–Muskegon line was 35 miles long, and Grand Haven was reached by an 8-mile branch from Fruitport. The main line operated by third rail, but trackage over city streets and on the Grand Haven branch was equipped with overhead wire. Schedules and tariffs were closely coordinated with Lake Michigan steamship lines, the Crosby Line at Muskegon for Milwaukee, and the Goodrich Line at Grand Haven for Chicago. The interurban had a heavy traffic in fruit, mainly in connection with the steamers. Between 1912 and 1925 the road was controlled by the United Light and Railways Company. In 1925 the line was purchased by S. L. Vaughan, its president, and W. K. Morley, its general manager. The line began to incur deficits in 1924, and went into receivership in 1926. In its first full year of receivership it lost $24,768, exclusive of fixed charges, and by the end had run up an indebtedness to the state and county governments of over $20,000. Continuation was impossible, and the line was abandoned on April 18, 1928. Parts of the right-of-way were used for widening U.S. Highway 16.

GRAND RAPIDS HOLLAND AND CHICAGO RAILWAY

Like Grand Rapids' other interurban connection with Lake Michigan, the Grand Rapids Holland and Lake Michigan Rapid Railway was opened in 1902. In addition to its line from Grand Rapids to Holland (29 miles), the interurban had extensions to Macatawa Beach (6 miles, built by the Holland and Lake Michigan Railway, 1899) and Saugatuck (17 miles, 1902). Throughout the road's history, it worked closely with the Graham & Morton Line's Chicago–Holland steamer service. The promoters had been unwise enough to double-track the main line in expectation of traffic that never appeared. Partly owing to the heavy capital expenditure on track and overhead, the company failed and its assets were sold to the newly formed Grand Rapids Holland and Chicago Railway in 1904.

In 1913, the Saugatuck branch was relocated to the west and converted to 1,200-volt DC.

In 1916 the line was leased by the Michigan Railway, which operated it until January 1, 1924, when the lease was terminated and the property returned to its owners. Deprived of revenues from the lease, the GRH&C defaulted on its interest payments on February 1, 1924, and went into receivership. At the same time the road was under court order to repair its track in the streets of Granville. The only bidder at a receiver's sale in 1926 was the Hyman-Michaels Company, a Chicago scrap dealer, which purchased the property for $227,500. Hyman-Michaels sold the right-of-way to the Consumers Power Company to be used for a transmission line, and scrapped the track west of Jenison together with the rolling stock after abandoning operation on November 15, 1926. The track east of Jenison (8 miles) was preserved as the United Suburban Railway and operated with city-style equipment until June 25, 1932.

BENTON HARBOR–ST. JOE RAILWAY AND LIGHT COMPANY

The street railway in Benton Harbor and St. Joseph operated two interurbans, one to a connection with the Michigan Central Railroad at Dowagiac and the other to the resort area at Coloma, Watervliet, and Paw Paw Lake. The former was built to Eau Claire (14.5 miles) in 1906 and extended to Dowagiac (11 miles) in 1911. The Watervliet line (15 miles) was built in 1910, and included a leased branch of the Pere Marquette Railroad (3 miles) from Coloma to Paw Paw Lake. The interurban lines were heavily dependent on interchange of passengers and freight, mainly fruit, with steamers of the Graham & Morton Line at Benton Harbor.

Control over the company passed in 1922 to the Indiana and Michigan Electric Company of South Bend, which shortly sold it to the American Gas and Electric Company. AG&E soon tried to divest itself of the property, and in 1928 abandoned the two interurban lines to facilitate the sale of the street railway to a new group called the Twin City Railway, which operated the streetcar lines until 1935.

SAGINAW–BAY CITY RAILWAY

In 1896 the Inter-Urban Railway built a line between Saginaw and Bay City (13 miles) along the west bank of the Saginaw River. The road became the Saginaw Valley Traction Company in 1899, and in 1910 it was merged into the Saginaw–Bay City Railway Company, which thereafter operated the street railways in both cities. The physical plant was inferior to the Michigan Railway's line built in 1914 between the same cities. After 1914 the Michigan Railway also controlled the S-BC.

In 1921 the S-BC went bankrupt, mainly because of jitney competition, and at the same time became embroiled in a franchise dispute with the city of Saginaw. When the city refused to grant a fare increase for city service as a condition of extension of the franchise, the railway discontinued service in August 1921. It was not until November 1923 that a new firm, the Saginaw Transit Company, was organized to restore the street railway to service. The new company abandoned the Bay City street railway and the interurban line, except for about 4 miles from Saginaw to Carrollton and Zilwaukee. The entire Saginaw street railway system was converted to bus operation in 1931.

ESCANABA TRACTION COMPANY

The street railway in Escanaba built an extension to Gladstone (11 miles) in 1910. The Escanaba Traction Company became the Escanaba Power and Traction Company in 1920, and abandoned its rail operations in May 1932.

HOUGHTON COUNTY TRACTION COMPANY

The Houghton County Street Railway operated an interurban line from Houghton to Mohawk (23 miles) on the Keweenaw Peninsula, with a branch from Red Jacket to Hubbell (8 miles). The road first offered service between Houghton, Hancock, and Wolverine in 1901, and was expanded through the copper-mining towns, reaching its full extent about 1908. The road became the Houghton County Traction Company in 1908. It went into receivership in 1921 because of the decline of mining in the area, but managed to survive until 1932. This interurban was one of the most isolated in the United States, but was part of the Stone and Webster system of electric lines.

Kentucky

APART FROM short extensions of electric lines from Ohio, Indiana, or West Virginia, Kentucky had only two interurbans, one serving Louisville and the other serving Lexington (see map, pp. 256–57). Surprisingly, there were no small local lines of the sort found in other areas.

LOUISVILLE AND INTERURBAN RAILROAD

By means of this wholly owned subsidiary, the street railway in Louisville operated seven interurban lines into the hinterland of the city. The Louisville and Eastern Railroad, acquired in 1911, built two lines, one to La Grange (opened to Crestwood in 1901, completed in 1907), and the other to Shelbyville (1910). The La Grange line was projected to Cincinnati and the Shelbyville line to Frankfort. The L&I itself built lines to Jeffersontown (1904), Okalona (1905), Orell (1907), and Fern Creek (1908). In addition, in 1904 the Louisville and Interurban electrified the Prospect branch of the Louisville & Nashville Railroad.

All the lines of both companies were built to the 5'-0" gauge of the street railway in Louisville, with the exception of the Prospect line, which was standard gauge. This line had been built to 3' gauge by the Louisville Harrod's Creek & Westport Railroad, but converted to 4'-8½" by the Louisville & Nashville. The 11-mile branch was first leased to the interurban for passenger service, and the L&N for a time continued to provide freight service with steam locomotives by night. The Louisville and Interurban eventually acquired title to the trackage, but never converted it to broad gauge, and always maintained a separate set of equipment for it.

The company's most important line ran to Shelbyville, and was in part double-tracked. Had it been completed to Frankfort (about 24 miles) it would have provided a connection to Lexington via the standard-gauge Kentucky Traction and Terminal Company. Passenger service on all lines was operated by heavy wooden equipment of orthodox design. Except on the Prospect line, railroad interchange was impossible, but LCL freight hauling was developed extensively; the company had some of the heaviest milk traffic of any interurban.

These interurbans all expired in the depression: the Okalona line in 1931, the Jeffersontown in 1932, the Fern Creek in 1933, the Shelbyville in 1934, and the rest— La Grange, Orell and Prospect—in 1935. All freight service was discontinued in 1934.

KENTUCKY TRACTION AND TERMINAL COMPANY

The Lexington and Interurban Railways Company was chartered in 1905 to acquire the street railways and interurbans of Lexington. In 1911 the properties passed into the hands of the Kentucky Traction and Terminal Company, which operated them thereafter. The company also operated the street railway in Frankfort.

The company had four interurban lines, of which the most important ran to Frankfort. The Central Kentucky Traction Company had opened this line to Versailles in 1905 and the affiliated Frankfort and Versailles Traction Company extended it to Frankfort in 1907. The Georgetown and Lexington Traction Company built to Georgetown in 1902 and the Blue Grass Traction Company to Paris in 1903. The Lexington and Interurban itself built to Nicholasville in 1910.

In the early 1920's, the International Utilities Corporation, which controlled the company, instituted a modernization program that received a great deal of publicity. In 1921 the company's interurban services were provided by wooden cars, the heaviest of which weighed 76,000 pounds, operating on 90-minute headway. Maintenance expenses on this equipment had increased greatly since 1918, and bus competition was attracting passengers from the rails in substantial numbers. In February 1922, the road took delivery of 10 lightweight cars from the Cincinnati Car Company, the first of the curved-side design that was to become common in the 1920's. Headway was reduced to an hour, fares were cut from 3.6 cents per mile to 3 cents on tickets and 3.25 cents cash. The new cars weighed only 25,100 pounds and cut power consumption 18.1 per cent in their first year of service, in spite of the increase in frequency. Consumption per car hour fell about 41 per cent. Each car had four motors of only 25 horsepower each. Track-maintenance and car-maintenance costs each fell by about 35 per cent. The company later bought 2 more interurban passenger cars, 2 Cincinnati lightweights fitted out as box motors, and 27 single-truck city cars, all using the same wheel, axle, and motor design.

Despite the fact that traffic was falling at the rate of 5 per cent annually, the new

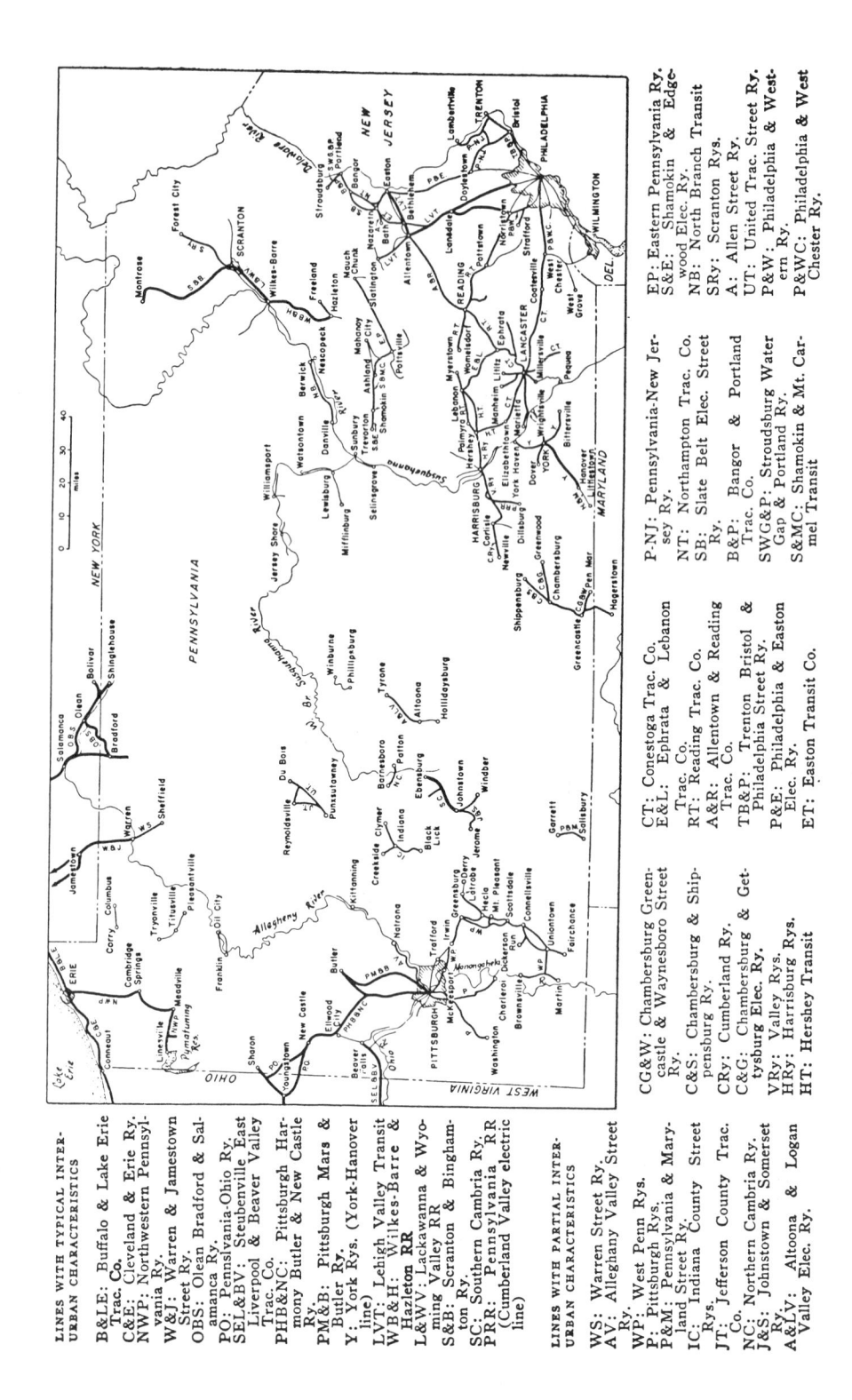

LINES WITH TYPICAL INTERURBAN CHARACTERISTICS

B&LE: Buffalo & Lake Erie Trac. Co.
C&E: Cleveland & Erie Ry.
NWP: Northwestern Pennsylvania Ry.
W&J: Warren & Jamestown Street Ry.
OBS: Olean Bradford & Salamanca Ry.
PO: Pennsylvania-Ohio Ry.
SEL&BV: Steubenville East Liverpool & Beaver Valley Trac. Co.
PHB&NC: Pittsburgh Harmony Butler & New Castle Ry.
PM&B: Pittsburgh Mars & Butler Ry.
Y: York Rys. (York-Hanover line)
LVT: Lehigh Valley Transit
WB&H: Wilkes-Barre & Hazleton RR
L&WV: Lackawanna & Wyoming Valley RR
S&B: Scranton & Binghamton Ry.
SC: Southern Cambria Ry.
PRR: Pennsylvania RR (Cumberland Valley electric line)

LINES WITH PARTIAL INTERURBAN CHARACTERISTICS

WS: Warren Street Ry.
AV: Alleghany Valley Street Ry.
WP: West Penn Ry.
P: Pittsburgh Rys.
P&M: Pennsylvania & Maryland Street Ry.
IC: Indiana County Street Rys.
JT: Jefferson County Trac. Co.
NC: Northern Cambria Ry.
J&S: Johnstown & Somerset Ry.
A&LV: Altoona & Logan Valley Elec. Ry.
CG&W: Chambersburg Greencastle & Waynesboro Street Ry.
C&S: Chambersburg & Shippensburg Ry.
CRy: Cumberland Ry.
C&G: Chambersburg & Gettysburg Elec. Ry.
VRy: Valley Rys.
HRy: Harrisburg Rys.
HT: Hershey Transit
CT: Conestoga Trac. Co.
E&L: Ephrata & Lebanon Trac. Co.
RT: Reading Trac. Co.
A&R: Allentown & Reading Trac. Co.
TB&P: Trenton Bristol & Philadelphia Street Ry.
P&E: Philadelphia & Easton Elec. Ry.
ET: Easton Transit Co.
P-NJ: Pennsylvania-New Jersey Ry.
NT: Northampton Trac. Co.
SB: Slate Belt Elec. Street Ry.
B&P: Bangor & Portland Trac. Co.
SWG&P: Stroudsburg Water Gap & Portland Ry.
S&MC: Shamokin & Mt. Carmel Transit
EP: Eastern Pennsylvania Ry.
S&E: Shamokin & Edgewood Elec. Ry.
NB: North Branch Transit
SRy: Scranton Rys.
A: Allen Street Ry.
UT: United Trac. Street Ry.
P&W: Philadelphia & Western Ry.
P&WC: Philadelphia & West Chester Ry.

interurbans paid for themselves in three years, the city cars in five. The company's experience widely influenced other interurbans to adopt Cincinnati lightweight cars, but its success was short-lived. Passengers continued to be lost to the automobile, and the company's important milk traffic was lost to trucks. Kentucky Traction and Terminal, then a property of Insull's Middle West Utilities Company, went bankrupt in 1934. On January 12, 1934, all interurban lines were discontinued. City service in Frankfort had ceased 6 days earlier as a result of a strike.

Pennsylvania

PENNSYLVANIA, with its dense population and heavy industrial development, was an obvious area for building a large network of electric railways. The roads ranged from rural trolley lines of the New England style to interurbans of Midwestern technology. The typical line in eastern Pennsylvania used New England style equipment on a side-of-the-road right-of-way. There is no rigorous distinction between interurbans and other electric railways in Pennsylvania, and classification is arbitrary. For convenience, we have divided the state's electric lines into roads that were unquestionably interurbans, roads that had some interurban characteristics (private right-of-way for long distances, freight interchange, affiliation with an interurban or railroad, and the like), and rural trolley lines. We have included the first two categories in our tabulations of mileages, but not the third. We do not claim any exactitude in our differentiation; undoubtedly some lines in the third category are as worthy of inclusion as many in the second.

INTERURBANS

CLEVELAND AND ERIE RAILWAY

The Conneaut and Erie Traction Company connected the cities of its name in 1903 (33 miles), and quickly proved itself to be a weak property. It failed in 1907, and was succeeded by the Cleveland and Erie Railway in 1909. The company was notorious for the poor quality of its service.

The C&E was one of the few electric lines driven into bankruptcy by a fellow interurban. In 1920 George Bullock, receiver of the Buffalo and Lake Erie Traction Company, brought the Cleveland and Erie into receivership because its payments for use of the B&LE's trackage approaching the terminal in Erie were in arrears. The C&E never emerged from the receivership and was sold for junk in 1922, thus ending the connection between the interurbans of New York State and the Midwestern network.

NORTHWESTERN PENNSYLVANIA RAILWAY

This interurban, which operated a standard-gauge line from Erie to Cambridge Springs, Meadville, Conneaut Lake, and Linesville, was formed in 1911 and 1912 out of three predecessor companies. The Meadville Traction Company had operated from Meadville to Linesville and Conneaut Lake (11 miles) since 1898. The Erie Traction Company had connected Erie with Cambridge Springs in 1901, and the gap between the two was filled by the Meadville and Cambridge Springs Street Railway (15.5 miles) in 1903. The road was the only rail route from Erie to Meadville, shop city of the Erie Railroad. The company did an excursion business to Conneaut Lake and to the Pymatuning Reservoir west of Meadville.

In 1923 the Northwestern Pennsylvania was absorbed by the Northwestern Electric Service Company of Pennsylvania, which operated the property for its five remaining years. The Linesville and Conneaut Lake lines were abandoned in 1927, and the Erie–Meadville trackage in 1928.

The Northwestern Pennsylvania organized a subsidiary, the Erie Cambridge Union and Corry Traction Company, later known as the Erie Southern Railway, that proposed to build an alternative line between Cambridge Springs and Erie along the Erie Railroad main line and the Pennsylvania Railroad's Erie branch, together with a branch to Union City and Corry. These lines were never built, but were shown as projected in the company's literature for many years. They were, in fact, shown as extant on the Central Electric Railway Association's maps, and subsequently have erroneously appeared on other maps.

LACKAWANNA AND WYOMING VALLEY RAILROAD[8]

Scranton and Wilkes-Barre, the two principal population centers of Pennsylvania's anthracite-mining area, were connected by three railroads and two street railway lines by the early years of the century, but service was generally considered inadequate. Consequently, the Lackawanna and Wyoming Valley Railroad was incorporated and, in 1903, was completed. Wishing to build entirely on private right-of-way, the proprietors incorporated under the statutes governing steam railroads, and thus secured the right of eminent domain. The completed line had no street running, and used third rail except for the approach to the terminal in Wilkes-Barre. The right-of-way was 60 to 150 feet wide, heavily graded, and equipped with 40 bridges, the most notable being a viaduct at Avoca 682 feet long. At first the road left Scranton on severe grades, but in 1905 a tunnel of 4,747 feet was drilled at South Scranton. Railroad freight cars could be handled, and there was a short branch at South Scranton to Dunmore which made a connection with the Erie. Passenger service on this branch was offered from 1904 to 1945. There were also connections to the Lackawanna and the Lehigh Valley.

The promoters of the Lackawanna and Wyoming Valley envisioned a large network of heavy electric lines amounting to some 200 miles, including high-speed lines to Nanticoke and Carbondale. Scranton and Carbondale were connected only by the local trains of the Delaware & Hudson Railroad and by a suburban extension of the Scranton Railways, but the expenditure on the Scranton–Wilkes-Barre line was so heavy (about $6 million) that further expansion was impossible.

In spite of its exceptional initial expenditures, the company (usually known as "The Laurel Line") was highly successful. Virtually no other interurban avoided receivership and maintained passenger service so long. For a time, the company operated local service on 20-minute headway with a limited every hour. Traffic density far exceeded that of most other interurbans. Heavy multiple-unit equipment, at first wood and later steel, provided the service. Frequency was cut first to every half hour, and then to every hour, but it was never reduced further. Limiteds were discontinued in 1931, but one was reinstated in 1946. The company had one major accident, a collision of three trains on July 3, 1920, in which 17 people were killed and 40 injured.

Although the company's efforts to build up freight traffic were fairly successful, the line was deriving 60 per cent of its revenue from passengers as late as the period following World War II. The time had passed when a road so dependent on passengers could survive, and in 1949 the company was put in trusteeship. Believing its freight operations to be viable, the road wound up its passenger service on December 31, 1952. The third rail was removed in 1953, and freight was thereafter hauled with a leased diesel locomotive of the Delaware Lackawanna & Western.

WILKES-BARRE AND HAZLETON RAILWAY[9]

One of the most heavily built interurbans, this company began in 1903 to operate from an elevated terminal in Wilkes-Barre to Hazleton, a distance of 31 miles. Except for street running in Hazleton over a subsidiary, the Lehigh Traction Company, the property was entirely operated by third rail. The line paralleled no railroad, but struck out boldly over the mountains between the two cities. As the route was sparsely populated, most passengers rode the length of the interurban. Consequently, in spite of the heavy gradients en route, schedules were faster than those of most interurbans—1 hour for limiteds and 70 minutes for locals. Passenger service was provided mainly by a series of ten steel combination cars built by Brill in 1915. The company handled carload freight in interchange with the railroads, but not in sufficient volume to survive. Permission to abandon was granted in 1933.

The company's subsidiary, the Lehigh Traction Company, operated a 22-mile trolley line between Hazleton and Freeland, serving an anthracite-mining area. It was built in 1893 and abandoned in 1932.

YORK RAILWAYS

The street railway in York operated four suburban lines of typical Pennsylvania style from York to Dover (8 miles, opened 1901), Bittersville (12 miles, built mainly in 1901), York Haven (13 miles, opened 1904), and Wrightsville, across the Susquehanna River from Columbia (11 miles, opened 1904). In 1907 it added a heavy interurban line to Hanover (17.5 miles), equipped with single-phase AC overhead and cars of the Midwestern type. In 1921 the company rebuilt the Hanover line for 660-volt DC to be consistent with the rest of the system. Rail operations were quite long-lived, surviving until 1939. The company went bankrupt in 1937, and converted its suburban and interurban lines to bus service within two years. Unlike most electric lines in its area, the York Railways used standard gauge. The company was noted for its high standards of maintenance of its equipment.

WARREN AND JAMESTOWN STREET RAILWAY

The Siggins brothers of Warren, Pennsylvania, who controlled the Warren Street Railway (as well as the Union Traction of Kansas), opened this 21-mile interurban in 1905. About half the line was in Pennsylvania, half in New York. The road was the second single-phase AC interurban, but was converted to 600-volt DC in 1911. The interurban used heavy wooden cars at the outset, Kuhlman center-door steel cars after 1916, and Kuhlman lightweight cars after 1924. Abandonment occurred on December 2, 1929.

The Warren Street Railway itself operated an interurban of 13 miles to Sheffield, opened in 1902. Unlike the Jamestown interurban, the Sheffield route used 600-volt DC from the beginning. The two roads worked closely together, and the Warren Street Railway provided an entrance into Warren for the Jamestown interurban. The Sheffield interurban was abandoned in 1928.

PITTSBURGH HARMONY BUTLER AND NEW CASTLE RAILWAY

The most important interurban in western Pennsylvania, this property consisted of two lines between Pittsburgh and Butler, with a major branch from Evans City on the west line to New Castle. The west line was built in 1908, together with the New Castle branch, and a 10-mile branch between Elwood City, Beaver Falls, and Morado was added about 1914. The east line was opened in 1907 by a rival firm, the Pittsburgh and Butler Street Railway. The west line, called the Harmony Route after one of its on-line towns, used 1,200-volt DC power, but the east line, called the Mars Route, used 6,600-volt AC until 1912-13, when it was converted to 1,200-volt DC. Both lines used Pittsburgh Railways as an entry into Pittsburgh, the Mars line having 5.4 miles of its 38.5-mile route on city streets. Both roads used the Pittsburgh gauge of 5'-2½".

The consolidation of the two interurbans followed the failure of the Mars line in 1917. The company was reorganized as the Pittsburgh Mars and Butler Railway in 1917 in expectation of a sale to the Harmony Route. When permission for the sale was denied by the Pennsylvania Public Service Commission in 1918, a holding company, the Pittsburgh Butler and Harmony Consolidated Railway & Power Company, was formed to control both roads. They shared officers and general offices, but retained separate superintendents. A joint terminal was built in Butler in 1921. In 1928 the holding company was succeeded by the Harmony Short Line Railway Bus and Land Company, which undertook bus service in the area. The railway companies went bankrupt in April 1931, and were quickly abandoned, but the bus company is still in operation.

SOUTHERN CAMBRIA RAILWAY

This standard-gauge 1,200-volt interurban ran northeast from Johnstown up the north side of the Conemaugh River valley and over the mountains to the towns of Ebensburg and Nanty Glo. Track reached South Fork (12 miles) in 1910, and Ebensburg (11 miles) in 1912. The branch to Nanty Glo (3.5 miles) was added in 1914. The road was affiliated with the Northern Cambria Street Railway, but the management was never able to extend track north to a connection.

Partly because of the heavy grades the company encountered, its safety record was one of the poorest in the industry. Its worst wreck, one of the most serious on any interurban, was a head-on collision in 1916 that killed 28 people and injured 80. The company was particularly troubled by derailments in Conemaugh at the foot of the long grade out of the valley; runaways in Conemaugh resulted in at least four major accidents in the company's history.

The Southern Cambria suffered losses in the mid-twenties, failed, was sold at a sheriff's sale in December 1928, and was scrapped.

PENNSYLVANIA RAILROAD

In February 1906, the Pennsylvania Railroad's subsidiary, the Cumberland Valley Railroad, purchased a short line, the Mechanicsburg and Dillsburg Railroad (7.5 miles), which it proceeded to electrify. Orthodox interurban passenger service was provided with a pair of open-platform railroad combines, equipped for electric operation in 1906 and 1907 in the Cumberland Valley's shops. The electrification used a side trolley, for which each car carried four poles. This odd electrification survived until January 15, 1928.

SCRANTON AND BINGHAMTON TRACTION COMPANY

A. J. Connell and W. L. Connell of Scranton promoted the Northern Electric Street Railway, which opened a line north to Lake Winola (18.6 miles) in 1908. In

1910 the property was leased to the Scranton and Binghamton Traction Company, which proposed to extend it north to Binghamton, mainly along the Delaware Lackawanna & Western Railroad. Between 1914 and 1918, this company controlled the Binghamton Railway, over which the interurban was to enter Binghamton. By 1916 the interurban had been extended northward through the mountains to Montrose, terminus of a Lehigh Valley branch, but it could never be built farther. Few interurbans suffered more from the failure to reach their goals, since the tributary territory was sparsely populated and well served by railroad. The road served farming communities in the foothills together with some small anthracite-mining towns, and carried a considerable amount of milk from rural areas.

The company failed and was succeeded by the Scranton Montrose and Binghamton Railroad in 1919, which in turn failed in 1930. Operation was discontinued on July 20, 1931, and the property sold for scrap October 27 of the same year.

LEHIGH VALLEY TRANSIT COMPANY

This company, which was mainly engaged in providing street railway service in Allentown and Bethlehem, operated an important interurban south to the Philadelphia area, and major suburban lines to Easton, Portland, and Slatington. The interurban was completed in 1903 between Allentown and Chestnut Hill, a Philadelphia suburb. The line was a lightly graded side-of-the-road route, but between 1905 and 1912 it was largely relocated onto private right-of-way, and its power system was improved. At the same time, an alternative entry into Philadelphia was built from Lansdale to Norristown, whence LVT cars ran to the Philadelphia terminal of the Philadelphia & Western, beginning in 1912. For this service, an excellent series of composite steel and wood cars was ordered from Jewett, based on the design of the Cleveland–Lima cars of the Lake Shore Electric and the Western Ohio Railway. The Lansdale–Chestnut Hill line was abandoned in 1926.

The interurban was heavily patronized because of the large tributary population and the little direct Philadelphia–Allentown railroad service; most trains on the Reading required a change at Bethlehem. Trains as long as three cars were run regularly. The company took advantage of the availability of modern equipment on the second-hand market from 1938 through 1941 to purchase lightweight, high-speed cars from the Cincinnati and Lake Erie and the Indiana Railroad, which thereafter provided most of the main-line service.

In 1949 the company ceased sending its cars to the 69th Street Terminal over the Philadelphia and Western. In the same year the Easton service, operated with Cincinnati lightweight cars originally built for the Dayton and Troy, was discontinued. Finally in 1951 the Norristown–Allentown main line was abandoned. It was probably the last example of a pure interurban, dependent entirely on passenger traffic and freight in interurban equipment, without railroad interchange.

LINES WITH SOME INTERURBAN CHARACTERISTICS

CONESTOGA TRACTION COMPANY

The street railway in Lancaster operated over 130 miles of rural extensions, largely patterned after street railway technology, but to a great extent on private right-of-way or at the side of the highway. The street railway was itself electrified in 1890, and rural extensions were built to Millersville (1891), Marietta (1894), Lititz (1895), Ephrata (1900), Manheim (1901), Strasburg (1901), Adamstown (1903), Rocky Springs (1903), Terre Hill (1905), Quarryville (1905), Elizabethtown (1908), and Coatesville (1909). The Conestoga Traction Company was itself chartered in 1899 as successor to the Pennsylvania Traction Company (after foreclosure) and several other predecessors. Much of the building was undertaken by subsidiaries.

The company was reorganized in 1931 as the Conestoga Transportation Company. In 1932 the company abandoned its weakest routes: Coatesville, Elizabethtown, Quarryville, Terre Hill, Adamstown, Strasburg, Manheim, and the segment of the Marietta line beyond Columbia. The remainder of the Columbia line and the Lititz line were discontinued in 1938, but the short Rocky Springs line, which went just beyond the city limits, and the long Ephrata line lasted until 1947. A combination of World War II and the inadequacies of nearby highways perpetuated the Ephrata line until virtually all other operations of this kind were extinct. The company remains a local bus operator in Lancaster and its environs.

HERSHEY TRANSIT COMPANY

The Hershey Transit Company was formed out of predecessor companies in 1913 by the Hershey family, proprietors of the chocolate-manufacturing firm at Hershey. The original line was built by the Hummelstown and Campbellstown Street Railway from Hummelstown to Palmyra via Hershey in 1904. Lines from Hershey to Elizabethtown and Lebanon were built in 1907 and 1911, respectively. By connections at Elizabethtown with the Conestoga Traction and at Hummelstown with the Harrisburg Railways, which also used a gauge of 5'-2½", the Hershey Transit was part of a continuous broad-gauge line from Philadelphia to Harrisburg. Passenger traffic was mainly local, and a considerable amount of milk was handled for the chocolate factory.

The entire property was long-lived. The Elizabethtown line was converted to bus operation in 1940, as was the Lebanon line in 1941, but the original main line survived the war, and was not converted until 1946.

CHAMBERSBURG GREENCASTLE AND WAYNESBORO STREET RAILWAY

A rural trolley line in southern Pennsylvania, this company was opened in 1903 between Greencastle, Waynesboro, and Pen Mar Park, a resort of some prominence. In 1908 the line was extended from Greencastle to Chambersburg. Short extensions from Chambersburg to Red Bridge Park and from Pen Mar to Blue Ridge Summit were added in 1912. The company used a private right-of-way and east of Waynesboro had heavy gradients and sharp curves. The line was scenic, and excursion business on open cars in the summer was important.

In 1918 the Hagerstown and Frederick Railway, with which the line connected at Shady Grove, Pennsylvania, gained control of the company, but because the H&F used standard gauge and the CG&W a broad gauge, interchange was impossible. Since the broad-gauge line could not participate in the carload freight operations that perpetuated much of the H&F until the forties and fifties, the Pennsylvania track was abandoned much earlier. Operations ceased on July 31, 1928, except on a segment between Ronzerville and Waynesboro that survived until January 16, 1932.

CHAMBERSBURG AND GETTYSBURG ELECTRIC RAILWAY

This rural trolley line was built between Chambersburg and Caledonia Park in 1903 and projected across South Mountain to Gettysburg. Since the Gettysburg extension would have entailed heavy grading, it was never built, although the company offered connecting service to Gettysburg by bus in its later years. Even the Chambersburg–Caledonia section remained unfinished until 1905 because of the Pennsylvania Railroad's unwillingness to let the electric line cross the tracks of its subsidiary, the Cumberland Valley Railroad, at two points. In 1905 the Cumberland Valley Railroad secured control of the trolley line and effected the crossings. The road, which used 5'-2½" gauge, served a meager tributary territory in its completed form, and did well to operate until December 21, 1926.

CHAMBERSBURG AND SHIPPENSBURG RAILWAY

The third of the broad-gauge trolley lines in the Chambersburg area, the 11-mile Chambersburg and Shippensburg Railway was opened in 1914. The road had a short history; it was abandoned simultaneously with most of the Chambersburg Greencastle and Waynesboro on July 31, 1928.

PHILADELPHIA AND EASTON ELECTRIC RAILWAY[10]

The Philadelphia and Easton Railway opened a 5'-2½" line between Doylestown and South Easton in 1904. At Doylestown it met the Philadelphia Rapid Transit and the New Jersey and Pennsylvania Traction Company, thereby securing connections for both Philadelphia and Trenton. Since there is no railroad from Philadelphia to Easton, the interurban was more successful than most Pennsylvania lines in developing through traffic. In particular, it did a substantial summer business among Philadelphians going north to the Delaware Water Gap. The absence of railroad competition also secured for the company a railway post office, one of the few to operate on the Pennsylvania trolley lines. The company had 10 passenger cars, which made the Doylestown-Easton trip in 2 hours.

The company's name was changed to the Philadelphia and Easton Electric Railway in 1904, and it was reorganized as the Philadelphia and Easton Transit Company in 1921. When the track was cut back to the Easton city limits by highway construction, through traffic suffered, and the line was abandoned on November 25, 1926.

NEW JERSEY AND PENNSYLVANIA TRACTION COMPANY

This firm was formed in 1901 as a consolidation of several earlier properties, mainly built in the late 1890's. The company had lines (all 5'-2½") from Trenton,

New Jersey, to Bristol and Doylestown, Pennsylvania, and to Lambertville, New Jersey, via the west bank of the Delaware River. In 1901 the company built a 4'-8½" line to Princeton, New Jersey. In 1913 the Pennsylvania lines were reconstituted as the Bucks County Interurban Railway and in 1917 they became the Pennsylvania-New Jersey Railway. The Princeton line and the street trackage in Lambertville retained their original identity until 1922, when they became the Trenton-Princeton Traction Company. The Bristol-Doylestown line was discontinued in 1923 and the Pennsylvania lines were all abandoned by 1934, but the Princeton line survived until 1940, largely on traffic to and from Lawrenceville School and Princeton University. When the Princeton line lost its access to the streets in both terminals in 1939, patronage declined rapidly and passenger service was discontinued in the following year. The Reading Railroad, which was then in control of the company, retained the track for freight service, but shortly cut it back to Lawrenceville.

EASTERN PENNSYLVANIA RAILWAY

In 1906 several predecessor companies, some of which had been in service since the early 1890's, were consolidated into the Eastern Pennsylvania Railway; the lines were connected and converted to a common gauge (4'-8½") to provide a continuous trolley line from Pottsville to Mauch Chunk, 35 miles. The road served an anthracite-mining area, as well as a resort development around Mauch Chunk at the east end of the line. The road was quite scenic. It succumbed to the usual causes in 1931.

EPHRATA AND LEBANON TRACTION COMPANY[11]

This company opened a 5'-2½" trolley line between the towns of its name (23 miles) in 1915. The track had been laid between 1912 and 1914 by a predecessor, the Ephrata and Lebanon Street Railway, which provided passenger service with Edison-Beach battery cars. The line crossed South Mountain via a gap along Clear Creek, and did not parallel a railroad. Because of sparse population along much of the line, the company was a weak one and failed in 1923. In 1925 it became the Lancaster Ephrata and Lebanon Railway Company, controlled by the Conestoga Traction Company. Milk destined for the chocolate plant in Hershey in interchange with the Hershey Transit Company at Lebanon was a principal source of revenue to the company. When the Hershey Chocolate Company canceled its milk contract in 1929, the electric line's position became extremely difficult, and after two more years of falling passenger revenues, it was abandoned in May 1931.

CUMBERLAND RAILWAY

The Cumberland Railway was chartered in 1908 by businessmen in Carlisle to run west along the Hagerstown branch of the Pennsylvania Railroad. Construction began immediately, and the line was built to Newville (12 miles). Had it extended farther to Shippensburg, it would have provided a continuous 5'-2½" line from Harrisburg to Chambersburg, Greencastle, and Waynesboro. Because of the gap between Newville and Shippensburg, the lines in the Chambersburg area remained isolated from the rest of the Pennsylvania rural trolley lines, although they were connected with the standard-gauge Hagerstown and Frederick.

In 1909 the Cumberland Railway acquired control of the Carlisle and Mount Holly Railway (7 miles), built in 1901. The entire operation was a particularly weak undertaking; it failed in 1918, was sold under foreclosure in 1920 and soon afterwards was scrapped.

VALLEY RAILWAYS

The Valley Traction Company was proprietor of four 5'-2½"-guage trolley lines, which all terminated in Market Square, Harrisburg, and crossed the Peoples' Bridge to the west bank of the Susquehanna. The most important was a line to Carlisle, opened on January 1, 1904. A suburban line to Marysville was completed in 1903. The other lines were short routes to White Hill and New Cumberland.

The Valley Traction Company failed and was replaced by Valley Railways in 1913. The new company's history was marked by a particularly slow attrition. In 1922, when the Carlisle municipal government presented the road with a bill of $11,000 for repaving, the company immediately gave up local service in Carlisle and ceased using the city streets. This caused the interurban to be cut back to Mechanicsburg. In 1931 the company abandoned the remainder of the main line west of a point called Eichelberger's Curve, abandoned the White Hill line, and cut the Marysville line back to Enola. In 1936 the road lost its entry into Harrisburg, and in 1938 the remaining rail operations were converted to bus.

PHILADELPHIA SUBURBAN TRANSPORTATION COMPANY

The main line of this company was completed by the Philadelphia and West Chester Railway in 1899, built to the Philadelphia guage of 5'-2¼". The line originally was an interurban, but as its tributary area became part of the Philadelphia suburbs, it lost its interurban character and became a suburban electric line. Suburban lines to Ardmore, Media, Colindale, and Sharon Hill were added between 1903 and 1917. Service was provided initially with interurban-style equipment, but cars of the street railway type geared for somewhat higher than street railway speeds became standard about 1916. The Philadelphia and West Chester Railway was replaced by the Philadelphia Suburban Transportation Company in 1936. The new company continued purchasing rail equipment; the last purchase was of 14 St. Louis cars of modified street railway design for the West Chester line in 1949. Although this line had adequate traffic, it was abandoned west of Westgate Hills in 1954 when the West Chester Pike, which it paralleled, was widened. The company believed the expense of relocating the track was unwarranted, and substituted buses (it was already operating a large network of bus lines in the Philadelphia suburban area).

In 1953 the Philadelphia Suburban Transportation Company absorbed the Philadelphia and Western Railroad, which it had controlled by stock ownership for some years. The P&W was a standard-gauge suburban line, operated by third rail on private right-of-way. It had been completed between 63d Street (Philadelphia) and Strafford in 1907, and a branch, which became the main line, was built from Villanova to Norristown in 1912. The road served the "main line" suburban area, and was quite successful, in spite of virtually complete dependence on passenger service. Freight service was limited to such items as sand for a local golf course.

In 1926 the joint terminal of the two suburban roads was moved from 63d Street to 69th. In 1932 the Philadelphia and Western was reequipped with 10 high-speed streamlined cars designed by Felix Pavlowsky of the University of Michigan at the instigation of Dr. Thomas Conway, Jr., who was then in control of the company. The road used the odd voltage of 730-volt DC, but after the merger was converted to 600-volt for uniformity with the Philadelphia Suburban Transportation Company. The Strafford branch was abandoned in 1956, but the Norristown line remains in service. As of 1960 the company has no plans to end the Norristown line, but expects to convert its other rail lines to bus by the early 1960's.

NORTHERN CAMBRIA STREET RAILWAY

A standard-gauge trolley line high in the Alleghenies, this company opened 13 miles of track between Patton and Barnesboro in 1906. It was succeeded after foreclosure by the Northern Cambria Railway Company in 1918, sold at a receiver's sale in 1926, and subsequently scrapped.

PITTSBURGH RAILWAYS

The street railway in Pittsburgh, one of the largest and most prosperous in the United States, operated two interurban lines, one to Washington (29 miles) and the other to Roscoe, just south of Charleroi (35 miles). A short branch of 3.5 miles ran from Black Diamond on the Charleroi line to Donora. The Washington line was begun in 1903 and completed in 1909, for the most part built on private right-of-way and, for street railway, heavily graded. Just south of Pittsburgh, the track was laid on the grade of the former Pittsburgh & Castle Shannon Railroad, a narrow-gauge road. The Charleroi line, which left the Washington line 7.8 miles south of Pittsburgh, was completed in 1910, although portions of its street trackage had been in service since 1895. The Donora branch was added in 1911.

The two lines were notable for their use of a wide variety of equipment over their history: heavy wooden interurban cars, standard streetcars equipped with multiple unit control, single-ended, center-door interurban cars, and finally PCC cars. The company, largest user of PCC's in the United States, converted some standard PCC's for interurban use in 1946, and then bought 25 for interurban service in 1949. Although the lines were heavily patronized, and offered half-hourly service much of the day, they could not survive and were cut back to city car lines in 1952. Freight service had ended in 1941, when the city of Pittsburgh condemned the company's LCL house.

WEST PENN RAILWAYS

This important company at its peak owned 339 miles of electric railway in three states, incorporating 62 predecessor companies, some of which were built as early as 1889. Most of the trackage was built in the late 1890's and during the interurban building booms. Zone fares were standard, and schedule speeds of about 16 miles per hour were customary on the rural lines. The company was one of the major buyers and builders of center-entrance equipment, most of which it later rebuilt for front entrance and one-man operation. The system was composed of six unconnected operations, all but one built to a 5'-2½" gauge:

1. Cowanshannock–Kittanning–Lenape Park. This was a short line at Kittanning, built to 4'-8½" (1899–1936).
2. Apollo–Leechburg (1906–36).
3. Oakdale–McDonald. This short suburban line was at the west end of the Pittsburgh suburban area, parallel to the St. Louis line of the Pennsylvania Railroad. It was opened about 1907 and abandoned in 1927.
4. Allegheny Valley Street Railway. This was a major suburban street railway line opened in 1906 from a connection with the Pittsburgh Railways at Aspinwall along the north bank of the Allegheny River for about 23 miles to Natrona. The route operated from 1906 to 1937.
5. The Wheeling Traction Company of West Virginia (*q.v.*), which the West Penn controlled from 1912 to 1931.
6. "The Coke Region," a large network of lines extending from connections with the Pittsburgh Railways at McKeesport and Trafford to Greensburg, thence south to Connellsville, Uniontown, Fairchance, Martin, and Brownsville. A major branch ran to Latrobe, and there were alternative main lines between Greensburg and Scottdale and between Connellsville and Uniontown. Greensburg and Uniontown were first connected in 1903.

The Coke Region lines were always looked upon as the company's principal interurban operation, particularly the Greensburg-Uniontown main line, on which half-hourly service was offered. The volume of traffic as late as the 1950's was exceptional. The roads in the area were poor, the number of automobile owners was small, and coal mining, the principal activity in the region, left the miners so dirty that those who owned automobiles frequently preferred not to drive them in working clothes. The company was exceptionally successful in protecting itself from parallel motorbus service in actions before the Public Service Commission.

The West Penn was an American Water Works and Electric Company subsidiary, and thus allied to the Hagerstown and Frederick in Maryland and the Monongahela–West Penn in West Virginia. The Public Utility Holding Company Act caused American Water Works to be dissolved in 1948. The connections with Pittsburgh Railways at McKeesport and Trafford were given up in 1938 and 1942, respectively, and the Greensburg–Scottdale west line was abandoned in 1939. Most of the other Coke Region lines remained intact as late as 1950, when the West Penn converted its branches south of Uniontown to bus service. The West Penn was one of the few interurbans that survived long enough to be adversely affected by television; when television came to the Pittsburgh region, evening ridership fell drastically. There had been some doubt among the company's officers that buses were practicable on the narrow, winding roads of the area, but the substitution was successful enough that the remaining rail operations were converted to highways in 1952.

Partly because of its long life, and partly because of its pleasant scenery and odd technology (described in Chapter 2), the West Penn had a peculiar fascination for the population in its area. Abandonment of most interurbans scarcely moved the population at all, but when the West Penn's last car left Connellsville for Uniontown at 11:30 P.M., August 9, 1952, a crowd of 5,000 appeared for a civic ceremony in its honor.

JEFFERSON COUNTY TRACTION COMPANY

The Jefferson County Traction Company operated 35 miles of trolley line between Big Run, Punxsutawney, and Reynoldsville, mainly in very mountainous country. The trackage was built between 1902 and 1905 and abandoned in 1927.

UNITED TRACTION STREET RAILWAY

A neighbor of the Jefferson County Traction Company, this road was built from Du Bois to Sykesville in 1906 and extended to Big Run in 1907. About 3 miles of track were on the abandoned right-of-way of a branch of the Buffalo Rochester & Pittsburgh Railroad. The sparse population of the area was the primary cause for its abandonment in 1928.

PENNSYLVANIA AND MARYLAND STREET RAILWAY

This railway was a short trolley line (12 miles) between Salisbury, Meyersdale, and Garrett, near the summit of the Alleghenies along the main line of the Baltimore & Ohio. The property was completed in

1908, but its owners proposed to extend it north through the mountains to Johnstown, more than 40 miles. The extension was never built and the line between Meyersdale and Garrett was abandoned in 1924. The remainder of the property passed into the hands of the Pennsylvania Electric Company in 1927 and was abandoned.

JOHNSTOWN AND SOMERSET RAILWAY

One of the last interurbans to be undertaken, this firm proposed to build south (mainly along the Baltimore & Ohio) from a connection to the Windber suburban line of the Johnstown Traction Company to Somerset and Rockwood, virtually the same route projected by the Pennsylvania and Maryland Street Railway. The company sold bonds to local residents in 1921 and managed to build about 5 miles to Jerome. It was unable to build further, and had a short life, surviving only until 1933.

ALLENTOWN AND READING TRACTION COMPANY

The Allentown and Kutztown Traction Company completed a 20-mile standard-gauge line between the communities of its corporate title in 1902. In the same year it leased a 5'-2½"-gauge line from Kutztown to Reading (also 20 miles) and changed its name to the Allentown and Reading Traction Company. The two gauges were never reconciled; the company had two sets of equipment, and throughout its history passengers changed cars at Kutztown. Running time was 2 hours and 40 minutes, and there was little through traffic. The line was broken in 1929, when the standard-gauge portion was cut back to East Texas, just outside Allentown. In 1930 the broad-gauge line was abandoned, and in 1934 the remaining segment of the standard-gauge line was discontinued. The company's equipment—orthodox street railway cars—had deteriorated to an unusual extent by the end.

NORTHAMPTON TRACTION COMPANY

The Northampton Traction Company was one of several standard-gauge electric lines in the vicinity of Allentown, Bethlehem, and Easton. It was opened in 1903 between Easton and Bangor (22 miles), and in 1915 was extended to Portland (9 miles) by means of the acquisition of the Bangor and Portland Traction Company, which had also been completed in 1903. The company hoped to arrange physical connection with the Easton and Washington Traction Company in New Jersey, but was never able to do so. The Northampton Traction Company went into receivership in 1919 and was reorganized as the Northampton Transit Company in 1922. The new corporation reequipped the line with lightweight cars; it was one of the few Pennsylvania interurbans to do so. The road survived until 1933.

SLATE BELT ELECTRIC STREET RAILWAY

This standard-gauge trolley line between Nazareth and Bangor was chartered in 1899 and probably opened in the following year. At Nazareth, the Slate Belt connected with the Allen Street Railway (1908–27) for Bath. The Lehigh Valley Transit leased the Slate Belt in 1904, but when the lease was soon after abrogated, the loss of revenue forced the company into bankruptcy. Reorganization followed in 1908. In 1921 the name was changed to the Slate Belt Transit Company, and in 1925 to the Bangor and Nazareth Transit Company. The line was abandoned in 1926.

STROUDSBURG WATER GAP AND PORTLAND RAILWAY

The predecessor Stroudsburg and Water Gap Street Railway opened a 4-mile line in 1907 and in 1911 merged with the Water Gap and Portland Street Railway to expand to a total of 10 miles of road. The completed line was part of a through route of standard-gauge electric lines from Philadelphia through the Lehigh Valley communities to the Delaware Water Gap. Because of the attraction of the Water Gap as a resort, summer travel was heavy. The company was succeeded by the Stroudsburg Traction Company in 1917. Bus operation began in 1925, and the railway was abandoned in 1928.

ALTOONA AND LOGAN VALLEY ELECTRIC RAILWAY

This company, the street railway in Altoona, operated two rural extensions, both built to the company's odd gauge of 5'-3". The earlier of the two was a line to Hollidaysburg (7 miles), opened in 1893. Although this route was double-tracked and mainly on private right-of-way, it was operated with street railway equipment and was treated as one of the streetcar lines. The later extension (14 miles) was a line northward along the Pennsylvania Railroad, opened to Bellwood in 1894 and completed to Tyrone in 1902. The Tyrone line was less heavily traveled, but was of more general interurban technology.

Both routes had long lives—the Tyrone line lasted until April 1, 1938, and the Hollidaysburg line until August 7, 1954.

READING TRANSIT COMPANY

The street railway in Reading, which underwent several changes in name, operated five rural lines, each with a 5'-2½" gauge. The most important was the former Oley Valley Railway, which pursued a rambling path from Reading to Boyertown where it connected for Pottstown with a short extension of the local street railway (1902–32). Shorter lines ran to Womelsdorf (1895–1932), Adamstown (1905–33), and Birdsboro (1904–34). The company also controlled an isolated line between Palmyra and Meyerstown via Lebanon (1892–1930), but the gap between Womelsdorf and Meyerstown was never closed. The street railway operation in Reading was particularly long-lived, and a suburban extension to Mohnton, part of the former Adamstown line, survived until January 7, 1952.

RURAL TROLLEY LINES

A very large number of other electric railways had substantial amounts of intercity track. Among the most important of these are the following:

Citizens' Traction Company. Franklin–Oil City (2 lines, ca. 1900–1928).

Corry and Columbus Street Railway (1906–24).

Titusville Electric Traction Company (1898–1924).

Beaver Valley Traction Company (1900 and earlier–1941), parallel to the Ohio River in the Beaver Falls–Rochester–Ambridge area.

Indiana County Street Railways. Black Lick, Clymer, Creekside (various dates around 1907–33).

Shamokin and Mount Carmel Transit Company (1894–1936).

Shamokin and Edgewood Electric Railway (1891–1938).

North Branch Transit Company (various dates before 1911–26).

Pottstown and Reading Street Railway (1899–1931).

Schuylkill Valley Traction Company (ca. 1895–ca. 1932).

Lewisburg Milton and Watsontown Passenger Railway (1911–28).

West Chester Kennett and Wilmington Electric Railway (1903–23).

West Chester Street Railway (1891–1927).

Trenton Bristol and Philadelphia Street Railway (1897–1933).

Schuylkill Railway (1893–ca. 1931).

Hanover and McSherrystown (1893–ca. 1931).

Lancaster and York Furnace Street Railway Co. (1903–ca. 1930).

Centre and Clearfield Railway (1903–27).

Scranton Railways — Forest City line (1893–1929).

Delaware

STRICTLY SPEAKING, Delaware had no interurbans. The street railway in Wilmington — the Wilmington and Philadelphia Traction Company—operated a trolley line to Chester (where it controlled the street railway) and to Philadelphia (1899–1934). Shorter suburban lines owned by the W&P ran to Stanton and to Delaware City via New Castle.

A trolley line connected the small towns of Middletown and Odessa for a short period, about 1906–9.

West Virginia

WEST VIRGINIA had two major interurbans, both affiliates of the West Penn Railways, and several smaller lines, most of which served limited populations.

WHEELING TRACTION COMPANY

The broad-gauge (5'-2½") street railway in Wheeling was proprietor of a standard-gauge interurban along the east bank of the Ohio to Steubenville, and for many years it endeavored without success to complete another along the west bank. The line on the east bank was a side-of-the-road operation which the company considered inadequate, and the line on the west bank was to be more heavily built. The Pan Handle Traction Company built most of the east line, and opened the Wheeling–Wellsburg segment (18 miles) in 1903. The Tri-State Traction Company reached Wellsburg from Steubenville in 1906, and the entire enterprise came under control of the West Penn Railways (*q.v.*). Wheeling Traction, also a West Penn property, leased the road in 1918, but the lease was canceled in 1931 when the Wheeling Traction Company failed. The interurban was returned to be operated by Pan Handle Traction and the Steubenville Wellsburg and Weirton Railway, successor to the Tri-State Traction, under the control of the West Penn. Pan Handle Traction went bankrupt in 1936, and the interurban line was abandoned on October 25, 1937. Service had been provided with heavy steel center-door cars of the West Penn's own style on local schedules of 90 minutes for the 23-mile run. Limiteds made the trip in 60 minutes, three times daily. The interurban had a branch from Steubenville to Weirton (6 miles), opened in 1911.

The unfinished line on the west bank was owned by a subsidiary of Wheeling Traction, the Steubenville and Wheeling Traction Company, which had standard-gauge lines from Steubenville to Brilliant and from Wheeling to Rayland and Warrenton. Beginning about 1901 the company endeavored to complete the line, but the 7 miles from Warrenton to Brilliant were never built. The company went so far as to relocate part of its entrance to Steubenville, and it announced on many occasions that the gap was about to be filled. Several maps show the interurban as completed, but it was operated as two suburban lines throughout its history.

Wheeling Traction operated broad-gauge suburban lines to Moundsville (1896–1941), Barton, and Shadyside. After the bankruptcy of 1931, the company was reorganized as the Co-operative Transit Company, owned by its employees. The Barton and Shadyside suburban lines survived until shortly after World War II.

WELLSBURG BETHANY AND WASHINGTON RAILROAD

H. G. Lazear, who had been the leading figure in the Pan Handle Traction Company, opened this trolley line from Wellsburg on the Wheeling–Steubenville interurban to Bethany (7.7 miles) on June 2, 1908. The company expected to build to Washington, Pennsylvania, but owing to the mountainous terrain and the increasing difficulty of financing electric railway projects, never did so. The road used open equipment in the summer months, and otherwise used the technology common to the Pennsylvania rural trolley lines. It was a standard-gauge line, however. The road survived until 1926.

MONONGAHELA WEST PENN PUBLIC SERVICE COMPANY

By far the most important West Virginia interurban was this large enterprise centered in the mountainous Clarksburg-Fairmont area. The Fairmont and Clarksburg Electric Railroad Company was begun to connect the two cities (25 miles) in 1901 and reported completed in 1907. The successor Monongahela Valley Traction Company extended the main line 24 miles from Clarksburg south to Weston in 1913. Branches from Fairmont to Mannington and Fairview were built in 1910 and 1911, respectively, and the company built a large number of short branches or spurs to mines and mining communities along the main line. The company provided street railway service in both Fairmont and Clarksburg. The main line was heavily graded and capable of handling railroad equipment; the company developed a small interchange of coal in hopper cars with the railroads.

The Monongahela Valley Traction Company changed its name in 1921 to the Monongahela Power and Railway Company, and in 1923 to the Monongahela West Penn Public Service Company, indicating the growth in importance of the auxiliary power business. Monongahela West Penn was part of the extensive network of public utility properties of the American Water Works and Electric System, along with the West Penn Railways.

Monongahela West Penn also operated an interurban from Parkersburg to Marietta, Ohio (14 miles, completed by the Parkersburg and Marietta Interurban Railway in 1903), along the east bank of the Ohio River. A 23-mile extension to Beverly, Ohio, had been built by the Muskingum Traction Company about 1908 in an unsuccessful effort to connect the Parkersburg area with Zanesville, and thus with the general Ohio-Indiana interurban network. No serious effort is known to have been made to connect the two West Virginia systems of the company.

Rolling stock was remarkably diversified: heavy wooden interurbans, steel center-entrance cars similar to the West Penn's own, and finally Cincinnati lightweight cars.

In 1944, during the period of dissolution of American Water Works holdings under the Public Utility Holding Company Act, the two railways were sold to the

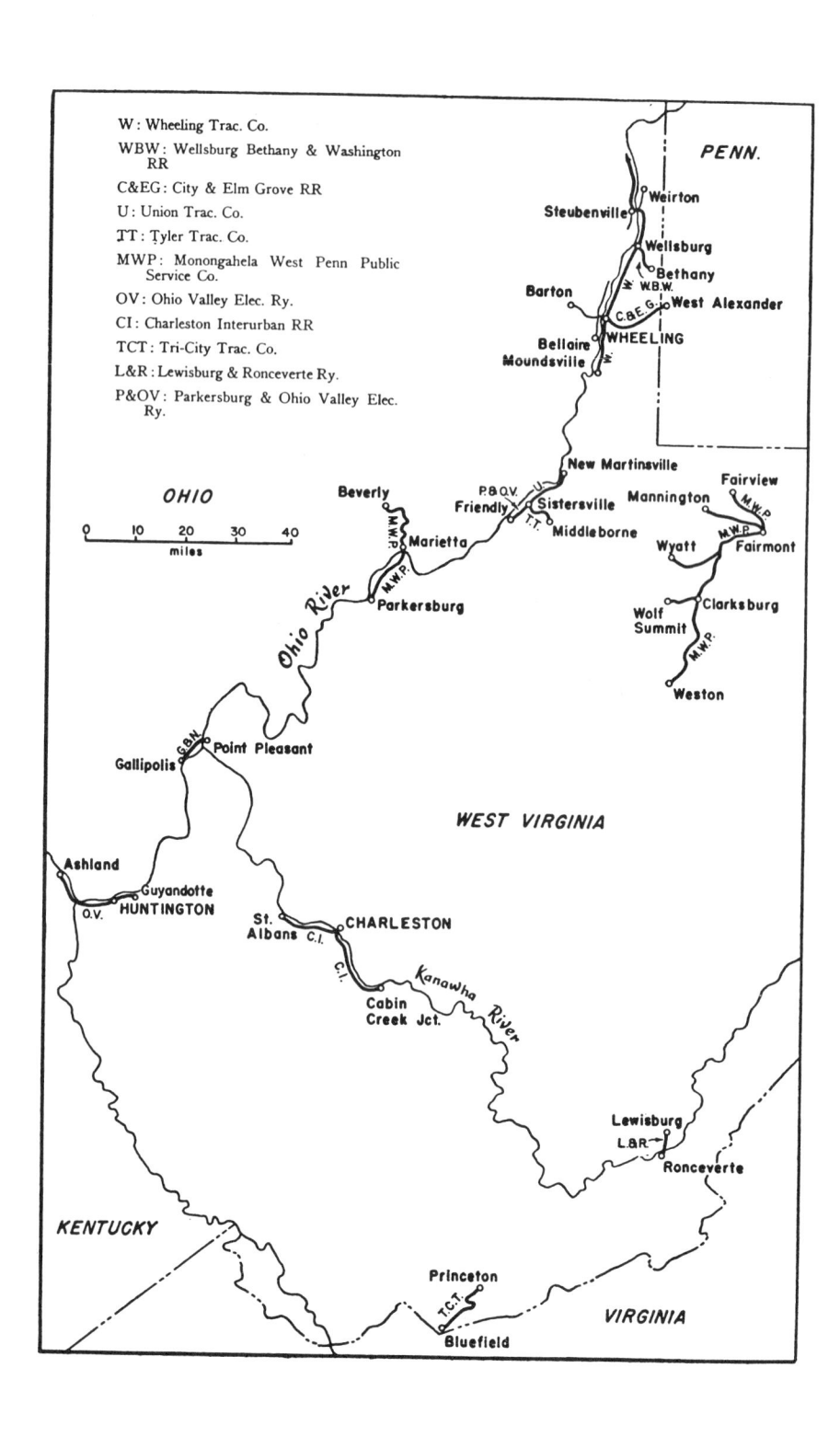

W: Wheeling Trac. Co.
WBW: Wellsburg Bethany & Washington RR
C&EG: City & Elm Grove RR
U: Union Trac. Co.
TT: Tyler Trac. Co.
MWP: Monongahela West Penn Public Service Co.
OV: Ohio Valley Elec. Ry.
CI: Charleston Interurban RR
TCT: Tri-City Trac. Co.
L&R: Lewisburg & Ronceverte Ry.
P&OV: Parkersburg & Ohio Valley Elec. Ry.

City Lines of West Virginia, which, in spite of its name, was not an affiliate of National City Lines. The new operator intended to convert operations to bus immediately after the war, and in 1947 the Fairmont-Clarksburg-Weston and the Parkersburg-Marietta lines were converted. The Marietta-Beverly extension had been abandoned in 1929, and the Mannington and Fairview branches in 1933.

CHARLESTON INTERURBAN RAILROAD

The Charleston Interurban Railroad, which was integral with the street railway in Charleston, operated two interurban lines, one to St. Albans built in 1912 and the other to Cabin Creek Junction built in 1916. At a receiver's sale in 1935, the property passed into the hands of the Charleston Transit Company, which converted the entire operation to buses on June 29, 1939.

CITY AND ELM GROVE RAILROAD

This road, whose history is particularly obscure, had its origin in a steam railroad, the Wheeling & Elm Grove, opened in 1877 and reported completed to West Alexander, Pennsylvania (13 miles), in 1890. It is believed to have been electrified about 1898. As the City and Elm Grove Railroad, it was a standard-gauge suburban electric line, running beside what is now U.S. Highway 40. A proposal to extend the track about 16 miles to a connection with the Pittsburgh Railways' interurban at Washington was never executed. Together with some street railway lines in Wheeling, the property was sold under foreclosure to the Wheeling Public Service Company in 1920. The city lines were sold to the municipal government in 1925, but the Public Service Company continued to operate the suburban line. The track was cut back from West Alexander to Roney's Point in 1929, and to Elm Court in 1931. The remainder of the road was converted to a bus line in 1937, when it was threatened with a relocation as a consequence of improvement in the parallel highway.

UNION TRACTION COMPANY OF WEST VIRGINIA

Sistersville, a town on the Ohio River with a population of 2,684 (1910), was the hub of three small electric lines, of which the most important was an 11-mile interurban to New Martinsville, built by the Wetzel and Tyler Railway in 1903. The company provided service with three single-truck convertible cars—an unusual type for the interurbans. When the original company failed, it was succeeded by the Union Traction Company of West Virginia in 1908, and by the Sistersville and New Martinsville Traction Company in 1919. The road was abandoned in 1925.

PARKERSBURG AND OHIO VALLEY ELECTRIC RAILWAY

This corporation was chartered in 1903 to build a major interurban about 95 miles long from Parkersburg north along the east bank of the Ohio River to Wheeling. The promoters began building at Sistersville and managed to reach only the little town of Friendly (pop.: 217) 5 miles south, when they encountered financial difficulties. The completed line served one of the smallest populations of any interurban and was clearly hopeless. The property was reported dismantled in 1918.

TYLER TRACTION COMPANY

The Tyler Traction Company was the last of Sistersville's three electric lines to be built, being incorporated in 1911 and put into service in 1913. The eastern terminus of the road was the town of Middlebourne, which, having no railroad service, produced a small amount of carload freight traffic. The West Virginia Public Service Commission authorized the company to discontinue passenger service effective July 27, 1929, but freight service survived into the following year. The Commission approved suspension of freight operations on March 26, 1930, and permitted the track to be removed effective December 1, 1930.

LEWISBURG AND RONCEVERTE RAILWAY

This short line (5.7 miles) was chartered in 1906 and built between the towns of its name. It connected the main line of the Chesapeake and Ohio Railway at Ronceverte with Lewisburg (pop.: 803). The line interchanged carload freight with the C&O. The road failed and was reorganized with minor changes in name in 1918 and 1927. It failed again and was scrapped after a foreclosure sale in 1931.

TRI-CITY TRACTION COMPANY

The Princeton Power Company connected Princeton and Bluefield with this 12-mile interurban in 1916. It was single-track, built on private right-of-way, and was operated together with the street railways of the terminal cities. The road adopted the name Tri-City Traction Company in 1928. Service was provided mainly with six double-ended Cincinnati lightweight cars of 1924, and an earlier (1917) Cincinnati car of semi-lightweight design. The company applied for bus conversion in 1942, but was refused permission to convert by the Office of Defense Transportation. The conversion took place in 1946.

OHIO VALLEY ELECTRIC RAILWAY

This company operated the street railways in the Ironton-Ashland-Huntington area, and operated intercity lines from Ashland to Huntington and from Ironton to Hanging Rock. From the road's opening in 1900 down to 1908 the property was operated by the Camden Interstate Railway, and thereafter by the Ohio Valley Electric Railway. In its later years it was controlled by the American Railways Company, which also owned the electric power system in the area.

Railway service was provided with equipment of the street railway type, and lightweight cars were used beginning about 1924. The line in Ohio was abandoned in 1930 and the Ashland-Huntington line in 1938.

MORGANTOWN AND DUNKARD VALLEY RAILROAD

This road was projected as a direct line from Morgantown through formidable mountains to Wheeling. It was opened to Cassville by 1911 and to Price by 1915. By 1920 it was reported to have reached Brave, Pennsylvania. Only a short distance, variously reported as 3 or as 8 miles, was ever electrified, and steam locomotives handled the traffic throughout the line's history. The original company was replaced by the Morgantown-Wheeling Railway in 1912 and by the Scotts Run Railway in 1923. The property was acquired in 1933 by the Monongahela Railway, which continues to operate it as a branch.

New Jersey

NEW JERSEY had little trackage that could be unambiguously termed interurban, but had a good many miles of electric railways of all sorts.

PUBLIC SERVICE CORPORATION OF NEW JERSEY

This vast enterprise operated a dense network of street railways in Newark, Jersey City, and throughout northern New Jersey. Many of these car lines were intercity, and some had substantial lengths of private right-of-way, but the lines were never considered interurbans. Two of the company's lines, however, had distinct interurban characteristics. Between 1899 and 1904, the company built the first of these, the Camden and Trenton Railway, also known as the Public Service Riverside Line. It was built to the 5'-0" gauge of the Public Service Camden lines, and completed in 1903, but a delay in securing the right to cross the Pennsylvania Railroad at East Trenton postponed the opening of through service until 1904.

Beginning in 1902 Public Service was able to offer street railway service all the way from Trenton to Jersey City, and between 1904 and 1906 it ran the service without change of cars. Since a through trip from Jersey City to Camden with a change of cars at Trenton required 8 hours and 47 minutes, the company decided to build a new line on private right-of-way from the North Jersey area to Trenton, to be called the Public Service Fast Line. In 1912 Public Service acquired the right-of-way of the New Jersey Short Line Railroad, which had failed in 1908 after building between Bayway and Bonhamtown. Public Service rehabilitated the track and tied it in with the street railways in the Newark-Jersey City area and in Trenton. The Fast Line was opened July 1, 1913, and branches were built to Perth Amboy and Carteret in 1914 and 1915, respectively. Both the Fast Line and the Riverside Line were operated with heavy steel equipment of the street railway type, equipped with multiple unit control. Since the Fast Line and the street railways in northern New Jersey were standard-gauge, through service to Camden was impossible.

The Fast Line proved unsuccessful, although a major terminal was built for it in Newark in 1916. Running time was 2 hours and 45 minutes for a 55-mile trip, including about 8 miles of street running in Newark and Elizabeth. Because of declining revenues, through service between Camden and points north of New Brunswick was discontinued in 1924, and after 1926, lightweight equipment was used on the line south of New Brunswick. The Newark-New Brunswick segment was replaced by buses in 1931, and the Perth Amboy and Carteret lines were abandoned in 1933. Electric equipment on the south end of the Fast Line was replaced in 1931 by gas-electric cars made out of former streetcars, and in 1934 the gas-electrics were superseded by standard motor buses equipped to run partly on the highway, partly on the railway. This unsatisfactory arrangement was discontinued in 1937, and the history of the Fast Line was ended. The Riverside Line had been abandoned in 1931.

ATLANTIC CITY AND SHORE RAILROAD

The Atlantic City and Shore Railroad, usually known as the Shore Fast Line, had its origin in a steam "dummy" line, the West Jersey Railroad, between Atlantic City and Somers Point. This line was electrified in 1906 and extended to Ocean City in 1907. A short extension to the Boardwalk in Ocean City was added in 1908. As the road left Atlantic City over the electrified line of the Pennsylvania Railroad it used a third rail, but it used an orthodox pole trolley in the streets of Atlantic City and on its own line south of Pleasantville. Large Brill and Stephenson wooden cars provided service throughout the company's history. The company also owned the street railway in Atlantic City.

Base service on the interurban line was offered every 20 or 30 minutes until 1931, and hourly thereafter. Additional trips were provided in the summer months. In 1946 the long trestle from Somers Point to Ocean City burned and was not replaced. The interurban cars continued service from Atlantic City to Somers Point in connection with a shuttle bus to Ocean City, but on January 18, 1948, interurban operation was abandoned in favor of bus service.

Atlantic City and Somers Point were also connected by a suburban trolley line, the Atlantic and Suburban Traction Company, built in 1904, two years before the electrification of the Atlantic City and Shore Railroad. The line also had a branch from Pleasantville to Absecon. The Atlantic and Suburban was handicapped by an inferior physical plant and by lack of access to Ocean City, a major resort, but it survived until 1929.

NORTH JERSEY RAPID TRANSIT COMPANY[12]

Chartered in 1908 and opened in 1910, this company operated an interurban from Ridgewood Junction (East Paterson) to Ho-Ho-Kus. In 1912 it was extended northward from Ho-Ho-Kus to Suffern, New York, but proposed extensions from Suffern to Greenwood Lake and Ho-Ho-Kus to Spring Valley were never built. Neither was the company able to build south from Ridgewood Junction to Newark, where it hoped to connect with the Hudson and Manhattan Tubes. In its finished form, it suffered from serious inadequacies at both terminals.

Service was provided with eight Jewett cars fitted with multiple unit control; trains as long as three cars were run. The road was built on private right-of-way except for about 1,000 feet at Suffern, and all the track was protected by block signals.

Public Service acquired the property in 1927 and abandoned it in 1929.

NEW JERSEY INTERURBAN COMPANY

The Easton and Washington Traction Company in 1906 opened a standard-gauge electric line from Phillipsburg, across the Delaware River from Easton, Pennsylvania, through Washington, New Jersey, to Port Murray. About 13 of the 18 miles were on private right-of-way. In 1913 the road was purchased by the owners of the Northampton Traction Company and the Bangor and Portland Traction Company, two lines on the Pennsylvania side of the Delaware. The name was then changed to the Northampton–Easton and Washington Traction Company. Unsuccessful efforts were made to join the line to the network immediately across the Delaware and to extend it east to Port Morris on Lake Hopatcong.

In 1923 the road was sold under foreclosure to the New Jersey Interurban Company, a name under which it operated for less than two years. It was abandoned on January 27, 1925.

BRIDGETON AND MILLVILLE TRACTION COMPANY

This trolley line, which was of borderline interurban character, was opened in the period 1892–95 between the two principal towns in south-central New Jersey. A branch was completed in 1902 from Bridgeton to Bivalve, a small port with an extensive oystering fleet. The road was a subsidiary of American Railways Company.

The Bivalve line was abandoned in 1922, and in the same year the road became the Cumberland Traction Company. In 1926, the company leased the Millville Traction Company, which had been completed be-

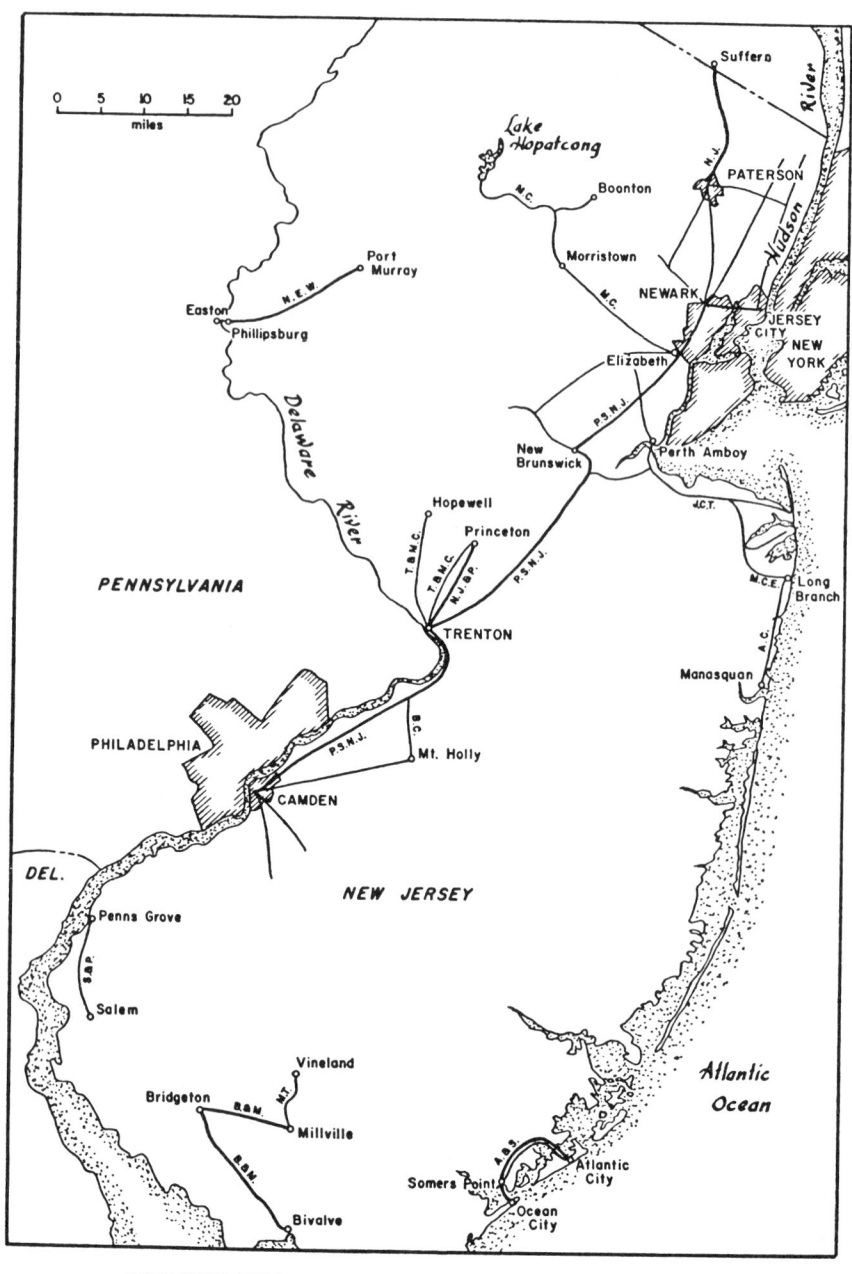

INTERURBAN LINES

NJ: North Jersey Rapid Transit Co.
PSNJ: Public Service of New Jersey
NJ&P: New Jersey & Pennsylvania Trac. Co.
B&M: Bridgeton & Millville Trac. Co.
A&S: Atlantic City & Shore RR
NEW: Northampton-Easton & Washington Trac. Co.
 Only a few major streetcar lines of the Public Service Corporation of New Jersey are shown.

MAJOR INTERCITY AND SUBURBAN
STREETCAR LINES

MC: Morris County Trac. Co.
T&MC: Trenton & Mercer County Trac. Corp.
BC: Burlington County Transit Co.
S&P: Salem & Pennsgrove Trac. Co.
MT: Millville Trac. Co.
AC: Atlantic Coast Elec. Ry.
JCT: Jersey Central Trac. Co.
MCE: Monmouth County Elec. Co.

tween Millville and Vineland in 1901. Cumberland Traction operated its new acquisition only a short period, and abandoned it in 1927. The Bridgeton–Millville line was itself abandoned in 1931.

*

In addition to the extensive network of trolley lines operated by Public Service in northern New Jersey and at Camden, there were several other intercity operations of streetcar technology. The *Morris County Traction Company* (1903–28) operated streetcars over 53 miles of track, running generally west from Elizabeth, and there were several street railways along the Atlantic Coast, of which the most important was the *Monmouth County Electric Company* (1896–1922) at Long Branch and Atlantic Highlands. A similar operation was the *Jersey Central Traction Company* (1901–23) at Red Bank and South Amboy. In 1906 the Pennsylvania Railroad laid third rail along its subsidiary, the West Jersey and Seashore Railroad, from Camden to Millville and Atlantic City, and provided local passenger service with wooden multiple-unit cars. This electrification was not entirely discontinued until 1949. At Trenton, the *Trenton and Mercer County Traction Corporation* operated suburban lines of 5'-2" gauge to Hopewell, Princeton, Hamilton Square, and Yardville. The Princeton line (1901–31) slightly antedated the standard-gauge Trenton-Princeton Fast Line. (See the New Jersey and Pennsylvania Traction Company of Pennsylvania, pp. 297–98.) The *Salem and Pennsgrove Traction Company* established a railway between Salem and the Wilmington–Pennsgrove ferry in 1916 and received permission to convert it to bus operation in December 1930.

New York

Upstate new york had an extensive network of interurbans, amounting to 1,129 miles.[13] Most of this was concentrated in a long series of properties that ran from the Pennsylvania state line roughly parallel to the main line of the New York Central Railroad through Buffalo, Rochester, and Syracuse to Little Falls.

The effect of the depression on the New York interurbans was particularly severe, and by 1933 little of the state's mileage was left in existence.

BUFFALO AND LAKE ERIE TRACTION COMPANY

This long (92 miles) and important interurban connected Buffalo with Erie, Pennsylvania, and thus joined the interurban networks of upstate New York with those of Ohio. The road was completed in 1909, but most of the line had been in service considerably earlier, beginning with street railway service by the Dunkirk and Fredonia Railroad in 1891. Buffalo had been connected with Dunkirk and Erie with Westfield in 1906. Fredonia and Brockton had been joined in 1903. The interurban entered Buffalo (where it terminated in Lafayette Square) over a subsidiary, the Buffalo and Lackawanna Traction Company. Between 1906 and 1920, the B&LE controlled a suburban line at Buffalo, the Hamburg Railway.

Upon completion, the B&LE was left with fixed charges too heavy for its traffic to bear. In 1915, a poor year for the industry, the company was put in receivership. In the early 1920's serious thought was given to abandoning the road, but the International Utilities Corporation, on the basis of its experience in modernizing the Kentucky Traction and Terminal Company, decided to reorganize the property, re-equip it with Cincinnati lightweight cars, and continue it in service. On January 1, 1925, the interurban was reorganized as the Buffalo and Erie Railway, managed by Chandler and Company. The lightweight equipment, which was immediately introduced, cut operating expenses about 20 per cent and was looked upon as a great success; 1925 was said to be the first year since the interurban's completion that it had shown a net profit.

The modernization proved only a palliative, and the secular decline in traffic continued. In 1932 the management decided to dispose of the property. The trackage from Buffalo to Angola and from the state line to Erie was discontinued in December 1932, and on January 27, 1933, the rest of the interurban was abandoned. The subsidiary Buffalo and Lackawanna Traction Company was abandoned November 14, 1933. The local service between Dunkirk and Fredonia, which the interurban had provided with 4-wheel cars, was perpetuated under the name of the Dunkirk and Fredonia Railroad, but in 1934 it was converted to bus operation. The Company's street railway operations in Erie had become the independent Erie Railways Company in 1925, and were abandoned in 1935.

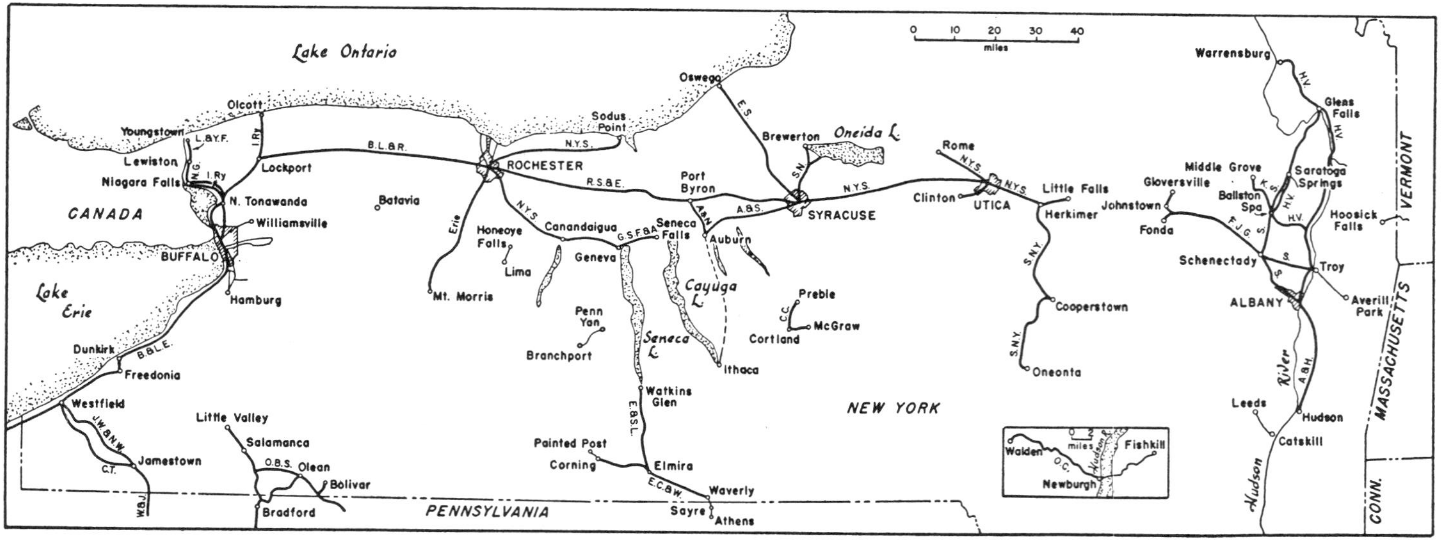

L&YF: Lewiston & Youngstown Frontier Ry.
NG: Niagara Gorge RR
IRy: International Ry.
B&LE: Buffalo & Lake Erie Trac. Co.
JW&NW: Jamestown Westfield & Northwestern Ry.
W&J: Warren & Jamestown Street Ry.
CT: Chautauqua Trac. Co.
OBS: Olean Bradford & Salamanca Ry.
E&SL: Elmira & Seneca Lake Trac. Co.
EC&W: Elmira Corning & Waverly Ry.

CC: Cortland County Trac. Co.
BL&R: Buffalo Lockport & Rochester Ry.
Erie: Erie RR electric lines
NYS: New York State Rys.
RS&E: Rochester Syracuse & Eastern RR
GSF&A: Geneva Seneca Falls & Auburn RR
A&N: Auburn & Northern Elec. RR
A&S: Auburn & Syracuse Elec. RR
ES: Empire State RR
SN: Syracuse Northern Elec. Ry.
SNY: Southern New York Ry.

FJG: Fonda Johnstown & Gloversville RR
S: Schenectady Ry.
HV: Hudson Valley Ry.
A&H: Albany & Hudson RR
OC: Orange County Trac. Co.
K: Kaydeross RR

Suburban and rural streetcar lines are shown by thin lines. Roads planned to be interurbans but never electrified are shown by broken lines.

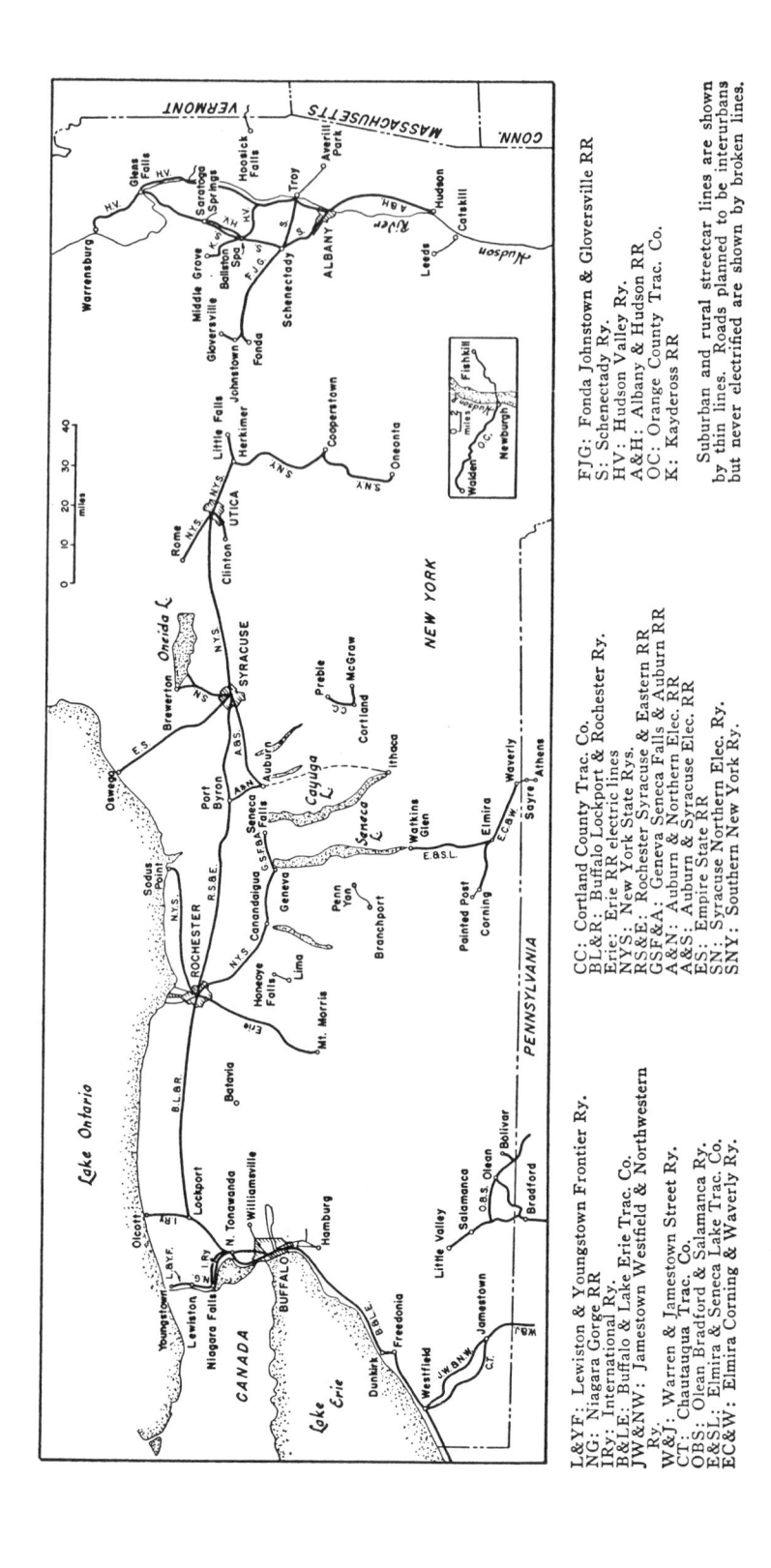

The Hamburg Railway, after 12 years of independence, was abandoned in 1932.

WESTERN NEW YORK AND PENNSYLVANIA TRACTION COMPANY

This interurban consisted of a triangle of track near the cities of Salamanca and Olean in New York and Bradford in Pennsylvania, together with several branch lines. The Olean Street Railway built extensions to Allegany in 1894, Bolivar in 1902, and Shingle House in 1903. The Olean Rock City and Bradford Electric Street Railway built from Bradford to Lewis Run in 1901. These companies were consolidated in 1906 into the Western New York and Pennsylvania Traction Company, which completed the system by building from Salamanca to Allegany in 1907 and both from Salamanca to Little Valley and from Bradford to Seneca Junction in 1908.

The Bradford-Olean line, which contained grades up to 6 per cent, was partly built on the right-of-way of a former narrow-gauge road, the Olean Bradford and Warren Railroad. The Western New York and Pennsylvania did fairly well financially, considering its severe gradients and curvatures. The road was able to handle carload freight in interchange with the railroads. As a consequence of declining revenues after World War I, the company was reorganized in 1921 as the Olean Bradford and Salamanca Railway, which operated the property for six years. The interurban was handicapped throughout its history by relatively unproductive branches. The Salamanca–Little Valley branch was abandoned in 1925, the Ceres–Bolivar branch in 1926, and all the rest of the system in 1927.

CHAUTAUQUA TRACTION COMPANY

The Broadhead family, who owned the Jamestown Street Railway, promoted an interurban to run along the west shore of Chautauqua Lake, through the town of Chautauqua, and beyond to Westfield on the main lines of the New York Central and the Nickel Plate Road. The track reached Chautauqua, home of the Chautauqua Institution, and Mayville, at the northern tip of the lake in 1904, but was not completed to Westfield until 1906. A 1-mile branch from Westfield to Barcelona was added in 1909.

After 1914, when the Broadhead family opened a second interurban between the same termini — the Jamestown Westfield and Northwestern (q.v.) — the Chautauqua Traction Company assumed a subordinate position. Traffic to Chautauqua was not enough to sustain the road, and in the 1920's the line declined rapidly. The Barcelona branch was abandoned in 1920, and the main line from Mayville to Westfield in 1925. The remainder of the line was abandoned March 19, 1926, except for the entry into Jamestown (2.6 miles), which was taken over by the street railway.

JAMESTOWN WESTFIELD AND NORTHWESTERN RAILWAY

In 1913 the Broadhead family (see above) acquired the Jamestown Chautauqua & Lake Erie Railway, a bankrupt steam railroad between Jamestown and Westfield, formerly controlled by the Buffalo and Lake Erie Traction Company. Electric operation was begun in 1914 with heavy steel passenger equipment. Interchange of railroad freight cars continued, and the line handled mail in considerable volume. The road, which operated along the east shore of Chautauqua Lake, was the stronger of the two Broadhead interurbans between Jamestown and Westfield, and survived the Chautauqua Traction Company by more than twenty years. For many years six passenger trains per day were provided. Passenger service continued until 1947, and freight operations behind diesel locomotives until 1950. In its last years the road was controlled by the scrap-metal merchant Murray Salzburg. This long survival is remarkable in the light of the company's meager earnings. The company was considerably helped by revenues from mail movements between New York Central trains at Westfield and the city of Jamestown, but carload freight revenues supported the road.

NEW YORK STATE RAILWAYS

The New York Central Railroad, which could hardly have been more hostile to the Midwestern interurbans, was in the anomalous position of itself controlling a major system of interurban and street railway lines, called the New York State Railways. It operated the city lines in Rochester, Syracuse, Oneida, Utica, and Rome, and four interurbans, all of which retained their identities under NYS operation. The city lines also owned short suburban routes. The four interurbans are described below.

Rochester and Sodus Bay Railway

This line, completed in 1900, was the principal example outside of New England of an interurban built on the highway. Of its 44.5 miles, only about 10 were on private right-of-way. The line used Jackson and Sharp monitor-roof cars of the style of the 1890's, generally considered obsolete by about 1903. The line's territory was lightly populated, and neither Sodus Bay nor Sodus Point, the eastern termini, produced much traffic apart from a modest resort business in the summer months. The line was acquired by the New York State Railways in 1909, which continued to operate it until after the New York Central divested itself of the NYS in 1928. The line was abandoned in 1929, except for the double-track portion from Rochester to Glen Haven, which continued as a suburban line of the Rochester street railway until 1933. The survival of the Sodus Bay line until 1929 in the face of its light traffic and obsolete technology (it was never modernized) is something of a wonder.

Rochester and Eastern Rapid Railway[14]

The R&E was an interurban of 45 miles built with typical Midwestern technology, opened from Rochester to Canandaigua in 1903 and from Canandaigua to Geneva in 1904. All but about 3.5 miles of the track in rural areas was on private right-of-way. The line had interchanges with the New York Central, the Lehigh Valley, and the Pennsylvania, but it was unable to develop any substantial volume of carload freight. In the early years it carried a heavy summer passenger traffic to the Finger Lakes, but this traffic was particularly vulnerable to automobile competition. The company early in its history maintained a local service with one car in Canandaigua.

The R&E became part of the New York State Railways in 1909, and remained in operation until July 31, 1930. After 1928 it entered Rochester by means of the subway.

Oneida Railway

In 1907 the New York Central electrified 49 miles of the West Shore Railroad between Syracuse and Utica under the name of the street railway in Oneida, the principal intermediate town. A covered third rail was laid, identical to the one used in the New York Central's New York terminal electrification, and it was expected that the Oneida line could be utilized in a general electrification from New York to Buffalo, if it were ever made. Most of the cars were heavy wooden multiple-unit interurbans, but in 1912 the company bought a pair of steel cars fitted with parabolic ends. Local trains ran on the streets in Oneida, but limiteds ran by the town to the south. All trains entered Syracuse and Utica on the street, using overhead trolley. A limited and a local were run every hour at the outset, but by the late 1920's only a single car was run each hour, except during the morning and evening rush periods. The entire operation was abandoned on December 31, 1930, and the track returned to freight service only.

Utica and Mohawk Valley Railway

This subsidiary of New York State Railways operated a double-track interurban from Rome to Little Falls (37.5 miles) via Utica, where the company had an extensive street railway. The line from Rome to Herkimer was completed in 1902, and the remaining 7.5 miles to Little Falls in 1903. From 1905 to 1913 the interurban used tracks of the West Shore Railroad for a short distance between Frankfort and Mohawk. In 1916 heavy steel cars were put in service, the most modern equipment bought for any of the NYS lines. In the peak years trains ran on the half hour, but service was considerably reduced in the twenties and early thirties. The interurban operated until 1933, and a segment from Utica to Whitesboro survived as a suburban line until 1938. The steel cars of 1916 were taken to Rochester in 1938, and thereafter operated in the Rochester subway until passenger service was discontinued in 1956.

BUFFALO LOCKPORT AND ROCHESTER RAILWAY

This interurban, completed in 1908 and put into regular service in 1909, paralleled the Falls Road of the New York Central Railroad for 59 miles from Rochester to Lockport, where it connected with the International Railway Company. The project failed during construction and was completed by the Woods-Nicholls interests of Toronto, who envisioned it as part of a high-speed Rochester–Toronto route. Accordingly, this was an exceptionally well built interurban, laid with 70-pound rail and crushed rock ballast, and equipped with heavy wooden high-speed, multiple-unit cars built by Niles. From 1914 to about 1919 these cars ran through to Buffalo over the IRC, but for the rest of the company's history a change at Lockport was required. However, the road regularly had through freight operations with the IRC. No connection for Toronto was undertaken.

In 1911 the company passed into the hands of Clifford D. Beebe of Syracuse, proprietor of one of the two main networks of interurbans in New York. The Beebe syndicate encountered financial difficulties at the time of World War I, and in 1919 let the BL&R pass into the hands of new owners in Rochester, who reorganized it as the Rochester Lockport and Buffalo Railroad Corporation. The road operated throughout the 1920's, but was abandoned on April 30, 1931. Between February 4, 1928, and abandonment, the company's cars entered Rochester by the municipal subway laid in the old bed of the Erie Canal.

LEWISTON AND YOUNGSTOWN FRONTIER RAILWAY

In 1896 this company built a 7-mile interurban from Lewiston to Fort Niagara on Lake Ontario. In 1904 the property was leased to the Niagara Gorge Railway, which owned a scenic line that formed a loop between Niagara Falls, Queenston, and Lewiston. Unlike the Gorge Railway itself, the Lewiston–Fort Niagara line handled carload freight in interchange with the railroads. When the Niagara Gorge line was abandoned in 1935, the L&YF continued in independent freight operation. It remains in service as a diesel freight line.

INTERNATIONAL RAILWAY

This company, which operated a large network of street railways in Buffalo and Niagara Falls, owned two interurbans between the two cities. The earlier was built by the Buffalo and Niagara Falls Electric Railway in 1895, and merged with other properties to form the International Railway in 1902. The line was double-tracked and mainly on private right-of-way, but street running in Buffalo, Tonawanda, North Tonawanda, and Niagara Falls was so lengthy and time-consuming that cars required 80 minutes for the trip of 24 miles. Traffic was so dense that the company undertook a new project, called "The Buffalo-Niagara Falls High Speed Line," to connect the two cities with an electric railway of quasi rapid-transit character. It was equipped with Kuhlman center-entrance cars capable of 60 miles per hour, and was built on private right-of-way, except for its entrances into the terminal cities.

The overhead right-of-way of 3.5 miles around the Tonawandas was particularly impressive. The new line was opened in 1918, and the former one abandoned in 1922. The high-speed line originally offered 60-minute service, but the introduction of local stops after 1922, plus a growing congestion in the streets of Buffalo, increased running time by about 12 minutes.

When the International Railway was formed in 1902, it also included an interurban from Buffalo to Lockport and Olcott Beach, a resort on Lake Ontario. The Buffalo and Lockport Railway (24 miles) had been opened in 1898, and the Lockport and Olcott Railway (13 miles) in 1900. As far as Lockport, the line was double-tracked, one track owned by the company and the other by the Erie Railroad, which provided it under lease for interurban operation.

Both interurban lines of the company suffered the general decline of the 1920's and 1930's, and by the end the high-speed line was reduced to two trips per day. Passenger service was discontinued on both lines in 1937. The Niagara Falls line was scrapped, but freight service continued on the North Tonawanda–Lockport line on the Erie Railroad's track until 1950, when the lease was terminated and the operation turned over to the Erie.

NEW YORK–AUBURN AND LANSING RAILROAD

In 1906 this line was begun as a direct route between Ithaca and Auburn (36 miles); it customarily used the name, "Ithaca–Auburn Short Line." Much of the track was laid on the rights-of-way of abandoned steam short-line railroads, and every third tie was elongated to provide for a third rail, which the company hoped to lay. Part of the line was in service by 1908 and all of it by 1909. The southernmost 7 miles between South Lansing and Ithaca were electrified with overhead trolley, but the remaining mileage was operated with steam locomotives and McKeen cars. The road proved so unsuccessful that further electrification was uneconomic; no third rail was ever laid.

The company went into receivership in 1912, and was reorganized in 1914 as the Central New York Southern Railroad, but the new company lasted only nine years. On October 31, 1923, the entire property was abandoned, except for about a mile in Ithaca that remained in switching service under lease to the street railway, with which the interurban had shared common ownership.

EMPIRE UNITED RAILWAYS

A system that was in some respects a counterpart of the New York State Railways was that headed by Clifford D. Beebe of Syracuse. In addition to the Buffalo Lockport and Rochester Railway (q.v.),

Beebe and his associates controlled interurbans from Syracuse to Rochester, Auburn, and Oswego. Between 1913 and 1916, three of these properties were consolidated into the Empire United Railways, but for most of their histories they were independently operated under the control of officers affiliated with Beebe. The interurbans of the Beebe syndicate were as follows.

Rochester and Syracuse Railroad

The principal Beebe road was this double-track, high-speed line of 87 miles between the largest cities of central upstate New York. It paralleled the New York Central Railroad main line and the Erie Canal, and had only one grade crossing with a railroad in its entire length. The road was completed under the name Rochester Syracuse and Eastern Railroad in 1909, although a number of miles had been in service since 1906. Construction costs had amounted to about $7 million, an exceptionally large sum. In 1913, largely in an effort to deal with the heavy fixed charges of the RS&E, Beebe merged it with two of his other interurban properties (not including the Buffalo Lockport and Rochester) into the Empire United Railways. The effort was unsuccessful; the Empire United failed in 1915, and was dissolved into its component interurbans in 1916. Beebe withdrew from interurban operation, and the RS&E was reorganized in 1917 as the Rochester and Syracuse Railroad. It existed throughout the twenties, went into receivership in 1930, and was sold for junk in the following year. It was abandoned on June 27, 1931.

While this road operated, it was notable for a high standard of service. Beginning in 1910 it operated three parlor cars on its limited trains, and continued to do so until World War I, when all three were converted to freight service. In 1927 the R&S rebuilt seven of its standard coaches for limited service, with double-width windows, bucket seats, and new flooring. Limiteds made the trip in about 2 hours and 40 minutes, some 50 minutes faster than local trains. After 1928 cars used the Rochester subway for their entrance to the city, saving about 12 minutes in running time. In spite of its excellent physical plant, this interurban was unable to induce the railroads to interchange freight cars.

Empire State Railroad

Beginning in 1898 trolley service from Syracuse north along the south shore of Onondaga Lake was provided by the Syracuse Lakeside and Baldwinsville Railway. The company failed because of excessive dependence on summer traffic, and in 1905 Beebe purchased it and reorganized it as the Syracuse Lake Shore and Northern Railroad. He relocated part of the track from the highway to private right-of-way and built northward toward Oswego, a major port on Lake Ontario. The line (38 miles) was not completed until July 26, 1911, but its physical standard was one of the highest of any interurban; it was double-tracked, strung with catenary overhead, and built to permit 60-mile-per-hour running. Schedules demanded more modest speeds, calling for 1 hour and 40 minutes for the trip.

The Syracuse Lake Shore and Northern was included in the Empire United Railways in 1913. In 1917, after the dissolution, the Syracuse–Oswego interurban and another former component, the Auburn and Northern Electric Railroad (Auburn–Port Byron, 9 miles, opened 1908) were combined as the Empire State Railroad. The merger was somewhat anomalous, since the two lines had no physical connection, and the Port Byron–Auburn line was essentially a branch of the Rochester–Syracuse interurban. In 1922 the Rochester and Syracuse Railroad acquired control of the Empire State Railroad, and in 1930 leased the Port Byron–Auburn line, after the abandonment of the direct interurban between Syracuse and Auburn. This arrangement was short-lived, and the Port Byron–Auburn line was abandoned with the rest of the R&S, June 27, 1931. The Oswego route of Empire State Railways had been abandoned three days earlier.

Auburn and Syracuse Electric Railroad

The Auburn Interurban Electric Railroad opened a line on the highway from Auburn to Skaneateles (7 miles) in 1901. In 1902 the company consolidated with the Auburn City Railway to form the Auburn and Syracuse Electric Railroad, which in 1903 built an interurban on private right-of-way from Skaneateles to Syracuse (20 miles). The new line was double-tracked in 1906. The company operated a steamboat on Skaneateles Lake and owned an amusement park on Owasco Lake. Passenger traffic was heavy in the summer months and the interurban carried substantial amounts of express. It handled occasional freight cars in railroad interchange.

Although the company was a Beebe property, it was not included in the Empire United Railways, and operated to the end without change of name. The road went bankrupt in 1927, and then gave up its street railway operations in Auburn. It strove to survive as an interurban, but failed to do so, and met an unorthodox end in 1930. The Enna Jettick Shoe Company was interested in its amusement park, and bought the entire interurban on March 20, 1930. Bondholders were paid off at about 25 per cent of the value of their holdings, and the property was abandoned on April 15, 1930.

Syracuse Northern Electric Railway

This Beebe line connected Syracuse with South Bay and Brewerton on Oneida Lake. The track had been laid to South Bay in 1905 by a predecessor company, but financial difficulties prevented operation until the Syracuse and South Bay Electric Railroad was organized in 1907. Service began in 1908. A branch to Cicero and Brewerton was opened by a subsidiary in 1912. Beebe had hopes of extending the Brewerton line to Watertown, but nothing came of them. The expense of building the Brewerton branch threw the property into receivership, from which it emerged in 1917 as the Syracuse Northern Electric Railway. The interurban was heavily dependent on summer traffic to Oneida Lake, but in the 1920's it developed a small commutation business in North Syracuse. Operations were abandoned on January 11, 1932. The line maintained its independence throughout its history, and was never a part of Empire United Railways.

SOUTHERN NEW YORK RAILWAY

In 1900 the street railway in Oneonta adopted the name Oneonta Cooperstown and Richfield Springs Railway, and began building an interurban northward. In 1901 the track reached Cooperstown (28 miles), and in 1902 a branch was opened from Index to Richfield Springs (16 miles). The line was pushed north from Richfield Springs to Mohawk (15 miles) in 1904. In 1906 the line became the Oneonta and Mohawk Valley Railway and in 1908 the Otsego and Herkimer Railroad. In 1916 it became the Southern New York Power and Railway Company, and in 1924 the Southern New York Railway, when the company's flourishing power business was separated from the interurban.

The interurban did not parallel a railroad, and early in its history gained access to railroad interchange. In its dependence on freight revenues in later years, the road resembled some of the Western interurbans. Passenger traffic declined relatively early, and by 1930 service was reduced to two round trips a day. In the early years a shuttle car ran between Cooperstown and Index, meeting mainline trains, but later through cars made the 3-mile trip on each run. The road served hilly country, and there were many impressive views of lakes and mountains. Passenger cars ran over the Utica and Mohawk Valley into Herkimer to make connections for Utica, and there were occasional through passenger movements. There were through interurban freight movements between Oneonta and Utica regularly. The road operated a railway post office.

For persistence in the face of adversity, this company had few rivals. After its separation from the power business it never covered its operating costs, but nonetheless continued operating. In 1926 it gave up its city lines in Oneonta, and in 1930 it began terminating its interurbans in West Oneonta. In 1933 it ceased carrying passengers and abandoned the track north of Jordanville, where a quarry controlled by the interurban's owners was the road's principal source of revenue and its reason for survival. Freight service from the quarry to Oneonta continued under electric power until 1941, when all the mileage was abandoned except for a short distance from an interchange with the Delaware & Hudson at Oneonta to West Oneonta, which remained in switching service with a diesel locomotive.

Upon the abandonment of passenger service, two of the passenger cars—large wooden Cincinnati combines—were sold to the Cedar Rapids and Iowa City, where one became a line car and the other remained in passenger service. The latter served during World War II on the Des Moines and Central Iowa.

ERIE RAILROAD

The Erie Railroad electrified one of its lines for operation under its own name with typical interurban technology. The Erie chose its Rochester-Avon-Mount Morris branch (34 miles) for this project, and equipped it with catenary overhead and current at 11,000 volts AC, the first such installation in America. Beginning in 1907 eight motor cars and four trailers, all equipped for multiple unit operation, provided the service. The over-all scheduled speed of trains was 29 miles per hour, appreciably higher than the ordinary interurban that had to engage in street running. Freight trains and a few through passenger trains continued to be hauled by steam locomotives.

The Erie electrification survived until November 29, 1934, when it was replaced with a gas-electric motor car. Passenger service on the branch was abandoned entirely on September 30, 1941, and the track was cut back from Mount Morris to Avon.

FONDA JOHNSTOWN AND GLOVERSVILLE RAILROAD[15]

This company was and continues to be a railroad in the area of the cities of its corporate title, but between 1894 and 1938 it operated electric railway service. In 1894 it secured control of the Cayadutta Electric Railroad between Johnstown and Fonda (8 miles) and the Johnstown Gloversville and Kingstown Horse Railroad (4 miles). The two electric lines were merged into the FJ&G in 1903, and were extended in the same year east to Amsterdam, Scotia, and Schenectady. Local service was provided in the Gloversville-Johnstown area, and between Scotia and Fort Johnson. The interurban provided hourly service with excellent St. Louis heavy wooden equipment, and was relatively successful.

In 1932 the company bought five lightweight, high-speed cars, some of the best interurban equipment ever built. In 1935 the road cut its fares drastically and gave every impression that it intended to continue service. But in 1938, when the state condemned the bridge over the Mohawk River (between Scotia and Schenectady) over which the interurban cars entered Schenectady under trackage rights on the Schenectady Railway, the company decided to abandon its interurban operations, and sold its lightweight cars to the Bamberger Railroad.

GENEVA SENECA FALLS AND AUBURN RAILROAD

The Geneva Waterloo Seneca Falls and Cayuga Lake Traction Company was formed in 1895 out of four predecessor companies, of which the most important, the Waterloo Seneca Falls and Cayuga Lake Railway, had been operating between Geneva and Cayuga Lake with steam "dummy" engines since 1886. The new company began operation with electric cars in 1895. The line was a side-of-the-road interurban, 18 miles long, including a short extension from Seneca Falls to an amusement park at Cayuga Lake.

The company, which had unfulfilled ambitions to build to Auburn, was reorganized in 1909 as the Geneva and Auburn Railway and in 1913 as the Geneva Seneca Falls and Auburn Railroad. The road provided city service in Geneva until 1925, and then operated its interurban until December 5, 1928. Wason steel combines, built in 1914, provided most of the service in the line's last years.

SCHENECTADY RAILWAY

The street railway in Schenectady built three interurban lines between 1901 and 1905. In 1901 it opened a double-track line to Albany (16 miles) and in 1902 a similar line to Troy (16 miles). In 1904 a line was built to Ballston Spa, which was extended in the following year to Saratoga Springs (21 miles) by electrifying the track of the Delaware & Hudson Railroad, joint owner of the electric railway with the New York Central. Service on the Albany and Troy lines was as frequent as four cars per hour in peak periods, but hourly service was usual on the Saratoga line.

Oddly enough, the company's three routes survived in inverse proportion to the size of their termini. The Albany line was replaced by buses on July 30, 1933, the Troy line on July 15, 1934, but the Saratoga line not until December 6, 1941. In that year the company's extensive city operations were in the process of conversion to buses, but because of the war were not entirely converted until 1946.

HUDSON VALLEY RAILWAY

This interurban, a subsidiary of the Delaware & Hudson Railroad, ran from Troy north to Warrensburg. Between Mechanicville and Glens Falls, there were alternative main lines, one along the Hudson River via Northumberland and the other via Ballston Spa and Saratoga Springs. The interurban originated as a horse car line between Glens Falls and Fort Edward, built in 1885 and electrified in 1891. The rest of the system was built in an exceptionally large number of short stretches, and completed in 1903 with the building of 18 miles between South Glens Falls and Saratoga Springs. Total mileage was about 102 miles. The D&H acquired control in 1907. In 1918 the Hudson Valley abandoned its own line between Ballston Spa and Saratoga Springs and began to use the tracks of the D&H, which had already been electrified by the Schenectady Railway. In 1925 the Hudson Valley gave up this arrangement, abandoned its track from Mechanicville to Ballston Spa, and discontinued its city service in Saratoga Springs. In 1927 it abandoned its northern tip from Lake George to Warrensburg and the branch from Northumberland to Greenwich. The rest of the system was abandoned in 1928, except for a short segment of the main line between Troy and Waterford, which was taken over by the United Traction Company and operated as part of the Troy city system until 1933.

ALBANY AND HUDSON RAILROAD

The Albany and Hudson Railway and Power Company was created in 1899 by the merger of three companies: the Hudson Street Railway, the Kinderhook and Hudson Railway, and the Greenbush and Nassau Electric Railway. The first was the street railway in Hudson, the second a steam railroad between Hudson and Niverville (16 miles), and the third an electric line incorporated to connect the Kinderhook and Hudson with Rensselaer and Albany, on which work had barely been started. The new company built the line from Niverville to Rensselaer (19 miles) and established trackage rights on the United Traction's line for the entrance into Albany. Two miles of track at Hudson were built to replace trackage rights the K&H had formerly held on the Boston & Albany Railroad. When the line was completed in 1900, it was the first third-rail interurban in the United States. It used trolley overhead at both termini and in the town of Valatie, where cars ran on the streets.

In spite of the excellent physical plant, the road was not a success and was reorganized on several occasions. In 1903 it became the Albany and Hudson Railroad; in 1909 the Albany Southern; and in 1924 the Eastern New York Utilities Corporation. The new management in 1925 put in service a pair of Cincinnati lightweight cars and converted some of the older rolling stock to one-man operation. But the cost savings from this conversion were insufficient, and revenue from a modest interchange of freight with the railroads was inadequate to support the company. In 1929, the road was abandoned. The two lightweight cars later served on the Fonda Johnstown and Gloversville and on the Portland Electric Power Company in Oregon.

CORTLAND COUNTY TRACTION COMPANY

In 1895 the Cortland and Homer Traction Company built a 5-mile line from Cortland to McGrawville. At the same time, a line built north from Cortland to Homer (4 miles) in 1885 was electrified. The road was reorganized as the Cortland County Traction Company in 1901. The Homer route was extended to Little York Lake in 1905 and to Preble in 1907, a total of 11 miles from Cortland. A proposal to build north to Syracuse was never executed. The company operated mainly in street railway fashion, but it interchanged freight cars at McGraw (formerly McGrawville) with the Lackawanna. City service in Cortland was abandoned in 1928, the Preble line in 1929, and the McGraw line in 1931. The Homer portion of the Preble line also survived until 1931.

PENN YAN KEUKA PARK AND BRANCHPORT RAILWAY

This company connected Penn Yan and Branchport (9 miles) in 1897 with a line partly on private right-of-way, partly on the highway. It charged zone fares, operated in the summer with open equipment and in the winter with closed, and was otherwise similar to the New England trolley lines. Since Branchport was without railroad service, the company hauled boxcars behind electric locomotives, mainly outbound from several wineries in the area. The line was served by a railway post office. Keuka College on the line provided some passenger traffic. The road became the Penn Yan and Lake Shore Railway in 1913, and retained the name until its demise. Passenger service was discontinued in 1927, and the road abandoned in 1928.

ELMIRA CORNING AND WAVERLY RAILWAY

This road was begun by the Waverly Sayre and Athens Traction Company, a streetcar line, but passed into the hands of the Erie Railroad early in its history. The line between Waverly and Wellsburg (11 miles) was opened in 1907 and extended to Elmira (24 miles) in 1909. The Elmira–Corning line was completed in 1911. Service was hourly on both lines, and schedules were somewhat faster than on most interurbans. The property was abandoned on April 1, 1930.

ELMIRA AND SENECA LAKE TRACTION COMPANY

The Elmira and Seneca Lake Railway was opened between Elmira and Watkins Glen (23 miles) in 1900, a mixture of on-the-highway, side-of-the-road, and private right-of-way operation. In 1906, as a result of flood damage, the company failed and was reorganized as the Elmira and Seneca Lake Traction Company. The new company was purchased in 1907 by the Elmira Water Light and Railroad Company, but operated separately from the street railway in Elmira until 1916, when it was merged. The line was regularly served by two interurban cars, but street cars were frequently used on it in the summer months. The decline of passenger traffic on this road was particularly rapid, and abandonment occurred in 1923.

KAYDEROSS RAILROAD

In 1898 the Ballston Terminal Railroad opened 7 miles of electric line from Ballston Spa northwest up Kaydeross Creek. The line was extended 2 miles in 1899 and 3 miles in 1902, when track reached Middle Grove. Although the road was built with typical interurban technology, and operated passenger cars, it was intended principally to serve paper mills along the creek, and regularly derived over 85 per cent of its revenue from carload freight interchanged with the Delaware & Hudson Railroad at Ballston Spa. The road was reorganized in 1906 as the Eastern New York Railroad, and as the Kaydeross Railroad in 1918. When the paper mills along the line converted to motor transport, traffic declined sharply, and the electric line deteriorated badly. The road was abandoned in 1929.

*

There were several companies in New York state that were, for one reason or another, on the borderline of the interurban industry:

LIMA HONEOYE ELECTRIC LIGHT AND RAILROAD COMPANY

One of the shortest and least successful electric lines was this 5-mile road between the town of Lima and an interchange with the New York Central at Honeoye Falls. The track had been laid by a steam short line in 1892, but abandoned in 1895. In 1899 the project was revived as an electric railway, but was again highly unsuccessful. It was reorganized in 1910 but continued to run substantial deficits, and was abandoned in 1915.

NEW PALTZ HIGHLAND AND POUGHKEEPSIE TRACTION COMPANY

The New Paltz and Walkill Valley Railroad in 1897 opened a 9-mile electric line between Highland and New Paltz, center of a resort area in the Catskill Mountains. Originally, some of the cars were handled over the Philadelphia Reading and New England Railroad's bridge into Poughkeepsie, but around 1900 this arrangement was replaced with a shuttle between the West Shore Railroad tracks in Highland and the ferry slip.

The road was unsuccessful from the outset, and was reorganized in 1900 as the New Paltz and Poughkeepsie Traction Company, and again in 1903 as the New Paltz Highland and Poughkeepsie Traction Company. It survived until 1925.

ORANGE COUNTY TRACTION COMPANY

A suburban extension of the street railway in Newburgh was built to Walden (10 miles) in 1895. It ran by the side of the highway and had three 5-cent-fare zones. The line was a pioneer in hauling milk and LCL freight, but was a weak enterprise and was abandoned in 1925.

WALKILL TRANSIT COMPANY

The Middletown–Goshen Traction Company connected the towns of its name in 1895 with a 12-mile electric line, mainly on private right-of-way. The road went bankrupt twice in its first decade, and was reorganized in 1899 as the Middletown–Goshen Electric Railway and in 1905 as the Walkill Transit Company. The entire property was thoroughly rebuilt in 1906. Operation was integral with the street railway in Middletown, and the company was controlled for most of its history by the Erie Railroad. Operations were unprofitable after 1921, and both city and interurban service were ultimately abandoned in 1924.

KEESEVILLE AUSABLE CHASM AND LAKE CHAMPLAIN RAILROAD

In 1890 this little road (6 miles) was opened to connect Keeseville, center of a resort area, with the main line of the Delaware & Hudson Railroad at Port Kent. It was electrified in 1905 with a third rail— probably the smallest third-rail line in America. The electrification was removed in 1911, but the railroad survived until 1924.

PAUL SMITH'S ELECTRIC LIGHT POWER AND RAILROAD COMPANY

This electric line served principally to connect Paul Smith's Hotel, a major resort in the Adirondacks, with the New York Central Railroad station at Lake Clear Junction, a distance of 7 miles. The road was notable for using a side trolley and a unique power system described in Chapter 2: 5,000-volt AC overhead with conversion on the cars to DC for the traction motors. The line was operated for 30 years, 1906–36.

NIAGARA GORGE RAILWAY

The Niagara Falls and Lewiston Railroad built a double-track trolley line from Niagara Falls to Lewiston at the bottom of the Niagara Gorge in 1895–96. The road became the Niagara Gorge Railway in 1899. Service was provided with double-truck open cars, and the great majority of passengers were sightseers. The road provided service on a loop between Niagara Falls and Lewiston, using the track of the Niagara Falls Park and River Railway Company, an International Railway affiliate, along the bluffs on the Canadian side.

The round trip was a great tourist attraction for more than thirty years, but by its very nature it was highly vulnerable to automobile competition. In addition, ice conditions during the winter months, when service had to be suspended, inflicted almost annual damage to the property. Falling rocks menaced the right-of-way each spring.

In 1932 the Niagara Falls Park and River Railway failed to renew its contract with Niagara Parks Commission, and suspended operations. A combination of the loss of the Canadian connection, the depression, the secular downtrend of traffic, and the difficulty of maintaining the physical plant caused the Niagara Gorge to abandon its line at the end of the 1935 season. An affiliate, the Lewiston and Youngstown Frontier (q.v.), remained in freight service.

New England

NEW ENGLAND was served by the most extensive network of rural trolley lines of any area. We have felt it impracticable to attempt a detailed history of the New England street and rural electric railways in this book, feeling that these companies require a separate study. Here, as in the section on Pennsylvania, we shall distinguish between interurbans, roads having some interurban characteristics, and rural trolley lines, but only the first group is included in the tabulations.

INTERURBANS

PORTLAND-LEWISTON INTERURBAN RAILROAD[16]

Portland and Lewiston, the two principal population centers in Maine, were the goals of several interurban builders in the period 1901–7, but no firm managed to build a direct line between them. A roundabout route through Brunswick via rural trolley lines was available after 1902. The Portland Gray and Lewiston Railroad, chartered in 1907, finally built the direct line, although seven years elapsed before its opening. Grading began in 1910 and was completed in 1912, but first operation was delayed until 1914. The project was financed privately by W. Scott Libbey and Henry M. Dingley without public sale of securities. When Libbey died just before the opening in 1914, the property passed into the hands of the Androscoggin Electric Company and was renamed the Portland-Lewiston Interurban Railroad.

It was a pure interurban of the Midwestern style in its technology. The right-of-way was 50 feet wide, had a ruling grade of 4 per cent, and did not parallel a railroad, although the Maine Central connected the terminals. Since there was little intermediate population, the company initially operated limited service almost exclusively, but in 1915, in response to an order of the Maine public utilities commissioners, the management began to run alternate limiteds and locals. Limiteds made the 31-mile trip in 1 hour and 20 minutes, locals in 20 minutes longer. Service was hourly. The road was designed for railroad interchange, but the Maine Central removed the connecting track on completion of the interurban and refused to restore it. Two box motors per day handled LCL.

Not only was the Portland–Lewiston Interurban the most heavily built New England electric line, but it was one of the most progressive American interurbans in technology—all the more remarkable since the company had only nine passenger cars. It was the first interurban to use the trolley shoe (1916), and was a pioneer in use of the Westinghouse automatic coupler (1914) and of the air horn (1924). The company never adopted lightweight equipment, but was planning to do so shortly before its abandonment. In spite of losses after 1931, the company made a serious effort to continue. It cut the Portland–Lewiston fare to one dollar and in 1932 sent its superintendent to the Midwest to examine the lightweight cars of the Indiana Railroad. While he was on his trip, the Maine legislature required separation of the interurban from the Androscoggin Electric Company, which was then controlled by the Insull system. The separation made it impossible for the interurban to continue, and abandonment occurred on June 29, 1933—19 years to the day after completion. The same crew and, indeed, many of the same passengers, made the first trip and the last.

AROOSTOOK VALLEY RAILROAD[17]

Senator Arthur R. Gould, owner of a lumber mill in Presque Isle, Maine, organized the Aroostook Valley Railroad, and in 1910 opened it between Washburn Junction, Washburn, and Presque Isle. Extensions to West Caribou and the small town of New Sweden were made within the next three years, bringing total trackage to 33 miles. The road was intended from the outset to be mainly a carrier of freight, and was rumored to have been built as an electric interurban mainly to avoid problems connected with getting a charter as a steam railroad. The road always worked closely with the Canadian Pacific Railway and utilized some of its track.

Although the tributary population was so small that the company never operated more than four passenger round trips daily, the road proved to be one of the most successful interurbans, and is still in existence as a freight hauler. Lumber, expected to be the principal cargo, was rapidly replaced by potatoes as the chief freight support of the railroad. A military air base at Presque Isle was the road's principal source of passenger traffic during World War II.

Passenger service was provided with two wooden Wason combines of Midwestern style. Passenger cars ceased serving the New Sweden branch in the late 1930's, and passenger service was discontinued entirely in 1946. The 1,200-volt overhead was then removed and the road dieselized. Since 1931, the line has been controlled by the Canadian Pacific.

SPRINGFIELD TERMINAL RAILWAY[18]

The Springfield Electric Railway was chartered in 1894 and on August 1, 1897, opened an 8-mile line from Springfield down the winding Black River Valley to Charlestown, New Hampshire, on the Connecticut River line of the Boston & Maine Railroad. To cross the Connecticut, the company acquired the Cheshire Bridge Corporation, which had been chartered in 1804, possibly the earliest antecedent of any interurban. The toll bridge remained a major source of revenue to the electric line. Passenger cars met trains of the Boston & Maine, and in spite of a ruling grade of 4.05 per cent and a curve of 35° 45', a relatively heavy interchange of carload freight developed. Springfield enjoyed a significant industrial development, particularly in the machine-tool industry, but it was not served by any steam railroad.

Although the company was generally prosperous, it failed during the difficult year of 1918 and was succeeded by the Springfield Terminal Railway in 1923. The new company continued passenger service until 1947, customarily with a pair of small steel Wason combines built in 1925. It was the last road to offer the train connections once common on New England electric lines. Freight service continued with two steeple cab electric locomotives until October 31, 1956, when the property was dieselized. Savings from the conversion were estimated at $15,000 per year. The Springfield Terminal remains a valuable freight feeder to the Boston & Maine, which controls it through stock ownership.

BOSTON AND WORCESTER STREET RAILWAY[19]

The only Massachusetts electric line to approximate interurban technology was the Boston and Worcester Street Railway, which operated heavy wooden equipment on a mixture of private right-of-way and street running. Some service was provided in open cars, however. The line was built in 1902 and opened for through service on June 30, 1903. Cars made the 44-mile trip in about 2 hours and 20 minutes, running on half-hourly headway. Additional half-hourly cars provided local service to South Framingham. In 1909 the company added a 2-mile branch from Natick to Natick Common. Cars terminated in Park Square, Boston, and spent 30 minutes in street running on Columbus and Huntington avenues and Boylston Street. Street running in Worcester occupied about 20 minutes.

The railway was generally profitable until 1918, when a deficit of $100,000 was reported, but it was frequently unprofitable thereafter. In 1925 the company was put into receivership, from which it emerged as the Boston Worcester and New York Street Railway in 1927. In the late 1920's several factors worked against the company. Abandonment of the Columbus Avenue streetcar line caused the interurban

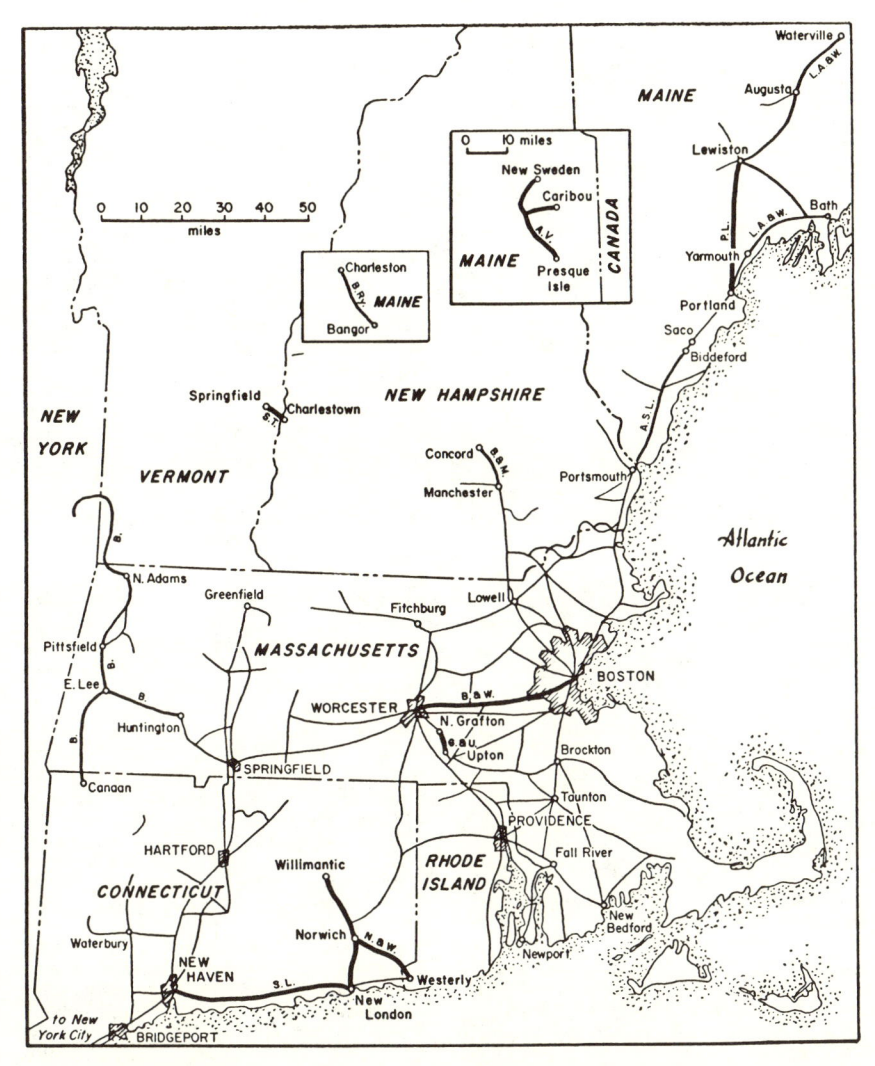

AV: Aroostook Valley RR
PL: Portland-Lewiston Interurban RR
ST: Springfield Terminal Ry.
B&W: Boston & Worcester Street Ry.
G&U: Grafton & Upton RR
N&W: Norwich & Westerly Trac. Co.
SL: Shore Line Elec. Ry.
ASL: Atlantic Shore Line Ry.
BRy: Bangor Ry.

B&M: Boston & Maine RR
B: Berkshire Street Ry.
LA&W: Lewiston Augusta & Waterville Street Ry.

Lightly drawn lines indicate the major intercity trolley lines. The Berkshire Street Railway's line from East Lee to Huntington operated only during the summers of 1917–18. Intermediate lines indicate roads with some interurban characteristics.

cars, which were then being operated hourly, to be rerouted via Berkeley Street. The short Hudson–Marlboro branch was abandoned in 1928, and in the same year, LCL freight service, which the company had promoted avidly, had to be discontinued in the face of highway competition. When the state highway authority in 1929 decided to locate a Boston–Worcester express highway on the west end of the company's right-of-way, the future became impossible. In 1931, the Worcester–Framingham Center segment of the main line was converted to bus operation and in 1932, buses took over all the company's traffic.

GRAFTON AND UPTON RAILROAD

This property had its inception in a 3-mile narrow-gauge railroad, the Grafton Center Railroad, opened between North Grafton and Grafton Center in 1874. In 1887 it was converted to standard gauge and in 1888 its name was changed to the Grafton and Upton Railroad. In the same period it absorbed the Upton Street Railroad, a 15-mile line, and in 1890 track was extended to Milford. The road was electrified in 1902 and passenger service provided by equipment of the Milford and Uxbridge Street Railway. Passenger service was discontinued in 1928, and the line was dieselized in 1946. An electric express and mail car was operated from 1922 until the removal of the electrification.

The road was always mainly dependent on carload freight interchange at the terminals, with the New Haven at Milford and the Boston & Albany at North Grafton. This freight traffic continues, serving mills and other industrial establishments along the right-of-way.

SHORE LINE ELECTRIC RAILWAY[20]

One of the few New England electric lines of genuine interurban technology, the Shore Line Electric was built in 1910 between Saybrook and a connection with the Connecticut Company at Stony Creek, just outside New Haven. In the following year, the company opened a more direct entrance into New Haven via North Branford, again using the Connecticut Company's tracks to reach the downtown area. A branch was built to Deep River in 1912 and extended to Chester in 1914. In 1913 the Shore Line leased the New London and East Lyme Street Railway (built in 1905) and built a connection from Saybrook to complete a through route between New Haven and New London. The Shore Line was built largely on private right-of-way with catenary overhead. The company had intended to install single-phase AC, but reconsidered and adopted 1,200-volt DC. The original cars were wooden center-entrance Jewett interurbans of distinctive appearance. Completion of the Shore Line made possible relatively direct electric railway connections between New York and Boston. Via the Shore Line, one could make the trip through Norwich and either Worcester or Providence.

In 1913 the Shore Line made two additional acquisitions that brought it to more than 250 miles and 200 pieces of equipment. It acquired stock control of the Norwich and Westerly Traction Company, an interurban opened in 1906. This road was built almost entirely on private right-of-way, and operated with multiple-unit equipment. Because its intermediate territory was relatively barren, the original firm, the Norwich and Westerly Railway, failed in 1909 and was reorganized, together with the Pawcatuck Valley Railway (Westerly-Watch Hill), in 1911. In 1912 the N&W leased and then bought stock control of the Groton and Stonington Railway, which had built a trolley line between Westerly and Groton in 1904. In the same year, the N&W built a branch of its subsidiary, the Pawcatuck Valley Railway, to the town of Weekapaug. Thus by 1913 the N&W operated about 60 miles of track, about half on private right-of-way.

The Shore Line's other major acquisition was the New London division of the Connecticut Company. The New London division, which was physically isolated from the rest of the Connecticut Company, provided city service in New London and Norwich, and rural trolley service from these cities to Willimantic, Central Village, Putnam, and North Grosvenordale. It connected at North Grosvenordale for Worcester via the Worcester Consolidated Street Railway and at East Killingly for Providence via the Providence and Danielson Street Railway, a division of the Rhode Island Company.

This large amalgamation of electric lines did not even last long enough for all its equipment to be painted in the company's standard green livery. On August 3, 1917, two of the Shore Line's center-entrance cars collided head-on at North Branford as a result of a violation of train orders, killing 19 and injuring 35. In 1918 the power house was shut down for three weeks, and June 21, 1919, the company had a second head-on collision. When a strike was called in July 1919, the company, weakened by these disasters, shut down operations completely and went into receivership in October. The New London Division of the Connecticut Company was returned to its owners in April 1920, and the Weekapaug line was abandoned in 1921. The Norwich and Westerly was abandoned in 1922, except for short segments at the terminals, and these were scrapped in 1923 and 1924. The Westerly–New London trackage was restored to service by a new Groton and Stonington Traction Company, which operated it from 1923 until it adopted buses in 1928.

After four years of idleness, the original New Haven–Saybrook trackage of the Shore Line was purchased by the Sperry Engineering Company, its builder, and restored to service in 1923 as the New Haven and Shore Line Railway Company. The new firm bought five Wason lightweight cars to operate the line, along with some former Shore Line cars and equipment from the Hartford and Springfield Street Railway, which had recently been abandoned. The restoration was a mistake, and operation lasted only until 1929. In 1928 the company replaced the track east of Guilford with bus service and in the following year completed the conversion. The company remains a bus operator between New Haven and New London. One of the Shore Line's center-entrance cars (No. 7) was sold to the Charles City Western Railway in 1915 and had a long service in Iowa.

LINES WITH SOME INTERURBAN CHARACTERISTICS

ATLANTIC SHORE LINE RAILWAY[21]

Several rural trolley lines at the southern tip of Maine, built between 1893 and 1907, were brought together into the Atlantic Shore Line Railway. The main line ran north from Kittery, opposite Portsmouth, New Hampshire, to Biddeford, where connection was made with the Biddeford and Saco, a trolley line that in turn connected with the Portland Railroad for Portland. The secondary route of the company ran east from the town of Springvale through Sanford to Cape Porpoise on the Atlantic. Another route ran northwest from Kittery to Dover and South Berwick. The tributary area had a population of only about 68,000, but there was a heavy summer resort business, from which the Atlantic Shore Line profited. Since in general the territory was not served by parallel railroads, the electric line was able to develop an interchange carload freight traffic that was a significant source of revenue. Otherwise the operation was almost entirely of the New England street railway style. The company operated a ferry between Kittery and Portsmouth, mainly with the small double-ended sidewheeler, *Kittery.*

The Atlantic Shore Line was not a financial success. It was reorganized in 1910 as the Atlantic Shore Railway, but after it again went bankrupt (1915), the York Utilities was organized in 1922 to take over the property. In 1923 the new company built an alternative line between Sanford and Springvale, but almost immediately began to discontinue the rest of the operations. In 1924 it abandoned the track between Kennebunk and York Beach and in 1925 the line between Town House, Kennebunkport, and Cape Porpoise. In 1927 the rest of the property was scrapped, excepting only the short York–Springvale trackage, which continued to carry passengers in streetcars until 1947.

BANGOR RAILWAY AND ELECTRIC COMPANY

The street railway in Bangor in 1906 absorbed a rural trolley line, the Bangor and Northern Railroad, which ran north 26 miles to Charleston. It had been opened as the Penobscot Central Railway in 1899, electrified in 1901, and extended from its original terminus at Corinth to Charleston (5 miles) in 1902. Since the line did not parallel a railroad, it was able to build up a carload freight traffic, mainly in potatoes (described in Chapter 4). The potato traffic was not sufficient to support the road after the development of motor transport, and passenger traffic was light from the beginning. The line was abandoned in 1930.

The company also operated suburban lines from Bangor to Old Town and Hampden Highlands.

LEWISTON AUGUSTA AND WATERVILLE STREET RAILWAY

One of the principal electric railways in Maine, this company operated city service in the Lewiston-Auburn area and rural trolley lines to Waterville, Augusta, Bath, and Yarmouth. The company was formed as the Auburn Mechanic Falls and Norway Street Railway, but changed its name to the Lewiston Augusta and Waterville Street Railway. The road acquired the Lewiston Brunswick and Bath Street Railway (opened 1898), the Augusta Winthrop and Gardner Railway (opened 1902), and the Auburn and Turner Railroad (opened 1905). It was brought to full size in 1913 with acquisition of the Brunswick and Yarmouth Railway (formerly the Portland and Brunswick Street Railway, opened 1902), which had a line between Brunswick and a connection with the Portland Railroad at Yarmouth. By threatening to build its own entry into Portland, it had induced the Portland Railroad to acquiesce to interline operations.

The Lewiston Augusta and Waterville failed in 1919 and was reorganized as the Androscoggin and Kennebec Railway. The new corporation did not undertake joint operations into Portland, but otherwise continued the road's services. In 1928 the Augusta-Winthrop branch was cut off, and in 1929 the main line was abandoned between Brunswick and Yarmouth. All lines east of Sabattus, including the main line to Augusta and Waterville, were abandoned on August 1, 1932. The remaining intercity line to Brunswick and Bath was cut back to Lisbon Falls on May 15, 1937, after becoming particularly deteriorated. All that remained were city lines in Lewiston and Auburn and suburban lines to Sabattus, Mechanic Falls, and Lisbon Falls. These were sold at auction on January 10, 1941, and scrapped, and the operations were converted to bus.

Operation throughout was of the New England style, but railroad freight cars were handled in interchange for short distances. The company handled LCL and interchanged it with coastal steamers.

BOSTON AND MAINE RAILROAD (CONCORD AND MANCHESTER ELECTRIC BRANCH)[22]

In 1902 the Boston & Maine built an electric line between Concord and Manchester (17 miles), two of the three largest cities in New Hampshire. The grading was somewhat heavier than was usual in New England, the track was more heavily ballasted, and there was some private right-of-way; but zone fares and open and closed equipment of the orthodox New England style were used. The road was said to be the second in New England (the Boston Elevated was the first) to adopt multiple-unit control. After 1903 the Concord Street Railway was incorporated into the system. The interurban line was less profitable than the city lines, but it survived until April 29, 1933, when the entire operation was replaced by buses.

BERKSHIRE STREET RAILWAY

The New York New Haven and Hartford Railroad formed this line out of predecessors in 1910, paying about triple what the earnings were to justify. When the Hoosick Falls Railroad was acquired and electrified as a northern extension, the road ran from Canaan (Connecticut) through Pittsfield (Massachusetts) and Bennington (Vermont) to Hoosick Falls (New York). This is believed to have been the only American electric line to have operated in four states simultaneously.* Much of the right-of-way was private, but equipment was of the typical New England model. The company owned a line with one of the shortest lives of any in the industry, a branch between Huntington and East Lee that operated only for the summers of 1917 and 1918. While this branch existed, the Berkshire was connected with the rural trolley lines of the Connecticut valley and of eastern Massachusetts, but otherwise the line was isolated. The company provided street railway service in Pittsfield.

The Berkshire Street Railway abandoned rail operations between Great Barrington and Canaan in 1919, and discontinued the Hoosick Falls extension in 1922. The remainder of the main line between Great Barrington and North Adams was abandoned in 1930, and the company completed its conversion from rail to bus operation, November 12, 1932.

RURAL TROLLEY LINES

Among the most important of the rural trolley lines were the following.

MAINE

1. *The Rockland Thomaston and Camden Street Railway* (1892–1931).
2. *The Portland Railroad* (suburban lines from Portland to Yarmouth, Old Orchard, South Windham, and Cape Elizabeth).
3. *The Biddeford and Saco Railroad* (1892–1939).

VERMONT

1. *Rutland Railway Light and Power Company* (1902–24).
2. *Mount Mansfield Electric Railroad* (1898–1932).
3. *Barre and Montpelier Traction and Power Company* (1898–ca. 1925).
4. *Bellows Falls and Saxtons River Electric Railroad* (1900–1924).
5. *St. Albans and Swanton Traction Company* (1904–21).

---

* The Indiana Railroad operated in Indiana, Kentucky, Illinois, and Ohio; but its Illinois mileage had been abandoned before its Ohio mileage was acquired.

Vermont was the site of an important abortive interurban, the Burlington and Southeastern Railway, which proposed to build from Burlington to Windsor, an industrial town below White River Junction. It graded 15 miles from Burlington to Hinesburg and laid some track, but apparently neither electrified nor offered service.

NEW HAMPSHIRE

1. *Berlin Street Railway* (1902–38).
2. *Manchester and Derry Street Railway* (1896–1928).
3. *Dover Somersworth and Rochester Street Railway* (ca. 1901–26).
4. *Exeter Hampton and Amesbury Street Railway* (1898–1926). The abandonment of this road is of interest. The company sought to abandon in 1918, but the Public Service Commission prevented closing the road until 1919. In the interim, the towns along the line secured a statute enabling them to buy the property. The town of Hampton assumed title to the company and Exeter and Seabrook agreed to contribute $2,500 and $500 per year, respectively, as subsidies to keep the line operating. When the line ran up deficits of $30,000 in five years, the municipal governments decided the project was hopeless. At a town meeting in March 1926, Hampton voted to abandon the railway.
5. *Manchester and Nashua Street Railway* (ca. 1907-1931).
6. *Portsmouth Electric Railway* (1899–1926).
7. *Claremont Railway* (opened 1903). The West Claremont line of this road remains in service as part of the dieselized Claremont and Concord Railway. Passenger service was abandoned in 1930.

Almost all of New Hampshire's trolley lines availed themselves of a state tax remission for electric railways in unprofitable years. This policy did not significantly prolong the life of the state's trolley lines; aside from the short portion of the Springfield Terminal in New Hampshire, all intercity passenger operations had ceased by 1938.

MASSACHUSETTS

Massachusetts had the densest network of electric railways of any state, relative both to area and to population. It was reported to have 3,056 miles of all track in 1917, about 358 miles of main track per thousand square miles, and 80 miles per hundred thousand people. Massachusetts was the only state to have a greater mileage of electric railway than railroad. Not only is it impractical to attempt any history of these companies here, but it would to some extent be redundant in view of Edward S. Mason's *The Street Railway in Massachusetts* (Cambridge: Harvard University Press, 1932).

Most of the state's railway mileage was concentrated around Boston in the area bounded roughly by Lawrence, Lowell, Fitchburg, Worcester, Providence, Fall River, and New Bedford. Rural extensions of the Worcester Consolidated Street Railway and the Springfield Street Railways Company (both New York New Haven & Hartford Railroad properties) provided a continuous route from the Boston area to the Connecticut Valley, where there was a network operated by several companies between Springfield, Holyoke, Northampton, and Greenfield. The Berkshire Street Railway was the only large property in the western portion of the state.

Much of the state's mileage was built in the late 1890's, and the network was virtually complete by the panic of 1907. Some street railway trackage in Boston is still in service, but mileage declined rapidly after World War I and almost the entire rural network had been swept away by 1933.

CONNECTICUT

1. The *Connecticut Company*. This company, one of the largest operators of electric cars in America, was formed by the NYNH&H in 1907 to consolidate the extensive street railways and rural trolley lines in Connecticut that the railroad had acquired in the previous few years. Charles S. Mellen, on assuming the presidency of the New Haven in 1903, launched a campaign of purchasing steamboat lines in Long Island Sound and electric railways in southern New England, both of which he considered to be serious rivals to the New Haven's virtual monopoly of transportation in the area. The New Haven paid prices that reflected the excessive optimism among electric railway officials during the building booms, and weakened itself to the point of failure by the acquisitions.[23]

The Connecticut Company controlled the street railways in New Haven, Hartford, Meriden, Wallingford, New London, Norwich, Stamford, Middletown, and other Connecticut cities. The principal rural routes were a line along the New Haven Railroad from Stamford to New Haven, with a branch from Stratford to Waterbury, and two routes from New Haven to Hartford, one via New Britain and the other via Meriden. An isolated route from New London north to North Grosvenordale comprised the New London division. There were many branches. These rural routes were never considered interurbans, but there was some private right-of-way, particularly on the New London division, where cars ran on electrified track of the New Haven between Taft's and Central Village. The continuity of the company's operations was less than its map would lead one to expect. Few passengers rode the cars for long distances, and it was frequently necessary to break one's journey en route; for example, a through passenger from Stamford to New Haven had to change cars at Norwalk and Bridgeport.

The rail lines were abandoned slowly and in piecemeal fashion. The Stamford–New Haven line was severed by the abandonment of the Stamford–Norwalk segment in 1933, and the remainder was discontinued in 1935 and 1937. The lines in central Connecticut were abandoned at various times from 1924 to 1937. The New London division was cut back to Norwich in 1925, but the Norwich–New London line survived until 1934. Although intercity rail operations had been wound up by 1937, the company continued to operate city streetcars, and did not give up rail operations in New Haven until after World War II. Bus service replaced trolleys in almost all the rail abandonments, and the Connecticut Company remains a major bus operator.

2. *Hartford and Springfield Street Railway* (1896–1926).

RHODE ISLAND

Rhode Island Company. This firm was the New York New Haven and Hartford Railroad's counterpart for Rhode Island of the Connecticut Company. Its principal property was the street railway in Providence, but it also operated virtually all the rural trolley mileage in the state, including suburban lines from Providence to Woonsocket, Pawtucket, Clephachet, North Scituate, Washington, East Greenwich, and Hope. By leasing the Providence and Danielson Railway in 1911, the Rhode Island Company gained a connection with the Connecticut system. All the suburban rail operations had been discontinued by the successor United Electric Railways by 1929. The Rhode Island lines, it might be noted, were among the worst of the New Haven's investments, and by 1914 were reported to be losing about $650,000 per year.

The Southern States

THE SOUTHERN states east of the Mississippi had very few interurban lines outside of Virginia and Maryland. The only line of consequence in the Deep South, the Piedmont and Northern, followed the pattern of the lines of the Far West much more than the pattern of the Midwestern and Eastern lines. The absence of interurbans was somewhat surprising, in light of population densities and other factors, but for some reason development never got underway. Some of the lines actually built, such as those in Tennessee, served much less promising territory than many other possible routes.

MARYLAND AND NORTHERN VIRGINIA

Maryland had two major systems, the Washington Baltimore and Annapolis, built to high-speed, typical interurban standards, and the rural trolley Hagerstown and Frederick. The H&F was connected with the Pennsylvania lines in the Chambersburg area, but no link was ever built between Baltimore and Wilmington, to connect the eastern Maryland and Pennsylvania routes. Suburban lines extended into Maryland from Washington, but the principal interurbans from the District (except for the WB&A) ran southward and westward into Virginia. The other major Virginia lines extended north and south from Richmond to Ashland and Petersburg.

WASHINGTON BALTIMORE AND ANNAPOLIS ELECTRIC RAILWAY[24]

One of the most important of the high-speed, high-traffic-density interurbans that concentrated on passenger service was the Washington Baltimore and Annapolis, which connected the three cities of its corporate name with very frequent service and very extensive through and suburban traffic. The system consisted of two distinct, and for many years separate, parts. The original WB&A operated the main line from Washington to Baltimore (38 miles) plus the electrified Annapolis Baltimore and Washington, an old steam road that crossed the main line at Naval Academy Junction with service eastward to Annapolis (14 miles) and westward to Odenton and Fort George G. Meade (6 miles). The other segment was the Annapolis Short Line, operating directly from Baltimore to Annapolis (25 miles).

The Washington-Baltimore line was planned as early as 1899 and construction started in 1902, under the ownership of the Pomeroy-Christy group, which built a number of Midwest lines. But financial difficulties caused receivership, and the ownership passed into the hands of the Bishop syndicate, also of Cleveland, which completed the line. Service was established from Washington to Annapolis in February 1908, and to Baltimore on April 3 of that year. The southern terminus was originally at 15th and H streets, N. E., with transfer to streetcars, although at the Baltimore end a downtown terminal was reached, with relatively little street running. The cars for Annapolis connected with north- and south-bound trains at the junction, rather than running through. The private-right-of-way line was built to high standards, with high-speed cars, and 6,600-volt AC single-phase power. Not only did the power system suffer from the usual weaknesses of AC, but the cars were so heavy that the archways on which the conduit-operated Washington streetcars ran would not support them. Finally, on February 15, 1910, operations were shifted to 1,200-volt DC, and cars were run through to the Treasury over the Seat Pleasant car tracks.

The Annapolis Short Line segment was an old steam road, which operated from Baltimore directly to Annapolis. This line was taken over in 1907 by the Maryland Electric Railways, which controlled the Baltimore transit system; it was electrified (also with AC), and trains were operated into Baltimore on Baltimore & Ohio trackage, terminating at the road's Camden Station. Thus Annapolis, which has no main-line railroad, almost simultaneously gained two electric lines. For more than a decade these two companies operated separately, but in 1921 the Short Line was absorbed by the WB&A, although both routes to Annapolis were still operated.

The system, widely publicized when it was built, was one of the country's better lines, with a gross annual revenue in excess of $2.5 million. The company's cars (some of the later of which were articulated) were among the best in the country, and its track was well maintained, although the long slow trip into downtown Washington was a serious handicap (see Chapter 2). The depression hit the road hard, and it entered receivership in 1931; nonetheless, the future seemed relatively secure, and substantial amounts were spent on improvements. But losses increased in 1934, and unexpectedly the road made the decision to abandon, ending service on August 20, 1935, despite gross revenues of nearly $1 million the year before.

When the WB&A proper was abandoned, the old Short Line was reorganized as the Baltimore and Annapolis Railroad and taken over by the Baltimore & Ohio. This line thenceforth provided Annapolis with its only rail service. Although passenger traffic was substantial, the line's equipment deteriorated, and finally, in 1950, bus operations replaced all rail passenger service. The track is still operated for freight service, with diesel power.

HAGERSTOWN AND FREDERICK RAILWAY COMPANY[25]

One of the most extensive interurban systems in all the Middle Atlantic states was the Hagerstown and Frederick, which operated 76 miles of line in central Maryland. These were not high-speed lines, and typically light single-car units were operated. But important freight business developed, and the line was to earn the distinction of being the last passenger-carrying interurban east of the Chicago area, on a route that by all logic should have abandoned service two or three decades earlier. The system consisted of two main lines, one connecting Frederick with Hagerstown, and the other going north from Frederick to Thurmont. In addition there were several branches, as noted below. The Hagerstown line crossed the Blue Ridge Mountains on very steep grades, to provide one of the most scenic interurban rides in the country. The company was a subsidiary of Potomac Edison, and in later years was operated under the parent company's name. Potomac Edison, an American Waterworks property, was the parent of the important Blue Ridge Lines bus system which connected Washington with the Ohio Valley.

The corporate history of the H&F is very complex, since the system was built piecemeal by a number of companies, which were consolidated as the Hagerstown and Frederick in 1913. There were two basic parts, one centering on Hagerstown, one on Frederick. The line eastward from Hagerstown reached Boonesboro (12 miles) in 1902 as the Hagerstown and Boonesboro. In 1906 the connection to the subsidiary Chambersburg Greencastle and Waynesboro was built northward 11 miles from Hagerstown to Shady Grove, Pennsylvania, and the important suburban line to Williamsport (6 miles) was completed in 1907. Meanwhile, a line had been built out of Frederick westward to Middletown (10 miles) in 1899, and extended westward to Myersville (6 miles) in 1904. The 5-mile Braddock Heights–Jefferson branch was built in 1907, and in that year the main line was pushed across the Blue Ridge from Boonesboro Junction to Myersville (7 miles) to allow through service. The last link was the line northward from Frederick to Thurmont (18 miles) built as a steam road and electrified in 1910.

The company also operated street railway service in Hagerstown and Frederick. Intercity passenger business was largely local, and there were also both through business between the two cities of the corporate title and the business gained from the Thurmont connection with the Western of Maryland. The Thurmont line handled considerable carload freight business in interchange with the WM, and other parts of the system around Frederick handled carload freight, but the Hagerstown portion could not, for reasons of track layout.

The coming of the automobile brought the inevitable decline; the first section to go was the Shady Grove line in 1932, after the abandonment of the connecting Pennsylvania road. But the main lines and other branches had a remarkably long life. The main line was not broken until 1938, when the Hagerstown–Myersville segment was abandoned, together with the Boonesboro branch. The Jefferson line went out in 1940, the portion of the old main line from Middletown to Myersville in January 1945, followed by the remainder later in the year. The Williamsport line lasted two more years, and the Frederick–Thurmont line continued passenger service until 1954, the old combine meeting Western Maryland trains. When the WM announced its plans to end passenger service, the Potomac Edison Company discontinued its passenger service on February 20 (although the WM did not in the end stop service at that time). Freight service was continued with diesel power until final abandonment in 1958 (except for the switching tracks in Frederick).

CUMBERLAND AND WESTERNPORT ELECTRIC RAILWAY

The only interurban in the westernmost part of Maryland was the Cumberland and Westernport, which followed a winding route from Cumberland via Lonaconing and back to the Potomac River at Westernport. This 25-mile line was more a typical rural trolley line than an interurban. It was completed in 1902, and for many years was a Cities Service subsidiary. Abandonment came in 1926.

WASHINGTON AND VIRGINIA RAILWAY

The Washington and Virginia, with its network of lines connecting Arlington and Fairfax counties with downtown Washington, was the most important suburban operation in the Washington area. The main line was essentially interurban in its characteristics.

The original company, the Washington and Mt. Vernon, was incorporated in 1890, and completed its line from Mt. Vernon to Alexandria in 1892, and to Washington in 1896. The road originated at 12th Street and Pennsylvania Avenue in downtown Washington, crossed the highway bridge, and extended past Potomac Yard to Alexandria, and thence on private right-of-way to Mt. Vernon (16 miles). Another line (built in 1891 as the Washington Arlington and Fairfax) extended from the end of the Rosslyn Bridge to Fairfax via Clarendon and Vienna (21 miles), paralleling the Old Dominion in part. A third line extended from Rosslyn southward to Fort Myer and Nauck (3 miles), and a fourth ran from Arlington Junction (near the present Pentagon) to Rosslyn, with a branch to Clarendon Junction to connect the two main lines. A very heavy suburban traffic was carried, plus the tourist business to Mt. Vernon.

The Washington and Virginia Railway Company was incorporated in 1910 to consolidate the previously independent companies. But owing to several years of losses caused by the rise of auto traffic, the company went into bankruptcy in 1924 and was reorganized in 1927, the southern portion becoming the Washington Alexandria and Mt. Vernon, and the northern the Arlington and Fairfax Electric Railway Company. The WA&MV was brought to an abrupt end on January 17, 1932, when the government forced abandonment in order to get the Washington terminal properties for new buildings. The A&F carried on until 1939, experimenting between 1936 and 1939 with rail buses. But the continued growth of auto use and regulatory difficulties led to abandonment, after 8 years of operating losses. These roads were almost entirely passenger carriers, generally operating single cars (except to Mt. Vernon).

WASHINGTON AND OLD DOMINION RAILWAY[26]

This line went through the complete cycle from a steam road to an interurban and back to nonelectrified (diesel) operation, and was one of the few interurbans ever to operate passenger service after the removal of electric facilities. The original

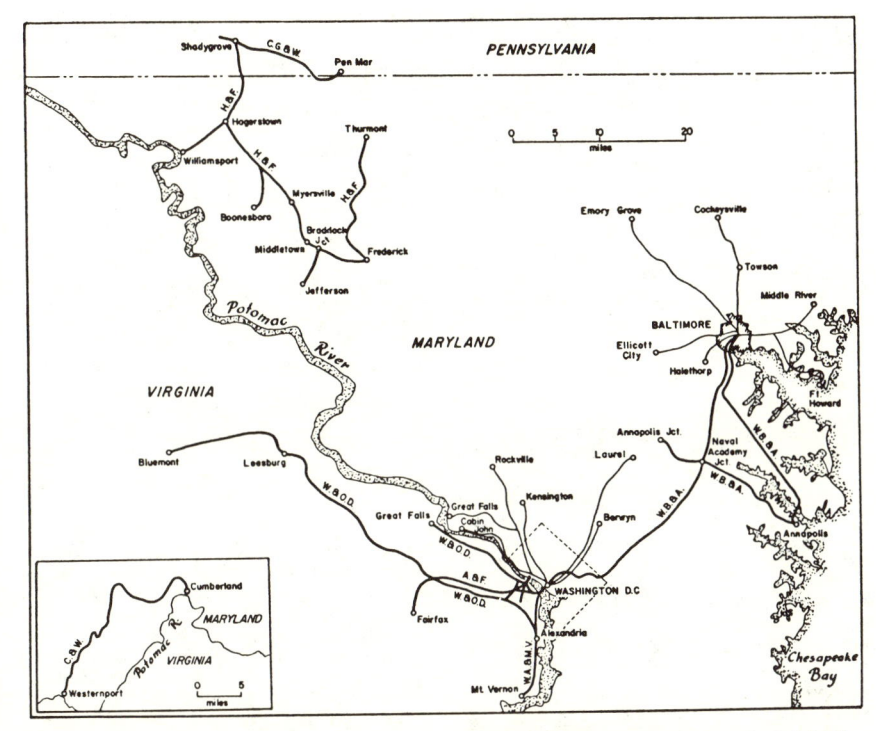

CG&W: Chambersburg Greencastle & Waynesboro Street Ry.
H&F: Hagerstown & Frederick Ry.
WB&A: Washington Baltimore & Annapolis Elec. Ry.
WA&MV: Washington Alexandria & Mt. Vernon Elec. Ry.
A&F: Arlington & Fairfax Elec. Ry.
W&OD: Washington & Old Dominion Ry.
C&W: Cumberland & Westernport Elec. Ry.

line was built as a steam road in 1858 from Alexandria to Leesburg, as the Alexandria Loudon & Hampshire, bound for Cumberland. The line reached Round Hill in 1874, passed into the hands of a predecessor of the Southern Railway, was merged into the Southern in 1894, and finally built on to the village of Bluemont in 1900, as the Washington Ohio & Western.

In 1912 the line was leased by the new Washington and Old Dominion, incorporated in 1911; it was initially developed by the McLean interests of Washington, and subsequently controlled for many years by the Elkins family of West Virginia. The entire leased line was electrified in 1912, and the road was merged with the Great Falls and Old Dominion Railway Company, which had been built as an electric line from Georgetown via the Aqueduct Bridge to Rosslyn and Great Falls (14 miles), beginning operation on March 7, 1906. A link was built between the Great Falls line at Thrifton and the main line at Bluemont Junction, and thereafter main-line passenger service operated from Georgetown (Rosslyn after 1923) to Bluemont (52 miles), the main freight route being the Alexandria–Bluemont sector. The road continued its substantial carload freight business, and developed both a commuter passenger traffic as the Virginia suburban area grew and some resort traffic to the Bluemont area.

The development of the automobile brought a decline in traffic, and the depression forced the road into bankruptcy and reorganization. The negligible passenger service from Alexandria to Bluemont Junction was discontinued in 1932, and the Great Falls line was abandoned in 1935. Four years later the main line was cut back from Bluemont to Purcellville, and in 1941 all passenger service was discontinued and freight operations converted to diesel. Meanwhile the company bought the line from the Southern for the nominal sum of $70,000. Under pressure from residents and public authorities, the road reestablished passenger service with gas-electric equipment in 1943. Heavy increases in freight traffic—stone, building materials, farm crops, and the like—soon earned the company the best profits in its history. Passenger traffic, which the company did not want, declined after the war, and the diesel service was finally discontinued on May 31, 1951, after the mail contract failed to be renewed.

The independent ownership of the road came to an end in 1956, when it was purchased by the Chesapeake & Ohio. As of 1960, it was still operated as a separate entity, with 47 miles of track from Alexandria to Purcellville and the 5-mile Rosslyn–Bluemont Junction line.

WASHINGTON AND BALTIMORE SUBURBAN LINES

The Washington and Baltimore areas had an unusually large number of suburban car lines, some of which used heavy interurban types of equipment. One major Washington route extended from M Street in Georgetown via the Wisconsin Avenue car tracks and private right-of-way through Bethesda to Rockville. Distinctive heavy wooden equipment was used until abandonment in 1935. This line was a subsidiary of the Washington Railway and Electric Company, and was built in 1893. The City and Suburban, an affiliated property, operated a long suburban line to Branchville, Beltsville, and Laurel. This route was built in 1893 as the Washington Berwyn and Laurel. The Beltsville–Laurel segment was abandoned in 1925, but the remainder continued in operation until after World War II; it was essentially a streetcar type of service in later years. Service was discontinued to Beltsville in 1949 and to Branchville in 1958.

The Washington and Great Falls Light and Power Company operated a 15-mile line from Tennallytown to Great Falls from 1913 to 1922, in competition with the Old Dominion across the river in Virginia.

The Kensington Electric Railway operated from Chevy Chase Circle to Kensington from 1895 until it lost its power source in 1935 when the Connecticut Avenue streetcar line was discontinued.

The Washington Interurban Railway extended from 15th and H streets, N.E., to Berwyn, paralleling the Laurel line for 12 miles (about 1 mile to the east). Service was cut back to Riverdale in 1918, and the whole line was abandoned in 1925.

The Baltimore area likewise had several very long suburban routes, operated as a part of the city transit system, with a broad gauge. The Ellicott City line, the Emory Grove line to the north (abandoned in 1938), the Towson–Timonium–Cockeysville lines, and the Halethorp line to the south (abandoned in 1937) were the most important.

WESTERN AND CENTRAL VIRGINIA

BRISTOL TRACTION COMPANY

The line was originally a narrow-gauge steam railroad, built to haul logs, which subsequently gained substantial resort traffic. It was electrified in 1912, and operated as an interurban for only 6 years (abandoned in 1918). The road connected Bristol, Tennessee, with Big Creek, in the Holston Valley in Virginia.

VIRGINIA ELECTRIC POWER COMPANY

The Virginia Electric Power Company operated an integrated power and transit system, including the street railways in Norfolk and Richmond and the 21-mile interurban line between Richmond and Petersburg. Originally owned by George Gould, this system became a Stone and Webster property, and as usual was well managed and well maintained. The interurban was built as the Richmond and Petersburg Electric Railway Company in 1902 on private right-of-way. High-speed service was maintained, and substantial through and suburban business developed. The volume was sufficient to permit continuation of all service until 1936, when abandonment occurred.

The affiliated Virginia Public Service operated a long suburban route to Hampton and Phoebus from Newport News.

RICHMOND AND CHESAPEAKE BAY RAILWAY[27]

Northward from Richmond extended a 15-mile line to Ashland, placed in service on October 28, 1907. The road was built to high standards, with a long concrete viaduct carrying the track out from downtown Richmond. The road used 6,600-volt AC power, one of the few General Electric AC installations. Cars carried pantographs. The project was started by George Gould, who also had an interest in Virginia Electric Power, but the road was independent of the power system. The company was caught by rising costs during World War I and was liquidated in 1918. However, a new enterprise, the Richmond–Ashland

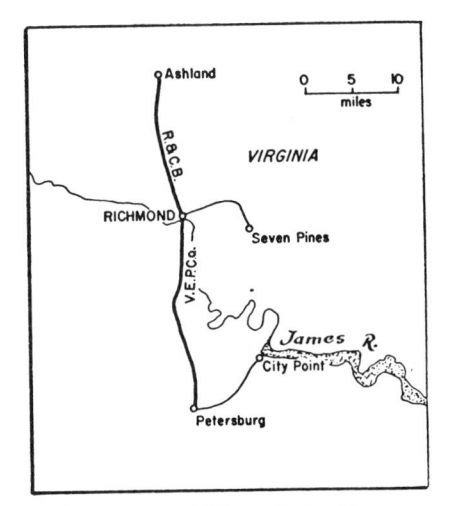

R&CB: Richmond & Chesapeake Bay Ry.
VEPCo.: Virginia Elec. Power Co.

Railway, was established, and operations were resumed, after conversion to DC. The new company did surprisingly well, considering the limited traffic possibilities, and continued to operate until 1938, two years after the much more important line to Petersburg was gone.

*

Virginia had a few other lines that might be classed as interurbans. A 9-mile line extended from Petersburg to Hopewell and City Point, built at the relatively late date of 1916, abandoned after only a few years, and then reorganized and operated until 1940. The Richmond and Rappahannock extended from Richmond to Cold Harbor. The Norfolk Southern, a railroad, operated 48 miles of electrified trackage, making a loop from Norfolk to Virginia Beach and back to Norfolk, serving the important resort area of Virginia Beach and nearby points. This operation was converted to gasoline rail-bus service in 1935, which was provided until all passenger service on the line was abandoned, November 8, 1947.

THE DEEP SOUTH

The Deep South had one major system, the Piedmont and Northern (in the Carolinas) plus a very few scattered lines.

PIEDMONT AND NORTHERN RAILWAY[28]

Although scarcely a typical interurban because of its heavy reliance on freight from the beginning, Piedmont and Northern was the most successful, financially, of all intercity electric railway projects. The system was a project of James B. Duke of the famous tobacco family of North Carolina, who developed the line between 1910 and 1916. The system consists of two disconnected lines. The southern, and longer, line extended 89 miles from Greenwood to Spartanburg, South Carolina, together with a 12-mile branch from Belton to Anderson, which was the first segment built, completed in 1910 by the Anderson street railway system. The main line, built as the Greenville Spartanburg and Anderson, was completed from Greenwood to Greenville in November 1912, and to Spartanburg in April 1914. The northern line, originally the Piedmont Traction Company, which extended westward 24 miles from Charlotte to Gastonia, in the North Carolina textile country, was completed on July 3, 1912. The 3-mile Belmont branch off of this line was completed in 1916. The two companies were merged in 1914 under the management of Edgar Thomason.

This was one of the early 1,500-volt DC systems, built to steamrailroad standards on private right-of-way, except for some street running in the cities. Heavy steel passenger equipment was used, often run in multiple units and in some cases drawn by electric locomotives, but trains did not operate with high frequency. Stress was placed on carload interchange freight business, and from the earliest days freight revenue exceeded passenger revenue. The road had been originally projected from Durham to Greenwood (320 miles), and after a delay caused by the war, the road began in the mid-twenties to fill the 51-mile gap between its two segments, together with a line from Charlotte to Winston Salem (72 miles), which would have completed a new north-south route in connection with the Norfolk Western and the Georgia Florida. As noted in Chapter 5, the I.C.C. denied permission to build.

During the late twenties the automobile drastically cut into passenger revenue, although a reduction in passenger rates from 3 cents per mile to 1 cent per mile resulted in a tenfold increase in passenger traffic. Passenger service with a few trains a day continued on down through the forties (except on the Belmont and Anderson lines, on which service was discontinued in 1932 and 1938), but by 1950 total passenger revenue was only $24,000, out of $5 million gross. Finally, in 1951, the passenger service was discontinued (February 28 on the northern division, October

THE CAROLINAS

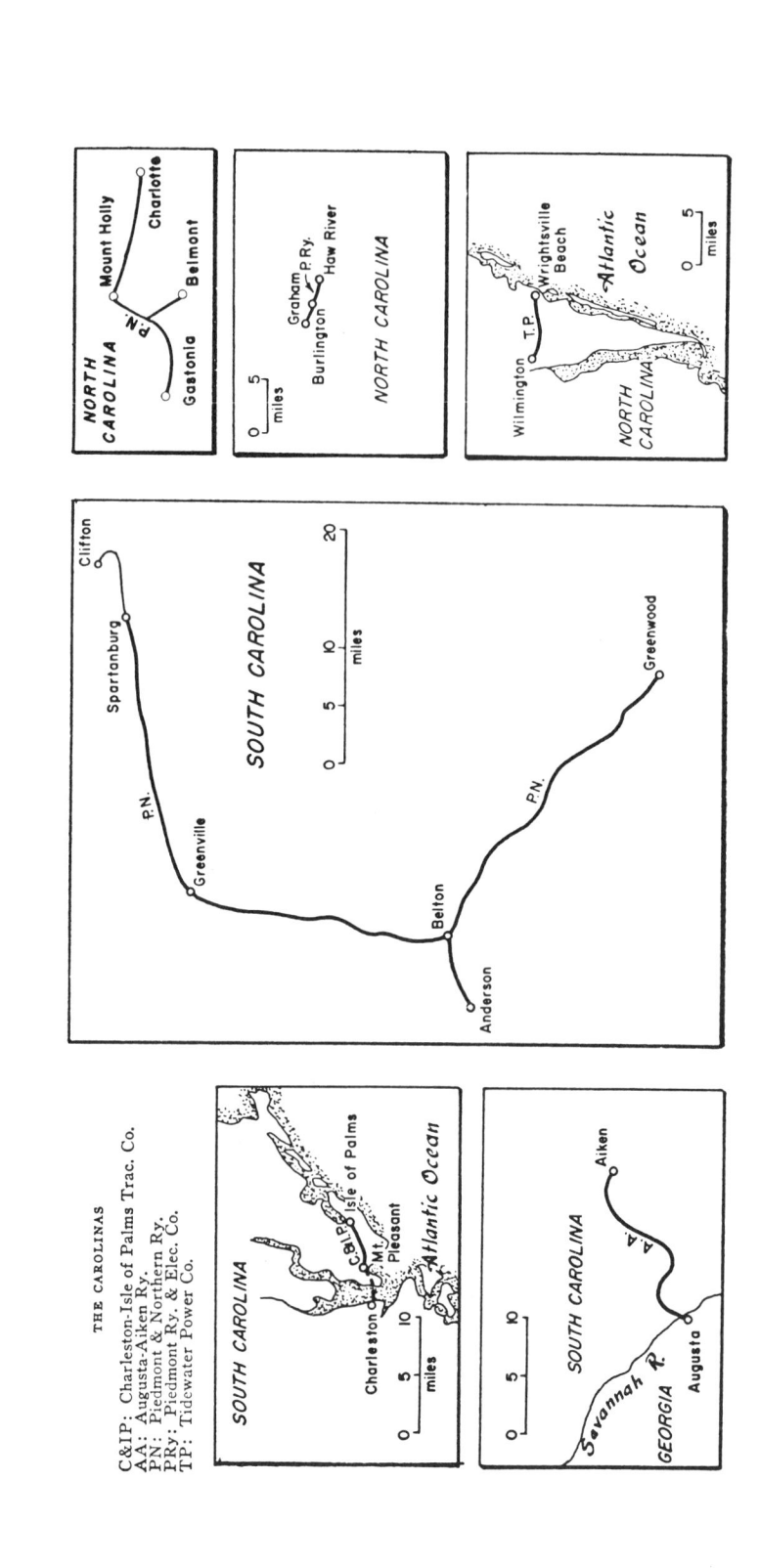

C&IP: Charleston-Isle of Palms Trac. Co.
AA: Augusta-Aiken Ry.
PN: Piedmont & Northern Ry.
PRy: Piedmont Ry. & Elec. Co.
TP: Tidewater Power Co.

31 on the southern). But the road continues as an important and profitable freight operation, still owned, as it has been from the beginning, by the Duke family and their associates. Dieselization began in 1950 and was completed in 1954.

AUGUSTA–AIKEN RAILWAY[29]

The Deep South had one interurban typical of the Midwestern variety, namely the 26-mile Augusta–Aiken Railway, a subsidiary of the Georgia–Carolina Power Company, which connected the two cities of the corporate name, most of the trackage being in South Carolina. The company also operated the Augusta city lines and a park at Lake Olmstead. The road, opened September 8, 1902, was a private right-of-way operation, built to typical standards of the 1900 period as the Augusta and Columbia Railway Company (the Augusta–Aiken after 1911), by interests seeking to develop land in the area served. The decline followed the typical pattern, with abandonment in 1929.

CHARLESTON–ISLE OF PALMS TRACTION COMPANY

This road operated 10 miles of line, from Mt. Pleasant, South Carolina, where it connected with a ferry operated by the company, to Isle of Palms, north of Charleston. Prior to 1913 the line was the Seashore division of Charleston Consolidated Railway, Gas, and Electric Company, opened in August, 1898. The company entered receivership in 1924 and was abandoned in 1925.

PIEDMONT RAILWAY AND ELECTRIC COMPANY

An 8-mile line from Burlington to Haw River in North Carolina, this road was completed on October 1, 1911, and abandoned in 1928.

TIDEWATER POWER COMPANY

The Tidewater Power Company, which operated the Wilmington (North Carolina) street railway system, also built a 15-mile interurban line from Wilmington to Wrightsville and Wrightsville Beach, largely to carry holiday traffic to the beaches. It was completed in 1902, and operated until April 1940. The system was an Insull property for a time. The beach resort was widely publicized, and the line hauled Pullmans to the beach resort from connecting steam roads.

GEORGIA RAILWAY AND POWER COMPANY

Two long electric suburban lines extended outward from Atlanta, with operating standards that qualify them as interurbans. Both used private right-of-way outside of the city, and high-speed interurban-type cars, in later years many of them acquired from other roads. Both were subsidiaries of Georgia Railway and Power Company, which supplied Atlanta with street railway and power service.

One, a 16-mile line known as the Atlanta Northern, extended northward from Atlanta to Marietta, using 3 miles of street railway track. The line was placed in operation on July 17, 1905, and developed a heavy volume of suburban traffic. It survived the coming of the automobile and the depression, but was abandoned in 1947 during the conversion of the Atlanta street railway system to buses.

The parent company operated the other interurban, 16 miles from Atlanta eastward to Hopewell and Stone Mountain, under its own name. This route was placed in service in November 1913, and was also abandoned in 1947.

A third line, more typically suburban, extended westward from Atlanta to Fairburn, built as the Fairburn and Atlanta. About half of the line, to College Park, was strictly a streetcar operation.

THE BIRMINGHAM SUBURBAN LINES

The states of Florida and Alabama had no lines that could be called interurbans, although there were some short intercity routes, one of which, from Tuscaloosa to Holt, handled considerable carload freight business. Three suburban car lines operated out of Birmingham, all terminating in Bessemer. Two of these were built shortly after 1900, the last in 1912. The last lines were replaced by buses in 1952.

GULFPORT AND MISSISSIPPI COAST TRACTION COMPANY

This interurban operated a line built to relatively high standards along the Mississippi coast, very close to the beach, extending eastward from Gulfport to Biloxi (13 miles, completed in 1906) and westward from Gulfport to Pass Christian (11 miles, built in 1907). The area was thickly settled, and a substantial passenger service devel-

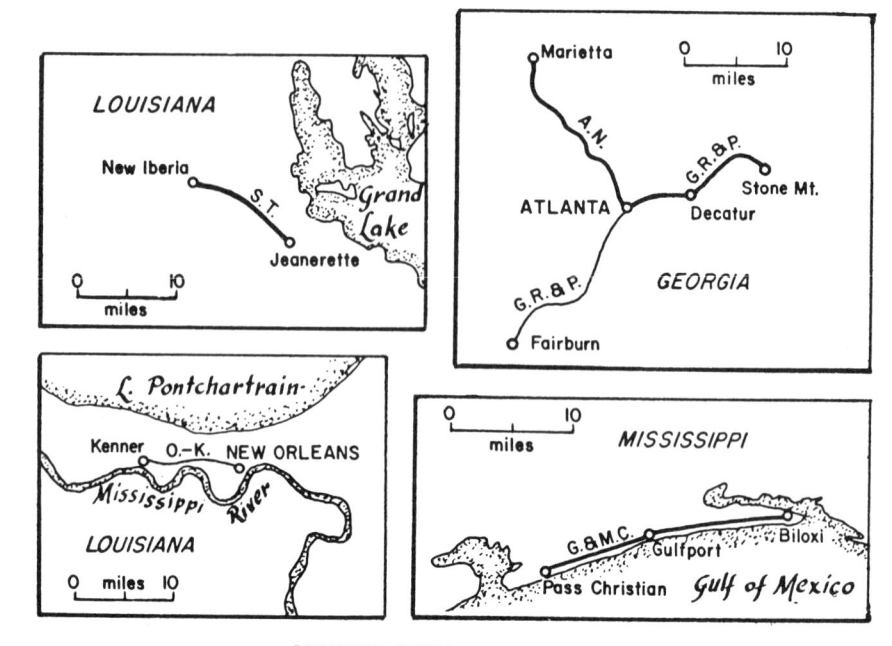

LOUISIANA, GEORGIA, AND MISSISSIPPI

ST: Southwestern Trac. Co.
O-K: Orleans-Kenner Elec. Ry.
AN: Atlanta Northern Ry.
GR&P: Georgia Ry. & Power Co.
G&MC: Gulfport & Mississippi Coast Trac. Co.

oped, as well as some freight carload switching service. But the development of the automobile resulted in the abandonment of passenger service in 1926. Portions of the track were continued in operation for many years for carload freight service. The line was a subsidiary of Mississippi Power Company.

ORLEANS–KENNER ELECTRIC RAILWAY

New Orleans had only one intercity electric line, the Orleans–Kenner, which extended on a private right-of-way along the Mississippi on the north side from the city to the suburb of Kenner. The road was not completed until late in 1914. It was ultimately operated by the New Orleans Public Service Company. All service came to an end in 1930.

SOUTHWESTERN TRACTION COMPANY

This line extended from New Iberia to Jeanerette (12 miles, completed in 1912). Service was discontinued in 1918, but the line was not dismantled until the mid-twenties. See p. 426 for another Louisiana line.

TENNESSEE

Tennessee had two true interurban lines, plus one that was little more than a suburban operation. Both interurbans operated out of Nashville.

NASHVILLE–GALLATIN INTERURBAN RAILWAY

In 1913 a 27-mile interurban was built northeastward from Nashville to Gallatin, using street railway tracks to enter the former city. The road passed through receivership in 1917 and was reorganized as the Union Traction Company of Tennessee. The earnings record in the twenties was fairly good, but automobile use took away enough business so that abandonment occurred in 1932.

NASHVILLE–FRANKLIN RAILWAY

The line, originally the Nashville Interurban Railway Company, was completed in 1909 between Nashville and Franklin, 19 miles. In 1933 it was reorganized with the name of Nashville–Franklin. In 1922 the road leased the 43-mile Middle Tennessee Railway from Franklin to Mt. Pleasant, and operated it until 1928 with gas-electric cars. The interurban eventually acquired a few Cincinnati lightweight cars secondhand, and managed to retain enough freight and passenger business to continue through the thirties. In 1940 passenger service ended when the Nashville streetcars were discontinued, and on February 4, 1943, the Interstate Commerce Commission authorized abandonment, which followed immediately.

MEMPHIS AND LAKEVIEW TRACTION COMPANY

A 12-mile line extended southward from Memphis to Lakeview, Mississippi. This was originally the Lakeview Traction Company, which passed into the hands of the Memphis Street Railway Company in 1913, and was renamed the Memphis and Lakeview. It was abandoned on April 30, 1928, after 5 years of losses. The road was the first link in a long-projected interurban to Clarksdale, Mississippi, but the remainder was never built.

N-F: Nashville-Franklin Ry. (Nashville Interurban Ry.)

N-G: Nashville-Gallatin Interurban Ry. (Union Trac. of Tennessee)

Illinois

ILLINOIS RANKED fourth in interurban mileage, with a total of 1,422 miles of line.[30] The state contained the largest single truly interurban system that remained under one management over a long period of years (the Illinois Traction), as well as some of the highest traffic density lines. But it also had an unusually large number of small disconnected roads, far more than had Ohio or Indiana. The two big networks in the state, one in the Chicago area, and the other the mid-state system, were themselves never connected, and the mid-state system was not joined with the Indiana lines, although the gap between them was only twenty miles. The Chicago area roads were joined to the great Indiana-Ohio network only by the roundabout route of the Winona. These gaps, more notable than any in the states to the east, were partly due to the location of population centers, particularly to the fact that Chicago, unlike Indianapolis and Columbus, was not in the center of its state, and thus lines could not radiate out from it in all directions to reach a large number of cities.

The larger Illinois lines demonstrated a much greater vitality than their neighbors to the east. One factor was the high degree of traffic density of the Chicago area roads that reached the Loop, and their lesser vulnerability to auto competition because of their greater potential speed. The other primary reason was the fact that from early years the big Illinois Traction system had succeeded in building up a large carload freight interchange business with the steam roads. Otherwise, the Illinois interurbans trod the same path to abandonment as their neighbors, although the pace was slowed down a little in some instances by the more restrictive policy of the Illinois utilities commission, which checked the development of bus competition.

THE CHICAGO AREA HIGH-SPEED ROUTES

CHICAGO NORTH SHORE AND MILWAUKEE RAILWAY[31]

The North Shore began in 1895 as the Bluff City Electric Interurban Street Railway (successor to the Waukegan and North Shore Transit, chartered in 1891), which in 1895 completed a short line from downtown Waukegan to 10th Street in North Chicago. In 1896 this was pushed south to 22d Street, and in 1898, 9 miles were built to Highland Park—disconnected from the first section by the Northwestern tracks—and the company was reorganized as the Chicago and Milwaukee Electric Railroad, in recognition of its enlarged ambitions. A year later a 10-mile line from Highland Park to Evanston was completed. A subway was built under the Northwestern and through service was opened from Waukegan to Evanston on August 6, 1899, the southernmost section being on Milwaukee tracks. In 1902 a branch was built westward from Lake Bluff to Libertyville (6 miles), opened for service on August 30, 1903, and extended to what is now Mundelein in 1905. Also in this year the northward extension was begun from Lake Bluff. In September 1906 service was established to Racine, and by 1907 the tracks reached Milwaukee. But the panic of that year forced the road into bankruptcy, and not until November 3, 1908, was the line actually completed and service established to Milwaukee.

Excessive debt brought bankruptcy in 1908; in 1916 the reorganization was completed under Insull ownership, and the road became the Chicago North Shore and Milwaukee. An entrance into downtown Chicago was urgently needed, and was obtained via operating rights over the Milwaukee road and the Chicago Elevated system to the Loop; through service began on August 6, 1919. The next improvement was to build a cutoff via the Skokie valley from Howard Street to North Chicago Junction to eliminate street running; the new service opened on June 5, 1926. The shore line was thereafter used only for local service.

The later years of the twenties were relatively profitable ones, the high-speed service minimizing the effects of bus and car competition. But the margin over fixed charges was slight, and the depression soon brought bankruptcy and the collapse of the Insull empire. The road covered operating expenses, and in 1946 a plan of reorganization was finally worked out, which involved the elimination of most of the debt. In 1941 two new streamlined articulated trains were bought, but a series of strikes in the forties severely injured the road.

After completion of the Skokie line in 1926, the road consisted of a high-speed, 74-mile main line from Howard Street via the new line to Milwaukee, a 23-mile local line from the Loop to Waukegan via the elevated tracks and Wilmette, and a 9-mile branch from Lake Bluff to Mundelein. The shore line handled a heavy local commuter traffic. The main-line traffic consisted of extensive commuter traffic and some through business, with military traffic important after 1940. Service was typically hourly. Freight operations, which never yielded more than 25 per cent of revenues, and in later years only 15 per cent, were largely confined to switching operations to on-line plants. The high ratio of passenger revenue squeezed the road severely after 1950, as wages continued to rise.

The weakest link in the system was the shore line, with short-distance traffic, problems of heavy peak loads, and excessive manpower requirements under union agreements. The original request to abandon in 1949 was denied, but a renewed request was granted in 1955, and service on this line came to an end in that year, track north of Highland Park being retained for freight service, and for access to the Highwood shop. However, operating losses continued, and in May of 1958 the company applied for complete abandonment of the whole system. In November 1959 the ICC examiner recommended approval of abandonment, but the Illinois Commerce Commission rejected the request. After a lengthy legal battle the road was abandoned on January 21, 1963.

The road was a pioneer not only in offering passenger service at very high speeds, but in providing dining-car service, and in introducing bus operation, which spread as far as Rockford. The line also pioneered piggyback freight service in the twenties, and introduced joint air-rail service in the same period with the air lines operating out of Chicago.

CHICAGO AURORA AND ELGIN RAILWAY
(AURORA ELGIN AND CHICAGO)

The second of the Chicago area lines that had high-speed routes into the Loop was the Chicago Aurora and Elgin. This road was built as the Aurora Elgin and Chicago shortly after 1900 by the Pomeroy-Mandelbaum syndicate of Cleveland, which had developed a number of the Ohio roads. The suburban area west of Chicago, including the Fox River Valley, was a natural setting for interurban building. In 1902 service was established from Laramie Avenue in Chicago through Wheaton to Aurora and Batavia. In the following year a branch was built from Wheaton to Elgin. In 1907 a spur was built from the Elgin line into Geneva, and service extended to St. Charles on Fox River trackage. Trackage rights over the elevated lines into Chicago were obtained in 1905. In 1906 the Fox River lines and the local lines in Aurora and Elgin were absorbed into the AE&C. The completed system totaled 61 miles of line, much of it double-track.

In 1919 the road passed into receivership, was reorganized under control of the bondholders in 1922, and renamed the Chicago Aurora and Elgin. The bonds were held largely in Philadelphia, and the bondholders sent Dr. Thomas Conway, Jr., to take charge of the reorganized line. Under Conway's direction track was rebuilt, new equipment obtained, and service greatly improved. In 1925 the road was sold to Samuel Insull, who was then building his great traction and power empire in the Chicago area. At the time of reorganization the Fox River lines were permanently divorced from the CA&E.

Except for the improvements made under the Conway regime and for increases in speed, the road operated in much the same fashion for more than forty years. Half-hourly service on the main line was typical, with alternate trains going beyond Wheaton. There were additional rush-hour trains. Wheaton was the center of operations; hourly limited trains operated between Chicago and Wheaton as a unit, and then divided into various branches. The trains terminated at Wells Street on the Loop, not actually going around the Loop. Freight motors handled the relatively limited freight service; the road, like the North Shore, was never able to develop much freight volume in an area blanketed by steam-road trackage. The road operated with third rail, and 650-volt DC. A portion of its trackage was used by the Chicago Elevated system.

As was typical with the heavy-traffic, suburban type of operation, the CA&E suffered from a relatively high operating ratio. But nevertheless it was able to earn a reasonably satisfactory return on investment rather consistently, and was not plagued by overindebtedness and long periods of receivership as was the North Shore. Its high-speed entrance into Chicago and private-right-of-way operation, plus the rapid growth of the west-side suburban area, protected it from the impact of the growth of the auto and the bus that destroyed the typical interurban. But despite its stable and heavy traffic, the road found it increasingly difficult to meet its expenses after World War II, as labor costs rose more than fares could be increased, and business became more heavily concentrated in peak hours. Nevertheless some new equipment was ordered in 1941 (delivered in 1945), and tracks were maintained to high standards.

The blow that finally destroyed the CA&E was the building of the west side superhighway into Chicago. The highway had been designed with tracks in the center for rapid-transit operation, and plans called for operation of the CA&E over them; certainly the governments involved had no intention of running the railway out of business. But during the several years of construction the line chose to terminate its trains in the outskirts of the city, as it regarded street operation, proposed by the city for the interval while the subway line was being built in place of the old "L" line, as too hazardous, although it had operated on the streets elsewhere. The result was drastic loss in passenger business, and in 1956 the company petitioned to abandon service.

The communities involved protested strongly, and a number of efforts were made by city and state officials to develop some plan, perhaps involving government operation, to keep the service going. When nothing was accomplished, and after several postponements, all service stopped in June 1957, leaving a large number of commuters to find other means of transport. However, plans for resuming operation by a Transit Authority were authorized by the Illinois legislature in 1959, and were still under consideration at the end of 1959. The road continued its limited freight operations for a time, but these too were discontinued, in the summer of 1959. Prior to 1957 only two abandonments had occurred, that of the light-traffic Geneva Junction–St. Charles line, which had been replaced by bus operation in 1937, and the Bellwood–Mt. Carmel suburban branch.

CHICAGO SOUTH SHORE AND
SOUTH BEND RAILROAD[32]

The most successful of the Chicago area roads in its later history is the South Shore line, extending 90 miles from Randolph Street in Chicago to South Bend, Indiana, using Illinois Central electric-line trackage from Randolph Street to Kensington. One of the ironies of the industry is the fact that for many years the South Shore was one of the weakest interurbans and was close to abandonment in 1925—yet it will almost certainly outlive all the other firms in the industry. Today it resembles electrified main-line suburban service; however, the portion of the line between Michigan City and South Bend retains many of the characteristics of the old-time interurban operation.

The line was incorporated in 1901 as the Chicago and Indiana Air Line, promoted by a Cleveland syndicate headed by J. B. Hanna, and constructed during 1907 and 1908 by J. G. White and Co., with service opened to South Bend in 1909. This was the period in which a number of companies were lured by the apparent advantages of high-voltage single-phase AC operation, and the road adopted this in preference to

DC, using 6,600 volts in the country and 800 volts (as required by franchises for safety purposes) in Gary, Michigan City, and South Bend. Consequently, five trolley changes were necessary en route to South Bend, as well as the use of both trolley and pantograph. To avoid turning the cars, the pantograph was placed in the center, with trolley poles on each end. The cars were of typical railroad-roof design, capable of multiple unit operation. The track terminated at Kensington, where connection was made with Illinois Central steam suburban trains for downtown Chicago, eventually with trailer cars attached to the steam trains for through service. The company's original name was changed to the Chicago Lake Shore and South Bend before its operations began.

The line was one of the most unprofitable of all the interurbans; in 1914, for example, when most lines were doing comparatively well, the road was earning less than 1 per cent on its investment. By the end of World War I it was in receivership, and was barely covering operating expenses. When the road was offered for sale in 1925, Insull purchased the road, barely outbidding a junk dealer who planned to scrap it. There were several difficulties—the unsatisfactory AC operation, the lack of an entrance into Chicago, and the competition of the old and powerful Northern Indiana and its affiliates.

Immediate and drastic changes were made by the new management, under the direct supervision of Insull's son, Samuel Jr. First came a new name, the Chicago South Shore and South Bend. Then the line was rebuilt, with additional doubletracking, and all new passenger equipment (68 steel cars) was purchased to replace the old wooden cars. At the same time the AC system was abandoned and replaced by a modern 1,500-volt DC system. The most important change, however, was the gaining of trackage rights over the newly electrified Illinois Central suburban trackage to downtown Chicago, giving the road a more satisfactory high-speed entrance to the Loop than that of either the North Shore or the Chicago Aurora and Elgin. The result was a spectacular fourfold increase in operating revenue between 1924 and 1930, and the conversion of a deficit into a $700,000 operating profit. The road was able to pay dividends through the first years of the depression. But the effects of the depression and the collapse of the Insull empire brought the road into receivership in 1933. Jay Samuel Hartt became receiver, representing the bondholders, and after reorganization in 1938, became the president of the new road.

There has been no change in ownership or management since 1938.

Recovery aided the road materially, as did expansion of the East Chicago-Gary industrial area. In the postwar period, the road's passenger operations were inevitably squeezed by the wage-fare relationship, but this was offset in part by continually increasing commuter business. For many years about half the road's revenue has come from passenger service, about half from freight. In 1956 the road netted over $1 million before taxes, more than the gross revenue of 1925.

In September 1956 the line placed in service a new 6-mile cutoff replacing the very troublesome street running in East Chicago that had plagued it for years.

In 1960 service on the line was much the same as it was in the late twenties, with higher speeds and somewhat more frequent service from Chicago to Gary. Twenty trains a day each way were operated for the full 90 miles to South Bend, or roughly on an hourly basis, with 34 trains each way to Gary. About 10,000 passengers were handled on weekdays. Cars were capable of speeds up to 79 miles an hour. Extensive freight service was provided, with trains up to 70 cars. The largest electric motors were three 800-class units acquired in 1949 from a group originally built for the USSR. A very large part of the traffic consisted of commuters from the south-side suburbs bound for Chicago, and others going to various industries in the towns along the south end of the lake. Freight traffic was highly diversified, although there was a substantial volume of coal. The road maintained joint freight and passenger rates with steam routes, with through tickets and joint billing.

OTHER CHICAGO AREA ROADS

CHICAGO AND SOUTHERN TRACTION COMPANY

This road completed its line from 79th and Halsted streets to Kankakee (54 miles) on October 5, 1907; the original segments had been built to Blue Island in 1897 and to Harvey in 1899 as a storage-battery line, and were electrified in 1901. The road was planned as a link in a system to St. Louis. In 1911 the company was reorganized as the Chicago and Interurban Traction (the local lines in Chicago being transferred to the city system) under Insull control. Large wooden cars operated on 90-minute schedules from 63d and Halsted to downtown Kankakee, reached over streetcar tracks.

The line suffered from its lack of a high-speed entrance into Chicago, and from the inadequate population in the area south of Crete; the small profits of the period before World War I gave way to operating deficits by 1921, after a highway had been built to Kankakee. The final blow was struck by the Illinois Central electrification, and the line was abandoned on April 23, 1927.

CHICAGO AND JOLIET ELECTRIC RAILWAY

The Chicago and Joliet also lacked a high-speed entrance into Chicago, but it served a more populous area than the Kankakee line, and hence lasted six years longer. This was one of the earliest interurbans, an outgrowth of the Joliet street railway system. The latter was taken over by the American Railways Company of Philadelphia, which built the interurban line northward to Lemont in 1900 and on to Chicago in 1901, service being opened on September 25. The line paralleled the Illinois River, extending from downtown Joliet (reached via streetcar tracks) to Archer and Cicero avenues in Chicago, where a connection was made with city cars. The property passed into Insull hands in 1915 and became a subsidiary of Central Illinois Public Service.

Cars were operated in single units, usually at hourly intervals. The road was among the first to use simple arched-roof cars (1911), and later acquired a group of lightweight cars (1927). Despite the substantial cost reduction gained from the new equipment, which helped to maintain a good rate of profit in the late twenties, the road was hit very hard by the depression, losing half of its revenue between 1929 and 1932, and was abandoned, November 16, 1933, after two years of deficits.

CHICAGO OTTAWA AND PEORIA RAILWAY (CHICAGO AND ILLINOIS VALLEY)

One of the longest lines in the state was the "Illini Trail," which extended westward down the Illinois Valley north of the river from Joliet to Princeton, with branches to Ladd and Streator. It was planned as a link in a Chicago–Peoria–St. Louis system, but the link from Streator to Mackinaw Junction was never closed.

The line was built piecemeal, starting from the relatively thickly settled area in the center of the system, with several separate companies involved. In 1902 the first segment was built from Ottawa through Spring Valley to Ladd (Illinois Valley Traction Company; after 1904 the Illinois Valley Railway), and the section eastward from Ottawa to Marseilles was completed in the same year. Then, under McKinley control, extensions were pushed westward from Marquette to Princeton and eastward from Marseilles to Seneca in 1906. A year later the western line reached Princeton. Known as the Chicago Ottawa and Peoria after 1908, the line reached Morris in 1909 and, finally, Joliet in 1912. The Streator line, begun by a separate company in 1906, was finished in 1908. After 1923 the road became the Illinois Valley Division of the Illinois Traction.

After 1924, the line operated relatively lightweight equipment compared to that of the parent company, and only a limited amount of freight service was ever developed. Service was hourly out of Joliet, the trains alternating beyond Spring Valley to Ladd and to Princeton, with two-hour service to Streator. The passenger service connected at Joliet with the Chicago and Joliet.

The contraction of the CO&P came slowly. First to go was part of the original line, the Spring Valley–Ladd branch, in 1924. In 1929 the Streator branch was cut off, as was the main line beyond Depue to Princeton. In the same year the company was reorganized as the Chicago and Illinois Valley Railroad, and in 1930 a belt line was completed around Ottawa. But the depression was too much for the road, and the entire line was abandoned, May 13, 1934. Considerable CO&P equipment went to the Illinois Traction for branch and suburban services.

JOLIET PLAINFIELD AND AURORA RAILROAD (JOLIET AND SOUTHERN; AURORA PLAINFIELD AND JOLIET)

The JP&A was an element in a semicircle around Chicago from Chicago Heights to Carpentersville, made up of a number of roads. The JP&A, which connected Joliet and Aurora, was a Fisher road, developed by the Fisher Construction Co., which had built a number of Ohio lines, including Columbus Delaware and Marion. The Joliet–Plainfield segment was opened for traffic on December 7, 1903, and the remaining segment to Aurora on October 22, 1904. About half of the 20-mile line was on a private right-of-way, the other half on highway property. Downtown Joliet was originally reached by street railway tracks, and later by the company's own line. The road used typically interurban equipment; the railroad roofs in some cases were later replaced by standard arched roofs. The road acquired the famous parlor car Louisiana, which was later destroyed by fire.

WISCONSIN
To Janesville
Beloit
Fontana
Harvard
C.H.&G.L.
To Milwaukee
Zion
Waukegan
N. Chicago
Mundelein
Freeport
R.&I.
Belvidere
Marengo
ROCKFORD
E.&B.
W.&S.
A.E.&F.R.
Carpenters-ville
Elgin
Sycamore
St. Charles
C.A.&E.
C.N.S.&M.
D.S.
De Kalb
C.A.&D.
Geneva
Wheaton
CHICAGO
IOWA
Dixon
S.D.&E.
Sterling
Middlebury
L.C.C.
Amboy
Lee Center
Batavia
Aurora
C.&J.E.
C.S.S.&S.B.
Yorkville
To South Bend
Harvey
A.P.&J.
F.&I.U.R.
J.&E.T.
Joliet
Chicago Hts.
Davenport
Rock Island
Sherrard
Cable
Aledo
Kewanee
K.&G.
Galva
Alexis
R.I.S.
Princeton
Ladd
La Salle
Ottawa
Bureau
Peru
C.&I.V.
Morris
C.&I.T.
Streator
Dwight
B.P.&J.
Pontiac
Kankakee
INDIANA
Monmouth
Galesburg
P.T.
Abingdon
Farmington
Fairview
Norris
I.C.E.
Canton
Lewiston
PEORIA
P.P.T.
Pekin
I.T.S.
Bloomington
Keokuk
K.E.
Hamilton
Warsaw
Paxton
K.&U.
Lincoln
Clinton
Champaign
Urbana
Danville
Homer
Catlin
Ridge Farm
Springfield
Mechanicsburg
Decatur
Rochester
S.C.L.&R.
Paris
To Indianapolis
T.H.I.&E.
Terre Haute
Charleston
C.I.T.
Mattoon
Mississippi River
Sante Fe
M.
Mexico
Carlinville
Hillsboro
Jerseyville
A.&J.
Staunton
Alton
A.G.&S.L.
Florrisant
St. Charles
Edwardsville
E. St. Louis
Missouri River
ST. LOUIS
Lebanon
E.S.L.&S.
S.L.&B.
Belleville
Meramac Highlands
Waterloo
E.S.L.C.&W.
ILLINOIS
Centralia
MISSOURI
Flat River
S.F.C.
Farmington
De Lassus
Murphysboro
C.&E.
Herrin
Carterville
Marion
M.&S.I.
Carbondale
Eldorado
S.I.R.&P.
Harrisburg
Carrier Mills
Ohio River
Anna
Jonesboro
20 0 20 40
miles
C.&S.L.
Mounds
Cairo

Illinois

The company went through several reorganizations. In 1907 the line was purchased by the newly incorporated Joliet and Southern (*q.v.*), which had plans for an extensive network of lines designed to connect Chicago with St. Louis, including the Bloomington Pontiac and Joliet. All that was ever built was the line to Chicago Heights. After the J&S went into receivership in 1914, the JP&A became the Aurora Plainfield and Joliet, separate from the Chicago Heights line. The road had enjoyed more or less typical interurban profits prior to 1912, but even as early as 1914 it was showing only a 2 per cent return, and a high operating ratio. The coming of the automobile quickly converted the small profit to losses, and the road ceased operations on September 1, 1924, thus becoming one of the first lines in Illinois to be abandoned.

ILLINOIS

CNS&M: Chicago North Shore & Milwaukee Ry.
CA&E: Chicago Aurora & Elgin Ry.
CSS&SB: Chicago South Shore & South Bend RR
C&IT: Chicago & Interurban Trac. Co.
C&JE: Chicago & Joliet Elec. Ry.
C&IV: Chicago & Illinois Valley Ry. (Chicago Ottawa & Peoria Ry.)
AP&J: Aurora Plainfield & Joliet Ry. (Joliet Plainfield & Aurora RR)
J&ET: Joliet & Eastern Trac. Co.
AE&FR: Aurora Elgin & Fox River Elec. Ry.
CH&GL: Chicago Harvard & Geneva Lake Ry.
CA&D: Chicago Aurora & De Kalb RR
DS: De Kalb-Sycamore & Interurban Trac. Co.
F&IUR: Fox & Illinois Union Ry.
E&B: Elgin & Belvidere Elec. Ry.
R&I: Rockford & Interurban Ry.
LCC: Lee County Central Elec. Ry.
SD&E: Sterling Dixon & Eastern Trac. Co.
K&G: Kewaunee & Galva Ry.
RIS: Rock Island Southern Ry.
PT: Peoples' Traction Co.
KE: Keokuk Elec. Co.
PPT: Peoria & Pekin Terminal Co.
ICE: Illinois Central Elec. Ry.
BP&J: Bloomington Pontiac & Joliet Elec. Ry.
SCL&R: Springfield Clear Lake & Rochester Ry.
ITS: Illinois Traction system (Illinois Terminal RR)
K&U: Kankakee & Urbana Trac. Co.
ESL&S: East St. Louis & Suburban Ry.
SL&B: St. Louis & Belleville Elec. Ry.
A&J: Alton Jacksonville & Peoria Ry.
AG&SL: Alton Granite & St. Louis Ry.
ESLC&W: East St. Louis Columbia & Waterloo Ry.
CBE: Coal Belt Elec. Ry.
CIT: Central Illinois Trac. Co.
M&SI: Murphysboro & Southern Illinois Ry.
SIR&P: Southern Illinois Ry. & Power Co.
C&SL: Cairo & St. Louis Ry.
THI&E: Terre Haute Indianapolis & Eastern Ry.
W&S: Woodstock & Sycamore Trac. Co. (never electrified)

EASTERN MISSOURI

SFC: St. Francois County RR
M: Mexico Investment & Construction Co.

JOLIET AND EASTERN TRACTION COMPANY

One of the weakest of all Illinois interurbans was the 20-mile Joliet and Eastern, the easternmost link in the arc route around Chicago. It was built in 1909 as a portion of the Joliet and Southern and operated as a constituent part of that road until the receivership of 1914. It was a side-of-the-road operation to New Lenox from Joliet, then a private-right-of-way line via Matteson to Chicago Heights, entering the town on the tracks of the local street railway. This line served a thinly populated area, and ran opposite to main flows of traffic; rarely did it operate cars more frequently than on 90-minute intervals. The development of the automobile quickly brought the road to the point of operating losses. The decision to abandon was made in 1923, directly prompted by the Illinois Central grade-separation project at Matteson, which necessitated major changes in the J&E's bridge-crossing of the Michigan Central at that point. The owners concluded that the expenditure was not justified, and the road was torn up. Two cars went to the Sand Springs, in Oklahoma.

AURORA ELGIN AND FOX RIVER ELECTRIC COMPANY

The Fox River Valley, about 35 miles west of Chicago, was built up at an early date and soon after 1900 became the western fringe of the Chicago commuting area, the towns being the termini not only of the lines of the electric Chicago Aurora and Elgin, but also of the steam commuter runs of the Burlington, the Milwaukee, and the Northwestern. It was inevitable that in time an interurban would be built north and south through these towns. The first segment, from Elgin to Carpentersville, was completed in the early nineties—one of the country's first interurbans. In July 1896 service was extended southward from Elgin to Geneva, and in 1899 the remaining link, from Aurora to Batavia, was completed. The road also operated a branch from Aurora southwest to Yorkville, completed in 1901. These lines had been largely built by local capital, the owners affiliated with the street railway systems in Elgin and Aurora. The roads were later acquired by the Pomeroy-Mandelbaum syndicate, which built the Aurora Elgin and Chicago (*q.v.*), and in 1901 were consolidated as the Elgin Aurora and Southern. In 1906 this line was merged into the Aurora Elgin and Chicago.

When the system went into bankruptcy in 1919, the CA&E divested itself of the weaker Fox Valley lines before it was rebuilt as a modern high-speed line. The separated 37-mile segment became the Aurora Elgin and Fox River. Consequently, the road never came under Insull control; it was purchased by the Western United Corporation, a Chicago holding company, which was primarily interested in natural gas enterprises, and the line was operated by Stone and Webster under contract.

The AE&FR was not a high-speed line comparable to the CA&E, although apart from street running in the towns it was built on private right-of-way. Light single-unit cars were employed, with hourly service typical, and much of the traffic was very short haul. It never developed much freight business except carload freight (mostly coal) to the Elgin state hospital.

The traffic volume was adequate to cover costs until the depression came, although the road did abandon its light-traffic line to Yorkville in 1924 (September 1) following the abandonment of the Yorkville–Morris road. The remainder of the system remained intact until a tornado struck the Dundee–Carpentersville line in 1933 and it was not rebuilt. Depression-induced traffic declines brought operating losses and the abandonment of the entire line on March 31, 1935. The property, including the city routes, was sold to the National City Lines for bus operation. The freight operation to the state hospital was retained by the new owners and later dieselized.

CHICAGO HARVARD AND GENEVA LAKE RAILWAY

In northern Illinois and southern Wisconsin, the 11-mile Chicago Harvard and Geneva Lake, although never connected with the Chicago-area electric roads, provided an important service to the Geneva Lake resort area as a connection for the Chicago & Northwestern. The road, completed on July 4, 1899, was one of the state's oldest interurbans. Its passenger business was subject to significant seasonal fluctuations, and the construction of a branch line by the Milwaukee through Walworth provided substantial competition. However, the Milwaukee line offered certain advantages, for the CH&GL was able to build up considerable carload interchange freight business with it, primarily in milk, ice for Chicago cut from Geneva Lake, and livestock.

The development of the automobile as the primary method of reaching resort areas seriously reduced the road's revenue and gave rise to operating deficits after 1928. Passenger service ended in 1930 but freight service was continued two more years, until the loss of business to trucks brought complete abandonment. For a time this road was a McKinley property.

CHICAGO AURORA AND DE KALB RAILROAD

The first significant Illinois interurban to be abandoned was the Chicago Aurora and De Kalb, extending 25 miles northwestward from a connection with the CA&E at Aurora to the town of De Kalb. It was built for gasoline motor-car operation and was electrified in 1910. Three relatively small cars of typical interurban design, patterned after the equipment of the nearby Joliet and Southern, were employed on 90-minute schedules.

The CA&D was a weak line from the beginning; the territory simply did not offer enough traffic for profitable operation. Bankruptcy in 1913 terminated in reorganization, but a second bankruptcy in 1922 resulted in the abandonment of all service on January 31, 1923.

DE KALB–SYCAMORE & INTERURBAN TRACTION COMPANY

The CA&D had one connecting line, the 8-mile De Kalb and Sycamore, a link between Sycamore and the larger road at De Kalb, opened in 1902. The equipment was essentially of the streetcar model, and most of the line operated on the side of the highway. The line controlled the De Kalb–Sycamore Power Company and with this affiliate passed into the hands of the Commonwealth Power system, which also owned the Rockford Interurban. The abandonment of the Chicago Aurora and De Kalb left the Sycamore line stranded—abandonment was inevitable and occurred on August 31, 1924.

FOX AND ILLINOIS UNION RAILWAY

Another small line that constituted an extension of the Chicago-area roads was the 20-mile Fox and Illinois Union, built in 1911, which connected the towns of Yorkville and Morris. Thus it linked the CA&E and the Chicago and Illinois Valley, forming a loop in conjunction with the C&IV and the Aurora–Plainfield line. The name of the road was derived from the two valleys served. The road had only two passenger cars, relatively large McGuire-Cummings products, which were never turned, since the road lacked wyes. Even in the best days of the line, only five trains a day were operated in each direction. The sparse passenger revenue was supplemented by the more reliable business of handling grain for five elevators on the line; this revenue kept the road operating until February 3, 1931, much longer than most of the other small, weak roads. The farm cooperative elevators then bought the line, and continued to operate it for carload freight service with the old freight motor equipped with a gasoline engine. Final abandonment occurred on October 21, 1938.

ELGIN AND BELVIDERE ELECTRIC COMPANY

Northwestward from a connection at Elgin with the CA&E extended an interurban route 78 miles long to Rockford and Freeport. The route was made up of two companies, the eastern portion being the 36-mile Elgin and Belvidere. This road was famous for the fact that it was completed and managed by Bion J. Arnold, the most distinguished city transit expert of the period between 1900 and 1925.

The road was built in 1906 to connect the Rockford lines with the Chicago area, to the standards typical of the period—relatively well graded private right-of-way in the country, and street running in Elgin (on city system tracks) and in other towns. Service began on February 2, 1907; the line had typical interurban clerestory-roof cars which ran on hourly intervals. The cars were relatively short, but occasionally operated in 2- or 3-car trains. Through service on a few limited runs a day was operated from Elgin to Rockford with the heavier cars of the Rockford system.

In 1927 the Rockford-Belvidere line of the old Rockford Interurban was merged with the E&B to form the Elgin Belvidere and Rockford. Lightweight one-man cars were borrowed from the Rockford city system and operated from Rockford through to Elgin. But the results were not financially successful, the new cars were returned to their owner, and the old E&B cars were remodeled for one-man operation.

Under the progressive Arnold management, the road was the first user of an automatic substation, and one of the few to install gasoline generators to provide electric power.

Passenger revenue per mile was never very great; the towns directly served were not large, and effective competition with the Northwestern for the Chicago–Rockford business was virtually impossible. The operating ratio was high and the rate of return rarely better than 2 per cent, even in the best years. Considerable milk and express-freight business was obtained until the coming of the motor truck, but the road never handled standard freight cars in any magnitude. The increased use of automobiles brought the road into serious financial difficulties in the late twenties, and on March 9, 1930, the company (still under Arnold ownership and management) discontinued all service. However, not until 1935 was all the track removed.

ROCKFORD AND INTERURBAN RAILWAY[33]

In northwestern Illinois the Rockford and Interurban operated 3 lines out of Rockford: (1) a 13-mile line to Belvidere, completed on November 15, 1901, as the Rockford and Belvidere, and after 1906 connecting with the Elgin and Belvidere; (2) a 28-mile line westward to Freeport, completed as the Rockford and Freeport, April 7, 1904; (3) a 34-mile line northward to Janesville (Wisconsin), completed as the Rockford Beloit and Janesville by the Newcomb-Nutt syndicate of Cleveland in 1902. The Rockford and Interurban was formed in 1902 under the control of Judge R. N. Baylies of Chicago, who had bought the old Rockford city system when it was in bankruptcy in the nineties. The R&I absorbed the city system and the Belvidere and Freeport lines, and in 1906 bought the Janesville route. The system passed into the control of the Union Railway Gas and Electric in 1909, which in turn was absorbed by Commonwealth Power.

The road was a typical interurban, built to relatively low standards, the original light rail of 1901 being used to the end of service. Hourly service out of Rockford on all lines was usual; cars reached the center of town on streetcar tracks. Most of the business was local, except on the two daily limiteds to Elgin, but even on these through business was not heavy, because of the severe competition from the steam roads. Freight was almost entirely limited to package and milk business, and was later lost to trucks.

The road had done well financially until 1917, paying regular dividends to the parent company. As automobiles developed, the business dropped rapidly and after 1918 the road was unable to meet interest payments. The parent holding company advanced it more than a million dollars between 1918 and 1925 to avoid bankruptcy. But by 1925 the road was no longer able to cover operating expenses, and the holding company finally permitted it to go into bankruptcy. The receiver appointed in

1926 sought to abandon all interurban operations at once, but this request was denied by the courts. A reorganization plan was worked out, under which the city property and each of the three interurban lines were separated, although in practice they were coordinated for operating purposes. The original names of the three interurban lines were resurrected. Technically the properties were sold to T. M. Ellis, Jr., son of the man who had headed the operations of the company for three decades, and a representative of A. E. Pierce and Co., which had bought a large proportion of the bonds.

The city company, now Rockford Public Service, bought 7 new lightweight, one-man cars, and leased them to the interurban lines, which used them from 1927 to 1930. None of the three properties was able to cover operating expenses, and business continued to drop. By 1930 it was obvious that the future was hopeless, and the tracks had deteriorated badly. The Rockford and Belvidere was abandoned on March 9, 1930, the Freeport line on September 30, 1930, and the Rockford Beloit and Janesville in two steps, the Beloit–Janesville segment in July 1929, the remainder the same date as the Freeport line. The lines were not dismantled until 1931.

LEE COUNTY CENTRAL ELECTRIC RAILWAY
(NORTHERN ILLINOIS ELECTRIC RAILWAY) [34]

The Northern Illinois Electric Railway Co. was incorporated in 1901 to build from Steward to Lee Center and Dixon. Some grading was done, but the company could not raise capital for the project, and not until 1910 was construction actually started. Construction involved a much more restricted project, primarily one to connect the pioneer town of Lee Center, which had no railroad, with nearby towns. The promoter was George H. T. Shaw, a railroad construction engineer, whose home was Lee Center. Service was opened from Lee Center to Amboy (5 miles) on December 10, 1910, with a second-hand streetcar. In 1911 a large car was obtained from Kentucky Railway and Terminal Company of Louisville, but the road lacked sufficient power to operate it satisfactorily. Likewise inadequate power prevented the handling of freight cars by electricity, and a series of ancient steam locomotives was used until the twenties when a Whitcomb gasoline locomotive was acquired. In 1912, 7 miles of additional line from Lee Center to a point called Middlebury (which consisted of an elevator and a schoolhouse) were placed in operation. For the next several years three trips a day were operated, some of the runs going beyond Lee Center "if there were passengers," according to the timetable.

The road went into bankruptcy in 1913 and was reorganized the following year as the Lee County Central Electric Railway. Passenger service was discontinued in 1915, and the trolley wires removed in 1916. But the road had developed considerable carload freight traffic in grain, interchanged with the Burlington at Binghampton, and its freight operations continued. The road deteriorated badly, and in the thirties the section east of Lee Center was abandoned; the service was so bad that the elevators had given up trying to use this section of the line. Finally in 1946 the road was purchased by the Lee County Grain Association, which has maintained the portion from Lee Center to Binghampton in good enough condition to allow the movement of grain cars. The road still operated in 1960; one of the poorest of all interurbans, it outlived most of the industry as a freight carrier. It was the first interurban to discontinue passenger service.

STERLING DIXON AND EASTERN TRACTION COMPANY

Another one of the isolated Northern Illinois lines was the Sterling Dixon and Eastern, whose 16 miles of line between Sterling and Dixon was placed in operation in May 1904 on an hourly schedule. In terms of the limited traffic potentialities, the road was able to show a surprisingly good operating ratio (around 60) before World War I, and a return on investment of over 3 per cent. But this type of operation was particularly vulnerable to the automobile, and traffic fell sharply after 1920. All operations ceased on September 17, 1925.

Southwest of this line was the Dixon Rock Falls and Southeastern, eventually reorganized as the Hoopole Yorktown and Tampico. This was designed to be an interurban, and was so listed in many reports, but it was never electrified. Steam operation on a limited scale continued until the 1950's.

KEWAUNEE AND GALVA RAILWAY
(GALESBURG AND KEWAUNEE RAILWAY)

The 9-mile line between the industrial towns of Kewaunee and Galva was completed on December 7, 1906, as part of a projected line to Galesburg. The road, locally promoted and owned, operated streetcars in Kewaunee in addition to the interurban line. Originally named the Galesburg and Kewaunee, the road was reorganized as the Kewaunee and Galva Railway in 1924, following receivership; the change in name reflected an acceptance of reality. In 1927 the company passed into McKinley's control. All service was abandoned on December 31, 1932. Beside purely local business, the road provided a connection from Kewaunee to Rock Island trains at Galva.

ROCK ISLAND SOUTHERN RAILWAY

Few interurbans died a slower and more painful death than the Rock Island Southern, although the road began life with great promise. It began in two segments; the older was built as the Western Illinois Traction between Galesburg and Monmouth (19 miles) paralleling the Burlington tracks. Before its completion on May 30, 1906, the enterprise was reorganized as the Rock Island Southern Railway Company. The other segment, a 60-mile line, was technically the Rock Island Southern Railway, built northward from Monmouth; it used the single-phase AC Westinghouse system and pantograph, and was completed in November 1910. The sections from Rock Island to Southern Junction and from Milan to Sherrard used track leased from the Rock Island. Five big Niles cars from the Washington Baltimore and Annapolis served on the line. Actually, however, this second segment of the line, with its branches to Alexis and Aledo, Sherrard and Cable, was from the beginning primarily a freight carrier, and its freight trains used steam locomotives. The southern portion became the Galesburg and Western after reorganization in 1919, but the two roads were always affiliated. Unlike the Sherrard branch, the Aledo and Alexis branches had regular passenger service connecting with all through trains.

The development of the automobile brought an end to most of the passenger traffic, and in 1926 all regular passenger service ceased, although the road showed mixed train service in the Official Guide up until the time of complete abandonment. The AC portion was converted as soon as passenger service ended, and steam power was continued for freight; however, electric freight operation was continued on the DC segment. During the thirties the road barely covered operating expenses. World War II brought temporary profits, but from 1943 on increased trucking soon caused losses of substantial magnitude. By 1950 the operating expenses exceeded the revenues by $30,000 a year. How the road kept going at all was a mystery—the track had deteriorated to an incredible degree. The Galesburg–Monmouth line was finally abandoned, March 30, 1951. The exact history of the disintegration of the upper portion is difficult to trace. The branches were gradually abandoned, except the one to Aledo, which was retained to the end. The main line itself was broken in two at Burgess in 1929 when fire burned a trestle. Gradually both ends shrank back toward Monmouth and Rock Island, as one by one the bridges rotted through and collapsed. In February 1952 the old steam locomotive made its last run into Rock Island.

For many years the road was owned and managed by various members of the Walsh family of Clinton. One peculiarity of the road was the failure to correct the listing in the Railway Guide; the line was shown as continuous for many years after it was broken, abandoned branches were shown intact, and lines were still shown as projected to Burlington and to Macomb.

KEOKUK ELECTRIC COMPANY

The Keokuk Electric Company's 7-mile line was chiefly notable for operating across the Mississippi River, on the Wabash–Toledo Peoria & Western railway bridge, on the way from Keokuk to Hamilton and Warsaw. An extension to Carthage was never completed. TP&W tracks were used for much of the route. This company also provided street railway service in Keokuk, and sold electric power; in 1913 it became a Stone and Webster property. Traffic possibilities were always limited, and the coming of automobiles brought losses and abandonment on May 11, 1928. One big steel interurban car was sold to Toledo and Indiana, and eventually went to Georgia Railway and Power for the Atlanta interurban service.

PEORIA AND PEKIN TERMINAL COMPANY

This line, before 1899 the Peoria and Pekin Traction Company, was completed from Peoria to Pekin (8 miles) on the west side of the Illinois River (except in Pekin) in 1900 and placed in operation on April 2. After reorganization in 1907 it became the Peoria Railway Terminal Company. For most of its years of operation it used five big wooden railroad-roof interurbans, run at half-hour intervals. The road passed into the hands of the Rock Island and the Alton, which developed it as an important terminal property, using steam power for switching. This became the road's primary business, and the passenger operations a nuisance; with the rise of the automobile and the bus, the volume of business dropped, and service was suspended on August 30, 1924. The road was eventually absorbed into the Rock Island, by which it is still operated. The road must not be confused with the Peoria & Pekin Union, which was never electrified.

ILLINOIS CENTRAL ELECTRIC RAILWAY

In the area directly west of Peoria, about halfway to Galesburg, the 28-mile Illinois Central Electric Railway operated a T-shaped line: the north-south portion extended from Lewiston to Farmington, and the other segment ran west from a junction north of Canton to Fairview. The line was built outward from Canton in three directions, construction beginning in 1907 and ending in 1912 when the Lewiston line was completed.* A great variety of equipment was used, some of streetcar design, but including old railroad-roof cars and one big arched-roof combine, built in 1913. Service on the Farmington–Lewiston line was typically on a 2-hour schedule; 5 (and in later years, 2) runs a day were made from Canton to Fairview. For a time the road did fairly well financially, but dependent on shorthaul passenger business and with only limited freight operations, its business was disastrously affected by the coming of the automobile. Revenues in 1925 were only 40 per cent of the 1922 figure. Operating losses had appeared by 1925, and on July 25, 1928, all operations ceased and the tracks were torn up.

BLOOMINGTON PONTIAC AND JOLIET ELECTRIC RAILWAY

Intended as a part of a line from Chicago to St. Louis, but never more than an isolated short line, the BP&J was completed from Pontiac to Odell (10 miles) on March 15, 1905, and to Dwight (8 miles) in June 1906, on private right-of-way except in the towns. The enterprise was locally promoted, passed into the hands of the Fisher syndicate, and finally, as a subsidiary of Northern Illinois Public Service, became a part of the Insull empire. This road was

* The lines were completed as follows: Canton–Norris (5 miles), 1909; Norris–Fairview (7 miles), 1910; Norris–Farmington (6 miles), 1911; Canton–Lewiston (10 miles), 1912.

one of the first single-phase General Electric AC systems, with 3,300 volts, and was widely publicized at the time of building. But the power system was not successful and was replaced by DC in 1915.

The traffic potential was very limited, and confined to passenger service, with 2-hour headway common. Highway development and World War I inflation squeezed the road; by 1924 only 21,000 passengers were carried compared to 154,000 in 1919. Operations ceased on November 24, 1925.

SPRINGFIELD CLEAR LAKE AND ROCHESTER RAILWAY

This line was completed in 1909 with 11 miles of track from Springfield to Rochester and a branch line to Clear Lake. Total mileage was 15. The line became the Springfield Suburban, and after 1910 the Mississippi Valley Interurban Railway; it was affiliated with some of the predecessor companies of Illinois Terminal. The road was in large measure designed for traffic between Springfield and the resort of Clear Lake. But the seasonal traffic was inadequate to keep the line going, and track deteriorated to the point that on July 18, 1912, the state commission ordered service suspended, pending improvements. These were not made, and operations ceased permanently.

ILLINOIS TRACTION AND OTHER CENTRAL ILLINOIS ROADS

ILLINOIS TRACTION COMPANY (ILLINOIS TERMINAL RAILROAD)[35]

The largest single midwestern interurban system that remained directly under one management over a long period of time, and the largest in the United States outside of the essentially suburban Pacific Electric, was the 400-mile Illinois Traction system, in later years the Illinois Terminal Railroad. In its early days it did not differ basically in track, equipment, or service from the typical Indiana-Ohio line. But at a very early date it began to develop carload interchange business with the steam roads, not to the liking, incidentally, of some of those roads. The success that it met was the primary factor in the long life of the road. But it enjoyed other advantages as well, notably: the absence of steam-road passenger-train competition on some of its best runs; its high-speed entrance into downtown St. Louis; the inadequate steam-road service to Peoria from the south; various industrial developments in Decatur, in Peoria, and in the area east of St. Louis, which were of particular benefit to it; and a substantial volume of coal and grain traffic, which was not highly vulnerable to truck competition.

The system's corporate history is complex. Although the lines were built by a number of companies, all were McKinley projects except for those acquired at a relatively late date in the St. Louis area. The original lines centered on Danville; of these the Danville-Westville segment, completed in 1901, was the oldest. This line was extended to Georgetown in 1902, and to Ridge Farm in 1905. The Catlin branch was also built in 1902. The main line was started eastward from Champaign, reaching St. Joseph in 1902 and Danville in 1903. The Homer branch was built in 1904. By 1903 McKinley had definite plans to build to St. Louis, and construction was started from Decatur and Springfield. The Decatur-Springfield line was built in 1904, the line north from Decatur to Clinton in 1905 and on to Bloomington in 1906, and the Decatur-Champaign line, which connected the earlier lines with those farther west, was placed in service in 1907. In the same period, the Springfield-St. Louis line was under construction, being completed from Springfield to Carlinville in 1904, to Staunton and Edwardsville in 1905, and to Granite City in 1906, whence trackage rights were obtained over the East St. Louis and Suburban into St. Louis. The Hillsboro branch was opened in 1905. Finally, the company's own bridge across the Mississippi was ready for use on November 10, 1910, and operation over the EStL&S ceased.

Lines were also being built north from Springfield, reaching Lincoln in 1906, and Mackinaw in 1908, where connection was made with a line built in 1907 from Bloomington to Peoria. These northern lines were built to operate with AC power, but shortly converted to the 600-volt DC employed by the rest of the system.

All the properties mentioned above were controlled by the Illinois Traction Company, incorporated in 1904, and operated as the Illinois Traction system. In 1923 a technical change was made; direct control was transferred to a new company, Illinois Traction, Inc., which was a subsidiary of Illinois Power and Light Company, whose capital stock was owned by the original Illinois Traction Company. As McKinley became increasingly interested in politics (becoming Congressman and then Senator from Illinois), direct management of the company passed into the hands of Clement Studebaker of the South Bend automobile family. Eventually both Insull and the North American Company became interested in the enterprise and purchased stock in it; in 1926 they reached an agreement on joint ownership, leaving the management in the hands of the Studebaker group. Following the collapse of the Insull system, North American took over complete control. To conform with the terms of Federal legislation, the property was sold to local St. Louis interests in 1945, which in turn sold it to a group of 11 main-line railroads in 1956.

In the mid-twenties the company made its last great expansion when it acquired a number of terminal properties in the area east of St. Louis. It acquired (1) the Alton Granite and St. Louis (by then St. Louis and Alton) from the East St. Louis and Suburban, thus gaining a high-speed passenger route to Alton and a second line to Edwardsville; (2) a portion of the Lebanon line of the same road; and (3) two steam lines, the St. Louis Troy and Eastern and the Alton and Eastern, a segment of the dismembered Chicago Peoria & St. Louis. These two lines, never electrified, were operated by steam power and later dieselized. Another short terminal line acquired was the Illinois Terminal Company, whose name was given to the entire system in 1928.

The company built belt lines around the major cities to avoid street running and to facilitate the handling of carload freight. This was done in Champaign in 1927 through use of Illinois Central branch-line trackage, in Decatur in 1931, in Springfield in 1933, and in Urbana and Edwardsville in 1937. (Earlier examples of the company's building of belt lines for freight trains are mentioned in Chapter 4.) These changes lessened the convenience to passengers so far as access to the downtown area was concerned, but greatly speeded service. Such changes were never made in Bloomington, Clinton, or Danville, and street running into the centers of the cities continued to the end. Street running was particularly troublesome in Bloomington, but fortunately little freight was handled on this line. In 1933 a new St. Louis station was completed, permitting street running to be eliminated.

The completed system consisted of three major routes. The most important was the 172-mile line from St. Louis to Peoria via Carlinville and Springfield, a route that was not duplicated by steam-line passenger service north of Springfield. The second line extended from Springfield eastward through Decatur and Champaign to Danville (123 miles). The third route extended northward 66 miles from Decatur through Clinton and Bloomington to a junction with the main line at Mackinaw, trains operating through from Decatur to Peoria. Various branches operated suburban and connecting service. Frequent suburban service was operated from St. Louis to Alton and streetcar service to Granite City. Street railway service was operated by affiliated companies in Decatur, Bloomington, Champaign-Urbana, and Danville. The Peoria system was controlled by the same interests. Nonelectric rail-bus service was operated from Alton to Grafton.

The IT lines were built to typical interurban standards, and except for the belt lines noted above, remained of this character throughout their history. Primarily they were built on private right-of-way, typically paralleling steam roads, highways, or both. This was true of the Danville line almost in its entirety, less so of the St. Louis–Springfield segment. In addition to the $3-million bridge into St. Louis, the most costly bridge venture ever attempted by an interurban, there were major bridges at Decatur and Peoria. The St. Louis–Springfield line was built through hilly country but most of the rest of the trackage was relatively level. The entire system was protected by a block-signal system of railroad standards.

As was inevitable with its diverse operations, the line used a wide variety of equipment. The early cars were typical railroad-roof wooden interurban cars, but by 1910 the road shifted to heavy arch-roof steel-sheathed cars with distinctive arched windows in front. A number of these, built between 1906 and 1913, provided the bulk of main-line service for more than three decades. Most of these cars were modernized and air conditioned during the thirties, and blue paint eventually replaced traction orange. The line bought no lightweight cars, and purchased no new passenger equipment of any consequence for mainline service between 1915 and 1948. In 1948, 8 streamlined cars were built for the road by the St. Louis Car Company, the last interurban cars ever built. These were used on the St. Louis–Peoria and Decatur service until passenger service ended. Apart from the coaches, the road had a number of parlor cars, and nine sleeping cars used on St. Louis–Peoria and St. Louis–Champaign runs, as noted in Chapter 3. A number of suburban-type cars were owned for use on the Alton line and various branches. Many of these came from the East St. Louis and Suburban and the Illinois Valley lines. For freight service, the early box and steeple cab units gave way to heavy articulated units, and finally to the Class D motors, among the most powerful ever used by interurban lines. The road also had a number of steam locomotives on its freight lines in the East St. Louis area.

The Illinois Traction passenger service was comparable to that of other large Midwestern interurbans, except for greater multiple-unit operation (usually two), and for the extensive use of parlor cars. However, many trains consisted of single units. For many years, hourly service was provided on most lines, some of the trains being limiteds and others locals. After the traffic declined as automobile use increased, the basic service was reduced to six trains a day each way for a number of years on all lines.

Although the Traction was built primarily as a passenger carrier and initially did not handle freight, the company recognized at an early date the possible advantages of carload freight. Considerable steam-road interchange business was obtained as early as 1910, but it was not until the loss of most of the package freight to trucks in the twenties that the road began to push its carload business and to build its belt lines. Freight revenue of $1.6 million in 1924—a very large figure for an interurban in this period—was increased to $2.2 million in 1926. Total annual revenue was about $6 million in this period. By 1954 the freight revenue was nearly $11 million, and passenger revenue $600,000. In terms of revenue the system was about the size of the Monon.

The road was fortunate in obtaining a diversified freight business. Coal, very important in earlier years, declined with the industry, and the gasoline business, which became of great importance for a time because the line's active solicitation of freight business coincided with the building of bulk stations, was almost totally lost to trucks after World War II. But the grain business remained relatively stable, and a substantial volume of traffic in manufactured goods of various sorts was built up. A number of plants, such as that of the C. S. Johnson Company in Champaign, were served only by the Traction lines. The Terminal was one of the few interurbans to own large numbers of standard freight cars regularly interchanged with steam roads.

The coming of motor transportation inevitably affected the road, but it was able to withstand competition better than most interurbans, largely because of the heavy carload freight business. However, some curtailments were made at an early date on the light-traffic branches. In 1929 passenger service to Mechanicsburg ended, but the line was retained for freight purposes. In the same year the passenger trains were taken off the Homer branch, and the track cut back to an elevator at State Road. In 1933 local passenger service was removed between Granite City and East St. Louis, and segments of the Ridge Farm, Catlin, and Hillsboro lines (abandoned beyond Georgetown, Tilton, and Litchfield, respectively). The remainder of the Georgetown line (the first to be built) was abandoned in 1936, the Tilton line in 1937, and the Litchfield line in 1939. But the main lines remained intact at the end of the thirties, with reduced but still substantial passenger service, in sharp contrast to the Ohio-Indiana situation.

In 1942, to the great surprise of the communities served, the road asked permission to abandon the Danville–Decatur and Decatur–Mackinaw lines (some 200 miles), and the War Production Board requisitioned the rails for defense purposes. It has never been clear whether the initiative came from WPB or the line, which was annoyed because the state had approved additional bus competition on these routes. In any event the company did not object. As a result of violent protests the I.C.C. denied permission to abandon, and in a major court case was upheld over the objections of the WPB.

In practice few changes were made during the forties. The road did well financially in the war period, with heavy defense traffic to the big ordnance plant at Illiopolis, and on other lines. Just after the war the management was optimistic enough to order the new streamlined trains (noted above) for main-line service and new cars for local service. After 1948, however, the passenger traffic declined sharply, and in 1950 there began a series of contractions in service and mileage that was to culminate in the complete abandonment of passenger service and electric operation. First, the number of passenger trains was reduced to half in the summer of 1950, thus greatly reducing the convenience of the service to the remaining users—commuters and shoppers. At the same time the Peoria service was cut back to East Peoria, largely because the streamliners could not negotiate the curves on the track into the Peoria station. In 1952 the Danville line was abandoned east of a point near Ogden, to facilitate the paving of Main Street in Danville. For no apparent reason passenger trains were run on to the end of the track for nearly a year, before being cut back to Champaign in 1953. Also in 1953 (February 21) came complete abandonment of the entire Clinton–Bloomington line, from Forsythe, north of Decatur, to Mackinaw. The Alton passenger line and the Alton–Grafton line were cut out on March 7, 1953. Finally, in 1954 the company requested permission to abandon all remaining interurban passenger service. The Illinois Commerce Commission initially denied the request, requiring continued operation of one train to Champaign and two on the Springfield line. This served no useful purpose, and passenger service to Champaign ended in June 1955 and to Springfield in April 1956. The St. Louis–Granite City streetcar service alone remained until 1958, when it too was discontinued.

With this series of abandonments completed, the road consisted of two main lines, from St. Louis to Peoria, and from Springfield via Decatur to a point east of Ogden, plus the various freight lines in the East St. Louis–Alton area. All freight service was dieselized before passenger service ended, at which time the trolley wire was removed.

KANKAKEE AND URBANA TRACTION COMPANY

One of the last interurbans to be built was the ill-fated Kankakee and Urbana, the "University Route." A local Urbana enterprise, headed for some years by Dr. C. A. Van Doren, father of the well-known writers, the company was chartered in 1909, and by 1913 (January 13) was able to open service from Urbana to Rantoul. Construction was pushed on north at snail's pace, reaching Paxton, 10 miles farther, on May 1, 1916. This was the end of construction, although Kankakee and the planned connection with the Chicago and Interurban were still 25 miles away. Chanute Field at Rantoul provided considerable business for a time, but deficits soon appeared, particularly after the parallel highway was paved, and on March 26, 1926, service came to an end with court approval when the receiver demonstrated that he had no funds with which to continue operations. One of the company's two modern cars, both double-truck Birneys, became a streetcar of the Third Avenue Railway in New York City.

EAST ST. LOUIS AND SUBURBAN RAILWAY

The second most important network of electric lines radiating out from St. Louis was that of the East St. Louis and Suburban, which at its peak operated 90 miles of road. Unlike Illinois Traction lines, these lines were all less than 30 miles in length, and were all in a sense suburban carriers. But the nature of their operations was such as to warrant their classification as interurbans.

The lines terminated at the end of the Eads Bridge in St. Louis, crossed the river and passed through East St. Louis on street railway tracks. Beyond the city they operated on private right-of-way, in part on embankments because of the swampy nature of the area. There were four major lines. The first extended through Edgemont southeastward to Belleville, a double-track line, paralleled by the affiliated freight-only St. Louis and Belleville Electric. The second line forked off the Belleville line at Edgemont and ran eastward through O'Fallon to Lebanon. The third ran in a northeast direction out of East St. Louis via Collinsville to Edwardsville. A short link from Edgemont to a junction above Caseyville connected this line with the Lebanon and Belleville lines. The fourth, operated under the name of the Alton Granite and St. Louis (later St. Louis and Alton), extended northward via Mitchell and Wood River to Alton. From Mitchell, a branch of this road extended into Edwardsville, to give the latter two routes to East St. Louis. A few city routes were operated in Alton, Venice, Madison, and Belleville, and the East St. Louis Railway city system was an affiliated enterprise.

The track was for the most part built to high standards. The O'Fallon–Lebanon segment was originally the main line of the Baltimore & Ohio, purchased by the EStL&S when the B&O relocated its route. The Belleville line, with service intervals of 15 minutes during the day and 7 minutes in rush hours, was the most heavily traveled route, and essentially most clearly a suburban type of operation. The other lines generally operated on hourly service, with service every half-hour to Edwardsville because of its two lines. Cars on this route were operated around the loop that the lines created. A wide variety of equipment was used, with a large number of typical railroad-roof interurban cars. Whereas the road lacked a high-speed entrance into East St. Louis, it did reach the downtown areas of both this city and St. Louis and the street running was not as laborious as in larger cities. The road conducted a general freight interchange business with the steam roads, and its own subsidiary, St. Louis and Belleville, was an important originator of coal movements, in addition to the handling of cars to industrial plants from the steam roads.

The EStL&S was incorporated in 1892, and gradually took over the various independent companies; not long after 1900 it passed into the hands of the Clark interests in Philadelphia and was supervised by the E. W. Clark Management Corporation.* In 1914 the East St. Louis and Suburban Company was formed as a holding company to unify control over the road and its affiliates, such as the East St. Louis Street Railway. In 1922 control was obtained by the North American Company, which later gained domination over Illinois Terminal and brought the two systems under common control. By this time, however, the EStL&S was on the way downhill.

The system, despite its heavy traffic volume compared to typical interurbans, was never as profitable as many smaller lines; it suffered from the same difficulties as roads such as the Pacific Electric, with high operating ratios and a relatively low return on investment. However, the business was at first less affected by the automobile than the typical line serving small cities, and not until the depression struck did the road fail to meet interest obligations. After 1928 the system began to disintegrate. The Alton Granite and St. Louis was sold to the Illinois Traction and merged into the latter system as part of the new Illinois Terminal Railroad. This portion was operated by IT until 1953, when the trackage was abandoned. The Mitchell–Edwardsville section, cut to a few runs a day and badly deteriorated, was abandoned by the Illinois Terminal in 1932. The IT also served Edwardsville and Collinsville by its own main line. Also in 1928 the EStL&S abandoned its light-traffic Edgewod–Lebanon and Edgemont–Caseyville lines. A portion of the Lebanon line to O'Fallon was taken over for steam-operated freight service by the Illinois Terminal. Finally in 1932, the remaining lines —the main routes to Belleville and to Col-

---

* The lines were completed as follows: East St. Louis–St. Louis via Eads Bridge, 1896; East St. Louis–Belleville (freight line), 1897, (passenger line) May 15, 1898; Edgemont–Collinsville, 1899; East St. Louis–Collinsville, 1901; Collinsville–Edwardsville, 1902; Edgemont–Lebanon, 1903; East St. Louis–Alton, 1905; Mitchell–Edwardsville, 1905.

linsville—were abandoned. The Collinsville–Edwardsville line was abandoned in 1928. The only segment that remained was the St. Louis and Belleville Electric, the freight line that had not operated passenger service except in its very earliest years. This was acquired by the Union Electric Company of St. Louis, and eventually sold to the Peabody Coal Company interests, which were still operating it in 1960, under the name of the Peabody Short Line Railroad.

ALTON JACKSONVILLE AND PEORIA RAILWAY

This road, later the Alton and Jacksonville, was one of the most complete failures of all interurbans. Incorporated in 1904 with the plan of building from Alton to Peoria, the company placed in operation its first 5 miles of track (from Alton to Godfrey) in August 1905. In 1911 an extension to Jerseyville was started through hilly unproductive country, reaching Jerseyville in 1912, and bankrupting the weak company. Reorganized as the Alton and Jacksonville in 1914, the road was soon at the point of operating losses, and service was abandoned on February 1, 1918.

EAST ST. LOUIS COLUMBIA AND WATERLOO RAILWAY

One locally owned, independent road served the East St. Louis area, operating 22 miles of line southeastward from the Eads Bridge terminal to Waterloo. The enterprise was incorporated in 1906, but construction was not completed until December 1912. Service was operated on a 90-minute basis throughout the road's history, and extensive carload freight traffic was developed, much of it bridge traffic between connecting steam roads. Passenger business fell rapidly after highways were paved in 1925, and passenger service was discontinued on June 1, 1932. Although this action reduced losses, freight service could not cover its costs, and complete abandonment occurred in the spring of 1936, when the road reached the point at which it was not able to meet its current bills.

SOUTHERN ILLINOIS LINES

COAL BELT ELECTRIC RAILWAY

The important coal-mining area around Marion was served by a suburban-type electric line, the only Illinois interurban that throughout most of its life was a steam road subsidiary. The road, promoted by the Illinois Midland Coal Co., and acquired in 1906 by the Missouri Pacific system, was completed on July 1, 1902. The line extended from Herrin to Marion (8 miles) with a 3-mile branch from Energy to Carterville. In early years there were additional short branches. Streetcar-type equipment operated, typically on hourly schedules. The road discontinued all freight service in 1914, giving the parent road the right to provide such service on its tracks. The heavy but very short-haul traffic fell sharply after 1922 as mining declined and automobiles developed, and late in 1926 all service was abandoned, although much of the track was retained by the parent company for freight. The rolling stock went to Houston North Shore, another Missouri Pacific subsidiary built during this period.

CENTRAL ILLINOIS TRACTION COMPANY

This line was built between Mattoon and Charleston (10 miles) in 1904, by the Mattoon City Railway. It began as a local enterprise, in conjunction with the local power system, but eventually passed into the hands of the Central Illinois Public Service Company, which consolidated a number of local power enterprises in central Illinois, and also owned the Southern Illinois Railway and the Chicago and Joliet. CIPS itself in turn passed under Insull control. Following the formation of CIPS in 1910, the interurban assumed the name of Central Illinois Traction Co. In 1912 it purchased the Paris street railway line as the first step in projected construction of a line from Charleston to Paris and a connection with the THI&E. This plan never materialized. For many years the line operated heavy old McGuire-Cummings cars ill-suited for this type of service. In 1924 these were sent to Southern Illinois Railway and were replaced by St. Louis lightweight cars, with arched roofs and distinctive arched windows. These went on to the Chicago and Joliet when the line was abandoned.

On the night of August 30, 1907, on a curve west of Charleston, two of the line's trains, one with two cars, met head-on. The wooden cars telescoped; 18 persons were killed and 50 injured; this was one of the worst interurban wrecks. The company was placed in receivership to protect the affiliated power company from damage claims.

Like other roads of this type, the Central Illinois was very hard hit by auto competition and virtually destroyed as soon as improved roads were completed between points served. By the mid-twenties operating expenses were 50 per cent greater than revenues. The power company carried the losses for a time, and then on March 1, 1927, abandoned the line and substituted buses.

MURPHYSBORO AND SOUTHERN ILLINOIS RAILWAY

In 1909 the Murphysboro Electric Railway and Light Company completed its little 3-mile street railway system, and the same local interests incorporated the Murphysboro and Southern Illinois to build the 7-mile line to Carbondale, which was completed on private right-of-way through the hills characteristic of this portion of Illinois. The volume of business remaining after the advent of the automobile was insufficient to allow the road to cover expenses, and all operations were discontinued on January 26, 1927.

SOUTHERN ILLINOIS RAILWAY AND POWER COMPANY

Another CIPS interurban was the Southern Illinois Railway and Power Company, whose 15-mile line from Eldorado through Harrisburg to Carrier Mills, in the Saline county coal area, was brought into service at the relatively late date of April 1913. The line used 1,200-volt DC from the beginning, and its medium-sized cars had arched-roofs. Harrisburg, the largest city on the line, was the center of the business, which moved into and out of this city in both directions, rather than through from Eldorado to Carrier Mills. Cars, however, ran through, usually at hourly intervals.

Unlike most of the Illinois short-line interurbans, the SI was able to develop considerable carload freight business, primarily in coal, handled by freight motors. The road owned a number of gondolas of its own. As a consequence the road outlasted most of its fellows. As late as the early thirties the road continued its passenger service, which was listed in the Official Guide. But the depression seriously affected the already declining coal industry of the area, and the loss in both freight and passenger traffic led to complete abandonment of the line in 1933. Since the track paralleled the New York Central throughout, there was little economic need for its retention.

*

Despite its ambitious name, the *Cairo and St. Louis* never got farther than Mounds, using Illinois Central tracks except for street running in the two towns serviced. This line was a McKinley property, operated in conjunction with the street railway system. The line was completed in 1910 and abandoned in the summer of 1931.

The *Southern Illinois Power Company* operated a 2-mile line from a connection with the Illinois Traction at Hillsboro to Taylor Springs, essentially a street railway operation. Of the same character were the lines of the Centralia and Central City Traction line between the two towns of its corporate name, and the Centralia Traction line south to Wamac.

The *North Kankakee Electric Light and Railway* operated from Kankakee through Bradley to Bourbonnais (5 miles).

A line built by the Moline East Moline and Watertown Railway, and later operated by *Tri-City Railway and Light Company*, connected Moline with Watertown, 9 miles. The line was completed in 1902 and abandoned in the late thirties.

There were two short routes out of Galesburg, one the 12-mile line of the *Peoples' Traction Company* to Abington, completed December 1, 1902. This line used interurban-type cars. The other route was that of the city system, the *Galesburg Railway and Light Company*, which had one suburban line to Knoxville. These were both McKinley properties.

One of the smallest intercity lines was that of the *Fruit Growers' Refrigeration and Power Company*, from Anna to Jonesboro in Southern Illinois. The 3-mile line, which was essentially a streetcar operation, was placed in operation early in 1907. The company eventually became a part of the Central Illinois Power Company system. In the summer of 1925 the line was replaced by bus service, a portion of the track into the state mental hospital on the outskirts of Anna being retained for freight service (mostly coal).

The *Woodstock and Sycamore Traction Company*, designed to be an interurban, was completed in 1911 northward from Sycamore to Marengo, on the Elgin & Belvedere. The 26-mile line was operated with McKeen gasoline motor cars, and later with a Fairbanks-Morse gasoline motor. Plans for electrification were never carried through, and the line was abandoned in 1918. The line called itself an "interurban" and operated with typical interurban standards.

Wisconsin

OF Wisconsin's 383 miles of interurban trackage, 52 miles consisted of portions of three Illinois lines—the North Shore, the Rockford and Interurban, and the Geneva Lake line—that extended into the state. Two short lines from Michigan also crossed the border. More than half the state's total mileage belonged to the Milwaukee Electric Railway and Light Company, which had one of the finest interurban systems in the country. Of the remainder, 76 miles consisted of a network in the Lake Winnebago area. A large portion of the Wisconsin mileage was built at an early date (over one third was completed before 1900).

THE MILWAUKEE ELECTRIC RAILWAY AND LIGHT COMPANY[36]

The TMER, as it was traditionally abbreviated, operated 198 miles of interurban line, after its absorption of the Milwaukee Northern in 1928, as part of an integrated interurban, transit, and electric power service. The company had its origin in the Milwaukee horse-car system, which was electrified in 1890; in the same year it passed into the control of the North American Company, one of the first of the large holding company systems. The North American Company was promoted in this period by H. H. Villard, who had completed the Northern Pacific Railway and was a founder of Edison General Electric. The Milwaukee Electric Railway and Light Company was incorporated in 1896, and immediately thereafter began plans to build interurban lines, under the direction of John I. Beggs, for a number of years the dynamic if eccentric figure dominant in the Wisconsin utilities field. Most of these lines were built under separately controlled corporations and later absorbed into the parent company.

With adequate financial backing, the company was able to proceed relatively quickly with construction. It acquired the Milwaukee–Wauwatosa Electric Railway, which in 1895 had built a 12-mile line to the suburb of Wauwatosa, and in 1898 (June 2) completed a line to Waukesha, 18 miles from Milwaukee. This line connected at Waukesha with a 5-mile line to Waukesha Beach, built in 1895 by an independent company. Meanwhile, the company had also begun to build south, reaching Racine on March 16, 1897, and Kenosha (34 miles from Milwaukee) in June, a decade before the North Shore built through this area.

A new downtown station in Milwaukee was opened in 1902, at 3d and Sycamore. Meanwhile construction was begun on a third line, which reached Hales Corners (13 miles) on June 27, 1903, St. Martins on June 21, 1904, Muskego Lake on September 1 of the same year, and finally East Troy (36 miles from Milwaukee) on December 13, 1907. Also in 1907 the Waukesha line was pushed westward from Waukesha Lake to Oconomowoc (completed June 3), and to Watertown, 50 miles from Milwaukee (opened July 31, 1908). Except for a 21-mile branch built from the East Troy line to Burlington, completed on October 1, 1909, expansion was at an end, since control of the North American Company passed from Beggs's hands to persons unsympathetic to his dreams of a great interurban empire. Projected extensions to Chicago, Madison, Lake Geneva, and elsewhere were never built. The western lines had been built to 3,300-volt AC, but as this proved unsuccessful, they were converted to 1,200-volt DC. Eventually (1927) all the company's lines were standardized to 600-volt DC.

While new construction ended in 1909, many improvements were made, various segments were converted from street running to private right-of-way, partly to meet continued complaints of the cities, and lines were double-tracked. In the twenties the company embarked on a $6 million improvement project, which provided a 7-mile, private-right-of-way entrance for the western lines to downtown Milwaukee, with 3 and 4 tracks in some places. A subway begun in 1930 from this line to the station was never completed, nor was a project begun in 1929 to bring the northern line downtown on private right-of-way. But the Kenosha line was completely rebuilt, mostly on private right-of-way. The high-speed, double-track routes offered service of the highest quality, and as a consequence were less vulnerable to the automobile than many lines. The company had entered the bus business at a very early date, with routes as far as Fond du Lac, Madison, and Beloit. In part this policy was necessitated by the failure of Wisconsin to protect interurbans against bus competition. But the result was a highly coordinated rail-bus system rarely duplicated elsewhere in the country.

For many years Milwaukee was also

served by one other independent interurban property, the Milwaukee Northern Railway Company. This line was incorporated in 1905; 29 miles to Port Washington were built in 1907 (placed in operation on November 2), and the remaining 28 miles to Sheboygan were completed in 1908 (September 22). This was likewise a high-speed, well-built line, although with considerable street running in Milwaukee. It connected in Sheboygan with a line of Wisconsin Power and Light that went west to Plymouth. The Northern, owned by a small group of Michigan and Wisconsin investors, resisted for many years the attempts of three groups to gain control over it—Insull's North Shore, the connecting Wisconsin Power line (which itself eventually became an Insull property), and the TMER. Finally, in 1922, the North American Company bought the controlling stock, and in 1928 the line was merged with the TMER.

Both the TMER and the MN in earlier years operated a variety of wooden railroad-roof interurbans, many designed for multiple-unit operation. The MN's cars were built by Niles in 1907, and most of TMER's cars by Kuhlman and St. Louis in 1909. These were later given steel sheeting on the sides and completely rebuilt, and many operated until the end of service. Only a handful of all-steel cars were ever used by the road; 4 were acquired from St. Louis in 1927, and 8 cars of 1923 construction were purchased from the Indianapolis and Cincinnati in 1929. In 1928 two articulated diner-coaches were built in the company shops, but the dining car experiment proved unsuccessful.

The frequency of service varied considerably, the outer portions of the lines receiving less frequent service than the inner portions. For example on the double-track route to Waukesha trains ran every thirty minutes, but cars went on to Watertown only on a one-hour (and later a two-hour) schedule. The Kenosha line service was usually hourly. The speed varied among the lines, but in general was good. The road was primarily a passenger carrier, but some carload freight business, mostly coal, was obtained.

The decline of the system essentially began with the depression, although the automobile had already had some effect on business, especially on the outer lines. But not until 1938 did the company begin to cut the lines back; in that year, the Burlington branch was abandoned, and on August 13, 1939, the East Troy line was cut to Hales Corners. The Watertown line was abandoned beyond Oconomowoc on February 1, 1940, and September saw the end of the northern line beyond Port Washington. In 1941 the western line was cut back to Waukesha. Thus at the beginning of the war, the system consisted of the Kenosha line, and the inner segments of the other three routes—to Hales Corners, Waukesha, and Port Washington. All carried a heavy volume of wartime traffic.

The company had been reorganized as the Milwaukee Electric Railway and Transport Company in 1938 as a result of Federal public utility legislation, but was still affiliated with the power company (now the Wisconsin Electric Power Company). At the end of the war a decision was made to eliminate all interurban operations. But the road had little interest in operating bus service itself, and found it advantageous to sell the interurban lines before abandonment to the Kenosha Motor Coach lines. The Port Washington line had been sold in 1942 (although still operated by the TMERT), and the Waukesha line in 1946. On September 13, the new owners abandoned the portion of the southern line from Racine to Kenosha, and the remainder of this line December 31. The Milwaukee–Port Washington line was abandoned on March 28, 1948. This left the Waukesha and Hales Corners lines, which had been sold by Kenosha to Greyhound. In 1949 these were resold by Greyhound to the newly formed Milwaukee Rapid Transit and Speedrail Company, organized by Jay Maeder of Cleveland in order to continue rail operation. Lightweight cars were acquired from various sources, and for a time it appeared that the new company might succeed. But on Labor Day in 1950, two specials, operated for the members of the National Model Railroad Association, collided head-on, killing 10 and injuring 47. President Maeder himself was at the controls of one of the trains. As a result of the Public Service Commission's investigations, insurance difficulties, and loss of traffic, the road was placed in trusteeship. A strenuous attempt was made to cover costs but to no avail, and on June 30, 1951, the two lines were abandoned.

The Milwaukee Electric Railway and Transport retained only one piece of track, a 5-mile, freight belt line on the south side of the city from Lakeside to Powerton, to handle coal to the Lakeside power plant. As of 1960, this is still in operation. When the line to East Troy was abandoned in 1939, the 6-mile segment between the Soo interchange at Mukwonago and East Troy was purchased by the Village of East

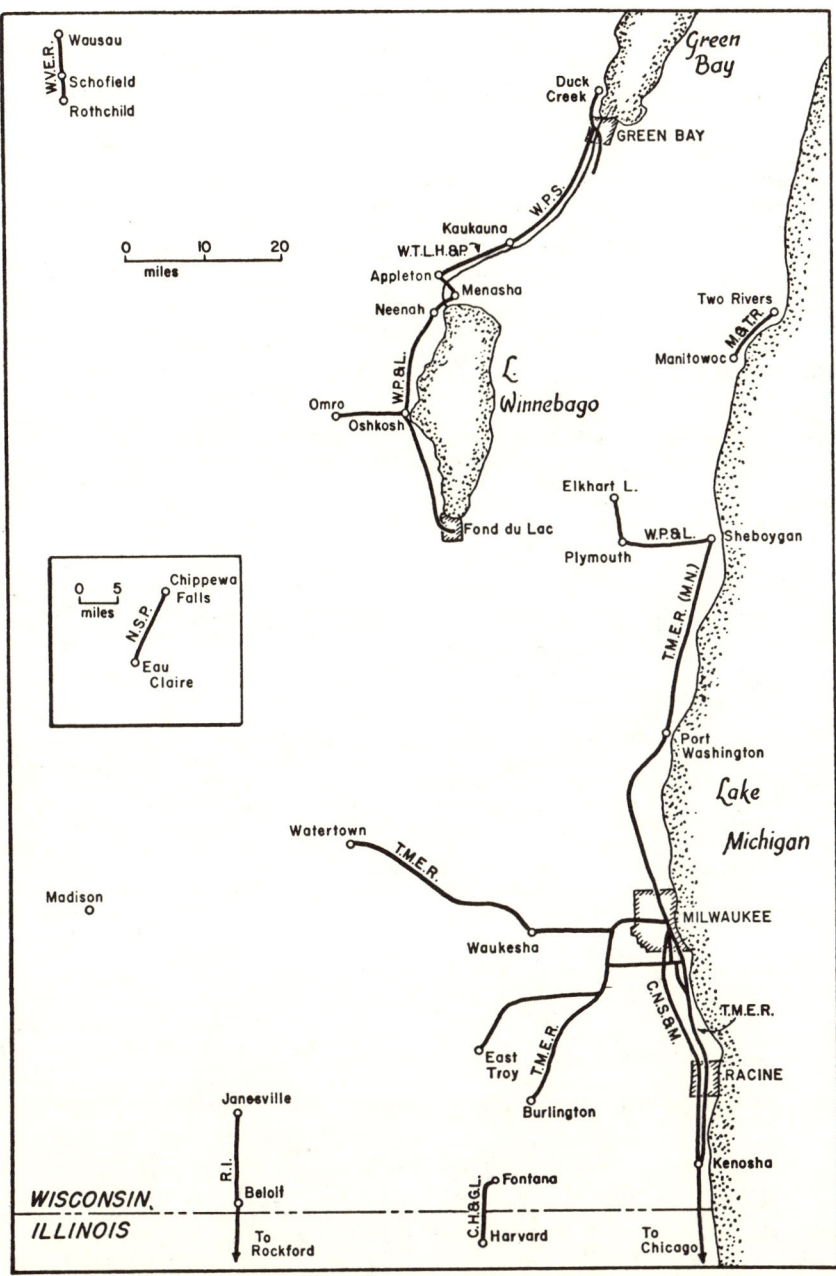

TMER: The Milwaukee Elec. Ry. & Light Co.
(MN: Milwaukee Northern Ry. Co.)
CNS&M: Chicago North Shore & Milwaukee Ry.
CH&GL: Chicago Harvard & Geneva Lake Ry.
RI: Rockford Interurban Ry.
WP&L: Wisconsin Power & Light Co.

WTLH&P: Wisconsin Trac. Light Heat & Power Co.
WPS: Wisconsin Public Service Co.
WVER: Wisconsin Valley Elec. Ry.
NSP: Northern States Power Co.
M&TR: Manitowoc & Two Rivers Ry.

Troy, and has since been operated by the village for carload freight service.

WISCONSIN POWER AND LIGHT COMPANY
(SHEBOYGAN LIGHT POWER AND RAILWAY COMPANY)

The Wisconsin Power Company, which was formed by the merger of a large number of small power and transit systems in central Wisconsin, and which eventually passed into Insull control, owned two unconnected sets of interurban lines. The first of these, originally the property of the Sheboygan Light Power and Railway Company, connected with the Milwaukee Northern in Sheboygan, and extended 16 miles westward via Kohler and Sheboygan Falls (reached in 1899) to Plymouth (1904) with a 7-mile extension northward from Plymouth to the resort of Elkhart Lake (built in 1909). A projected line to Fond du Lac was never built. Elkhart Lake was the most distant point that could be reached by interurban from Chicago except via the Winona in Indiana.

Business on the scenic Elkhart Lake line was largely seasonal, but the main line to Plymouth carried a steady volume of regular business, and hourly schedules were maintained even up into the thirties. The line developed substantial freight business, primarily serving as a connection for the Milwaukee Railroad to the Sheboygan industrial area, and for the Goodrich-West Ports Steamship Company. For many years the road used typical wooden interurban cars, with open cars operated to the lake in the summer months. Eventually the road inherited the 1924 lightweight cars built for the Wisconsin Power Company's Fond du Lac line.

The automobile quickly destroyed much of the business on the line to Elkhart Lake, and this segment was abandoned in 1927. But the main line, supported by its carload freight business, continued until 1939, a decade after the other Wisconsin Power lines had been torn up.

THE LAKE WINNEBAGO-GREEN BAY LINES

From Fond du Lac, at the lower end of Lake Winnebago, there extended a continuous 67-mile interurban route up the west side of the lake and the Fox River Valley to Green Bay. This route, however, was made up of three different systems, which had no financial connection whatsoever; all were at the outset separate local companies, and each became subject to control of a different holding company system. There was little cooperation among them; for many years there was no physical connection at Neenah between the two systems meeting there.

WISCONSIN POWER COMPANY

The southernmost portion of the route consisted of 29 miles of line from Fond du Lac to Neenah. The Oshkosh–Neenah portion was built in 1899 by Winnebago Traction, which was reorganized in 1908 as Wisconsin Electric Railway. In 1902 the company had built a 9-mile branch west from Oshkosh to Omro. The southern portion was built by the Fond du Lac and Oshkosh between the cities of the corporate title, completed on January 28, 1903, on private right-of-way in an almost straight line inland from the lake. The roads were consolidated as the Eastern Wisconsin Electric Company in 1917, and became part of Wisconsin Power in 1924, in which year five new lightweight cars were acquired. The road was hard hit by auto and bus competition, and as a result the Omro branch was abandoned in 1924 and the main line in 1927. Like its neighbors, the road had not developed carload freight service.

WISCONSIN TRACTION LIGHT HEAT AND POWER COMPANY

The middle segment of the network, extending through a thickly populated area from Neenah, Menasha, and Appleton to Kaukauna, was operated by Wisconsin Traction, successor (1900) to the Fox River Valley Electric Railway Company. The section from Neenah to Appleton, much of it through urban areas, was completed in June 1898 and the extension to Kaukauna in 1902. The Appleton city portion, built in 1886 with the Van Depoele system, was one of the first commercial electric railways in the United States.

Wisconsin Traction had the highest density of traffic of any of the central Wisconsin lines, but the bulk was of very short-haul business. Despite the nature of the operations, the line acquired 6 large interurban passenger cars in 1909, built to the same pattern as a group of Milwaukee interurban cars. These were traded to the Milwaukee system for a group of lighter cars in 1924. The Traction was controlled for many years by John Beggs, and was acquired in 1923 by North American. Thus it was an associate of Milwaukee Electric. The line suffered severely from auto and bus competition, and lacking freight traffic, was abandoned in 1928 in favor of bus service.

WISCONSIN PUBLIC SERVICE COMPANY LINES[37]

The northernmost segment of this route was the 23-mile line of the Green Bay Traction Company, later the Wisconsin Public Service Company; the line extended from a connection with Wisconsin Traction at Kaukauna to Green Bay. The same company, taken over in 1905 by the Murphy brothers, wealthy lumbermen, operated the Green Bay transit system, and suburban lines to Duck Creek and East De Pere. The through line to Kaukauna was completed in 1904. The equipment consisted of the usual wooden railroad-roof Niles cars of the period. Wisconsin Public Service was developed by Clement Smith; it later became a Standard Gas and Electric (Byllesby) property, thus being one of the few interurbans that this holding company system ever owned. Like the neighboring lines, the Green Bay line was hard hit by the development of the automobile, and all operations were abandoned in 1928.

NORTHERN STATES POWER COMPANY

In northwestern Wisconsin, east of Minneapolis, the Northern States Power Company operated a 14-mile line from Eau Claire to Chippewa Falls, completed on September 2, 1898, as the Chippewa Valley Light Railway and Power Company in conjunction with the street railway in Chippewa Falls. This was an Appleyard property prior to 1905, when it was taken over by local lumbermen. A 3-mile extension to Altoona was built in 1914. The system was abandoned in 1926 because of auto and bus competition, after 5 years of losses. It was reported that in the year preceding abandonment, an average of 1.5 passengers had been carried per interurban run.

WISCONSIN VALLEY ELECTRIC RAILWAY

In north-central Wisconsin, the Wisconsin Valley Electric operated a 9-mile line from Wausau to Schofield, originally with wooden railroad-roof cars, later with lightweight arched-roof steel cars. The road was built in 1909 and lasted until 1934, several years longer than its upstate Wisconsin neighbors.

MANITOWOC AND NORTHERN TRACTION COMPANY

The Manitowoc and Two Rivers, later the Manitowoc and Northern, completed on May 1, 1902, connected the two cities of its corporate name; despite the short distance (8 miles), the line was essentially an interurban in equipment and operating methods. It was designed to be a link in a line from Sheboygan to Green Bay, but no connecting links were ever built. It was abandoned late in 1926. This was originally a strictly local enterprise owned by the Higgins family, but later it became a part of the Wisconsin Public Service (*q.v.*).

Minnesota and the Dakotas

THE AREA between Wisconsin and Washington state had extremely little interurban mileage, as would be expected in light of the limited population of the area. There were three interurban companies in Minnesota (plus two other companies that had great but unrealized ambitions to become interurbans), none in North Dakota, and one in South Dakota.

MINNESOTA

Minnesota's three interurbans operated 77 miles of line; of the three, two were long-distance suburban lines out of St. Paul-Minneapolis, and the third, in the Mesaba mining country, was a typical interurban.

MINNEAPOLIS ANOKA AND CUYUNA RANGE RAILROAD

This line was built from Minneapolis to Anoka (15 miles) as the Minneapolis and Northern, and opened service in 1913 with McKeen motor cars. The line replaced a spasmodic bus operation between the two cities. It went into bankruptcy in 1914, was taken over by the bondholders, and was reorganized in 1915 as the Minneapolis Anoka and Cuyuna Range. Since the McKeen cars had been repossessed, the line operated with borrowed steam equipment until electrification was completed on October 13, 1915. The road acquired three cars from the Twin Cities system, one of the few street railways that built cars extensively. An agreement was reached to run the cars into downtown Minneapolis over street railway tracks. In 1923 the line began to use the Luce line depot at 3d Avenue and 7th Street. The line always operated with essentially streetcar equipment, and simply rented more cars from Twin Cities when needed. Freight was operated with steam power until 1922 and then by electric motors.

The loss of business to the automobile and the destruction of the Pillsbury mill in Anoka by fire caused serious financial problems, bankruptcy in 1926, and another reorganization. The line deteriorated into an extremely bad state of repair, and passenger service was finally discontinued August 23, 1939.

In 1943 the Northern Pump Company bought the line to facilitate transporting workers to a defense plant at Fridley; it abandoned the portion beyond Fridley and rebuilt the remaining segment from a connection with the city-system line at 30th Avenue and Grand. This passenger service (free, for employees only) was continued until 1948. This section of the line is still operated for freight service.[38]

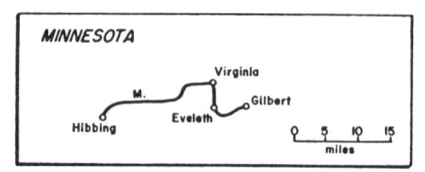

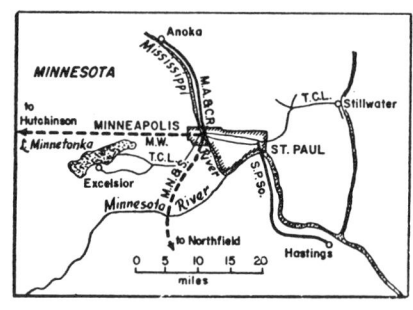

M: Mesaba Elec. Ry.
MA&CR: Minneapolis Anoka & Cuyuna Range RR
SPSo: St. Paul Southern Ry.
TCL: Twin City Lines (Twin City Rapid Transit Co.)
MW: Minnesota Western RR (never electrified)
MN&S: Minneapolis Northfield & Southern Ry. (never electrified)

ST. PAUL SOUTHERN RAILWAY

One of the least successful of the interurban ventures was the St. Paul Southern, built in 1914 southward from the suburb of Invergrove, parallel to the Mississippi, to the town of Hastings (18 miles). Four heavy Niles interurban cars of typical railroad-roof wooden design were employed. The cars operated under trackage rights on the Invergrove city car line to downtown St. Paul. The road was almost solely a passenger carrier. It was in financial difficulties almost from the first, and entered receivership in 1918. Conditions grew worse rather than better, partly because of unrestricted bus competition, and by 1924 the financial condition was desperate. The road managed to keep going until July 31, 1928. Initially the road operated hourly service, but this fell to 6 daily runs.

MESABA ELECTRIC RAILWAY[39]

One of the most isolated interurbans in the United States was the Mesaba, whose 36 miles of line between Hibbing and Gilbert, via Buhl and Virginia, were placed in operation in March 1913, using 750-volt DC power. The line was built on private right-of-way to high standards, with arch-roof interurban equipment typical of the period, and served a well-populated mining area, with many small intermediate villages. Hourly schedules were operated, often with 2-car trains. Boston interests chiefly owned and financed the road.

Owing to the good traffic potential, even though its freight revenues were limited, the road prospered in its earlier years and was able to pay dividends on preferred (but not common) stock. After 1920 revenues began to fall; interest was not earned after 1922, and an operating deficit appeared in 1924. The road was placed in receivership in that year, and was abandoned in 1927.

*

Three other Minnesota lines, two of which eventually came under common control, regarded themselves as electric railways, using gasoline motor cars. The first was the *Electric Short Line Railway*, now the Minnesota Western, which built westward out of Minneapolis, under the control of W. L. and E. D. Luce, in 1914. The other was the *Minneapolis St. Paul Rochester and Dubuque Electric Traction Company*, named the "Dan Patch Line" for the famous race horse owned by its promoter, M. W. Savage. The line, now the Minneapolis Northfield & Southern, had great ambitions, as the name implies, but never got beyond Northfield.* It was projected to Mankato, to Austin and Albert Lea, and to Rochester and Dubuque. The road was operated with gas-electric motor trains. The *Minnesota Northwestern*, operating 18 miles from Thief River Falls to Goodridge, built in 1914 and abandoned in 1940, used gasoline motor cars, and classified itself as an interurban.

---

* It did operate gas-electric cars for a time to Mankato over Chicago Great Western trackage.

The *Twin City Rapid Transit Company*, which operated the city lines in Minneapolis and St. Paul, long one of the finest city systems in the United States, had several long suburban lines which in earlier years at least were virtually interurbans. The main line from St. Paul to Minneapolis, built in 1890, ran through much open country, and was known generally as the Interurban, long before Charles Henry popularized this term. It ran for the most part on University Avenue, and always, to the day of its abandonment in 1953, was the most important of the car lines (it had long ceased to be an interurban, of course).

The longest rural line was the one to Excelsior Bay on Lake Minnetonka (14 miles), placed in service to Excelsior in September 1905. In the same year a branch was built to Deephaven by electrifying a Milwaukee Road branch. The Tonka Bay extension was placed in service in 1907, in part on a M&St.L branch. Standard streetcar equipment was used, with half-hourly service in the summer from downtown Minneapolis. These lines were discontinued in August 1932.

The other major route was built from St. Paul to Stillwater, completed in 1899. Branches were built to White Bear in 1904, and to South Stillwater in 1905. Interurban-type equipment, identical in appearance to the standard Minneapolis city cars, was originally used, typically on half-hour schedules. As business declined, the line was cut back to Wildwood (August 11, 1932). Service continued, with city cars, to Wildwood and Mahtomedi until November 3, 1951.

SOUTH DAKOTA

DEADWOOD CENTRAL RAILROAD

The Deadwood Central was a narrow-gauge steam road in the Black Hills of South Dakota, built in the 1880's, and absorbed by the Burlington. In 1902 a 4-mile segment of this road between Lead and Deadwood was electrified and passenger service provided with narrow-gauge interurban cars. The segment from Pluma into Deadwood was operated on Burlington tracks, with a third rail laid for the narrow-gauge cars. Part of the segment from Lead to Pluma was on an 8 per cent grade. In 1924, upon approval of the I.C.C., the line was abandoned, owing to operating losses and the deterioration of equipment.

Iowa

IOWA had 489 miles of interurban lines, the greatest mileage in any state west of the Mississippi except Texas and California.[40] The Iowa interurbans in general resembled West Coast lines much more than the Midwest lines; their development of substantial carload freight business at an early date enabled them to survive the coming of the automobile much more successfully. Many of the lines continued to operate passenger service until after 1950, and in 1960, 61 per cent of the mileage (30 miles) was still operating freight service. The two most important networks were those centering on Des Moines and in the Cedar River Valley. In addition there were several important unconnected lines.

CLINTON DAVENPORT AND MUSCATINE RAILWAY

Parallel to the Mississippi extended the 65-mile Clinton Davenport and Muscatine, made up of two segments built at different dates, which extended north and south out of Davenport and were operated independently.

The first of the two lines, from Clinton to Davenport, was built as the Iowa and Illinois Railway, and began operation on November 20, 1904. The southern line, the Davenport and Muscatine Railway, a 1,200-volt operation, was placed in service on August 1, 1912. The line cut inland from the Mississippi instead of following the river. In 1912 United Light and Railways acquired both lines and merged them in 1926 as the CD&M.

The two segments of the road were built to relatively high standards, on private right-of-way except in the cities. The arched-window wooden cars ran in single units, with hourly service for many years. Much of the business went through from Davenport to the two terminal cities, and many trains ran as limiteds. No interchange of equipment or through service on the two lines was physically possible. As passenger business declined, lightweight cars were introduced, and service was cut by the thirties to six runs a day on each line. Meanwhile, the freight traffic, instituted in 1912, had grown rapidly, especially on the Clinton line, and by 1934 over 10,000 cars were handled in interchange with the steam roads. But this was inadequate to keep the road going; the Muscatine line was abandoned in November

1938, and the Clinton line on March 31, 1940; the most important freight segment, from Davenport to LeClaire (14 miles), was taken over by the Davenport Rock Island & Northwestern, a joint subsidiary of the Burlington and the Milwaukee.

CEDAR RAPIDS AND IOWA CITY RAILWAY

One of the most financially successful interurbans over a long period of time was the Cedar Rapids and Iowa City,[41] known by its initials as the Crandic, a subsidiary of Iowa Railway and Light Company. The 27-mile private-right-of-way line from Cedar Rapids southward via the villages of Swisher and North Liberty to Iowa City was placed in operation on August 13, 1904. A decade later (1914) the road made the mistake of beginning to build a line to Davenport; it reached Mount Vernon and Lisbon, 17 miles from Cedar Rapids, before rising costs and falling profits led to the suspension of construction. There was inadequate traffic to support the branch as it stood, and it was abandoned in 1928.

The main line, however, prospered. Although there were no intermediate towns of any size, there was a substantial flow of traffic between Iowa City and Cedar Rapids; many a college student at the University of Iowa, for example, commuted on the Crandic. The typical hourly service was curtailed during the depression, but restored again during World War II, and as late as 1951 the road was operating 14 passenger trains a day, one of the last to operate typical high-frequency interurban service. Passengers were carried for many years in a series of wooden cars, some built by Stephenson in 1904, and two obtained from the Southern New York. In 1939 six modern steel cars were acquired from the abandoned Cincinnati and Lake Erie, and provided the bulk of the service for the remaining years. One additional lightweight car was obtained from the Indiana Railroad. Despite the drop in traffic after World War II, the total volume remained substantial for a time, but by 1952 the service had become so unprofitable that the road was forced to cut service drastically, and on May 30, 1953, all passenger operations were discontinued.

Meanwhile, however, the company had built up a very substantial carload interchange freight service, in connection with the Rock Island at Iowa City and the Milwaukee and the Northwestern in Cedar Rapids. Much of the business consisted of switching into industrial plants in Cedar Rapids. By 1950 freight service was grossing nearly $1 million a year, 90 per cent of all revenues. As soon as passenger service ended, freight service was dieselized.

WATERLOO CEDAR FALLS AND NORTHERN RAILWAY

The second largest of the Iowa systems, and the pioneer interurban in the United States in the development of carload interchange business, was the Waterloo Cedar Falls and Northern, known as the Cedar Valley Road.[42] The antecedent company was the Waterloo and Cedar Falls Rapid Transit Company, which was organized in 1895, and in 1897 completed an 8-mile line from Waterloo to Cedar Falls and electrified the Waterloo street railway system. The road was reorganized in 1904 as the Waterloo Cedar Falls and Northern. In 1901 it began to build north, reaching Denver (14 miles) in that year. In 1903 the line was extended to a junction with the Chicago Great Western at Denver Junction, and the road obtained trackage rights over the CGW to Sumner, 44 miles from Waterloo, and operated steam passenger service between the two cities. In 1910 it built its own electrified line from Denver Junction into Waverly, and discontinued the trackage agreement. Not until 1912 did the road begin to build the main line southward to Cedar Rapids. Track was completed to La Porte City in December 1912, to Urbana in December 1913, and to Cedar Rapids on September 14, 1914. The road was founded and owned by the three Cass brothers of Waterloo, one of whom, L. S. Cass, served as president until 1923, when he was succeeded by C. M. Cheney. In 50 years the company had only two presidents.

The private-right-of-way line, with some street running in the towns, was maintained to high standards. Because of the plans for high-speed freight operations, the main line was built to operate at 1,300-volt DC. Much of the equipment was designed to operate at full speed on either 1,300 or 650 volts, the latter current used in the main cities. The road began service with relatively small wooden equipment; near the time of completion of the main line it acquired 7 cars from McGuire-Cummings, which were destined to supply most of the main-line service from that time until the fifties. Three of these, designed for parlor car use with open-end observation platforms, were rebuilt as coaches when traffic proved inadequate for multiple-unit operation, and in later years provided all main-line service, with 8 trains a day in peak years, 3 in the 1930's, and 2 after 1948. The Waverly line, with 5 trains a day in

Iowa 361

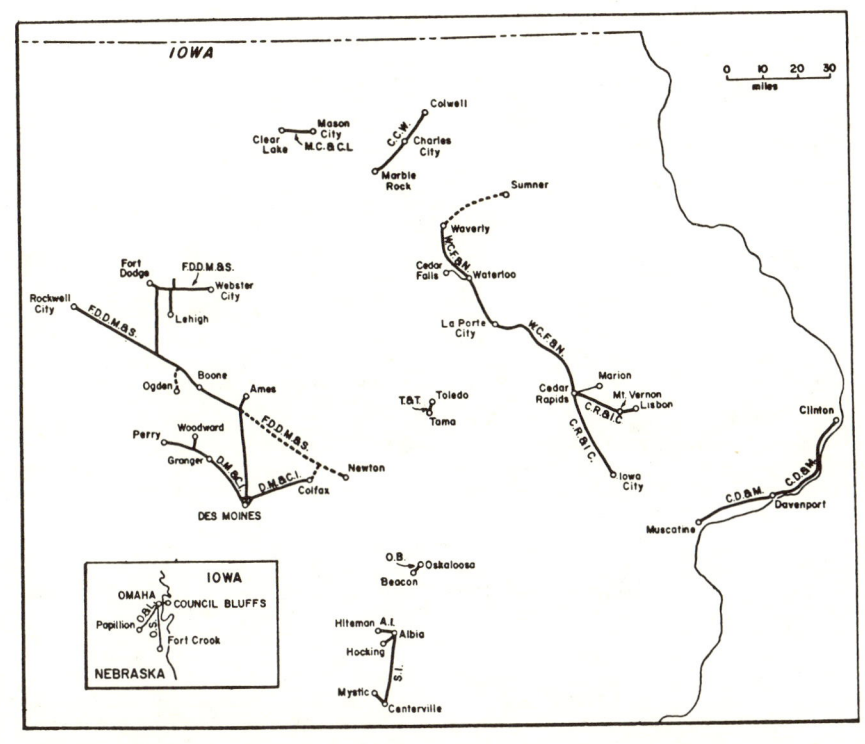

MC&CL: Mason City & Clear Lake RR
CCW: Charles City Western Ry.
WCF&N: Waterloo Cedar Falls & Northern Ry.
CR&IC: Cedar Rapids & Iowa City Ry.
T&T: Tama & Toledo Elec. Ry.
DM&CI: Des Moines & Central Iowa RR
FDDM&S: Fort Dodge Des Moines & Southern Ry.
OB: Oskaloosa-Buxton Elec. Ry.
AI: Albia Interurban Ry.

SI: Southern Iowa Utilities Co.
CD&M: Clinton Davenport & Muscatine Ry.

NEBRASKA SUBURBAN LINES

O&L: Omaha & Lincoln Ry. & Light Co.
OS: Omaha Southern Ry.
Broken lines indicate routes owned or operated by interurban companies, but not electrified.

peak years, was down to 1 daily train in the thirties. The Cedar Falls line, which used streetcar type equipment (in later years two cars from Knoxville, Tennessee), provided relatively frequent service, often at 30-minute intervals. The passenger service was gradually cut; on the main line, after 1952, one of the two trains began week-end operation only, and then the other daily train was taken off, leaving only the week-end schedule. Service to Waverly ended in August 1954. On October 31, 1954, a fire in the Waterloo roundhouse destroyed all remaining passenger equipment except car 100, one of the observation-end cars, which carried on passenger service alone for another 18 months, ending on February 19, 1956. The Waterloo–Cedar Falls service operated until July 31, 1958, the last electric passenger service in Iowa. In peak years the road had operated a through Pullman to Waterloo from Chicago in conjunction with the C&NW, one of the few interurbans ever to handle steam-road passenger equipment.

The Waterloo road was one of the first lines to push the development of carload interchange business. President Cass, in papers given at annual conventions, constantly exhorted his colleagues in the industry to do the same. The road was able to interest the Great Western in cooperative arrangements at an early date, and for many years much of its business arose from interchange with this road. The Waterloo also provided Cedar Rapids connections for CGW passenger trains. A large part of the freight traffic originated on the Waterloo belt line, which serves many Waterloo industries. It was the success of the freight policy that kept the road going; neither the main line nor the Waverly branch had nearly enough potential passenger traffic to support it, and without carload freight the road would not have lasted through the twenties. Before World War I the road did well financially, with a low operating ratio, but it was not able to restore a satisfactory cost-rate relationship after the war, and by the mid-twenties was not able to cover operating expenses. Bondholders set up a protective committee to safeguard their interests, but made no effort to oust the Cass management. An increase in freight traffic in the late twenties brought improved profits again. The depression affected the road somewhat less than many interurbans; while the revenue fell in half between 1929 and 1932, the company survived the depression with only two years of losses, and by 1940 its revenues reached an all-time high. But the margin over costs was still not good, and in 1940 the company entered receivership, with reorganization in 1944. The postwar situation was again one of relatively small margins over operating expenses and taxes. Shortly after main-line passenger service ended in 1956, the road was sold to the Illinois Central and the Rock Island, which renamed it the Waterloo Railroad. The Waverly line was abandoned.

CEDAR RAPIDS AND MARION CITY RAILWAY

One of the earliest lines to be built in the state, and one of the first in the country to be described as an interurban, was the Cedar Rapids and Marion, completed between those two cities (8 miles) in 1892. Even from the beginning, this was essentially a suburban operation, and an integral part of the local streetcar system. This property became a part of the United Light and Railways Company. Together with the other Cedar Rapids city lines, it was abandoned in 1938 and replaced by a bus system.

CHARLES CITY WESTERN RAILWAY

In the area northwest of Waterloo is located one of Iowa's smallest interurbans, the Charles City Western, extending 21 miles from Marble Rock through Charles City to Colwell. It was completed from Charles City to Marble Rock in 1911, for operation with a McKeen motor car and steam locomotives. In 1915 the Colwell line was built, and on July 30 of the same year the electrification of the entire line was completed, with the aid of a $120,000 subsidy from adjacent property owners, unusual in the history of American interurbans.

The line reached downtown Charles City by a line on city streets shared with the company's one and only streetcar, and operated on private right-of-way to Marble Rock and to Colwell. A belt line in Charles City was used for freight from the beginning, and the interurban car operated on this line following the abandonment of the city line in the early twenties. In 1915 the line acquired one arched-roof semisteel car, No. 50, from McGuire-Cummings, which performed the bulk of the line's interurban service from the day it was acquired until passenger service ended in 1952. The line was one of the first to operate one-man interurban service, although the cars were never adapted for this service, and when operating in one direction the motorman was separated from his passengers by the baggage compartment.

Passenger service never exceeded two round trips a day, and only one was operated in later years, the runs largely designed to connect at Marble Rock with Rock Island main-line trains. Freight service was of primary importance from the beginning, and the road owned a series of freight motors, mostly second-hand from the Shore Line. The strictly local enterprise developed carload freight interchange with the steam roads from the beginning, providing a connection into Charles City for the Rock Island and service to the Oliver Plow Company.

The line continues in freight service, using two electric locomotives for road hauls and two diesels for switching.

MASON CITY AND CLEAR LAKE RAILROAD

One of the smallest of the Iowa lines was the 11-mile Mason City and Clear Lake, opened for service on July 4, 1897, primarily to provide service for vacationers to Clear Lake. Because of the problem of heavy peak loads, the road acquired open trailers to operate behind its relatively powerful motors. From an early date, steam-road passenger cars were taken through to Clear Lake, and the road was one of the first to interchange equipment with steam roads. One of the major sources of freight traffic was ice from the lake, shipped out to various cities in the winter months. As automobiles took the bulk of the passenger traffic, the heavy equipment was replaced by lightweight cars in 1923, which in turn gave way to buses in 1936. Unlike most short lines, the company retained its bus service. This was a United

Light and Railway property. The road is still in existence as a freight carrier, and is still electrified.

TAMA AND TOLEDO ELECTRIC RAILWAY

One of the country's tiniest interurbans was the Tama and Toledo, which connected the two small towns of its name—each with a population of about 2,000—in east central Iowa, providing a connection for the Northwestern and the Milwaukee to Toledo. The road was owned, in conjunction with the power system, by Iowa Electric Power, the owners of Crandic. The line operated an open car in earlier years, and then a standard streetcar, providing connections for all C&NW and Milwaukee trains from 1894 until service was abandoned on June 17, 1925. But freight service, with a little industrial gasoline engine, was operated until the line's abandonment in 1954.

OSKALOOSA-BUXTON ELECTRIC RAILWAY

The town of Oskaloosa had not only a city streetcar system, but also a 3-mile line to Beacon operated with a conventional interurban car all out of proportion to the size of the line. The track was completed in 1907, but an extension to Buxton to connect with a proposed Southern Iowa line was never built. The line was abandoned in 1920.

SOUTHERN IOWA RAILWAY

The main line of this road, from Albia to Centerville, was built in 1879 as a portion of the Wabash system, and used by the line's Des Moines trains. It passed into the hands of the Iowa Central (M&StL) in 1890 under lease from the bondholders, who had taken it over when the Wabash entered bankruptcy. In 1910, under the name of the Southern Iowa Traction, the road undertook operation of its own line with steam power. In 1914 it was absorbed by the Centerville Light and Traction Company, which operated the street railway, electrified it, and united it with the Centerville road's Mystic line (built in 1909) under the name of the Centerville Albia and Southern. Improved freight facilities were provided in Centerville, with connections for the main lines in the area. The Mystic line served several mines.

Passenger service was never very extensive, rarely were more than 6 trains a day operated on the main line, with hourly service on the short route from Centerville to Mystic. Service on the main line was performed with a center-door American interurban car, and on the branch line with a suburban-type equipment. The road stressed its passenger connections with the Burlington's main line at Albia, as well as with the Wabash and the M&StL, and with the Milwaukee at Mystic. The coming of the automobile and the depression ended most of the passenger business, and all passenger service was discontinued in March 1933.

The road became the Southern Iowa Utilities Company in 1926, and the Southern Iowa Railway in 1941, but still owned by the local power-company interests. All track was retained until 1944, when the Mystic line was cut back to Appanoose, a connection being retained with the Milwaukee at Trask. In 1948 the 10-mile segment from Moravia to Albia was abandoned. Thus 18 miles of track from Appanoose via Mystic to Moravia were still in operation by electric power for freight service in 1960, providing connection for both the Wabash and the Milwaukee into Centerville.

ALBIA INTERURBAN RAILWAY

Distinct from the Southern Iowa property was another short-line electric, the Albia Interurban, which in 1908 placed in operation two lines out of Albia, to Hiteman and to Hocking, with a total of 11 miles of track. The company also operated the Albia local system. All operations were abandoned in 1925.

FORT DODGE DES MOINES AND SOUTHERN RAILWAY[43]

The largest Iowa system, the Fort Dodge Line, operated 147 miles of line, with an 85-mile main line from Fort Dodge southeastward via Boone to Des Moines, and branches to Ames, Rockwell City, Lehigh, and Webster City.

This company began life as a steam road, the Newton & Northwestern, which in 1905 had completed a line, almost straight, from Newton to Rockwell City, with a branch into Colfax. The Fort Dodge Des Moines and Southern Railroad Company was incorporated in 1906, and purchased the Newton line, as well as the Ames and College Street Railway. Actually the new company was promoted by the same interests as the Newton road, headed by Des Moines investor and coal-mine owner, Hamilton Browne. The company recognized that a line from Newton to Rockwell, as such, offered few possibilities; it electrified only the middle portion, from Hope to Midvale, in 1907, and built two extensions to this, one south from Midvale to a connection with the Des Moines and Central Iowa to provide service into the capital city, and one north from Hope into Fort Dodge. Through service over the new line, from Fort Dodge to Des Moines, was established on November 4, 1907, with high-speed Niles cars. A branch was built from Kelley into Ames. In 1911 the voltage was raised to 1,200 to facilitate freight operation when the Rockwell City line was electrified, and the steam-operated Midvale–Newton line was abandoned. Several changes were made in the entrance into Des Moines. A new line was built, and at first cars were operated into the Rock Island station over Rock Island trackage. Next, cars came in from Capitol Hill over city system trackage to the DM&CI station, and in later years terminated at the end of the private right-of-way at Capitol Hill.

The last expansion came in 1916, when the steam-operated Crooked Creek Railroad from Webster City to Lehigh was purchased, connected with the main line at Fort Dodge by the purchase of a Great Western branch, and electrified. This group of lines serves a large gypsum-producing area, and has been a major source of traffic for the line since that time, in later years yielding about half the freight revenue.

The entire line was built to high standards, with a bridge 800 feet long and 156 feet high across the Des Moines Valley north of Boone, which replaced a wooden trestle of the old Newton road. Except for a limited amount in Des Moines and Fort Dodge, there was no street running. Much of central Iowa is hilly, and the road was much more picturesque than many Midwestern lines. The road had some of the best equipment of its day, the original 10 wooden Niles cars with clerestory roofs being supplemented by steel arched-roof cars built in 1915 and 1916. A number of freight motors were acquired from GE in 1911, and in 1947 three motors that had been built in 1942 and 1944 were purchased from the Oregon Electric when it was dieselized. The road, like the Waterloo, owned a number of standard freight cars, at times as many as 500.

Passenger-service schedules resembled those of a steam road more than a typical Midwest interurban. During the peak years 8 trains a day were operated on the main line (2-hour intervals), with connections for the various branches. The branch-line revenue was never large, and after the development of the automobile revenue fell sharply. As a result, branch-line passenger trains to Rockwell City were eliminated in 1926, to Webster City in 1927, and to Ames in 1928. Service on the main line was cut down to 4 trains each way a day, and remained at this level for twenty years, being cut to 2 in the early fifties and operated in later years largely to facilitate the handling of freight crews. In 1954 the road began systematically to dieselize its freight operations, starting with the branch lines. In June of that year a flood of the Des Moines River wrecked the power plant at Fraser, and for four months all freights were operated with diesels borrowed from other roads. However, the electric system was restored, and passenger service resumed. At the end of August 1955, all passenger service was ended, and the main line was dieselized.

From early days the road depended primarily on freight for revenue. The road was planned as an electrified freight and passenger operation, not merely as a typical passenger and package-freight interurban. In addition to the important gypsum business (which the road served for the most part without competition), substantial interchange with the steam roads to industrial plants in the cities served was developed. The growth of the freight business gave the road a very favorable operating ratio and return on investment by 1914, and although the ratio had risen sharply by 1924, the return was still relatively good. However, the depression forced the road into receivership, and in the postwar period, despite annual revenues in excess of $2 million, difficulties were encountered in covering operating expenses. In 1956, for example, a relatively good year, the road had an operating deficit before taxes of over $100,000. The Fort Dodge line was, like the Waterloo, strictly a local railroad enterprise, never affiliated with other systems. In 1954 the line was sold to the Salzburg interests, a scrap-metal firm which has continued to operate for long periods several small railroads that it has purchased.

DES MOINES AND CENTRAL IOWA RAILROAD (INTER-URBAN RAILWAY)

One of the earliest Iowa lines was the road extending from Des Moines northwestward to Perry (35 miles) and eastward to Colfax (26 miles), built by the Inter-Urban Railway, incorporated in 1899. The first line built was the one to Colfax, opened in 1902. The cars on this line entered Des Moines on city-system tracks, but freight service, largely coal from mines on the line, was handled by a belt line around the edge of the city. Colfax was a resort area of some importance, and the passenger business was largely seasonal. The line up the Beaver Valley to Perry, with a short branch to Woodward, was completed in 1906.

The DM&CI was one of the weaker Iowa lines, the potential passenger business being severely limited, except for the operation of Camp Dodge during the two world wars. The towns served were too small to generate enough flow of traffic to Des Moines to make passenger service profitable, even under the most favorable conditions. Only the steam-road interchange kept the road going. Unfortunately the Milwaukee, with which the road connected at its western terminal, had its own line into Des Moines. For many years 9 passenger trains a day were operated to Perry (with two or more side trips to Woodward), and 9 to Colfax. By the early thirties the Colfax service was down to 3 trains, and in 1941 these were eliminated, the line being abandoned in 1946. Mainline passenger service was discontinued to Woodward in 1941, from Granger to Perry in 1948, and entirely in 1949. In 1949 all operations were dieselized. The Woodward branch was torn up in 1946, and the Granger–Perry segment in 1954. Thus all that remained for freight operation in 1958 was the line from Des Moines to Granger and the industrial belt in Des Moines, part of the old Colfax line.

The ancient wooden equipment dating back to 1906 was supplemented with two equally old Air Line cars, bought from the Gary and Interurban in 1917 to handle Camp Dodge traffic, and finally, in 1939, with three big steel interurbans, which had been built in 1918 by Jewett for the Lake Shore.

The original Inter-Urban was reorganized as the Des Moines and Central Iowa in 1922. It was developed by and affiliated with the Des Moines Street Railway for many years, and for a period operated directly by it. Both companies were almost wholly owned by N. W. Harris of Chicago. The city system, itself chronically in financial difficulties, was of little aid to the weak interurban, and in 1949 the road was sold to Salzburg. The city system operated two long suburban lines, to Fort Des Moines and to Urbandale—the last car lines operated, which were replaced by buses in 1950 and 1951.

Nebraska

It is rather surprising that the state of Nebraska had no strictly interurban lines, although many were projected.[44] The *Omaha Lincoln and Beatrice* had great plans for connecting the three cities of its corporate name, but in practice it never became more than a suburban car line and a freight-switching road in Lincoln, although it still served in the latter capacity in 1960. There were two suburban lines out of Omaha. One was the *Omaha and Southern Interurban Railway* (see map, p. 361), which operated 8 miles of line from Omaha southward to Fort Crook. This line, essentially a suburban streetcar line, and a subsidiary of the street railway system, was placed in operation on October 20, 1906, and abandoned twenty-five years later, in 1931.

The other suburban line, the *Omaha and Lincoln Railway and Light Company* (see map, p. 361), originally the Nebraska Traction and Power Company, operated 8 miles of line from Omaha to the suburb Papillon. This line was placed in operation on May 19, 1909, to Ralston, and in 1914 to Papillon. The road was a power company affiliate, and passed into the hands of the McKinley interests. It was abandoned in 1926.

Missouri, Kansas, and Oklahoma

A belt extending southward from St. Joseph through Kansas City and Joplin to Oklahoma City and Tulsa contained several quite extensive networks of interurbans, more than might be expected in terms of the population. The largest of these networks centered around the area in which the states of Missouri, Kansas, and Oklahoma meet, the second radiated out from Kansas City, and the third was located in the Oklahoma City-Tulsa area. In addition there was substantial mileage in the Arkansas Valley in Kansas, and a few scattered lines in other parts of the three states.

EASTERN MISSOURI

Surprisingly, the entire state of Missouri, except for the far western fringe, had only a negligible mileage of interurban lines. There were no truly interurban lines operating out of St. Louis to other points in the state, although there were several suburban car lines, operating in conjunction with the St. Louis transit system (a North American Company property) to street railway standards. The longest of these was the line to St. Charles, originally the *St. Louis St. Charles and Western*. This line was abandoned in 1932. The second major route was that to Florissant, completed in 1891 as one of the earliest inter-city trolley routes in the country.

ST. FRANCOIS COUNTY RAILROAD

The only interurban in the area south of St. Louis was the St. Francois County, completed between De Lassus and Flat River via Farmington on December 22, 1904, in the lead- and zinc-mining area of southeast Missouri (see map, p. 340). For many years it was operated by the Mississippi River & Bonne Terre, a steam railroad affiliated with the Missouri & Illinois, and extending southward from a connection with the M&I at Riverside to the Bonne Terre mining area. Trains of the St. Francois County connected with MR&BT trains at Esther for Farmington and De Lassus, where a connection was also made with the Missouri Pacific.

In 1926 the steam-road parent line was abandoned south of Elvins and the St. Francois resumed independent operation, after it was sold to local businessmen. Its connections were now with the Missouri Pacific at De Lassus, and the Missouri & Illinois at Hurryville, the paralleling segment from Flat River to Hurryville being abandoned in 1927. Passenger service was discontinued in 1927 and freight trains operated with the two interurban passenger cars. Most of the business was to and from Farmington, which now had no other railroad. Diesel power eventually replaced electricity. In 1957 the road was finally abandoned when most of its remaining business, handling coal to a hospital, was lost when gas was substituted.

MEXICO INVESTMENT AND CONSTRUCTION COMPANY

One of the most ill-fated lines was the road completed from Mexico, Missouri to the village of Santa Fe (16 miles) in 1915 (see map, p. 340). The 9-mile segment to Molino had been built in 1908 as the Mexico Santa Fe and Perry. The road was intended as a link to connect with the St. Louis and Hannibal at Perry, and thus establish a through route from central Missouri to Hannibal, but funds were lacking to complete the project. As a local road the company was hopelessly unprofitable, as only a few hundred persons lived in the towns connected by the line to Mexico. In 1917 the entire road was abandoned, and after attempts at reorganization failed, was torn up the following year.

KANSAS CITY AREA ROADS

Five interurbans operated out of Kansas City: one company, with two routes, serving Missouri points, and the other four extending westward into Kansas.

KANSAS CITY CLAY COUNTY AND ST. JOSEPH RAILWAY[45]

The largest Kansas City system was that of the Kansas City Clay County and St. Joseph, whose 79 miles of line were brought into operation at the relatively late date 1913. A 28-mile line, completed January 13, extended eastward through Avondale and Liberty to Excelsior Springs. The 51-mile line to St. Joseph on the Missouri side of the river, via Dearborn and Faucett, opened May 5, 1913, was for many years operated on hourly schedules. Two hours were required for the run, 20 minutes of which were used to travel the 2 miles from the Kansas City terminal at 13th and Walnut on streetcar tracks across the Missouri River bridge. The two terminal cities were large enough to provide substantial through traffic. The road was built on a private right-of-way, to relatively high standards, with 1,200-volt power. In the mid-twenties the road was relatively profitable, with gross revenues of over $700,000 annually, and net before interest of $150,000. Despite increased car usage, revenue fell only slightly up to 1929. The depression, however, caused a disastrous drop in business, the 1932 gross being well under half that of 1929. The road entered receivership in 1930, and was abandoned on March 10, 1933. This line without question would have lasted for many years had it not been so severely affected by the depression, or if the owners had been willing to hold out another year or so. This is one of the few cases in which owners deliberately liquidated a road early in the period of decline in order to withdraw as much money as possible. The road was owned largely by New York interests, but was not affiliated with power or other enterprises in the area.

ST. JOSEPH AND SAVANNAH ELECTRIC RAILWAY

An 11-mile interurban line extended from St. Joseph to Savannah; it was built in 1911 by the St. Joseph and Savannah, and owned and operated by the St. Joseph Railway Light Heat and Power Company. Three wooden Brill cars, somewhat larger than would be expected in terms of the size of the line, were acquired when the line was built. The track was on private right-of-way except for street operation in St. Joseph, the line terminating on the square in Savannah. Strangely, the obscure little line outlived the St. Joseph city lines and most of the big Kansas City interurbans—it was not abandoned until the late thirties.

MISSOURI AND KANSAS INTERURBAN RAILWAY

In 1907 the Missouri and Kansas, known as the Strang line (incorporated in 1904), completed its line 20 miles southwestward from Kansas City to Olathe, Kansas, via Overland Park (the cars entering Kansas City, Missouri, over street railway tracks). The line was owned by W. B. Strang and his associates, and operated at first with an invention of the president, a gasoline motor car known as the Strang car. This did not prove successful and the road was electrified in 1909. For many years hourly service was operated, with additional cars at rush hours. Three modern arched-roof lightweight cars were obtained in 1925 from American. Carload freight was interchanged with the Frisco and the Santa Fe, for delivery to industries on the line.

The company encountered financial difficulties in the late twenties and was reorganized in 1929, but it managed to survive the depression, earning a small margin over operating expenses up until 1938. In later years freight and passenger revenue were of about equal importance. All service was abandoned on July 24, 1940.

KANSAS CITY KAW VALLEY AND WESTERN RAILWAY (KANSAS CITY–KAW VALLEY)

The 35-mile line extending westward from Kansas City to Lawrence was the last interurban in this area to be built, reaching Bonner Springs in 1914 and Lawrence in 1915. The destination was Topeka, but this goal was never realized. Hourly service was provided to Lawrence for many years, with additional local trains to Bonner Springs. The cars reached the station at 10th and Main Street in Kansas City, Missouri, over streetcar tracks from Kansas City, Kansas. As with all Kansas roads, a freight interchange business was built up, primarily to industries in the Kansas City, Kansas, area. The road had bought the terminal properties and rights-of-way of the Kansas City Mexico & Orient, which were of great benefit to it in developing freight traffic. This portion is now the Kansas and Missouri Railway and Terminal Co., jointly owned by the Kaw Valley and the Kansas City Southern.

Despite the considerable volume of business to Lawrence, the road was in financial difficulties by the late twenties as autos and buses cut into its revenue and made it

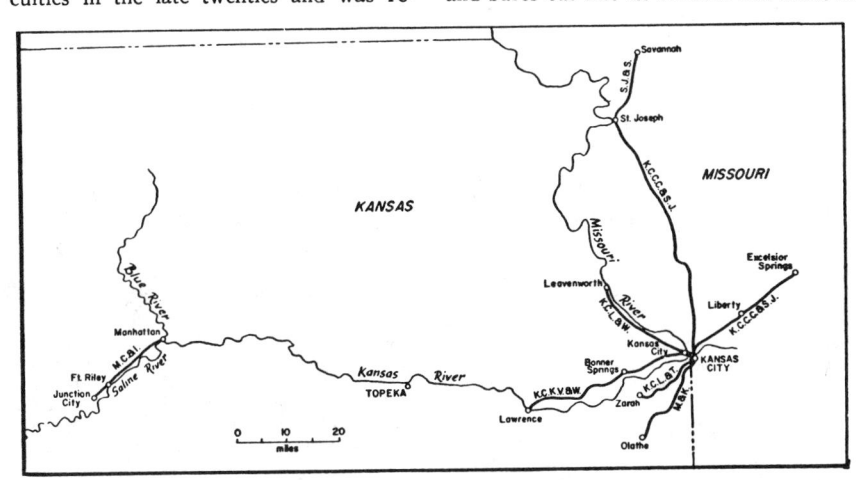

KCL&W: Kansas City Leavenworth & Western Ry.
KCKV&W: Kansas City Kaw Valley & Western Ry.
KCL&T: Kansas City Lawrence & Topeka Elec. RR.
SJ&S: St. Joseph & Savannah Elec. Ry.
KCCC&SJ: Kansas City Clay County & St. Joseph Ry.
M&K: Missouri & Kansas Interurban Ry.
MC&I: Manhattan City & Interurban Ry.

almost impossible for it to cover operating expenses. The company was soon in bankruptcy, and was reorganized in 1929. It barely survived the depression; in 1935 it eliminated all passenger service and was reorganized as the Kansas City–Kaw Valley Railroad, Inc. The 22-mile segment west of Bonner Springs was abandoned in 1949, largely at the insistence of Lawrence that the tracks be removed from city streets. The 13-mile remnant from Kansas City to Bonner Springs was still providing carload freight service in 1960.

KANSAS CITY LEAVENWORTH AND WESTERN RAILWAY

The first interurban to be built in the Kansas City area was completed in January, 1900, up the west side of the Missouri River via Wolcott and Lansing to Leavenworth, 26 miles. The line was built as the Kansas City–Leavenworth Railway, by the Cleveland Contracting Co., builders of the Toledo–Fostoria and Hamilton–Cincinnati lines, and was sold in 1905 to the Fisk-Robinson group, who renamed it the Kansas City Western. The company operated frequent passenger service with good equipment. Cars reached downtown Leavenworth over streetcar tracks also owned by the company, and Kansas City, Missouri, via the Public Service Company tracks and the Kansas City viaduct line. Unlike its neighbors the KCL&W was primarily a passenger carrier.

The road did well financially for many years, but the interest burden was relatively heavy, and insufficiency of earnings to meet fixed charges after World War I led to bankruptcy and reorganization in 1920, as the Kansas City Leavenworth and Western. During the twenties the net earnings, just about equal to the interest charges on the reduced debt, were remarkably stable, expenses declining roughly to the same extent as the gradual fall in revenue. The depression squeezed the road severely, but it managed to survive the worst years, continuing to operate until 1938, when the building of a dam flooded a portion of the line and funds were not available for track relocation.

KANSAS CITY LAWRENCE AND TOPEKA ELECTRIC RAILROAD (KANSAS CITY MERRIAM AND SHAWNEE)

The smallest of the Kansas City lines was the 12-mile line of the Kansas City Lawrence and Topeka, which stopped many miles short of the last two cities of its corporate title, extending only 12 miles from Kansas City to the town of Zarah.

It was incorporated in 1909 as a consolidation of the Kansas City and Olathe (which had built to Shawnee from Kansas City) and the Kansas City and Topeka. The 7-mile extension to Zarah was completed in 1910. The company entered bankruptcy in 1919 and abandoned all service in 1927. A new company, the Kansas City Merriam and Shawnee, formed by local interests to keep the line going for freight service, commenced operations in 1928 on the 7-mile portion from Rosedale to Rose Hill. The little road was barely able to cover expenses for a few years, and finally was completely abandoned in 1934.

THE NETWORK IN THE KANSAS-MISSOURI-OKLAHOMA CORNER

Over 230 miles of line spread out through the area in which these three states meet (see map, p. 370). Three of these systems were connected to form a triangle. These included the pioneer Southwest Missouri, the originally steam-operated Northeast Oklahoma, and the Joplin and Pittsburg. A few miles farther west, but not connected with these lines, was the 77-mile Union. A short line, the Iola, north of the Union completed the mileage in this area.

SOUTHWEST MISSOURI ELECTRIC RAILWAY[46]

One of the pioneer interurbans in the country, the Southwest Missouri built a network of lines out of Joplin in the last half of the 1890's. The system grew out of a mule-car line built in 1890 from Joplin to Webb City. This 6-mile segment, plus 2 miles to Cartersville, was electrified in 1893 as the Southwest Missouri Electric Railway. In 1895 a 12-mile line was built eastward from Carterville to the old city of Carthage, and a year later another 12-mile line went westward from Joplin to Galena, Kansas. The loop line via Duenweg was built in 1903, and a line from Webb City northward to Alba in 1906, as the Webb City Northern. This was the last extension for a decade; in 1917 the road acquired and electrified steam-road trackage from Galena to Baxter Springs and to Picher (completed 1918), and a connection with the Northeast Oklahoma. One of the early promoters was Charles L. Henry of the Union of Indiana, but the road was actually completed by a syndicate from Harrisburg, Pennsylvania.

The SWM was one of the very first interurbans in the country, and its development was widely publicized. The road served a thickly settled lead- and zinc-mining area, and frequent service carried a large volume of miners and shoppers, originally in little wooden cars, many built in the line's own shops. Half-hour service was usual on the main line west of Webb City, and hourly service east, even as late as 1930. The road was one of the first interurbans to provide limited service, established from Joplin to Carthage in the mid-1890's.

The road was relatively profitable, and paid dividends up until 1921. Thereafter it suffered a severe loss in traffic, both from increased car usage and from the decline in mining, and a long period of operating deficits (described in Chapter 8). The Duenweg line was abandoned in 1924 and the Alba line in 1927. The main-line passenger service was first cut in 1937, when operations from Carthage through Joplin to Galena were eliminated. The Baxter Springs–Galena service was cut out in 1938, leaving only the service from the Springs to Picher, which was abandoned in 1939, the track being sold to the Northeast Oklahoma (q.v.) for continued freight operation.

JOPLIN AND PITTSBURG RAILWAY[47]

The second of the lines in the area to be built, and the largest in terms of mileage, was the Joplin and Pittsburg, which at its peak operated 82 miles of line, all but 12 of them in Kansas. The J&P was incorporated in 1907 as a consolidation of the Pittsburg Street Railway and the Joplin and Pittsburg Street Railway. The main line, extending 27 miles northwestward from Joplin to Pittsburg, was completed in October of 1908. A second line (also 1908) extended southward from Pittsburg via Weir City and Scammon to Columbus. This line had two short branches, from Cherokee Junction to Cherokee (1909) and from Scammon to West Mineral (1908). The third line consisted of a Y with a bar across the top, going northward from Pittsburg to Dunkirk, and then forking, one line going northwestward via Ringo to Girard, and the second northeastward via Croweburg to Mulberry. The two legs of the Y were joined by a straight line, giving a direct route from Girard to Mulberry. The Girard–Mulberry line, most of the Croweburg line, and the Ringo–Dunkirk segment were built by the Girard Coal Belt Electric Railway in 1907 (Girard–Ringo) and 1908 (Dunkirk via Ringo to Croweburg). The GCBE was acquired by J&P in 1909, and the following year the lines from Pittsburg to Dunkirk and Franklin, and from Mulberry to Croweburg were built.

These lines served a major coal-producing area, and from the first carload freight was handled as well as passenger traffic. The passenger trains were operated in two major runs, from Joplin through Pittsburg to Mulberry, and from Columbus through Pittsburg to Girard, sharing the same track between Pittsburg and Dunkirk Junction. The other lines were served by connecting trains. For many years, hourly and hour-and-fifteen-minute service was provided on the two main lines. Streetcars were operated in Pittsburg (plus a line to Frontenac) and Joplin.

Like the Southwest Missouri, the road suffered severely from the combined effects of the automobile and the decline of mining, and finally, from the depression. Its revenue per mile had always been relatively low, and even the best years had never permitted more than a 2 per cent return on investment. By 1924 operating expenses were barely covered. Total revenue in 1930 was less than half the 1924 figure.

In 1928 the road began to cut back its passenger service, eliminating it from the Mineral and Cherokee branches. In 1930 much more drastic changes occurred. All passenger service was eliminated except the local service from Pittsburg to Frontenac, and the Girard line was totally abandoned. The 22 miles of track south of Cherokee Junction, including the Mineral branch, were sold to the Northeast Oklahoma (which continued passenger service north of Columbus to Scammon until 1933). This left only the main line from Pittsburg to Joplin, plus the northern line cut back to Croweburg and the segment to Cherokee Junction (Fleming), which the road continued to operate for freight service until 1951. Small segments, including that from Joplin to Waco, had been torn up before. Freight business was not unimportant—the road grossed about $100,000 a year from freight in later years.

The J&P was not affiliated with any of its neighbors, being promoted and owned by a group of Kansas City investors. Its long history of financial difficulties offered good evidence that even in the most favorable years, a road with extensive mileage serving small towns could not make a reasonable return on investment, even with some carload freight business.

NORTHEAST OKLAHOMA RAILROAD

The last of the Joplin-area roads to be developed and the last to operate was the Northeast Oklahoma. This road began life in 1908 as the Oklahoma Kansas and Missouri Inter-Urban Railway; its promoters planned a network of nonelectrified lines north from Miami, Oklahoma. But only 5 miles from Miami to Hattonville were completed until 1917 when the road built on north to Picher and thence southward to Century. This 13-mile line was operated on hourly intervals with gasoline motor cars. On November 1, 1919, the road was purchased by the Northeast Oklahoma Railroad (first called Northeast Oklahoma Traction), and in January 1921 electrification was completed and service began. Construction was also started northward in 1922, reaching Westville (3 miles from Picher) in that year, and early in 1923 service was established to Columbus (10 miles from Westville) where, in the city square, connection was made with the Joplin and Pittsburg. The NEO was a subsidiary of the Eagle-Picher Mining and Smelting Company, the major operator of the mines in the area.

In 1930 the Joplin and Pittsburg discontinued passenger service on the Columbus line, and later in the year the NEO purchased the portion of the J&P south of Cherokee, including the West Mineral branch, relocated the line off of the square in Columbus, and reestablished passenger service as far north as Scammon. In 1933 the portion of the West Mineral line west of Corona was abandoned. The NEO purchased the line primarily to ensure continued operation of the through freight route to the smelters from mines on the J&P. In 1939 the road bought the last segment of the Southwest Missouri, ex-

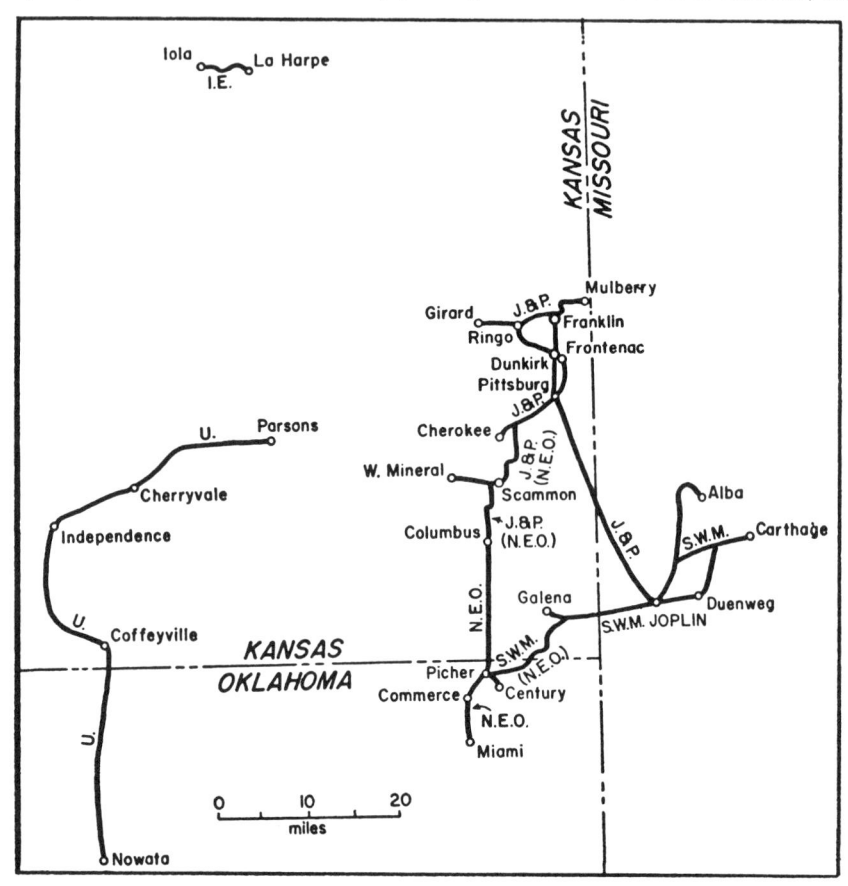

IE: Iola Elec. Ry.
J&P: Joplin & Pittsburg Ry.
NEO: Northeast Oklahoma RR

SWM: Southwest Missouri Elec. RR
U: Union Trac. Co.
(Union Elec. Ry.)

tending from Picher to Baxter Springs (7 miles) in order to continue service to several mines on the line.

The NEO operated very frequent passenger service in the early twenties, with half-hour service from Miami to Picher, and hourly service to Columbus, later cut back to a two-hour basis. As late as 1934 it acquired two 1923 Cincinnati lightweight cars from Northampton Transit. However, it eliminated passenger service from Scammon to Columbus in 1933, north of Picher in 1934, and the remainder in 1940. Eventually the road was dieselized, and continued through 1960 to provide freight service on more trackage than it had in 1925. Only the Corona–West Mineral and Scammon–Cherokee segments have been abandoned.

IOLA ELECTRIC RAILWAY

The 10-mile Iola Electric connected the small towns of Iola and La Harpe, north of the line of the Joplin and Pittsburg, with which it was designed to connect. The line was completed in 1901, and abandoned in 1919 owing to traffic decline.

UNION TRACTION COMPANY
(UNION ELECTRIC RAILWAY)

The Union of Kansas was a typical Midwestern interurban, its 77 miles of line serving no cities larger than 15,000 population, and operated with lightweight equipment over cheaply built track. Yet the Union survived until 1947, in many ways one of the last of its kind. It could easily have been abandoned 20 years before; for two decades it ran on a shoestring, barely able to pay its bills.

The line commenced in the little town of Nowata in northern Oklahoma, extended straight northward 25 miles to Coffeyville, and then swung westward to begin a great arc, through Dearing and Jefferson to Independence, and back eastward again through Cherryvale and Dennis to Parsons, 52 miles from Coffeyville (compared to the MKT's 31-mile line between the two cities). Four hours were typically required for the through trip from Nowata to Parsons—a trip that virtually no one ever made. The typical schedule called for 9 trains a day, and thus roughly 2-hour intervals. In the late twenties, the Parsons–Coffeyville service was increased to 75-minute intervals, and the Nowata service was cut back to 7 trains a day. As late as 1946 the road was running 11 trains each way a day north of Coffeyville, and 7 to Nowata. Streetcar service was provided in Coffeyville and Independence; the service ranked with that of Fort Collins, Yakima, and of Washington, Pennsylvania, as the last survivors of small city streetcar operations.

The road was promoted by the Siggins brothers of Warren, Pennsylvania. The Union Traction Company was incorporated in 1907, uniting together the little street railways in Coffeyville and Independence, and completing the interurban line between them on July 14, 1907. The extension to Cherryvale (10 miles) was placed in operation March 1, 1910, to Parsons in 1914, and south from Independence to Nowata (the Kansas and Oklahoma) in 1915.

The road earned sufficient profits in its early days to meet interest payments. But as we described in Chapter 8, it was in continuous financial difficulties after 1921 until its final abandonment on April 4, 1948; it covered operating expenses in only 2 of the 26 years. There had been no piecemeal disintegration; the mileage and operation in 1948 were almost identical to that of 1924, and not basically different from that of 1914. The road had always been protected from bus competition by the two state commissions. Freight business was developed at an early date, but there was little potential volume since the major towns were adequately served by the steam roads.

ARKANSAS VALLEY INTERURBAN RAILWAY[48]

In the Arkansas Valley of south-central Kansas the Arkansas Valley Interurban (the AVI) operated 59 miles of interurban line, built between 1910 and 1915. The line extended north from Wichita through Valley Center, paralleling the Santa Fe as far as Sedgwick (reached on December 18, 1910). At a junction point named Van Arsdale for the president of the road, the line forked, one segment going 6 miles northeastward into Newton, to which service was established on October 10, 1911. The other segment ran almost straight northwestward, paralleling the Santa Fe beyond Halstead (on the south side) into Hutchinson, which was not reached until December 22, 1915. Although the intermediate towns were small, the three terminal cities were of substantial size, even at the time the line was built. The road was projected northward from Newton through McPherson to Salina, westward from Hutchinson to Hudson and to Great Bend, and southward to Arkansas City. These extensions were never built.

The AVI was strictly a locally promoted Wichita enterprise, with capital raised by an extensive drive in the cities served, rather than by the usual syndicate method. The chief promoters were W. O. Van Arsdale, a Wichita stockbroker, and George Theis, Jr., described in the prospectus as a "capitalist," and for many years the road's principal owner. The road was conservatively financed, with a much lower ratio of debt to total cost of road than was typical; this was one instance in which the stock in large part reflected actual investment of cash. The city of Wichita provided $30,000 in aid.

Initially the downtown areas of both Wichita and Hutchinson were reached by trackage rights over the local street railway systems, although the AVI was not affiliated with either of these, the Wichita system being a McKinley property. In 1923 a private-right-of-way entrance was built into downtown Wichita, and in 1932, following the collapse of the Hutchinson Interurban, the AVI built its own entrance into Hutchinson, terminating at the Rock Island Station.

Passenger service—typically operated on 80-minute intervals, with connections made at Van Arsdale for Newton—was provided by a wide variety of rolling stock, all but one car being wooden, and not adapted for multiple-unit operation. The initial emphasis on package freight and cream eventually gave way to carload interchange business in cattle, grain, oil, salt, and sand, and by 1938, 95 per cent of the revenue came from freight, despite the restrictions on this service imposed by an inadequate power supply: voltage not infrequently dropped as low as 300 (from 625) between substations.

By the mid-twenties the road was encountering financial difficulties as automobile use increased, and also because the development of the combine was said to have lessened the number of harvest hands riding the line. The road proceeded to raise fares to 3.6 cents a mile (an extremely high figure for interurbans in the period) and to cut service, neither of which improved profits. The road suffered only spasmodically from bus competition, and for a time operated bus routes of its own. In the late twenties, the general boom in the area and greater oil business helped the line financially by increasing freight revenue. The depression, however, struck the area very hard, and in 1933 the road was in receivership. Operating deficits were incurred annually from 1931 on, and the road deteriorated badly. Passenger service continued to decline and finally ceased on July 31, 1938. In 1939 the road was offered for sale, and was purchased in November of that year by the H. E. Salzburg Company. The new owners immediately dieselized the road, and planned more or less permanent operation. But the war brought higher costs and a sharp increase in scrap-metal prices. Without objection by the owner, the line was requisitioned by the WPB, and all operations ceased on July 23, 1942. The 6-mile segment to Carey Mine from Hutchinson was acquired by Emerson Carey for the Hutchinson and Northern, an electric freight line serving the salt mines, and is still operated by that company.

The AVI had many advantages over the typical interurban. It operated out of a commercial center to cities of fair size. It had a well-built track on a private right-of-way, downtown stations reached without excessive street running, a potential carload freight business, few operating hazards, and a favorable capital structure. The road should have been able to do better financially than it did; the comparison has often been made between this road and the little Union, which lasted much longer with much less potential.

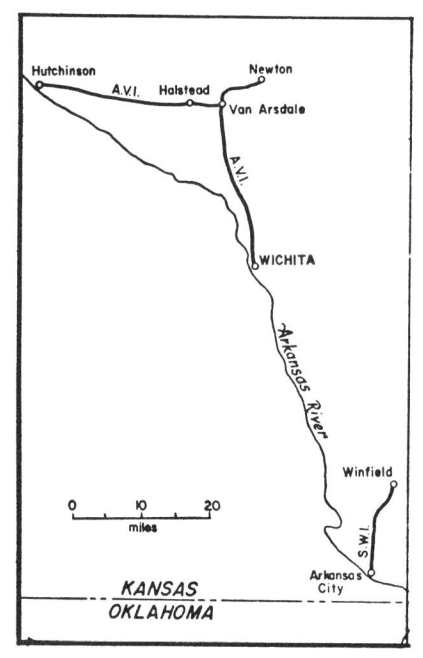

SWI: Southwestern Interurban Ry.
AVI: Arkansas Valley Interurban Ry.

SOUTHWESTERN INTERURBAN RAILWAY

To the south of the area served by the AVI was the Southwestern Interurban (not to be confused with four other lines—bearing the name of Southwestern in Texas, Louisiana, Ohio, and Ontario). This line was built in 1909 by D. H. Siggins, one of the brothers in the contracting firm that was simultaneously developing the Union. The equipment—typical wooden cars—came from the Union. The lightly built line, only 13 miles in length between Arkansas City and Winfield, had insufficient population to draw on and was never successful financially. In 1922 the road was purchased by George Theis, principal owner of the AVI, who intended to use it as a portion of the southern extension of the latter road, and renamed it the Arkansas City and Winfield Northern Railway. The line was reconstructed and otherwise improved, but could not cover its costs; the AVI extensions were not built, and upon Theis's death in an airplane accident the road was abandoned (June 8, 1927). The company had also operated the Winfield street railway system.

MANHATTAN CITY AND INTERURBAN RAILWAY

Among the least known of all Kansas interurbans were two lines which together formed a through route between Manhattan and Junction City, via Fort Riley, and operated the street railway lines in the two towns. The first interurban segment to be built was that of the Electric Railway and Ice Company, which completed its 5-mile line from Junction City to Fort Riley on August 10, 1901. The Manhattan City and Interurban had builts its city routes in 1908, but not until 1914 did it complete the 16-mile link westward to Fort Riley and a connection with the Junction City line. The latter had become a part of the Union Light and Power Company, which also gained control over the Manhattan line, and operations of the two roads were integrated after the through route was completed, cars running through from Manhattan to Junction City. Traffic fell sharply after World War I; the line substituted rail buses for electric cars in 1922, and abandoned the entire line in 1926. (See map, p. 367.)

OKLAHOMA

OKLAHOMA RAILWAY[49]

The largest Oklahoma system was the Oklahoma Railway, which operated a group of lines radiating out from Oklahoma City, west to El Reno (29 miles), north to Guthrie (31 miles), and south to Norman (18 miles). This system was an integral part of the Oklahoma city transit system. The western line was undertaken by the El Reno Interurban Railway Company, which also operated the El Reno city system, but was purchased by Oklahoma Railway before it was completed. The system was not a power company affiliate, but an independent enterprise, largely financed in St. Louis.

The first line was the Oklahoma City–El Reno, completed early in 1911 by the predecessor company as far as Yukon, and opened for service through to El Reno on December 3, 1911. The shorter line, but with heavier traffic density, to Norman was completed in 1913. The northern line was finished as far as Edmond in 1911, and through service opened to Guthrie in 1916. Much of the business was essentially suburban in character, but a considerable volume went through to the terminal cities, and especially to Norman, the location of the University of Oklahoma. Some freight business had been developed at an early date, but not until 1920 did the road begin to push the carload business, and in 1929 it purchased and electrified the Oklahoma Belt and the Oklahoma City Junction railways. In 1943, however, looking forward to the eventual abandonment of interurban operations, the freight trackage and rights over other lines were sold to the Rock Island and the Santa Fe for $525,000. For many years a major freight haul was handling through cars from Guthrie to Oklahoma City for the Fort Smith & Western, which terminated in Guthrie. When this road was abandoned in 1939, much of the longer-haul freight business was lost.

Passenger service was typically on an hourly basis on all lines, although in later years the interval was cut to 30 minutes on the Norman line and increased to 90 minutes on the other two lines, which had much lighter traffic density. It is impossible to determine the profitability of the lines because earnings data were not separated for the city and interurban properties. All lines reached downtown Oklahoma City via streetcar track but were on private rights-of-way in the country. A great variety of equipment was used, the earlier cars being gradually replaced by more modern arched-roof cars from abandoned lines—the lightweight Rockford cars, heavier cars from the Fort Wayne–Lima, and Dayton–Xenia and Schenectady equipment. The city system cars were all relatively modern, built in 1929 or later.

Plans had been made for abandonment of the interurban lines before World War II, after the system passed into the hands of new owners, and in 1946 the El Reno and Guthrie lines were eliminated. A year later service ended to Norman. All three lines were replaced by buses.

TULSA–SAPULPA UNION RAILWAY
(SAPULPA AND INTERURBAN; OKLAHOMA UNION)

Although no interurban was ever built between Oklahoma City and Tulsa, two lines were built out of Tulsa. The longer of these, the Sapulpa and Interurban was built southward from Sapulpa through Kiefer to Mounds, completed in March 1908. The little road barely made ends meet until an oil boom led to the rapid expansion of the area. The company had by then gone into bankruptcy (1912), and was eventually merged with the Oklahoma Union Railway, which had built a short line out of Tulsa toward Sapulpa. The new enterprise used the Oklahoma Union name, and completed its line between Tulsa and Sapulpa in 1918, thus creating a 25-mile through line. The company was now affiliated with three short-line steam roads, the largest of which was the Oklahoma Southwestern, and a network of lines connecting the various segments and covering much of eastern and central Oklahoma was planned. Nothing came of these hopes, and the steam roads were eventually abandoned, with the Oklahoma Union itself in bankruptcy in 1929. It was operated by receivers for several years, and in 1934 reorganized as the Sapulpa Union. The name was changed to the Tulsa–Sapulpa Union Railway about 1943.

The road provided both freight and passenger service from the beginning, the freight consisting largely of oil and oil products. Hourly passenger service through to Mounds was operated for a number of years, until the line beyond Sapulpa to Mounds—the original line—was abandoned in 1928. All passenger service was discontinued in 1933, but the road continued to supply freight service (still electrically operated) up to 1960, with revenues of around $100,000 a year and a small profit. The line was a pioneer in the use of buses, including lines radiating out from Sapulpa, and some local service in Tulsa in competition with the nonaffiliated street railway system.

SAND SPRINGS RAILWAY

The other Tulsa line was essentially a suburban streetcar operation which developed a tremendous volume of freight business because the area which it served became an important industrial center. The line was built in 1911 from downtown Tulsa to the newly developed suburb of Sand Springs (10 miles), mostly on private right-of-way, by Charles Page, millionaire Tulsa oil man. The road first used McKeen motor cars, but was electrified in 1911, generating the power with natural gas. Early wooden cars were eventually replaced by the pioneer Cincinnati Lawrenceburg and Aurora lightweight cars, then cars from the Tulsa–Sapulpa line, and finally the lightweight cars from Union when that road was abandoned in 1947. As industry grew in the area, a substantial freight business developed, as many plants were reached only by the line's tracks. The passenger business became essentially a suburban streetcar operation, on double tracks. When Page died he gave the line to the Orphan's Home as a source of income. Despite the heavy volume of passenger traffic the road found it difficult to make a profit from it, and finally discontinued it in 1955, the last electric passenger operation in the state of Oklahoma. With only 12 miles of track, the road had freight revenue of $742,000 in 1956.

PITTSBURG COUNTY RAILWAY

The Pittsburg County Railway extended 17 miles from McAlester through Haileyville to Hartshorne in the Oklahoma coal-mining area. The line was an outgrowth of the McAlester streetcar system, and was completed to Alderson, September 15, 1903, and to Hartshorne on November 14, 1904, as the Choctaw Railway and Lighting Company. It was owned by the Southwest Power Company, originally an Alfred Emanuel property (National Electric Power Company), and eventually taken over by the Insull interests. The system became part of the Public Service of Oklahoma. In later years the company was freed of power company ownership and operated as an independent enterprise.

The road operated hourly passenger service for most of its history, in later years with three Cincinnati lightweight cars purchased new in 1923, and ultimately operated with one man. The surprising feature of the line was its continuation of passenger service up until the complete abandonment of the line. The road profited from some carload freight business, primarily coal.

After deficits during the depression, small profits were earned up through 1944, but a sharp drop in business brought small losses in 1945 and a relatively severe loss

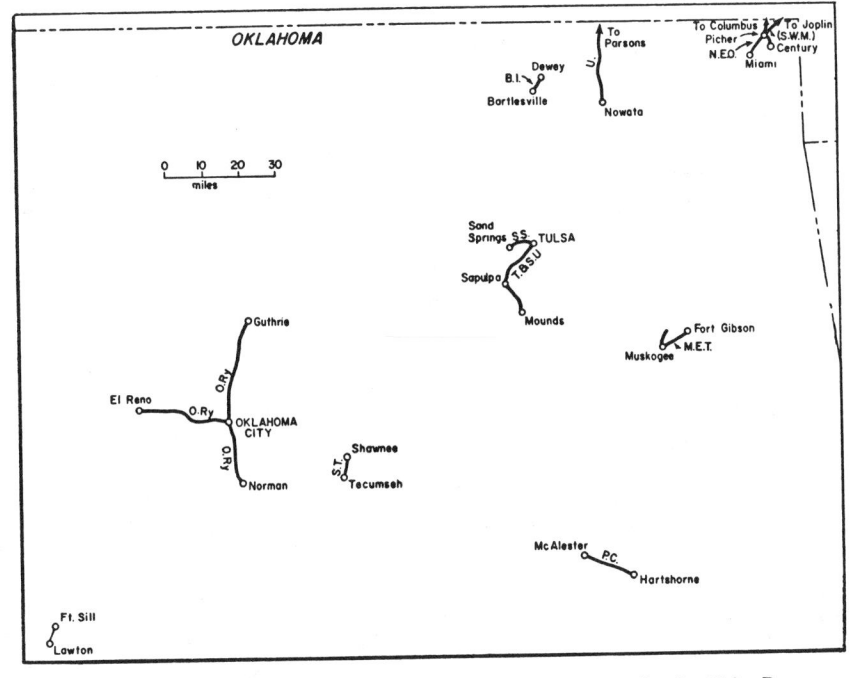

NEO: Northeast Oklahoma RR
BI: Bartlesville Interurban Ry.
SWM: Southwest Missouri Elec. Ry.
U: Union Trac. Co. (Union Elec. Ry.)
SS: Sand Springs Ry.
T&SU: Tulsa-Sapulpa Union Ry.
MET: Muskogee Elec. Trac. Co.
PC: Pittsburg County Ry.
ST: Shawnee-Tecumseh Trac. Co.
ORy: Oklahoma Ry.

($15,000 after taxes) in 1946. The road could go on no longer and ceased operations on April 27, 1947, after having been placed in receivership in 1946.

SHAWNEE–TECUMSEH TRACTION COMPANY[50]

The 6-mile intercity line of the Shawnee–Tecumseh Traction, which also operated the Shawnee city lines, connected the two cities of its corporate name. The line was completed on September 1, 1906, and together with the city lines, was replaced by bus service in January 1927. Even bus service was suspended in 1931. The road was controlled by New York interests. Despite the shortness of the line, it operated in typical interurban fashion on a private right-of-way.

MUSKOGEE ELECTRIC TRACTION COMPANY

The same interests that owned Shawnee–Tecumseh also owned the Muskogee Electric Traction Company. The company, in addition to the city lines in Muskogee, operated a 10-mile interurban line to Fort Gibson, built in 1911. The MET outlived most of the Oklahoma small systems as it continued in operation until 1934. Service was on a 90-minute basis by 1930, with greater frequency in earlier years. Carload freight service was handled on the line, as well as on the suburban line to Hyde Park, built in 1905 and also abandoned in 1934.

BARTLESVILLE INTERURBAN RAILWAY

Thirty miles west of Nowata was the 8-mile Bartlesville Interurban, extending from Smeltertown through Bartlesville to the village of Dewey, placed in operation on July 14, 1908. Operations were discontinued in 1921. The road was a Cities Service property.

*

At least three lines in Missouri and Kansas were often classified as interurbans, although they did not use electric power. One was the *Kansas City Ozarks and Southern*, with 15 miles of track from Mansfield to Ava. The second was *Westmoreland Interurban*, connecting Westmoreland, which had no other railroad, with the Union Pacific's Kansas Leavenworth & Western at Blaine. The *Oregon Interurban* connected Oregon and Forest City. These lines have all been abandoned, including the Union Pacific line with which the Westmoreland road connected.

The 5-mile *Cassville and Western*, built in 1896, was electrified in 1911 and operated with a Pullman interurban combine for a short period. As the Cassville & Exeter, it survived as a short line until 1956.

In Oklahoma, a line from Cushing to Drumwright, the *Cushing and Oil Fields*, was planned as an interurban, but was never electrified.

Texas

Texas contained almost exactly 500 miles of interurban lines, 350 miles of which were in the Dallas area, 104 in the Houston-Beaumont area of southeastern Texas, and the remainder scattered.[51] Of the Dallas mileage, 226 miles were operated by the Texas Electric, the largest single system between the Mississippi and the Pacific Coast. Much of the Texas mileage was built at a relatively late date (over 350 miles after 1910), when the building in other areas had largely ceased. This mileage included the last two new interurban systems to be developed in the country, the Texas Interurban and the Houston North Shore. One other feature of the Texas system was the control and management of several of the larger lines by Stone and Webster.

THE DALLAS AREA

TEXAS ELECTRIC RAILWAY

The Texas Electric property originally consisted of two separate but affiliated companies, the Texas Traction Company and the Southern Traction Company. The former was completed on July 1, 1908; it extended northward from Dallas 66 miles to Sherman, and included an additional 11-mile line from Sherman to Denison, which had been built in 1901 by the Denison and Sherman Railway and absorbed by Texas Traction in 1909. The line was built on private right-of-way, parallel and for much of the way adjacent to the line of the Houston and Texas Central (Southern Pacific). The Southern Traction Company (inc. 1912), built two lines—a 97-mile route to Waco via Waxahachie and Hillsboro, and a 52-mile line to Corsicana via Ferris and Ennis—which were built during 1912 and 1913 and placed in service on January 1, 1914. The two were merged as the Texas Electric Railway in 1916.

These lines were pioneers in the use of heavy arched-roof steel cars (with characteristic arched windows) capable of speeds up to 60 m.p.h., with single- or multiple-unit operation. The cars typically operated as single units except in rush periods. The private-right-of-way lines were also built to high standards, but the cars used streetcar tracks to reach the terminal in downtown Dallas. A new terminal was built for the interurban lines by the nonaffiliated Dallas city system. For many years the road scheduled trains at hourly intervals on all three lines, plus additional Sherman–Denison service. Many of the runs were expresses (known as Bluebonnets) that stopped only in the towns, and ran typically at 50 m.p.h. A few trains were eliminated around 1930, but even after World War II the line was operating essentially hourly service, with a few runs omitted in the middle of the day. Texas Electric was one of the few interurbans to operate RPO cars, running the next to the last of these. Although the road did not enter the carload freight business until 1928, it succeeded in building up a substantial volume, to offset the declining passenger business.

The system was a local Dallas undertaking, promoted by the J. F. Strickland Co., and not affiliated with power, transit, or other utility enterprises. It was headed for many years by J. P. Griffin, a leader in the activities of the American Electric Railway Association. Financially, the TE was one of the most successful of all interurbans, one of the few that more or less justified its investment. Although gross revenue fell from the high reached in 1921 of over $3 million, the operating ratio stayed at about 60 throughout the twenties, and the rate of return on investment at over 4 per cent, so the road's position was far more favorable than that of the industry as a whole. Fixed charges were easily earned, preferred stock dividends were paid through 1926, and common stock dividends were paid in several years. The depression caused a sharp drop in revenues and the company entered receivership in 1931, being reorganized as of January 1, 1936. Operating deficits were avoided, and with the coming of World War II the road flourished again; in 1944, for example, net after taxes was $510,000, on gross of $2,216,000.

In 1941 the light-traffic Corsicana branch was abandoned; the road pointed out that the deficits on this line impaired the financial stability of the whole system. After 1945 the traffic fell very sharply as car and truck use expanded, the 1947 gross being half that of 1944. In December 1948 the entire system was abandoned. A factor in the final decision was a head-on collision of two passenger cars, which killed a number of passengers.

NORTHERN TEXAS TRACTION COMPANY

The 35-mile line from Dallas to Fort Worth was one of the state's earliest lines, being completed and placed in operation on June 18, 1902. The location of two relatively large cities only 35 miles from each other in an area without adequate steam-road passenger service naturally prompted the building of an interurban. Despite the early date of building, the road was built to high standards, with nearly half of the line double-track. Service was of high frequency, with limiteds leaving on the hour and locals on the half hour, and with a running time of one hour for the limiteds—a fast run for interurbans. Operation of trains of several cars was common in rush hours, although only the cars acquired after 1910 were capable of running in multiple units. The cars resembled those of Texas Electric, with arched roofs and arched windows.

The line grew out of the old Fort Worth Street Railway Company, and the city lines and the interurban were operated as a single enterprise, with the Tarrant County Traction (*q.v.*) as a subsidiary. In 1905 the company itself became a subsidiary of the Northern Texas Electric Company, a Stone and Webster property, and the system was managed by Stone and Webster.

Despite its frequent service and high traffic potential, the Northern Texas was hard hit by the automobile and the depression, and in 1934 all service was discontinued, long before that of the potentially weaker Texas Electric. Part of the difficulty lay in the failure to develop carload freight business, and the important package freight of earlier years had largely disappeared as trucks developed.

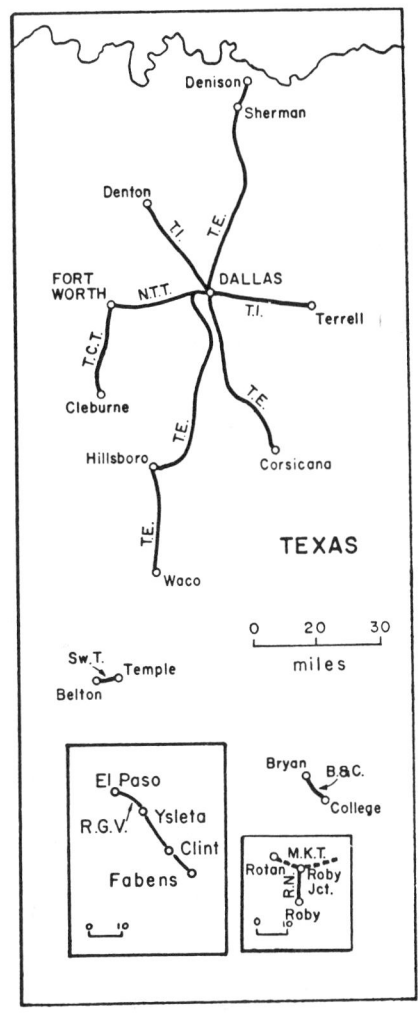

TE: Texas Elec. Ry.
RGV: Rio Grande Valley Trac. Co.
RN: Roby & Northern RR
TI: Texas Interurban Ry.
NTT: Northern Texas Trac. Co.
TCT: Tarrant County Trac. Co.
SwT: Southwestern Trac. Co.
B&C: Bryan & College Interurban Ry.

TARRANT COUNTY TRACTION COMPANY

An affiliate of the Northern Texas Traction, the Tarrant County Traction was built southward 31 miles from Fort Worth to the small city of Cleburne as the Fort Worth Southern Traction Company, and was placed in service on September 1, 1912. It was likewise a well-built private-right-of-way line, typically operated on hourly schedules. Reorganization as the Tarrant County Traction Company in 1914 was followed by the Northern Texas Electric Company's acquisition of the entire capital stock, and its subsequent operation of the road as a portion of its own line. The line had insufficient traffic potential to last beyond the depression, and it was abandoned in 1931.

TEXAS INTERURBAN RAILWAY

One of the last two interurban lines built in the country—and one which by any logic should not have been built—was the Texas Interurban. The first line, 33 miles from Dallas eastward to Terrell (the Dallas–Terrell Interurban Railway), was placed in operation on January 14, 1923. A year later, on October 1, 1924, the company completed electrification of a 29-mile line from Dallas northwestward to Denton (owned by the MKT), designed as the first link in a line to Wichita Falls. Both Terrell and Denton were small cities, with little population in between; Denton had only 7,000 residents, and Terrell 10,000. Lines serving similar areas had already been abandoned. The project arose from a commitment made by Electric Bond and Share to build two interurban lines in order to get the city of Dallas to renew the franchise of Dallas Railways. The company began service on the Terrell line with five double-truck Birney cars, operated on hourly headway. Following abandonment they went to the Dallas city system, where they were used as streetcars until the fifties. The interurban venture was hopelessly unprofitable from the beginning, and the lines were abandoned in 1931, after only 8 years of operation.

SOUTHEASTERN TEXAS

There were three lines in the southeastern portion of the state, two operating out of Houston, the third from Beaumont to Port Arthur.

GALVESTON–HOUSTON ELECTRIC RAILWAY

One of the best interurbans in the country, physically and financially, was the Galveston–Houston line, 50 miles in length, completed between the two cities of the corporate name in December 1911. This was another ideal location for an interurban—two cities of substantial size within easy interurban distance, provided with relatively little steam-railroad passenger service. This line was from the beginning a Stone and Webster property, operated in conjunction with the Galveston and Houston transit and power systems. The company developed a substantial volume of passenger business, providing highspeed, frequent service. In time it provided the connections to Galveston for the MKT, and through tickets were sold.

During the depression the line fared better financially than virtually any interurban, earning substantial margins over operating expenses, even though the total business fell to less than half the 1928 figure by 1932, and in 1935 was one third the 1928 figure. But the Stone and Webster management was well aware of the long-run difficulties of the interurban, and on October 31, 1936, replaced rail service with bus service. This was one of the very few properties that was abandoned without ever incurring an operating loss. Under independent ownership, operations would probably have continued through World War II.

HOUSTON NORTH SHORE RAILWAY

The last interurban enterprise to be developed in the United States was the Houston North Shore, completed and placed in operation in 1927. The line extended 34 miles from downtown Houston eastward through Highlands and Baytown to the town of Goose Creek, and provided service to a growing industrial area not previously served by a rail line. It was promoted by Harry K. Johnson, and purchased (before completion) by the Missouri Pacific system, primarily as a freight feeder. Service was typically at 2-hour intervals, with additional local service from Houston to Highlands. Four combination passenger and baggage cars of modern lightweight design were built for the company by Brill, and named for the four main cities served. In addition the road was sent some equipment from the Coal Belt Electric, another Missouri Pacific electric line in southern Illinois.

The North Shore was not the fiasco that might have been expected in view of its late date. The road was designed in large measure to handle carload freight, and built up a substantial business of this type for its parent road. It was operated as an integral part of the parent road; the passenger cars were labeled Missouri Pacific Lines, and the schedules were carried in the main-line timetables, designated as the

TEXAS

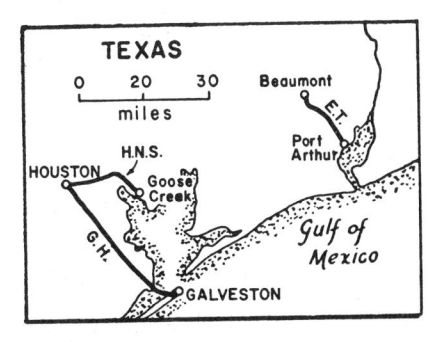

0 20 30
miles

HNS: Houston North Shore Ry.
GH: Galveston-Houston Elec. Ry.
ET: Eastern Texas Elec. Co.

electric division of the Beaumont Sour Lake & Western. Passenger operations in Houston terminated at the city limits, with connecting bus service to Union Station. At the end of World War II, 6 trains a day were operated in each direction. In 1949 electric freight operations were discontinued in favor of diesel power; several rail buses were acquired and substituted for electric passenger cars. Ultimately, however, service was cut to one run a day, operated only between the yards in Houston and Baytown. This service was still operating in 1960.

EASTERN TEXAS ELECTRIC COMPANY

In the thickly settled Port Arthur area on the Gulf coast in eastern Texas, the Eastern Texas Electric operated 20 miles of line between Beaumont and Port Arthur, opened for service on December 15, 1913, as the Jefferson County Traction Company. The road was built almost entirely on private right-of-way. The Eastern Texas was a Stone and Webster property, and also provided electric power in the area, as well as transit service in Beaumont. Since the line served a relatively thickly populated suburban area, and since there was substantial travel between the two terminal cities, the line was able to continue operations until 1935. The road had developed considerable freight business, and for a time several steam roads, particularly the Missouri Pacific, were reported to be interested in the line as a freight feeder. An application for extension of freight lines was denied by the I.C.C. in 1931, and nothing came of the plans.

ROBY AND NORTHERN RAILROAD

In west central Texas operated the tiny 4-mile Roby and Northern, one of the small number of interurban lines whose sole function was to connect a town with a nearby steam road. The Roby and Northern began life as a steam road built in 1915, connecting Roby, a town of about 1,000, with the MKT's long Waco–Rotan branch. The line was in bankruptcy in the early twenties, and was about to discontinue operations when it was taken over (apparently at the plea of local businessmen) by the West Texas Utilities Company, which electrified it in 1923. Thus it became a tiny segment in the great Insull empire, and a relative of such roads as the South Shore. The road scheduled three round trips a day to North Roby, two to connect with the Katy's lone passenger train to Rotan, the other a mid-day run. The passenger car towed such freight cars as might come along. The operations were among the smallest of any carrier in the United States, grossing from $5,000 to $7,000 a year with expenses of about the same amount. Finally, in 1941, operations were discontinued. (See map, p. 377.)

BRYAN AND COLLEGE INTERURBAN RAILWAY

This company operated 7 miles of line from Bryan to College Station (seat of Texas A. and M.), about halfway between Houston and Dallas. The company was chartered in 1910, completed its line in 1911, and electrified it in 1913. All operations ceased in 1923. (See map, p. 377.)

SOUTHWESTERN TRACTION COMPANY

The Southwestern of Texas operated 15 miles of line between Belton and Temple, in central Texas. The line was built as the Belton and Temple in 1905, and projected from Austin to Waco. It was reorganized as Southwestern Traction in 1911; operations ceased in 1923. (See map, p. 377.)

RIO GRANDE VALLEY TRACTION COMPANY

In far western Texas, the Rio Grande Valley Traction (later absorbed into the El Paso Electric Company) placed in service on August 30, 1913, a suburban line from El Paso southeastward to Isleta (13 miles). An extension to Clint and Fabens, 30 miles from El Paso, lost money from the start and was abandoned in 1918. The Isleta line was abandoned in 1932.

The service of the El Paso City Lines across the Rio Grande to Ciudad Juarez, still operated by electric cars in 1960, might be regarded as an interurban operation of a peculiar sort—the last electric railway to cross a U.S. border. (See map, p. 377.)

Colorado

FIVE INTERURBAN lines were built in Colorado, two operating out of Denver, one at Cripple Creek, one at Trinidad, and the fifth in the Grand River Valley in the westernmost part of the state.

DENVER AND INTERMOUNTAIN RAILROAD[52]

The older of the two interurbans out of Denver was D&IM, whose lines were operated for most of the period as a part of Denver Tramways. The first line built (standard-gauge) extended from Denver directly to Golden (23 miles); it was completed in 1893 as the Denver Lakewood and Golden by Samuel Newhouse, and was operated with steam. Not until 1909 was this route taken over by the Tramways and electrified. Meanwhile, in 1903 the Denver and Northwestern had completed a 26-mile narrow-gauge line from Denver to Leyden, electrically operated, but designed primarily to haul coal from the Leyden mines to the Tramways' power plant and coal yards in the city. The Golden branch off this line was completed in 1904. Technically, in 1902 the D&NW had acquired control of Denver Tramways, and from that date on the city and interurban lines were integrated, cars reaching downtown Denver over city tracks. The system was originally owned by the Clark interests of Philadelphia, but later taken over by the Boettcher family, prominent Denver industrialists.

The road numbered its standard-gauge interurban cars with integers and its narrow-gauge cars with decimals.

The Denver and Intermountain lines were both essentially suburban in character, employing zone fares, and running single units on relatively frequent headway, typically hourly on each line—thus providing Golden with half-hour service. The character of the service and the growth of the area west of Denver kept the road from suffering as badly as many roads from either the automobile or the depression, and service continued through World War II. But shortly after the war the decision was made to replace the antiquated street railway system (most of whose equipment was several decades old) with buses, and with this abandonment went the interurban lines as well. In 1950 passenger service was simultaneously discontinued on all lines, and the narrow-gauge tracks were torn up. The standard-gauge line to Golden was retained for freight purposes, but substantial operating losses were incurred and on March 15, 1953, all operations were discontinued.

The Denver Tramways also operated a suburban line extending 5 miles beyond the city limits to Englewood, completed in September of 1907 as the Denver and South Platte Railway, and abandoned in 1926.

DENVER AND INTERURBAN RAILROAD[53]

The second interurban out of Denver was the Denver and Interurban, a Colorado & Southern subsidiary. The 51-mile road operated northwestward from Denver to Boulder, on a track laid alongside the Colorado & Southern main line to Burns Junction, and thence on C&S trackage to Boulder by two routes that comprised a loop, one via Louisville and the other via Marshall. A spur, operated only in the summer, extended from Marshall to Eldorado Springs. Electrification of the line was completed and the road placed in operation in 1908. Originally the cars reached downtown Denver via Tramways tracks to 16th and Arapahoe, but in 1923 C&S trackage was electrified into Union Station, and the operation over the street-car tracks was discontinued.

The road employed 11,000-volt AC, with pantograph power collection, but the cars were also capable of running on DC, at 550 volts, with trolley poles, on the city lines in Denver and Boulder. The wooden 55-foot cars, 12 in number, were built in 1908 by the St. Louis Car Co.; they were distinguished by their tremendous weight (125,000 pounds), resulting from the heavy AC motors and the unusually heavy steel underframing. These were capable of multiple-unit operation, and 2-car trains were not uncommon. Normally 18 round trips per day were operated, half going one way around the loop and half the opposite way. A substantial volume of business between

Boulder and Denver was built up, since there was no effective steam-road competition, and the trip was widely advertised as a tourist route to the Rockies, connecting with stages for mountain resorts. The line was known as the Kite Route.

On September 6, 1920 an excursion train hit a regular train inbound from Boulder; 12 persons were killed and 100 injured as the two heavy cars telescoped. The wreck was apparently due to confusion over standard versus daylight saving time; the crew on the special had just been recruited from C&S main-line service, and were accustomed to standard time.

The road was not a financial success. Even in 1914 the operating ratio was 93 per cent, and the road was one of the half dozen in the country to show an operating loss in 1924. Deficits first appeared in 1920; expenses were drastically reduced, and losses avoided until 1923. Thereafter the deficits grew sharply year by year, as the volume of business fell—the 1926 revenues were only a third of the 1920 figure. The parent company finally concluded that the situation was hopeless, permitted the road to go into bankruptcy, and applied to abandon the line. All operations ceased on December 15, 1926.

COLORADO SPRINGS AND CRIPPLE CREEK DISTRICT RAILWAY[54]

Colorado's last great mining boom came in the 1890's, in the Cripple Creek area in the mountains west of Colorado Springs. Within a few years Cripple Creek itself had more than 10,000 residents, Victor 5,000, and the area as a whole about 30,000. In 1897 the Cripple Creek District Railway was incorporated to build electric lines in the area, to supplement the suburban service provided by the steam roads. The first line was the High Line, built from Cripple Creek via Poverty Gulch, Midway, the Portland Mine, and down Battle Mountain into Victor, with service established early in 1898. The line climbed up Poverty Gulch on a 7.5 per cent grade, and crossed the Midway divide at an elevation of 10,478 feet. The four wooden cars were built by Barney and Smith; one was among the first arched-roof interurbans.

The CCD was a strictly local enterprise. But in 1899 Colorado Springs interests, tired of the policies of the two steam roads that favored Florence mills for ore reduction, incorporated the Colorado Springs and Cripple Creek District Railway, which built a steam-operated, standard-gauge line from Colorado Springs to Cripple Creek (completed in 1901). In March 1899 the new road purchased the interurban, and in 1901 completed a shorter 5-mile electric line from Victor via Elkton to Cripple Creek, at lesser grade, known as the Low Line. The old High Line was relocated at the Victor end, swinging north from the Portland Mine through Independence, and entering Victor on an electrified steam line via Goldfield. This increased the length of the line to 10 miles. Eventually the Cripple Creek end of the High Line was relocated

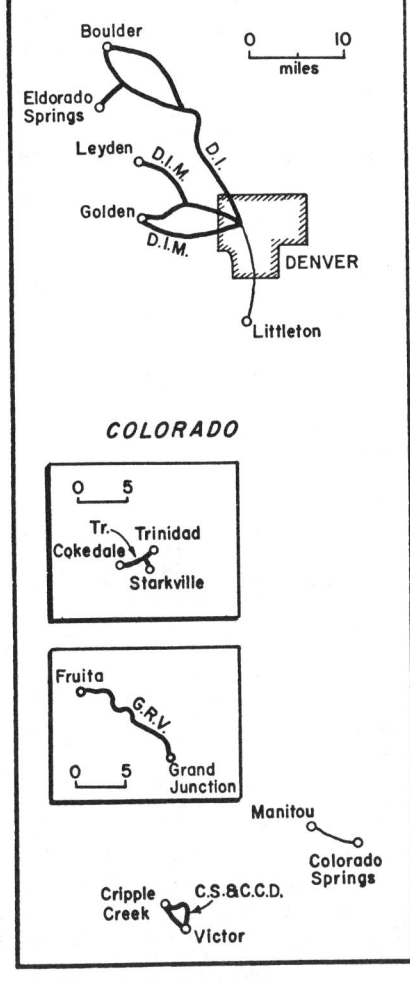

COLORADO

DI: Denver & Interurban RR
DIM: Denver & Intermountain RR
CS&CCD: Colorado Springs & Cripple Creek District Ry.
GRV: Grand River Valley RR
Tr: Trinidad Elec. Transmission, Ry. & Gas Co.

onto the steam road's main line over Hoosier Pass, and the grade was reduced, the total length of the High Line becoming 12 miles.

For the next decade, frequent service was provided on both lines, half-hourly on the Low Line and hourly on the High Line. Both routes entered the downtown areas of the two cities on tracks laid in the streets. The private-right-of-way lines were shared with steam-road switching operations, the electric division not handling carload freight itself. Later cars were specially geared for the mountain-climbing High Line. The lines' primary business was carrying miners to and from work and shoppers and commuters between towns, but in addition there was a very substantial summer tourist business. Cripple Creek was a major tourist attraction, and many visitors took time to ride the interurban, which climbed well above the timber line, and offered spectacular views of the Rockies. The cars were operated on strictly interurban and railroad standards.

In 1903 the other two steam roads in the area passed into the hands of the A. E. Carlton-Spencer Penrose interests of Colorado Springs, and in 1904 the Colorado Springs and Cripple Creek was purchased by the Colorado & Southern, a Burlington subsidiary; in 1905 all three of the area roads were united under common management, known as the Allied Lines, which operated the interurban as well as the steam roads. World War I hit the mining area very hard, population declined, and interurban service was cut to hourly on the Low Line and two-hourly on the High Line. The CS&CCD fell into receivership. On November 21, 1919, fire destroyed the car barn and six of the road's eight cars. Operations could not be continued without more cars; the profit situation was such that the receiver of the CS&CCD was reluctant to acquire them, and service was never resumed. The CS&CCD itself was abandoned in 1920. Over the years many employees had gone to the Denver and Interurban, also a C&S property.

GRAND RIVER VALLEY RAILROAD

In western Colorado the 16-mile line of the Grand River Valley, the "Fruit Belt Route," extended westward from Grand Junction in a series of steps (with nine sharp turns, most of them right angle) to the town of Fruita, through a fertile vegetable- and fruit-growing area. The line was completed on July 14, 1910, as the Grand Junction and Grand River Valley, the name being shortened in 1914. The company also provided electric power in the Grand Junction area. The road was owned by the Carlton-Penrose interests, who developed many of Colorado's industries and utilities.

From an early date much of the road's business consisted of carload freight interchanged with the steam roads at Grand Junction, largely shipments of fruit and vegetables. Up until the mid-twenties the road just about broke even, with annual revenues around $75,000. At the end of World War I the bankrupt Colorado Midland was taken over by Carlton and Penrose, and plans were revived to build it on to Salt Lake City, employing the Grand River Valley's line as far as Fruita. But nothing came of this; the Midland was abandoned, and eventually the GRV and its highly profitable power company affiliate were acquired by Cities Service Company.

By the end of the twenties, the passenger service—operated at two-hour intervals, and requiring almost an hour to make the 16 miles—had lost most of its business, and was discontinued in 1928. The road continued carload freight service, but this was reduced by the depression, and by 1932 revenue had fallen to $12,000 a year. After several years of operating deficits and continued deterioration of the line, the road was abandoned in 1935.

TRINIDAD ELECTRIC TRANSMISSION, RAILWAY, AND GAS COMPANY

On April 28, 1904, a 9-mile interurban line was completed from Trinidad to the mining communities of Sopris and Starkville, the route winding up through the foothills of the Rockies on grades up to 7 per cent. In 1908 the line was extended to Cokedale. Following several reorganizations, the company, which also supplied electricity and gas in Trinidad, became a subsidiary of Federal Light and Traction. All passenger service and much of the track were abandoned in 1923, but a short segment remained in operation for freight switching until the late forties.

*

The *Colorado Springs and Interurban Railway,* despite its name, can scarcely be classed as an interurban, but it did operate a suburban car line to Manitou. And the *Durango Railway and Realty Company,* one of the smallest street railway systems ever to operate in the United States (2 miles long), connected Durango with nearby Las Animas until it was abandoned in 1921.

Wyoming

THERE WAS only one interurban in Wyoming, the *Sheridan Railway and Light Company*, which extended 17 miles from Sheridan westward to Monarch, paralleling the line of the Burlington. The line was placed in operation on December 29, 1913, and operated with two interurban cars. City service, with five cars, was provided in Sheridan, a city of 8,000. The system was promoted by the Albert Emanuel syndicate of Dayton, Ohio. The potential traffic in this area was limited at best, and the company abandoned operations in 1924.

Utah

UTAH[55] contained one of the longest routes in the west (although made up of three separate companies), which extended 197 miles from Preston, in southern Idaho, via Logan, Ogden, Salt Lake City, and Provo, to Payson. All the larger cities in the state were on the line, and a high percentage of the total population of the state was served by it. In addition there were several branches. The Utah network lasted until a relatively late date—the major lines were all still providing passenger service until after the end of World War II. They were all strictly interurban transit lines, with no affiliation with railroads, power companies, or large holding companies.

BAMBERGER ELECTRIC RAILROAD

The Bamberger connected Utah's two major cities, Salt Lake and Ogden, and served the intermediate Davis county area as well. The road began life as the Salt Lake and Ogden, a steam road projected in 1891 by Simon Bamberger, pioneer Utah coal-mine operator, northward from Salt Lake toward Ogden and Coalville. Progress was slow; Ogden was not reached until 1908. It was decided to electrify because the building of a competing line threatened; electrified service was established on May 28, 1910, using 750-volt DC. The line was renamed the Bamberger Electric Railway in 1917, and in 1923 the company built a modern station in Salt Lake City across from Temple Square, in conjunction with the Salt Lake and Utah.

The road operated hourly passenger service for many years, after 1927 with coordinated buses. However, primary reliance was placed on rail service until the fifties. Much of the passenger business was of the commuter-shopper type between Davis county towns and Salt Lake and Ogden. But there was considerable through travel between the terminal cities and in conjunction with the Utah Idaho Central, heavy summer traffic to the resort at Lagoon, and school trains for the high school in Kaysville. For 40 years service was provided primarily by a group of heavy Niles and Jewett cars built between 1910 and 1916, some rebuilt with a capacity of 84. In the late thirties much of the double track was removed, an automatic block system was introduced, and cars were converted for one-man operation. Five almost new lightweight cars were acquired in 1938 from Fonda Johnstown and Gloversville. A tremendous volume of business was handled during World War II, but traffic fell steadily after 1945, although it was still substantial even as late as 1950. But after the destruction of the repair equipment and parts in 1952, when the shops in North Salt Lake were destroyed by fire, service was sharply curtailed, and on September 6, 1952, all passenger service ended.

Carload freight business, handled from the early years, grew steadily; the road provided exclusive service to a number of warehouses in Salt Lake City and to the U.S. Arsenal and Hill Field, near Kaysville. Some diesel power was acquired during the war when electric power was inadequate, and following the elimination of passenger service in 1952, the entire operations were dieselized. The road was generally profitable except for the early years of the depression when bankruptcy occurred (1933), followed by reorganization (1939). The line became the Bamberger Railroad, without change of control. Gross revenue and profit jumped sharply during the war, the former rising more than 7 times from 1939 to 1942. Postwar profits were moderate. In 1956 the road was sold by the Bamberger family to Texas interests affiliated with the Murchison group, and early in 1959 it was abandoned. The Salt Lake terminal properties were bought by the Rio Grande, and the line north of Hill Field by the Union Pacific.

On the whole, the Bamberger was one of the most successful of the interurbans, making the best of its advantages — its well-built track, the relatively high-speed entrances to the centers of the downtown areas of the two major cities, the large cities at each terminus with substantial intermediate population, the lack of damaging bus competition, and a heavy carload freight business. In the period after 1938 the line provided one of the best examples of the modern interurban, of what might have been typical had the industry not been destroyed. On the whole the service was far superior, in many respects, to that of some of the larger and more renowned interurbans, such as the Illinois Terminal.

SALT LAKE AND UTAH RAILROAD

Southward from Salt Lake City extended the Salt Lake and Utah — the Orem Road — incorporated in 1912 by W. C. Orem of Boston, builder of a number of mining roads in the West, and constructed by the famous woman contractor, Mrs. W. M. Smith. The line, extending down the west side of the Salt Lake Valley via Riverton and through Jordan Narrows into the Utah Valley, reached Provo in 1913; Hall-Scott motor cars provided service until electrification was completed July 14 of that year. Service was extended to Springville on July 18, 1915, to Spanish Fork on January 1, 1916, and to the terminus at Payson on May 20. The Granger–Magna branch was placed in operation on October 10, 1917. The numerous towns and farms provided substantial business for the road. The track was on private right-of-way in the country, but followed the main streets of the towns served, the great width of these streets in Utah diminishing the usual opposition to interurban street operation.

The line used steel passenger cars, among the best ever built and weighing 86,000 pounds, heavy for DC cars. Two observation cars were also acquired. Multiple-unit operation was usual. Service was hourly at first, but cut down to 2-hour intervals by the mid-twenties, and four trains each way daily in the thirties, supplemented by coordinated bus service. When the bus line was sold, rail service was increased again. In addition to its Red Arrow merchandise freight service, the road also built up a good volume of carload freight in coal, in sugar beets and other agricultural products, and in other items. The road also handled daily merchandise cars from the east, turned over to it by the Rio Grande. One of these came from Norfolk (with freight by steamer from New York) via

UIC: Utah-Idaho Central RR
ORT: Ogden Rapid Transit Co.
B: Bamberger Elec. RR
SLG&W: Salt Lake Garfield & Western RR
SL&U: Salt Lake & Utah RR
EC: Emigration Canyon Ry.

the Norfolk & Western, the Big Four, the Missouri Pacific, and the Rio Grande. The connection with the Utah Railway near Spanish Fork was an important interchange, since the two roads together formed a through route for coal to Salt Lake City independent of the Rio Grande. The road owned some standard freight cars, which passed into general service over the steam roads.

The road did moderately well financially up until the late twenties, when declining revenue (owing to automobile use) brought it into receivership. The receivers spurred freight business, and for a time finances improved. Even the depression did not result in operating deficits. The line was sold at a bankruptcy sale in 1938 to G. S. Eccles and M. A. Browning of Ogden, owners of the Utah-Idaho Central, essentially representing the bondholders. Management was coordinated with that of the UIC. By then, however, the road had badly deteriorated, and there was little chance of successful redevelopment. The war improved the road's profits somewhat, but by 1944 rising costs had exceeded revenues, giving rise to operating deficits, even though revenues were over $700,000 a year. The road was placed in receivership again in 1945 and the receiver applied for permission to abandon; the road was in exceptionally bad condition—the cars in a complete state of disrepair, the track so battered as to be unsafe. Without waiting for commission action, the Federal Court ordered suspension of operations upon request of the receiver, and March 1, 1946, saw the last run. The property was sold at public auction. The Bamberger was willing to buy the entire line north of Grundy (near Provo), but the receivers decided to ask for bids on separate portions. The Bamberger bought important switching lines in Salt Lake City, and the Rio Grande acquired segments reaching industries in a number of other cities. The lines bought by the Bamberger also passed to the Rio Grande when the Bamberger was abandoned in 1959.

On the whole, the Orem line did not make the most of its opportunities; bad labor relations, frequent accidents, and careless handling of equipment reduced profits, and few attempts were made to modernize. With more efficient management, the substantial volume of carload freight traffic might have carried the road on for a number of additional years.

UTAH-IDAHO CENTRAL RAILROAD
(OGDEN LOGAN AND IDAHO)

The northernmost and longest of the Utah lines, the Utah-Idaho Central, extended northward from Ogden into the Cache Valley, terminating at the town of Preston in southern Idaho. This road was an outgrowth of the city systems of Logan and Ogden. The southern portion was the older; a steam "dummy" line built from Ogden to Hot Springs in 1891 was electrified in 1907 and extended to Brigham, along the highway close to the mountains. In the Cache Valley, the Logan Rapid Transit Company placed a 7-mile line from Logan to Smithfield in operation in October of 1912. This was extended north to Preston and south to Wellsville in 1915. Later that year the link from Wellsville to Brigham across the Collinston Divide, using the abandoned Utah Northern grade, was completed, the old line from Ogden to Brigham was relocated away from the mountains, and through service was established on October 14, 1915. A branch was built from Lewiston to Kent in 1917, and extended to Quinney and Thaine in 1918. Another branch, built to Plain City as a steam road in 1909, was electrified in 1916 and two years later extended to Warren. The line shared the downtown Ogden station with the Bamberger, and operated on city streets in the other towns served.

Initially 16 trains a day were operated on the main line, using heavy steel cars, of which 18 had been purchased from the American Car Company in 1915—far more than the road had any use for. These cars were very similar to those of the Salt Lake and Utah, and painted with the same design, using green instead of red. The lines were supplied with 1,500-volt DC, even in cities. Connections were provided with the Bamberger, but through cars were not operated. Service was quickly cut back to 6 trains a day each way, plus additional school trips, and by 1940 there were only 3 daily runs. The Plain City branch had only 2 runs a day, and service on this line was discontinued in 1939; the Quinney branch provided school service only. Although passenger service was very limited, freight operations became highly important, handling primarily carload movements of coal, sugar beets, and other farm products in conjunction with the main lines at Ogden and the Bamberger. The road had a number of freight motors, but often pulled standard freight cars on its regular passenger runs.

The UIC was from beginning to end an Eccles venture, owned by the Eccles, Browning, and Scowcroft families, who controlled much of Utah's industry and banking (including Amalgamated Sugar and the First Security Bank system). But the venture was not very successful; despite the absence of significant steam-road competition, the area could not generate enough passenger business for profitable operation. In later years school service provided over 90 per cent of passenger revenues. Freight revenue alone was inadequate.

Before 1920 the road did reasonably well, but the growing use of the motor vehicle brought receivership and reorganization in 1926, with control shared with the Singleton interests of St. Louis, who held many of the bonds. Operating expenses were barely covered by 1938, and the war provided little aid; by 1945 the operating deficit was $245,000. The track had deteriorated so badly that a ride on the line was equivalent to a stage coach journey at 50 miles an hour over a plank road! Only one passenger trip a day was run the last two years. Service ended by court order on February 15, 1947, with a few Ogden spurs taken over by the Bamberger.

OGDEN RAPID TRANSIT COMPANY

Perhaps the most spectacular trolley ride in the country, even considering rides on the Victor-Cripple Creek line or the Southern New York, was provided by the 13-mile line up Ogden Canyon from Ogden to Huntsville. Both the Bamberger and Eccles interests sought to build up the Canyon, and the Eccles interests won out when in 1909 the Ogden Rapid Transit built as far as the Hermitage, a well-known resort, the line paralleling the river on grades up to 4 per cent. The line was extended to Idlewild in 1910, and finally in 1915, after the company had become a portion of the Ogden Logan and Idaho, to Huntsville. This line could have been extended to Logan but the much longer route via the Collinston Divide was employed instead.

The line carried two groups of passengers—regular travelers to and from Huntsville, and visitors to resorts and cottages in the Canyon, with heavy seasonal and week-end peaks. For a time the line was operated with the great steel cars of the UIC, but these were replaced by four suburban cars, sometimes all run in multiple units as a single train. In the off season, four single-car runs daily were usual. The development of the automobile cut passenger traffic to such an extent that service was discontinued in 1932, freight operations continuing until 1935, when the Ogden Dam inundated a part of the track. Business did not justify rebuilding. The end came the same day as that of the Ogden streetcar lines—December 26, 1935.

SALT LAKE GARFIELD AND WESTERN RAILROAD (SALTAIR LINE)

The smallest of the major Utah lines, but the last to supply passenger service, was the Salt Lake Garfield and Western, which began life as the Salt Lake and Los Angeles Railroad. The track was built straight west 16 miles from Salt Lake City, on the Salt Lake base meridian, to the resort of Saltair, as level as it was straight, across the salt flats. The road was steam operated, and not until 1916, when the road was renamed the Salt Lake Garfield and Western, were plans made for electrification. The Saltair Resort was purchased in 1918. Electrified service began on August 4, 1919, with six steel cars, operating on 1,500-volt DC. In the same year a 2-mile branch was built to Garfield, and regular year-round service established. Steam was used for freight until 1926, when the passenger motors began to handle the service; two of the powerful McGuire-Cummings cars, working in multiple, could pull the amazing total of 24 Pullman cars for the Salt Lake Air Force base on the perfectly level track. The passenger cars ran during the summer on hourly schedules, at times operating as many as 16 cars in a train, including open trailers. The line never reached the downtown area, largely because of the need for crossing the two steam-road main lines, and the problems of handling the long summer trains. The terminal near the fair grounds on West Temple Street was reached by city cars (and later, by buses). The fares were always extremely low, largely because of the desire of the management to stimulate business at Saltair. Substantial freight business was operated from the earliest years for the big Royal Crystal salt plant near the western terminal.

In 1930 the road abandoned the Garfield branch, which had never carried much traffic, and reverted to summer-only operation. In 1951 the decision was made to dieselize the road, and the electric car operation ceased August 16 of that year. However, a diesel car purchased from the Aberdeen & Rockfish and the diesel freight motors continued to pull the summer passenger trains in the summer of 1959. The line, owned originally by the Mormon church and after 1924 by the Snow family (which controls the Utah Portland Cement Company), had no affiliations with the other Utah interurbans, and did not connect physically with them, nor did it participate in their through-passenger ticketing arrangements. It did have joint freight rates with the steam roads, however.

EMIGRATION CANYON RAILROAD

The least known of the Utah lines was the Emigration Canyon Railroad, built in 1907 primarily to handle stone from Emigration Canyon to Salt Lake City. The line extended upward and eastward 14 miles from 5th and University to Pinecrest, with grades up to 8 per cent. Late in 1909 regular passenger service was installed to the lodges and resorts in the Canyon.

Most trains terminated in Salt Lake City near 5th South and 13th East, although some were operated on street railway trackage to the Hotel Utah, in later years via First South and 13th East. Trains operated only in the summer months; even freight service was suspended in winter.

The road was abandoned in 1916 as building stone was replaced by concrete for house foundations in the city. The line had 2 passenger motors (built by Danville) and 4 trailers, most of which went to the Tacoma city system upon abandonment. The line was reportedly owned by the Mormon church.

*

The Salt Lake City street railway system—the *Utah Light and Traction Company*, an Electric Bond and Share property—had no affiliation with any of the other interurbans in the state, which entered Salt Lake City on their own rails. However, it operated three long suburban lines, one built in 1913, northward 10 miles to Centerville, on the edge of the highway, in competition with the Bamberger; one south on State Street to Midvale, Murray, and Sandy (built in 1910); and one built in 1912 southeastward into the East Mill Creek area. The Centerville line was abandoned in 1927, the other two some years later. All three of the suburban lines were operated with ordinary street railway equipment.

Idaho

IDAHO had a total of 133 miles of line, including the segments of the Utah-Idaho Central and the Spokane Coeur d'Alene and Palouse that extended into the state. Apart from the SC&P mileage, all but a few miles were concentrated in the most populous part of the state from Boise westward.

BOISE VALLEY TRACTION COMPANY[56]

The lines of the Boise Valley, serving the fertile agricultural area west of Boise, comprised a loop, a 35-mile line going west on the north side of the Boise River via Star and Middleton to Caldwell (crossing the Boise River on a 550-foot bridge), and a line of similar length extending from Boise to Caldwell via Nampa and Meridian, south of the river. The northern loop was completed and placed in service on August 8, 1907, by the Boise Interurban Railway. The history of the southern line is much more complex. In 1906, the Boise Valley Railway Company built from Boise to Meridian, with a branch going west from Onweiler toward Nampa. But funds ran out, and this line was not completed into Nampa until 1910. In 1911, Boise Valley passed into the hands of the Kessel-Kinnicut Company, which built from Nampa to Caldwell, placing the line in service on June 6, 1912. Also in 1912 the new company rebuilt the line from Boise to Nampa directly via Meridian, primarily to eliminate curves, and opened the new line for service in December. The old line was abandoned except for a 4-mile spur westward from Onweiler to McDermott, which the company continued in service until 1922 under a lease arrangement whereby local residents agreed to bear the losses.

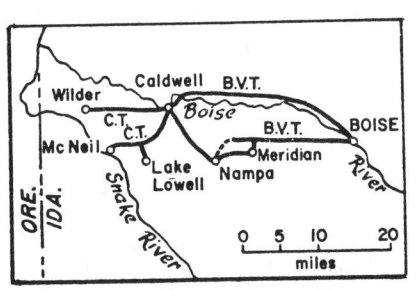

BVT: Boise Valley Trac. Co.
CT: Caldwell Trac. Co.

In 1912 the various properties, including the Boise transit system and the local power company, were merged into the Idaho Railway Light and Power Company, and the interurban lines were operated by a subsidiary, the Idaho Traction Company. In 1915 the properties were transferred to a new company, the Boise Valley Traction Company, owned by Idaho Power Company, and a subsidiary (through a pyramid of holding companies) of Electric Bond and Share. The system had been reasonably profitable up through 1920, but the volume of business fell in half in the next five years, and operating deficits appeared in 1924. After four years of operating losses, the system was abandoned in May 1928.

Although the bulk of the revenues had come from passenger service, the road had developed some carload freight business from very early days, mostly in sugar beets and other agricultural products, and although its line paralleled the Union Pacific, it served some plants not otherwise touched by rail. When the system was abandoned, a new company, the Boise Western, was formed by local interests and took over the sections from Boise to Onweiler (10 miles) and Boise to Star (22 miles) for freight service only. But the venture was not successful, partly because of the depression, and the lines were completely abandoned in 1931.

SANDPOINT AND INTERURBAN RAILWAY

A 5-mile interurban line was completed between Sandpoint and Kootenai, in northern Idaho, in April 1910, the first segment having been placed in operation in November 1909. The line paralleled the shore of Lake Pend Oreille. The road lasted only 8 years, and was abandoned in 1917. (See map, p. 390.)

LEWISTON-CLARKSTON TRANSIT COMPANY

This line operated a 3-mile interstate line between Lewiston, Idaho, and Clarkston, Washington, across the Snake River Bridge, placed in service on May 3, 1915, and abandoned on August 3, 1929.

CALDWELL TRACTION COMPANY

Local interests in Caldwell promoted a line extending westward from Caldwell, one line to McNeil (11 miles), with a 2-mile branch to Lake Lowell, and a second to Wilder (14 miles). The first line was completed in 1913; the second, brought about by electrification of a branch line of the Oregon Short Line (Union Pacific) leased by the company, was placed in operation in the summer of 1918. The road provided carload freight service as well as passenger service, but the traffic potential was strictly limited, and by 1920 the company was in serious financial difficulties. Because of the failure to meet rental obligations, the UP took back the Wilder line late in 1920 and resumed steam operation.

Service was suspended on the McNeil line, but after a receiver was appointed, operation was resumed, subject to speed limitations imposed by the state commission because of bad track. Freight business improved, and for the next several years the road covered operating expenses. But in 1924 the road was sold at sheriff's sale because of failure to meet obligations to the Tracy Loan and Trust Co. of Salt Lake City, and operations were discontinued on June 14. The Lake Lowell branch had been abandoned in 1918, partly to free equipment to complete the electrification of the Wilder line.

Montana

MONTANA had one line that might be regarded as an interurban. In 1909 a locally promoted enterprise took over the Bozeman street railway system and built an electric interurban line westward to Bozeman Hot Springs, and thence south to Salesville, 16 miles.[57] The primary aim was to provide freight connection with the Northern Pacific. But about the time the road was placed in operation (October 31, 1909), it was acquired by the Milwaukee road, which was building a branch from its main line at Three Forks toward Bozeman, and the electric line was incorporated into the new branch.

The Milwaukee operated through freight service to Bozeman with steam equipment, but continued to operate the interurban electric passenger service with the predecessor company's lone car. Not until 1930 were electric operations discontinued and the line reverted to steam freight-only service.

The Anaconda Copper Mining Company operated a suburban-type line from Anaconda to the mining property at Opportunity, primarily for the transportation of miners; the line continued to operate until 1951 with ancient wooden railroad-roof cars built in 1902.

The Butte Anaconda and Pacific is a heavy-duty steam road that was electrified but operated essentially as a main-line road; no interurban-type passenger cars were employed. This line is owned by Anaconda Copper Company.

Arizona

ARIZONA had one short interurban line, plus a suburban streetcar line from Phoenix to Glendale (10 miles) operated by the Phoenix Railway, built in 1910 and abandoned in 1927 when the city took over the transit system.

WARREN–BISBEE RAILWAY[58]

An 8-mile intercity line was placed in service on March 11, 1908 between Warren and Bisbee, in the copper mining area of southeast Arizona, near the Mexican border. An additional 4-mile "high line" out of Warren served a number of mines. The private right-of-way main line had grades up to 7 per cent. In earlier years, 30-minute service was operated, with a group of 42-foot McGuire-Cummings interurban cars. The decline of the mining area and the rise in car use brought several years of operating losses, and abandonment in 1928.

For a New Mexico line, see p. 426.

Washington

THERE WERE 381 miles of interurban line in Washington,[59] which earned it fifth place in total mileage among the states west of the Mississippi, following California, Texas, Iowa, and Oregon. The bulk of this mileage was located in the Spokane and Seattle-Tacoma-Everett areas.

EASTERN WASHINGTON

SPOKANE COEUR D'ALENE AND PALOUSE RAILWAY

Eastward and southward out of Spokane extended the two segments, at times independent, of the SC&P (see map, p. 390). The first segment built, Spokane–Coeur d'Alene (32 miles), was placed in operation on December 28, 1903, as the Coeur d'Alene and Spokane, promoted by F. H. Blackwell, Coeur d'Alene lumberman. This was a typical interurban passenger operation, using 600-volt DC, with frequent service (hourly for a number of years), handling commuters, shoppers, and resort travel to Lake Coeur d'Alene, and even providing a boat and train connection for Wallace, Idaho, from the morning Shoshone Flyer. The line was completed on to Hayden Lake on August 14, 1906, and a branch was built to Liberty Lake in June 1907. The Liberty Lake branch was operated in conjunction with a new suburban line from Spokane via Vera and Opportunity, completed on November 14, 1909. The early small wooden cars gave way to large Brill equipment, including several open-end observation coaches. Coordinated bus service was started in 1926, whereupon rail service to Coeur d'Alene was cut to two runs a day.

The southern lines were very different in character, designed primarily for freight service from the beginning. The rolling Palouse wheat country was very unpromising territory for an interurban, in terms of passenger traffic, but offered potential freight business. This line was built by the Spokane and Inland Empire Railway Company, promoted by the Graves interests of Spokane, which absorbed the Coeur d'Alene line in 1906. The 77-mile route to Colfax via Spring Valley was placed in service on October 8, 1907, and service was established to Moscow, Idaho, from the junction at Spring Valley (50 miles) on September 15, 1908. A 6,600-volt AC system with pantograph was employed, but the arched-window wooden cars, which provided service without change from 1907 to 1939, could also run on the 600-volt DC city lines. Typically only two round trips a day were operated on these lines, on essentially railroad standards, with an RPO car and one passenger car. By the thirties there was only one daily run, plus a mixed train connection from Colfax, unusual among interurbans. Freight service was emphasized from the first, with a number of standard boxcars bought when the road was built, and interchanged with the steam roads. One peculiarity of the line was the large number of wooden truss bridges with sides sheathed with wood.

The relatively unprofitable Palouse lines brought the system into bankruptcy in 1919, and when sold at foreclosure it was again split into two parts, the Spokane and Eastern and the Inland Empire Railroad, although both were controlled by the same group (headed by M. H. McLean and A. W. Harris of Chicago). The Inland Empire could scarcely keep going, and in 1927 the Great Northern bought both companies to avoid losing its freight feeders, and merged them as the Spokane Coeur d'Alene and Palouse. Operating deficits, which had developed in the late twenties, reached phenomenal proportions by 1941; in that year revenues were $330,000 and

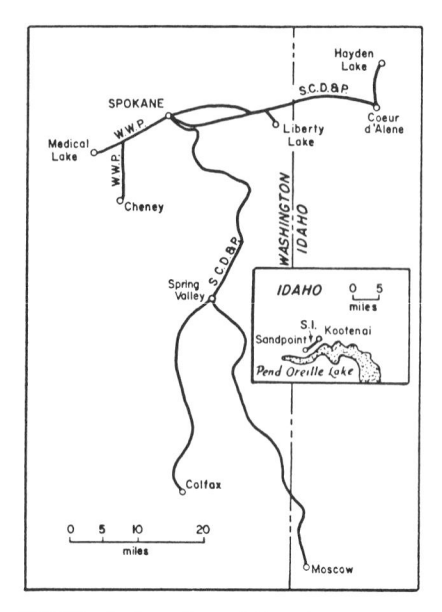

SCD&P: Spokane Coeur d'Alene & Palouse Ry.
WWP: Washington Water Power Co.
SI: Sandpoint & Interurban Ry.

operating expenses were over $600,000. But the GN apparently regarded the deficit as justified by the freight revenue (largely from wheat) that the line contributed to the system. Passenger service on the Opportunity and Liberty Lake line was abandoned on June 20, 1927, and on the Hayden line in 1929.

In 1939 the passenger service came to an end on the Palouse lines, and a year later on the line to Coeur d'Alene. In 1941 all freight service was dieselized. In 1960 the lines were still operated for freight service as a part of the Great Northern, the subsidiary company having been absorbed into the parent company in 1943.

WASHINGTON WATER POWER COMPANY

Westward out of Spokane extended the interurban line of the Washington Water Power Company to the small town of Medical Lake (17 miles), completed in 1905, with a branch from Cheney Junction to Cheney placed in service in September 1907 by the subsidiary Spokane Cheney and Southern. The WWP also operated a segment of the Spokane city system (and all of it after 1922, when it absorbed the Inland Empire local lines), as well as the power system. The road used the typical cars of the period, often run in multiple units in suburban rush-hour trips, plus open-end observation coaches. Trains generally ran separately on the two lines, on roughly 2-hour intervals. The road was primarily a passenger carrier, and the development of the automobile affected its traffic at an early date. Washington Water Power Company officials saw the handwriting on the wall more clearly than many other officials, and abandoned the interurban system in 1921, the first major interurban abandonment on the Pacific Coast.

YAKIMA VALLEY TRANSPORTATION COMPANY

This company, which also operated the Yakima streetcar lines, had two interurban routes. One extended northward to Selah and Speyers (9 miles), completed in 1913. The other ran westward into the Ahtanum area, which had no railroad service, reaching Wide Hollow on December 16, 1907, and Henrybro in 1910. A branch off of this line from Wide Hollow Junction to Wiley City was completed in 1911.

The YVT was from its earliest years a Union Pacific subsidiary; when the UP built up the Yakima Valley in competition with the strongly intrenched Northern Pacific, it was anxious to obtain feeder lines into the various fruit-growing areas, and developed YVT for this purpose. Over the years, much of the line's business was the handling of Pacific Fruit Express cars to cold storage plants in interchange with the UP. This is a highly stable business, and the little road (still in operation) has been relatively profitable.

The passenger service was always typically suburban in character, operated with two small Niles interurban cars built to the arch-window pattern of the period. These operated up Yakima Avenue, sharing trackage with the company's streetcars to the outskirts of town, and then ran on private right-of-way (much of it beside roads) to the towns served. None of these towns were large, but the area, thickly settled because of the relatively small orchards, provided susbstantial business until the automobile came. On the western line, cars typically ran on 3-hour schedules separately on each line, thus giving 90-minute service to points below the Junction. For years, Selah-Speyers cars ran 12 times daily, concentrated in the rush hours. In later years the schedules were reduced materially, and on the western line, cars ran first out one branch, then back to Wide Hollow, out the other branch, and in to Yakima. Finally, on May 15, 1935, the in-

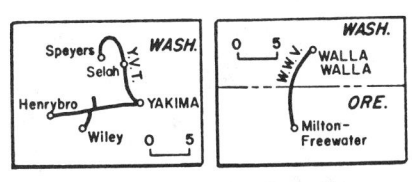

YVT: Yakima Valley Trans. Co.
WWV: Walla Walla Valley Ry.

terurban passenger runs were discontinued. However, the city system, operating modern Brill cars acquired in the late twenties, continued to provide passenger service until 1947, the last in the state of Washington. Freight service continues except on the portion of the Speyers line beyond Selah, which was abandoned in 1943.

WALLA WALLA VALLEY RAILWAY

The Walla Walla Valley extended 14 miles southward from Walla Walla to Milton-Freewater, Oregon. The line was completed on April 7, 1907, as the Walla Walla Valley Traction, and was renamed in 1910. It was for many years a subsidiary of the Pacific Power and Light Company, before the Northern Pacific acquired it as a freight feeder in 1921. All passenger service was abandoned in 1931, together with the city lines in Walla Walla. The line was dieselized in 1950, and still provides freight service. This line, like the YVT, serves a fertile fruit-growing area. The interurban service was provided primarily by car 22, of somewhat distinctive window design, which ran at hourly intervals.

WESTERN WASHINGTON

Western Washington contained one of the major systems on the Pacific Coast, consisting of two Stone and Webster properties which operated three major routes north and south in the Seattle-Tacoma area. In addition there were several short intercity routes.

PACIFIC NORTHWEST TRACTION COMPANY (NORTH COAST LINES)

The largest of the enterprises was the Pacific Northwest Traction,[60] operating a 29-mile route northward from Seattle to Everett, and a 27-mile line from Mt. Vernon north to Bellingham, with a branch to Sedro-Woolley. Plans to connect the two lines were never fulfilled.

The Seattle-Everett line was begun in 1906 by Fred Sander, a Seattle businessman, and completed that year to Lake Bollinger, 16 miles. It was taken over by Stone and Webster before its completion to Everett, May 1, 1910, as the Seattle-Everett Traction Company. In January 1912 it became the Pacific Northwest Traction, together with the Bellingham and Skagit, which was opened in 1913 between Mt. Vernon and Bellingham. Plans were immediately made for closing the gap from Everett to Mt. Vernon, and British Columbia Electric planned a line to Bellingham to connect with the system. These projects were checked by World War I, and were never undertaken. The other element in the system was a 6-mile light interurban from Everett to Snohomish, completed by the Everett Railway Light and Power Company on December 1, 1903, by the electrification of a Northern Pacific branch.

The system was well built, with private right-of-way except in the cities. Much of the road was very scenic, through wooded, rolling country, in part closely paralleling Puget Sound. A 4-mile trestle carried the line across tide flats (under water at high tide) between Blanchard and Clayton Bay. The cars reached the downtown areas of the cities on streetcar trackage, a very serious handicap in Seattle, because it required the use of the slow, high-frequency-service, Phinney line tracks. The two divisions used distinct types of cars. Through the life of the southern division, once the little cars of the pre-Stone and Webster days were replaced, six 52-foot typical Niles cars (built in 1910), with arches extending over two windows, provided the hourly service, with limiteds and locals alternating. The northern division used four larger arched-roof steel cars built by the St. Louis Car Co. in 1913. Apart from the two parlor observation cars purchased from Inland Empire, these were the only passenger cars the line ever owned. In 1921 coordinated rail-bus service was introduced to connect the two parts of its system, and Stone and Webster developed the North Coast Lines bus system which eventually operated throughout the area from Portland to Vancouver, B.C. In 1930 the interurban properties were merged into the North Coast Lines, the Stone and Webster management clearly recognizing the limited future of the interurbans.

The PNT had considerable interchange freight business from its earliest years. All freight service was operated at night. Between 1927 and 1929 the line ferried motor vehicles across gaps in the uncompleted Pacific Highway.

The northern line, with less traffic and greater maintenance expenses because of the numerous trestles on its shore-line location, was abandoned first (September 1931). The southern division trains, which handled extensive suburban business as well as through traffic to Everett, continued to operate until the Seattle Municipal system abandonded the streetcar lines in 1939, leaving the interurban without an access to the downtown area. The whole North Coast system was purchased by Greyhound in 1947. The Everett–Snohomish line ceased operations in December 1921, after flood damage, and the Sedro-Woolley branch was abandoned in 1925.

PUGET SOUND ELECTRIC RAILWAY[61]

As an affiliate of the Pacific Northwest Traction (though operated independently) the Puget Sound Electric Railway was also a Stone and Webster property. This line was built at a much earlier date, and despite its traffic potential, abandoned sooner (eleven years before the Everett line). The line was completed from Seattle to Tacoma via Kent and Auburn on October 5, 1902, a total of 36 miles, plus a 2-mile branch to Renton. The line was built as the Seattle–Tacoma Interurban Railway, promoted by the investment banking firm of Kidder-Peabody and Co. in Boston, and renamed the Puget Sound Electric Railway Company late in 1902, when it passed into Stone and Webster management. The Tacoma city system was a subsidiary, and the Seattle system was of course also a Stone and Webster property until acquired by the city. The last extension of the line was a branch into Puyallup, built in 1908.

The PSE was physically one of the best lines built before 1905, and one of the first third-rail lines. It operated on private right-of-way except in the cities, where it shifted to street running and to overhead trolley. The traffic potential in the days before the automobile was very substantial, and early earnings reports were extremely favorable. The passenger equipment was the standard wooden arch-window car, some built by Brill in 1902, others by Cincinnati in 1909, including open-end observation parlor cars. The line never had any modern equipment, but the old wooden cars, usually run in multiple units, were capable of high speed, the limiteds making the run in 70 minutes. Over most of the years, 30-minute-interval service was provided. Although freight was handled, the line's revenue came primarily from passenger service.

The road was hard hit by automobile and bus competition; it was permitted to go into receivership in 1928, and was abandoned on December 30, 1928. The Puyallup branch had been discontinued in 1918 after a bridge had been washed out. The early abandonment testifies to the Stone and Webster management's lack of sympathy

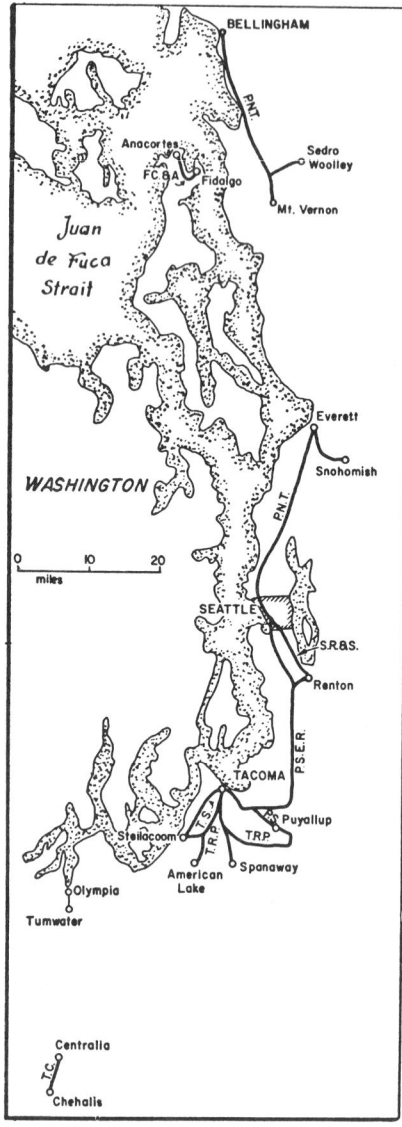

PNT: Pacific Northwest Trac. Co.
PSER: Puget Sound Elec. Ry.
TRP: Tacoma Railway & Power Co.
TS: Tacoma & Steilacoom Ry.
SR&S: Seattle Renton & Southern Ry.
TC: Twin City RR
FC&A: Fidalgo City & Anacortes Ry.

for a company that was not showing a profit, and pessimism about the future of the industry after the mid-twenties. The line certainly had greater potentialities than many roads that lasted for two decades longer.

TACOMA AND STEILACOOM RAILWAY

One of the first interurban lines in the United States was the Tacoma and Steilacoom, completed between the two cities via Chambers Creek in 1891, through a forest of giant firs. Whereas streetcar-type equipment was used, this line was a true interurban in its day. It was absorbed by the Tacoma Railway and Motor Company (Tacoma Railway and Power Company) the following year and operated as a portion of the Tacoma city system until abandonment on July 26, 1916. Meanwhile the city system had built a more direct line to Steilacoom, by then a suburb of Tacoma. The Tacoma system also operated suburban lines to Spanaway, to Puyallup, and to American Lake.

SEATTLE RENTON AND SOUTHERN RAILWAY (SEATTLE AND RAINIER VALLEY)

The suburb of Renton, south of Seattle, was served not only by a branch of Puget Sound Electric, but also by the direct line of the independent Seattle Renton and Southern, built much closer to Lake Washington. The line began as a street railway in Seattle, and was gradually extended, reaching Renton in 1896. A wide variety of suburban equipment was used over the years, including a group of Cincinnati center-door cars of unique design. The line encountered serious financial difficulties in the period before World War I, and spent a number of years in receivership. The city of Seattle negotiated for years for purchase, but never acquired the line. It was reorganized as the Seattle and Rainier Valley in 1916, benefited from the growth of the suburban area, and continued operations until 1937.

*

Western Washington had a number of other small systems, scarcely more than suburban car lines. These included the following.

FIDALGO CITY AND ANACORTES RAILWAY

On March 29, 1891, an 11-mile line was placed in operation between Anacortes, in the northwest, and the projected town of Fidalgo City. The origins of the line and its subsequent history are obscure; apparently it was built primarily to enable the promoters to obtain a large land grant. The road was completely abandoned in 1893; but it is reported that cars actually made only one or two round trips on the opening day and never ran again.

VANCOUVER TRACTION COMPANY

Vancouver's city system operated a 7-mile interurban to Orchards and Sifton, completed in 1910 and abandoned in 1925.

TWIN CITY RAILROAD

This small interurban company was also a subsidiary of Puget Sound Power and Light, and thus also a Stone and Webster property; it was built between the cities of Chehalis and Centralia in 1910, under the name of the Twin City Light and Traction Company. Passenger service was discontinued in 1929, but the track was retained for freight service until 1932, and 4 miles remained for freight switching until 1936. Passengers were carried in small city cars.

GRAYS HARBOR RAILWAY AND LIGHT COMPANY

A 9-mile line from Hoquiam to Cosmopolis via Aberdeen (on the coast) was placed in operation March 19, 1904. Despite the short length, this line used wooden combines built to interurban design, and in later years, modern two-truck Birney cars. This was a Federal Light and Traction property, acquired in the late twenties by Cities Service. The passenger service was operated until 1932, and the line kept in operation for freight service until 1941.

WILLAPA ELECTRIC COMPANY

Affiliated with the Grays Harbor, the WE operated a 6-mile line from South Bend to Raymond, south of Grays Harbor. The line, opened in 1912 as the Willapa Harbor Railway Company, was abandoned in 1930.

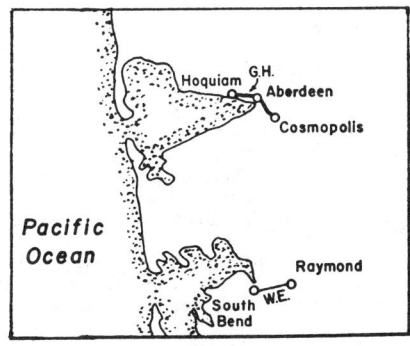

GH: Grays Harbor Ry. & Light Co.
WE: Willapa Elec. Co.

Oregon

OREGON had a surprising amount of interurban mileage, all but a few miles of which was concentrated in the Willamette Valley. The total, 432 miles, includes the 133 miles of Southern Pacific branch-line trackage that was electrified and operated as an interurban, but excludes the lines of the Oregon Electric which were never used for passenger service.

PORTLAND TRACTION COMPANY (PEPCO)[62]

Southward and eastward out of Portland, the Portland Traction Company and its predecessors operated two major routes. The older route, one of the first interurban lines in the United States, extended southward 14 miles to Oregon City, and was placed in operation February 16, 1893, as the East Side Railway. The second and longer route extended 36 miles southeastward to Cazadero. This was completed in 1903 after the East Side had been reorganized and absorbed by the Oregon Water Power and Railroad Company, with a new route built out of Portland parallel to the old line but closer to the river. The Cazadero line was projected in part to facilitate the parent company's construction of a power plant on the Clackamas River, and was designed to handle carload freight from the beginning. In 1909 a branch was built to Troutdale from a point just west of Gresham, and in 1912 the company acquired the Mount Hood Railway and Power Company, which on August 1, 1911, had completed an east-west line from Montavilla (northeast of Portland) to Bull Run, crossing the Troutdale branch at Ruby. The lines reached downtown Portland on their own tracks, crossing the Willamette on a street bridge.

The bulk of the passenger traffic was carried on the Oregon City line, which for many years offered 30-minute-interval service, and the Portland–Gresham portion of the Cazadero line. Only a few cars a day, plus Sunday picnic specials, went on to Cazadero. Cars from Montavilla went to Troutdale, whereas cars to Bull Run came through from Portland. Over the years a great variety of passenger equipment was acquired, beginning with three cars built in 1893 by the Columbia Car Company in Portland. A number of Holman cars were acquired shortly after 1900, and with the Mount Hood line came a group of heavy Kuhlman cars. As the old cars wore out and traffic, but not profits, increased, the road turned to the second-hand market, acquiring equipment from a number of lines, as noted in Chap. 7, with consequent maintenance headaches.

The road was less than a year old when it suffered the most serious accident of its history. A Columbia-built car named Inez, inbound from Oregon City on a morning early in November in 1893, came down the grade onto the Madison Avenue bridge in a heavy fog, the motorman failed to see that the span was open, and the car shot into the river. Fortunately, the captain of the steamer passing the opened bridge saw the accident, and all but 7 of the 27 passengers aboard were saved by small boats sent out from the steamer.

In 1906 the system was merged into the Portland Railway Light and Power Company, together with the city lines (Portland Railway) and the power system (Portland General Electric). For several decades thereafter the company, controlled by the E. W. Clark interests of Philadelphia, provided an integrated transit, interurban, and electric system. In 1924 the company was renamed Portland Electric Power Company (PEPCO). In 1946 PEPCO sold the city system to the Portland Transit Company (organized by California interests), and the interurban lines became the Portland Railway and Terminal Division of the Portland Traction Company, under the same ownership.

The development of the automobile inevitably affected the traffic, and as early as 1927 some cutbacks were made. In that year the Montavilla–Troutdale line was abandoned, followed in 1931 by the portion of the Bull Run line beyond Gresham, and in 1933 by the Cazadero line beyond Boring. Two years later passenger service was cut back from Boring to Gresham, and eventually rerouted on the Mount Hood line into downtown Gresham. In the late thirties, with serious operating losses and deteriorated track, the company asked for permission to abandon. But because of the cooperation of the employees, who accepted a wage cut at a time when wage levels were rising, the company managed to keep the lines going.

The war and rapid growth of the area quickly brought business back to profitable levels. But as automobile use revived, the volume dropped, although it was still very substantial. In 1949 the Gresham line passenger service was cut back to Bellrose, and two years later the company asked permission to abandon all passenger service. As noted in Chapter 5, this request was denied by the Utilities Commission. In 1955, however, the Multnomah County Board of Supervisors barred the cars from using the Willamette River bridge into downtown Portland. Service was cut back to the end of the private right-of-way, and with the need for transfer, business fell very drastically, leading to complete abandonment of passenger service in 1958. The Oregon City line was operated in passenger service longer than any other interurban in the United States—65 years.

WILLAMETTE VALLEY SOUTHERN RAILWAY

The Portland Electric Power system had one subsidiary road, the Willamette Valley Southern, which extended southeastward from a connection with PEPCO at Oregon City through Robbins, Mulino, and Mollala to Mount Angel (32 miles). This line was well to the east of the Oregon Electric and Southern Pacific main lines, especially at Mollala; the line swung back westward south of it. Mollala and Mount Angel were served by SP branches, but the rest of the towns on the line had no other rail service. The country, however, was a thinly settled lumber and farming area, and none of the towns served (except Oregon City) had a population of more than 1,000. The line was completed and placed in service in 1915, designed more to handle freight (forest products) than passengers, although typical interurban cars were operated, the three daily runs connecting with PEPCO trains at Oregon City. The road made a small operating profit in its earlier years, although the revenue per mile never exceeded $4,000; its freight business, however, was hit very hard by the depression (which shut down the lumber mills), and by 1935 gross revenue was less than one fifth of the 1929 figure. The weakest section, from south of Kayler (near Mollala) to Mount Angel (11 miles), had been abandoned in 1926. The passenger service on the remainder of the line was discontinued on April 9, 1933. The freight revenue continued to decline, and finally, in 1938, virtually all revenue vanished when the last of the logging camps served by the line closed down. Consequently, the line was abandoned on September 30; it had incurred operating losses in 7 of its last 8 years.

SOUTHERN PACIFIC ELECTRIC LINES[63]

One of the few instances in the United

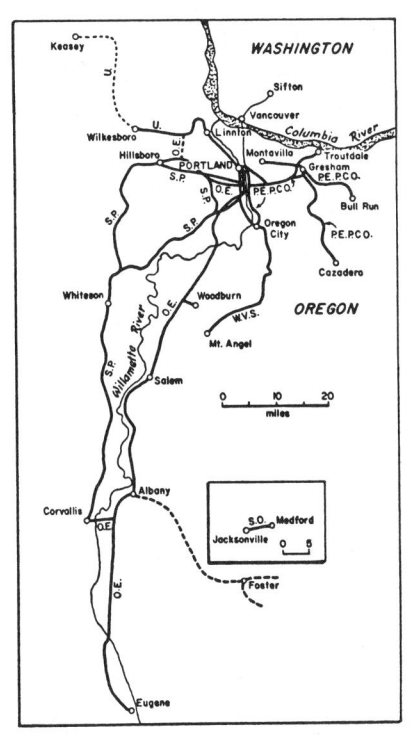

U: United Rys.
PEPCO: Pacific Elec. Power Co.
SP: Southern Pacific electric lines
OE: Oregon Elec. Ry.
WVS: Willamette Valley Southern Ry.
SO: Southern Oregon Trac. Co.

Interurban electrified lines that did not provide regular passenger service are indicated by heavy broken lines. Light, broken lines indicate interurban nonelectrified lines. Light solid lines indicate suburban streetcar lines.

States in which a steam railroad branch line was electrified and operated as essentially an interurban by the parent company was that of the Southern Pacific's lines on the west side of the Willamette Valley south of Portland. The decision to electrify these lines was prompted by the acquisition of the Oregon Electric by the Hill interests and their extension of it to Eugene. Electrification was also a convenient way to replace the relatively unprofitable local steam trains on the west side lines, and solve the problem of operation of steam locomotives on a long section of Fourth Street in Portland. The success of the electric lines in the Los Angeles area was another factor influencing the decision.

The first step was the acquisition of the Portland Eugene and Eastern, a local enterprise which had projected an interurban from Eugene to Portland, and had acquired the Eugene and Salem street railway systems. The SP planned to run the main electric line from Portland via Oswego to Salem, and thence via Corvallis to Eugene, and to develop an extensive network of branches to complete the system. Electrification of two west side steam lines was begun in 1912, and in January of 1914 service was inaugurated as far as Whiteson on two lines, one directly via Oswego, Tualatin, and Newberg (known as the East Side line), and the other via Beaverton, Hillsboro, Forest Grove, and Carlton. The second line closely paralleled the Oregon Electric's Forest Grove line, and the East Side line competed in part with PEPCO. In several cities new tracks were laid to bring the trains through the business districts. A line between Cook and Beaverton joined the two lines, but was not used for regular passenger service. The Portland Eugene and Eastern was dissolved in 1915, and the trains operated thereafter directly by the SP. Electrification was extended southward, and on June 17, 1917, through service to Corvallis was established. With the line completed, all East Side line trains went through to Corvallis, the West Side line trains terminating at Whiteson (and later at McMinnville). Electrification was never extended to Eugene.

The equipment on the line was the very distinctive Southern Pacific electric line design, as used in the East Bay and Northwestern Pacific electric service and in part on Pacific Electric. The Pullman-built all steel cars, with concrete floors, seated 60 passengers, and weighed more than 100,000 pounds. Like their East Bay cousins, they operated with pantographs, and used 1,500-volt DC. The characteristic feature was the set of great Owl Eye windows in front, three on cars with baggage compartments in front, two on others. The frequency of service varied. On the inner segments of the lines, frequent commuter service was operated, but never more than a few through trains a day were run on either line. Typically, in the twenties, four trains a day went to Corvallis and two to Whiteson. Gradually the extensive number of steam-operated branch-line connecting trains was reduced.

Passenger service (particularly the business beyond the commuter zones) was inevitably affected by the rise of the automobile. By 1925 the total loss in traffic had become substantial; in 1927 the SP organized the Oregon Motor Stages to take over the traffic in the area, and in early 1929 it announced that the trains would be eliminated. The last West Side line train operated in July 1929, and the last East Side train October 5. There was little opposition to the abandonment, despite the importance of the service to commuters. Two factors speeded abandonment: the unions' insistence on a standard three-man crew (completely ridiculous for this type of operation), and the desire of Portland to get the tracks off Fourth Street. Multiple-unit operation was common, although Portland prevented the operation of more than three-car trains during the day. RPO service was provided. Except for some switching, the freight trains were never handled by electric motors. After abandonment, a number of cars went to Northwestern Pacific and Pacific Electric. Following discontinuance of passenger service, some of the trackage in Portland was removed, and the remaining lines resumed their old non-electric status. A motor train was operated to Corvallis for a few years, and then all passenger service on the west side was discontinued.

OREGON ELECTRIC RAILWAY

One of the larger interurban systems in the country was the Oregon Electric,[64] whose main line extended 122 miles southward from Portland to Eugene, down the east side of the Willamette Valley. The road was developed by W. S. Barstow and Company, and completed and placed in operation as far as Salem on January 1, 1908. In 1910, however, it was acquired by the Spokane Portland and Seattle (jointly owned by Northern Pacific and Great Northern), and became an element in the struggle between the Hill and the Harriman lines. The Forest Grove line was completed in 1908, and the Woodburn branch in 1909. The main line reached Albany on July 4, 1912, and Eugene on October 17, 1912. The Corvallis branch was placed in service on March 25, 1913. At a much later date, the road built a 44-mile freight-only branch from Albany eastward to Foster and Dollar, in the Cascades, to handle lumber and log shipments.

The system was built to railroad standards, with private right-of-way throughout, and provided with the best high-speed interurban equipment of the period. Parlor observation cars were carried, and beginning in 1913 the line operated specially built sleeping cars for a few years, despite the fact that the run to Eugene required only 4 hours. The potential volume never warranted more than 4 or 5 runs through to Eugene daily, some operated as limiteds, some as locals. But 12 or more trains were operated each way as far as Tualatin, as the bulk of the business was always the suburban travel into Portland. Connections were made for Corvallis and Woodburn at the junction points. The Forest Grove trains ran through Portland, separately from the main-line trains. Oregon Electric was one of the few to provide through ticketing with steam roads (with all connecting lines except the competing Southern Pacific).

The passenger business on the line was seriously affected by the rise of the automobile and by bus competition. In 1931, the Corvallis branch was abandoned. Even earlier the main-line service was cut back, to morning and afternoon runs each way to Eugene, and additional service to Salem and Tualatin. The service on the Forest Grove line was down to two trains a day by 1930, and eliminated in 1932. The following year saw the end of all passenger operation. In 1945 the road was dieselized, and it has continued to provide freight service for its parent roads. The direct line into Portland was eventually removed, following the abandonment of passenger service, and connections were made via the Forest Grove branch and the Bowers–Orenco cutoff to the lines of the United and the SP&S.

The road was never very profitable, and during the depression operating deficits reached remarkable levels; for example, in 1932 total revenues were $261,000 (only $17,000 from passenger service), operating expenses $694,000, and the operating deficit $475,000. The situation improved as business conditions picked up, but even after passenger service was abandoned, the parent road had to meet annual deficits. On the other hand, the road contributed substantial through-freight business, and the losses in part merely reflected unfavorable rate divisions.

UNITED RAILWAYS

The United, which became a Hill property in 1909 and a subsidiary of the Spokane Portland and Seattle Railway in 1910, began life as a suburban carrier out of Portland, and then became primarily a steam- (later diesel-) operated freight carrier. The first predecessor company was the West Side and Suburban (Oregon Traction after 1904), which planned a line to Hillsboro and thence down the Willamette Valley. After several years of struggles to get franchises and raise money, the company was absorbed by United (inc. 1906), which finally began construction in 1908 and opened the line (April 18, 1909) from 2d and Stark in downtown Portland to Linnton and Burlington (12 miles). Construction was pushed westward, and the line opened to Wilkesboro and Banks, 28 miles from Portland, April 16, 1911, passing under Cornelius Pass through a 4,100-foot tunnel. The road was projected to Tillamook.

The line engaged in a bitter struggle to charge 10 cents on the Portland–Linnton run instead of the 5-cent fare allowed by the franchise; when permission was granted by the Oregon commission in 1915, the County Court canceled the road's franchise along St. Helens Road, and the Linnton–Portland section was abandoned. Thereafter, trains connected with SP&S main-line trains at Linnton. In 1922 the road absorbed the Portland Astoria and Pacific, which extended from Wilkesboro to Vernonia, and operated it with steam power. Connecting passenger service was operated, but a year later (1923) through steam-powered service was established from Portland to Vernonia, and electric passenger service came to an end. The line was de-electrified except for the Portland terminal lines. All passenger service ended in 1934. The road operated important terminal properties in Portland. Street improvements in the forties compelled abandonment of some of the trackage and the transfer of other segments to the Southern Pacific. United was absorbed into the SP&S in 1943.

SOUTHERN OREGON TRACTION COMPANY

The only other line in Oregon was the 6-mile Southern Oregon Traction, which connected Medford with Jacksonville, an old mining center in southern Oregon that had been bypassed by the Southern Pacific because of its location. In 1890 the Rogue River Valley Railway placed in operation a steam railroad to Jacksonville, later using for passenger service one of the earliest gasoline motor cars. In 1915, the road was sold to the Southern Oregon Traction Company, which the previous year had built two miles of streetcar line in Medford, electrified and operated with two streetcars. Jacksonville had been declining for many years and the road passed into receivership in 1918. Regular operation ended in 1920, but cars were operated on the line a few times thereafter, until the powerhouse burned in 1922. The line operated for freight until 1926. The city of Medford owned it for its last year.

For another Oregon line, see p. 426.

California

CALIFORNIA ranked third in the United States in interurban mileage (1,295 miles), and first among the states west of Indiana. More than half the total mileage figure consisted of the Pacific Electric's 700 miles of line, the remainder primarily of a system of lines in northern California. Most of the California roads developed carload freight business from the earliest years, and many became subsidiaries of steam roads; thus they survived as freight carriers, although passenger service was eventually discontinued.

NORTHERN CALIFORNIA

The greatest network of lines in Northern California was located in the Sacramento and upper San Joaquin valleys, with a connection to San Francisco; in addition there were several important, unconnected lines.

SACRAMENTO NORTHERN RAILWAY[65]

The largest of the systems was the Sacramento Northern, whose 183-mile run from San Francisco to Chico was one of the longest through runs anywhere in the country. The SN was one of the best interurbans, from the standpoint of service, and it utilized a wide variety of types of equipment. Unfortunately, its profits were never so notable as its service and equipment, and it probably would have been abandoned by the early thirties had it been an independent road.

The Sacramento Northern of later years represented a consolidation of two long separate, and in many ways, distinct types of lines. The northern lines, including those to Woodland and Vacaville, were originally the Northern Electric, a third-rail system of typical interurban characteristics. The line was promoted by H. A. Butters, who had built many railroads in South Africa and Mexico, together with the Sloss-Lilienthal (Pacific Gas and Electric) interests in San Francisco. The company purchased the Chico street railway system from the Diamond Match Co. in 1906; on April 26 of that year it completed the interurban line to Oroville, and in December it established service south to Marysville. This segment was built with a third rail, which subsequently was used on all of the Northern Electric lines. On September 7, 1907, through service was established to Sacramento, to give the east side of the valley its first frequent rail service, on a line more direct than that of the Southern Pacific. Next came the branches. The first (completed on October 31, 1907) ran from Chico to Hamilton, crossing the Sacramento River on a pontoon bridge, and operating only in the summer, mainly to haul sugar beets to the Hamilton refinery. A second branch was completed on July 4, 1912, from Sacramento to Woodland; and a third was completed on June 13, 1913, from Yuba City to Colusa. The disconnected Willota-Suisun-Vacaville line was also built in 1913, but was never extended to Vallejo and Woodland as anticipated, owing both to bankruptcy, and to the completion of the Oakland Antioch and Eastern.

The portion of the system between Oakland and Sacramento was built by the Oakland and Antioch (with the word Eastern later added to the name), promoted by a different San Francisco group.[66] The road was started from a connection with the Santa Fe at Bay Point, and built through the Ignacio Valley to Walnut Creek (1910) and to Lafayette (1911). A 3,500-foot tunnel was driven through the coast range, and on April 3, 1913, service was established to Sacramento from the Oakland connection with Key Route ferries. The Key System's trackage was used to 40th and Shafter, and the line climbed the coast hills on a 3 per cent grade to reach the tunnel. In 1914 a branch was built from Saranap to Danville and Diablo. Meanwhile construction had been completed on the line to Sacramento, which branched off at West Pittsburg, utilized a ferry crossing over the river, and set off in an almost straight line over the marsh land to Broderick where it joined the Woodland line of the Northern Electric, crossing the Yolo basin on an 11,000-foot trestle. Through service was established to Sacramento on September 3, 1913. In 1926 a Union Station was built in Sacramento in conjunction with the Northern Electric and the Central California Traction Company.

The OA&E went into receivership and was reorganized in 1920 as the San Francisco-Sacramento Railroad, known as the Sacramento Short Line. In turn, the stock of the new road was purchased in 1927 by the Western Pacific, which had bought the Sacramento Northern in 1922. In 1928 the two electric roads were merged. The WP was interested in these lines as freight feeders, although it did consider rebuilding the Short Line as part of its own main

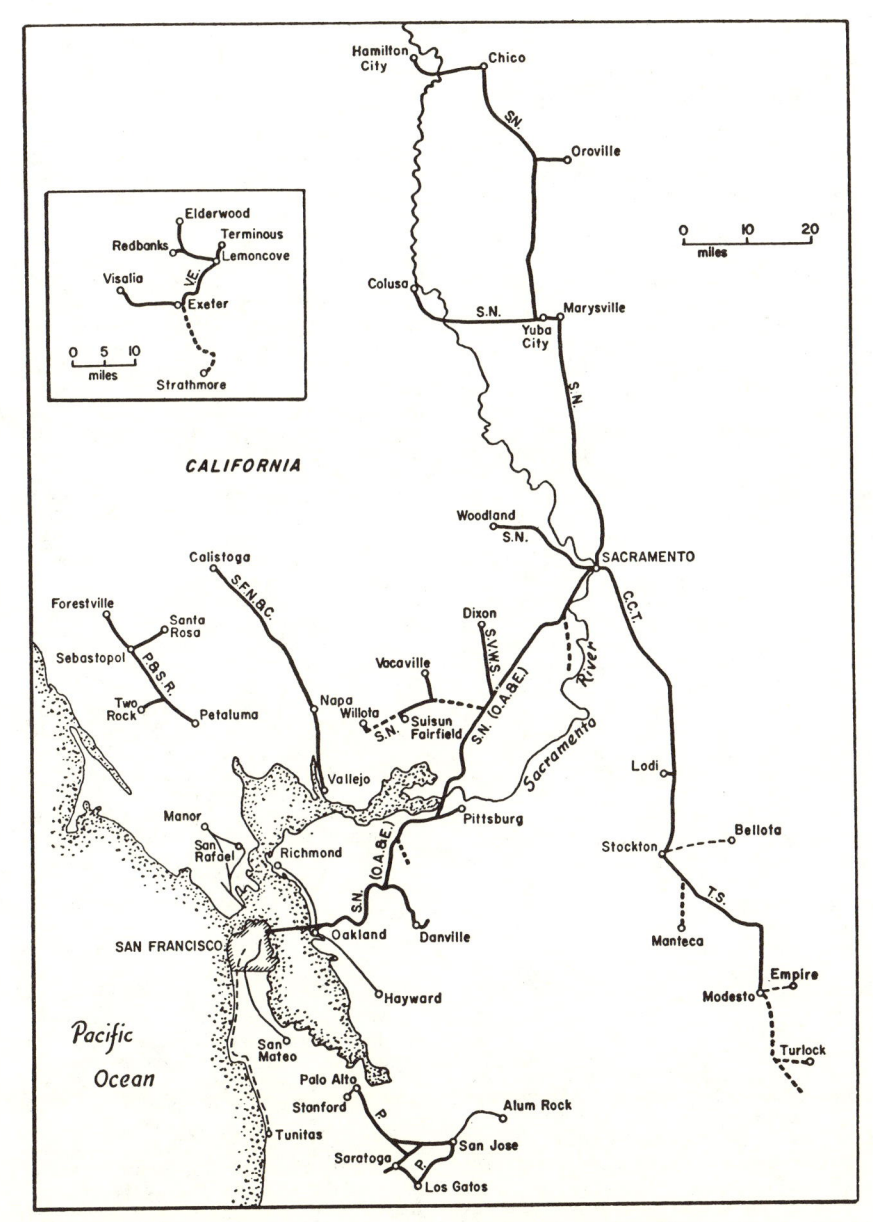

SN: Sacramento Northern Ry.
(OA&E: Oakland Antioch & Eastern Ry.)
CCT: Central California Trac. Co.
SVWS: Sacramento Valley West Side Elec. Ry.
TS: Tidewater Southern Ry.
SFN&C: San Francisco Napa & Calistoga Ry.
P&SR: Petaluma & Santa Rosa RR
P: Peninsular Ry.
VE: Visalia Electric

Suburban streetcar routes and the Northwestern Pacific electrified suburban system are shown by light solid lines. Freight-only lines of interurbans are shown by heavy broken lines. Roads planned as interurbans but never electrified are shown by light broken lines.

line, to replace the long route through the Altamont. However, this was never carried out. The new company built two new freight-only lines, one to reach farming areas around Clarksburg and Oxford, the other to connect with the Vacaville line (1930). The last extension occurred in January 1939, when passenger trains began to run into downtown San Francisco over the Bay Bridge.

Service was provided with a great variety of passenger equipment. The northern line had relied almost solely on wooden Niles or company-built cars, whereas the OA&E had used larger arched-roof equipment built by Holman, Wason, and Hall-Scott. Some southern division equipment could operate on the northern division, and in later years one of the two former OA&E cars comprising the typical Oakland–Sacramento train would go on through to Chico behind one of the Northern Electric's old Niles combines. For many years 7 trains a day operated on the main line south of Sacramento and 6 north, with connections to Colusa and Oroville. The Woodland line, operated separately, ran trains every hour for some years, and then at 2-hour intervals. Additional service was provided in rush hours from the pier to Pittsburg, to handle the commuter traffic. Some main-line trains carried observation-diner cars. Many cars were capable of speeds up to 73 m.p.h., and the Comet and the Meteor made the Sacramento run in less than 3 hours, despite the ferry crossing. Special school trains were operated in the Contra Costa area.

The line, especially on the southern division, was built to high standards, and the heavy cars provided one of the most comfortable interurban rides in the country. The line passed through very scenic territory between Oakland and Lafayette, and the river crossing provided additional interest. The cars were ferried across on the *Ramon,* an open-deck, distillate-driven vessel that could carry 6 cars. The trains operated on the streets of a number of the cities served, sharing the tracks with the company's streetcars in Chico, Marysville, and Sacramento. Freight belt lines were provided in some cities. Carload freight was an important source of revenue from early days.

The Sacramento Northern was affected by the rise of the automobile, by the speeding up of Southern Pacific service in the late twenties, and finally by the depression. The unprofitable Danville branch was abandoned in 1924 after years of losses, and in 1926 the road eliminated passenger service on the Vacaville branch. The major change came in 1931, however, when main-line schedules were cut sharply to three round trips a day, plus the Concord and Pittsburg local trains. Also, in that year, the freight-only Walwood line was abandoned. The Swanton suburban service was abandoned in 1932. The Oroville service was replaced by buses in 1938 when the bridge into the town was washed out. The extension of service into San Francisco had not aided business greatly, and in 1940 the management decided to eliminate all passenger service. On August 26, 1940, service was discontinued from West Pittsburg to Sacramento, and on October 31, 1940, all service north of Sacramento, including the Colusa branch, and the Woodland service. This left only the commuter service to Pittsburg, which was discontinued on June 30, 1941, after arrangements had been completed with Greyhound to supply bus service to the area. The last passenger operation of the company was the single-car Birney streetcar line in Chico, discontinued on December 14, 1947.

The line remained intact for freight service for several years. Then the *Ramon* was condemned, and the road discontinued service across the river; the long segment south of Dozier became almost useless, but was retained for possible future development. The line into Oakland served only the function of reaching the port of Oakland, and the city was anxious to get the rails off Shafter Avenue; when the Western Pacific was permitted to build a track on Union Street to the port, the SN abandoned its line west of Lafayette, including the tunnel. Gradually the electric freight operation was replaced by diesel service, beginning with the third-rail lines in 1944 and 1945. Despite these abandonments, the road continues to be an important freight feeder for the parent Western Pacific.

SACRAMENTO VALLEY WEST SIDE
ELECTRIC RAILWAY

This line was projected by Melville Dozier, the original promoter of the unbuilt Vallejo and Northern, from a connection with the OA&E at a point called Dixon Junction through Woodland to Marysville and up the west side of the Sacramento Valley. Twelve miles of track were laid on the line as far as the town of Dixon, and operated under contract by the OA&E. Operations began on January 1, 1915, with cars connecting at the junction for Dixon. But a town of 1,000 people could not support any sort of interurban service, and in August 1917 the OA&E received permission to abandon service. Shortly thereafter the line was torn up.

CENTRAL CALIFORNIA TRACTION COMPANY[67]

The second system to serve Sacramento was the Central California Traction Company, whose 53-mile main line connected the capital city with Stockton, with a branch from the main line to Lodi. The line reached the downtown sections of the terminal cities by street running on its own tracks, and operated on private right-of-way in the country, well to the east of U.S. Highway 99 and the Southern Pacific. Most passengers traveled through between Stockton and Lodi or Sacramento; for this reason service, typically at two-hour intervals on the main line and hourly to Lodi, was less frequent than that on roads with more local traffic.

The Stockton–Lodi line was built first, completed in September 1907. In August 1910 the main line from Lodi Junction into Sacramento was placed in operation. The road was promoted and owned for many years by the Fleishhacker group in San Francisco, prominent bankers and developers of other California utilities. Associated with the group were Walter Arnstein, H. A. Mitchell, and others who developed the OA&E. For a number of years the road was operated jointly with the separately owned Tidewater Southern. In the early twenties the Southern Pacific sought to buy control, and was opposed by the Santa Fe and the Western Pacific. Finally, each road was permitted by the I.C.C. to buy a one-third interest. Herbert Fleishhacker remained as president, a post which he held for 30 years.

Even in the peak years the road had only a minimum of rolling stock for the interurban lines. Service to Lodi was begun with four partially open American-built cars of Pacific Electric design. When the main line was opened, four motor cars and two trailers were acquired from Holman. Strangely, the line never purchased any modern freight motors, the extensive freight business being handled by a collection of old, wooden, box express motors and similar equipment, some of it from the Washington Baltimore and Annapolis, some from the Cincinnati and Lake Erie.

The well-built line employed 1,200-volt DC, except in Stockton (550 volt) and Sacramento (600 volt). The motors, however, simply ran at half speed on the lower voltages. The road was one of the first to use 1,200-volt electrification, and the first to use it with a third rail, which was employed outside of the cities. An under-running third-rail system was employed, in contrast to the Sacramento Northern's standard over-running subway-type third rail.

Almost from the first, the CCT built up a substantial freight business, largely in interchange with the steam roads, and was a financial success, one of the few interurbans that was never in bankruptcy. But passenger revenue was hit by the automobile and by bus competition between Stockton and Sacramento. First the through service to Lodi was reduced to shuttle operation; then on February 5, 1933, all passenger service was suspended. The net result was a substantial improvement in profits. However, even in the worst years of the depression, despite a drop in revenue of 50 per cent, the line never encountered operating deficits, and rarely was its net after taxes less than $100,000. The line continued to operate its suburban Sacramento streetcar service on the main-line track until 1944, when all streetcar service in Sacramento was taken over by the Pacific City Lines, and changed to bus in 1946. In 1946 the road also eliminated electric operation in favor of diesel service. Since that time virtually no changes have occurred.

TIDEWATER SOUTHERN RAILWAY[68]

The other line operating out of Stockton was the Tidewater Southern, built as an independent road, but a Western Pacific subsidiary after 1917. The road was never electrified in its entirety, and never used electricity for freight service except in Modesto; steam power was used until the acquisition of diesels in the late forties. The main line extended southeastward from Stockton to Escalon, running on private right-of-way alongside the Manteca–Oakdale road beyond Atlanta, and thence straight south into Modesto, passing close to the downtown area on city streets. The line originally entered Stockton east of the SP and the WP tracks, the cars reaching downtown via Sharps Lane and CCT tracks. In 1917 a new line was built west of the SP beyond the crossing at Ortega, terminating in a station on Weber Avenue, shared with the CCT. The company never operated streetcar service.

Construction was begun in 1911, and in October of 1912 steam passenger service was opened from Stockton to Modesto. Electrification of this line was completed on November 15, 1913, and service begun on a 2-hour schedule. In 1916 the line was exended to Turlock, and in 1917 to Hatch, but these lines were never electrified, and never operated passenger service. A freight-only nonelectric branch was built to Manteca in 1918. The TS operated at

1,200 volts, with trolley. The company owned only three passenger cars, an all-time low for a line with so much trackage; these three were 51-foot arch-roof cars built by Jewett. Service for a number of years was operated at 2-hour intervals, but was cut back in the late twenties to 5 trains each way daily. By 1931, passenger revenue, $11,000, was only 22 per cent of the 1920 figure and cars were averaging only four passengers a trip. The passenger revenue was always less important than the freight revenue, and was only 5 per cent of the total in 1931. All passenger service ended on May 26, 1932, and the section of track from Ortega into Stockton was abandoned.

The Tidewater Southern developed into an extremely significant feeder for the Western Pacific, serving an important fruit, vegetable, and wine-producing area, and supplying an extensive volume of carload freight to the parent road. Except for the short period around 1930 when the passenger service was dragging the road down, it continually showed (and still shows) a good profit, an unusual situation for what is essentially a branch-line operation.

PETALUMA AND SANTA ROSA RAILROAD[69]

In 1903 the Petaluma and Santa Rosa Railroad Company was incorporated, consolidating the street railways in the two cities of its corporate title. The line also acquired the steamer service that had operated for many years between San Francisco and Petaluma via Petaluma Creek, and built the interurban line as a connection to it. The line was placed in service between Petaluma and Sebastopol in October 1904, and was opened to Santa Rosa in December. The Northwestern Pacific, with which the road completed in its entirety, vigorously opposed the electric line's crossing its tracks to reach downtown Santa Rosa, and used force to prevent the connection from being made, until it was finally restrained by court order (see Chapter 1). Not until March 1905 did regular service into downtown Santa Rosa begin. The Sebastopol line was extended to Forestville (July 15, 1905). Plans for extension south to San Rafael and northward in several directions were ruined by the 1906 earthquake and never revived. The only addition ever built was a 5-mile line from Liberty to Two Rock, opened on July 28, 1913.

The company was promoted by J. A. McNear, Petaluma grain dealer and leading citizen of the California poultry center (whose son, many years later, was to rebuild the Toledo Peoria & Western), together with the Spreckels group of San Francisco, who had already made a fortune in sugar, and who had sponsored the San Francisco and San Joaquin Valley Railroad (now part of the Santa Fe). The P&SR was reorganized in 1918 without change in control, but when E. H. Maggard, President of the Northwestern Pacific, was admitted to the board, the bitter fight between the two roads ended. In the mid-twenties, as the Western Pacific developed plans for spreading into the area north of San Francisco, the NWP sought to tighten its grip on the P&SR to make sure it was not lost to the WP; an application to buy the road was strongly opposed by the WP, and thus the controlling stock was purchased by Maggard himself. In 1932 the control was transferred to the NWP; the two roads' terminals were coordinated and the NWP's Sebastopol branch abandoned. The P&SR has continued separate operation, however.

The line was planned as a freight and passenger carrier from the beginning. Nine combination express and passenger cars were obtained in 1904, from Holman and from Stephenson (whose cars were distinguished by center doors). The white paint of earlier years—very unusual for an interurban—was replaced by a bright yellow. Some of the runs from Santa Rosa went through to Petaluma, some to Forestville. Eighteen runs a day left Santa Rosa in the peak years. Cars were normally run in single units. Most of the business was local, although a limited amount involved connecting business with the NWP to and from Sebastopol (the steam road never offering much service on this branch), and via the steamer connection from San Francisco (which carried passengers until 1932).

The passenger business fell steadily as auto use developed, although the road never had direct bus competition. It made a strong effort to continue its service, converting to one-man operation to lower costs. Several times in the twenties, the annual reports of the company stated the belief that the expansion of auto use had ceased. The light-traffic Liberty branch lost its passenger service in 1925, but the main-line service continued until 1932. The road's freight business had grown steadily and the passenger revenue was only 5 per cent of the total by 1932. The steamer-rail service provided fast overnight service for hauling the eggs and fruit of the region to San Francisco, and for handling merchandise to the towns served, and managed to hold up well in the face of truck competition; the Sebastopol area, center of California's Gravenstein apple production, provided a steady stream of refrigerator-car business. Even in the worst years of the depression, the road showed a good margin over operating expenses. The freight service was operated with a group of steeple-cab motors with pantographs, most of them second-hand. In 1947 all electric operation was replaced by diesel motors. In 1953 the Two Rock branch was abandoned but the rest of the line remained in service in 1960.

The stern wheeler *Petaluma* continued for many years to paddle its way around San Francisco Bay and make its nightly run up Petaluma Creek, the last of the great fleet of stern wheelers that had once served the inland waters of California. In the late summer of 1950 it was replaced by barge and tug service.

SAN FRANCISCO NAPA AND CALISTOGA
RAILWAY (SAN FRANCISCO AND NAPA
VALLEY ELECTRIC RAILWAY)[70]

The fifth of the major Northern California interurbans resembled the other four lines in many ways, but unlike them it never became a steam-road subsidiary, and it did not develop enough freight business to enable it to continue operations beyond the thirties (except on the switching line to the Mare Island Navy Yard).

The line originated at the Vallejo docks of the Hatch (later Monticello) steamship line, which provided ferry connections to San Francisco for the trains, and extended northward 43 miles to Calistoga. Service was established to Napa on July 4, 1905, to Yountsville on August 23, 1907, to St. Helena on January 1, 1908, and to Calistoga, a pioneer resort city, on September 2, 1908. Street running was largely eliminated in Vallejo in 1925 by shifting the track to the never-used Vallejo and Northern grade, and in Napa in 1930 by use of SP trackage. The road was from beginning to end a local California enterprise, headed for many years by James Irvine of San Francisco. Several changes in name occurred; originally called the Vallejo Benicia and Napa Valley, it became the San Francisco Vallejo and Napa Valley in 1906 and the San Francisco Napa and Calistoga in 1911.

Service was typically at 2 hour and 15 minute intervals, dictated largely by the timing of the ferry service. High-voltage AC was used throughout the road's history, and the long wooden cars, built by American and by Niles weighed nearly 60 tons. The road also inherited a few steel cars from the Visalia Electric. Two-car trains, one an RPO car, were common, the line providing all mail service for the Napa Valley. Passenger traffic was substantial, partly local in the thickly settled fruit and vegetable area of the Napa Valley, partly through to San Francisco. For many years, even after the advent of the automobile, the road offered the best service to San Francisco, since the SP had only limited service, and driving required two auto ferry crossings. Carload freight service was operated, but compared to passenger revenue was never important, except on the spur line into the Mare Island Navy Yard. The road closely paralleled a Southern Pacific branch.

On June 19, 1913, the road experienced one of the worst interurban wrecks in California. Train No. 6, the morning Calistoga Flyer, running 17 minutes late because its ferry connection had been delayed by the tide, crashed head-on at full speed into No. 5, the 7:42 local out of Calistoga, on a blind reverse curve just north of the Vallejo city limits. Thirteen persons were killed as No. 5 overrode and telescoped No. 6's lead car, No. 41. The southbound train had received instructions to pass No. 6 at Hatch instead of Collins, but No. 6 had left the Vallejo wharf before receiving this word from the dispatcher.

The passenger traffic held up better than that of many lines, owing to the unusual nature of the San Francisco traffic and the lack of bus competition; the volume fell by only one third between 1925 and 1929. The depression, however, caused the loss of half the traffic, and the road found itself in serious financial difficulties. Then on January 22, 1932, a fire destroyed the Napa car barns, a large portion of the usable equipment, and the power plant. The road's bus subsidiary took over the schedule, and it was widely reported that the rail line would never operate again. But on May 29 facilities had been restored sufficiently to place cars in service as far north as St. Helena, and two new cars were ordered from the St. Louis Car Company. These were heavy steel cars, the last standard steel interurban passenger cars ever built in America.* They were placed in service on July 1, 1933, and rail operations extended to Calistoga. For the next 4 years the road operated 3 trains a day, plus some bus service. Revenues had stabilized, and despite the great decline from the twenties

---

* The ten cars received by Chicago Aurora and Elgin in 1945 were heavy cars, but not built to the standard patterns of the previous decades.

the road was able to cover its expenses on a remarkably low revenue-per-mile figure. The company had gone into receivership in 1934 and was reorganized in 1936 as the San Francisco and Napa Valley Railroad. Then on September 12, 1937, the final blow was struck; the connecting ferry, now operated by Southern Pacific Golden Gate Ferries, was discontinued. Without this connection the road could not survive, and on September 20 the last passenger trains were operated. The track north of Napa was abandoned in 1938, the Vallejo–Napa line in 1942, and the Mare Island line was dieselized. In 1957 the Navy Department took over the switching service, and the company was dissolved. Bus operations were sold to Greyhound in 1942.

There were many plans for uniting the Sacramento Northern with the Napa Valley; only a short gap from Willota to Napa Junction remained once the SN built its line from Creed. But nothing ever came of these plans.

PENINSULAR RAILWAY[71]

One of the least successful of the California interurbans was the Peninsular, which served the territory between San Jose, Los Gatos, and Palo Alto. During most of the road's life it was an SP subsidiary; the parent road kept it going for a number of years at a deficit, but had the road been independent, or a subsidiary of another steam road, it might have been more successful; it was severely damaged by absentee management.

The first portion was built in 1904 as the San Jose and Los Gatos by Santa Clara Valley promoters, with financial aid from St. Louis, and completed in March of that year from San Jose via Saratoga to Los Gatos. The road was soon acquired by SP interests, and placed under the management of Paul Shoup. On November 26, 1904, the direct route to Los Gatos via Campbell was opened. Plans for great expansions were never realized owing to the drain on SP finances imposed by repairs on the Sunset Route (damaged by the breakthrough of the Colorado River into Salton Sea), and by the panic of 1907. But in 1910 the route from San Jose to Palo Alto was finally opened, and in 1914 the steam line from Monta Vista to Congress Junction was electrified, to allow direct service to Los Gatos from Palo Alto. Short lines extended from Palo Alto to Stanford and to Ravenswood (part of a planned line to Oakland), and from Saratoga to Congress Springs, as well as one from San Jose through Berryessa to Alum Rock Park, operated much of the time by San Jose Railroads.[72]

The road typically operated hourly service, usually with single cars; it owned 12 medium-sized interurbans, built by American in 1903 for the original Los Gatos line, and 8 heavy Jewett cars built in 1913, far more equipment than it needed. The road did a fair amount of business through the relatively thickly settled area; it advertised an annual blossom tour, and handled recreation business to Congress Springs, as well as the routine commuter and shopping traffic. Although freight was handled from an early date, the volume was never great; only the short route from San Jose to Berryessa ever built up much volume. The road never earned interest on its grossly exaggerated capital structure (all of the securities being owned by the SP), and operating deficits began in 1919. There followed 16 continuous years of operating deficits, reaching $189,000 in 1927; operating expenses were clearly excessive relative to the traffic handled. Auto traffic cut into the business, but not as badly as most lines; the 1930 gross revenue was only one third less than that of the peak year of 1920. Under other management the road might have been relatively prosperous.

Much of the right-of-way was on the edge of the highways, unlike the usual California pattern, and the widening of the highways was a factor bringing abandonment. For this reason the line was abandoned north of Mayfield in 1929, and the Campbell line in 1932. The remaining lines were abandoned in 1933, except for the Mayfield–San Jose route, which went out in 1934. Only the trackage to Berryessa remained in service for freight operation, turned over to Visalia Electric management. The Jewett cars went to Pacific Electric, where they operated for many years. The Peninsular essentially had no separate management once it fell under SP control, having common officers with the other SP electric lines. There were many plans to extend the line to San Francisco, either directly or by connection with the San Mateo line of the Market Street Railway, but these were never carried out.

VISALIA ELECTRIC RAILROAD[73]

In the citrus-fruit area in Tulare county (in the southern part of the San Joaquin Valley), the Visalia Electric operated several lines, concentrating from early years on freight service in interchange with the parent Southern Pacific, which promoted the road. The line was built to Lemon Cove in 1905, but not until March 1908 was electrification of this line and the SP line from Visalia to Exeter completed and passenger service established. High-voltage AC power was chosen because of the plans for extensive long-distance electrification of SP lines in this area. This was the only road to use 15-cycle current. Service was extended to Terminus in 1909, to Redbanks on June 30, 1910, and to Elderwood on July 31, 1915. Most of the runs terminated at Woodlake, some cars going on to Elderwood and to Redbanks. Even in peak years only a few runs a day were operated. A nonelectrified line was built from Exeter south to Strathmore in 1916.

The passenger revenue reached its peak ($54,000) in 1912; by 1923 it had dropped to $15,000, before most electric lines had been affected drastically by the automobile. Meanwhile freight service had grown steadily, and in 1923 passenger revenue was only 7 per cent of the total. In 1924 the company requested permission to discontinue passenger service. The request was granted by the California commission —the first in a long line of decisions of this type—on the ground that the sharp drop in business showed the lack of need for the service. The Strathmore line was cut back to El Mirador in 1942 and to Fayette in 1953. The system was dieselized in 1944.

For a time the VE operated the nonelectric line from Chowchilla to Dairyland, in Madera County, and the freight operations of the Peninsular Railway in the San Jose area when that road was abandoned. Typically the VE has had the same officers as Pacific Electric.

PACIFIC COAST RAILWAY COMPANY

The Pacific Coast, a narrow-gauge steam road whose main line extended from Avila through San Luis Obispo and Santa Maria to Los Olivos, electrified in 1908 a line from Santa Maria to the connection with the Southern Pacific at Guadaloupe. The primary function of the electrified line was to provide passenger connections with the SP for Santa Maria, the largest city in the area, which the SP's coast route had bypassed by 11 miles. The frequency of service varied, but in the mid-twenties there were only three runs a day. The road also handled freight, mostly sugar beets, but carload shipments to Santa Maria came in over the standard-gauge Santa Maria Valley Railroad. The passenger service alone could not support the road, and in 1928 it was abandoned, replaced by bus service. The steam line to Los Olivos lasted a few years longer.

The Pacific Coast Railway was a subsidiary of the Pacific Coast Company, which owned, in addition to this road and the Pacific Coast Railroad in Washington State, a group of coal mines and steamship lines. (See Map, p. 408.)

*

NEVADA COUNTY TRACTION COMPANY

This line, scarcely more than a streetcar line, connected Grass Valley and Nevada City with its 6 miles of track. It was built in 1901, intended to be a link in a system that John Martin was promoting to connect the Grass Valley area with Sacramento. The line was abandoned in 1923.

WATSONVILLE TRACTION COMPANY

This line, later the Watsonville Railway and Navigation Company, operated a 6-mile line from Watsonville to Watsonville Beach for a time after 1910. Service was abandoned by 1917.

In addition to the lines noted, Northern California had several suburban electric railway operations, plus several long suburban car lines, which are beyond the scope of this study. The three suburban systems were: (1) *Northwestern Pacific* in Marin County, serving San Rafael, San Anselmo, Mill Valley, and intermediate towns, connecting with the Sausalito ferries, electrified in 1903, abandoned in 1941; (2) Southern Pacific East Bay electric service (electrified in 1911-12, abandoned in 1941), in its last years the *Interurban Electric Railway*, providing four lines to Berkeley, one through downtown Oakland to East Oakland, Melrose, Broadmoor, and Dutton Avenue, and two to Alameda; and (3) the *Key System*, serving the Oakland-Berkeley area, built in 1903 and 1904, and abandoned in 1959.

The *Oakland Traction Company* and its successors operated two long streetcar lines, one to Richmond, and one to Hayward. The former was completed in 1904 and abandoned in 1933. The latter, completed in 1893 and abandoned in 1935, was one of the pioneer intercity lines in the west, and essentially an interurban when it was built by the Oakland San Leandro and Haywards Electric Railway. It was the first electric railway to operate regular piggyback service, hauling wagons from the Oakland Ferry to Hayward on its flat cars and then taking them off for delivery of merchandise to the stores. This service, commenced in 1894, was not highly successful, and was abandoned a year later.

United Railroads of San Francisco (later

the *Market Street Railway*) completed a suburban line to San Mateo in 1903, which reached downtown San Francisco via Mission Street. This line was operated with interurban-type equipment, some of the original 1903 equipment still being used at the time the line was abandoned in 1949.

A line, electrified as the California Railway, built between East Alameda and Leona in East Oakland in 1896, had some characteristics of an interurban for a time operating both nonelectrified coaches behind an electric freight motor and individual cars. The road eventually passed into the hands of the Key System's predecessor companies, and cars were run on the line from downtown Oakland. The line became the Leona streetcar route, but freight service by electric motor continued until abandonment in 1936.

SOUTHERN CALIFORNIA

Southern California had one great system, the Pacific Electric, in the Los Angeles area, plus a few minor lines.

PACIFIC ELECTRIC RAILWAY

The largest intercity electric railway system in the United States was the Pacific Electric,[74] which, in its peak years, operated over 1,000 miles of track, and about 700 route miles of service.* Because routes overlapped, the true, non-duplicating line-mileage figure was closer to 520 miles. The investment was estimated by the California Railroad Commission to be about $100 million, far more than the investment of any other system, and nearly 10 per cent of the total interurban investment in the United States. In a sense, however, much of the operation was not typically interurban, but more like a suburban electrified main-line service.

The history of the system is very complex, and cannot be developed at length. The Pacific Electric was formed in September of 1911 by the merger of eight companies, which had all been under common control, although some had started life as independent roads. The predecessors date back to 1895, when a line was completed from Los Angeles to Pasadena, and 1896, when the line via Hollywood to Santa Monica was finished. The bulk of the mileage was built during the next decade.

The Pacific Electric, as a coordinated system, was largely the work of Henry Huntington, the nephew of one of the Central Pacific's Big Four, C. P. Huntington. Henry became president of the SP in the nineties and became very interested in the Los Angeles area. Later in the decade he began to build interurban lines in the area, and acquired several existing lines. He shared ownership of the interurbans with the Southern Pacific until 1911, but disagreements with Harriman (to whom he had sold controlling interest in the SP in 1901) and other factors led him to sell his stock to the railroad. Following the great merger in 1911, Harriman sent Paul Shoup to Los Angeles to head the system, a post that Shoup held for three decades. Shoup, who had risen from the job as Santa Fe ticket agent in San Bernardino to head the Peninsular Railway, became one of the interurban industry's leading spokesmen and one of the first to complain strongly of "subsidized motor competition" and taxation as the sources of the difficulties of electric railways.

The principal segments from which the system was built were:

1. The original Pacific Electric, chartered in 1901, and developed from the first by Huntington personally. This road acquired the Pasadena line from the Los Angeles Pacific, and built a number of the major routes, including the San Pedro, Long Beach, Covina, and Newport lines.

2. The Los Angeles Interurban Railway, also a Huntington project, which built the Glendale, Monrovia, and Santa Ana lines. The LAI bought the independent California Pacific (San Pedro via Gardena) in 1903. This enterprise was leased to the original PE in 1908.

3. The Los Angeles Pacific, a separate enterprise developed from 1895 on by M. H. Sherman and E. P. Clark; the LAP built the Hollywood, Santa Monica, Venice, and Redondo (via Playa del Rey) lines, which after the merger became the PE's western district. The LAP lost the Pasadena and Los Angeles to Huntington in 1898, and in 1906 the SP bought control of the entire company, although the road continued to operate separately until the merger; Huntington had no direct interest in LAP.

4. The Los Angeles and Redondo. The lines to Redondo, except the one via Playa del Rey, were built by the Los Angeles and Redondo, originally developed as a narrow-gauge steam road, and eventually electrified. The road was built by the Ainsworth-Thompson syndicate, a group

---

* If routes that operated entirely on lines also used by other routes are added, the figure is 760. Major examples were the Watts and Sierra Vista local service lines, and the routes operated to provide connections for S. P. trains to Pasadena and to Long Beach–San Pedro.

of West Coast promoters, and was acquired by Huntington in 1905.

In addition, four smaller Huntington properties in the San Bernardino area were absorbed, and later connected with the remainder of the system.

Most of the construction of the lines had been completed prior to the great merger of 1911, but the next several years saw the building of the San Bernardino line, and the making of numerous improvements in the system. By 1915 the PE was one of the finest electric railway properties in the country, with the most modern equipment, extensive private right-of-way, relatively high speeds, frequent service, and very complete coverage of the rapidly growing Los Angeles metropolitan area. No other area of the country ever had such an intensive network of lines built largely ahead of the growth of population. Over a thousand trains a day left from the Los Angeles stations, with headway as low as 7.5 minutes on some of the lines with the highest density.

The nature of the service, of course, varied with the type of line; the true interurban lines, such as the one to San Bernardino, had much less frequent service than the shorter suburban-type lines. The inner segments of the lines were double-track, and the two main routes out of the city, to Watts and Sierra Vista, used by a number of lines, had four tracks—two local and two express. The tracks reached the center of Los Angeles, and service on virtually all lines, except those out of San Bernardino, operated directly from the downtown area. Although there was some street running, mainly on the segments of the western lines leading out of downtown Los Angeles, in Hollywood, in Santa Monica, in Pasadena, and in Glendale, a large part of the system was operated on private right-of-way, with stations in the various towns. Street railway service was also operated in Pasadena, Long Beach, Glendale, and parts of Los Angeles. In 1925, in the last expansion program, a one-mile tunnel was built in downtown Los Angeles to eliminate some of the street operation for the western lines, but the overall program of relocation was stopped because of the falling off of business.

The road developed freight service at an early date, particularly carload interchange traffic with the SP in citrus fruits, oil, and inbound merchandise; most of this was carried on the Santa Monica Air Line, and on the San Bernardino, Stern, El Segundo, and Santa Ana lines. But most of the revenues (typically about 75 per cent, and 50 per cent even as late as 1953) came from passenger service. A wide variety of equipment was employed, most of the cars being acquired in large batches, from Jewett in 1913, Pressed Steel Car in 1915, Pullman in 1921, and Standard Steel Car in 1924. Some Northwestern Pacific equipment was acquired in 1941, and a group of PCC lightweight cars were bought for the Glendale–Burbank line. Two-man operation was usual, partly because of a Los Angeles ordinance. All lines except the 1,200-volt San Bernardino route used 600-volt DC, with trolley pickup rather than the usual SP pantograph.

Profits for a number of years were moderate but not high; traffic rose sharply up to 1923 as the area grew rapidly, and then fell as car use increased. However, traffic held up better during the twenties than on most interurbans, but the system was very hard hit by the depression, its revenues falling in half from 1929 to 1933. The Los Angeles area was particularly suited to the automobile, because of the widely scattered population and industry, good roads at an early date, and favorable weather. However, PE was never subjected to much bus competition after the initial difficulty with jitneys (see Chapter 7), except on the Venice–Santa Monica and Venice–Whittier lines. In 1923 it established its own bus system in cooperation with Los Angeles Railways.

Until the late thirties, the company continued to operate in much the same fashion as it had twenty years before. The service was still good, by comparison with what was offered in many areas, but it had not been modernized in any way, and the company seemed to have lost all ability to adjust to changing conditions. After the volume had fallen for a few years after 1923, the management began to lose interest in the whole venture. Cars became obsolete, track began to deteriorate, and few attempts were made to introduce improvements. Finally in the late thirties the first cutbacks of any consequence were made. An elaborate study by the California Railroad Commission suggested the company might eliminate much of its rail service, and make improvements in the remaining operations. The company took the former suggestion, if not the latter.[75] Between 1938 and 1941 a significant portion of the passenger service was abandoned, including the service to San Bernardino, Riverside and Pomona, San Gabriel and Temple, Yorba Linda, Fullerton and Whittier, Redondo (via both lines), and Newport Beach (temporarily restored during World War II). But the high-density traffic lines remained.

PACIFIC ELECTRIC RY.

1. Pasadena Short Line
1A. Mount Lowe
2. Pasadena-Oak Knoll
3. South Pasadena
4. Sierra Madre
5. Monrovia-Glendora
6. Alhambra-San Gabriel-Temple
7. San Bernardino
7A. Pomona
7B. Riverside

10. Whittier
10A. La Habra
10B. Fullerton
11. Santa Ana
12. Long Beach
13. Newport
14. San Pedro via Dominguez
15. San Pedro via Gardena and Torrance
16. Redondo via Gardena
17. Redondo via Hawthorne
17A. Hawthorne-El Segundo

20. Redondo via Playa del Rey
21. Venice Short Line
22. West 16th-Sawtelle
22A. Westgate
23. Santa Monica Air Line
24. Hollywood-Santa Monica-Venice
24A. West Hollywood (Colegrove)
25. San Fernando Valley
25A. San Fernando
25B. Owensmouth (Canoga Park)
26. Glendale-Burbank

101. Shorb
110. Santa Ana-Orange
111. Santa Ana-Huntington Beach
113. Long Beach-San Pedro
114. Long Beach-Seal Beach

201. Lagoon
231. Soldiers Home
232. Port Los Angeles
233. Inglewood

300. Redlands
301. Riverside-Corona

302. San Bernardino-Riverside
303. Colton
304. Arrowhead Springs
305. Patton-Highlands
306. Ontario-San Antonio Heights
307. Pomona-Claremont

P.C.: Pacific Coast Ry.
G.&M.: Glendale & Montrose Ry.

SAN DIEGO AREA LINES

SDE: San Diego Elec. Ry.
SDS: San Diego Southern Ry.

World War II brought a record traffic volume and a temporary financial improvement, soon lost because cost increases were not offset by rate increases. Basically the road was the victim of the productivity squeeze, and any attempts to avoid it were rendered difficult by union and municipal attitudes and by the cost of new equipment. Once the traffic volume began to fall again after the war, the road took steps to convert to freight-only operation. In 1950 all remaining passenger service was abandoned except to Long Beach and San Pedro, and to Bellflower, Hollywood, and Burbank. In 1954 these remaining lines were sold to the newly formed Metropolitan Coach Lines, the Pacific Electric retaining the tracks for freight service. The new company bought the passenger lines with the deliberate intent of converting them to bus service; this was done on the Hollywood and Burbank lines, and permission for it sought on the other lines, but this application was rejected by the state commission. An impasse had been created, since the company was determined to get out of rail operation; finally in 1957 the Los Angeles Metropolitan Transit Authority was formed and (as of April 1, 1958) purchased both the Metropolitan Coach Lines and the Los Angeles Transit Company. The Authority, however, proceeded to abandon the remaining rail lines except to Long Beach.*

Unlike the usual interurban, the Pacific Electric could have comprised the nucleus of a highly efficient rapid transit system, which would have contributed greatly to lessening the tremendous traffic and smog problems that developed from the population growth. In itself, the PE suffered serious limitations, particularly the excessive street running on the western district lines and the numerous grade crossings. But the system, with its extensive private right-of-way, was far superior to a system consisting solely of buses on the crowded streets, and was important as a potential element in a system involving subways in the downtown area. It is inevitable that such a system will fail to cover its costs directly; nonetheless, it may be entirely justified economically. But so long as PE was in private hands, it was virtually impossible to keep its unprofitable services going, regardless of how much they contributed to the solution of the traffic problem. The difficulty was aggravated by absentee control for many years, by the SP's general lack of interest after 1924 in local passenger service, by the considerable public hostility toward the company,

* The Long Beach Line was abandoned on April 9, 1961.

and by the management's failure to make any effort to modernize. It is regrettable that government units did not take over the system in the mid-thirties, while it was still intact, rather than two decades later, and recognize the importance of continued use of the rail facilities in the over-all solution to the transportation problem in the area.

A detailed review of the various lines would occupy a whole volume in itself; only a brief sketch is possible. The lines are numbered to correspond to the map key on p. 408; PE did not number its routes. Those numbered above 100 did not normally operate from downtown Los Angeles.

Northern District. The lines north and eastward from Los Angeles constituted the Northern District. These lines began at the station at 6th and Main in downtown Los Angeles, ran on the streets for about a mile, crossed the Los Angeles River and went onto private right-of-way, with four tracks to Sierra Vista. The San Bernardino line diverged at Valley Junction, the San Gabriel line at Sierra Vista, the Pasadena line at El Molino, and the Sierra Madre line from the Glendora line at San Marino.

1. *Pasadena Short Line,* the high-frequency-service main line to the Pasadena business district (12 miles), completed late in 1902, abandoned on September 30, 1951.

1A. *Mt. Lowe,* an extension of the Pasadena line to the summit of Mt. Lowe, strictly a tourist attraction. The portion as far as Rubio was completed in 1891, the second section, an incline railway, in 1893, and the last 4 miles to the summit in 1896. PE took over the line in 1902, and typically operated 5 round trips a day, the cars using the Short Line. The line was abandoned in 1938 after the Alpine Tavern was destroyed by fire, and a cloudburst tore out much of the line.

2. *Pasadena–Oak Knoll,* operating on the main line to El Molino and thence into east Pasadena, completed in 1906, abandoned in October 1950. For a time cars operated through to Altadena.

3. *South Pasadena,* the first line in the area, completed on May 6, 1895, by the Sherman-Clark group as the Pasadena and Los Angeles from downtown Los Angeles via Echandia Junction and Garvanza into South Pasadena and thence into Pasadena. After Huntington acquired it in 1898, and after the main Pasadena lines were completed, this line became a secondary route run in conjunction with the Watts local service, cars going on to Altadena on the northern end. The line was abandoned on January 2, 1935.

4. *Sierra Madre,* one of the lighter traffic routes, opened to Sierra Madre in 1906. Cars were operated on a shuttle basis except in rush hours after the thirties, and the line was abandoned on December 28, 1950.

5. *Monrovia–Glendora,* completed to Oneonta in 1902, Arcadia and Monrovia in 1903, and Glendora (26 miles from Los Angeles) in 1907. This was a heavy-traffic route west of Monrovia, with half-hour service typical. Passenger service was discontinued in September 1951, but the portion east of Arcadia was retained for freight service, joined to the San Bernardino line by a cutoff built at Rivas in 1951. The track between Azuza and Glendora was abandoned in 1959.

6. *Alhambra–San Gabriel–Temple,* a branch off the main line at Sierra Vista to Temple (14 miles). This route was completed to San Gabriel in 1902 by the Los Angeles and Pasadena, and a branch was built to Shorb (101) in 1904 to connect with Southern Pacific main-line trains and providing direct connecting service to Pasadena (until 1924). Not until 1924 was the San Gabriel line extended to Temple, in the system's last expansion. The line was abandoned on November 29, 1941, the portion to Alhambra retained for freight service until 1951. The Shorb spur is still in use for freight.

7. *San Bernardino,* the longest line in the system and the most typically interurban, from Los Angeles to San Bernardino (58 miles). The line was completed to Covina in 1907, to San Dimas in 1910, and to Pomona in 1912. A line built from Pomona via Claremont to Upland in 1910 by the Ontario and San Antonio Heights Company was incorporated into the system, the route was extended from Upland to San Bernardino, and through service established on July 11, 1914. This route, the only one to use 1200-volt power, was one of the best from a physical standpoint. Passenger service was discontinued east of Baldwin Park on November 1, 1941, except for rush hour service to Covina which was continued until 1947. Remaining passenger service ended on October 15, 1950, and the freight service was then dieselized.

7A. *Pomona,* a branch from La Verne on the San Bernardino line into Pomona, completed in 1912 with hourly service operated through from Los Angeles. Passenger service was discontinued on November 1, 1941.

7B. *Riverside,* service established from Los Angeles to Riverside via Rialto in March 1914, the line having been electrified from Riverside to Crestmore in 1908 and to Bloomington in 1911. A Union Pacific branch line was utilized for much of this route. For many years, one car for Riverside was attached to the San Bernardino trains and cut off at Rialto. Service was eliminated on June 9, 1940.

Eastern District. A number of rather short lines served the territory around Riverside and San Bernardino, important fruit-growing areas. Several lines were built before the main line by the San Bernardino Valley Traction Co. Cars were not operated through from Los Angeles, except for a time on the Redlands line.

300. *Redlands,* completed from San Bernardino in 1903 (9 miles). Passenger service was abandoned in 1936.

301. *Riverside–Corona,* electrified from Riverside to Arlington in April 1899, and to Corona (14 miles) in 1915 (February 17). This line had the most frequent service of all the lines in the area, but service was cut back to Arlington in 1931, and the remainder was eliminated in 1943.

302. *San Bernardino–Riverside,* 10 miles, completed on December 13, 1913, passenger service discontinued in 1939.

303. *Colton,* 5 miles, built 1902, abandoned 1942.

304. *Arrowhead Springs,* completed in 1907 largely to haul mineral water; passenger service abandoned, September 1932. Freight was dieselized in 1943.

305. *Patton–Highlands,* built 1903. The extension to Patton was abandoned in 1924, and passenger service to Highlands was abandoned 1936. Part of the route had been built in 1888 as a steam road.

In the area east of Pomona, the pioneer Ontario and San Antonio Heights, a local project later absorbed by Pacific Power and Light and sold to Pacific Electric in 1912, had built two routes, a portion of one becoming the Claremont–Upland section of the PE's main line to San Bernardino noted above.

306. *Ontario–San Antonio Heights,* built in 1887 as a mule-car line, the mules riding back down hill in a trailer attached to the car. The line was electrified in 1895. The portion north of Upland was abandoned in 1924, and the Upland–Ontario line in 1928, in two of PE's earliest abandonments.

307. *Pomona–Claremont,* a portion of the line built in 1910 between Upland and Pomona, and operated as a shuttle line by PE following acquisition. Passenger service was abandoned in 1933.

Southern District. The Southern District lines also operated from the 6th and Main Street terminal, with only a limited amount of street running, and with a four-track line as far as Watts (7 miles), the two additional tracks completed in 1902.

The Whittier line forked off at Slauson, while at Watts three major routes diverged, the El Segundo, Redondo-via-Gardena and Torrance–San Pedro lines going off to the west, the Santa Ana line to the southeast, and the main San Pedro and Long Beach–Newport Beach lines continuing straight south. The southern district consisted primarily of private-right-of-way lines able to operate at relatively high speeds, constructed for the most part after 1900 by Huntington. A separate local service was operated from Los Angeles to Watts, one of the last lines, continuing service until November 2, 1959.

10. *Whittier–La Habra–Fullerton,* a major route, opened to Whittier in 1903 (December 31) and offering high-frequency service for many years. Abandonment occurred in 1938.

This line was extended (10A) to La Habra in 1908 and Stern in 1911. Typically only 5 runs a day served this extension, but freight service was important. Passenger service beyond Yorba Linda to Stern was abandoned in 1933, and the track itself in 1938; on January 22, 1938, all passenger service on the entire line was eliminated. A branch to Fullerton (10B) had been built in 1917.

11. *Santa Ana,* a high-speed, private-right-of-way line, opened on November 6, 1905. The bulk of the travel was on the inner portion of the line, but service was continued to Santa Ana until July 2, 1950, when it was cut back to Bellflower. This service was eliminated May 25, 1958. The track has been retained for freight service.

Two branch lines extended from Santa Ana. One north to Orange (110), was built in 1887 as a horse-car line, and electrified in 1906. A line south 13 miles to Huntington Beach (111) was built in 1907. Passenger service on the Orange line was discontinued in 1930, and the track from Huntington Beach to the Santa Ana River was removed in 1930. Through service on the Huntington Beach line had ended in 1922 when a flood washed a bridge out. Much of the remainder of this line was abandoned in 1936, but some segments remain in freight service.'

12. *Long Beach,* 20 miles, the most important in terms of traffic of all the lines, and the first major Huntington project. The line was completed on July 4, 1902, with wide publicity. With high-frequency, high-speed service and the best equipment, this was the system's most profitable route. As of January 1960 it is still operated by the Los Angeles Metropolitan Transit Authority, the last intercity electric passenger line west of Chicago.

13. *Newport,* an extension of the Long Beach line from North Long Beach, which followed the shore line via Huntington Beach (1904) and Newport Beach (1905) to Balboa, reached in 1906. It was built largely to serve the beach resort area. Passenger service, never heavy beyond the Long Beach area, was discontinued in 1940, reestablished in 1942 for war needs, and abandoned again in 1950. Track has been retained for freight, except from Newport to Balboa (abandoned in 1941).

Two local interurban lines operated out of Long Beach, one to San Pedro via Wilmington (113) and one to Seal Beach (114). The lines were completed in 1910, and abandoned in 1949.

14. *San Pedro via Dominguez,* the direct line to San Pedro, using the same track as the Long Beach line to Dominguez. This was also a high-speed, heavy-traffic line. The route was placed in operation to Wilmington in 1904, and to San Pedro July 5, 1905. Passenger service ended Dec. 8, 1958.

15. *San Pedro via Gardena and Torrance,* built by the California Pacific, an offspring of Los Angeles Traction, via Vermont Avenue to Gardena and McKinley (December 30, 1901) and to San Pedro (January 1903). Control was obtained by the Southern Pacific in 1903, but not until 1912 was the line standard-gauged. At this time cars were rerouted over the cut-off to Watts, and the northern portion became a Los Angeles Railways car line. Also in 1912 a loop line was built into Torrance, location of the P.E. shops. Passenger service was discontinued south of Torrance in 1939 and north thereof in 1940.

16. *Redondo via Gardena.* Redondo Beach was served by three (and for a short time by four) routes, one of which was a portion of the western district and will be considered below (20). The principal route operated via Gardena; it was electrified (from a narrow-gauge steam road) west of Gardena in 1903. Originally cars reached Los Angeles via Vermont Avenue, after 1907 via Moneta Avenue, and finally after 1911 via Watts. The line was abandoned in 1940.

17. *Redondo via Hawthorne,* built by the Los Angeles and Redondo as a steam road and electrified in 1902. The route originally operated via Inglewood but in 1911 was rerouted via Watts north and east of Hawthorne, and the Inglewood line became a LARY car line. The through route to Redondo was cut in 1937 when the El Nido–Hawthorne segment was abandoned.

17A. *Hawthorne–El Segundo.* A line of minor importance for passenger service but one of the major freight routes extended westward from Hawthorne to El Segundo, cars using the route of the Redondo-via-Hawthorne line east and north of Hawthorne. This line was placed in service in August 1914, largely to serve the Standard Oil refinery in El Segundo. Passenger service was abandoned October 31, 1930.

Western District. The Western District consisted of the lines extending westward and southwestward from Los Angeles that had comprised the Los Angeles Pacific prior to the 1911 merger, plus the Glendale–Burbank and San Fernando lines. Most of the segments of this road were built under Sherman-Clark management, before Huntington acquired control of the road. The equipment used was painted green instead of the PE's red. The Western lines had their own terminal, the Hill Street terminal, used by the West-16th-Sawtelle cars until 1909. In that year Hollywood and Colegrove cars also began to use the terminal, and later in the year (following the completion of a tunnel) the Short Line cars did so as well. In 1925, when the subway was completed for the Hollywood and Glendale–Burbank lines, the new Subway Terminal was built on the same location. The only western district line to use the Main Street station was the Santa Monica Air Line, mainly a freight route, which connected with the Watts line at Amoco.

The Western lines may be classed into three groups: (1) the lines that turned south out of the subway terminal and operated via Vineyard, plus the Santa Monica Air Line; (2) the lines that operated to the west via the subway and Hollywood; and (3) the Glendale–Burbank line. These routes were all handicapped by a great amount of street running and congestion; none were able to maintain the speed of the other district lines, except outer segments of the Van Nuys and Redondo lines, which handled relatively little traffic.

20. *Redondo via Playa del Rey,* a narrow-gauge route from Los Angeles to Redondo, via Playa del Rey, running on the beach south of Playa. The line was built by the Los Angeles Pacific in 1903. It shared tracks as far as Vineyard with the West 16th line, and as far as Culver with the Venice Short Line. The track was standard-gauged in 1908. Abandonment occurred on May 12, 1940.

201. *Lagoon,* a 6-mile line connecting the Venice line with the Redondo-via-Playa route in Playa. The line was completed in 1905 and abandoned in July 1936.

21. *Venice Short Line,* which operated via Vineyard and Culver directly into Venice, and thence north to Santa Monica. This route, completed in 1902, was the fastest and most heavily traveled of the western lines. Abandonment occurred on September 17, 1950.

22. *West 16th–Sawtelle,* operated via Vineyard, and thence northwest to Santa Monica via Beverly Hills and Sawtelle, running much of the way on Santa Monica Boulevard. The line was completed from Los Angeles to Beverly Hills in 1897 to connect with the line built from Santa Monica via Hollywood the previous year. Through service was discontinued on July 7, 1940, and service as far as Olympic Boulevard ended in 1950.

22A. *Westgate,* a loop line off the Sawtelle route from Sawtelle to Santa Monica via Westgate, through service being operated only during rush hours. Completed 1906, abandoned on June 30, 1940.

23. *Santa Monica Air Line,* operated from the Main Street station via the Watts line to Amoco, and thence via private right-of-way directly to Santa Monica. This was always primarily a freight line, built in 1875 as the Los Angeles and Independence by Nevada mining millionaire John P. Jones, who developed Santa Monica. Purchased by the SP, it was leased to the Los Angeles Pacific and electrified eastward to Sentous in 1908 and into Los Angeles in 1911. For many years only one passenger trip a day was provided; this was discontinued in 1953 and the line dieselized.

231. *Soldiers Home,* a branch off 23, electrified in 1908, abandoned 1920.

232. *Port Los Angeles,* an extension of the Air Line, electrified 1911, abandoned 1924.

233. *Inglewood,* a line extending eastward from Santa Monica, utilizing a Santa Fe branch, purchased in 1902 and electrified that year. For many years one passenger trip a day (labeled "mixed") was operated; this was discontinued in 1928, but the line is still used for freight service.

24. *Hollywood–Santa Monica–Venice.* The first route to the west extended (after 1926) via the subway, Sunset and Hollywood boulevards via downtown Hollywood to Beverly Hills and thence on the same track as the West 16th line to Santa Monica and Venice. The line was completed in 1896 via Colegrove, and the main line rerouted via Hollywood Boulevard in 1900. This was little more than a streetcar service, with 390 runs a day to Hollywood, only about 20 going on to Venice. Service west of Beverly Hills ended in 1941, and to Hollywood in 1954. It was this line which

crossed the famous intersection of Hollywood and Vine.

24A. *West Hollywood (Colegrove),* a secondary line after the Hollywood Boulevard line was opened, abandoned June 1953.

25. *San Fernando Valley,* one of the last routes built. It left the West Hollywood line at Highland Avenue, and extended northward via Cahuenga Pass into the San Fernando Valley. The line forked at Van Nuys (reached in 1911), one line (25A) going north to San Fernando (completed 1913), the other (25B) west to Canoga Park (1912). Passenger service beyond Van Nuys was discontinued in 1938 and the remainder followed in 1952.

26. *Glendale–Burbank,* completed northward from Los Angeles to Glendale in 1904 and Burbank in 1911. This was a high-density line with frequent service, operated after 1940 with PCC cars—the only modern equipment the PE ever acquired. Service was abandoned by Metropolitan Coach Lines in 1955.

GLENDALE AND MONTROSE RAILWAY COMPANY

Glendale was also served by the independent Glendale and Montrose, built to Eagle Rock in 1909 and La Crescenta in 1913, abandoned in 1930. Four miles of Union Pacific track were used to reach Los Angeles.

THE SAN DIEGO LINES

A 13-mile interurban line extended southward from San Diego to Chula Vista and Otay. This was built as a steam road, in 1887, and electrified to Chula Vista in 1907 (service began on December 1) and to Otay in 1909. The line was originally the *National City and Otay,* becoming the *San Diego Southern* in 1908 and a part of the *San Diego Southeastern* in 1912. The road had passed into the Spreckels hands prior to electrification and was thus an affiliate of the San Diego city system. The road was operated with typical wooden Niles interurban cars. In 1916, following a serious flood, the interurban operations were discontinued. Service on the northern portion of the line was taken over by the San Diego city system, using city cars. The interurban equipment went to the PE.

Northward from San Diego to La Jolla extended the 18-mile *Los Angeles and San Diego,* which planned electrification but never succeeded, and in 1919 was abandoned. In 1923 a portion of the right-of-way was taken over by the *San Diego Electric Railway,* and an electric line was built to La Jolla, opened on July 1, 1924. This was operated with city-type equipment, employing pantographs. Abandonment occurred in 1940.

*

California had several lines which classified themselves as interurbans, although they never used electric power. These included:

Stockton Terminal and Eastern Railroad, completed from Stockton eastward to Bellota, in 1910. Lacking funds for electrification, the road purchased from the SP the old Mariposa, a steam locomotive built in 1864, which continued in regular service until after 1950, the longest active life of any steam locomotive in the United States.

Modesto and Empire Traction Company, completed in 1911 from Modesto to a connection with the Santa Fe at Empire, but never electrified.

Fresno Interurban Railway, completed in 1916, 19 miles from Fresno to Belmont Road, the city portion being electrically operated until 1921. The line was ultimately sold to the Santa Fe.

The Ocean Shore Railroad, projected down the coast from San Francisco to Santa Cruz, but the gap between Tunitas and Swanston was never closed. The road was abandoned in 1920, never having been electrified except in San Francisco.

Canada

ALTHOUGH the interurban developed simultaneously in Canada and the United States, Canada had no integrated system of lines. Canada's 25 companies, with a peak mileage of 850, were almost entirely isolated from one another. Over half the total mileage was in the province of Ontario. The term "interurban" was rarely used in Canada, the roads being referred to as electric railways or (particularly in Ontario) as radials. Canada's first intercity electric line, from Thorold to St. Catharines, began operations in 1887, two years before the Newark–Granville line, but several major lines were built well after the peak of U.S. construction.

The Canadian lines had several distinctive features: extensive government ownership, early emphasis on carload freight, and compared to Midwestern roads, long lives.

Directly or indirectly, a substantial portion of the total Canadian mileage passed into the hands of governmental units, an extremely rare occurrence in the United States. In part this was an accidental result of the fact that the predecessors of the Canadian National owned several interurbans, which passed to the government with their steam-road parents; but in part it resulted from deliberate action on the part of various municipalities. The extent of governmental control would have been far greater had the plans of Sir Adam Beck, founder of the Ontario Hydroelectric Power system, for a network of radials throughout southern Ontario been carried out.[76] But these plans foundered on the failure to get adequate cooperation of the municipalities involved, and on the rise of the motor vehicle.

Most of the Canadian lines pushed carload freight traffic almost from the first, partly because of the lines' extensive affiliation with the steam roads; the bitter antagonism between the steam railroads and the interurbans characteristic of the United States never developed in Canada. British Columbia Electric was a pioneer in long-distance carload freight traffic, and the Grand River lines, the London and Port Stanley, the Niagara St. Catharines and Toronto, and other lines as well became important freight haulers.

On the whole the Canadian lines lasted longer than their United States counterparts, for a variety of reasons, including their heavy freight business and government ownership. To be sure, one of the first abandonments in the industry's history occurred in Canada, that of the Beamsville–Vineland line of the Hamilton Grimsby and Beamsville in 1905 (after the company gave up hope of extension to St. Catharines), and two other lines, the Grand Valley and the London and Lake Erie, were discontinued prior to 1920, largely because new competing lines drove them out of business. But most of the roads lasted until after World War II; more than half the original mileage still provided passenger service in 1946, and in 1954 there were more passenger-carrying interurbans in Canada than in the United States. The Thorold–Port Colborne service operated until 1959—the last truly interurban passenger operation in either country. Because of the importance of freight revenues, a higher percentage of the total mileage (about 25 per cent) was retained when passenger service was finally discontinued.

In other respects the lines were much like their American counterparts. Some of the roads, such as the Lake Erie and Northern, were locally promoted, whereas others were developed by American and Canadian syndicates. One large system, British Columbia Electric, was strictly a British undertaking. Some lines, such as those in the Winnipeg and Toronto areas, were power and transit company affiliates; others, such as the Grand River, passed into railroad hands in early years. A number of the lines were acquired by Sir William Mackenzie, promoter of the Canadian Northern Railroad. Track and equipment were comparable to those of U.S. lines, ranging from the pioneer side-of-the-road Hamilton Grimsby and Beamsville to such electrified steam roads as the London and Port Stanley. Some cars were imported from the U.S., but most were built in Canada, primarily by Preston Car and Coach Co. (ultimately a Brill subsidiary) and by the Ottawa Car Co. Only one line used AC for any length of time, the Windsor Essex and Lake Shore, but several of the later lines used 1,500-volt DC. Lightweight cars were almost unknown, except for the four cars built in 1930 for Windsor Essex and Lake Shore.

Government control was comparable to that in the United States, although with somewhat greater jurisdiction on the part of the Dominion government. The provinces were rather slow to regulate bus service, but after 1925 Ontario established a highly restrictive policy, prohibiting bus competition so long as rail service was adequate. Governments supplied considerably more financial aid to the building of the lines than in the United States.

ONTARIO

The Ontario roads were located, with one exception, in the area between Toronto and Windsor, as would be expected in view of population density.

The Hamilton Lines

Four roads radiated outward from Hamilton, all eventually becoming subsidiaries of the Dominion Power and Transmission Company, a Hamilton enterprise. The lines reached the downtown area by street running, to a terminal on King St. East. In April of 1930 all property of Dominion Power was purchased by the Ontario Hydroelectric Power Commission and the remaining rail lines were abandoned.

HAMILTON GRIMSBY AND BEAMSVILLE ELECTRIC RAILWAY

One of the first interurbans built in America, this road was completed from Hamilton to Grimsby in 1896, built alongside the highway. Frequent but relatively slow passenger service was provided, and substantial fruit business was handled. In 1904 an extension was started to St. Catharines, the segment to Vineland placed in service late in the year. But the project fell through, and the Vineland extension was operated only one year before abandonment. In 1905 the company was acquired by Dominion Power; it passed into the hands of Ontario Hydro in 1930 and was abandoned on June 30, 1931.

HAMILTON AND DUNDAS STREET RAILWAY

In 1897 a 7-mile steam road from Hamilton to Dundas, built in 1876, was electrified, and frequent passenger service operated, with carload freight service provided by the Toronto Hamilton & Buffalo under trackage rights. Service was abandoned on September 5, 1923, but much of the track was acquired by the TH&B for continued freight service.

HAMILTON RADIAL ELECTRIC RAILWAY

Primarily a suburban carrier, this road was completed to Burlington via Burlington Beach in 1897, and a 14-mile extension to Oakville was opened on May 3, 1906. The extension, designed as a part of a through route to Toronto, never carried much traffic. Freight was negligible, and much of the passenger business was the very short haul seasonal traffic to the beach. The company ceased operations for two months in 1918 and 1919 when Burlington refused to approve a fare increase, but finally resumed. The Burlington–Oakville section was abandoned on August 3, 1925, and the remainder on January 6, 1929.

BRANTFORD AND HAMILTON ELECTRIC RAILWAY

The last of the roads in the Hamilton area to be built, and the only high-standard line, was completed between the two cities of the corporate name on June 1, 1908. The project was begun by the Von Echa syndicate, but completed under Dominion Power control. Hourly service was usual; like the Radial, freight traffic was negligible. The road passed to Hydro in 1930 and was abandoned on June 30, 1931.

The Windsor-Chatham Area Roads

SANDWICH WINDSOR AND AMHERSTBURG RAILWAY

This railway company opened the first commercial electric streetcar in Canada, in Windsor, on June 6, 1886. The 14-mile interurban line from Windsor to Amherstburg was completed June 10, 1903, and a 6-mile line northeastward to Tecumseh was built in 1907. In 1901 the SW&A was acquired by Detroit United Railways, under Everett-Moore control. In 1920 the property (including the Windsor car lines) was purchased by the municipalities served and operated by Ontario Hydro under contract as the Essex Division, Hydro Electric Railways; in 1934, the municipalities assumed direct operation. The Amherstburg line was replaced by buses on March 21, 1938, and the Tecumseh line on May 15.

It was reported that in the early twenties the road did a thriving business in handling carload shipments of beer from Walkerville to special sidings laid along the edge of the Detroit River, whence it was smuggled in small boats into the United States.

WINDSOR ESSEX AND LAKE SHORE RAPID RAILWAY

Although chartered in 1901, the road's construction was impeded by financial difficulties, and not until 1907 was service opened to Kingsville (27 miles); on April 10, 1908, an additional 9 miles (to Leamington) were put in service. This was the only Canadian line to employ AC over any length of time, the heavy cars using pantographs. When the owners threatened to abandon the line, the municipalities purchased it, as of September 8, 1929, and under Hydro management the line was rebuilt, converted to DC power, and four lightweight cars were acquired. But the depression brought such severe deficits that service was suspended on September 15, 1932, leaving the municipalities saddled with the debt incurred to purchase and modernize the road. Some were still paying this off in 1959.

CHATHAM WALLACEBURG AND LAKE ERIE RAILWAY

One of the weakest of the Ontario lines was the CW&LE, which extended northward from Chatham to Wallaceburg (18 miles, completed on November 20, 1905), and southward to Erie Beach (15 miles, completed in 1908). A 6-mile branch to

NC: Nipissing Central Ry.
SW&A: Sandwich Windsor & Amherstburg Ry.
WE&LS: Windsor Essex & Lake Shore Rapid Ry.
CW&LE: Chatham Wallaceburg & Lake Erie Ry.
L&LE: London & Lake Erie Ry. and Trans. Co.
L&PS: London & Port Stanley Ry.
WTV&I: Woodstock Thames Valley & Ingersoll Elec. Ry.
GR: Grand River Ry.
GV: Grand Valley Ry.
LE&N: Lake Erie & Northern Ry.
B&H: Brantford & Hamilton Elec. Ry.
H&D: Hamilton & Dundas Street Ry.
HR: Hamilton Radial Elec. Ry.
HG&B: Hamilton Grimsby & Beamsville Elec. Ry.
NStC&T: Niagara St. Catharines & Toronto Ry.
NFP&R: Niagara Falls Park & River Ry.
TS: Toronto Suburban Ry.
T&YR: Toronto & York Radial Ry.
T&E: Toronto & Eastern Ry. (never operated)

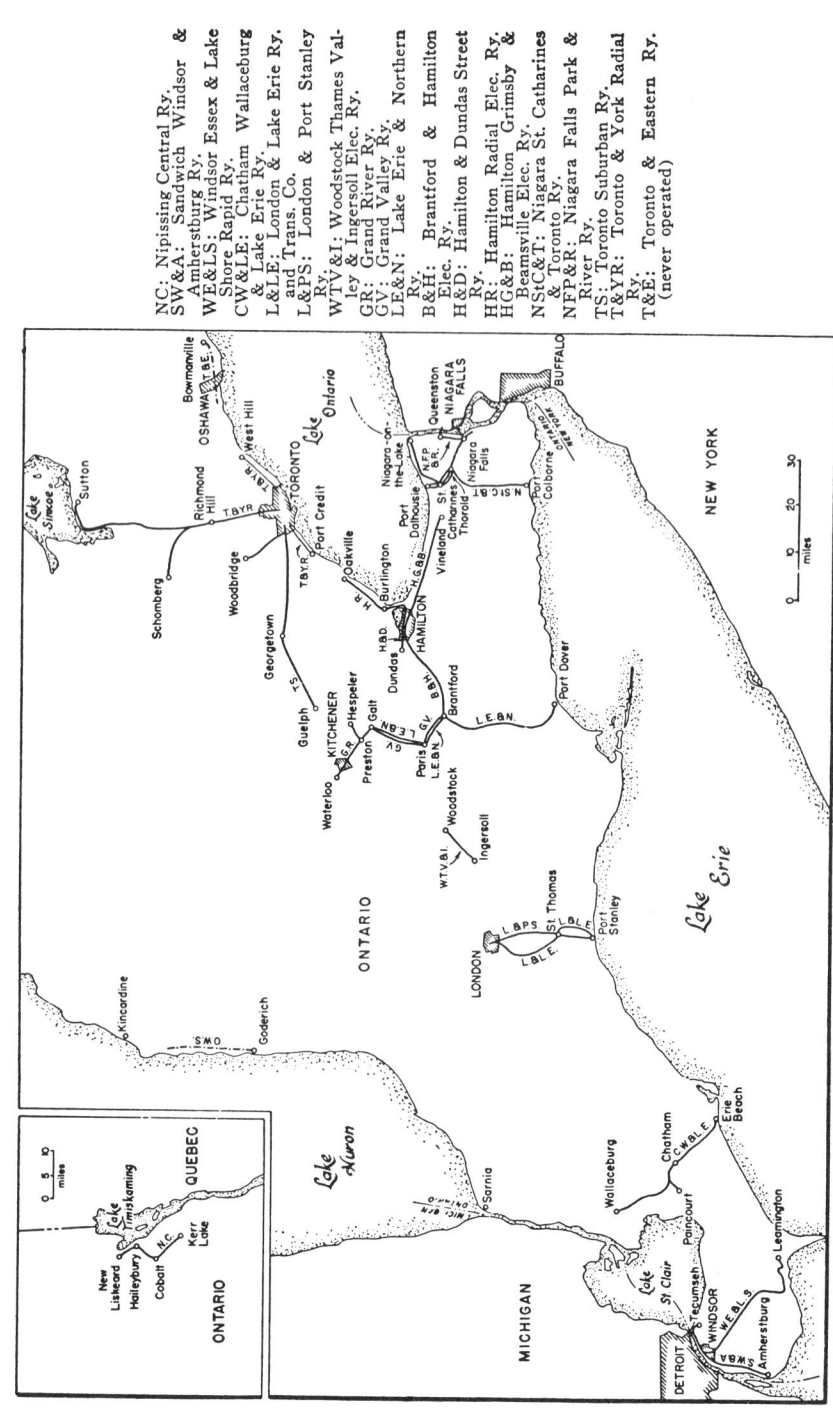

Paincourt from the northern line was placed in service in August 1910. In 1913 the company was acquired by the Mackenzie interests. The road had only limited traffic possibilities, and was hard hit by the coming of the automobile; only the handling of some carload freight business kept it going as long as it did. Passenger service was discontinued on July 2, 1927, and a long wrangle developed with the city of Chatham over the use of the streets for freight service. When the company refused to build a freight belt line, the city canceled its franchise, and operations ceased in March 1930.

The London Lines

SOUTH-WESTERN TRACTION COMPANY
(LONDON AND LAKE ERIE RAILWAY AND TRANSPORTATION COMPANY)

Operating only 12 years, this line was built southward from London to the lake by British capital, reaching Lambeth in 1906 (track having been laid in 1903 but not operated), St. Thomas later in the year, and Port Stanley in 1907. Part of the line was operated on the edge of the highway, and cars passed through St. Thomas on city-line trackage. In 1909 the road was acquired by G. B. Woods of Toronto and reorganized as the London and Lake Erie Railway and Transportation Company. For a few years the road prospered, aided by heavy week-end travel to the beaches, but the electrification of the parallel London and Port Stanley quickly drove the company into bankruptcy, and service was discontinued on October 15, 1918.

LONDON AND PORT STANLEY RAILWAY

The L&PS, a pioneer road in Canada, was completed from London south to Port Stanley (24 miles) on October 2, 1856, as a steam road. The road was promoted by London businessmen seeking lower freight rates, but most of the stock was eventually purchased by the city of London. The road was operated under lease for many years, first by the Grand Trunk and then by the Pere Marquette. The Pere Marquette's lease was not renewed when it expired in 1914, and under Sir Adam Beck's direction the road was rebuilt and electrified to the highest standards, with electric operation established July 22, 1915, under municipal management. The heavy volume of freight, particularly coal from the lake to London, made the road relatively profitable, but passenger traffic gradually declined. In 1953 voters rejected a plan to end the service, but finally in 1957 (February 1), passenger service came to an end after the city refused to advance necessary funds to enable the road's substation to use 60-cycle power in conformity with the change made by Ontario Hydro in the area. Freight service was dieselized.

The Grand Valley Lines

A considerable interurban network developed in the highly industrialized Grand Valley, midway between London and Toronto.

GRAND RIVER RAILWAY

Another one of the earliest pioneer interurbans, the Galt and Preston was completed between the two towns of its corporate title on July 26, 1894. In 1896 the line was extended to Hespeler and the road became the Galt Preston and Hespeler. The line from Preston to Berlin (now Kitchener) was opened October 6, 1903, as the Preston and Berlin. The companies had become Canadian Pacific subsidiaries at an early date, providing both freight and passenger connections for the parent to the Grand Valley towns from Galt. In 1918 the roads were merged as the Grand River Railway. All rail passenger service ended on April 24, 1955, but electric freight operation was continued. The original 600-volt electrification was raised to 1,500 volts in 1921 to conform with that of the Lake Erie and Northern.

LAKE ERIE AND NORTHERN RAILWAY

In 1911 Brantford interests incorporated the Lake Erie and Northern to build a steam road south to the lake. Before completion it was acquired by the CPR, which agreed to electrify it at the request of the city of Brantford; the city was anxious not only to obtain high-quality electric passenger service, but also to get rid of the derelict Grand Valley Railway (*q.v.*). The LE&N was built in 1914 and 1915, with passenger service established in 1916 (Brantford to Galt, February 7; Brantford to Simcoe, May 30, and on to Port Dover, July 22). A 1,500-volt system was employed. Freight traffic was dominant from the first, and passenger service provided at 2-hour intervals or less. Passenger traffic declined sharply after World War II, and cars made their last runs on April 24, 1955. The LE&N and the Grand River connected in Galt, and shared equipment extensively.

GRAND VALLEY RAILWAY

Not to be confused with the Grand River or the Grand River Valley was the Grand Valley, promoted by the Von Echa Co., of Harrisburg, Pennsylvania, which planned a great network of interurbans between Toronto and Detroit. The company acquired the Brantford street railway, and built 8 miles to Paris, opening service on May 22, 1904. The line was extended to Galt on October 6, 1905. After several changes in ownership, the road passed into the hands of G. B. Woods of Toronto. But traffic was limited, and the track gradually deteriorated until a snowstorm brought all operations to an end in 1912. Partial service was finally resumed, and in 1914 the city of Brantford bought the system, mainly to keep the streetcars in the city in operation. In 1915 Brantford sold the Paris–Galt portion to the Lake Erie and Northern for a nominal sum; this line was abandoned in 1916 as soon as the LE&N's own line, which paralleled the GV track but did not utilize it, was completed. The city operated the line from Brantford to Paris until 1929.

WOODSTOCK THAMES VALLEY AND INGERSOLL ELECTRIC RAILWAY

The smallest road in southern Ontario was completed from Woodstock to Beachville in 1900, and to Ingersoll (10 miles) in 1901, running alongside the highway. This was a Von Echa project, designed as a part of a through line to Detroit and London from Toronto. When the city of Brantford purchased the Grand Valley, the Woodstock line passed into the hands of the bondholders, who operated it until abandonment in 1925.

The Toronto Area Lines

The interurban network in the Toronto area was more limited than might be expected, and all the lines suffered from the lack of high-speed entrances into the city. Sooner or later all became Mackenzie properties, and were thus affiliated with the city street railway and power systems until the time that ownership passed to the city.

TORONTO AND YORK RADIAL RAILWAY

This system included three distinct lines, of which only the Metropolitan division, which extended 48 miles northward from Toronto to Lake Simcoe points, was a true interurban operation. The lines westward to Port Credit and eastward to West Hill in Scarboro were essentially suburban, and their inner portions eventually became streetcar lines.

The first segment, built up Yonge Street to Eglington as the Metropolitan Street Railway, was completed in 1885 and electrified in 1889. Track reached York Mills in 1890, Richmond Hill in 1896, Newmarket on April 14, 1899, and, under Mackenzie control, Jackson's Point on Lake Simcoe, June 1, 1907. The company became the Toronto and York Radial in 1898. The last extension, into Sutton, was built in 1909. A branch from a point near Aurora to Schomberg was built in 1904 but not electrified until 1916. The line never reached downtown Toronto; cars connected with city lines, originally at the CPR crossing of Yonge Street, then at Farnam Avenue, and finally at Deloraine Avenue. The southern portion followed the highway right-of-way (and included an 8 per cent grade out of Hoggs Hollow), while the northern portion was on private right-of-way. In addition to suburban business, the road carried a heavy summer traffic to Lake Simcoe resorts and cottages.

In 1922 the Toronto and York Radial passed into the hands of the city, together with other Mackenzie properties. The city portions were incorporated into the Toronto Transportation system, and the lines outside the city turned over to Ontario Hydro for operation. However, because of financial difficulties the city took over direct management in 1927, and the interurban gauge was changed from standard to the 4' 10⅞" of the city system for integrated operation, putting an end to carload interchange traffic. But losses became serious; the Schomberg line was abandoned on June 20, 1927, and the main line on March 16, 1930. Following an agreement with the municipalities, the 10-mile segment as far as Richmond Hill was placed back in service, and operated until October 18, 1948.

The two suburban lines of Toronto and York Radial were also built at an early date. The Toronto and Mimico built from the Humber to Long Branch in the late 1890's, and after absorption by Toronto and York Radial in 1904 extended the line to Port Credit in 1905. When Ontario Hydro took over operations in 1922, it changed the line to standard gauge, but when the city began direct management in 1927, it changed the gauge back to that of the city routes and turned operations over to TTC. The Long Branch–Port Credit line was abandoned on February 9, 1935, but the remainder was still being operated in 1960 as a streetcar route. The Scarboro line in the east was built in the late nineties along Kingston Road to Scarboro, and extended to West Hill in 1905. After the city took over direct operation in 1927, the outer portion was abandoned (June 25, 1936) and the remainder incorporated into the Kingston Road car line, still operated as far as Victoria Park in 1960. This route used the city system's broad gauge after 1904.

TORONTO SUBURBAN RAILWAY

For many years this road was merely a suburban car line, built by A. H. Royce in the mid-1890's from Keele and Dundas streets to Lambton Mills and to Weston. In 1911 the road was acquired by Mackenzie, and expansion undertaken. The route to Woodbridge was placed in service on October 10, 1914, and very slowly the main line was pushed westward, finally placed in service to Guelph (49 miles) on April 14, 1917. Cars terminated in Toronto at Keele and Dundas. The road was a Canadian Northern subsidiary, and passed with the latter into Dominion hands in 1917. The Canadian National shifted policy several times; the road was intended to become a link in Sir Adam Beck's Radial network; when this plan fell through, the CNR improved the road, rerouting the inner portion, and operating it as Canadian National Electric Railways, Toronto Suburban District. The Weston–Woodbridge line was abandoned on May 10, 1926 and the Weston portion taken over by the municipalities. Because of heavy losses, all service on the main line was abandoned on August 1, 1931.

Niagara Area Roads

The Niagara peninsula, with its dense population, extensive industry, and tourist trade, was a natural setting for interurbans.

NIAGARA ST. CATHARINES AND TORONTO RAILWAY

In the year 1888 a steam road, the St. Catharines and Niagara Falls, completed its line between the two cities of its title. Following bankruptcy in 1899, the road was taken over by the Haines syndicate of New York, reorganized as the Niagara St. Catharines and Toronto, and electrified, service beginning on July 19, 1900. In 1901 the company acquired the Port Dalhousie, St. Catharines and Thorold, which had built the first intercity electric line in Canada, placed in service between St. Catharines and Thorold in 1887. In May 1901 the line to Port Dalhousie was completed.

In 1905 the Nicholls-E. R. Woods group, affiliates of Mackenzie, acquired the road. Nicholls was a pioneer developer of electric equipment and President of Canadian General Electric. A new line was built southward from Thorold to Welland in 1907 and to Port Colborne in 1911, and a line to Niagara-on-the-Lake was completed in 1913. A high-speed route to Toronto was projected but never built. The system became a Canadian Northern subsidiary, and thus passed into the hands of the Dominion in 1917. Substantial modernization was carried out in 1923, and the Merriton–Port Dalhousie line of the CNR electrified.

In 1931, the Niagara-on-the-Lake line was discontinued, and the old local line from Thorold to St. Catharines was abandoned after a dispute with Merritton over franchise rights. Passenger service on the main St. Catharines–Niagara Falls line was suspended in 1940, reestablished in 1942, and finally abandoned, September 14, 1947. In 1950 passenger service was discontinued to Port Dalhousie. The Thorold–Port Colborne line continued in service, however, using chiefly the lightweight cars built for Windsor Essex and Lakeshore in 1930. In the summer of 1958, the company applied for permission to abandon this service, and the application was approved by the Board of Transport Commissioners in January, 1959. Service ended March 28, 1959. Carload freight service continues.

NIAGARA FALLS PARK AND RIVER RAILWAY

Strictly a tourist attraction, a 12-mile line was completed on May 24, 1893, between Queenston and Chippewa via Niagara Falls, closely parallel to the river. In 1899 the road began to operate across the upper bridge at Niagara and built a new bridge at Queenston. In 1901 International Railway purchased the line and operated it as a part of Buffalo's city and interurban system; arrangements were made with the independent Niagara Gorge Railroad (q.v.) for loop operation. For many years, cars went north down the river on the tracks of the Gorge line (which descended to the river at Whirlpool Rapids), crossed at Queenston, came down the Canadian side, and back across the river at Niagara.

On Wednesday, July 7, 1915, a greatly overloaded car with 154 persons aboard got out of control on wet rails as it came down off Queenston Heights, and shot over an embankment, killing 15 persons.

The company's 40-year contract with the

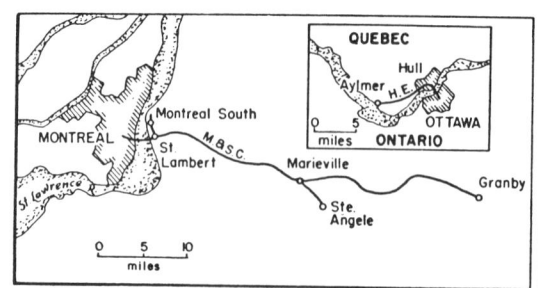

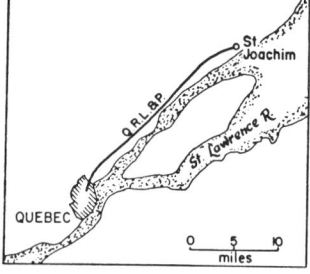

M&SC: Montreal & Southern Counties Ry.
HE: Hull Elec. Co.
QRL&P: Quebec Ry. Light & Power Co.

Parks Commission expired in 1932, and since the company did not seek renewal, operations ceased on September 11, 1932. The Commission was obligated by contract to pay the company for the assets of the line; however, an amazing decision of the Privy Council compelled the Commission to pay the reproduction cost—over $1 million—rather than the current salvage value.

NIPISSING CENTRAL RAILWAY

Far in northern Ontario, the little NC was built between the mining towns of Cobalt and Haileybury in 1910 (April 30), and extended to New Liskeard in 1912 (November 1). The line was purchased by the Temiskaming & Northern Ontario, and thus by the provincial government, in 1912. In 1914 the parent road's Cobalt-Kerr Lake branch was electrified, and operated by the interurban. When the T&NO built its nonelectrified line to Noranda in 1924, it did so under the name of the Nipissing Central, which had a Dominion charter.

The Kerr Lake service was discontinued in 1924, and all interurban operations ceased in 1935.

QUEBEC

QUEBEC RAILWAY LIGHT AND POWER COMPANY

The electric line along the St. Lawrence from downtown Quebec City via Ste. Anne de Beaupré to St. Joachim was built as a steam road (which was eventually extended to Murray Bay) and electrified in 1900 (to Montmorency) and 1901 (to St. Joachim). The road was operated for many years as the Montmorency Division of the Quebec Railway Light and Power Company, which also provided transit and power service in the city. Traffic was heavy, composed partly of suburban passengers, partly of pilgrims to the famous Catholic shrine at Ste. Anne. The steam-operated line from St. Joachim to Murray Bay passed into the hands of the Grand Trunk in 1919 and thus became a part of the CNR, through trains being operated over the electric line under trackage rights. In 1951 the CNR purchased the interurban outright when Quebec Railway abandoned the city streetcar lines, and continued to operate it, using heavy steel equipment purchased in the late twenties, with relatively frequent schedules. Application to abandon passenger operations was made late in 1958, and all electric passenger service ended on March 14, 1959.

MONTREAL AND SOUTHERN COUNTIES RAILWAY

The Grand Trunk's only venture into the interurban field was its acquisition of the Montreal and Southern Counties. The project was incorporated in 1897 to build to Sherbrooke, but no work was done for a decade; finally, 4 miles of line were built and service established to St. Lambert (November 1, 1909) over the Victoria Bridge. The Grand Trunk acquired the company in 1911 and extended the road to Richelieu and Marieville (1913), and to St. Césaire (May 2, 1914), by electrifying a Central Vermont line. A new line was then built to Abbottsford (1915) and Granby, and through service was opened in 1916 (April 30). On January 11, 1926, service was established from Marieville to St. Angèle on Central Vermont tracks. Trains operated from a station on Youville street in downtown Montreal.

The majority of the travel was suburban traffic to the St. Lambert-Montreal South area, which was provided with very frequent service.

The road passed into the hands of the CNR with the Grand Trunk, but few changes were ever made in its operation.

Losses began in the early thirties and continued year after year; no improvements were made, and track and equipment deteriorated badly. Finally, in 1951, the section from Marieville to Granby was abandoned and replaced by CNR diesel service from Central Station. In 1956 changes to the Victoria Bridge in conjunction with the St. Lawrence Seaway project necessitated alterations in the line, and the CNR decided instead to abandon it and free the space on the bridge for highway use. The M&SC operated many years—perhaps as much as two decades—beyond the date a private company would have been forced to liquidate.

HULL ELECTRIC COMPANY

This company, which operated the street railway lines in Hull, Quebec, acquired and electrified the Canadian Pacific's Hull-Aylmer line in 1897. Cars operated from a terminal under Confederation Square in Ottawa, turning on a loop under the Chateau Laurier, and crossed the Interprovincial Bridge on track laid alongside the CPR line. The line was a subsidiary of the CPR until 1926. Service into Ottawa ended in 1946 when fire at the Eddy Pulp plant damaged the bridge, and early in 1947 operations between Hull and Aylmer were abandoned.

THE MARITIME PROVINCES

The entire Maritime area had only two interurbans, both in Nova Scotia.

CAPE BRETON ELECTRIC COMPANY
(CAPE BRETON TRAMWAYS)

In 1902 the Sydney and Glace Bay was completed from Sydney to Glace Bay, with a loop back to Reserve Junction, giving the line the appearance of the figure 6. All cars operated counterclockwise around the loop, serving a mining and steel-producing area. The line was promoted by Cape Breton Electric Company, a Stone and Webster property, but ownership was shared with Dominion Coal Company, whose land was needed for right-of-way. CBE itself also operated a 6-mile interurban from its ferry connection at North Sydney to Sydney Mines, completed in 1903. In 1911 all the properties were merged as Cape Breton Electric Company.

In 1931 Stone and Webster permitted the company to go into bankruptcy; the power company was reorganized under local ownership, and permission was sought to abandon the interurban. The employees joined together to form Cape Breton Tramways, Ltd., and took over the line with a total investment of $5,000, intending to run it a year or so until the men could find other jobs. The enterprise did better than expected, wage cuts were rescinded, and relatively new cars obtained from the Greenfield and Montague, in Massachusetts. The line continued to operate for 16 years, one segment of the loop being abandoned in 1946 when fire destroyed a substation, and the remainder in 1947.

PICTOU COUNTY ELECTRIC COMPANY

A 10-mile line through an industrial section on the northern mainland of Nova Scotia, from Westville to Trenton, was opened on April 1, 1905, as the Egerton Tramways. The company was reorganized as Pictou County Electric Company in 1909, and in 1924 the railway was sold to the Pictou County Power Board. Operations were abandoned in 1929.

WESTERN CANADA

Only two interurbans operated in all of western Canada, but one of these, British Columbia Electric, was the largest single system in the Dominion.

WINNIPEG SELKIRK AND
LAKE WINNIPEG RAILWAY

This road, a subsidiary of Winnipeg Electric Company, and thus a Mackenzie property, was opened for service as a steam road from Winnipeg to Selkirk in 1904, and electrified in June 1908. In 1913 a freight spur from Middlechurch to Stony

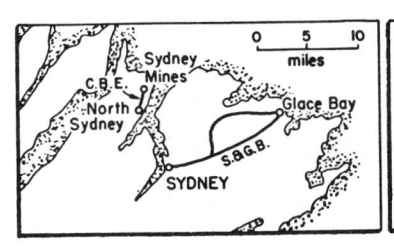

CBE: Cape Breton Elec. Co.
S&GB: Sydney & Glace Bay Ry.
PC: Pictou County Elec. Co.

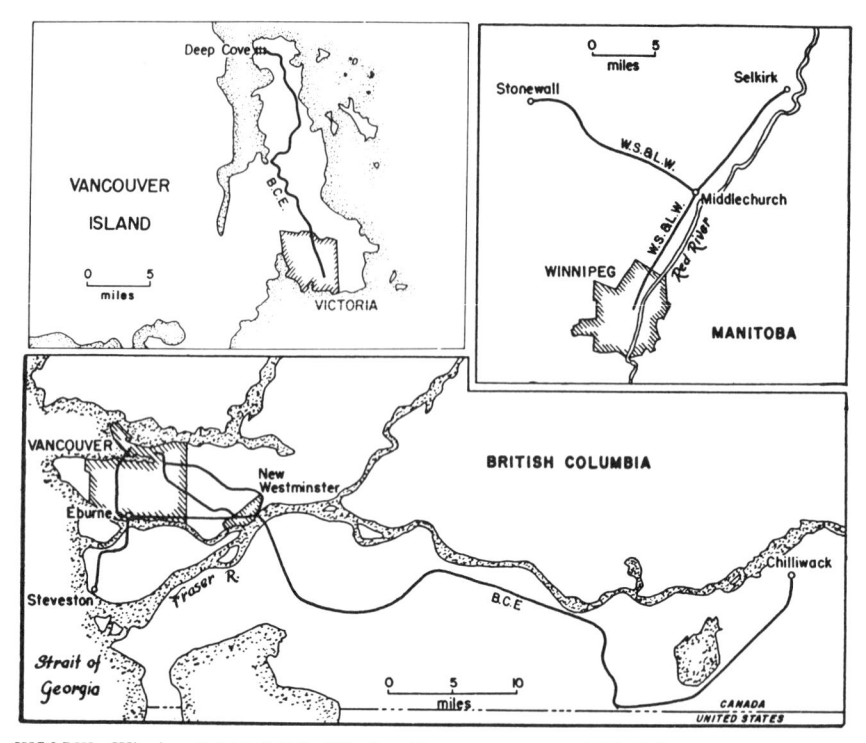

WS&LW: Winnipeg Selkirk & Lake Winnipeg Ry. BCE: British Columbia Elec. Ry.

Mountain was electrified, and in 1914, this line was extended to Stonewall. The system became a Nesbitt-Thompson property after Mackenzie's death, and for a time was controlled by Insull.

Service on the Stonewall line was discontinued in 1934 but resumed because of protests, and finally abandoned on May 1, 1939. The Selkirk line was replaced by buses on September 1, 1937.

BRITISH COLUMBIA ELECTRIC RAILWAY

This 125-mile system centering on Vancouver was the Dominion's largest system, providing extensive suburban service, plus a long-distance line with concentration on freight traffic. BCE was (and is) an integrated power and transit system, the electric rail lines having been built and maintained to high standards.

The first segment was built in 1891 as the New Westminster and Vancouver Tramways, Ltd., directly to New Westminster via Central Park, and absorbed by British Columbia Electric when the latter was formed in 1897. In 1905 the company leased the Vancouver and Lulu Island from the CPR and electrified it from Vancouver to Steveston for passenger service. In 1909 a link was completed from Eburne (Marpole) on the Steveston line to New Westminster, and on June 12, 1911, a third line was opened to New Westminster, via Burnaby. The company had built a 65-mile line from New Westminster up the Frazer Valley to Chilliwack, opened on October 3, 1910. This line was largely designed to handle logs and lumber but provided passenger service, usually three trains a day, compared to 20- and 30-minute service on the suburban lines. The last line, disconnected from the remainder, was built from Victoria to Deep Cove (22 miles), completed on June 19, 1913. The lines were almost entirely on private right-of-way, even in downtown Vancouver. Improvements in 1911 and 1912 provided extensive double track, and eliminated a 12 per cent grade on the original line into New Westminster. Extensive carload freight business was handled.

British Columbia Electric was for many years a British company, its policies directed from London. The guiding light was Sir R. M. Horne-Payne, Mackenzie's principal English associate, but direct management in the earlier years was in the hands of a Dane, Johannes E. C. Buntzen. In 1927 control passed from England to the Power Company of Canada (Nesbitt-Thompson-Gundy) interests.

The Saanich line was abandoned in 1924, but otherwise the system remained largely intact until after World War II. In the late forties, however, the management decided to abandon all rail passenger operations. The Frazer Valley line discontinued passenger service on September 30, 1950, and the line was dieselized. The New Westminster–Burnaby Lake line was cut back to Sapperton in 1937, and the remaining service abandoned in 1953. On the Steveston line, service was abandoned between downtown Vancouver and Marpole in 1952, the Marpole–New Westminster service November 17, 1956, and the old main line to New Westminster in 1953 (beyond Park Station) and 1954, after 63 years of service, the second longest term in either country. Marpole–Steveston service, the last to operate and retained so long only because of inadequacy of through streets, was abandoned in February 1958. Most of the lines, except the Burnaby route, have been retained for freight operations.

*

Several other lines operated intercity service, but largely on streetcar standards. The *Sudbury and Copper Cliffs Suburban Electric Railway* opened its 6-mile line between the two towns of its name November 11, 1915, and operated until after World War II. The *Mt. McKay and Kakabeka Falls* was projected from Fort William to the Falls, but only a 5-mile segment, largely used for hauling gravel, was ever built. *Levis County Tramways* in Quebec operated from Levis to nearby towns. The *Berlin and Bridgeport* operated 4 miles of line from Kitchener to Bridgeport and was projected to Guelph; it was operated as a part of the Kitchener city system after 1923 and abandoned in 1939. *Winnipeg Suburban,* a subsidiary of Winnipeg Electric, operated a 10-mile line from Winnipeg to Headingly.

Two lines, both in Ontario, never actually operated, although substantial track was laid. One was the *Ontario West Shore,* projected from Goderich to Kincardine, with 16 miles of track laid from Goderich to Kintail between 1908 and 1911. The company ran out of money, in part because one of the promoters absconded with funds (see Chapter 1), and was unable to complete and operate the road.

The *Toronto and Eastern* was a Canadian Northern project, designed to provide a high-speed interurban from Toronto to Bowmanville via Oshawa. Thirteen miles of track had been laid between Bowmanville and Whitby before the development of plans for a Radial line under Ontario Hydro sponsorship in the area led to the suspension of building. Then the war intervened, the CN fell into Dominion hands, and plans were made to use the road as part of the projected Radial network. When this project collapsed, the CNR started to complete the road in 1923, and did substantial additional work. This ceased in 1924, and in 1925 the government announced the abandonment of the entire project because of the increase in motor-vehicle use.

Principal Interurban Car Builders

Many firms built one or more interurban cars, but there were about 15 that can be considered specialists. A list of these follows, although it should be emphasized that no attempt has been made to make the compilation exhaustive.*

AMERICAN CAR COMPANY (1891–1931), St. Louis, Missouri

American built interurban cars for the Inter-Urban Railway, the Central California Traction Company, the Petaluma and Santa Rosa, and other roads. The company was particularly identified with double-truck Birney cars, which it produced extensively in the 1920's. Brill controlled the company after 1902.

BARNEY AND SMITH CAR COMPANY, 1849–1923, Dayton, Ohio

This company, which had been a builder of railroad cars since the mid-nineteenth century, produced a large number of interurban cars for the Midwestern lines.

J. G. BRILL COMPANY (1868–1941), Philadelphia, Pennsylvania

Brill had been a major builder of horse cars in the nineteenth century, and became one of the largest producers of electric cars of all types. For the interurbans Brill produced a great many suburban cars, especially for roads in Pennsylvania. Brill built the articulated units of the Washington Baltimore and Annapolis, the lightweight cars of the Fonda Johnstown and Gloversville, and in 1941, ten lightweight cars for the Philadelphia Suburban Transportation Company—Brill's last rail equipment. After the company merged with American Car and Foundry, Brill produced buses until 1954.

CINCINNATI CAR COMPANY (1903–31), Cincinnati, Ohio

This company was a subsidiary of W. Kesley Schoepf's Ohio Traction Company, and thus was an affiliate of the Cincinnati Street Railway and the Schoepf-McGowan interurban lines. Accordingly, it sold equipment in large volume to all these properties, and to other firms as well. In the 1920's the company had great success with its curved-side lightweight cars, but orders fell off rapidly around 1930 with the drastic decline in the fortunes of the interurbans. Car building ceased in 1931 and the firm went out of existence in 1938.

DANVILLE CAR COMPANY (1900–1913), Danville, Illinois

This small car builder produced street and interurban equipment for the Illinois Traction and other roads. In 1908 it came under Brill's ownership.

JEWETT CAR COMPANY (1894–1918), Newark, Ohio

This company was established in Jewett, Ohio, in 1894 but moved to Newark about 1900. The company built all kinds of electric cars, but specialized in interurban equipment for Midwestern roads. Its cars had an excellent reputation and were widely used, particularly by Ohio interurbans. The company's heavy dependence on the interurbans caused it to share the industry's own ill-fortune, and in the difficult year of 1918 the firm went bankrupt and was liquidated.

G. C. KUHLMAN CAR COMPANY (1892–1932), Cleveland, Ohio

Kuhlman was noted for producing center-door equipment both for city and for interurban service, but it built wood and steel cars of a wide variety, including a moderately successful lightweight car in the 1920's. Brill controlled the firm after 1904.

LACONIA CAR COMPANY (1881–1928), Laconia, New Hampshire

Laconia supplied equipment to rural trolley lines throughout New England, and shared the early decline of these roads.

MCGUIRE-CUMMINGS MANUFACTURING COMPANY (ca. 1888–1930), Chicago and Paris, Illinois

This company was a major producer of trucks for electric cars, but was also a car builder.

* For a detailed listing of car builders of all types, see E. Harper Charlton, *Railway Car Builders of the United States and Canada*, Interurbans, Special No. 24 (1957).

Niles Car and Manufacturing Company (1901–17)), Niles, Ohio

Like Jewett, Niles was a specialist in building the typical wooden interurban cars of the early years of the industry. Although the company produced rapid-transit equipment and other electric cars, it was unable to survive as a car builder after 1917, and began producing equipment for the trucking industry.

Osgood Bradley Car Company (1833–   ), Worcester, Massachusetts

This firm, which had a long history as a railroad car builder, built many cars for the New England rural trolley lines. As a major plant of the Pullman Standard Car Manufacturing Company, it is still in existence.

Ottawa Car Manufacturing Company (1891–1947), Ottawa, Ontario

This firm was one of the two principal Canadian interurban car builders.

Preston Car and Coach Company (1908–21), Preston, Ontario

The other of the two main Canadian interurban car builders, the Preston Company passed into Brill's control in 1921.

St. Louis Car Company (1887–   ), St. Louis, Missouri

This firm, one of the most important builders of electric cars of all sorts, is still in existence and continues to produce rapid-transit equipment. It produced both city- and interurban-style equipment for many interurban companies, including much of the rolling stock of the Illinois Traction Company. Following World War II, St. Louis was the only remaining American producer of street railway and interurban cars.

John Stephenson Car Company (1831–1917), New York City, New York, and Linden, New Jersey

This company, which had been one of the largest builders of horse cars, built electric streetcars and interurban cars for many companies, including the Aurora Elgin and Chicago, the Atlantic City and Shore, and several Indiana roads.

Wason Manufacturing Company (1845–1931), Springfield, Massachusetts

Another major New England producer, Wason became a Brill subsidiary in 1906.

Among the large number of firms that built one or more interurban cars, the following may be mentioned: Jackson and Sharp Company and Harlan and Hollingsworth, both of Wilmington, Delaware; the Holman Car Company of San Francisco; the Southern Car Company of High Point, North Carolina; J. M. Jones and Company of Watervliet, New York; American Car and Foundry Company; the Pullman Car and Manufacturing Company of Chicago; the St. Charles Car Company of St. Charles, Missouri; and the Pressed Steel Car Company of Pittsburgh. Several interurbans built their own cars, and many carried on very extensive reconstruction of equipment.

The Russell Car and Foundry Company of Ridgeway, Pennsylvania, was a major producer of snow plows, snow sweepers, and other work equipment. A specialist in supplying the interurban industry was the Ohio Brass Company of Mansfield, which produced trolley retrievers, couplers, trolley wheels, handles, and connections of various sorts, all of which were used by the majority of interurban companies.

Three Late Discoveries

Since the appearance of the first printing in 1960, the following small lines have been called to our attention as appropriate for inclusion:

WILLAMETTE FALLS RAILWAY

The Willamette Falls Railway, extending 9 miles along the west side of the Willamette River opposite Oregon City, Oregon, was built in 1893 by the Portland General Electric Company from West Linn to the village of Willamette, and later extended north and south to log hoists on the Tualatin and Willamette Rivers. While logs provided most of the traffic, regular passenger service was operated with two Brill interurban cars built in 1893. Passenger service was discontinued in 1930, and freight service in 1933. After 1912 the line was owned by the Southern Pacific.

ST. TAMMANY AND NEW ORLEANS RAILWAY AND FERRY COMPANY

This line extended 14 miles from Mandeville, Louisiana, on the north shore of Lake Pontchartrain, to Covington, with a steamer connection across the lake. The road was opened in 1909 and operated with gasoline motor cars until electrification in 1915. The line was abandoned in 1918.

LAS VEGAS RAILWAY AND POWER COMPANY

A railroad was built between Las Vegas, New Mexico, and the Montezuma Hotel at Las Vegas Hot Springs, 9 miles up Gallinas Canyon. It was absorbed into the Santa Fe system. In 1903, the Las Vegas and Hot Springs Electric Railway and Power Company developed a small street railway system and leased and electrified the Santa Fe line. Passenger service was provided to the hotel and a few other resorts, and an extensive traffic in ice for Santa Fe refrigerator cars and cold storage plants was handled by an electric locomotive. The operation was highly unprofitable; after two corporate reorganizations the interurban electric operation was discontinued (about 1909), and the Santa Fe resumed operation of the line. The resort declined, and the Santa Fe discontinued passenger service in 1913 and abandoned most of the line in 1937. (See *Street Railway Journal,* XXIX [1907], 130–34.)

Notes

NOTES TO CHAPTER ONE

1. Donald A. Moore, "The Automobile Industry," in Walter Adams (ed.), *The Structure of American Industry* (New York: Macmillan, 1955), p. 279.
2. See John B. Rae, "The Fabulous Billy Durant," *The Business History Review*, XXXII (1958), 255–71.
3. Robert Routledge, *Discoveries and Inventions of the Nineteenth Century*, 12th ed. (London: Routledge, 1898), p. 454.
4. Cf. Frank Rowsome, Jr., *Trolley Car Treasury* (New York: McGraw-Hill, 1956), pp. 17–34.
5. See J. Bucknall Smith, *A Treatise upon Cable or Rope Traction as Applied to the Working of Street and Other Railways* (London, 1892).
6. George W. Hilton, *Cable Railways of Chicago*, Bulletin of the Electric Railway Historical Society, No. 10 (1954), p. 4.
7. The most useful source on the beginnings of the streetcar is an address by Frank J. Sprague, "Growth of Electric Railways," published in the *Proceedings of the American Electric Railway Association*, 1916, pp. 273–317. See also Rowsome, *Trolley Car Treasury*, pp. 65–94, and John A. Miller, *Fares, Please!* (New York: Appleton-Century Co., 1941), pp. 54–69; both books contain extensive popular descriptions of the origin of the electric car.
8. Department of Commerce, Bureau of the Census, *Census of Electrical Industries: 1917; Electric Railways* (Washington: Government Printing Office, 1920), p. 11.
9. Edward S. Mason, *The Street Railway in Massachusetts* (Cambridge: Harvard University Press, 1932), p. 11.
10. *Giant's Causeway Electric Tramway, County Antrim, Ireland; Short Description of the First Electric Tramway in the United Kingdom* (London, ca. 1883). The best example of an interurban in the British Isles was the Manx Electric Railway, built in 1893–99 and still in service in 1959.
11. *Poor's Manual of Railroads*, 1896, p. 1191.
12. Randall V. Mills, "Early Electric Interurbans in Oregon," *Oregon Historical Quarterly*, XLIV (1943), 84.
13. James Greene and Stephen D. Maguire, "Lake Shore Electric," *Railroad Magazine*, LVI, No. 2 (November 1951), 79.
14. *Poor's Manual of Railroads*, 1898, p. 1071.
15. George S. Davis, "The Electric Railways of Ohio," *Street Railway Journal*, XVII (1901), 110.
16. *Cleveland Plain Dealer*, January 27, 1901.
17. For a description of the Everett-Moore syndicate's operations to control the street railway system in Detroit, see Graeme O'Geran, *A History of the Detroit Street Railways* (Detroit: The Conover Press, 1931), pp. 133–94, and Jere C. Hutchins, *Jere C. Hutchins: A Personal Story* (Detroit, 1938), pp. 161–76.
18. "The Winding Up of the Everett-Moore Syndicate," *Street Railway Journal*, XXI (1903), 660.
19. *Poor's Manual of Railroads*, 1901, pp. 942, 1018.
20. *Ibid.*, 1902, p. 1013.
21. *Street Railway Journal*, XVIII (1901), 778.
22. *Ibid.*, XX (1902), 278.
23. *Ibid.*, XVIII, 778.
24. "The Finances of Electric Interurban Railways," *Street Railway Journal*, XIX (1902), 154.
25. *Ibid.*
26. Ernest L. Bogart, "Economic and Social Effects of the Interurban Electric Railway in Ohio," *Journal of Political Economy*, XIV (1906), 586.

27. *Reports of the Secretary of State of Ohio*, 1900–1904.
28. Davis, "The Electric Railways of Ohio," *Street Railway Journal*, XVII, 114.
29. *Poor's Manual of Railroads*, 1903, p. 1055.
30. Carl C. Taylor, *Rural Sociology* (New York: Harper, 1926), pp. 136–37. Quoted by permission of Harper and Bros.
31. Ernest Gonzenbach, *Engineering Preliminaries for an Interurban Electric Railway* (New York: McGraw, 1903), p. 8.
32. W. C. Gotshall, *Notes on Electric Railway Economics and Preliminary Engineering* (New York: McGraw, 1904), pp. 56–57.
33. Roy Morris, "Trolley Competition with the Railroads," *Atlantic Monthly*, XCIII (1904), 730–36.
34. Bogart, in *Journal of Political Economy*, XIV, 590–91.
35. *Street Railway Journal*, XVIII, 108.
36. O. R. Cummings, *Boston and Worcester Street Railway*, Transportation, VIII (1954), 21.
37. Malcolm D. Isely, *Arkansas Valley Interurban*, Interurbans, Special Number 19 (1956), p. 13. This monograph contains an excellent description of the promotion and construction of a small interurban. An impassioned case for municipal subsidy, tax relief, and free rural rights-of-way can be found in Guy Morrison Walker, *The Why and How of Interurban Railways* (Chicago, 1904).
38. *Census of Electric Railways*, 1907, p. 272.
39. Bogart, in *Journal of Political Economy*, XIV, 597; cf. Walker, *The Why and How of Interurban Railways*, p. 4.
40. Glen A. Blackburn, "Interurban Railroads of Indiana," *Indiana Magazine of History*, XX (1924), 259.
41. *Ibid.*, p. 261.
42. See below, p. 42.
43. Gilbert H. Kneiss, *Redwood Railways* (Berkeley, Calif.: Howell-North, 1956), pp. 126 ff.
44. Blackburn, "Interurban Railroads of Indiana," *Indiana Magazine of History*, XX, 259.
45. Ann Arbor (pseud.), "Brief Sojourns," *Bulletin of the Railway and Locomotive Historical Society*, No. 35 (1934), p. 85.
46. A Brotherhood of Interurban Trainmen formed on the Lake Shore Electric seems to have accomplished little.
47. In this connection, see two articles by Walter Isard: "Transport Development and Building Cycles," *Quarterly Journal of Economics*, LVII (1942), 90–112; and "A Neglected Cycle: The Transport Building Cycle," *Review of Economic Statistics*, XXIV (1942), 149–58.
48. *Wall Street Journal*, December 11, 1902. The Detroit and Toledo Shore Line is still operated in this capacity, jointly by the Grand Trunk Western and the Nickel Plate Road.
49. *Street Railway Journal*, XXV (1905), 794; see also *Cleveland Plain Dealer*, 1902–5, *passim*.
50. *Street Railway Journal*, XXIII (1904), 406.
51. Frank T. Carlton, "The Electric Interurban Railroad," *Yale Review*, XIII (1904), 179–93.
52. Bogart, in *Journal of Political Economy*, XIV, 601.
53. *Wall Street Journal*, December 9, 1902.
54. *Ibid.*, December 17, 1902.
55. *Ibid.*, December 12, 1902.
56. John Keller, "Findlay's Interurban Golden Spike Ceremony," *Northwest Ohio Quarterly*, XVI (1944), 137–43.
57. *Street Railway Journal*, XXX (1907), 330.
58. Blackburn, in *Indiana Magazine of History*, XX, 437.
59. *Ibid.*, p. 438.
60. *Report of the Railroad Commission of Ohio*, 1908, p. 49.

61. *Ibid.*, p. 291.
62. See below, p. 213.
63. *Poor's Manual of Railroads,* 1912, p. 2182.
64. *Ibid.*, p. 2206.
65. *Traffic World,* XXXIII (1924), 739–40.
66. *Electric Railway Journal,* LXV (1925), 480.
67. *Street Railway Journal,* VIII (1892), 174.
68. *Railway Age,* XXXI (1901), 397.
69. Mary Crane, "Chicago–New York Electric Air Line Railroad," *Trains,* VI, No. 12 (October 1946), 15–19, 26–29; *Air Line News,* I–VII (1906–13), *passim.*
70. *Fourth Report of the Railroad Commission of Indiana,* 1909, p. 610.
71. The Martinsville line of the THI&E was aimed at Bloomington and Vincennes, and the Cincinnati Lawrenceburg and Aurora, among others, considered building to Madison.
72. *Street Railway Journal,* XXI (1903), 88.

NOTES TO CHAPTER TWO

1. For more detailed descriptions of interurban technology, see Albert S. Richey, *Electric Railway Handbook* (New York: McGraw-Hill, 1st ed., 1915, 2d ed., 1924); C. Francis Harding, *Electric Railway Engineering,* 3d ed. (New York: McGraw-Hill, 1926); Albert B. Herrick and Edward C. Boynton, *American Electric Railway Practice* (New York: McGraw, 1907); Rodney Hutt, *Electric Railway Dictionary* (New York: McGraw, 1911); A. Morris Buck, *The Electric Railway* (New York: McGraw, 1915); Sydney W. Ashe and J. D. Keiley, *Electric Railways* (3 vols.; New York: Van Nostrand, 1905); and the convention supplement for 1906 to the *Electric Railway Journal,* XXVIII (1906), 591–696.
2. *Street Railway Journal,* XXIX (1907), 631.
3. Gonzenbach, *Engineering Preliminaries for an Interurban Electric Railway,* p. 22.
4. It was used by the Scioto Valley, the Albany and Hudson, the Aurora Elgin and Chicago, the Michigan United, the Michigan Railway, the Lackawanna and Wyoming Valley, the Wilkes-Barre and Hazleton, the Philadelphia and Western, the Oneida Railway, the Sacramento Northern, the Central California Traction, the Puget Sound Electric, the Keeseville Ausable Chasm and Lake Champlain, the Grand Rapids Grand Haven and Muskegon, and (for short distances) the Atlantic City and Shore and the Chicago North Shore and Milwaukee.
5. William Bancroft Potter, "Economics of Railway Electrification," *Electric Traction Weekly,* VI (1910), 963–68.
6. In June 1903, there had been an experimental installation of single phase by Bion J. Arnold on the Lansing St. Johns and St. Louis Railway in Michigan, but the road operated commercially with 600-volt DC. See Bion J. Arnold, "Some Early Work in Polyphase and Single Phase Electric Traction," a paper presented to the International Electrical Congress at St. Louis, 1904.
7. *Ibid.* For a general treatise on single-phase electrification, see Edwin Austin, *Single Phase Electric Railways* (New York: Van Nostrand, 1915), especially 252–94.
8. *Street Railway Journal,* XXIII (1904), 330.
9. *Ibid.*
10. John R. Hewett, "The Indianapolis & Louisville 1200 volt Direct Current Line," *Street Railway Journal,* XXXI (1908), 4–9.
11. This description of the Sacramento Northern is based on information furnished by Addison H. Laflin, Jr.
12. "Electric Railway Signalling," *Electric Railway Journal,* XLII (1913), 607 ff.

13. For a description of the principal models of controllers, see Interurbans, Special No., forthcoming.

14. For a lucid description of the various air-brake systems of the interurbans, see Bulletin of the Central Electric Railfans' Association, Nos. 85 (1949) and 94 (1951), which are devoted to straight and automatic air brakes, respectively.

15. The various types of interurban trucks are described and illustrated in Bulletin of the Central Electric Railfans' Association, No. 78 (1948).

16. Open platform observation cars were used by the Sacramento Northern, Oregon Electric, Spokane Coeur d'Alene and Palouse, Puget Sound Electric, Salt Lake and Utah, Fort Dodge Des Moines and Southern, Waterloo Cedar Falls and Northern, Illinois Traction, Washington Water Power Company, Jamestown Westfield and Northwestern, Chicago North Shore and Milwaukee, and a few other companies.

17. *Forty-first Report of the Railroad and Warehouse Commission of Illinois* (1911), pp. 637–38.

18. *Fourth Annual Report of the Railroad Commission of Indiana* (1909), p. 402.

19. *Fifth Annual Report of the Railroad Commission of Indiana* (1910), pp. 381 ff.

NOTES TO CHAPTER THREE

1. Thomas Conway, Jr., "The Traffic Problems of Interurban Electric Railroads," a condensation of a doctoral dissertation at the University of Pennsylvania, reprinted from *The Journal of Accountancy* (March 6, 1909), p. 5.

2. *Traffic World*, XLVII (1931), 847 ff.

3. *Street Railway Journal*, XXVIII (1906), 668.

4. Felix E. Reifschneider, "The Long Drag Out of Town," *Interurbans*, IV, No. 2 (December 1946), 6.

5. *Report of the Railroad Commission of Ohio*, 1909, pp. 228–29.

6. Buffet service was also tried for a short period on the Muncie Meteor and the Marion Flyers.

7. "Limited Service and Interline Business," *Street Railway Journal*, XXV (1905), 198 ff.

8. *Street Railway Journal*, XXX (1907), 868.

9. *Census of Electric Railways*, 1907, pp. 250–51.

10. *The Railway Age*, XXXII (1901), 747.

11. *Proceedings of the Federal Electric Railways Commission* (Washington: Government Printing Office, 1920), I, 700.

12. "Annual Indexes of Electric Railway Fares and Costs, 1913–1932," *Transit Journal*, LXXVII (1933), 18.

13. *Proceedings of the First Annual Meeting of the Central Electric Railway Association*, Indianapolis, 1907. Hereafter this Association will be referred to as the C.E.R.A. Please note that we do not use C.E.RA. to indicate the Central Electric Railfans' Association, an enthusiasts' organization founded in 1938.

14. The last map was published in *Traffic World*, XLVII (1931), 848.

15. *Central States Guide*, September 1924.

16. *Electric Traction and Bus Journal*, XXVIII (1932), 127.

17. *Record of Proceedings of the Central Passenger Association*, 1904, p. 371.

18. *Ibid.*, 1906–12, *passim*.

19. *Proceedings of the Federal Electric Railways Commission*, I, 700.

20. *Hearings before the Subcommittee on Domestic Land and Water Transportation of the Senate Committee on Interstate and Foreign Commerce pursuant to Senate Resolution 50, 81st Congress, 2nd Session; Study of Domestic Land and Water Transportation*, p. 13.

21. *Hearings before the Subcommittee on Surface Transportation of the Committee on Interstate and Foreign Commerce, 85th Congress, 2nd Session. Problems of the Railroads*, Part I, p. 61.

22. *Railroad Passenger Deficit,* Interstate Commerce Commission Docket Number 31954, p. 69.

NOTES TO CHAPTER FOUR

1. *Electric Railway Journal,* LVI (1920), 1161.
2. Bryant Alden Long and William Jefferson Davis, *Mail by Rail* (New York: Simmons-Boardman Publishing Company, 1951), pp. 231 ff. Mr. Earl Moore of Chicago furnished additional information.
3. *Electric Railway Journal,* LIII (1919), 927.
4. *Ibid.,* LIV (1919), 992.
5. *Proceedings of the Federal Electric Railways Commission,* I, 711.
6. *Electric Railway Journal,* XLII (1913), 588; XLIII (1914), 1022.
7. *Ibid.,* LIII (1919), 397.
8. *Ibid.,* LXV (1925), 147.
9. *Ibid.,* LXIII (1923), 142.
10. *Ibid.,* LXXIII (1929), 250. His figures are based on the data in Table 5.
11. *Ibid.,* LVI (1920), 127; LX (1922), 46.
12. *Ibid.,* LXXIII (1929), 250.
13. *Ibid.,* p. 963 ff.
14. *Street Railway Journal,* XI (1895), 517.
15. *Electric Railway Journal,* LVIII (1921), 133; LXVIII (1926), 402-3.
16. This information is drawn from an address given before the Western Regional Meeting of the American Short Line Railroad Association, April 29, 1954, by H. J. Phillips, Traffic Manager of the CNS&M Ry. We are indebted to the North Shore Line for making the text available.
17. The highway portions of this traffic were held to be subject to state motor-carrier regulation. *Lake Shore Electric Ry. Co. v. Public Utilities Commission,* 125 O.S. 588 (1932).
18. *Report of the Public Utilities Commission of Ohio,* 1931, pp. 134, 167.
19. *Census of Electric Railways,* 1907, p. 266.
20. *The State ex rel. Wear v. Cincinnati and Lake Erie Railroad Company,* 128 O.S. 95 (1934). This doctrine had been enunciated in an earlier case arising out of a franchise dispute at Bellevue: *Lake Shore Electric Railway Company v. Public Utilities Commission,* 125 O.S. 588 (1932).
21. *Farmland Stone Company v. C. C. C. & St. Louis Railroad Company and Indiana Union Traction Company, Report of the Railroad Commission of Indiana,* 1907, pp. 92–97.
22. George H. Gibson, "High Speed Electric Interurban Railways," *Annual Report of the Board of Regents of the Smithsonian Institution for 1903,* p. 312.
23. *Proceedings of Meetings and Circulars of the Central Freight Association,* 1913, pp. 56, 121; 1914, pp. 14, 83.
24. "Discrimination against Electric Railway Freight," *Electric Railway Journal,* XLV (1915), 3.
25. *Ibid.,* XLVII (1916), 76.
26. *Ibid.,* LXXIII (1929), 561.
27. See below, p. 162.
28. "Carload Freight on Small Lines," *Electric Railway Journal,* XLV (1915), 1114.

NOTES TO CHAPTER FIVE

1. See the article by C. S. Collier, "Franchise Contracts and Utility Regulation," *George Washington Law Review,* I (1933), 172, 299.
2. For example, in *Kalamazoo Motors v. Michigan Railways* (PUR 1920C 888), the Michigan commission upheld parcel dispatch freight rates of the Michigan Railways (which were set at twice the Railway Express rates) as reasonable, in terms of the service rendered.

3. See above, p. 141.

4. The right of the state to control construction of new lines was upheld in *Re Shelton* (69 Conn. 626), involving an application of Shelton Street Railway to build a line in the Bridgeport area in competition with the New Haven.

5. See F. P. Hall, "Discontinuance of Service by Public Utilities," *Minnesota Law Review,* 13 (1928), 181.

6. California Railroad Commission, *Report on Engineering Survey of Pacific Electric Railway Company* (Los Angeles, 1939).

7. Colorado, Indiana, Kansas, Kentucky, Minnesota, Montana, New Jersey, North Dakota, Ohio, Oklahoma, South Dakota, Washington, West Virginia, and Wyoming.

8. New York was the only major state in which no grandfather clause rights were provided.

9. In a major case involving the Waterloo Cedar Falls and Northern, the right of the bus subsidiary of this road to a certificate under the grandfather clause in the Iowa law was upheld, even though it was evident that the subsidiary had been established for the primary purpose of running independent bus operations out of business.

10. A position more extreme than that of the Illinois commission was taken by the Illinois Supreme Court in the case of *Egyptian Transportation Co. v. L&NRR* (321 Ill. 580, 1926), in which a commission authorization for bus operation in competition with the Louisville & Nashville Railroad was overruled, despite the limited passenger service of the railroad, on the ground that if bus service was necessary, the railroad had prior right to provide it although in this instance the railroad had not sought to do so).

11. Policies of New England states relative to rural trolley lines were similar. Connecticut, in the basic *Re City of Bridgeport* case in 1921, denied jitneys the right to operate in competition with both city lines and the Bridgeport-Norwalk intercity line, arguing that their operation would lead to abandonment of the electric railway service, which was better suited to serve the public. Massachusetts and Rhode Island later took the same position. In 1923 the Maine commission, in turning down an application for operation of a bus line between Portland and Old Orchard (PUR 1923E 772), indicated that since it must take into consideration the welfare of the community as a whole, and not that of a few persons only, it could not permit the destruction of the electric railway, which provided year-round service. This doctrine was reaffirmed in 1924 (PUR 1925B 357), and in 1926 (PUR 1926B 545). The Vermont commission ruled likewise in 1923.

12. Wayne C. Broehl, *Trucks, Trouble and Triumph; The Norwalk Truck Line Company* (New York: Prentice-Hall, 1954), p. 47.

13. *Ibid.,* p. 30.

14. See J. F. Due, *Sir Adam Beck and the Hydro Radial Proposals,* Upper Canadian Railway Society Bulletin, 50 (1958).

NOTES TO CHAPTER SIX

1. See U.S. Bureau of the Census, *Street and Electric Railways for 1907.*

NOTES TO CHAPTER SEVEN

1. The Quebec–St. Joachim line, discontinued shortly before, was primarily a suburban operation.

2. Pre-1915 abandonments totaled 70 miles. These included the Fidalgo City and Anacortes (1893), one of the two lines from Dayton to Xenia, and the Middlefield line of Cleveland and Chagrin Falls.

3. See Harold Barger, *The Transportation Industries, 1889–1946* (New York: National Bureau of Economic Research, 1951), p. 120.

4. *Electric Railway Journal,* XLVII (1916), 403.

5. See *Reports of the Commission Appointed to Inquire Into Hydro-Electric Railways* (Toronto: Kings Printer, 1921).

Notes to pp. 240–322

NOTES TO CHAPTER EIGHT

1. The article by G. Shillinglaw, "Profit Analysis for Abandonment Decisions," *Journal of Business*, XXX (1957), 17–29, offers one of the few analyses of this question.
2. For example, the Portland Traction line in Oregon, one of the last to operate passenger service, was using, in later years, heavy 1924 steel cars from the Pacific Electric, lightweight city cars from Yakima rebuilt for interurban service, cars from the Indiana Railroad, the Fonda Johnstown and Gloversville, the Albany Southern, and the Key System.
3. Carl Van Doren, *An Autobiography of Carl Van Doren* (New York: Harcourt, Brace, 1958), pp. 41–42. Quoted by permission of Harcourt, Brace and Co.

NOTES TO PART II

1. James Greene and Stephen D. Maguire, "Lake Shore Electric," *Railroad Magazine*, LVI, No. 2 (1951), 76–90.
2. The Indiana interurbans are well documented: see Glen A. Blackburn, "Interurban Railroads of Indiana," *Indiana Magazine of History*, XX (1924), 221–79, 400–464; Bulletin of the Central Electric Railfans' Association, Nos. 91 (1950), 101 (1957), and 102 (1958); Robert M. Haley, "The American Electric Railway Interurban," an unpublished doctoral dissertation, mainly devoted to the Indiana interurbans (Northwestern University Library, 1936); George T. Oborn, "The Decline of Interurban Railways in Indiana," an unpublished paper delivered before the Indiana History Conference in Indianapolis, December 11, 1942; Roy M. Bates, *Interurban Railways of Allen County Indiana* (Fort Wayne: Public Library of Fort Wayne and Allen County, 1958); Jerry Marlette, *Electric Railroads of Indiana* (Indianapolis: Council for Local History, 1959).
3. The Bulletin of the Central Electric Railfans' Association, No. 84 (1949), contains a complete corporate history of this company.
4. Joseph A. Galloway and James J. Buckley, *The St. Joseph Valley Railway*, Bulletin of the Electric Railway Historical Society, No. 16 (1955).
5. George K. Bradley, *The Northern Indiana Railways*, Bulletin of the Electric Railway Historical Society, No. 6 (1953).
6. Eugene Van Dusen, "Winona Railroad," *Headlights*, XIV (April 1952), 1–3.
7. See *Electric Railways of Michigan*, Bulletin of the Central Electric Railfans' Association, No. 103 (1959); Robert E. Lee, "Car Tracks to Oblivion," *Detroit Historical Society Bulletin*, XIV, No. 7 (April 1958), 6–12; and A. Rodney Lenderink, "The Electric Interurban Railway in Kalamazoo County," *Michigan History*, XLIII (1959), 43–93.
8. W. F. Ellis and Edward S. Miller, "The Laurel Line," *Headlights*, XI, No. 12 (December 1949), 1–5.
9. F. E. Reifschneider, *Wilkes-Barre and Hazelton*, Interurbans, Special No. 7 (1949), p. 15.
10. *The Marker*, VI, No. 2 (December 1947).
11. Harry D. Lentz, *Trolley Roads in Lebanon and Lancaster Counties*.
12. *The Marker*, I, No. 4 (October 1942).
13. The electric railways of New York are well-covered by a series of careful monographs by Felix E. Reifschneider, *Toonervilles of the Empire State* (1947), *Interurbans of the Empire State* (1949), and *Trolley Lines of the Empire State* (1950), published by the author at Orlando, Florida. See also the Bulletin of the Central Electric Railfans' Association, No. 44 (1943).
14. William R. Gordon, *The Route of the Orange Limited* (Rochester, N.Y., 1953).
15. David F. Nestle and William R. Gordon, *Steam and Trolley Days* (Rochester, N.Y., 1958).
16. O. R. Cummings, *Portland-Lewiston Interurban*, Transportation, X (1956).
17. Bulletin of the Central Electric Railfans' Association, No. 65 (1946).

18. George W. Hilton, "Meets All Trains," *Trains*, VI, No. 10 (1946), 48–49; L. W. Moody and W. S. Young, "Six Miles and a Toll Bridge," *Short Line Railroader*, No. 35 (1958), pp. 6–8.

19. O. R. Cummings, *Boston and Worcester Street Railway*, Transportation, VIII (1954).

20. R. E. Mermet, "Shore Line Electric Railway," *The Marker*, V, No. 3 (December 1946).

21. O. R. Cummings, *Atlantic Shore Line Railway*, Transportation, IV (1950).

22. O. R. Cummings, *A Granite State Interurban*, Bulletin of the Electric Railway Historical Society, No. 12 (1954).

23. For histories of the New Haven's unwise acquisitions, see Henry Lee Staples and Alpheus Thomas Mason, *The Fall of a Railroad Empire* (Syracuse: Syracuse University Press, 1947); Louis D. Brandeis, *Business—A Profession* (Boston: Small, Maynard and Co., 1914), pp. 255–79; and Edward S. Mason, *The Street Railway in Massachusetts*, pp. 61–70.

24. See *Street Railway Journal*, XXXI (1908), 244–49.

25. See S. D. Maguire, "Hagerstown and Frederick," *Railroad Magazine*, XXXVII (March 1945), 107–11.

26. See R. H. Estabrook, "Washington and Old Dominion," *Trains*, VIII (April 1948), 42–47.

27. See *Street Railway Journal*, XXXI (1908), 364–68.

28. See T. G. Lynch, "The Piedmont and Northern Story," *Trains*, XIV (June, July 1954), 48–53 (in each issue).

29. See *Street Railway Journal*, XXI (1903), 21–25.

30. All Illinois interurbans except the large systems, for which specific reference are subsequently given, are noted in *The Smaller Electric Railways of Illinois*, Bulletin of the Central Electric Railfans' Association, No. 99 (1955).

31. See L. C. Harlow, "The North Shore Story," *Railroad Magazine*, LXII (October 1953), 72–90.

32. See R. White, "The South Shore," *Railroad Magazine*, XXXVIII (October 1945), 94–102; G. S. Moe, "South Shore Line," *Railroad Magazine*, LX (February 1953), 10–35; S. D. Maguire, "The Modernized South Shore Line," *Railroad Magazine*, LXVIII (April 1957), 50–55.

33. P. L. Keister, *The Rockford and Interurban Railway*, Bulletin of the Electric Railway Historical Society, No. 22 (1956), offers one of the most careful studies ever made of the history of a particular interurban road.

34. The authors are indebted to Mr. Frank Mynard of Urbana and Mr. Philip Keister of Freeport for information on this little-known road.

35. *Illinois Traction System*, Bulletin of the Central Electric Railfans' Association, No. 98 (1954).

36. A detailed account of the road is to be found in the Bulletin of the Central Electric Railfans' Association, No. 97 (1953), pp. xx–xxx, and in the article by W. V. Anderson, "Milwaukee Electric Lines," *Trains*, VII (August 1947), 44–54.

37. See *Street Railway Journal*, XXIV (1904), 1030–2.

38. See *Electric Railways of Minneapolis and St. Paul*, Interurbans, Special No. 14 (Los Angeles, 1953) for an account of the line and for a particularly good description of its operation in later years.

39. See *Electric Railway Journal*, XLIII (1914), 68–71.

40. See *Electric Railways of Iowa*, Bulletin of the Central Electric Railfans' Association, No. 100 (1956), for an invaluable description of the Iowa roads. See also Frank P. Donovan, Jr. "Interurbans in Iowa," *The Palimpsest*, XXXV, No. 5 (May 1954), 177–212.

41. W. D. Middleton, "Uncommon Interurban," *Trains*, XI (April 1951), 36–40.

42. See W. Schmidt, "A Steam Train with a Trolley Wire," *Railroad Magazine*, XLVIII (April 1949), 84–95; "Electric Line of Many Talents," *Trains*, IX (January

1949), 12–15; D. A. Strassman, "Destroyed by Fire," *Trains*, XV (February 1955), 24–26; *Electric Railway Journal*, XLII (1913), 99–104.

43. See "Fort Dodge, Des Moines and Southern," *Railroad Magazine*, LVIII (September 1957), 74–90.

44. See E. Bryant Phillips, "Interurban Projects in Nebraska," *Nebraska History*, XXX (1959), 163–82; and "Interurban Projects in and around Omaha," *ibid.*, pp. 257–85.

45. See *Electric Railway Journal*, XLII (1913), 212–20.

46. See *Street Railway Journal*, XV (1899), 281–84, and XVI (1900), 689–92.

47. See *Electric Railway Journal*, XXXII (1909), 54–58.

48. See M. D. Isely, *Arkansas Valley Interurban*, Interurbans, Special No. 19 (1956), an excellent account of the road's history.

49. See H. B. Thornton, "Oklahoma Traffic Boom," *Railroad Magazine*, XXXVIII (June 1945), 78–81, for an account of its later history.

50. See *Street Railway Journal*, XXIX (1907), 637–38.

51. See *Electric Railway Journal*, XVIV (1914), pp. 6–10. See also *Galveston-Houston Electric Railway*, Interurbans, Special No. 22 (1960).

52. See *Street Railway Journal*, XX (1903), pp. 164–66.

53. See *Denver and Interurban*, Interurbans, Special No. 5 (1947).

54. See M. Cafky, *Rails Around Gold Hill* (Denver: Rocky Mountain Railroad Club, 1955), an excellent detailed account of the railroads of the Cripple Creek area.

55. See *Interurbans of Utah*, Interurbans, Special No. 15 (1954).

56. The northern line is described in *Electric Railway Review*, XX (1908), 320–24. The authors are indebted to the Idaho Power Company for unraveling the obscure history of the southern line.

57. See Paul Busch, "Montana's Only Interurban," *Railroad Magazine*, LXII (December 1959), 29–30.

58. See *Electric Railway Journal*, XXXI (1908), 780–81.

59. See *The Electric Railroads of Washington State*, Bulletin of the Central Electric Railfans' Association, No. 95 (1951).

60. See *Pacific Northwest Traction Company*, Interurbans, Special No. 7 (1949).

61. See *Puget Sound Electric Railway*, Interurbans, Special No. 2. A new issue is in preparation.

62. See *Street Railway Journal*, XXIV (1904), 730–33; A. Allen "Willamette Valley Line," *Railroad Magazine*, LX (May 1953), 84–95; R. V. Mills, *Railroads down the Valleys* (Palo Alto: Pacific Books, 1950), chap. V, an interesting account of the road, despite a few errors. Note also J. T. Labbe and D. L. Stearns, "Portland Traction Company," *Western Railroader*, XXI No. 10 (August 1958).

63. See *The Red Electrics of Portland, Oregon*, Interurbans, Special No. 8 (1949).

64. See *Electric Railway Journal*, XLI (1913), 1050–53.

65. *Sacramento Northern*, Interurbans, Special No. 9 (1950). A new edition is planned for 1960. See also *Western Railroader*, XIII (June 1950); XV (December 1952); XVIII (November 1955).

66. See *Electric Railway Journal*, VLI (1913), 726–29.

67. See J. W. Dodge, *Electric Railroading in Central California*, Pacific Railway Journal (1956).

68. *Ibid.*

69. See *Western Railroader*, XV (February 1952).

70. See *Western Railroader*, Vol. XVI (February 1953).

71. See *Wheel Clicks*, Vol. V, No. 1 (1944).

72. A favorite resort of the San Jose area was Alum Rock Park, in the hills to the east of the city. The first electric line to this point was created by the electrification in 1901 of a narrow-gauge steam road, built in 1896, the San Jose and Alum Rock Park. The line was largely destroyed by floods in 1911 and cut back to Toyon; a new standard-gauge electric line was then built farther north via Berryessa Road by Peninsular, the cars reaching downtown San Jose by streetcar tracks. After 1921

all service was operated on the line by San Jose Railroads with city cars. Service to Alum Rock Park ended on July 11, 1932. Passenger service continued to Berryessa, however, until 1938; a part of the line (operated for freight service between 1934 to 1938 by the Visalia Electric) was taken over by the SP for continued freight operations. See *Western Railroader*, Vol. XXI, No. 3 (1958).

73. See *The Circuit Breaker*, Bay Area Electric Railroad Association, Vol. I, No. 50, Feb. 20, 1955. See also S. B. Renovich, "Visalia Electric Railroad," *Western Railroader*, XX (June 1959), 3–14.

74. References include: California Railroad Commission, *Report on Engineering Survey of Pacific Electric Railway Company* (Los Angeles: 1939). 10 vols.

Interurbans, Special Numbers on the Pacific Electric, including No. 16, "Pacific Electric" (four issues plus three supplements), No. 18 "Los Angeles Pacific" (1955); No. 20, "Los Angeles and Redondo" (1957).

D. Duke, *Pacific Electric Railway*, Pacific Railway Journal, II (1958) pp. 1–63. *Street Railway Journal*, XXIII (1904), 309–13.

75. See California Railroad Commission, *Report on Engineering Survey of Pacific Electric Railway Company*. The survey was the most complete one ever made of an interurban, and is invaluable as a source of information. The commission clearly recognized that many of the difficulties were of the company's own doing. But it failed to realize the importance of the depression as a source of the loss of traffic, and completely ignored the significance of growing traffic congestion in making bus service, which it recommended, an inadequate substitute for rail service, and the importance of retaining the private-right-of-way rail lines as an important element in a program for solving the traffic congestion problem.

76. See J. F. Due, *Sir Adam Beck and the Hydro Radial Proposals*, Upper Canada Railway Society Bulletin, No. 50 (1958).

Bibliographical Note

The primary source of information on the interurbans consists of the trade journals in the field, of which the *Electric Railway Journal* was much the most important. This periodical was founded in 1884 as the *Street Railway Journal*, and became the *Electric Railway Journal* upon its merger with the *Electric Railway Review* in June 1908. The *Electric Railway Review* had been founded in 1891 as the *Street Railway Review*, and operated under its original name until July 1906. The *Electric Railway Journal* became the *Transit Journal* in 1932 and was discontinued in 1942.

The other major trade journal of the industry was founded in 1905 as the *Interurban Railway Journal*, and became *Electric Traction Weekly* in 1906. From 1912 to 1932 it was known as *Electric Traction,* then as *Electric Traction and Bus Journal* until 1935, and subsequently as *Mass Transportation*. After 1930, this periodical paid little attention to the interurbans.

Substantial material on the development and financing of the lines is to be found in the railway and public utility volumes of *Poor's Manual* and *Moody's Manual*, and in the annual *McGraw-Hill Electric Railway Manuals*, as well as in the annual reports of the various companies.

Statistical data are to be found in the annual reports of the state public utilities commissions, and, after 1920, in the annual *Statistics of Electric Railways* issued by the Interstate Commerce Commission. Additional information appears in the volumes of decisions of the various state regulatory commissions (many of which are reproduced in *Public Utilities Reports*), and the *Decisions of the Interstate Commerce Commission.*

HISTORIES OF INDIVIDUAL COMPANIES

Bulletin of the Central Electric Railfans' Association (Box 503, Chicago 90, Illinois). Annual issues of recent years are devoted to electric railways of the several Midwestern states.

Bulletin of the Electric Railway Historical Society (7625 W. Gregory Street, Chicago 31, Illinois). Several of the bulletins of this society present histories of individual interurbans.

Interurbans, Special Numbers (1416 S. Westmoreland Avenue, Los Angeles 6, California). This is a series of detailed histories of particular companies, mainly in the Far West.

Transportation (Warehouse Point, Connecticut) is a series of short histories of New England electric lines.

The Marker (published by the North Jersey chapter of the National Railway Historical Society) is devoted to electric railways of New Jersey and neighboring states.

Headlights (Electric Railroaders' Association, 145 Greenwich Street, New York) has served the function of a trade journal in recording news items during the last years of the industry. It has frequently carried short histories of interurban lines, particularly at the time of abandonment.

Some issues of the *Pacific Railway Journal* (San Marino, California) and the *Western Railroader* (San Mateo, California) are devoted to histories of interurbans. *Trains* and *Railroad Magazine* carry articles on electric railways.

INDEXES

Index of Interurbans

The corporate histories of the principal interurban companies are indicated by italics. The index is not cross-referenced for minor changes in corporate name, such as "Pennsylvania & Ohio Elec. Ry." to "Pennsylvania & Ohio Tr. Co." This index also includes suburban lines, rural trolley lines, and a few steam railroad electrifications.

Akron Bedford & Cleveland RR, 10, 71, 273
Akron & Cuyahoga Falls Rapid Transit Co., 273
Albany & Hudson RR, 57, 58, 122, 155, 191, 317, 429
Albany & Southern, see Albany & Hudson RR
Albia Interurban Ry., *363*
Algonac Transit Co., 288
Allegheny Valley St. Ry., 174, 300
Allen St. Ry., 301
Allentown & Kutztown Tr. Co., 301
Allentown & Reading Tr. Co., 52, 214, *301*
Alton Granite & St. Louis Tr. Co., 37, 347, 350
Alton & Jacksonville, 351
Alton Jacksonville & Peoria Ry., 95, 212, 250, *351*
Altoona & Logan Valley Elec. Ry., 200, *301-2*
Androscoggin & Kennebec Ry., 167, 324
Angola Ry. & Power Co., 286
Annapolis Short Line, 62, 327
Ann Arbor & Ypsilanti St. Ry., 287
Arkansas City & Winfield Northern Ry., 373
Arkansas Valley Interurban Ry., 17, 37, 48, 69, 70, 151, 183, 184, 198, 206, 210, *371-72*
Arlington & Fairfax Elec. Ry., 233
Aroostook Valley RR, 91, 148, 165, *320*
Athol & Orange, 180
Atlanta Northern, 62, 333
Atlantic City & Shore RR, *307*, 425, 429
Atlantic Shore Line Ry., 148, *323*
Atlantic & Surburban Tr. Co., 307
Auburn Interurban Elec. RR, 314
Auburn Mechanic Falls & Norway St. Ry., 323
Auburn & Northern Elec. RR, 314
Auburn & Syracuse Elec. RR, 46, *314*
Auburn & Turner RR, 323
Augusta-Aiken Ry., *333*
Augusta & Columbia Ry., 333
Augusta Winthrop & Gardner Ry., 323
Aurora Elgin & Chicago, see Chicago Aurora & Elgin RR
Aurora Elgin & Fox River Elec. Ry.,*341-42*
Aurora Plainfield & Joliet Ry., 86, *341*

Ballston Terminal RR, 318
Baltimore & Annapolis RR, 220, 327
Bamberger Elec. RR, 49, 54, 56, 61, 81, 82, 83, 86, 93, 94, 96, 114, 116, 117, 133, 142, 178, 183, 197, 198, 219, 220, 231, 243, 244, 316, *383-84*, 385, 386
Bangor & Northern RR, 323
Bangor & Portland Tr. Co., 301, 307
Bangor Ry. & Elec. Co., 148, *323*
Barre & Montpelier Tr. & Power Co., 324
Bartlesville Interurban, 204, *375*
Bay State St. Ry., 212
Beaver Valley Tr. Co., 302

Beech Grove Tr. Corp., 69, 81, 285, *286*
Bellows Falls & Saxtons River Elec. RR, 324
Benton Harbor–St. Joe Ry. & Lt. Co., 114, 115, 120, 139, 203, *290*
Berkshire St. Ry., 16, 206, 218, 249, *324*, 325
Berlin & Bridgeport, 422
Berlin St. Ry., 325
Biddeford & Saco RR, 323, 324
Bloomington Pontiac & Joliet Elec. Ry., 38, 62, 185, 341, *346*
Blue Grass Tr. Co., 291
Bluff City Elec. Interurban, 335
Bluffton Geneva & Celina Tr. Co., 147–48, 169, 212, *282-83*
Boise Interurban Ry., 387
Boise Valley Tr. Co., 154, 199, 203, 212, 214, *387-88*
Boise Western, 169, 388
Boston & Maine RR (Concord & Manchester elec. branch), *324*
Boston Worcester & New York St. Ry., 320
Boston & Worcester St. Ry., 16, 35, 96, 133, 134, 136, 218, *320-22*
Brantford & Hamilton Elec. Ry., *415*
Bridgeton & Millville Tr. Co., 92, *307*
Bristol Tr. Co., *330*
British Columbia Elec. Ry., 221, 248, 414, *421-22*
Brunswick & Yarmouth Ry., 324
Bryan & College Interurban Ry., *379*
Bucks County Interurban, 52, 120, 174, 298
Buffalo Batavia & Rochester, 38
Buffalo & Erie Ry., see Buffalo & Lake Erie Tr. Co.
Buffalo & Lackawanna Tr. Co., 309
Buffalo & Lake Erie Tr. Co., 47, 80, 131, 150, 196, 293, *309-11*
Buffalo Lockport & Rochester Ry., 33, 43, 164, 196, *312-13*, 314
Buffalo & Lockport Ry., 313
Buffalo & Niagara Falls Elec. Ry., 313
Burlington & Southeastern Ry., 325

Cairo & St. Louis Ry., 201, 352
Caldwell Tr. Co., 164, 249, *388*
California Pacific, 406
California Ry., 406
Cambridge Power Lt. & Tr. Co., *272*
Camden Interstate Ry., 306
Camden & Trenton Ry., 306
Canton–Akron Consolidated Ry., 273
Cape Breton Elec. Co. (Tramways), *421*
Carlisle & Mount Holly Ry., 298
Cassville & Western, 376
Cayadutta Elec. RR, 316
Cedar Rapids & Iowa City Ry., 57, 72, 82, 93, 113, 161, 199, 220, 315, *360*, 363
Cedar Rapids & Marion City, *362*
Centerville Albia & Southern, 363
Central California Tr. Co., 57, 154, 173, 179, 207, 218, 248, *401*, 424, 429

Centralia & Central City Tr. Co., 352
Centralia Tr. Co., 352
Central Illinois Tr. Co., 38, 88, 189, 198, 200, *351–52*
Central Kentucky Tr. Co., 291
Central Maine Power Co., 200
Central New York Southern RR, 313
Centre & Clearfield Ry., 302
Chagrin Falls & Eastern Elec. Ry., 272
Chambersburg & Gettysburg Elec. Ry., 206, *297*
Chambersburg Greencastle & Waynesboro St. Ry., 202, *297*, 327
Chambersburg & Shippensburg Ry., *297*
Charles City Western Ry., 85, 214, 220, 240, 323, *362*
Charleston Consolidated Ry. Gas & Elec. Co., 333
Charleston Interurban RR, 166, *305*
Charleston–Isle of Palms Tr. Co., 333
Chatham Wallaceburg & Lake Erie Ry., 230, *415–17*
Chautauqua Tr. Co., 14, 112, 212, *311*
Chicago Aurora & De Kalb, RR, *342*
Chicago Aurora & Elgin RR, 11, 14, 28, 50, 58, 73, 75, 79, 93, 96, 100, 102, 104, 146, 180, 196, 200, 232, 266, *336–37*, 338, 331–42, 425, 429
Chicago Harvard & Geneva Lake Ry., 141, *342*, 353
Chicago & Illinois Valley Ry., see Chicago Ottawa & Peoria Ry.
Chicago & Indiana Air Line, 337
Chicago & Interurban Tr. Co., see Chicago & Southern Tr. Co.
Chicago & Joliet Elec. Ry., 174, 184, 200, 218, 231, 232, *339*, 351
Chicago Lake Shore & South Bend Ry., see Chicago South Shore & South Bend RR
Chicago & Milwaukee Elec. RR, see Chicago North Shore & Milwaukee RR
Chicago–New York Electric Air Line RR, 38–41, 48, 275, 365
Chicago North Shore & Milwaukee RR, 47, 49, 54, 56, 63n, 67, 69, 73, 75, 82, 84, 85, 86, 98, 99–100, 102, 104, 106, 107, 114, 116, 134–35, 146, 153, 156, 157, 161, 163, 185, 192, 197, 200, 201, 213, 218, 220, 223, 229, 232, 248, 283, *335–36*, 338, 353, 428
Chicago Ottawa & Peoria Ry., 36. 162, 201, *339*, 342; see also Illinois Traction Co.
Chicago & St. Louis Elec. Ry., 39
Chicago South Bend & Northern Indiana Ry., see Northern Indiana Ry.
Chicago & South Shore Ry., 276
Chicago South Shore & South Bend RR, 33, 49, 53, 59, 61, 62, 67, 72, 75, 78, 80, 83, 85, 88–89, 99–100, 102, 107, 111, 114, 115, 146, 197, 200, 201, 205, 213, 215, 222, 232, 248, 276, 283, *337–38*
Chicago & Southern Tr. Co., 151, 196, 200, 212, 214, 250, *338–39*
Chicago & West Towns Ry., 174
Chippewa Valley Lt. Ry. & Power Co., 189, 357
Choctaw Ry. & Lighting Co., 374
Cincinnati & Columbus Tr. Co., 57, 161–62, *255*
Cincinnati Dayton & Toledo Tr. Co., 13, 26, 28, 30, 31, 32, 46, 265, 266, 368
Cincinnati & Eastern Elec. Ry., 258

Cincinnati Georgetown & Portsmouth RR, 24, 47, 52, 72, 80, 92, 93, 120, 146, *255*, 258, 286
Cincinnati Hamilton & Dayton Ry., 83, 138, 155, 232, 266
Cincinnati & Hamilton Elec. St. Ry., 265
Cincinnati & Hamilton Tr. Co., 258
Cincinnati Interurban Co., 258
Cincinnati & Lake Erie RR, 52, 72, 81–82, 108, f11, 134, 138–40, 197, 198, 219, 232, 241, 242, 259, 265, *266*, 288, 296, 401
Cincinnati Lawrenceburg & Aurora Elec. St. RR, 52, 80, 134, *255*, 374, 428
Cincinnati & Miami Valley Tr. Co., 265
Cincinnati Milford & Blanchester Tr. Co., 18, 78, 80, 94–95, 183, *258*
Cincinnati Milford & Loveland Tr. Co., see Cincinnati Milford & Blanchester Tr. Co.
Cincinnati Northern Tr. Co., 265
Citizens Elec. Lt. & Power Co., 268
Citizens Tr. Co., 200, 302
City & Elm Grove RR, *305*
City Lines of West Virginia, 305
City & Surburban Ry., 330
Claremont Ry., 148, *325*
Cleveland Alliance & Mahoning Valley Ry., 24, 32, 130, *272–73*
Cleveland & Chagrin Falls Elec. Ry., 431; see also Eastern Ohio Tr. Co.
Cleveland & Eastern Tr. Co., see Eastern Ohio Tr. Co.
Cleveland Elyria & Western Ry., 13
Cleveland & Erie Ry., 131, 210, 213, 274, *293*
Cleveland Painesville & Ashtabula, see Cleveland Painesville & Eastern RR
Cleveland Painesville & Eastern RR, 10, 11, 25, 94, 111, 120, 122, 131, 214, *274*
Cleveland & Southern, see Cleveland Southwestern & Columbus Ry.
Cleveland Southwestern & Columbus Ry., 13, 16, 26, 28, 32, 43, 49, 54, 55, 72, 73, 80, 81, 120, 122, 130, 196, 218, 241, 259, *268–69*
Cleveland Southwestern Ry. & Lt. Co., see Cleveland Southwestern & Columbus Ry.
Cleveland & Southwestern Tr. Co., see Cleveland Southwestern & Columbus Ry.
Cleveland Youngstown & Eastern Ry., see Eastern Ohio Tr. Co.
Clinton Davenport & Muscatine Ry., 63, 143, 144, 204, *359–60*
Coal Belt Elec. Ry., 206, 210, *351*, 378
Coeur d'Alene & Spokane, 389
Colorado Springs & Cripple Creek District Ry. (elec. div.), 54, 207, 213, *381–82*
Colorado Springs & Interurban Ry., 382
Columbus Buckeye Lake & Newark Tr. Co., 13, 265
Columbus Clintonville & Worthington St. Ry., 17, 269
Columbus Delaware & Marion Ry., 13, 17, 32, 35, 43, 48, 53, 73, 79, 80, 92, 123, 125, *269–70*, 339
Columbus Delaware & Northern, 17
Columbus Grove City & Southwestern Ry., 29, 265
Columbus London & Springfield, 13, 16, 28
Columbus Magnetic Springs & Northern Ry., 35, 43, *270*
Columbus Marion & Bucyrus RR, 32, 35, *269*

Columbus New Albany & Johnstown Tr. Co., 275
Columbus Newark & Zanesville Elec. Ry., 13, 265, 266
Columbus Urbana & Western Ry., 270, 275
Concord Maynard & Hudson, 159
Conestoga Tr. Co., 51, 199, 203, 218, *296*, 297, 298
Conneaut & Erie Tr. Co., 293
Connecticut Co., 133, 206, 322, 323, *325–26*
Cook Transit Co., 286
Co-operative Transit Co., 303
Corning & Painted Post, 206
Corry & Columbus St. Ry., 302
Cortland County Tr. Co., 317
Cortland & Homer Tr. Co., 317
Covington & South Western RR, 41
Cripple Creek District Ry., *see* Colorado Springs & Cripple Creek District Ry.
Cumberland County Power & Lt. Co., 148
Cumberland Ry., *298*
Cumberland Tr. Co., 307–8
Cumberland Valley RR (elec. line), 295
Cumberland & Westernport Elec. Ry., 204, 328
Cushing & Oil Fields, 38, 376

"Dan Patch Line," 358
Davenport & Muscatine Ry., 359
Dayton Covington & Piqua Tr. Co., 54, 71, 75, 91, 92, 109, 121, 198, *261*
Dayton & Muncie Tr. Co., 31, 33, 265, 280, 281
Dayton & Northern, 29, 33, 265
Dayton Springfield & Urbana Ry., 13, 28–29, 265
Dayton Springfield & Xenia Southern Ry., *see* Dayton & Xenia Transit Co.
Dayton Spring Valley & Wilmington Transit Co., 259
Dayton & Troy Elec. Ry., 26, 31, 48, 54, 57, 67, 68, 78, 80, 83, 95, 99, 122, 184, 243, 259, *260–61*, 296
Dayton & Western Tr. Co., 20, 27, 29, 99, 100, 104, 210, *259*, 265, 266, 269, 279, 283–84
Dayton & Xenia Transit Co. (D&X Rapid Transit), 17, 22, 34–35, 91, 93, *259–60*, 373
Deadwood Central RR, 169, 207, *359*
De Kalb-Sycamore & Interurban Tr. Co., 203, *342*
Delaware & Magnetic Springs Ry., 270
Denison & Sherman Ry., 376
Des Moines & Central Iowa RR (Inter-Urban Ry.), 33, 77, 85, 104, 106, 199, 210, 315, 363, *364–65*, 424
Denver & Intermountain RR, 51, 136, 137, 199, 246, *380*
Denver & Interurban RR, 58, 59, 62, 196, 212, 214, *380–81*
Denver & Northwestern, 380
Denver & South Platte Ry., 380
Detroit Almont & Northern Ry., 287
Detroit Flint & Saginaw Ry., 289
Detroit Jackson & Chicago Ry., 210, 249, 288
Detroit Lake Orion & Flint Ry., 287
Detroit Lake Shore & Mount Clemens Ry., 287
Detroit Monroe & Toledo Short Line, 31, 35, 48, 185, 210, 249, 287
Detroit & Northwestern Ry., 287

Detroit Plymouth & Northville Ry., 287
Detroit & Pontiac Ry., 287
Detroit Rochester Romeo & Lake Orion Ry., 287
Detroit & Toledo Shore Line, 11, 27–28, 38
Detroit United Ry., 11, 15, 16, 25, 27–28, 46, 48, 56, 68, 79, 86, 95, 100, 107, 123, 125, 126–27, 129, 130, 134, 140, 142, 160, 181, 192, 199, 212, 214, *287–88*, 415
Detroit Ypsilanti Ann Arbor & Jackson Ry., 48, 93, 287
Detroit Ypsilanti & Ann Arbor Ry., 287
Dixon Rock Falls & Southeastern, 344
Dover Somersworth & Rochester St. Ry., 325
Dunkirk & Fredonia RR, 309
Durango Ry. & Realty Co., 382

East Bay St. Ry., 177
Eastern Massachusetts St. Ry., 133
Eastern Michigan–Toledo RR, 99, 218, 238, 266, 288; *see also* Detroit Monroe & Toledo Short Line
Eastern Michigan Rys., 218, 238, 241, 288; *see also* Detroit United Ry.
Eastern New York RR, 318
Eastern New York Utilities Co., 169, 317
Eastern Ohio Tr. Co., 10, 34, 35, 36, 43, 55, 71, 100, 116, 120, 122, 196, 212, *272*, 274
Eastern Pennsylvania Ry., 218, 298
Eastern Texas Elec. Co., 99, 165, 202, *379*
Eastern Wisconsin Elec. Co., 356
East Liverpool & Wellsville St. Ry., 270
East Lorain St. Ry., 267
Easton & Washington Tr. Co., 301, 307
East Penn Tr. Co., 167
East St. Louis Columbia & Waterloo Ry., *351*
East St. Louis & Suburban Ry., 24, 201, 347, *349–51*
East Side Ry. Co., 9, 10, 394
East Troy, Village of, 180, 354–56
Edgerton Tramways, 421
Emigration Canyon RR, 249, *387*
Electric Ry. & Ice Co., 373
Electric Short Line Ry., 358
Elgin Aurora & Southern, 341
Elgin & Belvidere Elec. Ry., 55, 217, 343
Elgin Belvidere & Rockford, 343
Elmira Corning & Waverly Ry., 206, 317
Elmira & Seneca Lake Tr. Co., 317–18
El Reno Interurban Ry. Co., 373
Elwood & Alexandria Ry., 280, 281
Empire State RR, 314
Empire State Rys., 206, 312
Empire United Rys., 142, *313–15*
Ephrata & Lebanon Tr. Co., *298*
Erie Cambridge Union & Corry Tr. Co., 293
Erie RR (Mt. Morris elec. line), 25, 58, 62, 205, *315*
Erie Southern Ry., 293
Erie Tr. Co., 293
Escanaba Tr. Co., 290
Evansville & Eastern Elec. Ry., 17, 285
Evansville Henderson & Owensboro Ry., 286
Evansville & Mount Vernon Elec. Ry., 285
Evansville & Ohio Valley Ry., 115, *285–86*
Evansville & Princeton Tr. Co., 44, 285
Evansville Princeton & Vincennes Interurban Ry., 285
Evansville Rys., 49, 115, 285–86
Evansville & Southern Indiana Tr. Co., 285

Evansville Suburban & Newburgh Ry., 91, 198, 285, *286*
Exeter Hampton & Amesbury St. Ry., 168, 325

Fairmont & Clarksburg Elec. RR, 303
Felicity & Bethel, 255
Fidalgo City & Anacortes Ry., 9, 10, 248–49, *393*
Findlay Forest & Marion Ry., 20
Findlay & Marion Elec. Ry., 43
Fonda Johnstown & Gloversville RR, 47, 82, 218, 238, *316*, 317, 383, 424
Fort Dodge Des Moines & Southern Ry., 24, 33, 49, 63, 73, 77, 85, 92, 113, 121, 139, 144, 214, 220, 246, *363–64*
Fort Wayne & Decatur Tr. Co., 58, 59, 61, 62, 91, 93, *277–78*, 282
Fort Wayne–Lima RR, *see* Fort Wayne Van Wert & Lima Tr. Co.
Fort Wayne & Northern Indiana Tr. Co., 280
Fort Wayne & Northwestern Ry., 59, 62, 91, 201, 263, 280, *281–82*
Fort Wayne & Springfield, *see* Fort Wayne & Decatur Tr. Co.
Fort Wayne Van Wert & Lima Tr. Co., 31, 32, 47, 78, 92, 103, 218, 250, *264–65*, 283, 373
Fort Wayne & Wabash Valley Tr. Co., 22, 26, 32, 50, 73, 88–90, 97, 104, 123, *280*, 282
Fort Worth Southern Tr. Co., 377
Fostoria Arcadia & Findlay Ry., 99, 261
Fostoria & Fremont Rys., 32, 98, 261, *262–63*
Fox & Illinois Union Ry., *342*
Fox River Valley Elec. Ry., 356
Frankfort & Versailles Tr. Co., 291
Fresno Interurban, 413
Fruit Growers Refrigeration & Power Co., 352

Galesburg & Kewaunee, 345
Galesburg Ry. & Lt. Co., 352
Galesburg & Western, 345
Gallipolis & Northern Tr. Co., *271*
Gallipolis & Point Pleasant Ry., 271
Gallipolis St. Ry. Co., 271
Galt & Preston, 417
Galt Preston & Hespeler, 417
Galveston–Houston Elec. Ry., 99, 202, 242, 250, *378*
Gary Connecting Ry., 40
Gary & Interurban, 365
Gary Rys., 40, 41, 107, 176, 201, *275–76*
Geneva & Auburn Ry., 316
Geneva Seneca Falls & Auburn RR, *316*
Geneva Waterloo Seneca Falls & Cayuga Lake Tr. Co., 316
Georgia Ry. & Power Co., 81, 136, 203, *333*, 345
Girard Coal Belt Elec. Ry., 369
Glendale & Montrose Ry., 155, 169, 413
Grafton & Upton RR, *322*
Grand Rapids Grand Haven & Muskegon Ry., 115, 162, 214, *289*, 428
Grand Rapids Holland & Chicago Ry., 49, 56, 113, 115, 143, 203, 214, *289–90*
Grand Rapids Holland & Lake Michigan Rapid Ry., 289
Grand River Ry., 79, 220, 414, *417*
Grand River Valley RR, 156, 170, 191, 204, 210, 214, 241, 246, *382*

Grand Valley Ry., 184, 414, *418*
Gray's Harbor Ry. & Lt. Co., 204, *393*
Green Bay Tr. Co., 357
Greenbush & Nassau Elec. Ry., 317
Greenfield & Montague, 180
Greenville Spartanburg & Anderson, 331
Groton & Stonington Ry., 322, 323
Gulfport & Mississippi Coast Tr. Co., 203, *333–34*

Hagerstown & Boonesboro, 327
Hagerstown & Frederick Ry. (Potomac Edison Co.), 114, 148, 199, 202, 219, 232, 244, 297, 298, 300, 326, *327–28*
Hamburg Ry., 309, 311
Hamilton & Dundas St. Ry., *415*
Hamilton Grimsby & Beamsville Elec. Ry., 185, 249, 414, *415*
Hamilton Radial Elec. Ry., *415*
Hanover & McSherrystown, 302
Harrisburg Rys., 297
Hartford & Springfield St. Ry., 323, 326
Hershey Cuban Ry., 223n
Hershey Transit, 198, *296–97*, 298
Hocking–Sunday Creek Tr. Co., 255, *271–72*
Holland & Lake Michigan Ry., 290
Houghton County Tr. Co., 202, 205, *290*
Houston North Shore Ry., 207, 213, 219, 221, 236, 351, 376, *378–79*
Hudson St. Ry., 317
Hudson Valley Ry., 126, 140, 154n, 160, 206, 212, 214, *316–17*
Hull Elec. Co., *420*
Hummelstown & Campbellstown St. Ry., 297
Huntington Columbia City & Northern Tr. Co., 34
Hutchinson Interurban, 38, 372
Hutchinson & Northern, 372

Idaho Tr. Co., 387
Illinois Central Elec. Ry., 11, 198, *346*
Illinois Terminal RR, *see* Illinois Traction Co.
Illinois Traction Co., 27, 33, 35, 36, 38, 46, 48, 49, 59, 62, 67, 68, 69, 72, 73, 75, 77, 79, 81, 82–83, 84, 85, 86, 87, 88, 91, 92, 98, 108, 110, 113, 114, 100–101, 102, 121, 124, 127, 130, 133, 136, 137, 139, 144–46, 147, 154, 162, 163, 165, 174, 179, 183, 198–99, 201, 205, 206, 219, 220, 232, 246, 248, 335, 339, *346–49*, 424, 425
Illinois Valley Tr. Co., 339
Indiana Columbus & Eastern Tr. Co., 29, 32, 33, 115, 138, 196, 212, 232, 236–37, 259, *265*, 266
Indiana County St. Ry., 302
Indiana Elec. Ry., *276*
Indiana Northern Tr. Co., 33, 280, 281
Indianapolis & Cincinnati Tr. Co. (Indianapolis & Southeastern), 26, 35, 49, 58, 59, 62, 67, 80, 81, 107, 123–24, 196, 212, 238, 273, 283, *284–85*, 286, 354
Indianapolis Coal Tr. Co., 23, 278
Indianapolis Columbus & Southern Tr. Co., 279
Indianapolis Crawfordsville & Danville Elec. Ry., 278
Indianapolis Crawfordsville & Western Tr. Co., 18, 25, 35, 278
Indianapolis & Eastern Ry., 278
Indianapolis Greenwood & Franklin RR, 279

Index of Interurbans

Indianapolis & Louisville Tr. Co., 33, 62–63, 163, 184, 279
Indianapolis & Martinsville Rapid Transit Co., 278
Indianapolis Martinsville & Southern RR, 20
Indianapolis New Castle & Eastern Tr. Co., 281
Indianapolis New Castle & Toledo Elec. Ry., 281
Indianapolis & Northwestern Tr. Co., 18, 278
Indianapolis & Plainfield Elec. RR, 278
Indianapolis Shelbyville & Southeastern Tr. Co., 284
Indianapolis & Southeastern RR, *see* Indianapolis & Cincinnati
Indianapolis Traction & Terminal Co., 69
Indianapolis & Western Ry., 278
Indiana RR System, 72, 77, 81, 82, 84, 85, 90, 100, 102, 108, 111–12, 120–21, 134, 146, 147, 156–57, 169, 197, 201, 218, 219, 232, 241, 242, 243, 244, 259, 265, 277, 279, 280, 281, 282, *283–84*, 296, 324n, 360
Indiana Ry. Co., 276
Indiana Rys. & Lt. Co., 282
Indiana Service Corp., 70, 96, 199, 201, 218, 232, 265, 278, 280, 282, 283, 284; *see also* Fort Wayne & Wabash Valley Tr. Co.
Inland Empire RR, 59, 61, 62, 71, 103, 119, 121, 212, 235, 250, 389; *see also* Spokane Coeur d'Alene & Palouse Ry.
Inter-City Rapid Transit, 81, 273, 285
International Ry., 83, 99, 113, 177, 185, 199, 211–12, *313*
Interstate Public Service Co., 49, 54, 56, 63, 78, 90, 94, 97, 100, 101–2, 115, 129, 131, 132, 137–38, 200, 201, 210, 232, 249, 277, *279–80*, 283
Interurban Elec. Ry. (SP RR), 405
Inter-Urban Ry. (Iowa), *see* Des Moines & Central Iowa RR
Inter-Urban Ry. (Michigan), 290
Interurban Ry. & Terminal Co., 52, 68, 212, 258
Iola Elec. Ry., *371*
Iowa & Illinois Ry., 144, 359
Iowa Southern Utilities, 199
Ithaca Auburn & Lansing (Ithaca–Auburn Short Line), 38, *313*

Jackson & Battle Creek Tr. Co., 289
Jackson Consolidated Tr. Co., 289
Jamestown Westfield & Northwestern Ry., 14, 24, 148, 155–56, 170, *311*
Jefferson County Tr. Co., 300
Jersey Central Tr. Co., 213, 309
Johnstown Gloversville & Kingstown Horse RR, 316
Johnstown & Somerset Ry., *301*
Joliet & Eastern Tr. Co., 213, *341*
Joliet Plainfield & Aurora RR, *339–41*
Joliet & Southern, 339, *341*
Joplin & Pittsburg Ry., 258, 368, *369*, 370

Kalamazoo Lake Shore & Chicago Tr. Co., 18, 289
Kanauga & Gallipolis Tr. Co., 271
Kanauga Tr. Co., 271
Kankakee & Urbana Tr. Co., 38, 81, 183, 198, 210, 250–51, *349*
Kansas City Clay County & St. Joseph, 15, 143, 218, *366*
Kansas City Kaw Valley & Western Ry. (KC-KV RR), 37, 107, 157, *367–68*
Kansas City Lawrence & Topeka Elec. RR, 368
Kansas City Leavenworth & Western Ry. (KC-L Ry.), 126, *368*
Kansas City Merriam & Shawnee, 368
Kansas City & Olathe, 368
Kansas City Ozarks & Southern, 376
Kansas City & Topeka, 368
Kansas City–Western, *see* Kansas City Leavenworth & Western Ry.
Kansas & Oklahoma, 371
Kaydeross RR, 119, 164, 170, 198, *318*
Kesseville Ausable Chasm & Lake Champlain RR, *318*, 428
Kenosha Motor Coach Lines, 354
Kensington Elec. Ry., 330
Kentucky Tr. & Terminal Co., 80, 200, 232, *291–93*, 309
Keokuk Elec. Co., 24, 201, *345*
Kewaunee & Galva Ry., 344
Key System, 405–6; *see also* General Index
Kinderhook & Hudson Ry., 317
Knox County Elec., 120
Kokomo Frankfort & Western Tr. Co., 282
Kokomo Marion & Western Tr. Co., 73, 282

Lackawanna & Wyoming Valley RR, 15–16, 47, 48, 93–94, 99, 154n, 215, *293–94*, 428
Lafayette & Indianapolis Rapid Transit Co., 20
Lake Erie Bowling Green & Napoleon Ry., 14, 17, 22, 74, 167–68, 212, 250, *263*, 268, 362
Lake Erie & Northern Ry., 220, 244, 414, *417*
Lake Shore Elec. Ry., 10–11, 12, 20, 25, 28, 37, 46, 48, 49, 55, 67, 69, 71, 73, 74, 75, 79, 81, 86, 88, 90, 91, 92, 93, 96, 98–99, 103, 104, 112, 115, 122, 129, 130, 135, 178, 189, 192, 197, 212, 214, 219, 237, 238, 241, 242, 249, 261, 262–63, *267–68*, 269, 288, 296, 365, 427
Lakeside Napoleon & Western, 17
Lakeview Tr. Co., 335
Lancaster Ephrata & Lebanon Ry., 298
Lancaster & York Furnace St. Ry., 302
Lansing & Jackson Ry. Co., 289
Lansing St. Johns & St. Louis Ry., 428
Lansing & Suburban Tr. Co., 289
Las Vegas Ry. & Power Co., 426
Lebanon & Franklin Tr. Co., 212, *258–59*
Lebanon–Thorntown Tr. Co., 40, *286*
Lebanon Valley, 204
Lee County Central Elec. Ry., 38, 212, 233, *344*
Lehigh Tr. Co., 167, 294
Lehigh Valley Transit, 71, 79, 81, 82, 114, 203, 219, 220, *296*, 301
Levis County Tramways, 422
Lewisburg Milton & Watsontown Passenger Ry., 302
Lewisburg & Ronceverte Ry., 305
Lewiston Augusta & Waterville St. Ry., 126, 148, *323*
Lewiston Brunswick & Bath St. Ry., 323
Lewiston–Clarkston Transit Co., *388*
Lewiston & Reedsville, 200
Lewiston & Youngstown Frontier Ry., 169, *313*, 319
Lexington & Interurban Rys., 291

Index of Interurbans

Lima–Honeoye Elec. Lt. & RR Co., *318*
"Lima Route," 31, 32, 99, 122, 130, 260–63
Lima & Toledo Tr. Co. (L-T RR), 18, 29, 32, 212, 232, 262, 264, 266
Lockport & Olcott Ry., 313
Logan Rapid Transit Co., 385
London & Lake Erie Ry. & Transportation Co., 212, 414, *417*
London & Port Stanley Ry., 83, 181, 244, 414, *417*
Lorain & Cleveland Elec. Ry., 10, 267
Los Angeles Interurban Ry., 406
Los Angeles Metropolitan Transit Authority, 171, 223, 409
Los Angeles Pacific, 406, 412
Los Angeles & Redondo, 406
Los Angeles & San Diego, 413
Louisville & Eastern RR, 291
Louisville & Interurban RR, 33, 127, 199, 279, *291*
Louisville & Northern Ry. & Lighting Co., 279
Louisville & Southern Indiana Tr. Co., 279

Mahoning & Shenango Ry. & Lt. Co., 25, 159, 272, *274*; see also Penn-Ohio Public Service Co.
Manchester & Derry St. Ry., 325
Manchester & Nashua St. Ry., 200, 325
Manhattan City & Interurban Ry., *373*
Manitowoc & Northern Tr. Co., 151, *357*
Manitowoc & Two Rivers, 357
Mansfield Public Utility & Service Co., 268
Mansfield Ry. Lt. & Power Co., *268*
Manx Elec. Ry., 426
Marion Bluffton & Eastern Tr. Co. (M&B Tr. Co.), 147–48, 280, *282*, 283
Marion Elec. St. Ry., 280, 281
Market St. Ry., 204, 406
Mason City & Clear Lake RR, 25, 144, 185, 204, *362–63*
Massachusetts Northeastern, 204
Mattoon City Ry. 351
Maumee Valley Rys. & Lt. Co., 262
Meadville & Cambridge Springs St. Ry., 293
Meadville Tr. Co., 293
Memphis & Lakeview Tr. Co., *335*
Mesaba Elec. Ry., 214, *358*
Metropolitan Coach Co., 170, 221, 409
Mexico Investment & Construction Co., *366*
Miami & Erie Canal, towing-railway on, 13, 28, 53
Miamisburg & Germantown Tr. Co., 265
Miami Valley Ry., 260
Michigan Elec. Ry., *see* Michigan United Ry.
Michigan RR, *see* Michigan United Ry.
Michigan Ry., *see* Michigan United Ry.
Michigan Tr. Co., 46, 289
Michigan United Ry., 24, 35, 37, 49, 65, 127, 129, 131, 153, 162, 196, 203, 210, 214, 234, 237, 241, *389*, 429
Middlesex & Boston St. Ry., 159
Middletown & Goshen Tr. Co., 318
Midland Power & Tr. Co., 272
Milford & Uxbridge St. Ry., 222
Millville Tr. Co., 307
Milwaukee Elec. Ry. & Lt. Co., The (TMER & Transport Co.), 33, 42, 46, 48–49, 53, 58, 59, 61, 62, 71, 75, 81, 83, 88, 100, 102, 114, 159, 176, 179, 180, 199, 201, 219, 220, 231, 232, 233, 285, *353–57*; failure to reach all destinations, 35
Milwaukee Northern, 18, 353–54
Milwaukee Rapid Transit & Speedrail Co., 243, 355
Milwaukee–Wauwatosa Elec. Ry., 353
Minneapolis Anoka & Cuyuna Range RR, 155, *357–58*
Minneapolis & Northern, 357
Minneapolis St. Paul Rochester & Dubuque Elec. Tr. Co., 358
Minnesota Northwestern, 358
Minster & Loramie Ry., 261
Mississippi Valley Interurban Ry., 346
Missouri & Kansas Interurban Ry., *367*
Modesto & Empire Tr. Co., 413
Monmouth City Elec. Co., 309
Monongahela Power & Ry Co., 303
Monongahela Valley Tr. Co., 303
Monongahela West Penn Public Service Co., 148, 157, 179, 202, 218, 300, *303–4*
Montreal & Southern Counties Ry., 181, *420*
Morgantown & Dunkard Valley RR, 306
Morgantown–Wheeling Ry., 306
Morris County Tr. Co., 189, 309
Mount Hood Ry. & Power Co., 394
Mount McKay & Kakabeka Falls, 422
Mount Mansfield Elec. RR, 324
Muncie Hartford & Fort Wayne Ry., 33, 280, 281
Muncie & Portland Tr. Co., 18, 44, 183, 281
Murphysboro & Southern Illinois Ry., *352*
Muskingum Tr. Co., 303
Muskogee Elec. Tr. Co. *375*

Nashville–Franklin Ry., 81, 191, 244, 285, *334–35*
Nashville–Gallatin Interurban Ry., *334*
Nashville Interurban Ry., 287, 334, 338
National City & Otay, 413
Nelsonville–Athens Elec. Ry., 272
Nevada County Tr. Co., *405*
Newark & Granville St. Ry., 9, 21, 56, 71, 265
New Haven & Shore Line Ry., 323
New Jersey Interurban Co., 307
New Jersey & Pennsylvania Tr. Co., *297–98*
New Jersey Short Line RR, 306
New London & East Lyme St. Ry., 322
New Paltz Highland & Poughkeepsie Tr. Co., 22, 46, *318*
New Paltz & Walkill Valley RR, 318
New Westminster & Vancouver Tramways, 421
New York & Stamford, 206
New York State Rys., 121, 175, 204, *311–12*
Niagara Falls & Lewiston RR, 319
Niagara Falls Park & River Ry., 319, *419–20*
Niagara Gorge Ry., 313, *319*
Niagara St. Catharines & Toronto Ry., 115, 181, 208, 221, 414, *419*
Nipissing Central Ry., 181, *420*
Northampton–Easton & Washington Tr. Co., 307
Northampton Tr. Co., *301*, 307, 371
North Branch Transit Co., 302
North Coast Lines, 202, 244, 391–92
Northeast Oklahoma Ry., 24, 155, 165, 198, 213, 214, 236, 258, 368, *369–70*
Northern Cambria St. Ry., 295, *299*
Northern Elec. Ry. (Cal.), 30–31, 35, 74,

115, 184, 196, 398; *see also* Sacramento Northern Ry.
Northern Elec. St. Ry. (Pa.), 295
Northern Illinois Elec. Ry., 344; *see also* Lee County Central Elec. Ry.
Northern Indiana Power Co., 125, 199, 201, 232, *282*, 283
Northern Indiana Ry., 27, 81, 86, 107, 115, 128, 218, *276*, 282
Northern Massachusetts, 180
Northern Ohio Tr. & Lt. Co., 9, 10, 11, 25, 26, 28, 43, 47, 49, 51, 75, 77, 81, 84, 86, 93, 96, 107, 122, 129–30, 131, 189, 199, 203, 218, 241, *273*
Northern States Power Co., 168, *357*
Northern Texas Tr. Co., 69, 202, 218, *377*
North Jersey Rapid Transit Co., *307*
North Kankakee Elec. Lt. & Ry Co., 352
North Shore Line, *see* Chicago North Shore & Milwaukee RR
Northwestern Electric Service Co. of Pennsylvania, 293
Northwestern Ohio Ry. & Power Co., 267
Northwestern Pacific RR (elec. lines), 405
Northwestern Pennsylvania, 131, 214, *293*
Norwalk & Shelby RR, 268
Norwich & Westerly Ry., 45, 322, 323

Oakland Antioch & Eastern (O&A), 21, 37, 47, 50, 63, 83, 84, 97–98, 167, 398–400; *see also* Sacramento Northern Ry.
Oakland San Leandro & Haywards Elec. Ry., 134, 405
Oakland Tr. Co., 405
Ocean Shore RR, 38, 413
Ogden Logan & Idaho, 210, 385
Ogden Rapid Transit, *386*
Ohio Central Tr. Co., 23, 26, 269
Ohio Elec. Ry., 18, 31–32, 35, 37, 47, 73, 81, 94, 95, 99, 102, 122, 141, 197, 198, 258, 259, 262, 263, 264, *265–66*
Ohio Midland Lt. & Power Co., 271
Ohio Public Service Co., 72, 130, 179, 267, 268
Ohio River Elec. Ry. & Power Co., *271*
Ohio Service Co., 203, 272
Ohio & Southern Tr. Co., *275*
Ohio Tr. Co., *258,* 424
Ohio Valley Elec. Ry., 203, 204–5, *306*
Oklahoma Kansas & Missouri Inter-Urban Ry., 369–70
Oklahoma Ry., 199, 210, 219, 220, 265, *373–74*
Oklahoma Union Ry., 374
Olean Bradford & Salamanca Ry., 24, 189, 198, 214, *311*
Olean Rock City & Bradford Elec. St. Ry., 311
Olean St. Ry., 311
Oley Valley Ry., 204, 302
Omaha Lincoln & Beatrice, 38, 365
Omaha & Lincoln Ry. & Lt. Co., 365
Omaha & Southern Interurban Ry., 365
Oneida Ry., 25, 42, 57, 63, 121, 205, 206, *312,* 428
Oneonta Cooperstown & Richfield Springs Ry., 315
Oneonta & Mohawk Valley Ry., 315
Ontario West Shore Ry., 41, 422
Orange County Tr. Co., *318*

Oregon Elec. Ry., 24, 63, 85, 100, 102, 113, 119, 151, 154, 165, 196, 207, 210, 212, 218, 225, 246, 250, 364, 395, *396–97*
Oregon Interurban, 376
Oregon Tr. Co., 397
Oregon Water Power & RR Co., 394
Orleans–Kenner Elec. Ry., *334*
Oskaloosa–Buxton Elec. Ry., *363*
Otsego & Herkimer RR, 315

Pacific Coast Ry., *405*
Pacific Elec. Ry., 49, 52, 56, 63, 69, 71, 75, 77, 85, 86, 87, 100, 114, 121, 133, 142, 155, 157, 166, 169, 170, 173, 180, 210, 212, 214, 219, 221, 235, 246, 248, 250, 398, *406–13*
Pacific Northwest Tr. Co., 35, 199, 202, 231, 244, *391–92*; *see also* North Coast Lines
Painesville Fairport & Richmond St. Ry., 274
Pan Handle Tr. Co., 302–3
Parkersburg & Marietta Interurban Ry., 303
Parkersburg & Ohio Valley Elec. Ry., *305*
Pasadena & Los Angeles, 406
Paul Smith's Elec. RR, 56, 60, *318*
Pawcatuck Valley Ry., 322
Peninsular Ry., 71, 156, 196, 207, 212, 218, 241, 244, *404,* 406
Pennobscot Central Ry., 323
Penn-Ohio Public Service Co., 129, 130, 131, 151, 158, 160, 203, 231, 274; *see also* Mahoning & Shenango Ry.
Pennsylvania & Maryland St. Ry., *300–301*
Pennsylvania–New Jersey Ry., 167, 298
Pennsylvania–Ohio Elec. Co., 274
Pennsylvania & Ohio Elec. Ry., 131, 213, *274*
Pennsylvania RR (Cumberland Valley elec. lines), 56, *295*
Pennsylvania Tr. Co., 296
Penn Yan Keuka Park & Branchport Ry., *317*
Penn Yan & Lake Shore Ry., 317
Peoples' Tr. Co., 352
Peoria & Pekin Terminal Co., *345–46*
PEPCO, *see* Portland Trac. Co.
Petaluma & Santa Rosa RR, 23, 164, 173, 179, 198, 207, 210, 214, 218, 248, *402–3,* 424
Philadelphia & Bristol Passenger Ry., 23
Philadelphia & Easton Elec. Ry., 51, 120, *297*
Philadelphia Suburban Transportation Co., 65, *299,* 424
Philadelphia & West Chester Ry., 299
Philadelphia & Western RR, 82, 218, 223, 296, *299,* 428
Phoenix Ry., 389
Pictou County Elec. Co., *421*
Piedmont & Northern Ry., 35, 84, 107–8, 148, 155, 156, 165, 214, 219, 246, 249, *331–33*
Piedmont Ry. & Elec. Co., 333
Piedmont Tr. Co., 331
Pittsburg County Ry., 200, 220, *374–75*
Pittsburgh & Butler St. Ry., 62, 295
Pittsburgh Harmony Butler & New Castle Ry., 33, 47, 107, 130, 136, 140, 178, 218, 232, *295*
Pittsburgh Mars & Butler Ry., 295
Pittsburgh Rys., 24, 87, 150, 199, 202, 204, *299,* 305
Pittsfield & Lenox St. Ry., 45
Plymouth & Shelby Tr. Co., 268
Portland & Brunswick St. Ry., 324
Portland Elec. Power Co., *see* Portland Tr. Co.

Portland Eugene & Eastern (SP RR), 25, 63, 71, 205, 214, 229, *395–96*
Portland Gray & Lewiston RR, 319
Portland–Lewiston Interurban RR, 19, 77, 78, 148, 200, 218, 319–20
Portland RR, 200, 323, 324
Portland Ry. Lt. & Power Co., 394
Portland Tr. Co., Portland Ry. & Terminal Div. (Portland Elec. Power Co.), 151, 171, 179, 199, 205, 221, 230, 244, 248, 317, *394–95, 433*
Portsmouth Elec. Ry., 325
Portsmouth Public Service Co., 271
Portsmouth St. RR & Lt. Co., 210, 271
Potomac Edison Co., see Hagerstown & Frederick Ry.
Pottstown & Reading St. Ry., 302
Preston & Berlin, 417
Princeton Power Co., 305
Providence & Danielson St. Ry., 322, 326
Public Service Co. of Evansville, 285
Public Service Co. of Indiana, 280, 283
Public Service Corp. of New Jersey, 46, 52, 94, 218, *306–7*
Puget Sound Elec. Ry., 99, 160, 198, 202, *392–93, 429*

Quebec Ry. Lt. & Power Co., 181, 221, *420*

Rapid Railway (Mich.), 54, 176–77, 287; see also Detroit United
Rapid Railway (Ohio), 258
Reading Tr. Co., 163, 199, 204, *302*
Rhode Island Co., 206, 322, *326*
Richfield Springs Ry., 315
Richland Public Service Co., 268
Richmond–Ashland Ry., 330–31
Richmond & Chesapeake Bay Ry., 62, 168, *330–31*
Richmond & Petersburg Elec. Ry., *330*
Richmond & Rappahannock, 331
Richmond St. & Interurban Ry., 278
Richwood & Magnetic Springs Ry., 270
Rio Grande Valley Tr. Co., *379–80*
Roby & Northern RR, 198, 200, *379*
Rochester & Eastern Rapid Ry., 206, *312*
Rochester Lockport & Buffalo RR, 313
Rochester & Sodus Bay Ry., 46, 206, *311–12*
Rochester Syracuse & Eastern RR (R&S RR), 49, 164, *314*
Rockford Beloit & Janesville, 343
Rockford & Freeport, 343
Rockford & Interurban Ry., 83, 134, 203, *343–44*, 353, 373
Rock Island Southern RR, 61, 62, 85, 198, *345*
Rockland South Thomaston & St. George, 168
Rockland Thomaston & Camden St. Ry., 324
Rutland Ry. Lt. & Power Co., 324

Sacramento Northern Ry., 63–64, 67, 71, 74, 75, 78, 81, 86, 93, 94, 100, 102, 115, 117, 137, 139, 153–54, 165, 170, 173, 177, 179, 207, 213, 219, 221, 225, 232, 244, 248, *398–400, 429*
Sacramento Valley West Side Elec. Ry., 167, 212. *400–401*
Saginaw–Bay City Ry., *290*
Saginaw & Flint Ry., 289
Saginaw Transit Co., 290
Saginaw Valley Tr. Co., 290

St. Albans & Swanton Tr. Co., 324
St. Francois County RR, *366*
St. Joseph & Savanna Elec. Ry., 204, *366–67*
St. Joseph Valley Tr. Co. and Ry., 19, 38, 44, 68, 212, 263, *276*
St. Louis & Alton, 347, 350
St. Louis & Belleville Elec., 350–51
St. Louis St. Charles & Western, 366
St. Paul Southern Ry., *235*
St. Tammany & New Orleans Ry. & Ferry Co., 426
Salem & Pennsgrove Tr. Co., 309
Salisbury & Spencer, 204
Salt Lake Garfield & Western RR, 220, 221, *386*
Salt Lake & Utah RR, 22, 37, 71, 85, 91, 93, 117, 125, 169, 197, 210, 220, 232, 248, *384–85*
San Diego Elec. Ry., 413
San Diego Southeastern, 413
San Diego Southern, 413
Sandpoint & Interurban Ry., 249, *388*
Sand Springs Ry., 87, 191, 246, 255, 341, *374*
Sandusky & Interurban Elec. Ry., 10, 267
Sandusky Milan & Norwalk Elec. Ry., 9, 10, 71, 267
Sandusky Norwalk & Mansfield Elec. Ry., 14, 18, 31, *268*
Sandusky Norwalk & Southern, 112
Sandwich Windsor & Amherstburg Ry., 11, 181, 288, *415*
San Francisco Napa & Calistoga, 61–62, 114, 121, 173, 210, 218, 238, 244, 247, 249, *403–4*
San Francisco–Sacramento RR, 398
San Francisco Vallejo & Napa Valley, 403
San Jose & Los Gatos, 404
Sapulpa & Interurban, *374*
Schenectady Ry., 126, 204, 206, *316*, 373
Schuylkill Ry., 302
Schuylkill Valley Tr. Co., 204, 302
Scioto Valley Tr. Co., 11, 27, 28, 47, 48, 49, 50, 54, 56, 57, 68, 77, 93, 95, 103, 104, 175, 217, 242, 255, *271*, 272, 428
Scotts Run Ry., 306
Scranton & Binghamton Tr. Co., 24, *295–96*
Scranton Montrose & Binghamton, 296
Scranton Rys., 200. 294, 302
Seattle & Rainier Valley, 393
Seattle Renton & Southern Ry., 79, *393*
Seattle–Tacoma Interurban Ry., 392
Shamokin & Edgewood Elec. Ry., 302
Shamokin & Mount Carmel Transit Co., 302
Sharon & New Castle, 95
Shawnee–Tecumseh Tr. Co., *375*
Sheboygan Lt. Power & Ry. Co., 356
Sheridan Ry. & Lt. Co., 38, 383
Shore Line Elec. Ry., 60, 81, 212, 249, *322–23*, 362
Sistersville & New Martinsville Tr. Co., 305
Slate Belt Elec. St. Ry., 301
South Bend Northern Ry., 276
Southeastern Ohio Ry., 267
Southeast Ohio Ry. & Lt. Co., *266–67*
Southern Cambria Ry., 88, 243, *295*
Southern Illinois Power Co., 352
Southern Illinois Ry. & Power Co., 198, 200, 351, *352*
Southern Indiana Ry., 284
Southern Indiana Gas & Elec. Co., *285*
Southern Indiana Power Co., 199, 203

Index of Interurbans

Southern Iowa Ry., 218, *363*
Southern Michigan Ry., 276
Southern New York Ry., 42, 104, 106, 148, 204, 212, 241, 242, *315*, 360
Southern Ohio Public Service Co., 133, 214, 265
Southern Ohio Tr. Co., 265
Southern Oregon Tr. Co., 38, *397*
Southern Pacific RR (Oregon elec. lines), *see* Portland Eugene & Eastern
Southern Pennsylvania Tr. Co., 174
Southern Tr. Co., 376
South Shore Line, *see* Chicago South Shore & South Bend RR
Southwestern Interurban Ry., 184, *373*
Southwestern Tr. Co. (La.), *334*
South-Western Tr. Co. (Ont.), *417*
Southwestern Tr. Co. (Tex.), *379*
Southwest Missouri Elec. Ry., 241, 242, 249, *368–69*, 370
Spokane Coeur d'Alene & Palouse Ry., 77, 154, 207, 246, 387, *389–90*; *see also* Inland Empire
Spokane & Eastern, 389
Spokane & Inland Empire, *see* Inland Empire RR
Springfield Clear Lake & Rochester Ry., 164, *346*
Springfield Elec. Ry. (Vt.), 320
Springfield South Charleston Washington Court House & Chillicothe Tr. Co., 21, 260
Springfield St. RR (Mass.), 136, 206
Springfield Suburban RR (Ohio), 147, 260
Springfield Suburban Ry. (Ill.), 346
Springfield Terminal Ry. (Vt.), 69, 87, 148, 206, *320*, 325
Springfield Terminal Ry. & Power Co. (Ohio), 260
Springfield Troy & Piqua Ry., 114, 147, 213, *260*
Springfield & Washington Ry., 185, 213, *260*
Springfield & Xenia Ry., 28, 241, *259*
Stark Elec. RR, 48, 50, 55, 68, 81, 83, 86, 93, 107, 130, 136, 176, 242, 250, 270, *273–74*
Sterling Dixon & Eastern, 200, *344*
Steubenville East Liverpool & Beaver Valley Tr. Co., *270–71*
Steubenville Wellsburg & Wierton Ry., 202, 303
Steubenville & Wheeling Tr. Co., 303
Stockton Terminal & Eastern, 413
Stroudsburg Tr. Co., 301
Stroudsburg Water Gap & Portland Ry., 301
Suburban Tr. Co., 258
Sudbury & Copper Cliffs Suburban Elec. Ry., *422*
Syracuse Lake Shore & Northern RR, 60, 314
Syracuse Lakeside & Baldwinsville Ry., 314
Syracuse Northern Elec. Ry., *315*

Tacoma & Steilacoom Ry., *393*
Tama & Toledo Elec. Ry., 46, *363*
Tarrant County Tr. Co., 202, 218, *377–78*
Terre Haute Elec. Co., 278
Terre Haute Indianapolis & Eastern Tr. Co. (THI&E), 23, 33, 44, 46, 47, 68, 69, 86, 90, 92, 99, 101, 103, 104, 129, 130–31, 134, 147, 176, 179, 189, 192, 199, 201, 214, 217, 232, 241, 258, 259, *278–79*, 283, 286, 351, 428
Terre Haute Tr. & Lt. Co., 55, 278
Texas Elec. Ry., 63, 81, 121, 143, 156, 157, 212, 215, 219, 241, 242, 243, *376–77*
Texas Interurban Ry., 57, 87, 203, 213, 218, 236, 249, 376, *378*
Texas Tr. Co., 376
THI&E Lines, *see* Terre Haute Indianapolis & Eastern Tr. Co.
Tidewater Power Co., 333
Tidewater Southern Ry., 119, 151, 207, 218, 226, 247, 248, *401–2*
Tiffin Fostoria & Eastern Elec. Ry., 13, 71, 136–37, 262, *263*
Tiffin & Fostoria Elec. Ry., 263
Tiffin & Interurban Consolidated Ry., 263
Titusville Elec. Tr. Co., 302
TMER&L, TMER&T companies, *see* Milwaukee Elec. Ry. & Lt. Co., The
Toledo Ann Arbor & Detroit RR, 21, 33–34
Toledo Ann Arbor & Jackson, 34
Toledo Bowling Green & Fremont Ry., 261
Toledo Bowling Green & Southern Tr. Co., 26, 31, 32, 43, 79, 82, 91, 93, 99, 114, 129, 137, 260, *261–62*
Toledo & Chicago Interurban Ry., *see* Fort Wayne & Northwestern Ry.
Toledo & Defiance Ry., 18
Toledo–Detroit RR, 34
Toledo & Eastern RR, 267, 268
Toledo & Eastern Ry., 14
Toledo & Findlay RR, 262
Toledo Fostoria & Findlay Ry., 79, 98–99, 137, 191, 261, *262*, 263, 368
Toledo Fremont & Norwalk St. RR, 10, 11, 267
Toledo & Indiana RR, 18, 21, 34, 47, 81, 123, 125, 130, 146, 204, *263–64*, 282, 345
Toledo & Maumee Valley, 134, 262
Toledo & Monroe Ry., 11, 287
Toledo Napoleon & Defiance, 17
Toledo Ottawa Beach & Northern, 204
Toledo Port Clinton & Lakeside Ry., 14, 21, 22, 35, 48, 50, 51, 55, 56, 67, 115, 116, 123, 146, *267*
Toledo Urban & Interurban Ry., 34, 262
Toledo Waterville & Southern Ry., 17, 262
Toledo & Western Ry., 37, 44, 50, 67, 72, 80, 81, 84, 91, 120, 137, 146, 162, 169, 204, 206, 212, 218, *264*, 276
Toronto & Eastern Ry., 181, 422
Toronto Suburban Ry., 83, 181, *419*
Toronto & York Radial Ry., 52, 181, 199, *418–19*
Trenton Bristol & Philadelphia St. Ry., 302
Trenton & Mercer County Tr. Corp., 52, 309
Trenton–Princeton Tr. Co., 52, 157, 166, 206, 298
Tri-City Ry. & Lt. Co., 352
Tri-City Tr. Co., *305–6*
Trinidad Elec. Transm. Ry. & Gas Co., *382*
Tri-State Ry. & Elec. Co., 270–71
Tri-State Tr. Co., 303
Tulsa-Sapulpa Union Ry., 212, *374*
Tuscarawas County Tr. Co., 28; *see also* Northern Ohio
Twin City Rapid Transit Co., 359
Twin City RR (Wash.), 393
Tyler Tr. Co., *305*

Union Elec. Ry. (Kan.), 87, 184, 212, 219, 241, 295, *371*, 372, 374

450   Index of Interurbans

Union Traction Co. (of Indiana), 26, 33, 48, 49, 54, 55, 56, 68, 69, 70, 71, 72n., 73, 75, 79, 86, 88–89, 91, 93, 96–97, 103, 112, 113, 125, 128, 129, 137, 140, 141, 147, 176, 183, 189, 196, 198, 201, 212, 214, 217, 232, 276, 277, *280–81*, 282, 285, 373
Union Tr. Co. of Kansas, *see* Union Elec. Ry.
Union Tr. Co. of Tennessee, *334*
Union Tr. Co. of West Virginia, *305*
United Elec. Rys. (R.I.), 326
United RRs of San Francisco, 405
United Rys. (Ore.), 47, 151, 153, 169, 191, 207, 212, 213, 244, 250, *397*
United St. Rys. (N.Y.), 206
United Tr. Co. (N.Y.), 126, 204, 290
United Tr. St. Ry. (Pa.), 300
Upton St. RR, 322
Urbana Bellefontaine & Northern, 29, 265
Urbana Mechanicsburg & Columbus Elec. Ry., 275
Utah-Idaho Central RR, 24, 37, 68, 92, 93, 116, 117, 156, 198, 215, 220, 231, *385–86*, 387
Utah Lt. & Tr. Co., 387
Utica & Mohawk Valley Ry., 121, 206, *312*, 315

Vallejo Benicia & Napa Valley, 403
Valley Rys., 203, *298*
Valparaiso & Northern, 40
Vancouver Tr. Co., 393
Virginia Elec. Power Co., 199, 202, 330
Visalia Elec. RR, 62, 119, 170, 173, 184, 207, 213, 214, 247, 248, *404–5*

Wabash & Rochester Ry., 34
Walkill Transit Co., *318*
Walla Walla Valley Ry., 203, 207, 246, *391*
Warren–Bisbee Ry., *389*
Warren & Jamestown St. Ry., 59, 60, 62, 107, 184, *295*
Warren St. Ry., 184, 295
Washington Alexandria & Mount Vernon, 328
Washington Arlington & Fairfax, 328
Washington & Baltimore, 11
Washington Baltimore & Annapolis Elec. Ry., 48, 59, 60–61, 62, 77, 83, 94, 95, 99, 105–6, 107, 116, 120, 180, 184, 185, 192, 196, *326–27*, 345, 401, 424
Washington Berwyn & Laurel, 330
Washington & Great Falls Lt. & Power Co., 330
Washington Interurban Ry., 330
Washington & Mount Vernon, 328
Washington & Old Dominion Ry., 24, 65, 120, 148, 221, 246, *328–29*
Washington Ry. & Elec. Co., 330; *see also* General Index
Washington Tr. Co., 260
Washington & Virginia Ry. Co., 328
Washington Water Power Co., 67, 213, *390*
Water Gap & Portland St. Ry., 301
Waterloo Cedar Falls & Northern Ry., 37, 93, 113, 143–44, 198, 207, 220, 244, 246, *360–62*
Waterloo & Cedar Falls Rapid Transit Co., 360, 430
Waterloo RR, *see* Waterloo Cedar Falls & Northern Ry.
Waterloo Seneca Falls & Cayuga Lake Ry., 316
Watsonville Tr. Co., *405*
Waukegan & North Shore Transit Co., 335
Waverly Sayre & Athens, 206, 317
Wellsburg Bethany & Washington RR, *303*
Wellston & Jackson Belt Ry., 56, 206, *271*
West Chester Kennett & Wilmington Elec. Ry., 302
West Chester St. Ry., 302
West End Terminal Ry., 52
Western Illinois Tr. Co., 345
Western New York & Pennsylvania Tr. Co., 196, *311*
Western Ohio Ry., 13, 18, 26, 28, 31, 44, 48, 55, 56, 98–99, 101, 103, 122, 129, 218, 260, *261*, 262–63, 296
Westmoreland Interurban, 376
West Penn Rys., 51, 65, 69, 76, 103, 133, 136, 140, 174, 179, 202, 219, 220, 248, *299–300*, 302–3
West Side & Suburban, 397
Wetzel & Tyler Ry., 305
Wheeling & Elm Grove, 355
Wheeling Public Service, 205, 305
Wheeling Tr. Co., 36, 111, 136, 151, 153, 160, 202, 300, *302–3*
Wilkes-Barre & Hazleton Ry., 47, 84, 168, 218, *294*, 428
Willamette Falls Ry., 426
Willamette Valley Southern Ry., 205, 246, *395*
Willapa Elec. Co., *393*
Wilmington & Philadelphia Tr. Co., 302
Windsor Essex & Lake Shore Rapid Ry., 59, 62, 181, 414, *415*
Winnebago Tr., 356
Winnipeg Selkirk & Lake Winnipeg Ry., *421*
Winnipeg Suburban, 422
Winona Interurban, 21, 36, 44, 97, 116, 128, 183, 201, 218, 237, 248, 276, *277*, 283, 286
Winona & Warsaw Ry. Co., 277
Wisconsin Elec. Ry., 356
Wisconsin Power Co., *356*
Wisconsin Power & Lt. Co., 42, 200, 201, 214, 354, *356*
Wisconsin Public Service Co., 167, 168, 204, 214, *357*
Wisconsin Tr. Lt. Heat & Power Co., 201, *356*, 357
Wisconsin Valley Elec. Ry., *357*
Woodstock & Sycamore Tr. Co., 38, *352*
Woodstock Thames Valley & Ingersoll Elec. Ry., 184, *418*
Worcester Consolidated St. Ry., 136, 206, 322
Worthington Clintonville & Columbus, 17
Wyandotte & Detroit River Ry., 287

Yakima Valley Transportation Co., 119, 207, 246, *390–91*
York Rys., 62, 199, 200, *294*
York Utilities, 323
Youngstown & Ohio River RR, 32, 107, *270*
Youngstown & Southern Ry., 32, 146, 156, 200, 206, *270*
Youngstown & Suburban, *see* Youngstown & Southern Ry.

General Index

Abandonment, 212-13, 240-51; early examples, 35; ICC control of, 165-66, 169-70; state control of, 166-69; statistics relating to, 215, 222, 240; *see also histories of individual roads*, Index of Interurbans
Aberdeen & Rockfish RR, 386
Adams Express Co., 122-23
Adrian, Mich., 146, 264
AC electrification, 53, 58-62; *see also* Electrification
Agents, 123
Agricultural depression of 1920's, 251
Ahab, Capt., 124
Ainsworth-Thompson syndicate, 406
Air horn, 90, 319
Air Line News, 39
Air Line Stockholders' Assn. of the World, 40
Air lines, joint ticketing with, 336
Akins, A. E., 31
Akron, Ohio, 10, 26, 43, 93, 96, 131, 273; — Tr. & Elec. Co., 273
Alabama Power Co., 157
Albany, N.Y., 122, 316, 318
Alexandria, Ind., 26, 33, 283
Alexandria Loudon & Hempshire RR, 329
Alko Express Lines, 133
Allegan, Mich., 65, 289
Allentown, Pa., 52, 79, 296, 301
Alliance, Ohio, 68, 272, 273, 274; — Elec. Ry. Co., 273; — Power Co., 273
Almont, Mich., 16, 287
Alton & Eastern RR, 347
Alton RR, *see* Chicago & Alton RR
Altoona, Pa., 51, 301
Amboy, Ill., 233, 344
American Car Co., 363, 367, 385, 403, 404; history, 424; specialty in Birney cars, 87
American Car & Foundry, 82, 97, 280, 425
American Elec. Ry. Assn., 109, 123, 132, 376
American Express Co., 122
American Gas & Elec. Co., 202, 290
American Locomotive Co., 73
American RR Assn., 143
American Ry. Express Co., 123
American Rys. Co., 304, 339
American St. & Interurban Ry. Assn., *see* American Elec. Ry. Assn.
American Waterworks & Elec. Co., 201-2, 300, 303, 327
Ames & College St. Ry., 363
Amsterdam, N.Y., 47, 316
Amusement parks, 116
Anaconda Copper Co., 388
Anderson, Ind., 26, 33, 55, 96, 140, 147, 244, 280, 281, 283
Anderson's Ferry, Ohio, 52, 255
Androscoggin Elec. Co., 319
Annapolis, Md., 60, 61, 120, 326-27
Annapolis Baltimore & Washington RR, 326
Ann Arbor, Mich., 15, 24, 33
Ann Arbor RR, 24
Anti-climbers, 90
Antioch College, 259
Appleyard, Arthur E.: syndicate of, 13, 19, 21, 26, 31, 265, 266, 357; its failure, 28-29
Arizona, 389; motor-carrier policy, 171
Arkansas, motor-carrier policy, 171

Arlington, Cal., 210
Arnold, Bion J., 21, 55, 343
Arnold Elec. Power Station Co., 21
Arnstein, Walter, 401
Ashtabula, Ohio, 10, 131, 274
Assn. of Ry. Executives, 143
Associated Gas & Elec. Co., 203
Atchison Topeka & Santa Fe Ry., 165, 179, 207, 367, 371, 373, 401, 402, 413
Atlanta, Ga., 41, 203, 333
Atlas, Mich., 142
Auburn, N.Y., 43, 313, 314, 315
Automatic train stop, 67
Automobile: development of, 3; rivalry of, 37, 108, 227-28, 234-36

Baggage: fees, 110; revenues from, 120
Baker Wood Preserving Co., 260
Balch, W. E., 117
Baldwin Locomotive Works, 73, 84
Ballast, 48
Ball family (Muncie), 183
Ballston Spa, N.Y., 119, 316, 318
Baltimore, Md., 51, 60-61, 94, 120, 326, 327, 330; — Tr. Co., 199
Baltimore & Ohio RR, 24, 40, 61, 99, 106, 161, 258, 272, 282, 301, 326, 350
Bamberger, Simon, 183, 198, 383
Bangor, Me., 148, 323
Barger, Harold, 228
Barney & Smith Car Co., 73, 74, 102, 381; history, 424
Barstow, W. S., 396
Bartonville Bus Line, 174
Bascomb, Ohio, 136
Batavia, N.Y., 43
Battery cars, 5
Battle Creek, Mich., 65, 289
Bay City, Mich., 43, 288, 289, 290
Baylies, R. N., 343
Bay Point, Ohio, 115
Bay State St. Ry., 150
Baytown, Tex., 213
Beaumont Sour Lake & Western RR, 379
Beaumont, Tex., 99, 165, 202, 379
Beck, Sir Adam, 236, 237, 414, 417, 419
Beebe, Clifford D., 312, 313-16
Beech Grove, Ind., 41, 286
Bee Line, 175
Beer, smuggling of, 415
Beggs, John I., 353, 356
Bellefontaine, Ohio, 18, 26, 32, 88, 178, 265, 266
Bellingham, Wash., 35, 391
Beloit, Wis., 35, 344
Bentley and Knight, 5
Benton Harbor, Mich., 115, 128, 290
Berea, Ohio, 13
Berlin Heights and Berlinville, Ohio, 178
Bethel, Ohio, 43, 52, 258
Big Four RR, 32, 49, 96, 99, 112, 141, 279, 280, 286, 385
Binkley Mine, 147, 284
Birney, Charles O., 86; Birney cars, 86-87, 202
Bishop syndicate, 327
Bivalve, N.J., 92, 307
Blackwell, F. H., 389

452 General Index

Blissfield, Mich., 50, 264
Bloomington, Ill., 36, 38, 145–46, 347–49 *passim*
Bloomington, Ind., 42, 275
Blue Ridge Lines, 231, 327
Blue Star Auto Stages, 172
Bluffton, Ind., 33, 88, 89, 97, 147, 282, 284
Boettcher family (Denver), 380
Bogart, E. L., 20
Bonner Railwagon, 135
Bono, Ohio, 14
Bosenbury, J. M., 73, 77
Boston & Albany RR, 317
Boston & Maine RR, 206, 320, 324
Boston, Mass., 93, 103, 320–22 ; — Elevated, 324 ; money market, 19, 27, 184
Bowling Green, Ohio, 14, 137, 262, 263
Box motors, 83–84, 125
Bracket arms, 56
Brady, Arthur, 281
Brakes, 75–76
Brantford, Ont., 184, 417, 418
Brazil, Ind., 47, 278, 283
Bridges, 49
Bridgit (ferry), 50
Brill, J. G. Co., 82, 294, 378, 389, 392 ; history, 424
Bristol, Pa., 120, 167
Broadhead family (N.Y.), 311
Brookdale, Pa., 88
Brooks-Scanlan case, 168
Brown, F. W., 129
Browne, Hamilton, 363
Browning, M. A., 385
Bryan, Ohio, 263, 264, 282
Bucklen, H. E., 276
Bucyrus, Ohio, 13, 26, 28, 32, 43, 92, 268–69
Buffalo, N.Y., 43, 83, 94, 99, 113, 177, 274, 309, 313
Buffalo Rochester & Pittsburgh RR, 300
Buggies, limitations of, 8
Buntzen, Johannes E. C., 423
Burlington, Wis., 35, 353
Burnham, D. H., & Co., 69
Burton, Ohio, 116
Buses, 227–28 ; competition of, 106, 171, 234–36 ; interurban operation of, 177, 231–33
Bushnell, Asa S., 260
Butte Anaconda & Pacific RR, 388
Butler, Pa., 43, 178, 295
Butters, H. A., 398

Cable cars, 5
Cab signals, 67
California, 31, 42, 398–413 ; characteristic equipment in, 71, 75 ; maps, 399, 408 ; state policy, 152, 164, 166–67, 169, 170–73 *passim*, 177, 221, 235
California Northwestern RR, 23
Calumet area, Ind., 44, 275–76
Camden, Me., 120
Camden, N.J., 51, 93, 306, 309
Camp Dodge, Iowa, 106, 365
Camp Meade, Md., 106, 326
Canada, 42, 180–81, 413–23 ; maps, 416, 420–22
Canadian National Rys., 181, 414, 419, 420–21, 423
Canadian Northern Ry., 419
Canadian Pacific Ry., 41, 206, 320, 417, 421, 422
Cannelton, Ind., 114, 285

Cannonball bus line, 175
Canton, Ohio, 9, 10, 51, 275
Cape Breton Elec. Co., 421
Capital market, 19, 27, 184 ; choice of projects by, 42–43
Carey, Emerson, 372
Cargo Transport, Inc., 134
Carload freight, 136–40 ; *see also* Freight
Carlton-Spencer-Penrose syndicate, 382
Cars, 70–83 ; builders, 424–25 ; cannibalization of, 230 ; lightweight, 80–83 ; orders, 191 ; rebuilding, 81 ; second-hand market, 246
Cascade Tunnel, 53
Cass, L. S., 143, 360
Cassville & Exeter RR, 376
Catalina Island, boat trains, 75
Catenary overhead, 59, 63n
Catholic Church, 28th Eucharistic Congress (1926), 116
Cedar Point, Ohio, 115
Cedar Rapids, Iowa, 24, 161, 360–62
Celina, Ohio, 18, 44, 261, 278, 281, 282, 286
Census of Elec. Rys., 8, 188, 189
Centerville Lt. & Tr. Co., 363
Central Electric Ry. Accountants Assn., 111
Central Electric Ry. Assn. (C.E.R.A.), 69, 77, 109–11, 124, 129, 132–33, 146, 275, 276, 286, 287, 293 ; dissolution, 111 ; founding, 109
Central Electric Railway Master Mechanics Assn., 77, 84, 111, 129, 145
Central Electric Traffic Assn., 110, 112, 113, 128
Central Freight Assn., 128, 141
Central Illinois Power Co., 198
Central Illinois Public Service Co., 200, 351
Central Ohio Lt. & Power Co., 261
Central Passenger Assn., 109, 113, 141 ; boycott of interurbans, 112
Central Public Service Co., 202, 203, 204
Central States Guide, 111
Central Transit Equipment Assn., 111
Chagrin Falls, Ohio, 212, 272
Champaign, Ill., 27, 36, 86, 101, 145, 183, 347–49 *passim*
Chandler & Co., 309
Chanute Field, Ill., 349
Chapman signals, 65, 66
Charles River Bridge case, 171
Charleston, Ill., 38, 88, 351
Charlestown, N.H., 148, 320
Cheney, C. M., 360
Chesapeake & Ohio Ry., 113, 114, 206, 271, 305, 330
Cheshire Bridge Corp., 320
Chester, Pa., 174
Chesterton, Ind., 40
Chicago, Ill., 23, 35, 36, 39, 41, 42, 44, 53, 101, 102, 112, 114, 128, 134–35, 146, 184, 200, 219, 222, 223, 250, 335–39 *passim* ; — Elevated, 57, 73, 75, 82, 114, 116, 134, 336, 337 ; — Symphony Orchestra, 116 ; — Transit Authority, 180
Chicago & Alton RR, 98, 144, 145, 345
Chicago Burlington & Quincy RR, 39, 144, 207, 341, 345, 359, 360, 363, 382, 383
Chicago Cincinnati & Louisville RR, 112–13
Chicago Claims Conference, 143
Chicago & Eastern Illinois RR, 144–45
Chicago Great Western RR, 113, 143, 358, 360
Chicago Milwaukee St. Paul & Pacific, 85,

General Index

144, 161, 284, 341, 356, 360, 363, 365, 388
Chicago & Northwestern Ry., 161, 335–36, 341, 360–61, 363
Chicago Peoria & St. Louis RR, 145, 347
Chicago Rapid Transit (Chicago Elevated), *see under* Chicago
Chicago Rock Island & Pacific RR, 24, 145, 161, 207, 345, 360, 362, 364, 372, 373
Chicago & South Haven SS Co., 289
Chicago World's Fair (1893) Intramural Ry., 26, 57
Chico, Cal., 35, 63, 64, 86, 398
Children's fares, 110
Chillicothe, Ohio, 175, 258, 271
Chippewa Falls, Wis., 168, 357
Chris-Craft Corp., 288
Chrisney, Ind., 17
Christy, Will and James, Jr., 21, 327
Cincinnati, Ohio, 13, 26, 31, 32, 35, 42, 43, 51, 52, 81, 94, 102, 108, 122, 232, 255, 258, 265, 266, 284–85, 288; dual overhead, 52; gauge, 52; — St. Ry. 26, 258; — Subway, 52, 284; — Tr. Co., 175
Cincinnati Bluffton & Chicago RR, 38, 147
Cincinnati Car Co., 73, 138, 259, 261, 262, 280, 285, 286, 393; history, 424; its lightweight cars, 80, 81, 82, 87, 269, 274, 291, 293, 303, 306, 309, 317, 335, 374
Cincinnati Hamilton & Dayton RR, 260–61, 284
Cities Service Co., 204, 267, 328, 375, 382, 393
City streetcar systems: control of interurbans, 199; operation by interurbans, 86; equipment, 86–87; *see also* Street railways
Claremont, N.H., 148, 325
Clark, E. W., Management Corp., 350, 380, 394
Clark, T. L., Truck Line, 174
Clarksburg, Cal., 213
Clarksburg, W. Va., 202, 303
Cleveland, Ohio, 10, 13, 14, 16, 25, 26, 27, 32, 35, 36, 42, 43, 44, 51, 53, 69, 93, 94, 96, 98, 100, 104, 112, 117, 121–22, 124, 128, 234, 263, 267, 268, 269, 272–74, 288; money market, 19, 28; street rys. of, 27, 28, 111; — Union Terminal, 69, 85
Cleveland & Buffalo Transit Co., 111, 130
Cleveland Exchange Banking Co., 263
Clinton, Iowa, 63, 144, 359–60
Coen, F. W. (vice-pres. of LSE), 237
Coeur d'Alene, Ida., 27, 389, 390
Coffey Creek, 40
Collisions, 88–89
Colorado, 380–82; map, 381; motor-carrier policy, 172, 176
Colorado Midland RR, 382
Colorado Springs & Cripple Creek District Ry., 207
Colorado & Southern Ry., 207, 380, 382
Columbus, Ind., 27, 279
Columbus, Ohio, 13, 17, 26, 43, 51, 52, 53, 81, 91, 101, 104, 117, 125, 128, 131, 133, 175, 232, 258, 265, 269, 271, 274–75
Columbus Hocking Valley & Toledo Ry., *see* Hocking Valley RR
Columbus & Lake Michigan RR, 29, 32, 141, 275
Combines, prevalence of, 71
Commonwealth Power System, 342, 343
Commonwealth & Southern Corp., 203, 273
Commuter traffic, 100, 229

Condemnation proceedings, 20
Coney Island, Ohio, 52, 255
Conneaut, Ohio, 131, 274, 293
Connecticut, 323–26; map, 321
Connell, A. J. and W. L., 295
Connersville, Ind., 35, 284
Construction of interurbans, 21–25; contracting for, 21; public regulation of, 164–65
Consumers Power Co., 290
Container cars, 134
Controllers, 74; type-K, 10
Conway, Dr. Thomas, Jr., 81, 82, 91, 111, 132, 133, 200, 232, 237, 238, 266, 299, 337
Cook, F. W., & Sons, 286
Cooke, Jay, III, 19
Corkwell, B. T. (motorman), 89
Corona, Cal., 210
Corsicana, Tex., 63, 376–77
Coshocton, Ohio, 13, 42
Costs: of construction, 184; trend of, 191–97
Council Bluffs, Iowa, 153
Couplers, 76–77
Covington, Ind., 41
Crawfordsville, Ind., 35, 41, 92, 130, 278, 279, 282
Creaghead Engineering Co., 22
Crescent Navigation Co., 115
Crestline, Ohio, 23
Crooked Creek RR, 364
Crosby Transportation Co., 115, 162, 289
Cross-bench open car, 70, 71
Crowell Collier Publishing Co., 260
Crown Point, Ind., 176, 275
Cumberland Valley RR, 295, 297
Cummings Car & Coach Co., 276–77; *see also* McGuire-Cummings
Curves, 47–48

Daft, Leo, 5, 6
Dallas, Tex., 121, 122, 213, 376–78 *passim*; Rys., 203
Danville, Cal., 172
Danville, Ill., 27, 36, 81, 86, 101, 130, 145, 174, 183, 219, 347–49 *passim*
Danville, Ind., 23, 279
Danville Car Co., 387, 424
Darby, Pa., 174
Davenport, Iowa, 144, 359–60
Davenport, Thomas, 4
Davenport Rock Island & Northwestern RR, 144, 360
Davidson, Robert, 4
Dayton, Ohio, 13, 26, 32, 34, 41, 42, 43, 44, 51, 52, 81, 99, 101, 104, 109, 115, 122, 259, 260–61, 265, 266, 279, 284
Dayton Lebanon & Cincinnati, 29
DC electrification, 53–54, 62–64; *see also* Electrification
Deadwood, S.D., 169, 359
Dean, W. L., re, 176
Decatur, Ill., 82, 86, 101, 144, 145, 346–49 *passim*
Decatur, Ind., 59, 278, 282
Deere, John, 144
Defiance, Ohio, 17, 18, 29, 42, 262, 263, 264, 265
Delaware, 302
Delaware, Ohio, 17, 270
Delaware & Hudson RR, 204, 206, 237, 316, 318
Delaware Lackawanna & Western RR, 294, 296

Demurrage, 142, 143
Denison, Tex., 63, 121, 376, 377
Denton, Tex., 213, 378
Denver, Col., 51, 220, 381 ; — Tramways, 52, 380
Denver & Rio Grande Western RR, 383, 384
Depression of 1930's, 62, 214–15, 238, 242
Deshler, Ohio, 29, 32
Des Moines, Iowa, 24, 104, 363–65 ; — St. Ry., 81, 365
Deterioration of plant, 48, 244
Detroit, Mich., 10, 15, 26, 27, 28, 42, 51, 94, 95, 99, 125, 127, 128, 176, 287–89 ; — St. Ry., 288
Detroit & Cleveland Nav. Co., 111, 130
Detroit River tunnel, 85
Detroit Toledo & Ironton RR, 34, 260
Detroit & Toledo Shore Line, 38
Diamond Match Co., 398
Dickey, Sol S., 277
Diesel operation, conversion to, 25, 221, 224–25
Dingley, Henry M., 319
Dispatching, 67–68
District of Columbia, 152
Dixon, Cal., 167, 400
Doherty, Henry L., 204, 263, 264
Dolan, Thomas, 26
Dominion Coal Co., 421
Dominion Power & Transmission Co., 414, 415
Dowagiac, Mich., 114, 290
Doylestown, Pa., 120, 297
Dozier, Melville, 400
Duke, James B., 331
Dundee, Mich., 34
Dunreith, Ind., 120–21, 279, 283
Durant, W. C., 3, 12
Durham, N.C., 165, 331
Dwight, Ill., 38, 346

Eagle Picher Corp., 198, 370
East Bay St. Rys., 199
East Chicago, Ind., 213, 338
Eastern N.Y. Utilities, 155
Easton, Pa., 120, 297, 301, 307
East Peoria, Ill., 83, 349
East Troy, Wis., 35, 180, 353, 354
East St. Louis, Ill., 36, 101, 347, 349–50, 351
Eaton, Ohio, 27, 259
Eau Claire, Wis., 168, 357
Eccles, G. S., 385
Eddy Pulp Co., 421
Edison, Thomas A., 5, 6
Edison General Electric, 353
Edwards, D. C., 113
Edwardsville, Ill., 144, 347, 350
Eel River RR, 277
Elder, Bowman, 283
Eldridge, Chauncey, 19
Electrical Installation Co., 21, 277
Electric Bond & Share, 199, 202, 203, 378, 388
Electric Express (Albany, N.Y.), 122, 126
Electric motor, development of, 4
Electric Package Company (Agency), 122, 124, 130
Electric Rys. Freight Co., 130, 135
Electric Rys. War Board, 105
Electric Traction Weekly, 31 ; speed award, 99

Electrification, 53–65 ; AC single-phase, 58–62 ; AC three-phase, 53 ; DC at 600 volts, 53–54 ; DC at 1,200–1,500 volts, 62–64 ; sales to outside buyers, 54, 139 ; transmission of power, 54–56
Elkhart, Ind., 27, 97, 276–77
Elkhart Lake, Wis., 42, 356
Elkins, George and William, 26
Elkins family (W. Va.), 329
Ellis, T. M., Jr., 344
Ellisville, Miss., 203
Elmira, N.Y., 164, 317 ; — Water Lt. & RR Co., 317–18
El Paso, Tex., 379, 380
El Paso Elec. Co., 379
Elway Transit, 130
Elyria, Ohio, 13, 43, 178
Emanuel, Alfred, 374, 383
Endicott, re, 178
Enna Jettick Shoe Co., 315
Enthusiasts and hobbyists, 103, 116
Epizootic, the Great, 5
Equipment trusts, 197
Erie, Pa., 31, 131, 178, 293, 309
Erie RR, 114, 123, 138, 147, 260, 269, 270, 293, 313 ; control of electric lines, 206, 317, 318 ; Mount Morris electrification, 25, 205, 315–16
Erie Stone Co., 147
Escalon, Cal., 151
Eugene, Ore., 63, 102, 296, 397
Evansville, Ind., 27, 43, 44, 49, 111, 276, 285, 286 ; — Rys., 49, 115
Everett, Henry A., 10 ; syndicate with E. W. Moore, 10, 11, 13, 14, 19, 31, 198, 199, 262, 264, 267, 273, 274, 287, 415 ; its failure (1902), 27 ; its reorganization, 28
Everett, Wash., 35, 392–93 ; — Ry. Lt. & Power Co., 391
Excursions, 107, 115
Express freight, 121–24

Fairmont, W. Va., 202, 303, 305
Fairport Painesville & Eastern RR, 274
Fares, 103–8 ; commission regulation of, 158–59 ; franchise regulation of, 150–51
Farmer, Moses, 4, 6
Farmers, acquisition of land from, 20 ; effect of interurban on, 91, 100, 117
Farmland Stone Co., 141
Federal Lt. and Tr. Co., 393
Fenders, 78
Ferdinand RR, 38
Finances, 183–207 ; public regulation of, 179
Findlay, Ohio, 13, 26, 32, 34, 43, 98, 261–62 ; driving of golden spike, 31 ; — St. Ry., 114, 261
Fires, 243–44
Fisher Construction Co., 183, 339, 346
Fisk-Robinson syndicate, 368
Fleishhacker, Herbert, 207, 401
Flint, Mich., 11, 27, 31, 131, 140, 288, 289
Fonda, N.Y., 42, 316
Fond du Lac, Wis., 356
Ford, Henry, 3, 12
Ford Motor Co., 3, 12
Forest, Ohio, 43
Fostoria, Ohio, 43, 262
Fort Dodge, Iowa, 363–64
Fort Harrison, Ind., 100
Fort Sheridan, Ill., 106

General Index

Fort Smith Tr. Co., 166
Fort Smith & Western RR, 373
Fort Wayne, Ind., 26, 32, 43, 44, 70, 82, 88, 102, 104, 112, 120–21, 128, 147, 263–64, 278, 280, 281, 282, 284; limited service to Indianapolis, 96–97
Fort Worth, Tex., 202, 377; — St. Ry., 377
Fostoria, Ohio, 44, 262–63
Franchises for street running, 16–19, 127, 130, 140, 149–51
Fraser, T. C., 237
Frederick, Md., 114, 327–28
Freight, 119–48, 231; carload, 136–48; equipment, 83–87, 129; franchise restrictions on, 130, 140, 150; freight-only trackage, 224–25; interchange with railroads, 140–48; less-than-carload (LCL), 124–36; rates, 126; tariffs, 128
Fremont, Ohio, 43, 99, 263, 267
Fresno Interurban Ry., 413

Galbraith, W. M., 270
Galesburg, Ill., 85, 344–45
Galveston, Tex., 99, 378
Gaps in interurban networks, 42–44, 130–31
Garland, Utah, 178
Garrettsville, Ohio, 36, 212, 272
Gary, Ind., 40, 41, 59, 176, 275, 338
Gauges, off-standard, 51–52, 134, 140
General Electric, 10, 84, 184, 202–3
General Gas & Elec. Co., 204
General Motors Corp., 3, 140
Genoa, Ohio, 22, 267
Georgetown, Ill., 174
Georgia: map, 334; motor-carrier regulation, 171
Georgia-Carolina Power Co., 333
Georgia & Florida RR, 165, 331
German Bank (Buffalo, N.Y.), 29
Giant's Causeway Elec. Tramway, 9
Glen Carbon, Pa., 167
Glover, Ill., 145
Goderich, Ont., 41, 423
Golden, Col., 51, 380
Gonzenbach, Ernest, 14, 142
Goodrich, Mich., 142
Goodrich Transit Co., 115, 289, 356
Goodrum, Ind., 39, 40
Goshen, Ind., 27, 34, 36, 97, 276, 277
Gotshall, W. C., 14
Gould, George, 330
Gould, Sen. Arthur R., 320
Graham, George M. (president of Pierce-Arrow), 236
Graham & Morton Line, 115, 128, 139, 143, 290
Grain elevators, 139
Gramme, Zenobe, 4
Grand Rapids, Mich., 37, 65, 114, 289, 290
Grand Rapids & Indiana RR, 278
Grand Trunk Ry., 28, 162, 417, 420–21
Grandview, Ind., 114, 285, 286
Granite City, Ill., 144, 347, 348
Gravel as freight cargo, 136–37
Graves syndicate, 389
Great Lakes Naval Training Station, 106
Great Northern Ry., 53, 61, 207, 389, 396
Green Bay, Wis., 35, 168
Greencastle, Ind., 47, 278
Greenfield, Mass., 180
Greensburg, Ind., 35, 284–85

Greensburg, Pa., 133, 300
Greenwood, Ind., 102, 279
Greyhound Lines, 232, 392, 400, 404
Griffin, J. P., 376
Guide Publishing Co., 111

Haines syndicate, 419
Hales Corners, Wis., 88, 353
Hall-Scott (car builder), 384, 400
Halsey Stuart & Co., 200
Hamilton, Ohio, 43, 59, 258, 265, 266, 284
Hamilton, Ont., 43, 184, 414
Hammond, Ind., 114, 275, 276
Hammond Township, Ind., 17
Hankey, John R., 43–44
Hanna, J. B., 337
Harlan & Hollingsworth (car builders), 101, 425
Harmony Short Line Ry. Bus & Land Co., 295
Harriman, E. H., 396, 406
Harris, A. W., 389
Harris, N. W., 365
Harrisburg, Pa., 298
Hartman, S. B., stock farm of, 275
Hartt, Jay Samuel, 146, 338
Hazleton, Pa., 167, 294
Heinz, H. J., 183, 277
Henderson (ferry), 50
Henderson, Ky., 49, 285, 286
Henry, Charles L., 26, 35, 109, 124, 128, 183, 235, 237, 280, 284, 368
Henry, John C., 5
Hershey Chocolate Co., 198, 296–97, 298
Higgins family (Manitowoc, Wis.), 357
Highland, N.Y., 22, 318
Highland Park, Ill., 146, 335–36
Hill, James J., 396–97
Hillsboro, Ill., 38, 347, 352
Hirsch, Patrick, 21
Hobbyists, 103, 116
Hocking Valley RR, 56, 104, 206, 271
Holcomb, James, 269
Holding Companies, 197, 199–205; *see also* Insull, Samuel; Cities Service Co., General Electric; North American Co.; Stone & Webster; United Corp.
Holland, Harris F., 101
Holland Palace Car Co., 101
Hollywood, Cal., 173; 412
Holman Car Co., 394, 400, 402, 425
Hoopole Yorktown & Tampico RR, 38, 344
Horne-Payne, Sir R. M., 423
Horse cars, 4
Hosmer, Howard (ICC examiner), 118
Houston, Tex., 99, 213, 378
Houston & Texas Central RR, 376
Hudson, N.Y., 42, 317
Hudson & Manhattan tubes, 132, 307
Huntingburg, Ind., 17
Huntington, Henry, 406–7
Huntington, Mass., 249
Huron, Ohio, 10
Huron Construction Co., 41
Hyman Michaels Co., 290

Idaho, 387–88; map, 387; state policy, 164
Idaho Power Co., 203, 387
Idaho Ry. Lt. & Power Co., 387
ICC, *see* Interstate Commerce Commission
Illinois, 27, 38, 42, 225, 335–52; map, 340; motor-carrier regulation, 171, 172, 174,

177; state policy, 144, 163, 168, 174; two-cent-fare law, 105
Illinois, University of, 23
Illinois Central RR, 23, 49, 144, 145, 151, 161, 207, 250, 337, 338, 339, 341, 362
Illinois Midland Coal Co., 351
Illinois Northern Utilities, 200
Illinois Power Co., 179, 199, 347
Indiana, 9, 12, 26, 32–33, 42, 119, 121, 141, 142, 200–201, 215, 234, 275–86; financial statistics, 216–17; map, 256–57; motor-carrier regulation, 172, 176; requirement of signaling, 67, 164; state policy, 89–90, 150, 151, 152, 159, 179; two-cent-fare law, 105
Indiana Chamber of Commerce, 142
Indiana Dunes State Park, 116
Indiana Elec. Ry. Assn., 109
Indiana & Michigan Elec. Co., 290
Indianapolis, 26, 27, 33, 43, 44, 53, 55, 59, 69, 93, 94, 99, 101, 102, 104, 112, 117, 120–21, 127, 128, 130, 131, 137, 147, 163, 277, 278–86 passim; freight terminal, 131; limited services from, 96–97; — St. Ry., 26, 69, 94, 278, 279, 286; Traction Terminal, 27, 69–70, 131, 286
Indianola, Iowa, 24
Insull, Samuel: utility enterprises, 163, 179, 199, 200, 205, 232, 275, 277, 279–81, 293, 337, 339, 346, 347, 351, 354, 356, 374, 379, 422; earliest interurban venture, 279; failure, 201; formation of Indiana Railroad, 283; rebuilding of CNS&M, 336; rebuilding of CSS&SB, 338
Insull, Samuel, Jr., 338
Interborough Rapid Transit Co., see New York Subway
International Utilities Corp., 291, 309
Interstate Commerce Act of 1887, 152, 157, 158
Interstate Commerce Commission, 37, 109, 111–12, 118, 126, 132, 149, 151, 152–79 passim, 183; abandonment policy, 169–71; jurisdiction, 152–59; rate control, 160–63
Interstate Motor Freight System, 284
Interurbans: abandonment, 240–51; average life of, 248; bankruptcy, 196–97; building after 1908, 36; building booms, 3, 25, 27, 30; capital structures, 184; contribution to urban growth, 117; decline of, 3, 92, 208–39; distinguished from rural trolley lines, 8; early earnings overstated, 11–12; estimated potential traffic of, 14–15; factors causing rise of, 7–8; finances of, 183–207; geographical pattern, 41; government ownership of, in Canada, 414; ICC definition of, 153–57; obligations as common carriers, 149; rate of return, 186; statistics relating to, 186, 190, 210, 223, 226, 249; total investment, 185; total mileage, 33
Interurban Elec. Ry. (SP RR), 64, 405
Interurban Ry. Journal, 31
Iowa, 77–78, 143, 219, 225, 359–65 ;map, 361; motor-carrier regulation, 176; reasons for survival of Iowa interurbans, 143–44; two-cent-fare law, 105
Iowa Central RR, 363
Iowa City, Iowa, 24, 161, 360
Iowa Elec. Power Co., 363
Iowa Ry. & Lt. Co., 360

Iowa, University of, 360
Irvine, James, 403

Jackson, Mich., 27, 288, 289
Jackson & Sharp Co. (car builders), 312, 425
Jacksonville, Ill., 36
Jamestown, N.Y., 14, 43
Jamestown Chautauqua & Lake Erie Ry., 311
Jamestown–Fredonia Transit Co., 175
Janesville, Wis., 35, 343
Janney, Eli, 76
Jasper, Ind., 17
Jewett Car Co., 73, 98, 258, 296, 307, 322, 365, 383, 402, 404; history, 424
Jitneys, 234, 274, 290
Johnson, C. S., Co., 348
Johnson, Harry K., 378
Johnson's Island, Ohio, 50
Johnstown Tr. Co., 301
Joliet, Ill., 36, 38, 86, 339, 341
Jones, J. Levering, 26
Jones, J. M., & Co. (car builders), 425
Justus, L. C., 282

Kalamazoo, Mich., 18, 24, 65, 288, 289
Kankakee, Ill., 23, 251, 338, 349
Kansas, 366–73; maps, 367, 370, 372
Kansas City, Mo.–Kan., 15, 37, 41, 85, 366–68; — Public Service Co., 368
Kansas City Mexico & Orient RR, 367
Kansas City Southern RR, 367
Kansas & Missouri Ry. & Terminal Co., 367
Kaukauna, Wis., 168, 201, 356–57
Kenosha, Wis., 35, 43, 146, 353
Kentucky, 291–93; map, 256–57; motor-carrier regulation, 172
Kentucky Derby, 115
Kentucky & Indiana Terminal RR, 49, 280
Kessel-Kinnicut Co., 387
Keuka College, 317
Key System, 64, 94, 98, 398, 405–6
Kidder-Peabody & Co., 392
Kimberley, D. H., 263
Kincardine, Ont., 41, 423
Kingman, Ind., 41
Kingsland, Ind., collision at, 88–89, 164, 280, 282
Kinney, conductor, 89
Kintail, Ont., 41
Kittery (ferry), 323
Kokomo, Ind., 26, 282, 283
Kroger family (Cincinnati), 183, 255, 258
Kuhlman, G. C., Car Co., 73, 74, 83, 87, 261, 269, 273, 295, 313, 354, 394; history, 424
Kutztown, Pa., 52, 301

Labor, productivity of, 228–29
Laconia Car Co., 424
Ladd, William, 4
Lafayette, Ind., 22, 27, 31, 276–80 passim
Lagoon Park, 116
Lake Erie Islands, 115
Lake Erie & Western RR, 96–97, 147
Lake Geneva, Wis., 35, 342
Lake Shore Coach Co., 268
Lake Shore & Michigan Southern RR, 11, 15, 263
Lakeside, Ohio, 116
Lake Wawasee, Ind., 34
Lamar, Alfred M., 30

General Index   457

Lancaster, Ohio, 104, 271, 272
Lansing, Mich., 288, 289
La Porte, Ind., 39, 40, 275, 276, 277
La Rue, Ohio, 43
Lattimer, J. E., 269
Laurel, Miss., 203
Lawrenceville School, 298
Lazear, H. G., 303
LCL, *see under* Freight
Lead, S.D., 169, 359
Lear, King, 44
Leavittsburg, Ohio, 36, 272, 274
Lebanon, Ind., 92, 286
Lebanon, Ohio, 52, 258
Lebanon, Pa., 163, 297, 298, 302
Lee Center, Ill., 233, 344
Lee County Grain Assn., 344
Le Claire, Iowa, 144, 360
Lehigh Valley RR, 24, 296, 312, 317
Lemon Cove, Cal., 173
Lenox, Mass., 16
Lewiston, Me., 319, 323–24
Lexington, Ky., 291
Leyden, Colo., 51, 380
Libbey, W. Scott, 319
Lightning, protection from, 56–57
Lightweight cars, 80–83, 87
Lima, Ohio, 13, 26, 29, 31, 32, 43, 44, 78, 98, 99, 101, 261, 263, 264, 265, 266, 267
Lincoln, Ill., 144, 347
Lincoln, Neb., 43, 365
Linnton, Ore., 151, 212, 397
Lisman, A. A., analysis of interurban earnings, 29–30
Litchfield, Ill., 81
Little Falls, N.Y., 42, 309, 312
Live Oak, Cal., 64
Lockport, N.Y., 43, 164, 312, 313
Locomotives: electric, 84–85; self-contained, 85
Logansport, Ind., 22, 280, 283
London, Ont., 10, 43, 181, 417
Long Beach, Cal., 166, 223, 406–13 *passim*
Long Island, N.Y., 175
Lorain, Ohio, 43, 267–68
Loree, L. F., 237
Los Angeles, Cal., 27, 41, 42, 51, 69, 78, 121, 142, 166, 170, 173, 180, 234, 235, 406–13
Los Angeles Ry., 52, 407
Louisiana, 334
Louisville, Ky., 33, 42, 49, 63, 82, 101, 102, 131, 137, 157, 255, 279, 280, 283–84, 291; gauge, 51, 94; limited service to Indianapolis, 97; Board of Trade, 163
Louisville Harrod's Creek & Westport RR, 291

McAdoo, Pa., 167
McAdoo, Wm. G., 105
McGowan, Hugh J., 26, 69; *see also under* Schoepf
McGuire-Cummings Manufacturing Co., 342, 351, 360, 382, 386, 389; history, 424
McKeen cars, 24, 38
MacKenzie, Sir William, 414, 418, 419, 421, 423
Mackinaw Jct., Ill, 36, 339, 347
McKinley, Wm. B., 27, 36, 144, 183, 201, 339, 342, 347, 352, 365, 372
McKinley Bridge, (St. Louis), 36, 49

McLain, J. B. re, 175
McLean family (Washington, D.C.), 329
McLean, W. H., 389
McNear, J. A., 402
Macomb Industry & Littleton RR, 38
Madison, Ind., 42, 255, 275
Madison, Wis., 35, 41, 42
Maeder, Jay, 354
Maggard, E. H., 179, 402
Mail, 120–21
Maine, 318–19; map, 321; state policy, 149, 167, 168
Maine, University of, 148
Maine Central RR, 23, 148, 319
Maitland, Ohio, 114, 147, 260
Mandelbaum, M. J., 13; *see also under* Pomeroy
Mange-Hopson system, *see* Associated Gas & Elec. Co.
Manitowoc, Wis., 35, 357
Mann-Elkins Act., 153
Mansfield, Ohio, 26, 28, 32, 43, 204, 268, 269
Maps; Canada, 416, 420–22; Cal., 299, 408, Colo., 381; Conn., 321; Georgia, 334; Idaho, 387; Ill., 340; Ind., 256–57; Iowa, 361; Kansas, 367, 370, 372; Ken., 256–57; La., 334; Maine, 321; Mass., 321; Md., 329; Mich., 256–57; Minn., 358; Miss., 334; Mo., 340, 367; N.H., 321; N.J., 308; N.Y., 310; N.C., 332; Ohio, 256–57; Okla., 370, 375; Ore., 395; Penn., 292; R.I., 321; S.C., 332; Tenn., 335; Tex., 377, 379; Utah, 384; Va., 321, 329; Wash., 390, 391–93; W.Va., 304; Wis., 355; C.E.R.A. map, description of, 110–11
Mare Island Navy Yard, 62, 403
Marion County Commissioners, Ohio, 20
Marion, Ind., 33, 96, 280, 282, 283
Marion, Ohio, 13, 17, 26, 43, 44, 55, 269, 270
Market St. Ry., 199, 205
Martin, John, 405
Martinsville, Ind., 27, 279
Maryland, 326–30; map, 329; motor-carrier regulation, 176; tax relief, 180
Maryland Elec. Rys., 327
Marysville, Cal., 64, 86, 398
Mason City, Iowa, 362
Massachusetts, 8, 150, 320–22, 325; map, 321; state policy, 16, 93, 159, 172, 179
Massillon, Ohio, 9, 10, 51, 273
Mattoon, Ill., 38, 88, 350
Maumee, Ohio, 17, 262
Maxville, Ind., 141
Mechanicsburg & Dillsburg RR, 295
Mellen, Charles S., 325
Memphis, Tenn., 335
Memphis St. Ry. Co., 335
Merchants and the interurbans, 16, 117
Michigan, 12, 42, 111, 287–90; early abandonment in, 177; map, 256–57; motor-carrier regulation, 172, 176; regulation of interurbans, 126–27, 142, 160; two-cent-fare law, 179
Michigan, University of, 15
Michigan Central RR, 15, 24, 114, 142, 289, 290, 341
Michigan City, Ind., 27, 43, 59, 114, 120, 222, 276, 277, 337, 338
Middlebury, Ill., 233, 344
Middlefield, Ohio, 35, 116, 272, 274
Middle Tennessee Ry., 335

458 General Index

Middletown, Ind., 33, 281
Middle West Utilities System, 269, 293
Midland United Corp., 200, 275, 279, 281, 283–84
Midwest Utilities Corp., 200
Mileage books, 109–10
Milford, Ohio, 118, 258
Milk, 126–27
Miller, Alexander C., 39
Miller trolley shoe, 78–79
Milwaukee, Wis., 18, 42, 43, 53, 86, 102, 114, 135, 146, 162, 201, 223, 336, 352, 356
Milwaukee Road, *see* Chicago Milwaukee St. Paul & Pacific
Minneapolis, Minn., 26, 357–59
Minneapolis Northfield & Southern, 38
Minneapolis & St. Louis RR, 104, 145, 363
Minnesota, 357–59; map, 358
Minnesota Western, 38
Mississippi, 335; map, 334
Mississippi Power Co., 334
Mississippi River & Bonne Terre RR, 366
Missouri, 366–69; maps, 340, 367
Missouri & Illinois RR, 366
Missouri-Kansas-Texas RR (M-K-T), 113, 371, 379
Missouri Pacific, 206, 207, 351, 366, 378, 379, 385
Mitchell, H. A., 401
Modesto & Empire Tr. Co., 38, 413
Monmouth, Ill., 85, 345
Monongahela Ry., 306
Monon RR, 15, 40, 112, 115, 138
Montana, 388
Montour RR, 206, 270
Monticello Steamship Co., 115, 121, 403
Montreal, Que., 10, 420
Montrose, Pa., 24, 296
Moore, E. W., 10, 11; *see also under* Everett
Moore-Mansfield Construction Co., 282
Morgan, Randal, 26, 265, 278, 279
Morley, W. K., 289
Mormon Church, 386
Morrisville, Pa., 167
Motor carriers: regulation of, 171–78; *see also* Trucks; Buses; Interstate Commerce Commission
Mt. Carmel, Pa., 167
Mt. Clemens, Mich., 176
Mt. Vernon, Wash., 35, 391
Moyes, J. W., 41
Multiple unit control (MU), 75
Muncie, Ind., 26, 33, 44, 55, 70, 93, 96, 97, 112, 147, 280, 281, 283
Mundelein, Ill., 116, 223, 336
Murchison, Clint, 383
Murdock, John, & Sons, 270
Muskegon Tr. & Lighting Co., 111

Nachod signals, 65–67
Napoleon, Ohio, 17, 262, 263, 264
Nashville, Tenn., 334–35
National Bureau of Economic Research, 228
National City Lines, 342
National Elec. Power Co., 200
National Model Railroad Assn., 354
Nebraska, 365; motor-carrier regulation, 171
Neenah, Wis., 201, 356
Nesbitt-Thompson syndicate, 422, 423
Networks, gaps in, 42–44, 130–31
Newark, N.J., 94, 306

Newark, Ohio, 13, 27, 47, 265, 266
New Brunswick, N.J., 94, 306
Newburgh, Ind., 43, 285, 286
New Castle, Ind., 33, 55, 96, 121, 280–81, 283, 284
New England, 319–26; equipment, 70, 75; express, 121; freight, 133,; interurbans' early decline, 212; map, 321; rural trolley lines, 8, 27, 159, 194, 199, 214–15, 324–26
New Hampshire, 324–25; map, 321; state policy, 168, 325
New Haven, Conn., 81, 93, 322–23, 325–26
Newhouse, Samuel, 380
New Jersey, 103, 306–9, map, 308; motor-carrier regulation, 172
New Lebanon, Ohio, 20
New Orleans, La., 334
New Richmond, Ohio, 52, 258
New Sweden, Me., 165, 320
Newton, Kansas, 16
Newton & Northwestern RR, 363
New Westminster, B.C., 248, 422, 423
New York, 39, 42, 85, 103; state policy, 160, 164; map, 310; motor-carrier regulation, 172, 174–75
New York, N.Y., 42, 93, 103; Elevated, 83; Subway, 67, 77, 79; money market, 19
New York Central RR, 39, 42, 73, 85, 97, 114, 145, 204, 264, 282, 284, 309, 312, 314, 318, 352; control of interurbans, 205, 206, 311; hostility to interurbans, 22–23, 42, 145, 311; Oneida electrification, 25, 312
New York New Haven & Hartford RR, 206, 324, 325
Niagara Falls, N.Y., 83, 99, 113, 313, 319
Niagara Falls, Ont., 115, 419
Nickel Plate Road, 15, 97, 98, 112, 114, 120, 147, 261, 263, 311
Niles Car & Manufacturing Co., 34, 39, 73, 74, 267, 312, 345, 354, 358, 364, 383, 390, 391, 400, 403; history, 425
Norfolk Southern RR, 331
Norfolk & Western Ry., 161, 165, 271, 331, 385
Norristown, Pa., 79, 223, 296, 299
North American Co., 201, 347, 350, 353, 354, 366
North American Lt. & Power Co., 201
North Carolina, 331, 333; map, 332
North Coast Lines, 231, 391–92
Northern Illinois Public Service Co., 346
Northern Illinois Tr. & Lt. Co., 168
Northern Pacific Ry., 203, 207, 353, 388, 390, 391, 396
Northern Pump Co., 358
Northern Texas Elec. Co., 377–78
North Shore RR (NWP), 67
Northwestern Pacific RR, 23, 179, 207, 396, 402, 405, 407
Norwalk, Ohio, 13, 43, 55, 268, 269
Norwalk Truck Line, 178
Notre Dame University, 115
Nova Scotia, 421

Oak Harbor, Ohio, 22
Oakland, Cal., 43, 47, 63, 64, 93, 94, 98, 115, 134, 172, 177, 405
Oberlin, Ohio, 13, 16, 269
Oborn, George T., 215, 237
Obsolescence, consequences of, 231
Ocean Park, Cal., 173

General Index

Ocean Shore RR, 413
Office of Defense Transportation, 306
Official Guide of the Railways, 111
Official Interurban Equipment Register, 129
Ogden, Utah, 93, 94, 96, 133, 178, 383–86
Ohio, 9, 12, 28, 31, 32, 41, 95, 115, 255–75; state policy, 137, 152, 161, 167–68, 175–76; map, 256–57; motor-carrier regulation, 172, 175, 178; revenue passengers (table), 106; tax relief, 180; two-cent-fare law, 105
Ohio Brass Co., 77, 425
Ohio-Indiana-Michigan network, 26, 27, 29, 31, 56, 68, 84, 86, 92, 103, 108–11 *passim*, 124, 129, 146, 147, 183; characteristic equipment, 75; corporate histories, 255-90; decline, 219; description of, 42, 43–44; map, 256–57
Ohio Interurban Ry. Assn., 31, 109
Ohio Methodist Conference, 116
Ohio & Morenci RR, 264
Ohio Power Co., 263
Ohio River & Western RR, 29
Ohio Ry. Museum (Worthington, Ohio), 267, 268
Ohio syndicate, 265
Ohl, Frank M., 44
Oklahoma, 373–75; map, 370, 375
Oklahoma, University of, 373
Oklahoma Belt Ry., 373
Oklahoma City, Okla., 373
Oklahoma Southwestern RR, 374
Olean Bradford & Warren RR, 311
Oliver Plow Co., 362
Omaha & Council Bluffs St. Ry., 153
Omaha, Neb., 43, 153, 365
Oneida, N.Y., 175, 311, 312
Oneonta, N.Y., 42, 315
Ontario, 42, 115, 236, 414–20; map, 416; proposals for publicly owned lines, 180, 191; — Ry. & Municipal Board, 41
Ontario Hydroelectric Power System, 62, 181, 185, 191, 236, 244, 414, 415, 417, 423
Operating ratios, 186, 190, 194–95
Operation at a loss, 240–43
Oregon, 394–97; map, 395; motor-carrier regulation, 172; — RR Commission, 151
Oregon City, Ore., 9, 27, 248, 394, 395
Oregon Short Line, 388
Orem, W. C., 384
Orestes, Ind., 147
Ortonville, Mich., 142
Osgood Bradley Car Co., 425
Ottawa Car Manufacturing Co., 414, 425
Ottawa, Ill., 36, 339
Ottawa, Ont., 421
Owensboro, Ky., 115, 285
Owosso, Mich., 131, 289
Oxford, Cal., 213
Oxford, Mich., 142, 160

Pacific City Lines, 401
Pacific Coast RR, 405
Pacific Fruit Express, 390
Pacific Gas & Elec. Co., 398
Pacific Great Eastern Ry., 102
Pacific Power & Lt. Co., 391
Pacinotti, Antonio, 4
Page, Charles (oil executive), 374
Page, Charles G. (inventor), 4
Painesville, Ohio, 10, 274

Palmyra, Pa., 163
Panic of 1903, 33; — of 1907, 33, 44
Paradox Land & Transportation Co., re, 176
Parallel services, 43
Paris, Ill., 38, 130–31, 279, 283, 351
Paris & Mount Pleasant RR, 38
Parke County coal field, Ind., 41
Pasadena, Cal., 27, 406–13 *passim*
Passenger traffic, 91–118; average haul, 95; dependence on, 91; effect of abandonment, 246–48; fares, 103–8; interline arrangements, 108–12; limited services, 96–100; types of, 91
Patoka, Ind., 44, 285
Paulista Ry., 85
Paving requirements, 18, 50, 149
Pavlowski, Felix, 299
Paw Paw Lake, Mich., 115, 290
Paxton, Ill., 251, 349
Peabody Short Line RR, 351
Pennsylvania, 8, 42, 103, 148, 200, 292–302; map, 292; motor-carrier regulation, 171, 172, 174, 178; state policy, 150, 167, 168, 177; two-cent-fare law, 105
Pennsylvania Elec. Co., 301
Pennsylvania RR, 61, 73, 99, 106, 108, 112, 138, 264, 273, 279, 284, 293, 298, 300, 301, 307, 312; Camden, N.J., electrification, 309; control of electric lines, 206, 270, 297; Cumberland Valley electrification, 56, 295; hostility to interurbans, 22–23, 145, 263, 306; pioneer in steel equipment, 79
Pennsylvania trolley gauge (5′–2½″), 51
Peoria, Ill., 36, 82, 86, 98, 101, 121, 145, 219, 345–49 *passim*
Peoria & Eastern RR, 130
Peoria & Pekin Union, 145, 162
Per diem agreement, 142, 143, 145, 147
Pere Marquette RR, 16, 40, 162, 289, 290, 417
Perry, Iowa, 104, 364–65
Peru, Ind., 26, 36, 55, 97, 112, 120–21, 277, 280
Petaluma (steamboat), 403
Petersburg, Mich., 34
Philadelphia, Pa., 79, 120, 296, 297, 299, 302; gauge, 51; money market, 27, 184
Philadelphia Rapid Transit, 297
Philadelphia Reading & New England RR, 318
Pictou County Power Board, 421
Pierce, A. E., & Co., 344
Piggy-backing, 134–35
Pilots, 78
Pioneer & Fayette RR, 264
Piqua, Ohio, 13, 43, 260–61
Pittsburgh, Pa., 32, 43, 107, 178, 202, 219, 295, 299; gauge, 51
Pittsburgh & Castle Shannon RR, 299
Pittsburgh & Lake Erie RR, 206, 270
Pittsburgh Lisbon & Western RR, 270
Pittsburg St. Ry., 369
Plainfield, Ind., 23, 27
Pomeroy, F. J., 13; syndicate with M. J. Mandelbaum, 13, 14, 19, 26, 28, 31, 32, 265, 268, 327, 336, 341
Pontiac, Ill., 38, 346
Pontiac, Mich., 11, 288
Port Arthur, Tex., 99, 202, 379
Port Clinton, Ohio, 13, 22, 204, 263, 267

General Index

Port Colborne, Ont., 181, 414, 419
Port Credit, Ont., 181, 418
Port Dalhousie, Ont., 115, 419
Port Huron, Mich., 11, 27, 288
Portland Astoria & Pacific RR, 397
Portland General Electric, 394
Portland, Ind., 44, 55, 261, 281, 283
Portland, Ore., 9, 27, 41, 63, 102, 151, 212, 248, 394–97 *passim*
Portland Ry. (Ore.), 394
Portsmouth, Ohio, 175, 271
Port Stanley, Ont., 43, 417
Pottsville, Pa., 167
Power Co. of Canada, 423
Pressed Steel Car Co., 425
President's Conference Committee (PCC) cars, 87
Preston Car & Coach Co., 414, 425
Preston, Ida., 93, 385
Princeton, Ill., 36, 339
Princeton, Ind., 27, 285
Princeton University, 298
Providence, R.I., 322, 326
Public Service of Oklahoma, 374
Public Utility Holding Company Act of 1935, 179, 267, 300, 303
Public utility regulation by states, origin of, 152
Puget Sound Power & Lt. Co., 198, 393
Pullman Car & Manufacturing Co., 82, 396, 425
Pullman Co., 101, 102
Purdue University, 230

Quebec (city), 181, 420, 423
Quebec (province), 420–21
Quebec Ry., 420
Quinney, Utah, 117, 385

Racine, Wis., 135, 140, 163, 336
Radial railways, 117, 413
Rail, 48; bonding of, 49
Railroads: affiliation with New York bankers, 19; attraction of LCL from, 131; attraction of passengers from, 15; competition of, 37, 117–18, 233–34; control over interurbans, 197, 205–07; emulation of interurban service, 23–24; hostility of, 22–23, 140–41, 160; inadequacy of local service, 8, 91; interurbans' use of plant, 19; rate-cutting, 104; rate divisions with, 141
Railroad Retirement Act, 156, 158, 159
Railway Accounting Officers Assn., 143
Ry. & Bus Associates, *see* Associated Gas & Elec. Co.
Railway Labor Act of 1926, 156, 158, 159
Railway Post Office (RPO), 120–21
Randall Race Track, 272
Rate of return: defined, 186; statistics, 186–87, 190
Ravinia Park, 116
Ramon (ferry), 50, 400
Reading Co., 166, 206, 298
Reading, Pa., 52, 301, 302
Reconstruction Finance Corp., 272
Red Bluff, Cal., 35
Refrigerator cars, 84
Reid, Harry, 97, 137, 280
Republic Ry. & Lt. Co., 274
Richey, Prof. Albert S., 107

Richfield Springs, N.Y., 315
Rich Man's Panic of 1903, 27
Richmond, Ind., 27, 44, 259, 278, 279, 283, 284
Richmond, Va., 7, 330–31; — Union Passenger Ry., 7
Ridge Farm, Ill., 130, 347
Rights-of-way: acquisition, 20–21; comparative types, 20, 46–47
River Auto Stages, 177
Rochester, N.Y., 41, 42, 43, 121, 164, 309, 311–14 *passim*; franchise restriction on freight, 127; subway, 53, 312–13
Rockford, Ill., 128, 343, 344; — Public Service Co., 344
Rock Island Lines, *see* Chicago Rock Island & Pacific
Rockland, Me., 120
Rockport, Ind., 115, 285, 286
Rockwell City, Iowa, 63, 363, 364
Rogue River Valley RR, 397
Romeo, Mich., 16, 287
Roosevelt, Theodore, 45
Royal Crystal salt, 386
Royce, A. H., 419
Rural trolley lines: decline, 212; distinguished from interurbans, 8; equipment, 70; fares, 8, 103; freight, 121, 133; handicaps of, 45; municipal ownership, 180, 325; in New England, 45–46
Rushville, Ind., 59, 120, 284–85
Russell Car & Foundry Co., 425

Sacramento, Cal., 63, 64, 69, 70, 86, 98, 115, 398–401 *passim*
Safety, 87–90, 164
Saginaw, Mich., 43, 288, 289, 290
St. Agatha, Me., 165
St. Catharines, Ont., 413, 415; — St. Ry., 9
St. Charles Car Co., 425
St. Joachim, Que., 181
St. Joseph, Mich., 276, 290
St. Joseph, Mo., 15, 204, 366–67; — Ry. Lt. Heat & Power Co., 367
St. Louis Car Co., 61, 299, 316, 348, 354, 380, 391, 403; history, 425
St. Louis, Mo., 36, 37, 38, 49, 81, 82, 98, 101, 112, 184, 219, 346–50 *passim*; Chamber of Commerce, 237; — Public Service, 199; suburban lines, 365–66
St. Mary's, Ohio, 55, 261
St. Louis–San Francisco Ry. (Frisco), 367, 376
St. Louis Troy & Eastern, 347
St. Paul, Minn., 26, 357–59
Salem, Ore., 63, 396, 397
Saltair Resort, 386
Salt Lake City, Utah, 69, 70, 93, 94, 96, 125, 133, 178, 198, 383–87 *passim*
Salt Lake & Ogden RR, 383
Saltonstall, C. L., 19
Salzburg, H. E. and Murray (scrap merchants), 311, 364–65, 372
San Bernardino, Cal., 63, 121, 173, 410
Sander, Fred, 391
San Diego, Cal., 42, 413
Sandusky, Ohio, 10, 13, 50, 115, 267, 268
San Francisco, Cal., 43, 63, 64, 98, 100, 115, 121, 134, 180, 213, 244, 398, 402–3, 406, 413
San Francisco & San Joaquin Valley RR, 402
San Jose, Cal., 43, 404; — RRs, 404

General Index

San Pedro, Cal., 142, 166, 173, 406, 411
Santa Clara Valley Auto Stages, 173
Santa Fe System, *see* Atchison Topeka & Santa Fe Ry.
Santa Rosa, Cal., 23, 402
Saratoga Springs, N.Y., 214, 316
Sawyer, W. H. 37
Saybrook, Conn., 81, 322
Scheduling, 91–93
Schoepf, W. Kesley, 26; syndicate with Hugh J. McGowan, 26, 28, 29, 31, 32, 33, 69, 73, 102, 109, 201, 258, 265, 266, 275, 276, 278, 280
Schonthal Co., Joseph, 264
School trains, 116–17
Scottsburg, Ind., 101
Scowcroft family, 385
Scranton, Pa., 99, 293–94
Seagrave, Frank E., 264, 282
Seat Pleasant, Md., 60, 327
Seattle, Wash., 27, 35, 41, 42, 99, 391–93
Securities & Exchange Commission, 179, 284
Sellersburg, Ind., 33, 62, 163, 279
Seville, Ohio, 13, 32, 33, 269
Seymour, Ind., 33, 62, 163, 279, 284
Shaker Heights Rapid Transit, 81
Shamokin, Pa., 167
Shaw, George H. T., 344
Sheboygan, Wis., 35, 354, 356; — Lt. Power & Ry. Co., 356
Shelbyville, Ind., 27, 284–85
Sherrill, N.Y., 175
Shoup, Paul, 235, 404, 406
Siemens, Werner von, 4
Siggins brothers, 184, 295, 371, 373
Signals and signaling, 65–67, 86; compulsory installation in Indiana, 90, 164; *see also* Safety
Sistersville, W.Va., 305
Sleeping cars, 100–102
Sloss–Lilienthal syndicate, 398
Smith, Clement, 357
Smith, Mrs. W. M., 22, 384
Snow family, 386
Soo Line, 114
South Bend, Ind., 27, 43, 59, 86, 97, 115, 222, 276, 277, 337, 338
South Carolina, 331, 333; map, 332
South Dakota, 359
Southeastern Express Co., 138
Southern Car Co., 425
Southern Ohio Express Co., 122
Southern Pacific Company (SP RR), 22, 24, 85, 98, 114, 155, 205, 376, 394, 397, 398, 401, 403, 405; control of interurbans, 142, 179, 184, 207, 404, 406–13 *passim*; — Golden Gate Ferries, 404; Oregon electrification, 25, 395–96
Southern Ry., 145, 329
South La Porte, Ind., 39
Southwest Power Co., 374
Span wires, 56
Sperry Engineering Co., 323
Spokane, Wash., 27, 213, 389, 390
Spokane Portland & Seattle, 207, 396, 397
Sprague, Frank J., 6, 7, 75
Sprecher, Peter (motorman), 261
Spring, Edward C., 109
Springfield, Ill., 36, 91, 101, 121, 144, 219, 346–49 *passim*
Springfield, Mass., 128

Springfield, Ohio, 26, 114, 147, 151, 259–60, 278; effort to eject the C&LE, 138
Springfield, Vt., 148, 320
Ste. Anne, shrine of, 420
St. Lawrence Seaway, 421
Standard Gas & Elec. Co., 204, 357
Stanley Construction Co., 34
Stations, 68–70
Staunton, Ill., 88, 347
Steam "dummy" engines, 5
Steamboats, 117–18; Great Lakes, 104, 111, 115, 130, 162, 276, 289; local river steamers, 8; Sacramento River, 115
Stedman, N. H., re, 176
Steubenville, Ohio, 36, 158, 202, 271, 302–3
Stephenson, John, Co. (car builder), 78, 260, 360, 402; history, 425
Stockbridge, Mass., 16
Stockton Terminal & Eastern RR, 413
Stoffel, T. H., 129
Stone & Webster, 202, 290, 330, 342, 345, 376, 377, 378, 379, 391, 392, 421; development of Birney car, 86
Strang Construction Co., 28
Strang, W. B., 367
Strathmore, Cal., 213, 405
Streator, Ill., 36, 339
Street railways, electric: development of, 4–7; gauges, 51–52; power systems, 53; ICC jurisdiction over, 166; *see also* City streetcar systems
Street running, 50–53, 93–95; franchises for, 16–19, 127, 149–51; municipal regulation of, 75
Street Railway Journal, 11–12, 31, 45
Strickland, J. F., Co., 376
Studebaker, Clement, 201, 347
Studebaker, J. M., 277
Subsidies to construction, 16–17
Substations, 54–55
Suburban traffic, 229
Sudbury, Ont., 423
Suisun Bay, 50, 93, 98
Sullivan, Ind., 44, 285
Sunday, Rev. William, 277
Sutherland Commission (Ontario), 237
Sutton, Ont., 181, 418
Sydney, Nova Scotia, 421
Syracuse, N.Y., 10, 42, 43, 164, 309, 311, 312, 314

Tacoma, Wash., 27, 42, 51, 99, 392, 393; — Ry. & Power Co., 393
Tarrytown, N.Y., 42
Tax relief, 180, 325
Teamsters, Brotherhood of, 135
Telephone, use of in dispatching, 67–68
Television, 300
Temiskaming & Northern Ontario Ry., 420
Tennesssee, 334–35
Terminal RR Assn. of St. Louis, 145
Terre Haute, Ind., 23, 130, 131, 147, 278, 279, 282, 283, 284, 285; first all-Birney system, 86
Terrell, Tex., 213, 378
Texas, 142–43, 202, 218, 367–80; maps, 377, 379; motor-carrier regulation, 172
Theis, George, Jr., 373
Third Avenue Ry., N.Y., 349
Third rail, 57–58
Thomason, Edgar, 331

General Index

Thorold, Ont., 9, 181, 413, 414, 419
Thurber, James, 275
Thurmont, Md., 114, 327–28
Ties, 48
Tiffin, Ohio, 13, 43, 263
Timetable, C.E.R.A. consolidated, 111
Tipton, Ind., 89, 283
Toledo, Ohio, 10, 11, 13, 14, 24–28 *passim*, 32, 33, 34, 41–44 *passim*, 51, 53, 55, 73, 78, 81, 93, 94, 96, 99, 102, 104, 108, 112, 117, 137, 204, 232, 255, 261–67 *passim*, 281, 287; projected interurban to Napoleon and Defiance, 17, 43, 262; — Edison Co., 267; — Ry. & Lt. Co., 27
Toledo Peoria & Western RR, 345
Toledo Ry. & Terminal Co., 146
Toledo St. Louis & Western RR, 28, 112, 147, 282
Tonawanda, N.Y., 177, 313
Toronto, Ont., 10, 43, 115, 181, 312, 413–19 *passim*; gauge, 51, 52, 418; — Transportation Commission, 418
Toronto Hamilton & Buffalo Ry., 415
Track, 48
Trailers, 128–30; C.E.R.A. standard design, 129–30
Trailways System, 232
Transmission lines, 55
Transportation Act of 1920, 153
Transportation Securities Co., 274
Trenton, N.J., 94, 297, 306, 309; multiplicity of gauges, 52
Trolley contact signals, 85
Trolley poles, 78
Trolley wheels, 78
Trolley wire: suspension of, 56; height of, 57
Troy, N.Y., 175, 316, 317
Trucks (highway), growth of, 132–33; rivalry of, 236; protection from by commissions, 178
Trucks (of cars), 78
Tucker, Anthony & Co., 21, 30
Tunnels, 47
Turners Falls, Mass., 180
Tuscaloosa, Ala., 157
Twin City Rapid Transit Co. (Minn.), 359
Twin City Ry. (Mich.), 290
Two-cent-fare laws, 37, 105

Uhrichsville, Ohio, 26, 273
Union City, Ind., 88, 176, 265, 281
Union Lt. & Power Co., 204, 373
Union Pacific RR, 22, 207, 376, 383, 388, 390, 410
Union Ry. Gas & Elec. Co., 343
Union Trust Co. of Cleveland, 261
United Corp., 199, 203
United Lt. & Power Co., 205
United Lt. & Rys. Co., 289, 359, 362
United States Electric signals, 65, 66
United States Express Co., 122–23
United States RR Administration, 105, 123–24, 144
United States Steel Co., 41
Upper Sandusky, Ohio, 44
Urbana, Ill., 36, 145, 183, 349
USSR, locomotives designed for, 85, 338
U.S. Supreme Court, 153, 155, 157, 160, 165, 166, 168, 176
Utah, 84, 108, 137, 219, 234, 383–87; equipment, 75; joint traffic arrangements, 110, 114, 386; map, 384; motor-carrier regulation, 178; — Lt. & Tr. Co., 199
Utah Northern RR, 385
Utah Ry., 385
Utica, N.Y., 42, 63, 311, 312, 315

Vallejo, Cal., 115, 121, 244, 403
Vallejo & Northern RR, 400
Van Arsdale, W. O., 372
Vancouver, B.C., 248
Vancouver & Lulu Island Ry., 422
Van Depoele, Charles J., 5, 6, 9, 356
Van Doren, C. A., Dr., 183, 250–51, 349
Van Doren, Carl, quoted, 250–51
Varley, C. F., 4
Vaughan, S. L., 289
Venice, Ill., 36, 350
Vermont, 320, 324–25; map, 321
Victoria, B.C., 422
Villiard, H. H., 352
Vincennes, Ind., 42, 44, 275, 285
Vineland, Ont., 249, 415
Virginia, 330–31; maps, 321, 329; state policy, 168
Visalia, Cal., 173, 405
Von Echa syndicate, 184, 415, 418

Wabash, Ind., 33, 280, 283
Wabash Ry., 17, 24, 40, 89, 104, 145, 277, 345, 363; control of Toledo & Western, 146, 204, 206, 264
Waco, Texas, 63, 376, 377
Wadsworth, Ohio, 43
Wall Street Journal, 19, 29
Walsh family, 345
Wapakoneta, Ohio, 13, 32, 261
Ward signals, 65, 66
Warren, Ohio, 36, 272, 274
Washington, 389–93; maps, 390, 391–93; motor-carrier regulations, 176; RR Commission, 166
Washington, D.C., 60–61, 94, 199, 326–30 *passim*
Washington Ohio & Western RR, 329
Washington Ry. & Elec. Co., 60, 201
Wason Manufacturing Co. (car builders), 87, 320, 323; history, 425
Waterloo, Ind., 120, 263, 281, 284
Waterloo, Iowa, 143–44, 360–62
Watertown, Wis., 35, 42, 353
Waterville, Ohio, 17, 262
Watervliet, Mich., 115, 290
Waukesha, Wis., 114, 353, 354
Wedgewood, re, 178
Weed control, 48
Wellington, Ohio, 13
Wells–Fargo Express Co., 122–23
Wesson Co., 284
West End Ry. of Boston, 7
Western Maryland Ry., 114, 328
Western Pacific RR, 22, 153, 154, 179, 207, 398, 401, 402
Western United Corp, 342
Western Weighing & Inspection Bureau, 143
West Hill, Ont., 181
Westinghouse, 10, 84; introduction of single-phase AC, 58
West Jersey RR, 307
Weston, Mass., 16
West Shore RR (NYC), 22, 312

West Texas Utilities Co., 379
West Virginia, 303–6; map 304; motor-carrier regulation, 176
Wheatstone, Sir Charles, 4
Wheeling, W. Va., 10, 13, 27, 32, 36, 202, 273, 300, 302–3, 305
Wheeling & Lake Erie RR, 113, 273
White, J. G., Engineering Co., 21, 237, 337
Whitney, Henry M., 7
Wichita, Kansas, 69, 70, 183, 371
Widener, George and Peter, 26
Wilder, Ida., 249, 388
Wilkes-Barre, Pa., 47, 99, 293–94
Willingson, W. E., 125
Willys–Overland Corp., 146, 204, 264
Wilson, Del (conductor), 89
Winchester, Ind., 141
Windsor, Ont., 11, 59, 415
Winnipeg, Man., 10, 421
Winnipeg Elec. Co., 421
Winona Assembly, 36, 116, 277
Wisconsin, 176, 353–57; motor-carrier regulation, 172, 176; state policy, 163, 167, 168; two-cent-fare law, 105

Wisconsin Elec. Power Co., 354
Wolverine Transportation Co., 176
Woods, G. B., 417, 418
Woods–Nicholls Syndicate, 312, 419
Woodville, Ohio, 22, 263
Wooster, Ohio, 13, 26, 269
Worcester, Mass., 320–22
Worcester Construction Co., 22
Work motors, 85
World's Columbian Exposition, *see* Chicago World's Fair, 1893
World War I, 33, 70, 86, 94, 107, 108, 110, 123, 144, 188, 209, 230; effect on interurbans, 105–6
World War II, 92, 209, 215, 219–20, 242
Wyoming, 383

Xenia, Ohio, 34, 43, 259

Youngstown, Ohio, 32, 36, 131, 270, 272, 274
Yuba City, Cal., 64, 86

Zanesville, Ohio, 13, 26, 47, 99, 101, 133, 265, 266, 303
Zone fares, 103, 108, 159